Praise for
A Matter of Honor

"In a well-researched book, Summers and Swan demonstrate that Admiral Kimmel does not deserve the blame he's been assigned. Americans have found it easier to blame Kimmel than to admit to the prejudice which allowed the attack to proceed. Americans drew comfort from the preferred stereotype of the incompetent oriental. Bigotry obscured the Japanese threat."   —*The Times* (London)

"Summers and Swan make the case for Admiral Kimmel being a scapegoat who was wronged, humiliated, and flimflammed."   —*New York Post*

"An unflinching look at the bombing of Pearl Harbor. . . . The authors convincingly contend that Kimmel was scapegoated . . . sober yet captivating."   —*National Book Review*

"Persuasive evidence that Admiral Kimmel suffered gross injustice . . . passionately developed."
                                              —*World War II Magazine*

"Thought-provoking . . . a dramatic rendering of the investigations into the attack, which laid accountability squarely on Kimmel's shoulders and which—the authors argue—ignored other players."
                        —*Proceedings*, journal of the U.S. Naval Institute

"This is historical biography that you will want to read. . . . Summers and Swan take us a long way toward understanding more completely what happened leading up to December 7, 1941 . . . persuasive, exhaustive research, and detailed insights."   —*Cryptolog*, journal of former Navy codebreakers

"Duplicity and betrayal in Washington, which turned to someone who sacrificed himself for the country, only to be sacrificed when it needed a scapegoat."
—Intelligencer, journal of the Association of Former Intelligence Officers

"Fascinating look at our defense, diplomatic, and intelligence policies leading up to the war and its effect on one person, aptly described as an 'American Dreyfus.' . . . Excellent."
—Steven Z. Freiberger, author of *Dawn over Suez*

"Demonstrates how Pearl Harbor was the result of systematic unpreparedness and of human error up and down the chain of command. . . . Exhaustive analysis."   —Barnes & Noble

"Outstanding."   *—Christian Science Monitor*

"A stirring indictment of government officials . . . the worst intelligence failure of the twentieth century."
—Manhattan Book Review

"Reads like a thriller. . . . An airtight case that Admiral Kimmel should not have been blamed. . . . There were dots that American intelligence did not properly connect. Kimmel was scapegoated and slandered without basis."
—Publishers Weekly

"An exposé of the scapegoating of the commander in chief of the U.S. Pacific Fleet."   *—Kirkus Reviews*

"Important. . . . Within hours, the race to find someone to blame for the catastrophe was in effect . . . a saga of missed messages, faulty memories, long-classified documents, and official inertia."   *—Library Journal*

"A nailbiter. . . . Darkly humorous, galling, infuriating. . . . Imagine a James Bond novel in which the spies and intelligence agents are either incompetent or altogether ignored. . . . It's extremely hard to read this book and not think the President has a responsibility to restore Admiral Kimmel to his full rank."   —*Ordinary Times*

"The most comprehensive, accurate, and thoroughly researched book of events leading up to the Japanese attack on Pearl Harbor ever written. It provides new information never before revealed. . . . As a matter of honor, for the institution of the U.S. Navy, it is long past due to correct the injustice that has been imposed on Kimmel and Short. Their wartime ranks must be posthumously restored."

—Admiral James Lyons, former Commander
in Chief, U.S. Pacific Fleet

"Compelling, thoroughly researched. A much-needed objective look, especially, at the role of Admiral Husband Kimmel, who was in command of the U.S. Pacific Fleet on December 7 and whose name was forever tainted. Summers and Swan make complex history clear."

—Col. Kevin Farrell, former Chief of Military History,
U.S. Military Academy, West Point

"Streamlined, muscular, objective, and well-written—a sensitive examination of a vast constellation of source material. Summers and Swan dispose of the silly 'President Roosevelt had foreknowledge' conspiracy theory in a no-nonsense way. And they present a powerful argument in defense of Admiral Kimmel, who was blamed for the attack and forced into inglorious retirement. . . . Excellent."

—Martin Morgan, World War II historian and
author of *The Americans on D-Day*

"A fine book. Summers and Swan drive a stake through the heart of the outrageous theory which, like Dracula, has stubbornly refused to die—that villainous conspirators, including President Roosevelt—were somehow responsible for the attack on Pearl Harbor. Scrupulously researched and rigorously argued."

—David M. Kennedy, Pulitzer Prize–winning author of *Freedom from Fear: The American People in Depression and War, 1929–1945*

"Meticulous, eloquent, and compelling—and hugely readable. The seventieth anniversary of the Japanese attack is well served by *A Matter of Honor*."

—Simon Winchester, author of *Pacific*

"Anthony Summers' & Robbyn Swan's *A Matter of Honor* is a noble and right-minded portrait of Admiral Kimmel, the scapegoat for Pearl Harbor. The amount of fresh research is deeply impressive. Never again, too, can anybody claim that FDR knew about the bombing in advance. Highly recommended!"

—Douglas Brinkley, author of *Rightful Heritage: Franklin D. Roosevelt and the Land of America*

"Meticulous research . . . thorough-going . . . provides a great deal of insight into the ordeal of Admiral Husband Kimmel, who served his nation well but was treated shabbily by its leaders."   —Paul Stillwell, author of *Battleship Arizona*

A MATTER OF HONOR

A MATTER OF HONOR

PEARL HARBOR: BETRAYAL, BLAME, AND A FAMILY'S QUEST FOR JUSTICE

Anthony Summers and Robbyn Swan

HARPER

NEW YORK · LONDON · TORONTO · SYDNEY

A hardcover edition of this book was published in 2016 by Harper, an imprint of HarperCollins Publishers.

A MATTER OF HONOR. Copyright © 2016 by Anthony Summers and Robbyn Swan. All rights reserved. Printed in the United States of America. No part of this book may be used or reproduced in any manner whatsoever without written permission except in the case of brief quotations embodied in critical articles and reviews. For information, address HarperCollins Publishers, 195 Broadway, New York, NY 10007.

HarperCollins books may be purchased for educational, business, or sales promotional use. For information, please e-mail the Special Markets Department at SPsales@harpercollins.com.

FIRST HARPER PAPERBACK EDITION PUBLISHED 2017.

Frontispiece courtesy of Everett Historical/Shutterstock, Inc.

Library of Congress Cataloging-in-Publication Data has been applied for.

ISBN 978-0-06-240552-4 (pbk.)

17 18 19 20 21   LSC   10 9 8 7 6 5 4 3 2 1

For the seven members of our families who, in World War II, served in the U.S. Army and Navy, and in the British Royal Air Force.

Contents

Authors' Note

FOR AMERICANS IN modern times, two events resonate like none other: Pearl Harbor and 9/11. They resonate because of the enormous loss of life involved, and because the attacks took place on U.S. territory and were aimed at the heart of the homeland itself. Both events catapulted the United States into war. Pearl Harbor marked the start of a world war that would last four years and cost half a million Americans their lives.

Both events initiated a tsunami of official records, books, academic papers, films, and—in the case of 9/11 especially—seemingly inexhaustible discourse on the Internet. As when we were working on our book on 9/11, *The Eleventh Day*, we have plunged deeply into the facts—and factoids—about Japan's strike on Pearl Harbor. This has included pulling at the multiple strands of conspiracy theory in which the story of the catastrophe has for so long been entangled. They center on the notion that President Roosevelt, or British Prime Minister Churchill, or members of their governments and staffs, had foreknowledge that Japan was going to strike Hawaii. Yet for cynical reasons, some have suggested, it was decided not to warn the commanders there.

None of the supposed evidence of treachery that we examined proved solid. We have reported on much of it, usually not in the text but in the Notes. (Should readers wish to ask us about a lead they may think we have not explored, they may contact us through our publisher.)

What we have found during our work is a tragedy replete with human error and lapses—some understandable, some inexcusable—many of them at a high level in Washington. There was a cover-up, a necessity at the time. But there was also blame, unjustly placed.

A.S., R.S.
September 2016

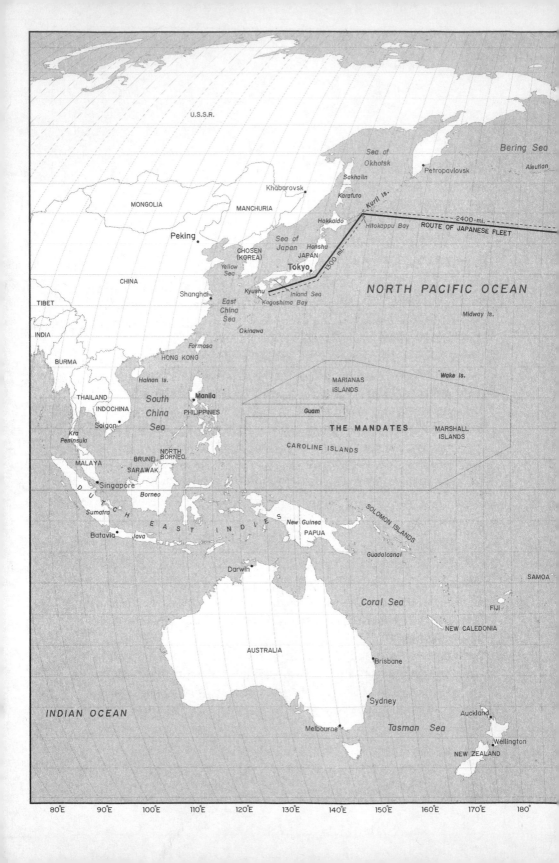

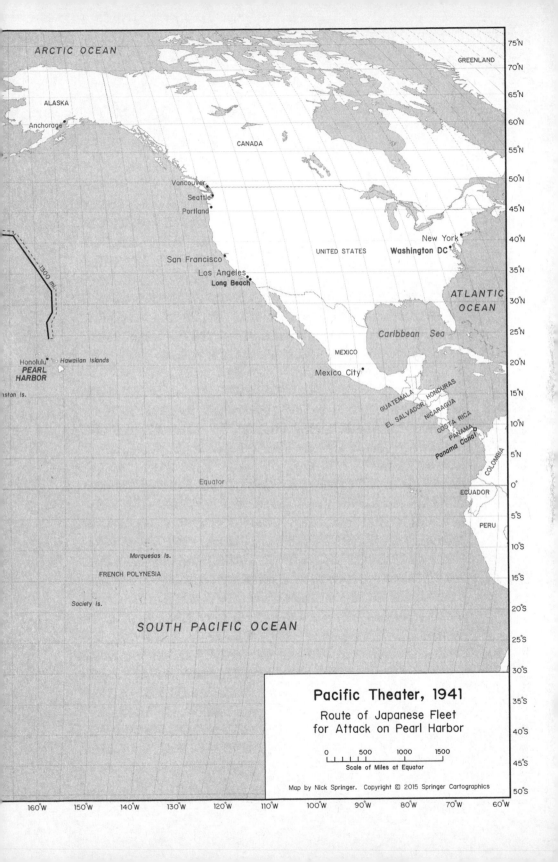

A MATTER OF HONOR

Prologue

IN THE EVENINGS, when the old man was in his eighties, he liked to sit up playing solitaire. Sometimes, when he wanted company, his daughter-in-law would sit with him and they would talk a little—she would mostly listen—until he fell asleep. The old man had had no daughters, only sons, and they held each other in great affection.

On one such fall night in the 1960s, it was chilly in the clapboard ranch house in New England. The old man was sitting at his desk, bundled up in a heavy maroon robe, with a thick scarf around his neck. On his head, pulled down low, was the blue knitted sailor's watch cap he liked to wear. For he had been a sailor, at heart always would be.

That night as he sat with his daughter-in-law, the man wanted to reminisce, to share memories and memorabilia. He pulled out a packet of papers tied together with a ribbon; they were faded and crumbling, some of them dating back to the nineteenth century: letters between his grandfather and his father, who had fought in the Civil War; letters from the two world wars; letters from the wife he had married fifty years earlier; and letters from his three sons.

Earlier, he had entrusted his daughter-in-law with other treasures. Now, as he gave her the letters, he admonished her to keep them safe. Then, settling back in his barrel-shaped chair and pulling out a deck of cards, he talked on. As she listened, the daughter-in-law looked past him, across the desk, at a painting.

It was a portrait of a man in his prime, a U.S. Navy officer in full-dress uniform, pristine white, with a high collar. On his chest, the white was broken only by the ribbon denoting his medals. In his lap, the officer held his gold-encrusted hat. On the shoulders, making broad shoulders seem broader, were the epaulets indicating his rank.

Four stars. For the officer in the portrait had once been one of the most senior, most distinguished admirals in the U.S. Navy.

"Had been" because, soon after it was painted, the portrait became an anachronism. Accused of "dereliction of duty" and "errors of judgment," the Admiral had been relieved of his command and lost his four-star rank. In the eyes of millions, it was his personal failure that had led to the deaths of more than 2,400 men, and to the injuries of more than a thousand others. The Admiral had borne the lion's share of the blame for one of the greatest military disasters in U.S. history.

Pearl Harbor.

After his fall, the Admiral had fought on, year after year, to convince the world that he was innocent of the allegations. There had been no fewer than nine investigations into the debacle that led to his disgrace. The famous and the less famous had testified, some reluctantly, as to what—they claimed—had really happened. Books had been published. Americans had argued. Had others made the Admiral the scapegoat for their blunders? Had the Admiral been the victim of a grotesque official conspiracy, as even he surmised in his less restrained moments? Nothing had been resolved.

Two decades on, beneath the portrait of himself as he had once been, the old man sat talking into the night with his daughter-in-law. Time was running out for him, and he knew it. In the past, when anniversaries of Pearl Harbor came around, he had given press interviews. Eventually, however, he began turning reporters away. "Please don't try to make me talk," he told one of them. "Pearl Harbor is all in the history books. You don't want to see me. I'm dead."

The truth of the matter, an intimate said, was that the Admiral still thought about Pearl Harbor "every moment of the day." His mind was still sharp, his sense of humor intact. There was bitterness, though, behind his smiles. Bitterness over the injustice he believed had been done to him, bitterness toward one man in particular, a man he had thought was his friend.

A letter he had not given to his daughter-in-law, one he never mailed, would be found in a desk drawer when death did finally claim the Admiral. In it, he told the former friend, the man who had been Chief of Naval Operations at the time of Pearl Harbor, that he had "betrayed the officers and men of the Fleet by not giving them a fighting chance for their lives . . . May God forgive you for what you have done to me, for I never will."

The Admiral's three sons had all served in the U.S. Navy in World War II. One, a submarine skipper, had been killed in action. The other two were to carry on the fight to clear their father's name until and after the millennium.

Today, led by two grandsons, the family continues the struggle. For them, it is a matter of honor.

PART I

CATASTROPHE

1

DECEMBER 1941. FRANKLIN Roosevelt is President, almost a year into his third term in office. World War II is not yet America's war—not quite. More than two years after Britain and France declared war on Nazi Germany, the United States remains officially neutral. Faced with strong opposition to U.S. involvement, the President has assured the country: "We will not participate in foreign wars . . . We will not send our army, navy, or air forces to fight in foreign lands outside of the Americas, except in case of attack."

The President has nevertheless been tiptoeing toward involvement. When Hitler's armies rolled across Europe, when in 1940 Britain fought off a massive German air bombardment, Roosevelt pulled the political levers to get "surplus" American war supplies to the British. He has told his countrymen that Britain's struggle with the Nazis is "a fight that will live forever in the story of human gallantry."

He and British Prime Minister Winston Churchill have for more than two years been exchanging secret correspondence—there will eventually be some two thousand such communications between them. In the messages, Roosevelt addresses Churchill as "Former Naval Person" while Churchill calls him POTUS, for "President of the United States." "Former Naval Person" has long since implored POTUS to send an even greater supply of munitions and ships—and food.

The President has called on Americans to produce "more ships, more guns, more planes," not only for export but for defense of the homeland. The situation, Roosevelt has said, is "an emergency as serious as war itself." He has warned of the threat posed by three nations that aim at "world control": Germany, Mussolini's Italy—and Japan.

Tension between Washington and the Land of the Rising Sun, on the increase for years, is now at breaking point. Japan's empire has long been expanding militarily: pushing on deeper into China; seizing strategic islets in the South China Sea; thrusting into Indochina—the future Vietnam. In 1941, it threatens territories controlled by three western nations: the Philippines, a key outpost of U.S. influence in the western Pacific; the Netherlands East Indies, today's Indonesia; and Britain's Malaya and Singapore.

As part of its ongoing effort to restrain Japan, the United States has cut off exports of vital supplies. For several months the embargo has included oil, a commodity absolutely essential to the Japanese military—a military that now controls the government in Tokyo. Now, months of diplomatic shadowboxing appear to be ending. By land and by sea, Japanese forces are on the move.

On the night of Saturday, December 6th, President Roosevelt sends a message to his counterpart in Tokyo, Emperor Hirohito, whose title—"Showa"—means "Enlightened Peace." Together, Roosevelt tells Hirohito, they have "a sacred duty to restore traditional amity and prevent further death and destruction."

2

THE HOUR AFTER DAWN, SUNDAY, DECEMBER 7TH, HAWAII. The waters of Pearl Harbor, from its narrow entrance to its inner reaches, are warming in the early sunlight. The sound of church bells drifts across from nearby Honolulu.

At 7:54 a.m., perched high on a water tank at the Navy Yard, sailors prepare to raise a blue-and-white flag, the signal requiring that—in six minutes precisely—the Stars and Stripes is to be hoisted.

Who sees what first will become lost in the clamor of memory? Bandsmen forming up aboard the battleship USS *Nevada* spot "dots in the sky" to the southwest. At the Marine Barracks, men changing the guard glance up as a line of planes, flying low, swoops over the main gate of the Navy Yard. Admiral William Furlong, waiting for the breakfast call on the quarterdeck of the minelayer USS *Oglala*, watches as a solitary aircraft flies low over an islet in the center of the harbor. Logan Ramsey, a lieutenant commander at the Naval Air Station, possibly sees the same plane.

It should not be there, Ramsey thinks, not at the moment of the little ceremony with which the U.S. Navy greets every day of the year: this must be some madcap U.S. pilot "flathatting," flying recklessly low, and he attempts to make out the plane's number. He does not see what falls from the aircraft before it pulls up and away. Then he hears an explosion, and suddenly understands.

The airplane they have been watching, Ramsey snaps to the duty officer at his side, is Japanese. Then he runs—it is no distance—to the radio room across the hall. He orders an immediate broadcast in plain English, eight words that will galvanize the nation:

AIRRAID ON PEARLHARBOR X THIS IS NO DRILL

At virtually the same moment, the reality dawns on others. At the changing of the guard at the Marine Barracks, a veteran sergeant tells his commanding officer, "Sir, those are Japanese war planes." The officer, realizing he is right, orders the bugler to sound the call to arms.

"Over near the dry dock," a Marine colonel will recall, "there is a terrific blast, and flames and smoke shoot hundreds of feet into the air . . . Men are stumbling out of the barracks, wide-eyed, dazed. Some are dressed. Some are lurching into pants and shorts on the run. Two or three are wrapped in towels.

"Someone screams: 'Get out of the building—take cover under the trees!' Someone else yells: 'Get inside! Get inside! They're gonna strafe!'" Bombs whistle to earth. There are thunderous explosions. "You can see the morning sunlight glisten on the bombs as they fall," the colonel remembers, "silvery flashes, like trout or mackerel jumping . . . A few stray machine guns begin to bark. A few riflemen aim their pieces skyward and let fly. God knows why."

Elsewhere, the atmosphere is surreal. Hastening to his post, a senior officer finds his workplace filled with church music. "The Japanese were bombing the hell out of things on the outside," he will recall, "and here is this officer's radio launching forth with 'Rock of Ages Cleft for Me' and 'What a Friend We Have in Jesus.'"

Many mistake the din outside for the noise of a training exercise. Players on golf courses are displeased. "Christ!" grouses an admiral. "Why doesn't anyone tell me anything around here? I didn't know we'd invited the Russians for fleet maneuvers." One disgruntled golfer exhorts the military to go play its war games elsewhere.

Some, though, are not disturbed at all. One Army wife will slumber on for hours. In his Honolulu hotel room, *Christian Science Monitor* correspondent Joseph Harsch wakes his wife to tell her sagely—he is a war correspondent—that the racket sounds like a "good imitation" of an air raid. Then they both doze off again.

In his quarters, Admiral Husband Kimmel, commander in chief of the Pacific Fleet, is very much awake. About twenty-five minutes earlier—at about 7:30 a.m.—a duty officer has phoned to report messages, from a destroyer and a patrolling plane, that a suspected Japanese submarine may have been sunk outside Pearl Harbor. Kimmel has said he will get right over to the office. Now, during a second call to the Admiral about the incident, the duty officer is interrupted. A yeoman has rushed into headquarters with news that Pearl Harbor is under attack.

Outside his house, waiting for the car that will rush him the two hundred yards to headquarters, the Admiral can only watch as Japanese aircraft pulverize his ships. To Navy wife Grace Earle, a neighbor, he looks "stricken, white as a sheet." Kimmel has understood at once, from the sheer number of aircraft involved, that this is no hit-and-run raid. It is, rather, "something terrible."

An air armada of more than 350 Japanese airplanes— dive-bombers, horizontal bombers, and swarms of fighters—is executing a bombardment that has been planned for a year, rehearsed for months. The purpose is to cripple the U.S. Pacific Fleet and remove it as a significant force for months to come, winning Japan time to impose its rule on Southeast Asia.

The punch is delivered with stunning effect. At the U.S. Navy and Army airfields, explosives rain down on airplanes, hangars, and living quarters. The eventual tally will be 169 aircraft destroyed and 159 damaged: the virtual obliteration of American airpower in the Hawaiian islands. The enemy achieves control of the skies, clearing the way for the devastation of the Pacific Fleet, the primary target.

A supply officer at the Navy Yard, working on his morning shave near a window, is jolted by the sight of "a plane with Rising Sun markings flying down the street at eye level, headed for Ten-Ten."

Ten-Ten Dock, so named because it was 1,010 feet long, offers a commanding view of Battleship Row, the home base for ships that have been the pride of the Navy for twenty years. There is the USS *Pennsylvania*, Admiral Kimmel's flagship; and there—in a line—are silhouetted the other battleships: *California*, *Oklahoma*, *Maryland*, *West Virginia*, *Tennessee*, *Nevada*, and—the leviathan that has become synonymous with horror—*Arizona*.

Dozens of other vessels, fighting and support ships alike, lie immobile around the harbor—easy prey. First to be hit, with two aerial torpedoes, is the training ship *Utah*, an old battleship that, ironically, the U.S. Navy has routinely used for target practice. The *Utah* herself matters little, but fifty-eight men on board are killed. Twenty men die on the cruiser USS *Helena*. None die on the minelayer *Oglala*, but she will eventually capsize.

Worst hit are the capital ships. USS *Pennsylvania*, which is in dry dock, is hit by two bombs. Eighteen men are killed and thirty injured. *California*, holed by two torpedoes and hit by two bombs, gradually sinks. Ninety-eight men are killed, fifty of them in the explosion of an ammunition magazine.

Twelve torpedoes strike the USS *Oklahoma*, the last and most destructive of them at main deck level. Lighting systems fail, leaving men below blundering around with flashlights. As the ship rolls upside down, some of those not trapped escape by sliding down the hull into the water. Crewmen who later cut into the hull with acetylene torches will succeed in extracting only thirty-two of their comrades. "We could hear tapping all through the ship, SOS taps, no voices, just those eerie taps," a would-be rescuer will recall. "There was nothing we could do for most of them. I still hear that tapping in my dreams." Four hundred and fifteen men will die.

USS *Maryland*, which has been shielded by the *Oklahoma*, is far more fortunate. Hit by two bombs, she floods but stays afloat—with the loss of only four men. Some *Oklahoma* survivors get aboard the *Maryland*, then help out on the antiaircraft guns.

USS *West Virginia*, affectionately known as the "Wee Vee," is struck by seven torpedoes and two bombs. She sinks until only her top deck shows above the water. One hundred and six men perish, including the captain. The *Tennessee* is hit by two bombs, neither of which fully explodes. She stays afloat, and there are no fatalities. The crewmen of the *Nevada*, hit by a torpedo and several bombs, manage to get her under way. When she is punished by further bombing, however, headquarters orders that she be run aground. Fifty crewmen die, and 109 are wounded.

It is the USS *Arizona* that will come to symbolize the catastrophe.

Of eight Japanese bombs that strike the battleship, just one seals its doom. About a thousand men are killed in the cataclysmic blast and the inferno that instantly follows. To a distant onlooker, the ensuing firestorm is a display—but for the result—of "the most beautiful piece of fireworks." The detonation of the *Arizona* ejects tons of debris skyward. "Legs, arms, and heads of men" rain down on a nearby vessel. Of the ship's company of 1,512, only 335 survive.

The *Arizona*, long a symbol of American sea power, settles gradually into the mud. Only the superstructure protrudes from the water, the flag at the stern still flying.

A worker at Dry Dock One recalls the scene. "Each of the great battleships is in agony. The *Arizona*, tilted at a crazy angle, amid oil clouds rising like thick black cauliflowers . . . only the cage-like top sections of the masts on the *West Virginia* and *Tennessee* visible through the roiling filth . . . The *California*, half-sunk, listing on one side in snapping fires." Of the capsized *Oklahoma*, all that can be seen is its underside, whale-like, in the muck.

It is "like looking into hell on a sunshiny day."

At headquarters onshore, Admiral Kimmel and his senior staff have the grandstand view. There is, an ensign will recall, "no panic, only a sense of helplessness and dismay." The Admiral paces back and forth, "shocked by the enormity of the thing" but "composed . . . cool and collected." He and another admiral are heard to agree, grimly, that the enemy's plan has been "very effectively executed."

At one point, told that his staff still has no idea where the attackers came from, Kimmel explodes in frustration. "Goddamn the intelligence! You don't even know if they're north or south? Chrissake!" He later apologizes for the outburst.

So close are the enemy planes that the watchers at headquarters can from time to time see an "exultant look on the faces of the Japanese pilots as they dive past our window. We worry about the Admiral exposing himself." They worry with good reason. Marine Colonel Omar Pfeiffer will recall the "slight ping as a spent and tumbling 50-caliber bullet breaks through the window glass and strikes Admiral Kimmel on the left breast, in the area where the service ribbons are usually worn."

But for a bruise on his chest—the Admiral has been protected by the eyeglass case in his uniform jacket pocket—Kimmel is unhurt. Glancing down at the bullet on the floor, according to communications officer Maurice Curts, Kimmel says quietly: "Too bad it didn't kill me."

Outside still, and for hours to come, the horror continues.

A mechanic: "There is a vast amount of fire. Sailors jumping off ships. Burning, so I guess they had to jump. Oil, thick, on the water."

A gunner's mate: "The oil from the *Arizona* kept coming . . . a sea of fire."

A Marine, one of the men swimming: "Bomb splashes nearby. Strafing in the water . . . feeling the impact of the bullets . . . confusion and noise . . . oil, bubbling up and congealing, a glob-like carpet about six inches thick, gelatinous . . . catching fire slowly and incinerating."

A quartermaster aboard the *Maryland:* "Some of them are burned. Guys are screaming for help, really pitiful. Some of the *Maryland* boys jump in after the *Oklahoma* boys. Risked their lives . . ."

A gunner on the *Arizona:* "Wounded lying all over the place. One man crawling around without any clothes on. They have all been burned off. He falls into the water. The water covered with oil, some of it on fire."

A man who later boarded the *Arizona*'s superstructure: "She burned for two-and-a-half days. A lot of these men burned right down to the deck. I could not stop the ashes blowing away." The skipper, Captain Franklin von Valkenburgh, is one of those who burn "right down to the deck." When it becomes possible to reach the superstructure, all that is left of him is his Naval Academy class ring.

Many of those in the water fare no better. A coxswain on the *Tennessee*: "I can still see those poor guys, in groups of four or five, blasted, burned, and butchered by shrapnel, being towed by launches and whatever small craft is available. The worst part was when a body started to disintegrate, and we would have to stop in the middle of a tow and re-lash."

The worker on Dry Dock One recalls mooring a launch that comes in filled with wounded men, slick with oil, hard to hold. "Two or three are quite still . . . I know one is dead . . . his head rolls from side to side against my chest. I can tell from the eyes of the sailor helping me that he, too, knows his shipmate is gone. We put the boy down gently among the wounded by the side of the road."

Someone covers the faces of the dead with caps or pieces of clothing.

The Navy, the Army, and the Red Cross have contingency plans for dealing with casualties. No one, however, could have planned for this.

A nurse—her duty this day has been on the maternity ward—will remember the carnage at just one military hospital. "Injured men lie on hospital litters up and down the hall, and it is all red. A bloody mess. A nurse goes down the line giving them all shots of morphine and marking a red M—for 'medicated'—on their foreheads. The ones that have broken legs and things that can't set, they send them over to surgery and they do amputations right away. Which is the wrong thing to do. They should be treated for shock first, but they didn't know that in those days.

"The people that are really hurt they put in a room away from the other fellows . . . I stay with them until they die and then fix the bed up for another patient. They are all young, good-looking kids. I notice that most of them have beautiful teeth. I am busy, but I am scared."

Another nurse at the same facility: "We work all day and night, thirty doctors and about thirty-five nurses. Dentists come over to help by administering anesthesia." There are not enough nurses, but there are ready volunteers—some of them not the volunteers one might expect. Marion Leary, an admiral's wife who has the previous night hosted a dinner at the Halekulani, rolls bandages at Red Cross HQ. From the other end of the social scale, it is said, several of the whores from the red-light district turn up to help.

Surgeons working on the mangled bodies run out of sterile packs and steam sterilizers. Instruments and gloves are boiled. "Clean" replaces "sterile." People line up to donate blood, but there is not enough.

There are terrible injuries. A medic, John Snyder, will remember: "Limbs just hanging, or so shattered there is no hope of saving them. In a room off one of the surgical suites, there are several large cans filled with arms and legs, placed there for disposal. Some of the arms still have wrist watches on the wrists and rings on the fingers."

A Red Cross worker with only a little training in first aid can do no more than "hold the hand of a dying man, give him a drink. Or help the wrought-up hospital corpsman wiping up blood from the floor, so no one will slip."

A priest will recall: "I take care of more than five hundred young men. Many of them I gently close their eyes in death, while some I have to leave, leaving this duty to others."

One of the "others" is Mary Ann Ramsey, daughter of the officer who just hours earlier sent out first word of the attack. Mary

Ann, who is only sixteen, has—with her mother—made her way to a makeshift shelter in an old gun emplacement.

Her first memory: "A young man, filthy black oil covering his burned, shredded flesh, walks in unaided. The skin hangs from his arms like scarlet ribbons as he staggers toward my mother for help. He gestures to his throat, trying to speak—he must have swallowed some of the burning oil. His light blue eyes against the whites, made more so by the oil clinging to his face, are luminous in visible shock at what they have seen and experienced. When I see that first sailor, so horribly burned, personal fear leaves me."

The teenager ministers to men who are dying. She holds a man in her arms, lights a cigarette for him. He takes a puff or two, heaves a sigh, and dies. She covers him up, then moves on to another wounded man.

The corpses of men who never make it to the hospital lie scattered near one of the huge Army barracks. A colonel grapples with the fact that many "have not only been killed but don't have their identification tags on. It is exceedingly difficult to figure out who these men are."

Most casualties are servicemen, but civilians have also suffered. A young reporter will recall getting "to where there's a real commotion, to a store that's been bombed at an open-air market. Some little kids are badly burned. One has a jump rope she's holding, but the rope is gone. And she dies. People don't know what is going to happen next."

American commanders fully expect the Japanese will now invade. Reports say Japanese forces are already storming ashore at Waikiki Beach, Diamond Head, and elsewhere. Enemy paratroopers are said to be landing. Local radio stations are ordered to go off the air for fear their transmissions may aid the attackers' navigation. Rumors fly that the water supply has been poisoned.

Martial law is declared across Hawaii, and Army commanding general Walter C. Short is named Military Governor. He and the top brass head to an underground shelter to direct the defense against the expected invasion. Buses carry some four hundred women and children, members of military families, to another vast cave under the rock.

Admiral Kimmel and his staff remain at their headquarters at Pearl Harbor. As night approaches, to comply with the blackout that has been ordered, the windows are painted black. Kimmel, who expects a further attack, remains at his post.

At nightfall, a motley fleet of buses and trucks starts evacuating some two thousand family members to the city of Honolulu— only to be bracketed by shells fired mistakenly, by American gunners, at friendly airplanes.

Sporadic shooting continues through the night. "The guards shoot at anything that moves," a nurse recalls. "They give us blue paper to cover our flashlights." Hospital staff are told to equip themselves with pocketknives "in case we are captured—to slit our wrists."

From a bus in the evacuation convoy, an Army wife looks back. Oil fires, still burning on the waters of Pearl Harbor, are backlighting the superstructures of half-sunken battleships. This, she thinks, is a scene out of Dante's *Inferno*.

"Look!" someone exclaims, "a moonbow!" There is tonight indeed a "moonbow," a sort of lunar rainbow, produced when the moon's light is refracted off moisture-laden clouds. In Hawaii, one of the few places on the planet where moonbows are seen, the phenomenon is said to be a sign of good luck.

This day, by the most authoritative count, 2,403 men—and a few women and children—have died.

Come the dawn at Pearl Harbor on December 8th, launches crisscross the water picking up bodies and body parts. In one of the morgues, medics swab oil from body parts and try to link them to named servicemen. Entries on the list they compile read: "Charred remains. No identifications. No personal belongings." And: "Badly mangled and decomposed remains. Identification impossible." For the doctors of 1941, the only reference points are fingerprints and dental records.

Six hundred of those who died in the water or on land remain unidentified. The unknown American dead will long lie buried, intermingled, at a cemetery called the Punchbowl, a volcanic crater high above the harbor. As of this writing, seventy-five years on, experts are using DNA profiling to try to put names to the remains and bring the families closure.

3

THE NEWS HAD reached Washington, five thousand miles to the east, shortly after 1:30 p.m.—five and a half hours ahead of Pearl Harbor time—on the 7th. Secretary of the Navy Frank Knox had been talking with Admiral Harold Stark, the Chief of Naval Operations, when an officer entered with a message. It was a printed copy of "AIRRAID ON PEARLHARBOR," the broadcast that had been transmitted from Hawaii minutes after the bombs began to fall.

For a moment, Knox could not believe what he was reading. "My God!" he exclaimed. "This can't be true. This must mean the Philippines." Stark, though, pointed out that the signal's origin was the office of CINCPAC—commander in chief Pacific Fleet—Admiral Kimmel's headquarters at Pearl Harbor. Knox picked up the phone and called the White House.

The President was lunching with his aide Harry Hopkins, but Knox insisted on being put through. Hopkins, like Knox, doubted that the news could be true. Roosevelt, however, thought such an attack "just the kind of unexpected thing the Japanese would do . . . If this report is true," he said, "it takes the matter entirely out of my hands."

In rapid sequence, the President phoned Secretary of State Cordell Hull and Secretary of War Henry Stimson—the latter was at home having lunch. At about the same time, at the War Department itself, an enlisted man handed a colonel a scrawled copy of the Navy's signal from Pearl Harbor. A call went out to General George Marshall, the Army chief of staff, who was also at home. He hurried to the office.

Within an hour of news of the attack, on Roosevelt's orders, a signal went out to all ships and stations. It read:

URGENT URGENT URGENT
EXECUTE WPL-46 AGAINST JAPAN

WPL-46 was the Navy's war plan, its blueprint for war.

Already, from his embattled HQ at Pearl Harbor, Admiral Kimmel had informed the Pacific Fleet that:

HOSTILITIES WITH JAPAN COMMENCED
WITH AIR RAID ON PEARL

The news started to break across the country, what fragmentary news there was in the first brief "flash" from the White House to the wire services. First reports gave no sense of the scale of the catastrophe. Most Americans heard of it first on the radio— television was still in its infancy. CBS had the story for the top of its weekend edition of *The World Today*. In New York, a WOR announcer broke into the coverage of a football game between the New York Giants and the Brooklyn Dodgers.*

In Washington, at the White House, the peaceful Sunday atmosphere dissolved. The uniformed guard was doubled; machine-gun crews were ordered to the roof. Outside, knots of people began to gather. Reporters streamed in. The pressroom would soon be crammed with newsmen fighting for phones, newsreel cameramen, and clutter. Actual news, detailed information, was scant.

Away from the press, the President's secretary Grace Tully fielded the stream of incoming calls, most of them from Chief of Naval Operations Stark. So many calls were there, so great the crush of people coming and going, that she eventually retreated to the phone in the President's bedroom. There, she made shorthand notes of incoming information, typed them up, then took them in to Roosevelt, the man White House and other senior staff called "the Boss."

She would remember the afternoon as one of "anguish and

---

* In 1941, there were football and baseball teams thus named.

near hysteria . . . I could hear the shocked unbelief in Admiral Stark's voice . . . At first the men around the President were incredulous; that changed to angry acceptance as new messages supported and amplified the previous ones. The Boss maintained greater outward calm than anybody else, but there was rage in his very calmness. With each new message, he shook his head grimly and tightened the expression of his mouth."

To Secretary of the Navy Knox, who also spent time with Roosevelt that afternoon, the President appeared "visibly shaken."

Sometime after 4:00 p.m. Washington time, British prime minister Winston Churchill came on the line from his country residence in England. He and his dinner guests, U.S. Ambassador John Winant and military aid coordinator Averell Harriman, had heard—without paying full attention—the tail end of a BBC radio bulletin reporting a Japanese attack on ships in Hawaii. What exactly had happened? Was the report true? Now, on the phone to Washington, Churchill received confirmation from the President himself. "It's quite true," Roosevelt said. "They have attacked us . . . We are all in the same boat now."

"This," the Prime Minister told the President, "certainly simplifies things." The United States and Britain now had a common cause—in the open. After the call, the Prime Minister would one day write, he and his American guests "tried to adjust our thoughts to the supreme world event which had occurred, which was of so startling a nature as to make even those who were near the centre gasp . . . We had no idea that any serious losses had been inflicted on the United States Navy."

Earlier, over dinner, Harriman had thought Churchill looked "tired and depressed . . . immersed in his thoughts, with his head in his hands part of the time." News of the attack on Pearl Harbor changed everything. Churchill would write in his diary: "So we had won after all . . . American blood flowed in my veins. I thought of a remark . . . that the United States is like 'a gigantic boiler. Once the fire is lighted under it there is no limit to the power it can generate.' . . . I went to bed and slept the sleep of the saved and thankful."

For Roosevelt, with the number of casualties and scale of destruction at Pearl Harbor ever clearer, there was no such comfort. "My God," he muttered around this time, "How did it happen? I will go down in disgrace." For him, hours of work still lay ahead. About 5 p.m., he called in secretary Grace Tully. Pulling on a cigarette, he said: "I'm going before Congress tomorrow. I'd like to dictate my message. It will be short."

The President spoke slowly, incisively, pointing up every punctuation mark:

Yesterday comma December 7 comma 1941 dash a date which will live in infamy dash the United States of America was suddenly and deliberately attacked by naval and air forces of the Empire of Japan period paragraph . . . I ask that the Congress declare that since the unprovoked and dastardly attack . . . comma a state of war has existed between the United States and the Japanese Empire period end.

Throughout the afternoon and early evening, Roosevelt had been getting situation reports from the Chief of Naval Operations. Stark, in turn, was receiving updates from Hawaii from Rear Admiral Claude Bloch, Commandant of the 14th Naval District and Admiral Kimmel's base defense officer. The news got worse with every call.

The President's son James, who went in to see his father, found him sitting alone in a corner of his study. Roosevelt did not look up, merely murmured, "It's bad, very bad." At 8:30 p.m., Cabinet members began gathering in the study, to be joined a while later by congressional leaders. So absorbed was the President by incoming calls and messages that he seemed at first barely to notice his advisers. "Most of the evening," Secretary of Labor Frances Perkins would recall, his face remained "tense and screwed up around the mouth. His upper lip pulled down and his lower lip sort of pulled in . . . quite gray."

Roosevelt opened by saying it was the most serious meeting

of the Cabinet since the start of the Civil War eighty years earlier. The Japanese attack had been an act "almost without parallel in relationships between nations."

Though reports were still confusing, he told his colleagues, numerous ships had been sunk at Pearl Harbor. Casualties were "extremely heavy." Pearl Harbor had not been the only target. The U.S. garrisons at Guam and Wake, islands thousands of miles to the west of Hawaii, had also been bombed. "We believe," the President added, "that Manila was attacked, but that has not proved true . . . Those are merely reports."

As would become clear within hours, the reports were true. Though news of the attack on Pearl Harbor had been known in the Philippines since half an hour after it began, although sporadic early Japanese attacks on Philippines targets had provided early warning, and though commanders had received Washington's order to implement war plans, the U.S. response to the main Japanese attack in the Philippines had been utterly ineffective. Japanese bombing had devastated the U.S. Army's Far East Air Force, ending America's control of the skies in the Philippines. Japan had also begun assaults against the British-administered territories of Malaya and Hong Kong.

The situation, Roosevelt told his audience, was "awfully serious . . . The fact is that the principal defense of the west coast of this country, the whole west coast of the Americas, has been very seriously damaged today." America must deal with a threat to its "national existence."

Already, within two hours of its attack on Pearl Harbor, Japan had declared a state of war with the United States and Britain. Now, when the President read his Cabinet the draft of the speech he planned to make to Congress, no one demurred. Nor did congressional leaders who joined the group. The United States was going to war, a conflict that in the Pacific theater alone would cost more than a hundred thousand American lives.

———

There was anger at the meeting in the White House, not all of it directed at the perfidious Japanese. The senators and congressmen listened to the President "in dead silence," Secretary of War Stimson would recall. Afterward, Chairman of the Senate Foreign Relations Committee Tom Connally exploded in frustration. Connally was a Democrat, a supporter of the United States' entering the war, but he could not accept what appeared to have been American incompetence at Pearl Harbor.

"Hell's fire!" he asked Roosevelt, "Didn't we do anything?" To which Roosevelt could only reply feebly, "That's about it." Connally then directed his ire at Secretary Knox, whose responsibility the Navy was: "Well, what did we do? . . . Didn't you say last month that we could lick the Japs in two weeks? Didn't you say our Navy was so well prepared and located that the Japanese couldn't hope to hurt us at all?

"Why did you have all the ships at Pearl Harbor crowded in the way you did? . . . And why did you have a log chain across the mouth of the entrance to Pearl Harbor, so that our ships could not get out?"

Connally was not finished. "They were supposed to be on the alert . . . I am amazed at the attack by Japan, but I am still more surprised at what happened to our Navy. They were all asleep."

Assumptions were already being made about the Navy's supposed failures, Secretary Perkins would recall. "Before we left that room," she would say, "we knew that most of the high Navy personnel were not on board ship. I got a feeling that it was humiliating for the President to have to acknowledge the fact that it was Sunday morning and the naval officers were otherwise occupied . . . His pride in the Navy was so terrific that he was having actual physical difficulty in getting out the words that bombs dropped on ships that were not in fighting shape and [not] prepared to move, just tied up.

"Roosevelt was having a dreadful time," Perkins thought, "just accepting the idea that the Navy could be caught off guard. However, at that time there were no recriminations. There was no thought of anybody being blamed for this. Naturally, people asked what Admiral Kimmel was doing."

There it was, the name of the man with overall responsibility for America's Pacific Fleet, the man who—with the Army's Hawaiian commander Lieutenant General Walter Short—would be at the center of a slew of investigations into the catastrophe. Even before the end of the meeting at the White House that Sunday night, it was agreed that Navy Secretary Knox would fly to Hawaii on an immediate fact-finding mission.

The recriminations began the day Knox set out, with a demand in Congress that Kimmel and others be tried by court-martial. The stream of blame and denial, accusation and rebuttal, claim and counterclaim, was to flow on until long after Admiral Kimmel would be dead and gone. It flows on still in the second decade of the twenty-first century.

The effluent from the stream, which has become central to it, is the suspicion of a greater evil. Book after book, article after article, has entertained the notion that President Roosevelt and some of those around him knew in advance that Pearl Harbor would be attacked, that they allowed the attack to happen, that they were party to the deaths and destruction of December 7th.

Speculations include the notion that high officials in Washington knew, before the attack, that Japanese warships were steaming toward Hawaii; that U.S. codebreakers had days earlier intercepted a message hidden in a Japanese weather bulletin, which signaled the coming break in relations; that British intelligence learned the attack was coming and sent America advance warning; that President Roosevelt and members of his government concealed a meeting they had held, far into the night, on the eve of the onslaught. Roosevelt, according to one allegation, ordered that no timely warning be sent to those defending Pearl Harbor.

Seventy-five years later, is there any evidence to support suspicions about the role of the thirty-second President, a leader revered by generations of Americans?

And was Admiral Kimmel a failed commander or a man cynically maligned?

America has wrangled over these questions for three-quarters of a century.

4

HUSBAND KIMMEL DID not much like to talk about himself in public. He was not one for grandstanding. Once, when asked by a reporter about his background, he would emphasize that it included "no dukes or high-falutin' ancestors, just plain everyday Americans—preachers, soldiers, tradesmen, farmers, miners." He allowed, however, that his family had included "some interesting folks, common and plain."

The first Kimmels—they were probably "Kümmels" when they got off the boat from Germany—settled in Pennsylvania 250 years ago. The Husband family, two female descendants of which were to marry a Kimmel, are said to have come earlier from England. The Admiral's great-great-grandfather, Herman Husband—though a Quaker and pacifist—was a leader of pre-Revolution insurgencies against the British over high taxes, notably those on whiskey. A biography of Husband characterized him as a "sort of modern John the Baptist, making straight the path for the patriots who later took the first step that became the war of the Revolution."

The Kimmel who married into the Husband family, a grandson of the earliest arrivals, operated a forge, produced cannonballs for the federal government, and became the first sheriff of Pennsylvania's Somerset County. His son, the Admiral's grandfather, operated flatboats and barges on the Ohio and Mississippi rivers, was elected to the Illinois legislature, and started what is said to have been one of the nation's earliest chain stores. His son Marius, who would father Admiral Kimmel, had a very colorful life.

After a false start at Princeton—Marius was expelled for breaking college regulations—he graduated from West Point and then began an extraordinary military career. Even today, almost two hundred years later, his descendants tell and retell stories of his experiences while fighting the Comanche. One story features a comic battlefield exchange between Marius—whose hat had been pierced by a bullet—and his friend Fitzhugh Lee, Robert E. Lee's nephew, who had been shot through by an arrow. (Lee lived to fight again, with distinction.)

During the Civil War, after having fought on the Union side in the defense of Washington and at the battle of Bull Run, Marius switched his allegiance to the Confederacy, saw combat in nine battles, and rose to the rank of major. When the Confederacy went down to defeat, and on hearing that West Pointers who had fought for the South were to be hanged, he fled to Mexico on horseback.

It soon became safe to return, and Marius's luck held. He came into twenty thousand dollars' worth of gold, a fortune at the time, which had been hidden away in the attic through the years of war. Wealthy now, Marius moved to Henderson, Kentucky, became superintendent of a coal mine, married, and had seven children. The future Admiral Husband Edward Kimmel was the fourth of those children.

He was born on February 26, 1882, just weeks after Franklin D. Roosevelt, whose actions as President—he would one day come to believe—were to destroy his glittering career. Though he was christened Husband, his grandmother's maiden name, virtually everyone found the name awkward. Most people addressed him as "Hubbie" or "Kim."

Home for the Kimmel youngsters was 512 North Green Street in Henderson, a rambling house set well back from the road, with large rooms that offered relief from the summer heat. Downstairs, portraits of past generations of Kimmels lined the walls. For the boys in the family, there was ample opportunity for horseback riding, boating on the Ohio River, and hunting. Their military father taught them how to handle guns.

Marius's offspring, four boys and three girls, were born over a period of twenty-one years, and their age differences meant Husband did not grow up really close to any of his siblings. Half a century on, when he found fame, his brother Singleton—twelve years his senior—would be the best source of information on his formative years.

Of all the children, Singleton said, Husband took his schooling most seriously. When he was nine, a surviving report card shows, his grades averaged 97 percent. At seventeen, he graduated as valedictorian of his small high school class. In the middle of his carefully prepared graduation speech, his brother would recall, he suddenly appeared lost for words. He had not forgotten his lines, he insisted afterward. It was just that he could not get the words out. Even then, he did not like public speaking.

Already in his mid-teens, Husband had a yen for detail. When Singleton became city engineer, his younger brother proved useful by drawing accurate site maps. "He always wanted to know the whys and wherefores of everything," his brother recalled. The characteristic he would recall most, though—far in the future, when Husband was promoted to four-star admiral—was his honesty. "He'll either tell you the truth about something or say nothing at all. There's no deceit in him."

That, and an insistence on digging for the facts were traits that one day, after his fall and fight back, would inspire respect in many and irritation in those who would rather the matter just go away.

Initially, as he approached adulthood, the young Kimmel did not hanker after a life as a seafarer. In his teens, captaincy of a small sailboat ended in capsize and a chilly immersion in the Ohio, followed by ignominious rescue. The expectation was that he would follow his father to West Point, but it could not take him at the time he applied. There was an opening at the Naval Academy at Annapolis, however, and a Henderson-born congressman made the necessary nomination.

So it was that, on May 21st, 1900, eighteen-year-old Husband Kimmel, Record No. 5015, joined the Navy. He and his contemporaries—"cadets" as they were still called then—faced four years of rigid discipline.

"Controlled by an iron hand of authority in every sector of his life," an historian has written, "the cadet was understood not to be an individual aspiring to naval service but as one *belonging* to the service . . . The overall and intentional effect of discipline was mastery over self . . . Self-mastery was the development in each cadet of a deep personal sense of honor. Reputation and a good name were paramount values . . . Cadets were taught to 'guard their own honor and the honor of the service.' Death should be preferable to dishonor."

The man who four decades later would be blamed for the debacle at Pearl Harbor, and then fight for the rest of his life to clear his name, would not forget the tenets of the Annapolis creed.

Kimmel emerged from the course four years later ranked thirteenth in a class of sixty-two, with qualifications equivalent to a bachelor of science degree. His entry in the class yearbook noted that he had been Brigade Adjutant and "the best type of greaser"—Academy lingo for an especially proficient cadet.

Also noted was that he was "intensely in earnest about everything. Sometimes gets mad, but is soon over it." Though "somewhat in the social line," the entry continued, he "couldn't stand the pace." Kimmel never would be one for much gallivanting. He looks solemn, determined, in a contemporary photograph.

"Beyond a doubt," the yearbook declared, the members of the class of 1904 "will all win glory and fame for themselves in the days to come." He and many of his contemporaries were bound for the top. "The Class the Stars Fell On" is the phrase usually used to characterize not Navy men but the West Point graduates of 1915. More than a third of that extraordinary class, which included Dwight Eisenhower and Omar Bradley, would go on to attain a general's stars. More loosely, the "Stars" label has been attached to the Navy officers who graduated around the time Husband Kimmel won his officer's sword.

Future admirals included Ernest King, five stars; Harold Stark, four stars; William Halsey, five stars; Chester Nimitz, five stars; Raymond Spruance, four stars; Richmond Kelly Turner, four stars; Thomas C. Kinkaid, four stars; and Husband Kimmel—

four stars until he forfeited them after Pearl Harbor. Kimmel was close to Stark, would be an usher at Halsey's wedding, and was to marry Kinkaid's sister.

In the words of the newspaper in Kimmel's hometown, his progress after graduation was like "a balloon . . . up, and up. And up."

At home in Henderson, Kimmel received his first orders:

SIR:
Proceed to New York, N.Y., and report to the Commandant of the Navy Yard at that place on July 2, 1904, for duty on board the USS KENTUCKY.

Respectfully. . . .

A posting to a battleship named for Kimmel's home state proved a happy coincidence. He discovered gunnery, gaining expertise in which he would become preeminent. He then served on a destroyer commanded by then Lieutenant Thomas Hart, who would be an admiral in the Pacific at the time of Pearl Harbor. "I never saw anyone better," Hart recalled of the Kimmel of those early days. "He was doing his job better and better all the time."

As an ensign, the man who did better served as an aide to the captain of a new battleship, the USS *Virginia*. The *Virginia*'s 1906 mission to Cuba, part of a U.S. operation to install a new government, earned him his first medal. At the end of the decade, when President Theodore Roosevelt sent a fleet of battleships on a show-the-flag mission around the world, Kimmel served on the staff of one of the admirals.

The ostensible purpose of sending out the warships, their bows painted in peacetime white, was to demonstrate America's international goodwill. Equally important, the voyage was to impress on foreign governments that the United States was now a major sea power. The message was intended not least—even at that early date—for the government of Japan.

The journal Kimmel kept during the fourteen-month trip has survived, a scrawled record that is sometimes serious, as often entertaining. It covers a 1908 visit the Fleet made to Hawaii—and Pearl Harbor:

> July 15
> Lat = 22–54 N
> Long = 154–54 W
>
> July 16
> Molokai . . . The fleet steamed in about eight miles from the beach and with glasses we could see the building and the people . . . On the land side the cliffs are sheer and absolutely impassable . . . When we passed, several balloons were sent up and the people seemed to be cheering etc . . . Honolulu . . . Left ship at 8:30 a.m. to go in parade . . . More or less a frost—too early in the morning for these people. Parade finished at 10:00 when all the best people, girls and matrons, met the brigade at the landing and distributed "leis" to all . . . The dance at Waikiki beach was a beauty . . . Met several attractive girls, among others a Miss Fisher, Miss Sturgeon, Miss Wilcox and others . . . Waikiki is certainly beautiful by moonlight.

A day or two later, Kimmel told his diary that the "charming" Miss Wilcox and a friend took him and a friend on a tour of the island. Before he left Hawaii, they would spend an evening dancing together.

The next day, July 21st, foreshadowed Kimmel's and this country's future:

> Left the ship at 9:30, taking a tug at the foot of the dock for Pearl Harbor . . . We saw the site of the new Naval Station that is to be built, work beginning immediately.

Everything continued to go right for Kimmel. The USS *Louisiana*'s gunnery officer considered him, his 1910 Fitness Record noted, "one of the best turret officers I have ever served with, and he handles men with marked ability. I have never been shipmates with a more capable watch, division, and battery officer."

It was as a lieutenant that in 1912, just before his thirtieth birthday, Kimmel returned to Annapolis—to get married. The wedding and the marriage that followed were Navy through and through. The bride, twenty-one-year-old Dorothy Kinkaid, was the daughter of a Navy captain. Her brother Thomas would in 1944, as an admiral, vanquish the Japanese in the Battle of Leyte Gulf, the largest naval engagement of World War II.

Dorothy was to bear her husband three sons, all themselves destined for the Navy, in a marriage that would last more than half a century. Kimmel, a fellow officer would say, "never looked at any woman except his wife." Like everyone else, and more so because she was his spouse, Dorothy had no use for that unwieldy first name "Husband." Not for her, however, the pet names "Hubbie" or "Kim." Dorothy always addressed her spouse as plain "Kimmel."

Like so many other Navy couples, they were to live through prolonged absences—and be beset by tragedy. On one early occasion, Kimmel himself narrowly escaped death.

5

IN AUGUST 1914, Lieutenant Kimmel sat on the deck of a U.S. cruiser, penning a note home:

> *This picture was taken immediately after I was shot . . . Several shots were fired . . . One passed between Evans and me. The next struck the stanchion just in front and particles splattered, wounding me twice in the right arm and once in each leg.*

The accompanying photograph, which has survived, shows Kimmel, seemingly unfazed, standing on deck in his bloodstained uniform. In 1914, as faraway Europe was becoming engulfed by World War I, neutral America was interceding—not for the first time—in a war in Mexico. During the Mexican revolution, following a coup in which the United States had a hand, U.S. Navy ships were stationed off the coast of Baja California. The overt purpose was to protect American citizens, but the mission also involved making sensitive contacts.

Kimmel, now an aide to the commander in chief in the Pacific, had been ashore for consultations with a key Mexican commander, at that time an ally of Pancho Villa. Sometime later, while heading back to his ship in a barge, he had come under fire from the shore and suffered minor wounds. The Mexican military faction friendly to the United States claimed afterward that the man believed to have shot at him had been executed. Kimmel did not quite believe that. "Quien sabe?"—"Who knows?"—he wrote in the note to his family.

The incident got the attention of Kimmel's admiral. Despite the gunfire, he wrote in a letter of commendation, "Lieutenant Kimmel remained at his post, keeping the commander in chief constantly in touch with the situation by radio." Kimmel had earned himself another medal.

By 1917, with the United States increasingly drawn into World War I, he had risen to lieutenant commander, a promotion coincident with his proven talent with heavy guns. Late that year, he crossed the Atlantic to brief British naval gunners on the latest thing in range finders, a device for "plotting fall of shot by triangulation cameras." The British adopted the system Kimmel had helped develop.

In the cold early morning of November 21st, 1918, Kimmel was present to witness the surrender of the German fleet off the coast of Scotland. He wrote home:

> *Everyone on all ships was at battle stations, for we were taking no chances. We sighted the first German battle cruiser, escorted by a British light cruiser, about 9:20. The other heavy ships came gradually out of the mist until we counted five battle cruisers and nine of the latest type battle ships. Away off down astern and out of sight until the haze lifted were eight light cruisers and fifty destroyers . . . To have such a force as this surrender without a fight has no parallel in naval annals . . . We had anticipated a meeting under quite different circumstances—with them shrouded in the smoke and flame of gunfire and our own guns answering in kind. To see this perfectly harmless lot come tamely in to surrender was a shock to all seagoing men.*

Kimmel's promotions continued as the years passed. In short order, he was elevated to commander, then captain. There was a Pacific posting, in the Philippines; command of a destroyer division in the Far East; and an attachment to the Army War College. He was, in the judgment of the Navy's most senior officer, then Chief of Naval Operations William Pratt, "a humdinger . . . I expect to see him get to the very top."

Kimmel, Pratt thought, was a "driver . . . does it all without antagonizing people." Available information suggests that both officers and men enjoyed working under him—not least because of his dry sense of humor. One young pilot recalled being mortified about having landed his seaplane too far from the ship for easy recovery. "The book," intoned Captain Kimmel as he came to the rail, "says the plane is supposed to come to the ship, not the other way round." One look established that he was grinning broadly— and the pilot's embarrassment was over.

A radioman aboard the same battleship, the USS *New York*, would not soon forget the night the alarm sounded when— because of the heat—he was sleeping out on the deck virtually naked. As he struggled into his uniform, a voice far above on the bridge roared, "Leave your damn clothes alone and get to your station!" The radioman craned his neck upward, saw that Captain Kimmel was himself in his underwear, and knew he was not in trouble.

Kimmel, who turned fifty-three in 1935, had mellowed. The long hard grind of his Navy career aside, what opportunities there had been for a family life had seen to that. Family was impor- tant to him. He had taken pains to write to his boys from their earliest childhood, and to insist that they write back to him. Two of them—Manning and Tom—were grown now. The youngest, Ned, was in his teens.

Four years earlier, twenty-two-year-old Manning had written home:

Dear Mother, Dad, Ned and Tom,

Yesterday we reported to the administration building and received our orders . . . We were then given a list of things to get at the midshipmen's store. I've never made so many trips upstairs in a day. Five flights carrying a seaman's bag . . . The company commander cussed us right and left for our appearance . . . At 4:15 we were sworn in. We're in the Navy now!

Love to you all,
MANNING

Manning had followed his father to Annapolis, graduated, became something of a tennis champion, and was soon to get married. Both he and his younger brother Tom, who also attended the Naval Academy, were later to command submarines. Ned, the baby of the family, would not go to the Academy but—come World War II—join the Navy and serve as an officer on an aircraft carrier.

Dorothy Kimmel remained the dutiful Navy wife and mother. "It is a wonderful promotion for Husband," she was to say on one of the occasions that he moved up a rank—for a reporter's benefit using the awkward first name she never used at home. "He is thrilled about it and so am I." She added, however, that it would mean moving again. The Kimmels did a lot of packing and unpacking.

During the early years of Franklin Roosevelt's presidency, Kimmel's final assignments came rapidly: in 1935, to chief of staff to the admiral commanding Battleships; to Navy budget officer, a stint behind a desk in Washington; then, in November 1937, at fifty-five years of age, an elevation to rear admiral. With two stars on his shoulder boards, he headed back to sea as commander, Heavy Cruiser Division 7.

A colleague who watched Kimmel during exercises in the Caribbean would recall his handling of a task force assigned to locate and repulse an "enemy" invasion fleet. "By superb maneuvering and employing a smoke screen, he completely surprised and foiled the opposing forces—and reached a position to annihilate the enemy convoy without losing a single ship."

In the spring of 1939, with Europe on the brink of war, Roosevelt acted to shore up the United States' relationships in Latin America. The USS *San Francisco*, Kimmel's flagship, steamed out of Cuba's Guantánamo Bay accompanied by two other heavy cruisers. Their stopovers in seven countries—replete with grand ceremonies, courtesies exchanged with presidents, galas, and banquets—were billed as "goodwill" visits, as during the cruise back in 1908. This too, though, reminded host nations of U.S. sea power.

The cruise was not all smiles and handshakes. Cape Horn, legendary for its savage storms, outdid itself. Kimmel drove his men to the limit, winning praise from one of his peers for inspiring his crews to have "supreme confidence in the Admiral's seamanship and tactical prowess." The overall handling of the cruise, Secretary of State Cordell Hull declared when it was over, had been "exemplary." A posting later that year to the Pacific as commander, Cruisers Battle Force, brought more plaudits.

"Fitness Report," March, 1940: "Exceptionally able, efficient, and zealous. Fully qualified for any duty. Highly recommended for assignment to higher command. Strong, forceful, aggressive . . . rare quality." In September 1940: "An outstanding officer of great promise for high command . . . Strongly recommended for advancement."

Kimmel was now close to the summit of command in the U.S. Navy. The decision to raise him to the summit was one President Roosevelt had to consider with care. For all the vast number of people he had encountered in the course of his career, Franklin Roosevelt had some reason to remember the Admiral. Two decades earlier, when Roosevelt had been Assistant Secretary of the Navy, young Lieutenant Kimmel had been seconded to act as his temporary aide during a two-week visit to the West Coast. Later, when Kimmel had been posted to England, they had met again.

Courtesy letters from presidents, it is said, are usually drafted by staff members. The letter Roosevelt had sent to a Kimmel cousin at the time of her relative's appointment as commander, Cruisers Battle Force Pacific, however, suggests a real personal interest.

My dear Mrs. Kimmel,
    I can well understand the feeling of just pride that must have prompted you to write. For a great many years I have followed the progressive steps of your cousin's service

career . . . [He has had] a splendid record during almost a lifetime of faithful service to our country . . . His record of service distinguishes that type of naval officer for whom there is always a need in positions of great responsibility . . .

Very sincerely yours,
FRANKLIN D. ROOSEVELT

Eighteen months later, the President took him to the pinnacle.

6

Franklin D. Roosevelt

President of the United States of America

To All Who Shall See These Presents

Greeting:

Know Ye, that reposing special Trust and Confidence in the Patriotism, Valor, Fidelity and Abilities of

HUSBAND E. KIMMEL

I have designated him as Commander in Chief Pacific Fleet and Commander in Chief U.S. Fleet with the rank of Admiral from the 1st day of February 1941 . . .
This designation to continue in force until he is detached from such command.

Done at the City of Washington . . .

By the President
FRANKLIN D. ROOSEVELT

The proclamation made Kimmel the most senior officer in the U.S. Navy, answering only to the Washington-based Chief of Naval Operations. He was now not only CINCPAC, commander in chief Pacific Fleet, but also CINCUS, titular commander in chief of the U.S. Fleet worldwide, an honorific that distinguished him from the admirals heading the Atlantic and Asiatic fleets. From two-star rear admiral, he had been promoted over forty-seven more senior officers.

Kimmel was now entitled to wear the coveted four stars of a full admiral; he was only the fifty-fourth officer ever to have been so designated.

Kimmel had been summoned from a Sunday afternoon golf game to be told of the promotion. Shown the order on the deck of the battleship USS *Pennsylvania*, he felt—he would recall—"perfectly stunned." His golf partner of half an hour earlier, Captain Walter DeLany, thought Kimmel was "going to faint."

Surprised though he was, he could guess how the promotion had come about. Months earlier, on a visit to Hawaii, Secretary of the Navy Knox had stayed aboard Kimmel's flagship for several days. Having watched him direct maneuvers at sea, and having sounded him out on naval issues, Knox had been very favorably impressed. The Secretary's approval, however, was not the full explanation.

The President himself had a role in the decision. As CNO Harold Stark told Kimmel in a letter, the final decision on high-level appointments was always made at the White House. When Knox and Stark submitted Kimmel's name to him, Roosevelt had exclaimed: "Of course! Why didn't I think of him?" When he announced the promotion, Roosevelt praised Kimmel as "one of the greatest naval strategists of our time."

Kimmel's peers wholeheartedly approved. Then–Rear Admiral Chester Nimitz, the future victor of the war in the Pacific, was to say he too had recommended Kimmel for the job. There was not a flag officer in the Pacific, according to then–Vice Admiral William Halsey, whose achievements at Guadalcanal and the Battle of Leyte Gulf were to make him a legend, who did not "feel that Kimmel was an ideal man for the job."

The opinion of "the entire Navy," CNO Stark told Army Chief of Staff Marshall, was that Kimmel was "outstanding in his qualifications for command." The fact that war was likely, Stark wrote to Kimmel, was one reason "why I am thankful that I have your calm judgment, your imagination, your courage, your guts, and your good head, at the seagoing end. Also your CAN DO—rather than CAN'T . . . Good luck and God Bless You."

Stark and the new commander in the Pacific went way back. Their years at the Naval Academy had overlapped—he was Kimmel's senior by eighteen months. Stark's appointment as Chief of Naval Operations had advanced him, like Kimmel, over dozens of higher-ranking admirals. Stark's biographer would characterize him as a "first-rate seagoing sailor," a "skillful and competent administrator," and an "effective Navy representative before Congress," a man imbued with "modesty, kindness, consideration for others, and a great capacity for hard work." Officers who served under him praised what they deemed his "honesty" and "integrity." Stark worked on weekends and through holidays, sometimes until long after midnight.

Others had reservations. "Stark cannot be said to be the 'strongest' man," thought Admiral William Pratt, one of his predecessors as CNO. According to future Rear Admiral James Shoemaker, "It was the general opinion in the Navy at the time that Stark was a weak sister." His own aide, then–Lieutenant Commander William Smedberg, would say of Stark that he had been "a dear old man and I loved him very much, but he was not the man that I would have chosen as Chief of Naval Operations."

Stark's relationships with Secretary of the Navy Knox and with President Roosevelt were unusually close. Secretary of War Stimson, though, rated him "the weakest" of the President's advisers, "a little bit timid and cautious when it comes to a real crisis."

Like many of his peers, Kimmel addressed the CNO by his old Annapolis nickname "Betty"—an abstruse, somewhat inaccurate reference to the wife of a long-dead namesake, an army general of Revolutionary War days. Stark, for his part, often called Kimmel "Mustapha" because of a similarity between the name Kimmel and that of Mustafa Kemal, the founder of modern Turkey.

The new commander in chief was installed with great ceremony, more in line with British than American tradition. Brass bands played aboard the *Pennsylvania*, the "Grand Old Lady of the Fleet." Some 1,600 officers and crew members lined the deck, resplendent in white uniforms. The commanders of the many other warships in port, gold-braided admirals and captains, stood at attention on the quarterdeck.

To the shrilling of boatswains' whistles, Kimmel and his predecessor, Admiral James O. "Joe" Richardson, arrived aboard separate barges. There was a ruffle on the drums as they saluted Old Glory. Admiral Richardson spoke of the way ahead under his successor, extolled him as "a forthright man, an officer of marked ability and a successor of whom I am proud." For a brief moment, as Richardson's flag was lowered, no one was in command of the Fleet.

Admiral Kimmel spoke briefly, standing beneath the massive barrels of one of the battleship's gun turrets. "In light of what we all know," he noted, "the days ahead will be busy ones." Then, with the raising of a new four-star flag, the ceremony was over.

The handover had been broadcast on the radio, and there was major press coverage. The new commander, the Associated Press noted, was "5 feet 10, about 180 pounds; his hair is graying, his eyes are light blue . . . He swears like a trooper, according to his friends, when he gets mad . . . When he smokes, it's a cigarette. When he drinks, which is seldom, it's an Old Fashioned or a whiskey and soda. He is a man of few hobbies. He eats, sleeps and talks Navy, morning noon and night."

At fifty-eight, AP noted, Kimmel was "one of the youngest Fleet commanders in the history of our Navy . . . as modern as an anti-aircraft gun." He was "one of the first top men of the Navy to drill his men in anti-aircraft defense . . . wants more anti-aircraft guns on his ships . . . wants more airplanes, better aircraft carriers." He would get them, too, the AP correspondent wrote, "because he is a driver, and what he goes after he gets."

Things were not to turn out that way. In the weeks before the ceremony aboard the USS *Pennsylvania*, the new admiral had conferred at length with his predecessor. Richardson had from the start been unhappy that the Fleet was at Pearl Harbor at all.

———

Pearl's shamrock-shaped anchorage, though often called the "Gibraltar of the Pacific," had its deficiencies. So narrow was the entrance from the sea that large warships could arrive or exit only in vulnerable single file. It had long been used principally as a refueling and repair facility and submarine base. The Fleet's home since the end of World War I had been the harbors at Long Beach and San Pedro, in California. In late 1939, however, a number of warships had been dispatched to Hawaii for what was officially categorized as "training." To Richardson, this had been mere "double talk."

Then, in the spring of 1940, not long after Richardson had been appointed commander in chief, the Fleet proper had sailed for Hawaii on maneuvers. Little knowing that it was there to stay, Richardson took to asking repeatedly when his ships would be returning to California, where their support systems were. Washington only prevaricated. Then, on May 9th, he was told to issue a statement in his own name saying that he had asked to remain in Hawaii for some undefined purpose of his own. The statement was "phony" and looked it, Richardson would say much later. It had made him look like a "nitwit."

Though signed by CNO Stark, the messages keeping the Fleet at Pearl had been sent at the direction of President Roosevelt. The hope was that the ships' presence there would deter new Japanese military adventures in the Pacific. Richardson demurred, arguing that, cut off from its backup resources two thousand miles away on the U.S. West Coast, his force was inadequately equipped and geographically ill placed.

Twice in 1940, Kimmel's predecessor had taken his concerns to Washington and to the President in person. On the second occasion, in late fall, he delivered an audacious broadside that he had prepared in advance. "Mr. President," he was to recall saying, "I feel that I must tell you that the senior officers of the Navy do not have the trust and confidence in the civilian leadership of this country that is essential for the successful prosecution of a war in the Pacific." Roosevelt's response, not long afterward, was reportedly to phone CNO Stark and tell him: "Get rid of Richardson."

The commander in chief had been summarily fired, but he did not bleat about it. He had understood from the time of his appointment, he said privately, that it came to him "by the arbitrary power of one man, and I have always realized that I could be removed in the same way at any time." He intended, he said, to keep his mouth shut and "loyally pull my oar."

In late January 1941, an emissary from CNO Stark's office in Washington came to confer with the outgoing CINCUS and his replacement. This was Commander John McCrea, delivering the documentation for a crucial new U.S. war plan.

McCrea's journey to the Pacific had been cloak-and-dagger. "At night," he would recall, "I put the war plans under my mattress. I took them to the bathroom with me when I went to shave in the morning." The material he was carrying was the result of weeks of work by Admiral Stark and intense discussions with high officials, including President Roosevelt.

Military historians have rated the plan as perhaps the most important strategy document of World War II. At issue was how, given the prospect of confronting foes in both Europe and the Pacific, U.S. forces would conduct the coming conflict. Stark had come up with four options, plans A, B, C, and D, and D had been selected. "D" is rendered as "Dog" in the military radio alphabet, so it became known as Plan Dog.

Plan Dog envisaged that U.S. interests would best be served by a strong offensive posture in the Atlantic theater to confront Germany, the most serious potential threat. The strategy for dealing with Japan, which was perceived as a secondary threat, was to be essentially defensive—a deterrent.

A key element in the plan was to do everything possible to ensure that Britain remained undefeated and engaged in the conflict. Whatever could be done to ensure that, however, had to be handled with great sensitivity. Opposition to United States' participation in the war, voiced persistently by isolationist politicians and press, made even arm's-length involvement a very delicate matter. It was agreed that the American military would discuss military cooperation, secretly, with Britain and her allies.

Adopting Plan Dog, however, meant rethinking the existing war plan, which had been framed on the premise that U.S. military muscle would primarily be used to destroy Japan's forces in the Pacific. The Navy's role in the revised plan, Rainbow 5, envisaged restraining Japan by using the Fleet—operating out of Pearl Harbor—as a bulwark against Japanese aggression.

There was a problem. Admirals Richardson and Kimmel knew it, and CNO Stark knew it. In a letter to Richardson before he was replaced, Stark had expressed his concern about a possible "sudden attack in Hawaiian waters," and asked Richardson "what steps the Navy Department and the War Department should be taking to provide additional equipment and additional protective measures."

Shortly before handing command over to Kimmel, Richardson wrote to Stark saying he thought that—if Pearl Harbor were to be more secure—there would have to be increased airborne patrols and augmented antiaircraft defenses. That would involve allocating Navy assets to assist the Army, whose mission it was to defend Pearl Harbor. The Fleet, however, was already "severely handicapped" by "marked deficiencies."

He listed them:

- "The critical inadequacy of A.A. [antiaircraft] guns available for the defense of Pearl Harbor, necessitating constant manning of ships' A.A. guns while in port." Doing that on a permanent basis, Richardson wrote, was not practical.
- "The small number and obsolescent condition of land-based aircraft, necessitating constant readiness" of Fleet planes both for strikes and for local patrol missions.
- "Lack of suitable local defense vessels," requiring diversion of Fleet ships from other duties.
- "Lack of aircraft detection devices ashore."

"Immediate measures" should be taken, Richardson wrote, to put the situation right.

In a letter congratulating Kimmel on his new command, Stark
made clear his conviction that war was indeed coming. "I have
told the Gang here for months past," he wrote from Washington,
"that in my opinion we were heading straight for this war . . . It
may be a matter of weeks or days . . . We may become involved
in the Pacific and in the Atlantic at the same time; and to put it
mildly, it will be one H . . . of a job."

Kimmel replied, summarizing some of the reasons it would
indeed be a hell of a job, and made it clear that he agreed with
Richardson. It was of "paramount importance" that Pearl Harbor
be secure, Kimmel said, and he deplored the Army's lack of equipment to defend it effectively.

The lamentable situation had also been spelled out to Stark
by Rear Admiral Claude Bloch. Bloch was the Navy commander
responsible for the Hawaiian coastline, outlying islands—and
the base at Pearl Harbor. As Kimmel's "base defense officer," he
was—with the Army—responsible for the protection of the base.
The Army had no planes for distant reconnaissance, and those
pursuit planes and bombers it had were obsolete. Many more antiaircraft guns, up to perhaps five hundred such weapons, would be
required to provide "any semblance of defense" for Pearl Harbor.
He hoped the War Department was "proceeding vigorously" to
improve the situation.

From headquarters, Stark assured Kimmel that he was doing
all he could. Pressure had been brought to bear on the Army, he
reported, and Chief of Staff Marshall was prepared to "go to almost any length possible" to help the Navy out. In a postscript,
though, Stark pointed out that resolving some issues would take
time and that "dollars cannot buy yesterday."

That was the truth behind the to-and-fro. Kimmel could ask, but
Washington was unable to oblige. In a letter to the Army commander who took over the military's role in Hawaii that same
month, General Walter Short, Marshall defined the Army's primary mission: "The fullest protection for the Fleet is THE, rather

than A, major consideration for us." On the other hand, he was not encouraging about the Navy's requests for airplanes and antiaircraft guns. "What Kimmel does not realize," he observed, "is that we are tragically lacking in this matériel . . . We cannot perform a miracle."

Responding to the concerns coming out of Hawaii, Stark had approved a letter for Navy Secretary Knox to send to War Secretary Stimson. It was essential, Knox urged, that Stimson take every step to "increase the joint readiness of the Army and Navy to withstand a raid." A copy of the letter went to Admiral Kimmel, and Stark added a formal note of his own. In light of the "inadequacy of the Army defences," he wrote, the Fleet had a responsibility "for its own protection." That said, Kimmel should "constantly press" General Short to make all possible improvements.

In his letter to the Secretary of War, Knox wrote: "If war eventuates with Japan, it is believed easily possible that hostilities would be initiated by a surprise attack upon the Fleet or the Naval Base at Pearl Harbor." Written as it was ten months before the Japanese onslaught, Knox's letter was prophetic. It should not, however, have come as a revelation. The concept of an attack on Pearl Harbor was not new at all.

The Navy had run exercises based on that possibility for more than a decade—time after time, and long before the presence of the U.S. Fleet made Pearl Harbor an especially tempting target. In war games in 1932, "enemy" airplanes launched from carriers had swooped in at daybreak on a Sunday morning, just as the Japanese would in 1941. "We caught them completely off-guard," an officer with the mock "attacking force" would recall, although "they were supposed to be ready for anything."

The result had been the same four years earlier, in 1928, and would be again in 1933 and 1937. In short, the surprise "attack" in the exercises invariably succeeded, even when it did not come as much of a surprise at all. Everyone, moreover, knew the identity of the potential enemy.

Four thousand miles to the west, Japanese military men had long nurtured dreams of victory over America in the Pacific.

7

THIRTY YEARS BEFORE Admiral Kimmel was installed as commander in chief, Pacific, a thirty-year-old U.S. Army officer named William Mitchell had gone to Japan undercover to collect information on Japanese military activities. He reported on his return that Japan had expansionist ambitions and would at some point go to war with the United States. Defense of American territories in the Pacific, he wrote, should be greatly increased. Mitchell's 1911 report to the War College went nowhere—Congress lacked the will to spend the necessary money.

In 1923 Mitchell, by now a senior officer, returned to the Far East on his honeymoon, an interlude that covered for a further intelligence mission. The 323-page report he submitted on his return repeated his earlier view with emphasis. Japan, he wrote, "knows war with the United States is coming some day."

That war, Mitchell predicted, would start with a surprise attack, first on Pearl Harbor, then the Philippines. The attack would be launched as follows:

> Bombardment, attack to be made on Ford Island [where the Naval Air Station would be in 1941] at 7:30 a.m. . . . Attack to be made on Clark Field [in the Philippines] at 10:40 a.m.

His details were wrong, but Mitchell was chillingly prescient. He even foresaw that aerial torpedoes would be used in the future attack on Pearl Harbor. The year after his report, joint Army and Navy exercises showed that Hawaii's defenses were indeed inadequate. Again, however, no effective action was taken.

Mitchell, already a controversial figure, was later demoted and court-martialed for insubordination after publicly having accused officialdom of "criminal negligence" in relation to aviation safety; he then resigned.

Once, as Assistant Secretary of the Navy, Franklin Roosevelt had dismissed Mitchell's views on aviation matters as "pernicious." As President, after Pearl Harbor, he would call for Mitchell's posthumous promotion to two-star major general. Some regard Mitchell as the father of the U.S. Air Force.

Mitchell's prophetic 1923 report was not a public document. Already, though, a former British naval spy had come to similar conclusions and made them public. In a nonfiction book, Hector Bywater predicted a Japanese-American war at sea. Bywater is said then to have argued publicly with Assistant Secretary of the Navy Roosevelt, who at the time thought such a war unlikely. It was to "get in the last word," Bywater said, that he wrote a further book, a novel titled *The Great Pacific War*.

The novel, so filled with naval and military jargon that it reads like nonfiction, chronicles the complete destruction of a U.S. naval force—though in the Philippines rather than Hawaii. In the story, as would occur in 1941, the Japanese attack involves planes launched from aircraft carriers. In Hawaii, there is naval action and severe fighting around Pearl Harbor.

Bywater's earlier, nonfiction book attracted attention in an intriguing quarter. The Japanese General Staff arranged for it to be translated for distribution to senior officers. The second book, the novel, appeared at a time when an ambitious Japanese navy captain named Isoroku Yamamoto was serving in Washington as a naval attaché. He and Bywater attended the same naval conferences, and dined together on at least one occasion. Later, when Yamamoto delivered a lecture in Japan, he cited Bywater's ideas.

By January 1941, when Admiral Kimmel and his colleagues were trading letters on the vexing matter of the defense of Pearl Harbor, Yamamoto had been commander in chief of the Japanese Combined Fleet for a year and a half. On the 7th, in his cabin aboard his flagship, Yamamoto took brush in hand—a writing brush was routinely used for formal correspondence at that time—to compose a letter to the minister in charge of his country's navy. The way to win the coming war with the United States, he proposed, was to start by destroying the U.S. Pacific Fleet in a surprise preemptive strike on Pearl Harbor.

In the margin of the letter, Yamamoto wrote: "Minister's eyes only. To be burned. No circulation." Japanese security, however, may have been less than perfect. In the months leading up to the attack on Pearl Harbor, U.S. intelligence—like any intelligence service in any era—was confronted daily with a surfeit of information. Much of it may have been worthless, chaff blown on the wind of rumor. Some, though potentially of high value, was discarded.

In a sense, Japan's ambitions were an open book, literally so. The year 1940 saw publication of *Nichi-Bei Sen Chikashi,* which translated prosaically as *Japan–United States War Imminent,* by a Japanese lieutenant general, Kiyokatsu Sato. "In a war with the United States," Sato declared, "we must at all costs, even with the sacrifice of a few ships, take possession of Hawaii . . . The struggle for Hawaii constitutes the first stage."

His book received coverage in the U.S. press, though with a comforting reminder that the author "now has no official connection with the Japanese government or army." So far as one can see, there was no reporting at the time of the fact that there had long been a stream of novels, and what one historian has described as "penny thrillers," on the theme of a war to restore Japanese national honor—a war Japan always won.

Many Americans, meanwhile, may have bought the misleading concept that "Japs" or "Nips" belonged to an inferior race. Cartoons sometimes depicted them as having exaggeratedly slanty eyes and monkey-like faces. According to the head of the Far East section of U.S. Naval Intelligence, Commander Arthur McCollum, even some people in ONI had the deluded notion that the Japanese were no good at making war. "The problem that was constantly facing ONI," he recalled, "was the lack of knowledge on the part of our own people," the idea fostered by the press that, "'They're funny little people, they can't march and they can't work.' . . . Actually, at this time that we're talking about now, in 1940, Japanese armies had overrun any part of China they wanted to." Some in Naval Intelligence, McCollum went on, made the same mistake about Japanese pilots. "Anytime that we would send out something that said how good they were, we would get a storm of, I wouldn't say abuse, but . . ."

Nothing indicates that ideas of racial superiority influenced U.S. policy and strategic planning. Navy and Army intelligence officers, and many at the FBI, however, would have reason to rue one particular judgment call they made at this time.

On January 8th, 1941, the day after Admiral Yamamoto wrote his letter recommending a strike on Pearl Harbor, a Korean-born émigré, Kilsoo Haan, wrote a letter to President Roosevelt. Koreans had suffered terribly under decades of Japanese rule, and Haan now devoted his life to anti-Japanese activism. His letter to the President, he said, was motivated by his knowledge of a "war plan" book suggesting that, during peace talks with the United States, Japan intended to carry out a "surprise attack upon Pearl Harbor, Hawaii."

This latest book, which bore the ponderous title *The Triple Alliance and the Japan-America War*, had appeared in Japan three months earlier. Its author, Kinoaki Matsuo, has been described as an "intelligence officer" who functioned as liaison between the Japanese Navy and the foreign ministry. He was also a "high official" in an ultranationalist organization called Kokuryukai, a name usually translated as the Black Dragon Society. Its membership had links to Tokyo's political and military elite.

The "Triple Alliance" of the book's title referred to the recent pact between Japan, Germany, and Mussolini's Italy calling for a "new order of things." Matsuo's book exulted in the notion of "our naval flags, symbolic of the Rising Sun and of the Number 1 country of the world . . . fluttering over the Pacific, and submarines and pocket battleships flying the Hitler Swastika rampant over the Atlantic, [along with] the Italian colors of green, white and red." The book was a rambling mix of triumphalist bombast and evident naval knowledge.

Japan's destruction of U.S. naval power, Matsuo wrote, would include forcing the closure of the Panama Canal, to prevent American reinforcement of either ocean; invasion of the Philippines and other strategic islands; and—at Pearl Harbor—"an attack by the Japanese surprise-attack fleet."

According to a later assessment by the Un-American Activities Committee of the U.S. Congress, circulation of the book outside Japan was initially limited to "only the most trusted" pro-Japan activists within the United States. This was a propaganda tool, used to motivate such activists.

Eleven months before Pearl Harbor, when Korean émigré Haan first wrote to President Roosevelt, he received a predictable response. An aide reported, as government aides often typically do report, that Haan's suggestions had been "brought to the attention of the proper authorities in the defense organization."

Over the months that followed, Haan was to fire off letters to government officials, Naval and Army Intelligence, and members of Congress. Like the White House aide before him, Navy Secretary Knox sent a courteous reply. His department had heard from Haan before. "Some of your facts and predictions have indeed been borne out by the passage of time," Knox wrote in April. "I assure you that the information you have given us has always been highly appreciated."

What was Haan's background? The paper record shows that his parents had brought him to Hawaii as a child in 1905, when Japan tightened its grip on Korea. As an adult, he had served with the Hawaii National Guard before eventually becoming active with Korean exile political groups. In his late thirties, he had headed for Washington as a representative of one of the groups.

The FBI version of Haan's career, however, suggests he also had a shady side. While working as a real estate salesman, an agent reported, Haan had had his license revoked for obtaining money on false pretenses. FBI reports portrayed him as a "smooth talker," probably "a confidence man." As to his dire warnings about Japanese war plans, Haan had been merely "shooting his mouth off."

The FBI's dismissive attitude may be explained by something Haan mentioned during an interview with its agents. He had tried years earlier to bring information to the FBI, Haan said, but been "brushed off." After Pearl Harbor, when his warning of a Japanese attack had been proved right, it may have seemed expedient to paint him as unreliable.

An FBI agent reported having learned that Haan "had been making a practice in Honolulu of impersonating an officer of the military intelligence department . . . stating that he was engaged in confidential missions for military intelligence." Checks with Army and Naval Intelligence, a source said, gave the impression that Haan was "more or less persona non grata." All of this put Haan in a bad light, but it seems not to have been the whole story.

Years later, Haan named an officer, "Byron Meurlott . . . [of] U.S. Military Intelligence of Fort Shafter, Honolulu," with whom he said he had "many years of association." Meurlott was indeed a senior officer in G-2 in 1941, and his unit looked into the "war plan" book that Haan had obtained. Haan was to use a copy of a letter from Meurlott to help in establishing his own credentials.

Another clue to Haan's involvement with Army Intelligence comes from Senator Guy Gillette of Iowa. Gillette served on the Senate Foreign Relations Committee and the Naval Affairs Committee. The Senator would say after Pearl Harbor that—by late summer 1941—he had "understood" that "Haan was employed by the military officials as an informant." Army officials had indicated, however, that "they could not continue their association with him" once he began speaking out publicly. To distance itself from an operative once he becomes an embarrassment, an intelligence organization will often disown him. Hence, perhaps, the claim in the FBI file that Haan had become "persona non grata" with U.S. Intelligence.

For more than two years in the late 1930s, Haan was to say, he had been "placed" in a job at Japan's consulate in Hawaii. Even then, long before the Pearl Harbor attack, he said, the consular staff had acquired "blueprints and detailed technical information" on U.S. construction work at the Pearl Harbor naval base.

There seems, too, to have been more to Haan's acquisition of the book *Triple Alliance*, with its clues to current Japanese intentions. Haan "stole" it, he said, during a visit by two Japanese officers to California to cultivate pro-Japanese sympathizers. He named the officers—a Navy captain, Otojiro Endo; and an Army major, Masaichi Sujihara—and said he purloined several copies of *Triple Alliance* from one of them when he was staying at the Olympic Hotel in Los Angeles. Haan had done this, he said, "at risk of his life" following a meeting with the two officers. His overall operation, this suggests, had been mounted not merely to snatch a book but to acquire information.

Warned by Haan in the summer of 1941 about "the possibility of a Japanese invasion of the Hawaiian Islands and the West Coast," Senator Gillette was to deliver the book to the State Department. He got the impression, he said later, that State had "not translated the book or taken any action."

Haan himself would contact the State Department repeatedly. In a communication in late October, one he copied to both Secretary of State Hull and Secretary of War Stimson, he said he had learned from his "agent . . . in the Orient" that, according to a former high Japanese official and others, December 1941—or February 1942—had been decided on as the optimum date to start war with the United States.

At the State Department in fall 1941, special adviser Stanley Hornbeck did not dismiss Haan's warning. "In evaluating information given by Mr. Haan," he wrote to Secretary of State Hull, "we must take into account the fact that Haan is a Korean, a bitter enemy of Japan . . . At the same time, the Koreans do have certain contacts in Japan . . . Mr. Haan has from time to time furnished our military intelligence with information which proved authentic and also of value. We cannot dismiss Haan or information given by him."

There is no evidence, however, that anyone in the government took any action. Haan, who felt he was being ignored, tried to alert the press. The CBS newsman Eric Sevareid recalled that Haan "would often drop into my Washington office. He was in touch with the anti-Japanese Korean underground. 'Pearl Harbor,' he kept telling me, 'before Christmas.' He could get no audience at the State Department." Haan, Sevareid was to say, "always ended up seeing very minor officials who took a very minor view of his warnings."

In early October 1941, Senator Gillette would introduce a resolution calling for an investigation into "the activities of Japanese consular officials in Hawaii," but he was persuaded not to proceed; Secretary of State Hull asked him not to "rock the boat" while negotiations with Japan were continuing.

According to Gillette's nephew Thomas, citing his uncle, that was not the end of it. In late November, Haan made contact again—to warn that Japanese warships had left port "under battle orders . . . to attack Pearl Harbor or the Panama Canal." The Senator had been sufficiently concerned, he told his nephew, to make an appointment to see the President. Roosevelt had told him the matter would be followed up.

There is no record of such a meeting with Gillette in the President's appointment books—but that does not necessarily mean that it did not take place. A senior archivist at the Roosevelt Library told the authors that the President often had off-the-record meetings that were not recorded.

Whatever the truth about Haan's claims and Gillette's follow-up, the first warning of an attack on Pearl Harbor had been received in Washington as early as January 1941. It had come not from an exile with an anti-Japanese ax to grind but from the government's own man in Tokyo. It was wasted.

8

ON JANUARY 27TH, 1941, the U.S. ambassador to Japan, Joseph Grew, sent this telegram to Washington:

> *Tokyo*
> *Dated, January 27, 1941*
> *Rec'd. 6:38 a.m.*
>
> *KD*
> *This telegram must be closely paraphrased before being communicated to anyone. (D)*
>
> *Secretary of State,*
> *Washington.*
>
> *125, January 27, 6 p.m.*
> *My Peruvian Colleague told a member of my Staff that he had heard from many sources including a Japanese source that the Japanese military forces planned, in the event of trouble with the United States, to attempt a surprise mass attack on Pearl Harbor using all of their military facilities. He added that although the project seemed fantastic the fact that he had heard it from many sources prompted him to pass on the information.*
>
> GREW

Ambassador Grew had served in Tokyo for the previous nine years. His diary entry for the day he sent the above telegram, published later in a memoir, reads:

> There is a lot of talk around town to the effect that the Japanese, in case of a break with the United States, are plan-

ning to go all-out in a surprise attack on Pearl Harbor . . . Of course, I informed our Government . . . I rather guess that the boys in Hawaii are not precisely asleep.

In the mid-1940s, asked about the telegram in the course of the Pearl Harbor investigations, Grew said the information about a coming attack reached him as "a rumor." It had come from "the Peruvian Minister in Tokyo," a "close personal friend" whom he had known for years, who had his "full confidence." Grew passed the word to the Secretary of State, he said, because he thought it "of such utmost importance." The second time Ambassador Grew testified, however, he stated that the information had reached him, not directly from the Peruvian minister, but secondhand, passed on by an unnamed member of the American embassy staff.

The staff member's identity remains in doubt. Various accounts name him as having been Max Bishop, who served at the embassy as Third Secretary—and Bishop himself acknowledged this. He had detractors, though, who claimed he lied. Two books on Pearl Harbor, meanwhile, identify the staffer as having been not Bishop but First Secretary Edward Crocker.

The identity of the Peruvian diplomatic source, however, is crystal clear. He was, all agree, Ambassador Ricardo Rivera Schreiber, a distinguished diplomat who was to go on to become his country's minister for foreign affairs. Rivera Schreiber's postwar account, buttressed later by his widow's affidavit, differs radically from the version offered to the American public. He communicated what he learned, he said, not to any lesser member of the U.S. embassy staff, but to Ambassador Grew himself.

On receiving word of a coming attack on Pearl Harbor, Ambassador Rivera Schreiber said, he "immediately proceeded to telephone Mr. Joseph Grew and requested an urgent interview. I had developed a friendship with Mr. Grew, and he at once told me to take my car and go to see him." The two envoys met at the U.S. ambassador's residence, according to the Peruvian's widow, and they talked for more than an hour.

"I explained to him clearly and faithfully everything I knew,"

Rivera Schreiber was to recall, "without omitting the smallest detail. The American diplomat saw the gravity of what I told him, and he at once sent a cable."

The fact that Rivera Schreiber said he met with the American ambassador in person, while others say he passed the word through a third party, is not a lone anomaly. Witnesses' accounts of just how he acquired his information, and from whom, vary greatly.

In testimony to a congressional committee, Grew would say he did not "recollect" having asked Ambassador Rivera Schreiber the source of his information. Former Third Secretary Bishop, who claimed it was he who talked with Rivera Schreiber, said he did not ask where the information had come from. Charles Bohlen, who also worked at the embassy, said he heard that the information came from a Peruvian naval officer who "obtained the information from a Japanese naval officer who had too much to drink." Grew's secretary, Robert Fearey, suggested it came from "a Japanese admiral in his cups."

Rivera Schreiber himself, however, said nothing of the kind. He was clear about his sources and clear as to why he considered what they said significant. The first word of the Japanese plan to attack the U.S. Fleet, he said, had come from Yasuhisu Soganuma, a Japanese interpreter loaned to the embassy by the Japanese foreign office, whom the Peruvians suspected was linked to the Kempeitai, the military secret police. The longtime head of Rivera Schreiber's domestic staff told him—and this seems to be the origin of references to loose drunken talk—that Soganuma, while drinking, had mentioned information picked up from a cousin in the navy ministry. The cousin, Soganuma said on more than one occasion, had talked of Japanese plans for a naval operation to "destroy the U.S. Fleet" at a place unnamed "in the middle of the Pacific," using airplanes.

Ambassador Rivera Schreiber initially thought this interesting but perhaps no more than wild talk by an ultranationalist, not the sort of high-caliber information that justified raising an alarm. On January 26th, however, when a man he knew and respected came to see him, that changed. His visitor was Tokyo University's Professor Furukido Yoshida, who on occasion served as a translator for the ministry of war, and whom he knew opposed Japanese militarism. Yoshida said he had learned of a war plan that could have "catastrophic consequences" for his country.

"The professor told me," Rivera Schreiber would recall, "that Admiral Yamamoto had outlined the plan to attack the American Fleet in Pearl Harbor . . . The plan was, without the slightest doubt, ready to be activated." The strike was to involve aircraft flying off carriers.

This information, Ambassador Rivera Schreiber said, coupled with what he had been told of interpreter Soganuma's tipsy talk, led him to phone his U.S. counterpart. The Peruvian took the information very seriously. Why then did Ambassador Grew's cable to the State Department convey none of the "utmost importance" he would later say he ascribed to it?

It was apparently common practice in the U.S. Foreign Service for many messages initiated as brief cables to be followed by lengthier "dispatches" containing fuller information. These dispatches, sent by courier or by mail, often reached Washington many days if not weeks later. Available documentation, however, contains no follow-up dispatch about Grew's "warning." That, it has been claimed, is because files containing compromising information were culled after Pearl Harbor.

Claims that government files have been purged are common enough and typically come from conspiracy theorists. Rarely, though, is there substance to back them. But in this case there is some reason to think information may have been removed from the record. On December 16th, nine days after the Pearl Harbor attack, a memo to Secretary of State Hull recorded the creation of a team of "three or four" officials to "work upon compilation of documents" relating to U.S.-Japanese relations in the preceding decade. The undertaking was known in-house as "Bally's Project," after Joseph Ballantine, one of the four senior officials.

The State Department had long made "compilations" on foreign policy developments. The process, then, might seem innocuous enough. An affidavit signed by Helen Thomas, UPI's legendary White House correspondent, however, would suggest otherwise.

In a 1994 affidavit, Thomas put on record what she had been told by Helen Shaffer, a former secretary in State's Far Eastern Division. Shaffer, according to Thomas, said she had been "the secretary assigned by Ballantine to the project. She had been told it was a 'secret' project, admonished that she was not to tell anyone what she was doing, and [said] that she had worked in a locked room in which no one other than the few involved were permitted to enter; also that the room was filled with filing cabinets which had been transported there from the central files."

Asked by Thomas whether officials "rewrote documents" and whether she did the "retyping," Helen Shaffer replied: "Yes, I did. I got so tired of retyping those damned, long documents on those clumsy typewriters . . . I finally asked for a transfer out of the Division."

What may be corroboration that there was tinkering with the record came from the former Third Secretary at Tokyo, Max Bishop, who served at State following his stint in Japan.

In 1955, in a letter to former Ambassador Grew, Bishop wrote of returning to Hornbeck "all of his little 'personal memoranda.'" Two of the memos, he thought, were either among Hornbeck's originals or had been "destroyed." Bishop, who had contact with Admiral Kimmel in the 1950s, said some documents had been selectively removed, possibly destroyed.

Whatever the State Department in Washington may have learned as to the details of the Peruvian ambassador's warning to Ambassador Grew in Tokyo, there is no evidence it received serious attention. It did reach Naval Intelligence, according to Commander McCollum of ONI, writing long after the war. His people, however, dropped the matter when they learned that one of the sources was the Peruvian ambassador's "Japanese cook."

In fact, of course, the sources for the information were better than that. Rivera Schreiber's first source had been the head of his domestic staff, a trusted retainer of many years' standing. He, for his part, had reported what he was hearing from a Japanese man believed to be involved with the military secret police.

No decent intelligence professional would reject information merely because it originates with a servant—or indeed with someone who speaks while inebriated. Some of the best information comes in thanks to human weaknesses. The Peruvian ambassador's firsthand source, meanwhile, the professor who worked in the war ministry, was of real potential value.

The nascent plan to mount the Pearl Harbor attack was known to at least some members of the Japanese Navy's General Staff by the time Rivera Schreiber brought his information to Grew. "Already at the end of January and the beginning of February," an officer who served in the Operations Section said after the war, "I was writing up my own plans . . . plans which included my own ideas concerning the operation against Pearl Harbor." According to the officer, Commander Shigeshi Uchida, several fellow officers were also aware of the plan.

With hindsight, given that serious planning for the Pearl Harbor attack was beginning at the time, and given that—top secret though it was—a tight circle of Japanese officers knew it, there is no reason to think the leads Grew received were less than credible. This was hot information, and it was squandered.

Four days after Grew's message from Tokyo had come in, Mc-Collum in U.S. Naval Intelligence paraphrased it and added a comment of his own:

> The Division of Naval Intelligence places no credence in these rumors. Furthermore, based on known data regarding the present disposition and employment of Japanese naval and army forces, no move against Pearl Harbor appears imminent or planned for the foreseeable future.

Chief of Naval Operations Stark forwarded this assessment to Admiral Kimmel on February 1st, 1941, the very day he was installed as commander in chief Pacific Fleet. This would not be the last time the Admiral received inadequate information from Washington. In the weeks and months ahead, important information that would reach him was at times not only incomplete but misleading. Other, crucial intelligence would not be shared with him at all.

9

THE TASK FACING Admiral Kimmel was colossal, the responsibility daunting. In little more than a year, Congress had at first agreed that the U.S. Navy could grow by 11 percent, and then—as the Nazis marched on across Europe—by a dizzying 70 percent, at an estimated cost of four billion dollars. During the months Kimmel served as commander in the Pacific, with titular authority over the Fleet worldwide, the Navy would come to total well over three hundred fighting ships.

During Kimmel's installation ceremony, a reporter had noted a "clatter of riveting machines, trip hammers, and carpenter hammers," all the hubbub of a shipyard working round the clock. At Pearl Harbor, the focus was on keeping the Fleet seaworthy. In yards from the eastern seaboard to the Pacific, meanwhile, the push was on to build new warships.

The Pacific Fleet the Admiral controlled was to number four aircraft carriers, nine battleships, seventeen cruisers, forty destroyers, and twenty-two submarines. More than 100,000 men served under his command.

To enhance communications security, Kimmel moved his headquarters from aboard his flagship, USS *Pennsylvania*, to roomier accommodations at the submarine base. His office, about eighteen by fifteen feet, became the nerve center. A window offered a view over the harbor. A vast map of the Pacific dominated one of the walls. There was nothing grandiose, though, about the way the Admiral operated. Captain Walter DeLany, his operations officer, would remember him as "sort of a roamer," a boss who ventured forth regularly to confer with close aides. He made himself accessible, within reason, to all who wanted to see him.

Pearl Harbor veterans were to recall Kimmel as having been

ᴀ ᴴard taskmaster, tough but human. Then–Commander Ralph Christie, who served in submarines, thought he was "very efficient and held his officers and men up to very high standards, which he himself met. He had a reputation of being pretty hardnosed, but everyone respected him for it . . . a very strict man, but never harsh." Harold Pullen, then skipper of a destroyer, remembered a training schedule so rigorous that "we practically never went ashore."

When officers did get to go ashore, the Admiral did not let them sport colorful Hawaiian shirts. They were to wear shirt, tie, and hat at all times. In the Pacific Fleet, a man's hat soon came to be known as a "Kimmel." On board ship, certainly, the Admiral was a stickler for spit and polish—some thought overly so.

He was prone to losing his temper on occasion. Marine Colonel Omar Pfeiffer would recall a day when Kimmel, impatient over a delay in getting a report he had asked for, exploded in "boiling rage." "I believe," Pfeiffer said, "that in my whole career I have never been addressed in such colorful and foul language by a superior officer." (That, in the Navy, was saying something.) When it turned out that Pfeiffer was not to blame, however, the Admiral greeted him with "as beautiful a smile as I have ever seen . . . Any rancor that I had felt flowed away from me and from that moment I was a Kimmelite."

"Contrary to popular impression," said Kendall Fielder, a lieutenant colonel in Army Intelligence who liaised with the Admiral, "Kimmel was human and had a sense of humor." He was, though, "super-conscientious." "I have never known a naval officer," said Rear Admiral Robert Theobald, a destroyer flotilla commander and a colleague of Kimmel's for more than thirty years, "who gave more wholehearted, day by day, attention to his naval duties."

The pressure was great, the tension constant. The Admiral, moreover, could not leave his problems behind him at headquarters each evening. The Fleet's move to Hawaii had separated thousands of men from their families for longer periods than ever before. This greatly lowered morale. Though many officers had been able to bring their wives and children to Hawaii, Kimmel felt he should be seen to share the emotional burden of those who had not.

That meant being away from his wife Dorothy. With the exception of brief visits east, she had for some time been living in Long Beach, California. When the Fleet's base had been on the West Coast, she, like other Navy wives, had waited there for Kimmel to come home on shore leave. "Home," in Long Beach, meant a rented apartment.

Since her husband's elevation to commander in chief, and as first lady of the seagoing Navy, Dorothy had become something of a celebrity. With new warships and submarines pouring off production lines, she was called upon to officiate at launching ceremonies.

Her image in the press was of a woman committed to a life apart from her spouse. "Mrs. Husband E. Kimmel can make herself at home in any port," ran the caption under a set of photographs in the *Washington Post*. "She can't always put a finger on her husband." As and when the Fleet might return to California, readers were told, the Admiral's wife would be among the first to see it arrive. Her apartment had a commanding view of the ocean.

Dorothy's love and loyalty were important to Kimmel. Decades later, when both were long dead, a petty officer who had served in the Fleet post office at Pearl would recall a special service he rendered to the Admiral. "My first day, I was told to report to your grandfather," the sailor wrote in a 2002 letter to a Kimmel relative. "He told me how important your grandmother's letters were to him. I met the [Pan Am] Clippers, and the first thing off the plane was always the mail. The fastest way to find your grandmother's letters was to open a bag and smell for her perfume. If it was there, I would look for her pink envelopes."

None of the letters the couple exchanged during their sixty-year marriage have survived. They were probably destroyed by Dorothy following her husband's death. The vast family archive does, however, include correspondence between the Admiral and his three sons and other relatives. For a family separated by calling and circumstance, the mails were essential. The couple's eldest son, Manning, who turned twenty-eight in 1941, was by then a lieutenant serving in submarines, married, and with an infant daughter. He and his twenty-six-year-old brother Tom, also a submarine officer, had both been posted to the Pacific—to the Philippines.

Through the letters comes a sense of longing; hope for togetherness; and, from 1940 on, uncertainty about possible conflict with Japan. "The Japs are supposed to have been on the edge of collapse," Manning wrote in September 1940, "but they seem to be able to keep going . . . It would appear that somebody will have to stop the Japs' southern drive, and it will probably be us." Two months later: "If we all got together, it would be a grand Kimmel party. Well, 'war is hell,' but on the other hand I think we'll probably start earning our pay now . . . Best love." Hope lingered, though. "Maybe the Japs will calm down and let us lead a more peaceful life soon . . . Most of our thoughts are of home."

Ned, the youngest son, was in his junior year at Princeton, and the Admiral carefully monitored his progress. His letters were formal, sometimes paternally stern. "If at the end of this summer," he had written earlier, "you wish to take up either Politics or Economics, I shall interpose no objection. Your idea of taking a Law Course upon the completion of either the Politics or Economics Course I think an excellent one . . . I wish, however, to point out to you the necessity of making up your mind." And: "Those who are constantly shifting seldom reach any position of real responsibility."

Security, and the vagaries of the postal system, meant family members often had only the haziest idea of where others were at any given time. Manning again: "No information about the whereabouts of my mother. We think she might have gone to Honolulu with Dad . . . Dad might of course be in any one of a thousand and one places—no use in trying to keep up." In fact, Dorothy never did go to Hawaii.

Kimmel rarely failed to mention his wife in his letters. To one of his brothers, in Kentucky: "Dot is in Long Beach, wondering when the ships will return." To son Ned: "I was greatly disappointed when I realized that I would not see Mother for some time." And: "Mother does appear to be well and happy in California. I regret very much that I am not in Long Beach with her . . . You must not get irritated at Mother's criticisms." And: "Mother gives fine accounts of you . . . Go to see Mother as often as your studies permit . . . Keep her cheered up. I don't know when I will ever get home."

At the end of a long day at headquarters, the Admiral would be driven to the house he had rented high above the harbor, above the ships and men that were his professional family.

He talked with his next-door neighbor Grace Earle, a Navy captain's wife, about how much he missed Dorothy. "Admiral Kimmel was so very lonely," she recalled. "Our houses were identical in their construction and furnishings, but when he would come over he would look around and say, 'This is a *home*. Mine is only a *house*.' And he would tell us what a real homemaker Mrs. Kimmel was."

The Admiral's single-minded commitment, however, was to his formidable task. "Sitting out here in the middle of the Pacific," he wrote to Ned, "we wonder from day to day what the next move of the Administration will be . . . Meanwhile we have a very clear-cut job and are exerting all of our efforts to accomplish it. We have a force here which I believe will give a good account of itself."

The Navy's "clear-cut" job was to deter further expansionist moves by Japan, and to hit back should war come. Threatened American territories in the Pacific aside, there were discussions, too, about how the United States was to respond should the Japanese attack Allies in the region—British territories, or the Dutch East Indies. Under the Navy's revised war plan, WPL-46, the Fleet would be tasked with securing certain strategic islands in the central Pacific and destroying enemy communications.

Maximum time, CNO Stark told the Admiral, should be devoted to training and "to perfect the technique and the methods that will be required." The mission was complex and hugely challenging. With Washington's approval, Kimmel divided the Fleet into three task forces—carrier, amphibious, and battleship. One, often two, of the forces would normally be at sea. During maneuvers, virtually all ships left port. Contrary to the angry assumptions some would make after the Japanese attack, the entire Fleet was never in port at the same time.

The Admiral believed in rigorous training and efficiency. "On Kimmel's insistence," Admiral Halsey recalled, "we stepped up war-training exercises of all types. The carrier air groups staged gunnery, bombing, and torpedo runs almost daily, and practiced night takeoffs and landings. We arranged for submarines to maneuver with the carriers so that our pilots could learn to spot them at different depths. We experimented with our radars . . . Kimmel was an ideal man for the job."

Others agreed. "No one," then–Rear Admiral Kent Hewitt wrote in an unpublished memoir, "could have been more indefatigable than Admiral Kimmel in getting his cruisers ready to face what all felt sure was coming. We never knew what he was going to spring on us next. He was liable to come suddenly on board any ship of his command and hold any emergency or casualty drill that came into his head."

"The efficiency and training of the Fleet," Fleet gunnery officer Captain Willard Kitts would say, "was at its highest level in history."

Always, as the nonstop activity continued, a fundamental issue remained: how best to protect the ships when they were in port. Years earlier, the Navy and the Army had agreed on an edict they called FTP 155: "Strategic freedom of action of the Fleet must be assured. The Fleet must have no anxiety in regard to the security of its base." According to FTP 155, responsibility for Pearl Harbor's security lay not with the Navy but with the Army.

The reality at Pearl Harbor was different. While the Army was primarily accountable, the Navy was called on to contribute. Liaison with the Army high command fell to the base defense officer, Rear Admiral Claude Bloch—and to Admiral Kimmel himself.

Defense against the unpredictable, Kimmel knew, was a headache that would not go away and that he had to share. Close cooperation with the newly appointed commander of the 43,000-strong Army force in Hawaii, Lieutenant General Walter Short, was essential.

"I am either going to be good friends with the Army and get things done," the Admiral had said before he met the three-star General, "or I am going to have a hell of a fight with them . . . The defenses against aircraft for Pearl Harbor must be improved." He spoke with emphasis.

In the past, Navy commanders at Pearl had been at odds with their Army counterparts. There was no unity of command—a fact that belatedly, after the Japanese attack, would be seen as having been a major flaw. Within weeks of the attack, the Navy would essentially be allotted overall command. Until then, however, the situation remained as it had always been. Though codependent, Kimmel and Short answered to their separate departments in Washington. Kimmel did not take direction from Short, nor Short from Kimmel.

Chief of Staff Marshall, who well knew there had been interservice clashes in the past, sought to forestall similar problems. Kimmel, he told Short in a letter, was said to be "very direct, even brusque and undiplomatic in his approach to problems." The Admiral was, however, "entirely responsive to plain speaking on the part of the other fellow if there is frankness and logic" and "outstanding in his qualifications for command."

To Kimmel, Short was at first an unknown quantity. That was why, he was to recall, that the moment the General arrived, "I immediately got into my car . . . went out and paid a call on him. I told Short about the shortcomings which had existed and asked [for] his help. I established cordial relations." He was soon to report that he had found the General "highly cooperative." Short used the same words to describe his exchanges with Kimmel and Bloch. The professional relationship had obvious priority, but Kimmel and the General also became social friends—they played golf together almost every Sunday. Their cordial relationship would endure until and after the Japanese attack.

This is not a trivial matter because—among the calumnies that were later to be cast on the commanders—one would be the accusation that they did not cooperate, another the insinuation that they barely spoke to each other. The second claim would be made, most notably, by Senator Harry Truman before he became vice president. The claims were false. Both man-to-man, and through base defense officer Bloch, Kimmel and Short did work together. Kimmel thought the General "a man of sound judgment and a competent soldier."

Within a week of his first meeting with Short in February, the Admiral issued a four-page security directive to the Pacific Fleet. It specifically envisioned the possibility, before a declaration of war, of a "surprise attack on ships in Pearl Harbor." To guard against that possibility and other eventualities, he ordered no fewer than eighty-one measures. These standing orders applied immediately, and were to remain in force—as updated—until the Japanese indeed attacked ten months later.

Two months after General Short arrived, he and the Navy's Admiral Bloch agreed on a Defense Plan. CNO Stark approved it, so much so that he circulated it to other commands as a model for defense planning. It contained, however, a serious flaw: the Plan was not designed to take effect until war broke out, or there was mobilization for war, or until Short and Bloch deemed implementation necessary. As neither war nor mobilization would occur before the attack—and as Short and Bloch were never to conclude that the moment for implementation had come—the Plan essentially remained just a plan.

Major General Frederick Martin and Rear Admiral Patrick Bellinger, commanders respectively of the Army air force and Navy patrol planes in Hawaii, contributed their estimate as to what sort of attack was most probable—and how to confront the possibility. Their March 1941 report was prophetic:

> It appears that the most likely and dangerous form of attack . . . would be an air attack . . . Such an attack would most likely be launched from one or more carriers which would probably approach inside of three hundred miles . . . In a dawn air attack there is a high probability that it could be delivered as a complete surprise in spite of any patrols we might be using . . .

The air force commanders' report had only one suggestion for how to foil a surprise attack:

> Run daily patrols as far as possible to seaward through 360 degrees . . . This would be desirable but can only be effectively maintained with present personnel and matériel for a very short period and, as a practicable measure, cannot therefore be undertaken . . .

And:

> The aircraft at present available in Hawaii are inadequate to maintain, for any extended period . . . a patrol extensive enough to insure that an air attack from a [Japanese] carrier cannot arrive . . . as a complete surprise.

Admiral Kimmel and General Short did not have enough airplanes—or pilots to fly them. They would long plead with Washington to send what was needed—but largely in vain.

10

IT WAS THE long, lingering problem that—on its own—may well have ensured the Pearl Harbor catastrophe. Six months before Kimmel took command, plans had been approved to quadruple the number of the Navy's airplanes to a total of almost eight thousand. That was hugely ambitious. To build a new patrol plane—the plane Pearl Harbor needed to fly long-distance reconnaissance—took a minimum of six months. Equally important, the program called for sixteen thousand aircrew—pilots and replacement pilots. To train a patrol plane pilot took between sixteen months and two years.

The United States was playing catch-up, but not fast enough. It had been "urgently necessary" to increase overall patrol strength, in the words of an earlier commander in chief of the U.S. Fleet, long before Kimmel took over. What action had been taken by Washington, however, had been insufficient. "I always felt," Admiral Richardson, Kimmel's immediate predecessor, was to say, "the Hawaiian area was well down on the Navy Department's priority list for receipt of additional patrol squadrons." Priority was given, rather, to the Atlantic—and to getting aircraft to the British Navy.

Letter after delaying letter from Chief of Naval Operations Stark in Washington had persuaded Richardson that "the Navy Department viewed with considerable equanimity the inadequate patrol plane situation at Pearl." As far as patrol planes were concerned, Hawaii held out the begging bowl in vain.

"After taking over command," recalled Navy air forces commander Rear Admiral Patrick Bellinger, who served under both Richardson and Kimmel, "I was surprised to find that here in the Hawaiian Islands, an important naval advanced outpost, we were operating on a shoestring and the more I looked, the thinner the string appeared to be."

An effective search of the vast area of ocean around Pearl Harbor, Bellinger had told Richardson before Kimmel took command, would require flying fifty naval patrol planes, on a daily basis, in a 360-degree arc, to a distance of eight hundred miles. He had only sixty-odd VPB aircraft in total—and they could be operational only every second or third day. In testimony after the attack on Pearl Harbor, Bellinger was to increase the estimate he had given Richardson. To maintain thorough long-range reconnaissance, he would testify, he would have needed eighty-four planes, in operational condition, available daily. To meet that requirement, he would have needed an overall total complement of some two hundred planes.

In the later months of 1940, under Richardson, long-distance reconnaissance from Hawaii was limping along, overstretched, following confusing messages from Washington. A mere six patrol planes were ranging out to a distance of just three hundred miles and covering only a 180-degree arc to the west. This, Richardson knew, was merely a "token reconnaissance."

Even such limited patrols stretched men to the limit. "We were working hard seven days a week for many, many months," recalled future Admiral Thomas Moorer, who as a young pilot under Richardson and Kimmel flew patrols out of Pearl Harbor. "We had patrols nearly every day, and they lasted eighteen hours apiece. We'd go out in a wedge-shaped sector which looked like a thin piece of pie when you drew it on a chart . . . That meant the sector could be about 9 or 10 degrees wide . . . We usually had only about six [planes] available, and that meant we could do only about 60 degrees. The sectors of a given flight were picked at random."

"The fly boys," said Richardson's flag secretary, Commander George Dyer, "bitterly opposed" this schedule. "Pat Wing 2 would send in these letters asking that the daily air reconnaissance be canceled . . . The naval aviators we had on the staff . . . would tell about the horrendous effects that the tremendous air effort was having on the personal training of young aviators. And what deleterious effects it was having on the planes . . . The Admiral had to make the decision. Each time he said, 'No, we're going to continue it.' "

The toll that constant reconnaissance took on training loomed large for Richardson and Kimmel. Their principal mission, both men knew, was to prepare the Fleet for war. CNO Stark, Richardson noted, had "continued to accentuate the overriding nature of the flight training requirements." Flight training was to be given "first priority."

Kimmel's war plans officer, Charles "Socrates" McMorris, thought limited searches "would give only limited effectiveness, that training would suffer heavily, and that if we were called upon to conduct a war we would find a large proportion of our planes needing engine overhaul . . . The matter was given considerable thought." "It was a question," his assistant, Vincent Murphy, would recall, "of wearing out our planes over a considerable period of time, wearing out our pilots."

In the draft of the final security directive of his tenure, Admiral Richardson called for continuing reconnaissance patrols to three hundred miles out. CNO Stark in Washington, however, wrote saying that occasional sweeps by planes and ships might help, but continuous patrols were "not yet necessary." In light of this message, Richardson would recall, "the requirement for long-range naval patrol plane reconnaissance was stricken out of my order."

Kimmel did not resume routine long-distance patrolling. Stark told him in a letter that in general, "the force left with you will still be great enough to perform both the offensive and defensive tasks assigned you."

Washington never did send the additional planes required to mount truly effective distant reconnaissance. As Stark's key aide, Lieutenant Commander William Smedberg, acknowledged, "We had nothing like the number of planes that we had to have in order to fly proper reconnaissance." Not one of the hundred additional patrol planes authorized for the Pearl Harbor naval base was to arrive before the Japanese attack.

Two of Kimmel's peers, both of whom served at Pearl Harbor,

summed up his predicament. Rear Admiral Walter Anderson, who commanded Battleships, Battle Force, there, wrote that the Admiral "did not have the necessary planes. He repeatedly asked the Navy Department for them. The Department evidently considered there was more pressing need for the planes elsewhere, and refused to supply Kimmel with the planes."

"The Fleet's most desperate shortage," Admiral Halsey thought, "was patrol planes and their crews . . . Kimmel had neither sufficient planes nor an adequate scouting force. I am not exaggerating when I say that he did not have enough planes to maintain complete coverage of a 60-degree sector. As for crews, his original shortage was increased by orders to transfer twelve trained crews to the mainland every month . . . Even an ideal man can't do a job without proper tools, and Kimmel did not have them."

For the first time in history, there was another way perhaps to spot an approaching enemy in the vastness of the Pacific Ocean—radar. Effective radar was still on the cutting edge of technology, and Britain had the lead.

What the U.S. Navy called "radar"—radio detecting and ranging—the British called "RDF": radio direction finding. As of early 1940, the American version could not be relied on. Interviewed in 2014 at age one hundred, Vice Admiral David Richardson recalled his experience as a pilot at Pearl in 1940. "Radar was not trusted at that time. It could be right and it could be wrong. No one understood it or necessarily believed it."

Radar was a gizmo, a newfangled device. General Douglas MacArthur, commanding Army forces in the Far East, did not even know what it was. He had to have it explained to him. "The possibilities of such an instrument," Admiral Halsey reflected years later, at the time seemed "too tremendous to grasp."

In Europe, though, concern about impending conflict had spurred technological advances. This, as Winston Churchill was to write later, was the "wizard" war. As developed by his electronics whiz kids, radar had proved critical to fighting off the German

Luftwaffe in June 1940. Soon after, to their mutual advantage, Prime Minister Churchill had arranged with President Roosevelt for a reciprocal exchange of military secrets. Some U.S. military leaders, including Chief of Naval Operations Stark, had resisted this idea. The fear was that the risk of secrets leaking outweighed the potential advantages of sharing. In a memo for Chief of Staff Marshall, moreover, one U.S. general declared that America's "airplane detector . . . [was] more efficient than anything the British have."

Not so, and Britain had the additional advantage that its radar techniques had been honed in battle. At any rate, during the months before the technology exchange got under way, valuable information was already being exchanged.

Those who eventually investigated Pearl Harbor would be told nothing of the work of John "Jack" Opie and the covert mission he was assigned in May 1940. Opie, a thirty-seven-year-old lieutenant commander who had once served at the Naval Torpedo Station in Alexandria, Virginia, was pulled away from duty in the Pacific, ordered to Washington, briefed in Admiral Stark's office, and sent to England. He sailed from a Canadian port aboard a civilian liner, dressed not in uniform but in civilian clothes. The passport he carried bore a large pink reminder that the Neutrality Act barred U.S. citizens from travel in combat zones—a bar he would not observe. Officially, Opie was listed as an Assistant Naval Attaché at the London embassy, but his tasks were to be carried out undercover. He was one of the first of thirty U.S. "observers" soon to be embedded with the Royal Navy.

In late summer that year, Opie wrote a report aboard HMS *Illustrious*, an aircraft carrier. Having seen British radar in operation, he told the Chief of Naval Operations, he could report that it was far better than the corresponding American technology. It was "essential," in his view, to get the British version into service in the United States. In the months that followed, Opie would repeat how important this was.

By December 1940, at Pearl Harbor, there were plans for an "Aircraft Warning Service" to consist of three fixed and five mobile

Army radar stations. By February 1941, Secretary of War Stimson was telling CNO Stark that equipment for them would reach Hawaii "in June." First signs that installation was to be delayed, however, came in March, when the National Park Service raised objections. If located on high ground, it said, radar bases could spoil Hawaii's natural beauty. In Washington the next month, Special Assistant to the Secretary of War Harvey Bundy—who had special responsibility for scientific matters—noticed that the Army was "struggling with radar."

In May, when some radar did reach Hawaii, Admiral Kimmel thought it "excellent." "Delivery of RADAR should be accelerated," he told Stark. Not only did the Army require radar, for the land-based defense of Hawaii; so did the Navy—for its warships. In July, though, Stark would still be writing that he was "terribly disturbed about our lack of radar." By late September the five mobile units were functional. The three planned stationary sites were not—for lack of vital parts. Reporting to Washington on progress, Army air commander General Frederick Martin said he hoped the full Aircraft Warning Service would be up and running in a month.

Pious hope. To the end, the Army would continue to have a problem with the supply of parts. Equipment was being poached from the stationary sites to get mobile radar units working. Pearl Harbor would not have a fully functional, coordinated system when the Japanese attacked more than two months later.

"I was very conscious," Vice Admiral Wilson Brown, who commanded one of the Fleet's task forces, was to testify, "that the defenses of Pearl Harbor were quite inadequate in . . . radar and planes . . . I was also aware that these shortages had repeatedly been brought to the attention of the Department, and that we were informed that it was not possible to meet those shortages because of more pressing needs."

Frequently, Brown went on, he overheard Admiral Kimmel ask General Short what equipment the Army had to defend Pearl, against an air attack, and Short replied that "his equipment was wholly inadequate and that he had done everything possible to try to have it increased."

Kimmel's fleet aviation officer, then-Commander Arthur Davis would be asked whether a radar warning net, properly manned and fully efficient, would have contributed "toward the certainty of ample warning." It would, he replied, but the situation on December 7th was that "the Army's air warning net had not been fully developed. It was, broadly speaking, still in a status of test, completion, and training, rather than on a full basis of readiness . . ."

On the day the Japanese attacked, the one opportunity for the miracle of radar to have prevented the enemy from achieving total surprise was to be squandered. Two theoretically off-duty radar operators staring at their oscilloscope, one of them a trainee, would spot planes approaching when there was still time to trigger an alert. The young Army lieutenant they were to contact, a "pursuit officer," would be doing duty for only the second time, in an information center that was still not fully up and running. He would assume that the incoming radar blips represented a scheduled American flight of airplanes, and do nothing. Opportunity lost.

During the postattack investigations, Kimmel would be grilled about this failure. "The radar warning service," he told one questioner, "was the function of the Army and the Naval base defense officer"—Admiral Bloch. Not until two days later had Kimmel learned that the incoming enemy planes had been sighted—and that no action had been taken.

The nub of the matter, a questioner suggested, was whether Kimmel and General Short should not have had a "better understanding" on the procedure to be followed if incoming planes were spotted. Kimmel responded that he had thought he did know the procedure. "You have always got to depend on someone . . . You cannot do everything . . . I thought the radar was manned . . . I had confidence in General Short."

There was to be a not dissimilar failure with radar in the Philippines when the Japanese struck hours after the attack on Pearl Harbor—even though commanders there had been alerted to what had occurred in Hawaii. A two-hundred-strong Army radar company had arrived in August—but without equipment. The first mobile radar unit arrived only in October. In spite of requests to get the further necessary equipment delivered immediately, only that one unit was to be operational by the day of the attack.

At Pearl Harbor, U.S. forces had been taken totally by surprise; by contrast, those in the Philippines had prior warning—they learned of the Pearl Harbor onslaught little more than half an hour after it occurred. Consequently, the Army there was on combat alert for about nine hours before Japanese planes struck their main target, Clark Field, the principal base for the U.S. Far East Air Force.

The one functioning radar unit had begun to pick up flights of aircraft offshore even *before* news came in of the attack on Pearl. An hour before the attackers reached Clark, it would be claimed, the unit transmitted a warning that waves of airplanes were coming in. If a warning was indeed sent, however, it was not acted on. Later explanations would range from the statement that communications were less than adequate to a claim that a radio operator left his post to "go to lunch."

The enemy caught most of the U.S. planes at Clark on the ground. America's Far East Air Force was put out of action. Eighty men were killed and more than a hundred wounded.

Dwight Eisenhower, who had earlier served under MacArthur in the Philippines and was by December 1941 on the general staff in Washington, observed in his diary that he thought MacArthur "certainly should have saved his planes."

MacArthur, however, would not be removed from command following the debacle. Nor would there be a formal investigation. No senior commander in the Philippines would ever be held to account. There would be no fall guy—no one disgraced as Admiral Kimmel and General Short would be disgraced.

11

FOUR YEARS BEFORE Kimmel took command, one of his future patrol wing officers had written an essay, "Aerial Attacks on Fleets at Anchor," for a Naval Institute competition. Battleships at anchor in a large sheltered anchorage, Logan Ramsey reflected in the essay, were "a magnificent sight—but also a perfectly marvellous target for a squadron of hostile torpedo planes."

It was to be torpedo planes, of course, that would wreak devastation in December 1941. Battleships USS *California*, USS *Oklahoma*, USS *West Virginia*, and USS *Utah* went to the bottom, each struck by multiple torpedoes. The battleship USS *Nevada*, struck by a single torpedo, had to be grounded. Single torpedoes hit and damaged the cruisers USS *Raleigh* and USS *Helena*. The minelayer USS *Oglala* sank because of the back blast from the explosion on the USS *Helena*.

Torpedoes launched from aircraft, then, proved massively effective at Pearl Harbor. Of thirty-six torpedoes launched by enemy planes, twenty-five struck U.S. ships.

Air-launched torpedoes functioned by plunging into the ocean some distance from a ship, gradually ascending to their "run" depth, then speeding toward the assigned target. They had a tendency, however, to plunge too deep and wind up uselessly embedded in the mud on the seabed. Because the water at Pearl was so shallow, a mere thirty to forty-five feet, aerial torpedoes had not been considered a serious threat.

The terrible reality of December 7th would prove that to be a fatal misjudgment. But whose misjudgment? In the future, fingers would be pointed at Kimmel. Secretary of the Navy James Forrestal, who at war's end would tear into Kimmel for having failed to demonstrate superior judgment, asserted that Washington had told Kimmel Pearl was potentially at risk from torpedoes. Forrestal's observation was seriously skewed.

As recently as 1992, in his *History of the U.S. Navy*, which was promoted on the cover as being "the world standard text," Robert Love Jr. claimed that neither Kimmel nor his base defense officer, Rear Admiral Bloch, "took account" of a warning from Washington on the subject of antitorpedo nets. This was inaccurate.

A dig into what Kimmel called "this torpedo business" reveals a troubling sequence of events. Records available today offer a fuller picture of what the Navy learned about aerial torpedoes in the months before Pearl Harbor, how it processed the information it received, and what it did or did not tell the men with the most pressing need to know, the commanders in the Pacific.

Three naval actions in summer 1940, before Admiral Kimmel took command, had direct relevance to torpedoes and the depth of water in which they could successfully be fired. With France under the virtual control of Nazi Germany, the British government feared French naval power could be used against Britain. British ships confronted the French fleet at Mers el-Kébir, off what was then the French colony of Algeria. When the French commander failed to respond to a British attempt to negotiate, the British attacked.

On July 6th, 1940, Swordfish biplanes flown off the carrier HMS *Ark Royal* dropped a single torpedo at Mers el-Kébir. The weapon hit and sank a small ship, triggering an explosion that put the battleship *Dunkerque* out of action—she had already been grounded following an earlier artillery exchange. There were many casualties. Two days later, at Dakar in what was then the French colony of Senegal, a torpedo—dropped by airplanes from the carrier HMS *Hermes*—disabled the battleship *Richelieu*.

The truly big development, for those alert to the use of air-launched torpedoes, came four months later. On November 11th, two waves of British planes—Swordfish again, attacking at night with bombs and torpedoes—struck the pride of Mussolini's navy at anchor in the port of Taranto, in southern Italy. Five of the torpedoes dropped hit their targets, punching holes in three battleships. One, the *Conte di Cavour*, was sunk. Two others, the *Littorio* and the *Caio Duilio*, were out of action for many months.

These successes made news in the American press—but without the sort of detail that naval warfare specialists needed. "Unofficially," the *New York Times* reported, "it was believed that aerial torpedoes must have been used to inflict such heavy damage." There was no public mention of the water depths at Taranto. Existing charts, however, showed that—while depths in the Taranto harbor varied widely—some areas were very shallow, as at Pearl Harbor.

Navies worldwide wanted to know the crucial details. Exactly where at Taranto had the torpedoes been dropped? Where had the Italian ships been anchored? If the torpedoes had indeed been dropped in shallow water, how had the British made aerial-launched torpedoes work successfully in shallow water—a feat previously thought virtually impossible?

In Germany, Hitler promptly commissioned research to develop a torpedo that would be effective in shallow water. Within weeks, a Berlin-based Japanese officer flew to Taranto to discuss the attack. Months later, a Japanese naval mission headed to Italy to follow up. How did the United States respond? The question is important, not least because Pearl Harbor's maximum depth—forty-five feet, close to the depth at some points at Taranto—potentially placed it at serious risk.

At Pearl Harbor in November 1940, right after the Taranto raid, Kimmel's predecessor Admiral Richardson had been alerted to the implications. He ordered that the Fleet stop using an offshore anchorage southeast of Pearl—it now appeared to him to be very vulnerable. From headquarters in Washington, meanwhile, CNO Stark for some time expressed concern about Pearl Harbor itself. On November 22nd, in a letter to Richardson, he wrote: "My concern for the safety of the Fleet in Pearl Harbor has become even greater . . . Is it desirable to place torpedo nets within the harbor itself? I shall appreciate your comments."

Steel mesh antitorpedo nets or "baffles"—noncontinuous nets—hung from booms had in the past been used to protect warships. In the U.S. Navy, though, they had fallen out of favor. The nets were cumbersome, impeded ships' movements in crowded harbors, and delayed sortieing in an emergency. Having consulted with his staff, Richardson told Stark he thought nets "neither necessary nor practicable. The area is too restricted."

Shortly before Kimmel had in turn taken command, however, he raised the issue with Stark's emissary, Commander John McCrea. Kimmel suggested, rather, that Washington *should* consider supplying torpedo nets to Pearl Harbor—and barrage balloons to obstruct raiding aircraft. None were to be forthcoming.

In the Mediterranean two months earlier, the CNO's observer in place, Lieutenant Commander Opie, had been aboard the British aircraft carrier that launched the aerial attack on Taranto. He had exceptional access, listened to the briefing and debriefing of the Swordfish pilots involved, and been supplied with the British commander's postoperation report. Opie's own report, coupled with that of the British commander, arrived at the Office of Naval Intelligence in Washington on January 9th, 1941. The text of the reports did not refer to the water depths in which aerial torpedoes had been used with such success. Attached to Opie's report, however, was a postattack *chart*.

That chart, found during research for this book in the National Archives—it was among ONI's "Secret Reports of Naval Attachés"—has never surfaced publicly before. The information it contains, information that was available to ONI almost a year before the Pearl Harbor attack, is very significant. Symbols on the chart show the positions of Italian warships in the Taranto anchorage at the time of the British attack. Clusters of "T" symbols show where the British dropped torpedoes. The chart also shows the *depths of the water in those areas.*

Two torpedoes, marked on the chart at a position that lines up with the battleship *Conte di Cavour*, were dropped at a point at which most depths were identified as being only about four fathoms, just twenty-four feet, far less than the average depth at Pearl Harbor. The *Conte di Cavour* went to the bottom. Because of the obvious implications for the Pacific Fleet at Pearl Harbor, the chart Opie sent should have grabbed the immediate attention of ONI. Nothing in the contemporary record, though, or in that of later official investigations, indicates that the chart got attention from anyone at all in Washington.

Lieutenant Commander Opie, who had himself briefly served at Pearl Harbor, felt that his knowledge of the Taranto attack was very relevant. In mid-January 1941, as his stint in the Mediterranean was coming to an end, he sent in a suggestion. "I honestly feel," he wrote, "that I should fly to Hawaii and talk to the boys there on [my] war experiences and how to train to meet the lessons learned." No one took him up on the proposal.

A letter for the Secretary of War, written at Stark's request on January 24th following an in-house study, referred to overall concerns about security at Pearl in light of "reports from abroad" of successful "torpedo plane attacks on ships while in bases." The letter, however, made no mention of either Opie's information from Taranto or of the need for torpedo nets.

In February, in a letter to Kimmel about antitorpedo equipment, Stark bemoaned the drawbacks of torpedo nets—"very expensive, extremely heavy . . . take up about 200 yards . . . take a long time to lay." He hoped an efficient net could be developed "in the near future."

In the same letter, Stark told the Admiral that the depths of water in which the Taranto torpedoes had been launched was "between fourteen and fifteen fathoms"—or eighty to ninety feet. He also said: "A minimum depth of 75 feet may be assumed necessary to successfully drop torpedoes from planes. 150 feet of water is desired."

The Admiral and nine members of his senior staff saw both this and a similar letter Stark sent. What they read, Kimmel's gunnery officer Captain Willard Kitts would recall, indicated to them that "the water at Pearl Harbor was so shallow that the success of a torpedo attack on ships in Pearl Harbor was dubious."

Nets were considered nevertheless. Kitts recalled, however, "The difficulty of procuring these nets, on which there was a low priority, and the need of moving the Fleet on short notice from berths for a sortie, the difficulties of cluttering up the harbour with these nets . . . gave us the feeling that the risk of a successful torpedo attack was slight."

The aviation officer, Commander Davis, summed up the reaction. "I don't think Pearl Harbor need worry," he noted at the time; "too shallow."

In view of Stark's letter, Kimmel recommended that "no A/T nets be shipped this area . . . until a light efficient net that can be laid temporarily and quickly is developed." No such nets materialized.

Stark's suggestion that a successful drop required a minimum depth of seventy-five feet seems to have put the minds of Kimmel and his team at rest—given that the water depth never exceeded forty-five feet at Pearl Harbor.

The CNO's figures, of course, were grossly inaccurate. The actual depth at some of the anchorages at Taranto was not eighty to ninety feet but only forty feet. At none of the three locations where torpedoes had been dropped in recent months had the water been anything like as deep as the seventy-five feet Stark "assumed necessary."

Four months later, in June, Stark's deputy fired off yet another message to base defense officer Bloch, Kimmel, and all other major Navy commands. While stating that "no minimum depth of water . . . can arbitrarily be assumed as providing safety from torpedo plane attack," he considered an attack launched in a depth of sixty feet "much more likely." A number of the torpedoes at Taranto, the deputy added, were dropped in depths of from sixty-six to seventy-two feet. Again, the figures cited by Stark's office did not accord with the minimum depth in which torpedoes were dropped at Taranto.

Having considered these figures, Kimmel would recall, he and his staff agreed that the risk of a torpedo attack succeeding in the shallow water at Pearl was "negligible."

A week after Stark's deputy's letter went off, headquarters received a report from England with intelligence on another of the British attacks of the previous year. In the attack on the French battleship *Richelieu* at Dakar, the report noted, the water depth had been "only 7 fathoms"—forty-two feet. Receipt of that information alone would surely have alerted Admiral Kimmel and his aides at Pearl Harbor and caused them to reevaluate the possible risk to Pearl. A Navy review of the files conducted later, however, would note there was "no indication" that the document was sent to the Pacific Fleet.

Finally, in July, a further startling observation reached Naval Intelligence in Washington from a second U.S. observer who had served with the British Navy in the Mediterranean. Royal Navy records, Lieutenant Commander Albert Morehouse wrote, indicated that an aerial torpedo could be dropped in water "as shallow as 4 fathoms"—twenty-four feet. Morehouse's report matched the information on the chart sent months earlier by Jack Opie. This was a second opportunity to take note of this vital intelligence. If torpedoes could hit their marks in such shallow water, Pearl Harbor certainly was at risk.

Did this latest information reach Admiral Kimmel? A routing slip indicates that Naval Intelligence copied Morehouse's report not only to him, but to CNO Stark, to Stark's deputy, and to at least eight other departments at Washington headquarters. There is real doubt, though, as to whether most addressees received it. Though a stamp shows that it was received by Naval Intelligence, nothing in the record indicates that Stark or the many other addressees actually received the report. Had any of them done so, it would surely have gotten attention from one or more of them— and there is no evidence that it did. Nor, though the existence of the report would have been potent fuel for criticism of Admiral Kimmel, was the report's existence ever mentioned during the many investigations of Pearl Harbor.

The Fleet's commanders, the men at the sharp end, had been left in the dark. Kimmel's aviation officer, Commander Davis, would remember what must have seemed the ultimate cruel irony. "Shortly after 7 December," he was to testify, "I recall a dispatch from the [Navy's] Bureau of Ordnance which clarified its position in the matter. The general tenor of this dispatch was that, actually, torpedoes *could* [authors' italics] be effectively used in depths as shallow as Pearl Harbor."

This is a sorry record of inefficiency in Washington. Then–Commander Walter Ansel, who served in the War Plans Division at headquarters, well understood why the lapses occcurred. As the most junior member of his team, he was picked to work up a study of the British aerial torpedo attack on Taranto. "The fact that the junior man should get the assignment," he was to say three decades later, "is an indication of how unimportant the rest of them thought it was."

The Division's work in general, he said, "was done mostly off the top of the head whenever something came up . . . There was no continuing systematic planning. We met things as they came and did what we could . . . We were not fitted either to plan a war or conduct a war . . .

"I was a greatly disillusioned young commander . . . At sea, answers had been demanded of us. I now found out that not much was done with those answers when they arrived in Washington . . . I finally had to give up and treat this as the way things ran in Washington; they ran on expediency."

Ansel's views—he later rose to rear admiral—would have been highly relevant to the many later inquiries into the Pearl Harbor attack. He was never called to testify.

12

WASHINGTON'S COMMUNICATIONS WITH ADMIRAL KIMMEL, five thousand miles away, were often inept. What was required of him, moreover, often seemed unwise. So it was, in the spring of 1941, when the high command began bleeding the Pacific Fleet of both ships and men.

The previous year, when Roosevelt had moved the Fleet to Hawaii, he had done so on the premise that its presence would deter Japanese aggression. Now, with America increasingly involved in British efforts to run the gauntlet of Nazi U-boats, he wanted a number of ships and men moved to the Atlantic. The situation there was, as Stark told Kimmel, "obviously critical . . . hopeless" unless firm measures were taken.

No one seriously questioned that. Yet Kimmel knew—everyone had known from the start—that Japan's fleet was numerically superior to the Pacific Fleet. Just as he had been pushing for the additional planes he needed for reconnaissance, he had from the start pressed for more ships, men, and equipment to augment his command. Now, in April and May, the Admiral was being asked to *shed* one of his four aircraft carriers, three battleships, four cruisers, and eighteen destroyers—a quarter of his warships. There was to be no debating this. "I am telling you," Stark wrote, "not arguing with you."

The warships were duly moved to the Atlantic. Kimmel and his aides were acutely aware, though, that the transfers weakened the concept of the Pacific Fleet as a deterrent. Some of his officers called the changes the "kiss of death." "Suppose you had a fleet of taxicabs operating in a big city," Fleet intelligence officer Edwin Layton was to say. "Suppose that fleet of taxicabs were cut down by about a third, do you think you could operate as effectively as before the cut-down?"

At the White House, meanwhile, Roosevelt had a singular way of operating, based on the exceptionally close relationship he had built with his intensely loyal Chief of Naval Operations. To the President, Stark was "Betty," the curious nickname he had picked up in his youthful days at Annapolis. "Betty" was linked to Roosevelt by a direct phone line installed in Stark's office and at his home. Roosevelt would phone—often out of the blue, sometimes after midnight—frequently summoning him to the White House on weekends.

So unpredictably would the President call that Stark and his close aide Lieutenant Commander William Smedberg resorted to preserving phone conversations with Roosevelt—and others—on the best device available at the time (this was before the introduction of the tape recorder), a "wax cylinder." "The reason being," Smedberg would recall, "in the case of the President, that he talked so fast.

" 'Now Betty,' he would say, 'I want this and I want that and I want you to do this and do that, and this and this and this' . . . I monitored every conversation . . . As soon as the President hung up Admiral Stark would ring for me and I'd go in and he'd say, 'Did you get all that? . . . All right, get started on everything.'"

Those recordings would obviously have been a treasure trove for historians, not least in connection with the roles of Roosevelt and others before and after Pearl Harbor. From time to time, Smedberg said, "when it was a personal thing," Stark would tell him to destroy a recording. Later, when Smedberg left the CNO's office to take up another posting, he himself ordered that the recordings be destroyed. That, as he said understatedly, was a "bad mistake."

In the course of his Pearl Harbor testimony, CNO Stark was to be asked, "Did you ever keep any record of your conversations with the President during the year 1941?"

He replied, "No, I did not." He lied.

Surprisingly, given what he had been privy to over the months, Stark's aide Smedberg was called to testify only once during the official inquiries. He was at no point questioned on the details of his work for Admiral Stark.

Lost to history, at any rate, are all those recordings of exchanges between the President and Stark, recordings that could have cast dramatic light on developments in 1941: Stark as the chief executive's trusty adviser; Stark "wheedling"—as Smedberg would recall—to get more money, ships, or men out of Roosevelt; the President on the occasions he "blew his top, telling Stark he was giving him an order right now"; and, not least, the President when he came up with sometimes highly idiosyncratic notions as to how to use the nation's warships.

"I just want to keep them popping up here and there, and keep the Japs guessing," he told Stark during one discussion about the Navy's role in the Pacific. Stark's close aide Commander Charles Wellborn, who also handled contacts with the President, thought Roosevelt was "something of a 'lunger,' somebody who had a bright idea . . . without really thinking it through."

Secretary of War Stimson had a similar impression. He felt, he wrote in his diary, that Roosevelt's mind "does not easily follow a consecutive chain of thought . . . but hops about in his discussions from suggestion to suggestion . . . It is very much like chasing a vagrant beam of moonshine."

One of Stark's functions, Wellborn said, was "keeping the President from making precipitous mistakes and doing things he might regret the next day." Late in the summer of 1941, Stark told Admiral Kimmel he might be called upon to "send a carrier load of planes to one of the Asiatic Russian ports"—3,000 to 4,000 miles from Hawaii. Kimmel nixed the idea as "fantastic." "With the fuel we had," he recalled, "we couldn't have gotten back . . . I said that the plan was nuts, and I wouldn't do such a thing."

If ordered to do it, Stark told the Admiral, he might be obliged to obey. "No I wouldn't," Kimmel said he responded. "I would resign before I would do such a thing. I would never put the Fleet in such a position." Nothing came of the idea.

A favorite sign-off to the often rambling letters Stark sent Kimmel was, "Keep cheerful." Kimmel was resilient enough, but by mid-1941 he had reason to be less than cheerful. He was beset by a concern that had nothing to do with the arithmetic of ships and men—the worry that he was not being kept fully informed.

"I have recently been told by an officer fresh from Washington," the Admiral had written to Stark right after taking command, "that ONI [Office of Naval Intelligence] considers it the function of Operations to furnish the Commander-in-Chief with information of a secret nature. I have also been told that Operations considers the responsibility for furnishing the same type of information to be that of ONI. I do not know that we have missed anything, but if there is any doubt . . . will you kindly fix that responsibility so there shall be no misunderstanding?"

It may seem obvious that, as his nation's top seagoing naval officer, Kimmel should have been entrusted with all relevant secret matters. Replying, Stark told him that ONI was "fully aware of its responsibilities in keeping you adequately informed concerning foreign nations, activities of these nations, and disloyal elements within the United States."

With hindsight, however, and on a careful reading of the wording of this letter, Stark was not being forthright. To be "aware" of a responsibility is not necessarily the same as fulfilling it.

Stark's letter did not dispel Kimmel's unease. He continued to worry, his Assistant Chief of Staff Walter DeLany would recall, that he was not "getting the complete story of international affairs . . . that he was not being adequately informed."

By late May 1941, six months before the Japanese attack, the Admiral evidently decided he had had enough. In an eleven-page, almost five-thousand-word letter to headquarters, he listed familiar complaints—the lack of sufficient manpower, the hemorrhaging of the numbers of men he did have, the shortage of necessary aircraft and pilots in general, and the Army's lack of planes and radar for the defense of Pearl Harbor. Then, in an unusual step for a senior military officer, he broached matters that were more normally the preserve of the civilian administration.

While "largely uninformed as to day-by-day developments," Kimmel wrote, he could not escape "the conclusion that our national policies and diplomatic and military moves to implement them are not fully coordinated." To back into a war, he went on, "unsupported or only half-heartedly supported by public opinion, is to court losing it . . . To tell our people anything else is to perpetrate a base deception."

Near the end of this broadside, under the heading "INFORMATION," the Admiral complained that he was being kept in the dark. He was, he wrote,

> in a very difficult position . . . as a rule, not informed as to the policy, or change of policy, reflected in current and naval movements and, as a result . . . unable to evaluate the possible effect upon his own situation . . . This lack of information is disturbing . . . It is realized that, on occasion, the rapid developments in the international picture, both diplomatic and military, and perhaps even the lack of knowledge of the military authorities themselves, may militate against the furnishing of timely information, but certainly the present situation is susceptible to marked improvement. Full and authoritative knowledge of current policies and objectives, even though necessarily late at times, would enable the Commander-in-Chief, Pacific Fleet, to modify, adapt, or even reorient his possible courses of action to conform to current concepts . . .
>
> It is suggested that it be made a cardinal principle that the Commander-in-Chief, Pacific Fleet, be immediately informed of all important developments as they occur and by the quickest secure means available.

Kimmel apparently saw the situation in which he found himself as critical. Rather than send his letter to Washington by naval courier, he took it there himself. He made the journey—a long, laborious one in those days—accompanied only by his war plans officer, Captain Charles "Soc" McMorris. There, in early June, he met with Stark, alone or with others of the top brass, at least seven times. His friend Stark, he would recall long afterward, gave the impression he was "doing the best he could under the circumstances."

High on the wish list for Kimmel and McMorris was to get an assurance that they really were being kept fully informed. "They didn't give a damn who gave them the dope," then the head of ONI's Far East Section, Commander Arthur McCollum, was to remember long afterward, "just so long as they got it." They were told by the head of War Plans, Rear Admiral Kelly Turner—with Stark's approval—that he would indeed see that they were kept fully in the loop.

Captain McCollum would also recall, however, that headquarters' "complex on secrecy" was all very well but "tended to make people so secretive that they didn't tell anybody what was going on." Admiral Kimmel, as commander in chief Pacific, was not "anybody," but the promise he had been given was not kept—not then, and not as the weeks unwound to December 7th. For Kimmel, when he came much later to understand how he had been failed, that was the great betrayal.

On the afternoon of June 9, after several days in Washington, the Admiral and McMorris went to the White House to talk with the President. During their brief encounters during World War I, when Roosevelt was Assistant Secretary of the Navy, Kimmel had not been favorably impressed. Roosevelt, he had thought then, had "tried to equate military affairs with politics." He was, however, a "very engaging fellow and certainly quite charming," a man who "loved the Navy and would do anything to be with the Navy."

The surviving record does not make clear how well briefed Roosevelt had been on the letter of protest his commander in chief Pacific had brought to Washington. Stark would have told the President of the Admiral's naval concerns, but may have said nothing of his outburst about national policy: seven months earlier, Kimmel's predecessor had criticized the civilian leadership and been fired.

The only known formal record of the ninety-minute meeting with the President is a long memorandum that Kimmel lodged with the Navy Department. The President told the Admiral, in very general terms, that talks were under way with Japanese representatives. The discussions, he said, envisaged peace in the Pacific "for a hundred years." Kimmel had the impression, he wrote in his memo on the meeting, that this required "a considerable amount of wishful thinking."

He and Secretary of State Hull, Roosevelt said, were "daily 'taking it on the chin' for not putting an embargo on oil shipments to Japan" while there were oil shortages in the United States. The trade embargo was the big stick, the weapon—short of war—that the United States had used against Japan as long ago as World War I. When Japan bombed Chinese civilians in 1938, the United States had acted to restrict sales of aircraft. It had also used the embargo in 1940, when Japan's hostile moves included an advance into what is now Vietnam.

In June 1941, when Roosevelt and Kimmel met, Japan's occupation of China was continuing and further advances in Indochina were expected. Washington was only weeks away from freezing all Japan's assets in the United States—which would, crucially, cut off oil exports. Without oil to power warships and planes, Japan's armed forces would be crippled.

Now, week in and week out, the President and Secretary of State Hull were exchanging messages and negotiating points with Japanese ambassador Kichisaburo Nomura. This involved complex diplomatic sparring, for the well-meaning Nomura was himself being manipulated by the militant faction in Tokyo. When Admiral Kimmel visited the White House, Roosevelt gave him a glimpse of these complex exchanges.

Then the President changed the subject. What did the Admiral think, he wanted to know, of the notion of further reducing his force by three of his battleships? CNO Stark and Navy Secretary Knox, Roosevelt said, had told him that six battleships were enough both to defend Hawaii and to mount raids on Japanese communications. Could not three of them, the President wondered, be used to do "a lot of raiding"?

Kimmel's response was to "explode," he wrote in his formal memo. The idea was "crazy." Apparently without missing a beat, Roosevelt responded that it sounded "silly" to him too.

The President asked what the Admiral thought of mounting air raids on Japan, and the Admiral replied that there were few planes suitable for such missions. When Kimmel made the arguments against such tactics, Roosevelt seemed impressed. The President then went on to talk, though, of developing a bomber that could be carried aboard ship to within six hundred miles of Japan, be lowered over the side, and then "return to the parent ship to be hoisted in." Kimmel thought the portable bomber a "fanciful proposal," and they moved on to another subject.

Digressions aside, the meeting had been an opportunity for Kimmel to articulate his serious concerns. It had also produced what for the Admiral was a real breakthrough. The President relieved Kimmel of the impression he had that plans were afoot to transfer even more of his ships to the Atlantic. "Don't worry about it," said Roosevelt, "we have cancelled that." For this alone, the Admiral's journey to Washington had been worthwhile.

And that was that. From the White House, accompanied by ONI's Arthur McCollum, the Admiral and "Soc" McMorris headed for the Japanese embassy. Their exchange with diplomats there, as McMorris was to remember it, amounted to "a chat on banalities."

During Kimmel's visit, CNO Stark and his aides—and the President—had given the Admiral the impression that his views mattered. Stark and Roosevelt had heard him out. Whether they would respond to his many long-standing requests, of course, was another matter.

Kimmel broke his journey back to Hawaii in San Diego. He probably had an opportunity, however brief, to spend some time with his wife, Dorothy. He took time to address workers at Consolidated Aircraft, the company that made the PBY seaplanes he needed for long-range reconnaissance. "The Fleet needs, and needs badly, more of the planes which you are turning out," he told an audience of some eight thousand workers. "You must not permit a delay of one minute in the delivery of aircraft so vitally needed."

Many PBYs were indeed produced that year, to be allotted to units on the East Coast and to foreign Allies. None, however, were sent to Hawaii.

Shortly before Kimmel's visit to Washington, the President had asked Chief of Staff George Marshall for his views on the military's ability to defend Pearl Harbor. After two years in the post, sixty-year-old Marshall was on the way to becoming the towering American military figure of the twentieth century. The Chief of Staff had assured Roosevelt that the base at Pearl Harbor was "the strongest fortress in the world," that "with adequate air defense" an attacking enemy force would be intercepted "750 miles" before reaching its objective. Thanks to the airpower he said could be made rapidly available to Hawaii, attacking Pearl Harbor was considered "impracticable."

ONI's Arthur McCollum would recall thinking that those holding the reins of power had become complacent about the situation in the Pacific. From where he sat at headquarters, it seemed to him that they had come to the "grand conclusion . . . that if there was going to be a war, as far as the United States was concerned, it would be in the Atlantic and we could forget about the Pacific." Given the indications that the Japanese military seemed bent on seizing further territory, McCollum demurred. "Look here," he said he told colleagues; "we're underestimating these people."

In early spring, in Hawaii, Fleet intelligence officer Lieutenant Commander Edwin Layton had brought a book to Kimmel's attention. Layton, who had studied Japanese and served as Assistant Naval Attaché in Tokyo, had been mulling over translations he had made of a volume by a writer on naval matters, Shinsaku

Hirata. Hirata referred to U.S. war games that had showed it was theoretically possible for carrier-borne planes to strike Pearl Harbor in a "surprise raid." The book's title translated as *When We Fight*. "When," not "If."

Kimmel had asked Layton whether in his view the book reflected official or semiofficial thinking in Japan. Layton doubted it did, but said the Japanese might risk an attack "if they thought they could get away with it." "Soc" McMorris, for his part, thought it unlikely Japan would take such a gamble—but possible.

Weeks later came a glimpse of what the Japanese might be planning.

13

ON JUNE 9TH, 1941, the same day Admiral Kimmel met with the President, two Japanese men in Los Angeles were charged with espionage. One was a thirty-nine-year-old "language student," Itaru Tachibana; the other a "servant," Toraichi Kono. A third man, an American citizen named Al Blake, was held briefly in "technical custody," then released. Tachibana and Kono were charged with "conspiracy to obtain national defense information to be used for the injury of the United States."

It was an oddity about the characters involved that caught public attention; Kono had earlier been chauffeur-cum-valet to Charlie Chaplin. He had known Blake, a sometime street performer familiar to many as "Keeno, King of the Robots," back in silent film days. These details aside, though, the case was in fact a breakthrough in counterespionage. For the third member of the trio, Tachibana, was no ordinary language student.

He was, rather, a commander in the Japanese Navy working undercover. Ostensibly, over the past two years, he had been in the United States studying U.S. history and foreign policy. Sometime after enrolling at the University of Southern California, however, he had attracted the attention of the Office of Naval Intelligence in Los Angeles.

In part, what alerted ONI was the fact that he used the city's Olympic Hotel, a known haunt of suspected Japanese agents. It had been there, months earlier, that Kilsoo Haan, the Korean whistle-blower whose warnings of an attack on Pearl Harbor were to fall on deaf ears, had observed a meeting of other Japanese naval officers. Now, surveillance of Tachibana led Naval Intelligence to suspect he was monitoring the movements of U.S. warships.

What led to the agent's downfall, though, was a chance meeting between his driver Kono and Kono's old acquaintance from movie-making days, Al Blake. Kono then introduced Blake to Tachibana. On learning that Blake had once been in the U.S. Navy, the Japanese agent pumped him for current information. Blake had none but—sensing he could make big money—said he thought he knew how to get some. He pretended he had a friend serving aboard the battleship USS *Pennsylvania*, Admiral Kimmel's flagship, at Pearl Harbor. Could the "friend," Tachibana asked, come up with the sort of items he wanted—Navy code-books, plans of minefields, and so on? For that sort of thing, he promised, he would pay top dollar.

Realizing he was in over his head, Blake ran to the FBI—only to find that agents had no interest in his story. Naval Intelligence officers he contacted, however, did react. Seeing an opportunity for a sting operation, they contacted Admiral Kimmel's headquarters in Hawaii. Counterespionage was outside the Admiral's scope, but he gave the order that led to the trapping of Tachibana.

"We could easily arrange for Blake to get faked classified information," the Fleet intelligence officer recalled advising Kimmel. "That would bolster his position with Tachibana and at the same time feed bum dope to the Japanese . . . Kimmel approved, saying, 'Why not . . . I think it's a good idea. You go ahead with it.'"

A letter from the nonexistent friend was concocted, written on USS *Pennsylvania* stationery, telling "traitor" Blake that the "friend" had a grudge against the Navy and was keen to make money. Tachibana took the bait, and paid Blake to travel to Hawaii to see the imaginary buddy. He returned with bogus gunnery records—supposedly generated aboard the USS *Phoenix*, one of Kimmel's cruisers. Tachibana was now on the hook.

With the approval of the Japanese naval attaché in Washington, he offered Blake the vast sum of $6,000—that would be about $100,000 today—to return to Hawaii and obtain even more information. In the longer term, Tachibana suggested, Blake should set up a small business in Honolulu as a cover for gathering a stream of naval secrets. Following a second phony "spy mission,"

Blake passed Tachibana what appeared to be Admiral Kimmel's Fleet training schedules.

Caught red-handed, Tachibana was arrested. When they searched his effects, investigators found file cabinets and luggage containing a trove of information about defense: times of warships arriving and leaving, details of warships currently being built, information on naval airplanes, aerial photographs of naval bases.

Urgent Japanese diplomatic efforts, however, resulted in Tachibana's rapid release. This, Secretary of State Hull was to write, was because "our conversations with the Japanese were at a critical stage . . . The President and I figured that if there were the slightest possibility of inducing Japan to withdraw from the Axis alliance, we should pursue it." Tachibana was deported.

The operation had opened a window on the sheer scale of Japanese espionage. Papers found in Tachibana's possession linked him to a former British Royal Air Force officer, Frederick Rutland. Rutland had been on the Japanese payroll for years, urged, as he would later admit, to keep Tokyo supplied with information on the movements of U.S. warships.

Hawaii had long since also been part of the former squadron leader's focus. He, like Blake after him, had been urged to set up a business there as a cover—he had had in mind importing whiskey. Such a move, the Japanese Director of Naval Intelligence had explained to a colleague in a message, would "consolidate the ground for the future." What exactly Rutland had been up to in 1941 was never resolved. Because he was a British subject, and to avoid a noisy prosecution, he was quietly flown back to London.

There was a final irony of the Tachibana episode—something ONI learned even before arresting the spy. Though he had been caught trying to target the Pacific Fleet, that was precisely what he had originally been instructed *not* to do. His orders were to focus on American warships everywhere "except vicinity of Honolulu and Far East." The Japanese high command's plans for Pearl Harbor required, rather, specialized, high-caliber intelligence.

Nothing in the record, however, indicates that either U.S. Naval Intelligence or the FBI saw the possible implication—that operatives other than Tachibana might have been tasked for the work in Hawaii.

Following his expulsion from the United States, Tachibana went back to work for Japanese naval intelligence. He was to play a substantive role in intelligence planning for the raid on Pearl Harbor.

After World War II, the Joint Congressional Committee report on the attack would come out with an extraordinary statement: "The role played by espionage . . . may have been magnified out of all proportion to the realities of the situation." The evidence, as this and other chapters will show, is to the contrary.

A mass of detailed information establishes that Japan's spymasters did indeed concentrate on Pearl Harbor. They had done so long before the attack was even conceived, and the focus became sharper, month by month and week by week, as December 7th, 1941, approached. As the plan took shape, moreover, and once Japan forged an alliance with Hitler, agents acting on behalf of Germany weighed in.

The FBI and Naval Intelligence shared responsibility for counterespionage involving Japan, and Admiral Kimmel and his Fleet had to rely on them. Both agencies were to prove catastrophically inadequate, delinquent in failing to share with Kimmel's command key information that pointed to enemy plans to target Pearl Harbor. That is the stark conclusion to be drawn from the thousands of pages of government and military documents, books, and independent studies that have emerged—in some cases painfully slowly—since the war.

Japanese interest in the Hawaiian Islands did not ignite suddenly in early 1941. It had smoldered for nearly half a century since America took possession of them. As the U.S. Navy and Army footprint in Hawaii deepened, Tokyo had stationed agents in the islands and begun building files. By the mid-1930s, as tension between the two nations increased, so did the snooping.

On the eve of World War II, as many as 160,000 inhabitants, some 40 percent of the Hawaiian population, were ethnic Japanese. Wittingly or unwittingly, they were a fertile source of every sort of intelligence. Businessmen and ships' passengers could also be pumped for their observations. In Tokyo, the *joho kyoku*, the Third Bureau of the naval general staff, took the lead in commissioning and collating intelligence.

Nazi Germany, meanwhile, was cooperating with Japan on espionage. The arrangement had been in the works for years, as agreed at a secret 1935 meeting between Admiral Wilhelm Canaris, Hitler's military intelligence chief, and the Japanese naval attaché in Berlin. In the fall of 1940, when Germany, Japan, and Italy signed a military alliance that effectively carved up the world among the three countries, word went out that there was to be active cooperation on intelligence.

On the U.S. East Coast, U.S. intelligence intervened when a German agent met with a Japanese naval officer to pass him microfilm and purloined technical equipment for transmission to Germany. Neither of their nations was as yet at war with the United States, but routing through Japan was probably deemed more secure. Though the two men were caught and detained, the Japanese officer was allowed to leave for home. As in the Tachibana case weeks earlier, the State Department had asked that he not be prosecuted.

All the while, in Hawaii, a couple named Otto and Friedel Kühn were going about their seemingly ordinary lives—he growing fruit and vegetables, she running a beauty salon. Otto had left Germany, he was to say, because he wished "to study the Japanese language," and the couple sometimes traveled to Japan.

Otto Kühn's background spoke volumes. In Germany, he had joined the Nazi Party and consorted with a naval intelligence officer named Reinhard Heydrich, later to become second in command to SS leader Heinrich Himmler. Kühn had himself met

Himmler. Though he would claim he broke with the Nazis before leaving his homeland for the Pacific, he was reputed in Hawaii to lead the local German-American Bund, the organization of ethnic Germans that promoted the image of the Nazi regime in the United States. The German entertained lavishly, and his guests often included U.S. Army officers.

This detail did not escape the notice of the local office of the FBI. Nor did the fact that the Kühns were living way beyond their known means. Much later, after Pearl Harbor, the Bureau would calculate that Kühn over the years received the sum of $70,000— in today's currency, more than a million dollars—from "questionable sources." More than two years before the Japanese attack, a source told the FBI that the couple "may be espionage agents." The Bureau passed the word to Army and Navy Intelligence, but no action was taken.

On April 10th, eight months before the attack, a local FBI report proposed that the Kühns be "considered for custodial detention in the event of war." The previous month, in a wider-ranging report on the subject of detention, the same office had stated flatly that war would not come to Hawaii itself. "It is not conceivable," the report read, "that there could be a hostile attack on the Hawaiian Islands so long as the American Fleet is present in Pacific waters."

So embarrassingly inaccurate was this that after the war, when the FBI was preparing to share documents with one of the official inquiries into the Pearl Harbor attack, a senior aide would recommend to Director J. Edgar Hoover that the passage be "eliminated."

In 1941, as the months passed, the FBI continued to permit the Kühns to remain at large. Just two weeks before the attack, indeed, a new report would say there was nothing to indicate they were engaged in espionage, that Otto Kühn was due soon to be granted U.S. citizenship.

Not until after the attack would it become blindingly clear that the Kühns were indeed spies, and had taken money from the Japanese to help in preparations for the attack.

Long before the onslaught on Pearl Harbor, though, there would be other evidence—vivid evidence for anyone alert enough to pay attention—that German agents were gathering military information about Hawaii and the Pacific Fleet on behalf of the Japanese.

Nothing in the record indicates, however, that anyone paid real attention, or took the trouble to warn those in Hawaii.

14

IN EARLY 1941, 5,500 miles from Honolulu on the Atlantic island of Bermuda, a young woman named Nadya Gardner made
a discovery. Gardner, a former ballet dancer, was a staff member of Imperial Censorship—more prosaically, the mail-check
operation—that was based in the British colony during the war.
Bermuda was a routine stopover for civilian planes crossing the
Atlantic, and none were allowed to leave until all letters and pack-
ages had been checked. Contraband and traffic in currency aside,
the censors' crucial task was to identify communications between
enemy agents. If found, such mail would be photographed, perhaps altered, then sent on to its destination.

For months past, examiners had been giving special attention
to several letters mailed from New York to addressees in Germany,
Franco's Spain, and neutral Portugal. The sender, supposedly, was
a businessman who signed himself "Joe K." These were clearly covert communications, and the return addresses on the envelopes
turned out to be phony. Yet the text of the letters appeared vacuous, without significance. What was their real meaning?

The persistence of Nadya Gardner, the examiner assigned to
the letters, resulted in a major breakthrough. Laboratory tests for
secret writing time and again came back negative, but she insisted
on further testing. Then at last, when a rarely used chemical test
was performed, the hidden messages became visible. Some of the
letters contained information on American airplane production
figures and naval shipping movements. In March, a letter to one
of the suspect addressees reported on airplane shipments to Britain and U.S. Army training. The information about Joe K, and
more, was shared with the FBI.

As the months passed, on the orders of Winston Churchill and

with President Roosevelt's approval, British Intelligence had increased cooperation with its American counterparts. Following a
meeting between the British emissary William Stephenson and
FBI Director J. Edgar Hoover, Roosevelt had authorized what Stephenson said later was intended to be "the closest possible marriage between the Bureau and British Intelligence." With America
not yet in the war, this was a highly sensitive, top-secret arrangement. In New York, Stephenson set up an organization euphe-
mistically known as British Security Coordination (BSC). When
relevant to the United States, the discoveries made by Britain's
mail censors in Bermuda were reported through BSC to the FBI.

The writer of the "Joe K" letters turned out on investigation to
be Kurt Ludwig, a German spy fronting as a leather goods salesman. He and five associates would be caught, convicted of espionage, and sent to prison. Though British Intelligence had played a
central role in the case, this brought a burst of marvelous publicity
for the FBI.

The leader of the spy ring, a man who had used the name "Kon-
rad" in the correspondence, did not face justice: he had been killed
in a traffic accident in Manhattan before the case was broken.
His true name was Ulrich Von der Osten, and he had reported at
length on the U.S. base at Pearl Harbor.

An experienced professional, Von der Osten had been known
to Allied counterintelligence agencies since World War I. He was
an officer in German military intelligence and had served on the
general staff. His base in 1940 and 1941, when he was not in the
United States, was Shanghai, in China. The Far East connection
had been key to the overall operation. Team members had sent
duplicates of their messages, intended ultimately for the attention
of SS chief Himmler and his aides, to addresses in China and
Japan. When Von der Osten's accomplice Ludwig was arrested, he
was apparently trying to make his way to a West Coast port and a
ship bound for Japan.

Three documents that emerged during the case showed that
the spies had sought intelligence very relevant to Admiral Kimmel and his Pacific Fleet. A letter attributed by the FBI to Ludwig

contained a slip of paper that bore the words "Pacific insular defences" followed by a question mark and "Wake Island." Kimmel
was to reinforce Wake, a strategic outpost with a layover airstrip
for the Pan Am Clipper, shortly before the Pearl Harbor attack.
Two weeks after the attack on Pearl, however, Wake would fall to
the Japanese.

A second, truly remarkable document, written in longhand
by Von der Osten on the stationery of an American ocean liner,
provided detailed intelligence on Pearl Harbor itself. He reported
specific observations made while he was in Hawaii. It read:

AMERICAN PRESIDENT LINES

NEW YORK—CALIFORNIA—ORIENT—ROUND THE WORLD

ON BOARD

A. *Honolulu* (Island of Oahu)
  Strong concentrations of troops of all kind. Said to be
40000 Army and as many Navy. Lately arrived: 1500 technicians, more expected . . . Harbor SW MoKapu is being read-
ied as sea plane base. Barracks for army are being built . . .
esp. between Pearl Harbor-Honolulu. . . . 57 officers of the
F.B.I. are said to be in Oahu alone. Questioning can't be done
too openly . . . Navy: Said to be stationed in Pearl Harbor &
rest of islands 150 units of all kinds. Seen in harbor about
50 vessels at least: 5 armoured ships, big (battleships?), Saratoga and other, very small aircraft carrier. . . . several units of
destroyers . . . destr. No. 372, 383, 374, 375—1 drydock 1000
ft. stationary, other swimming [floating] dock of same length
said arrived recently . . . *Airforce*: Nothing to be seen, safe [sic]
a few planes in air. Main bases southwest Pearlharbor . . .
Seen 2 forts between Waikiki-beach and Honolulu . . . Crater
of Diamondhead said containing lots of guns, esp. howitzers.
Point farthest to right on photo has lookout . . .

Von der Osten had asked the person to whom he was sending
his letter—the unimaginative name he used was "C. W. Smith"—

to forward it on to "Carl—82, with map and photo." The segment dealing with Pearl Harbor ended with the note:

> This will be of interest to our yellow allies, are you interested? Might be a good idea to despatch observer, if you are. Want me to find somebody?

The postmark on the envelope shows that the letter had been mailed in February 1940, a year before Admiral Kimmel took command of the Fleet and almost a year before—unknown to all but the Japanese high command—the plans to attack Pearl Harbor began to take shape.

The third document, retrieved a year later in the spring of 1941, when the attack plan was very much on the drawing board, shows that Von der Osten evidently gathered more material of potential use to Germany's "yellow allies." His belongings, retrieved from his room at Manhattan's Taft Hotel after his death in the traffic accident, included a map featuring Pearl Harbor.

What had been intended as a "marriage" between U.S. and British Intelligence had been beset, from the start, by territorial skirmishes.

In May 1941, Britain's Director of Naval Intelligence, Rear Admiral John Godfrey, arrived in Washington accompanied by Commander Ian Fleming—the future author of the James Bond books. They, like Stephenson before them, went to see J. Edgar Hoover. The FBI chief, Fleming would recall, "expressed himself firmly but politely uninterested in our mission . . . Hoover's response was negative as a cat's paw. With the air of doing us a favor he had us piloted through the FBI laboratory and record department . . . Then, with a firm, dry handshake, we were shown the door."

As Admiral Godfrey saw it, the problem was not only at the FBI. Contact with military intelligence left him disconcerted. "After a fortnight," Godfrey recalled, "it became clear that I was up against a brick wall, and that by approaching only the Navy and

Army intelligence chiefs, and Federal Bureau of Investigation['s] Mr. Hoover, I should achieve nothing." Godfrey concluded that there was virtually no collaboration between the agencies.

In an effort to improve the situation, President Roosevelt would soon appoint a Coordinator of Information. U.S. Naval Intelligence and Army Intelligence, and the FBI, were displeased with the decision. FBI Director Hoover called the move "Roosevelt's folly."

In mid-1941, the FBI remained the U.S. agency responsible for liaison with the British on counterespionage matters. According to the official history of Britain's covert wartime intelligence operations in the United States, published in 1998, the price of Hoover's cooperation in the months before Pearl Harbor would be "always conditioned by his overwhelming ambition for the FBI."

Late that summer, the Germans would send to the United States a man who—they hoped—would supply hard intelligence about Pearl Harbor. He was, however, a double agent who was in reality loyal to British Intelligence. The FBI would be told in advance that he was coming and would handle him for many months. It and other U.S. agencies, however, were to squander the opportunity he offered.

15

IN JUNE 1941, FBI Director Hoover was advised that the British proposed to send to the United States a man named Dusko Popov. Popov, he was told in a staff memorandum, was:

> *presently of assistance to the English government, although actually in the employ of the Germans. He has been issued instructions to proceed to the United States . . . London thought there was no question concerning his honesty, his reliability, and no doubt existed as to his loyalty . . . The British would vouch for him 100%.*

Indeed they would. The legendary British Intelligence controller who ran Popov, John Masterman, would later describe him as having been "one of the chief figures in the double-cross world . . . a leading and highly placed agent." Masterman headed the XX— for Double-Cross—Committee, which used double agents to feed disinformation to the Nazi enemy, time and again causing the Germans to make disastrous mistakes. He and Stewart Menzies— head of MI6, Britain's foreign intelligence agency—forged a bond with Popov, who was to become godfather to Menzies's nieces.

Capping his various feats of counterespionage, Popov would be one of the team of agents who deceived the Germans over where the D-Day landings would be made, and when. The successful ruse is thought to have saved many Allied lives. After the war, Popov would be awarded the honorary rank of colonel, the Order of the British Empire, and the Distinguished Service Medal.

The businessman son of a wealthy, well-connected Yugoslav family, Popov had been approached by the Germans to spy on their behalf, had agreed to do so, then made contact with the British. The British encouraged him, in particular, to stay in touch with a German friend named Johann "Johnny" Jebsen, himself a seeming Nazi agent whose real sympathies—like Popov's—would also turn out to be with the Allies. Jebsen, for his part, introduced Popov to a loyal German agent who used the name "Major Ludovico von Karsthoff."

Complex checks on Popov, made during "business" trips to England from his base in neutral Portugal, eventually satisfied British interrogators that he could be the real thing—a double agent of great potential benefit to Britain's war aims.

Popov's German handlers made it their practice to send the man they thought to be "their" spy off to Britain with a list of questions, usually but not always on military matters, a routine that played neatly into London's double-cross system. Through Popov, the enemy would be fed answers that were a poisonous mélange—false information designed to mislead mixed in with true or half-true information that could cause Britain no serious harm.

In the summer of 1941, Popov's German handlers decided to send "their" agent on a mission to the United States. The British, his true controllers, accordingly sent word to the FBI. Knowledge of what intelligence information the Germans wanted Popov to deliver, London suggested, could prove valuable. At the FBI, Director Hoover approved the visit. Popov duly arrived in New York in the second week of August.

As on previous missions for the Germans, Popov brought a questionnaire with him. It reached America in the form of a two-page document—typewritten, in German—and, as befitted a spy mission, also in the form of "microdots" on seemingly innocuous telegram forms. Microdots—minuscule photographs that appeared on paper as periods or dots on the letter "i"—were a new technique. Their use by the Germans came as a revelation to intelligence personnel in both Britain and the United States.

The questionnaire Popov brought with him made clear that the Germans expected real results from their presumed spy during his time in the United States. They wanted information on U.S. aircraft production, delivery of planes to Britain, pilot training, naval movements, and the training of troops, as well as "reports regarding U.S. bases." One requirement, for Popov to report on bases in Florida, was summarized in a mere three words.

Of the ninety lines of the questionnaire, however, more than half were devoted to questions about Hawaii. German Intelligence wanted to know, in part:

Details regarding the Naval munitions and mine depot of the island of Kushua (Pearl Harbor). Sketches if possible . . . Is the crater Punchbowl (Honolulu) being used as a munitions store? If not, are there other military facilities there? . . . Airport Luke Field. Details (sketches if possible) regarding situation of the hangars (number?) workshops, bomb stores and fuel stores . . . Exact situation of the hydroplane station . . . Naval Air base Kaneohe. Exact information . . . Army Airports Wicham [sic—a mangling of Hickam] Field and Wheeler Field. Exact situation . . . underground facilities? Surface covering? (sketches).

Thirteen lines of the questionnaire were devoted to "Navy Base Pearl Harbor":

1. Exact information and sketches regarding the situation of the government shipyards, of the pier facilities . . . fuel facilities, situation of the drydock number 1 and of the drydock now under construction . . .
2. Details regarding the Submarine station (Layout-plan) . . .
3. Where is the station for mine-sweeper units located? How far has the dredging work progressed at the entrance . . . Water depths?
4. Number of mooring berths?
5. Is there a floating-dock located in Pearl Harbor? . . . Special Assignments
    Reports regarding torpedo-protective-net . . . To what extent already available in commercial and battle fleet?

Very evidently, four months before the attack that was to bring America into the war, the Germans wanted detailed military information on Pearl Harbor. In the German plain text version of the questionnaire, the fifty questions about Pearl Harbor appear almost at the top of the list of requests. (They also appear in full, though less prominently, in the FBI laboratory's random assembly of the text contained in the microdots.) To any 1941 reader, obtaining intelligence on Pearl Harbor would have appeared to be Popov's priority task.

Popov himself, moreover, was to insist years later—in a memoir—that he explained to FBI debriefers the additional reasons to pay attention to the questionnaire's items on Pearl Harbor. Before he set off for the United States, Jebsen—the German agent friend who had originally asked him to work for the Nazis—had mentioned a recent visit by a Japanese naval delegation to Italy. The Japanese visitors' special interest, said Jebsen, who had been assigned to act as liaison, had been to collect information on Britain's recent successful strike on the Italian fleet at Taranto. A distinctive feature at Taranto was the shallow depth of the water—as it was, too, at Pearl Harbor.

There was a further clue to what the Japanese might be planning, Popov was to recall having told the FBI. Before he left for the United States, his German controller von Karsthoff had told him he had received "specific instructions" on the need for information about Pearl Harbor "as soon as possible." The instructions, Popov remembered informing the FBI, were that it was "the first thing on my agenda." He was to report to von Karsthoff that he was making immediate "arrangements to go to Hawaii, perhaps next week."

Three decades later, when Popov's memoir was about to be published, the FBI rushed to deny the former agent's assertions. Its Director at the time, Clarence Kelley, insisted to Popov's publisher that the agent had not supplied information that "indicated the Japanese would attack Pearl Harbor." The spy's account, Kelley was told by his staff, was "fiction designed to sell his book."

Did Popov embroider or misremember events when, years later, he claimed his German contact Jebsen told him of the Japanese interest in the use of aerial torpedoes at Taranto? Was it true that, as Popov was to claim, his German handler von Karsthoff said his superiors wanted "rapid results" on Hawaii? Nothing in the U.S. record, now apparently released in its entirety, refers to his having discussed any of that with the FBI.

Various facts support the essence of what Popov claimed. A Japanese naval mission did go to Taranto at the relevant time in the spring of 1941. The admiral who led it, Koki Abe, would later take part in the Pearl Harbor attack. The Italian Admiral Giuseppe Fioravanzo, who after the war wrote at length about the mission, recalled that the Japanese team showed special interest in the British raid on Taranto using aerial torpedoes.

One thing the FBI could not deny was the authenticity of the questionnaire Popov brought to the United States. The very detailed military information on Pearl Harbor it requested—not least the question about "water depths"—was the very sort of intelligence an enemy force planning a strike would need. Oddly, though, there is nothing at all in the FBI record about Pearl Harbor as an aspect of Popov's mission, other than the text of the questionnaire itself.

The U.S. and British files combined, meanwhile, tell a melancholy tale of the agent's experience in America. Things started well enough. In his first days in the United States, a senior FBI agent deemed him "very enthusiastic and seemingly sincere." The British got word that Popov, for his part, was "quite satisfied with arrangements made."

Less than a month later, however, London heard that Popov's morale had plummeted. He "did not believe the American authorities trusted him . . . If they did not trust him, he wanted to return to England." Though London had "unhesitatingly" vouched for him before he arrived, the files vividly show, FBI agents bugged his living quarters, listened to his phone calls, relentlessly watched his every move.

Popov lived high on the hog, spending money like water, dallying with women, and gambling, behaving like a playboy. Back in England, his British handlers were familiar with this, and tolerated it. As a former colleague noted, his lifestyle—in which he reveled—was a cover for his espionage. In the FBI of 1941, an organization ruled by the famously puritanical J. Edgar Hoover, Popov's behavior was anathema. That, combined with a report at one point that something Popov had said raised "very serious doubt as to the informant's sincerity," irreparably damaged his relationship with the Bureau.

Popov was to stay on in the United States for more than a year, but his operation was a shadow of what had been intended. The FBI's aims and methods were very different from those of British Intelligence. Its handling of the Von der Osten spy case, in which British analysts had played a major role, had riled the espionage hierarchy in London. "Revelations in the American press," counterespionage chief Guy Liddell noted, were "very damaging to our work."

The British ran double agents in order to deceive a hostile intelligence service, to trick an enemy into making damaging mistakes. The FBI's concept of running a double agent had no such long-term goal. The Bureau's objective, in the words of a British internal review of the Popov fiasco, was merely to "get their double agent into contact with genuine agents, whom they can arrest and have tried in the full light of publicity."

From the start of the Popov operation, a memo shows, the FBI was leery of British "meddling," of London's not leaving the running of the spy entirely to the Bureau. The way the FBI ran him, however, was less than effective. The FBI did eventually set up a radio transmitter to relay bogus messages to Popov's German spymasters, but did so ineptly. The British had to complain that Popov "had not been taken to see the W/T station and had no idea of its location . . . There is very real danger here such as might arise if he were suddenly asked by one of his friends to transmit a message rapidly."

Responding to the requests in the German questionnaire Popov brought with him would have meant traveling to a number of places. He did make a brief visit to Florida, watched constantly by the FBI, but never did get to Pearl Harbor to go through the pretense of gathering the intelligence the Germans wanted. An FBI agent told him that the trip was off.

The paucity and poor quality of the reports Popov did manage to send back to Germany placed him in peril. There would come a time—months after the attack on Pearl Harbor—when the British realized "there were indications that the Germans had begun to recognise for the first time the possibility that Popov might be playing a double game"—might be disloyal to the Nazi cause.

When Popov eventually returned to Europe, the British told him the chances were that he had been blown, that returning to Portugal and his German handlers could be a fast route to arrest, torture, and probable execution. He could, they said, honorably end his work as a double agent.

Instead, Popov did go back to Portugal, continued the pretense that he was working for the Nazis, and went on to play his part in deceiving the Germans as to where and when the D-Day invasion would take place. The appalling risk he took in returning to the enemy camp, one of his British handlers was to write years later, was a supreme example of "cold-blooded courage."

Virtually every American agency had, one way or another, mishandled the Popov matter. Not even his arrival in August had gone according to plan. The officers who approached him and began pumping him for information were from Naval and Army Intelligence, not initially from the FBI, which was expecting him. The FBI had to step in to call off its military counterparts.

Some weeks later, the Bureau reached out to Navy and Army Intelligence. In order for Popov to respond to the German questionnaire, the military would have to supply information—albeit a mix of misleading and truthful but harmless information. About a month after the agent's arrival, the record shows, the Army began to oblige.

Naval Intelligence at first declined to help. Then, when Popov told the FBI it was vital that he receive credible information to feed to the Germans, a Navy liaison officer said he would take the request to the head of Naval Intelligence and to Chief of Naval Operations Stark.

At last, little more than a month before the Pearl Harbor attack, the Navy came up with a partial response to the questionnaire—on the matter of whether the United States was protecting its ships with torpedo nets. The proposed answer was concocted so as to suggest that such armored netting was in use. (In fact, it was not, least of all—as discussed in Chapter 11—at Pearl Harbor.)

That, however, was the extent to which any U.S. intelligence agency took advantage of the German requests for military information relevant to Hawaii. Hawaii, of course, was far away from Germany's theater of naval operations. It did not require a skilled analyst to realize that the Nazis did not need such intelligence for themselves. The responses to the questionnaire Popov brought to America were of real interest only to the Japanese.

Clearly, each of the U.S. intelligence agencies with knowledge of the questions about Pearl Harbor bore some responsibility for the way the matter was handled. Naval and Army Intelligence had been supplied by the FBI with paraphrased summaries of the questionnaire. Both summaries, especially the one sent to the Navy, made it obvious that the information requested was of use only to an enemy. Nothing in the record, however, suggests that Navy or Army Intelligence gave the matter serious attention.

Popov's former British handlers would years later assert that, on seeing the questionnaire, they had deduced that an attack on Pearl Harbor was being planned. Should they, then, have merely assumed that the FBI would reach the same conclusion? "We ought to have stressed its importance more than we did," John

Masterman, who headed the Double-Cross Committee, was to write: "should have risked a snub and have pointed out to our friends in the United States what the significance of the document might be." Major "Tar" Robertson, who had the closest personal contact with Popov, thought with hindsight that it had been a mistake "not to take the Pearl Harbor information and send it separately to Roosevelt."

FBI Director Hoover was a man who milked every opportunity to boast about the Bureau's achievements. Rather than bring attention to the peril to Pearl Harbor that was implicit in the questionnaire, he saw it as another opportunity to brag.

Within hours of receiving his laboratory's analysis of the microdot version of the German questionnaire, Hoover had rushed off a memorandum to President Roosevelt's military aide at the White House. "I thought," he wrote, "the President and you might be interested in the attached photographs which show one of the methods used by the German espionage system in transmitting messages . . . The microphotographs referred to above were secured in connection with a current investigation being made by the FBI."

The military aide, a two-star general, did pass Hoover's message to Roosevelt. Soon afterward, the Director wrote again, this time to crow about the fact that his technicians had managed to *improve* on the microdot technique. The FBI laboratory, he said, had managed to make microdots that were even more minuscule than the Germans'. Neither note acknowledged the fact that, far from having been obtained in the course of an FBI investigation, the microdots reached the FBI courtesy of British Intelligence.

There was, though, a greater irony, the most tragic aspect of Hoover's self-promotion. While attachments to his notes to the President included excerpts from the German questionnaire, they omitted entirely its long opening portion—the part with requests for intelligence on Pearl Harbor. When the Director's second message reached the White House, like its predecessor without the questionnaire's most significant content, only two months remained before the Japanese attack.

———

Future CIA Director William Casey, referring to the Popov episode, was one day to contend that it had shown Hoover's "total
incompetence for sophisticated wartime intelligence activity early
on." Admiral Kimmel's former Fleet intelligence officer, Edwin
Layton, thought the Director's failure "another American fumble
on the road to Pearl Harbor."

It was an unforgivably careless fumble, by Hoover and by every
official who handled the questionnaire and missed its ominous
significance. No mention of their incompetence, however, would
be made during postwar Pearl Harbor investigations. None of
those who failed to give the questionnaire proper attention would
be questioned about it, let alone held to account.

Admiral Kimmel, who never saw the questionnaire, was to be
treated very differently.

16

FROM THE MOMENT Japanese officers began considering the possibility of a strike on Pearl Harbor, access to solid, regular intelligence had become a priority. Should it come from their ally Germany, it was welcome. Primarily, however, Tokyo relied on its own resources. In Hawaii, its agents' mission was only too easy.

As one historian put it, the sprawling base where President Roosevelt had placed the U.S. Pacific Fleet was "one of the most open naval installations in the world . . . almost as open as a goldfish bowl." The bowl was the anchorage itself. The goldfish were Admiral Kimmel's ships and airplanes. For anyone with knowledge and powers of observation, the heights above the harbor were an ideal vantage point. As Kimmel himself would tell one of the official inquiries into the attack, a large part of the mission for a Japanese spy was merely to "go up in the hills and look down."

There is espionage and there is espionage. The practitioners of derring-do, from the real-world Dusko Popovs to the fantastic agents of *Mission: Impossible* and the James Bond movies, are in the minority. "Legal" espionage, the entirely legitimate practice of systematically watching, recording, and reporting—without breaking the law—goes on all the time, all over the world. The individuals tasked to carry it out may or may not have been trained in espionage. Their front, however, is as members of an internationally protected species: the world's diplomatic corps.

At Pearl Harbor, the base from which Japan's spies operated was no secret. "It was a matter of common knowledge," recalled Lieutenant General Charles Herron, who had commanded the Army's defense force in Hawaii before Kimmel arrived, that "the Japanese consulate in Hawaii was the hotbed of espionage."

The consulate, on Honolulu's Nuuanu Avenue, was a colonial-style building surrounded by exotic blooms and the obligatory palms. It had housed Tokyo's consular staff since the nineteenth century. With the Fleet's arrival in 1940, the Imperial Japanese Navy's intelligence department—the Third Bureau—required a more regular stream of information. Its requests were funneled to the consulate through Japan's foreign ministry.

America's open culture, with its newspapers, periodicals, and books, for a while sufficed as a resource. From late 1940, however, media coverage was no longer enough. The first "legal" observer sent out to scout Pearl Harbor, American investigators were eventually to learn, was consulate treasurer Kohichi Seki. He did so under the direction of the vice consul.

Sometimes by taxi, sometimes with a fellow staff member, Seki would drive to the anchorage, peer through the car windows, then return to the consulate to write up what he had seen. His reports, in code, were transmitted to Tokyo by commercial telegraph. Though he had some rudimentary naval knowledge, however, the Third Bureau wanted somebody more professional assigned to the work.

March 1941 saw two arrivals at the consulate. A new consul general, Nagao Kita, would henceforth sign most reports to Tokyo about Pearl Harbor. The second man's job description was "chancellor," a post that supposedly meant he would be dealing with "expatriation matters." The name under which he registered with the State Department was "Tadashi Morimura." His true name, however, was Takeo Yoshikawa, and he was a graduate of the Japanese naval academy who had spent four years training with the Third Bureau. In the nine months to come, he would supply the high-quality information required for the attack on Pearl Harbor.

Yoshikawa, who survived the war, would eventually spin stories that made him out to be a sort of master spy. His accounts graced the pages of the *Washington Post* and the U.S. Naval Institute's magazine *Proceedings*. To swallow them whole, however, one would have to believe that Yoshikawa spied by working as a dishwasher in a U.S. officers' mess, wandered near a prohibited military area posing as a peasant—once being shot at by a sailor on guard duty—and performed underwater espionage by breathing through a "hollow reed."

Such claims are ludicrous, not least because to have indulged in such follies would have risked arousing suspicion. Exposure of what he was doing could have wrecked Japan's entire Pearl Harbor endeavor. Yoshikawa's earliest interviews, and the accounts of those who knew him in 1941, are more reliable. For all the agent's later bombast, his work as a "legal" spy was remarkable.

The opportunity to do intelligence work had come Yoshikawa's way by chance, when he was twenty-seven and illness stymied his plan to become a naval aviator. He had since been deskbound, studying U.S. and British naval activity in the Pacific and Far East—and learning English. In Hawaii, Consul Kita provided him with a desk near his own office and living quarters within the compound. Standing instructions, Yoshikawa was to recall, were that a consulate staffer could "indulge only in such espionage activity as could be carried on without compromising diplomatic and consular relations."

The agent proceeded for a while much as had his predecessor Seki. Using one or the other of two drivers, he would simply cruise around by car. The newcomer, however, was more systematic. He identified spots with especially commanding views of particular locations: a spot useful for observing Pearl Harbor and the Hickam Field air base; a good place to watch the runway on Ford Island; a vantage point from which to see the submarine base.

One of the drivers who accompanied the "chancellor" on such trips sometimes carried a camera—a prop to suggest that the men were ordinary sightseers. The fundamental rule, the drivers had been told, was "not to get caught."

On occasion, but not too often, the "chancellor" would dress in laborer's clothes, then wander in sugarcane fields that offered a fine view of Pearl Harbor. He frequented a teahouse, the Shuncho-ro, which had a window that looked down on Pearl Harbor— and a telescope. The Shuncho-ro also employed geishas (hostesses and entertainers who offered female company, not the so-called "geisha girls" of postwar occupation days in Tokyo, who were whores).

Yoshikawa was, nevertheless, something of a womanizer and sybarite. Former associates at the consulate would recall that he was "frequently drunk, often had women in his quarters over-night, came to work late or not at all . . . generally conducted himself as if he were beyond penalty . . . a mystery man."

Talking with geishas, or with others who met U.S. servicemen, however, could be a way of gaining tidbits of information. Pausing for a drink at the soda stand near the main gate of the Navy Yard, without being too obvious about it, could also be profitable. The operator of the soda stand was a useful source on the comings and goings of American warships. Given the huge number of people with Japanese features in Hawaii, there was nothing especially noticeable about Yoshikawa.

Tokyo's "legal" spy even reportedly had opportunities to chat one-on-one with some of Admiral Kimmel's seamen. Yoshikawa is said to have frequented the Venice Café, a bar popular with men on shore leave. At the Dai Nippon Athletic Club, he may have talked about kendo, or other martial arts, with Americans. He was ever alert for snippets about naval activity. No one, though, would ever recall him having pumped people for information. He never overstepped the mark.

Through the spring and summer of 1941, Yoshikawa would sally forth to gather information, return to write up his notes, then pass them to Consul Kita for transmission to Tokyo. The reports went out as encoded telegrams, addressed to the foreign ministry but destined for study by the analysts in the Third Bureau.

"The key information," the spy would recall, "was always the number and type of ships present at Pearl Harbor and the number and type of aircraft present at the various island airfields." Essential, too, were his observations of the routines the Fleet's ships seemed to follow, and the number and timing of flights by reconnaissance airplanes—of which, Admiral Kimmel had long complained, there was such a shortage.

One day, at the consulate, Yoshikawa was present when the FBI Agent-in-Charge in Hawaii, Robert Shivers, came to visit Consul Kita. During the conversation, a sort of amiable verbal jousting, Shivers suggested that Kita himself venture out to "see what you can see." Kita smoothly declined the suggestion, noting that the FBI would follow his every move.

Shivers was under no illusions about the consulate staff's nefarious activities—he had even been tipped off as to what Yoshikawa, under the alias Morimura, might be up to. An FBI memo now available shows that, by early summer, agents were aware that the spy spent most of his time out of the office. An informant told them, moreover, that he "must be an outside man for the consulate." Apparently, however, the Bureau lost interest in him at that point—an investigative lapse that did not surface during any post–Pearl Harbor inquiry.

The subject of espionage by the consulate, though, came up regularly at the weekly meetings Shivers held with the Navy's District Intelligence chief, Captain Irving Mayfield; and the Army's chief local investigator, Lieutenant Colonel George Bicknell. For months, Mayfield's men had been tapping eight of the consulate telephone lines, including the phone at the Consul's home. The taps picked up some evidence of interest in the Fleet, but not much more.

What Mayfield could not have, and wished he had, was access to the Consul's cable traffic. Federal law prohibited the interception of cable or wireless traffic to and from foreign nations. The Kita cables that flashed Yoshikawa's espionage reports back to Tokyo remained beyond American investigators' reach.

In June 1941, it looked for a while as though action might be taken against Japanese consular staffers across the United States. Nationwide, German and Italian consulates were closed down. Yet in spite of the furor over Itaru Tachibana's arrest and deportation from Los Angeles—for directing espionage against Kimmel's Fleet from Los Angeles—Japanese consulates remained open. It was not a time, the State Department felt, to imperil delicate ongoing negotiations.

In Hawaii, the FBI's Shivers called a meeting with his military counterparts to discuss another way of bringing pressure to bear. Over and above the staff at the consulate, he thought, the more than two hundred "consular agents"—Japanese citizens who performed minor functions for the consulate—represented a potential security risk. As many of them had not registered as required, could they not be prosecuted? Shivers sought the views of his opposite numbers in the military, and legal advice.

The Navy's view on what to do about the consular agents, Admiral Kimmel would cheerfully recall, was essentially to "put them all in the jug." General Short demurred, however, arguing that prosecution would "unduly alarm" local Japanese.

In Washington in late summer and early fall, politicians lobbied for action to address Japan's espionage. The chairman of the House Un-American Activities Committee, Martin Dies, and—separately—Senator Guy Gillette, both called for investigations in Congress. Gillette's resolution specifically referred to the activity of "Japanese consular officials in Hawaii."

Neither investigation went forward. When Dies and Gillette pressed their initiatives, President Roosevelt and Secretary of State Cordell Hull told them this was no time to rock the boat. Following a further advance into Indochina by Japanese forces, a move that was being punished by even stiffer American economic sanctions, the United States' diplomatic exchanges with Japan were supersensitive. Dies and Gillette backed off.

In Honolulu, Consul Kita had brazenly denied the allegations being made in Washington. "The Japanese consulate here," he told the local press, was "not engaged in any such activities." Regardless, FBI observation of the consulate, and the tapping of its phones, continued. Behind the scenes, meanwhile, Bureau agents received authorization to conduct thorough, complete investigations of the Japanese consular agents. As the weeks slipped by, however, nothing actionable was developed.

Under the noses of the U.S. investigators, and even though the FBI had been tipped off about him, Takeo Yoshikawa aka "chancellor Morimura" would continue gathering vital intelligence until the very eve of the attack. As plans for a strike firmed up, the demands on his services increased.

Ten weeks before the attack, a new encoded message from Tokyo was delivered to Consul Kita. Nominally from the Foreign Minister, Teijiro Toyoda, it was in fact from Japanese naval intelligence. It was marked *shikyu*, "very urgent":

FROM: Tokyo (Toyoda)
TO: Honolulu
SEPTEMBER 24, 1941
83

Strictly secret.

Henceforth, we would like to have you make reports concerning vessels along the following lines insofar as possible:

1. The waters (of Pearl Harbor) are to be divided roughly into five sub-areas. (We have no objections to your abbreviating as much as you like.)

Area A. Waters between Ford Island and the Arsenal.

Area B. Waters adjacent to the Island south and west of Ford Island. (This area is on the opposite side of the Island from Area A.)

Area C. East Loch.

Area D. Middle Loch.

Area E. West Loch and the communicating water routes.

2. With regard to warships and aircraft carriers, we would like to have you report on those at anchor, (these are not so important) tied up at wharves, buoys and in docks. (Designate types and classes briefly. If possible would like to have

you make mention of the fact when there are two or more
vessels along side the same wharf.)

This message, expressed as it was with old-fashioned politesse,
would one day become a notorious historical document. For Consul Kita and his spy Yoshikawa at the time, it signaled a major
change in what their Tokyo spymasters wanted from them. They
were to report in a new way, one that required them to divide Pearl
Harbor into precisely specified segments, and send intelligence
not only on warships' movements but also where these ships were
moored and whether they were moored alongside other vessels. In
the end—three weeks before the Pearl Harbor attack—the orders
were to do this as often as *twice a week*.

The very existence of the message, meanwhile, would one day
have the effect of calling into question the reputations of some
of the most senior military officers and highest government officials in the United States. For a small circle of those officers and
government officials shared a hypersensitive secret—that American codebreakers had long since cracked some of the codes in
which Japan transmitted its most sensitive messages. The text
of encoded traffic to and from Tokyo and its diplomatic missions
around the world was available in Washington throughout 1941.

Those reading the intercepts of consular messages knew well
that Japanese Intelligence routinely collected basic information
on numerous harbors used by the U.S. Navy—not only Hawaii
but San Francisco, Panama, Seattle, Los Angeles, Manila, and the
base at Guantánamo in Cuba. There was nothing unusual about
that. No one, however, seems to have noticed that the Honolulu
consulate received more requests for information than any other
mission. Nowhere else, moreover, had Japanese missions been
told to provide information on the location of ships in specific
parts of harbors, or on where ships were moored together.

Any alert American privy to the secret intercepts should have
seen the potential significance of the very specific requests in the
September 24th message to Kita and Yoshikawa. The message
should have triggered several questions: What is the reason for

these requests? Why are these precise details required about Pearl Harbor, and about nowhere else? And, not least: Why are these requests being made *now*?

The only rational reason for making the requests was that the Japanese Navy was at least seriously considering an aerial or submarine attack on Pearl Harbor, and perhaps was even about to carry out such an attack.

Those with responsibility for thwarting espionage in Hawaii—the FBI and military investigators—were not told either of the September 24th message, or of the exchanges that were to follow. Nor were they made available to Admiral Kimmel, to the Army's General Short—whose force bore primary responsibility for the defense of Pearl Harbor—or to their intelligence staffs.

Years later, in a prepared statement to Congress' Joint Committee, the Admiral would not hide his outrage over the fact that Washington had withheld from him messages that—in his words—"pointed to an attack by Japan upon the ships in Pearl Harbor. The information sought and obtained, with such painstaking detail, had no other conceivable usefulness from a military viewpoint."

Kimmel pointed out to the Committee that at the very beginning of 1941, when Ambassador Grew in Tokyo had passed on word of a possible attack on Pearl Harbor, the Office of Naval Intelligence had told him the report had no credibility. "I was entitled to know," Kimmel went on, "when information in the Navy Department completely altered the information and advice previously given to me . . . No one had a more direct and immediate interest in the security of the Fleet in Pearl Harbor than its commander in chief."

Only much later would it become clear why the telltale Japanese consular traffic had not been shared with the Admiral and General Short in Hawaii. Rightly or wrongly, whether deliberately or by mistake, they had been excluded from one of the most closely held secrets the nation has ever had.

MAGIC.

THE MAGICIANS OF war, then as now, were the codebreakers. On the eve of World War II, a cohort of driven American men and women were laboring—under intense pressure—to read the secret messages of the nation's perceived adversaries. Years earlier, when he was Secretary of State, Henry Stimson had held the idealistic notion that "Gentlemen do not read each other's mail." Such reservations, soon to be backed by law, put the brake on work that—with the onward march of radio technology—was an absolute necessity.

The reality was that, then and into the 1930s, a handful of Army and Navy codebreakers worked on in secret, illegally, in an atmosphere of sometimes bitter interservice rivalry, underfunded and undermanned. They were a talented few, directed and inspired by a handful of experienced veterans.

"Most of the time," one of their number wrote, a cryptanalyst was "groping in the darkest night. Now and again a little flicker of light gleams across the darkness, tantalizing him with a glimpse of a path. Hopefully he dashes to it, only to find himself in a different labyrinth . . . Sometimes he is engulfed in an interminable polar night."

For years during the 1930s, there had been light. The U.S. Navy's Communication Security Section, OP-20-G—headed by a gifted veteran, Commander Laurance Safford—had been able to read Japan's primary naval operating code. Navy cryptanalysts and the Army's Signal Intelligence Service (SIS) had also broken a number of codes used by Japan's foreign ministry. The ministry's many codes broke down into four basic groups. The highest level, known as "RED," was for top-secret communications to and from embassies and consulates; the lowest was for routine administrative messages.

Darkness fell for the cryptanalysts in 1939 when, one by one, the Japanese introduced new codes. Once changed, their main naval ciphers would long remain impenetrable to the United States. So, for many months, did the new top-security diplomatic code, encrypted by a machine the Japanese called *97-skiki O-bun Injiki*, or "Alphabetical Typewriter 97." American cryptanalysts named this new challenge "PURPLE"—to distinguish it from its predecessor.

The effort to break PURPLE fell to the Army's team, working out of two small rooms, protected by steel doors and barred windows, in the Munitions Building on Washington's Constitution Avenue. The Japanese, we now know, thought the code was unbreakable. It was not, but the struggle to break it required marathon, brain-bending efforts.

Coming as it did after two decades of similar toil, the task took a brutal toll on the team's leader, legendary cryptanalyst Colonel William Friedman. By the time the problem was cracked, he would be hospitalized in a state of nervous collapse, never to return to his previous round-the-clock schedule. The Japanese-speaking analyst John Hurt was to recall that, by the time war was declared, the team members would reach "the psychological and physical end of our rope." At the end of the war, he too was to collapse and spend months in a hospital.

By late summer 1940, however, after labors that had lasted eighteen months, SIS had cracked PURPLE. The author David Kahn, who has perhaps come closest to explaining codebreaking for the layman, described the arduous process:

A cryptanalyst, brooding sphinxlike over the cross-ruled paper on his desk, would glimpse the skeleton of a pattern in a few scattered letters . . . tested the new values that resulted and found that they produced acceptable plain text . . . Experts in Japanese filled in missing letters. Mathematicians tied in one cycle with another . . . Every weapon of cryptanalytic science was thrown into the fray. Eventually, the solution reached the point where the cryptanalysts had a pretty good pencil-and-paper analog of the PURPLE machine.

Then there was another hurdle. How to build a machine that would replace the pencil-and-paper process, to make monitoring Tokyo's highest-level diplomatic traffic a practical proposition? In the event, SIS managed it in a matter of weeks, using readily available components. A veteran described the device they produced as "a rat's nest of wiring and chattering relays housed in a makeshift wooden box." The box disgorged its wonders accompanied by a "whizzing and occasional spewing of sparks."

This unlovely contraption became a weapon of enormous potential power, one that was to serve the United States for the duration of the war and beyond. As Kahn put it, "Solving the secret messages of a hostile power is like putting a mirror behind the cards a player is holding, like eavesdropping on the huddles of a football team. It is nearly always the best form of intelligence."

Some in the Army called the top-secret intelligence now being received "boogie-woogie." One senior officer, meanwhile, described the team that had broken PURPLE as "magicians." Soon, insiders took to referring to PURPLE, and other decrypted diplomatic intelligence, as MAGIC.

MAGIC yielded much valuable intelligence, and was a treasure not to be squandered. Chief of Staff George Marshall sought to hide it behind a rampart of secrecy. Those with access to MAGIC messages were in the main required to sign what more than one senior officer described as a "horrendous" security oath. A signatory of the oath, which was itself classified as "TOP SECRET," was required to:

> solemnly swear and declare upon my honor that I will not now or hereafter disclose or discuss the existence or context of such intelligence . . . that I will never in the future discuss the subject . . .

even after my retirement or release from the Service of my Country. So help me God.

Early in 1941, the heads of the military intelligence services decided on a basic list of just ten people permitted to read the information MAGIC provided. They were the President; the Secretaries of War, Navy, and State; the Chief of Staff; the Chief of Naval Operations; the heads of Army and Naval Intelligence; and the heads of the Army and the Navy War Plans divisions.

Numerous others, however, also saw MAGIC. They included, obviously, those who initially decoded the messages, and the officers who controlled them and distributed the take. The President's close adviser Harry Hopkins saw it, as did White House military and naval aides, the Assistant Chief of Naval Operations, and aides to the Chief of Staff and to the Secretaries of the Navy and State. Copies were destroyed once seen, and only two master copies were kept—one by the Navy, one by the Army.

To handle the PURPLE intercepts, the prized diplomatic traffic, additional decoding machines were built in a Navy machine shop. One went to the Army, over and above the original prototype. Two went to the Navy's cryptanalytic section, based in cramped office space in the Navy Department. Three, over the months, would be sent to Great Britain; in return, the British supplied cryptanalytic data to the United States. Those in Hawaii, however, who might have greatly benefited from PURPLE—and from MAGIC in general—went without.

The FBI, which shared responsibility for counterespionage in Hawaii, was not made privy to MAGIC. Nor were the Navy and Army Intelligence agents who worked with the FBI in the effort to detect Japanese spying. Most pertinently, and though the consular code had been broken, they knew nothing of the reports on Admiral Kimmel's ships that the professional spy assigned to the consulate, Yoshikawa, was regularly filing.

Like the vast majority of generals and admirals commanding U.S. forces abroad, Kimmel himself was—with one brief aberrational exception in July—excluded from PURPLE traffic and even from the gist of what it contained.

Exceptions were the commanders in the Philippines, General Douglas MacArthur and Admiral Thomas C. Hart. A Navy code-breaking unit in the Philippine islands, which unlike Hawaii had been sent a PURPLE machine, shared the take with both the Army and the Navy. The Philippines, located less than two thousand miles from Tokyo, were well placed for intercept operations. Because of their proximity to Japan, too, the islands were seen as especially vulnerable.

Hawaii, four thousand miles east of Tokyo, was not deemed to be at so great a risk. "The U.S. authorities," SIS cryptanalysis chief Friedman would write, "believed that the Philippines might be cut off—but not Hawaii. Manila needed MAGIC much more than Pearl."

It remains astounding, nevertheless, that it was not seen as essential that Admiral Kimmel, in his position as CINCPAC (commander in chief Pacific Fleet) and CINCUS (titular commander in chief of the U.S. Fleet worldwide), should be sent MAGIC. Comments on the subject by those in authority in Washington are a tangle of contradiction and confusion.

The Director of Naval Intelligence at the time of the attack, Captain Theodore Wilkinson, was to say in a memo that he had told early investigators that the Admiral had "had as much information as we had." The Director of War Plans, Rear Admiral Kelly Turner, was to assert—before and after Pearl Harbor—that Kimmel was receiving MAGIC. When asked whether that was so, according to an aide to Navy Secretary Knox, Turner had replied, "Of course he is. He has the same MAGIC setup we have here."

At the war's end, according to the Pacific Fleet's former intelligence officer Edwin Layton, Turner remained insistent that this had been the case. In the wardroom of the USS *South Dakota*, at a gathering to celebrate victory over Japan in 1945, Layton recalled, Turner truculently claimed that inquiries had found that "that goddamned Kimmel had all that information and he didn't do anything about it. They ought to hang him higher than a kite." This was not what the inquiries had found, and Kimmel had not been privy to MAGIC. Layton challenged Turner, said as much, and they nearly came to blows.

Chief of Naval Operations Stark, who had repeatedly assured Kimmel that he would be kept in the loop, would say in testimony that he "inquired on two or three occasions as to whether or not Kimmel could read certain dispatches when they came up . . . and I was told that he could." Asked who had told him that the Admiral had access to MAGIC, Stark replied, "Well, when Admiral Turner told me he could do it, I did not consider it necessary to go any further."

Turner acknowledged the exchanges with Stark. "On three occasions," he was to testify, "I think all three times at Admiral Stark's initiative, I asked Admiral Noyes as to whether or not Admiral Kimmel and Admiral Hart were receiving the same decrypted information that we were receiving here . . . On each occasion, Admiral Noyes assured me . . . that those officers had the same information that we had." He so reported, he said, to CNO Stark.

"Noyes" was Rear Admiral Leigh Noyes, the Navy's Director of Communications, the man in overall charge of its cryptanalysts. Asked during a later official inquiry whether he had ever told Turner that Kimmel was receiving MAGIC, he responded with a flat, "No." Asked again, he said he had "not intentionally" given Turner the impression that Kimmel was getting PURPLE. Quizzed again, he said that "to the best of [his] knowledge and belief" he never told Turner that Kimmel had access to PURPLE. If Turner misunderstood, he said, that might be because he "confused in his mind" two different streams of information.

Even key officers in Noyes's division, however, were misinformed. The head of the codebreaking unit, Commander Safford, would later say he thought until two years after the attack that Kimmel had received MAGIC. So did the officer assigned to distribute the MAGIC take for the Navy, Lieutenant Commander Alwin Kramer. They too were wrong.

This muddle of memory, all recorded in the formal record, indicates that no one took the trouble to discover for sure whether Kimmel really was in on MAGIC. Most of the testimony would seem to suggest the Admiral was omitted from the trusted circle by *accident*. If so, and given how the Japanese attack was to catch the Fleet totally unaware, the omission was tragic carelessness.

Finally, though, there is the testimony of Chief of Staff George Marshall. Major General Henry Russell, who questioned Marshall during each of his three appearances before the Army's investigation of Pearl Harbor, would remember him as having been "evasive and difficult to examine."

The Chief of Staff was asked whether it would have been possible, without risking exposure of the fact that the United States was reading Japanese codes, at least to send summaries of MAGIC messages to the Army's commander in Hawaii, General Short. This would have been possible, Marshall responded, but he had thought that to do so would be "unwise." That statement would suggest MAGIC was deliberately withheld from Hawaii.

Later, however, the Chief of Staff contradicted his own testimony. In an affidavit at the end of the war, Marshall said it had been his "understanding" before Pearl Harbor that Short *had* in fact been "aware of and was receiving" some MAGIC material "from facilities available in his command." He had not.

The head of Army Intelligence, General Sherman Miles, thought the Navy under Admiral Kimmel had been receiving MAGIC. It had not.

MAGIC was potentially of incalculable value. The way it was handled in 1941, however, was seriously flawed.

18

THE INADEQUACIES HAD been there from the start. By 1941, there were barely a thousand people working in Army and Navy code-breaking units. The vast majority of them manned the more than a dozen far-flung intercept stations where messages were grabbed from the ether.

Of the daily stream of potentially relevant Japanese messages, some were missed because of static or other reception problems. There were often lengthy delays in getting the messages to Washington. Except in the case of those deemed to be urgent—PURPLE had priority—intercepts were not radioed to Washington from the stations that had picked them up.

Most intercepts were forwarded by mail, preferably airmail but sometimes by surface mail—train and ship. It was not unusual for there to be a delay of two weeks or more between the date of interception of a message and distribution in Washington. In one case, there was a delay of nearly eight weeks.

When the cryptanalysts in turn had done their work, there remained the hurdle of translation from Japanese into English. Finding translators was an almost insurmountable task. Telegraphic Japanese, for reasons too arcane to explain here, was effectively a language within a language. "Any two sounds grouped together to make a word," one officer who wrestled with the process explained, "may mean a variety of things. For instance, 'ba' may mean 'horses,' or 'fields,' or 'old women,' or 'my hand.'"

Predictably, translations could be garbled. An extreme example—in a message that would be processed only after the Pearl Harbor attack—was a clause that initially came out of the mix as "the whole matter appears to have been dropped..." It should have read, "there is considerable opportunity to take advantage for a surprise attack . . ."

The Navy doubled its complement of translators in 1941—to a total of six. The Army found even fewer. Some worked sixteen-hour days, and they had little time off—least of all in December, when deteriorating relations between the United States and Japan led to unprecedented traffic.

A measure intended to make the process less burdensome served only to make it more complicated. To spread the load and ease the logjam, it was decided that the Army and Navy teams were to take turns working on the intercepts. The Army was responsible for tackling incoming MAGIC intercepts on even days of the month, the Navy on odd days.

In each service, one named officer had the responsibility of deciding which MAGIC messages were to be delivered to officials at the top at the War and Navy Departments, at State, and at the White House. The Army delivered to the White House during odd-numbered months—in January, March, etc.—the Navy during even-numbered months: February, April, and so on.

MAGIC material would be placed in a folder, and the folder would be carried, in a locked pouch, for delivery to recipients. During early 1941, summaries of salient points, written by the distributing officer, would accompany individual messages. Later, the Army officer charged with the task would simply red-pencil passages that he deemed important. The Navy's officer flagged them, according to his reading of their significance, with paper clips and asterisks.

This system had built-in flaws. As recipients of MAGIC were not required to sign, to indicate that they had seen material, there was no way of knowing who had or who had not seen a given message. It would be impossible, in the future, to hold anyone responsible for action taken, or for failure to have taken appropriate action.

The fundamental problem, though, was caused by the perceived need for great secrecy. Most recipients had a chance merely to look rapidly at the actual messages—or, just as often, the summaries—while the military officer delivering the material waited to retrieve it and head on his way. At times, there were more than a hundred messages a day. Nobody, therefore, was able to take time to consider messages or reflect on them in context.

Years later, the cryptanalyst William Friedman put his finger on this grave defect in the arrangement for assessing MAGIC. No person or persons, he wrote, had the responsibility of trying to:

> *put the pieces of the jigsaw together . . . The distribution of the MAGIC messages was so rigidly controlled that there was nobody in either of these intelligence staffs whose duty it was to study the messages from a long-range point of view. The persons, officers and civilians, in intelligence as well as in the White House, had the messages only for so short a time that each message represented only a single frame, so to speak, in a long motion picture film—a film which should have been intently studied as a continuous series of pictures, because they were telling a story. But the film was not there to be studied, and this was a very serious problem . . .*

A Joint Army-Navy Intelligence Committee, which might have led to a capacity for meaningful evaluation of MAGIC, was in the process of being formed in the fall of 1941. There was disagreement, however, over exactly what its task would be—and even over the mundane matter of office space. The Committee would not meet until after Pearl Harbor.

As it was, the system failed early on. In the spring of 1941, the State Department lost a document that referred to an intercept. At the White House, missing MAGIC material was found in the desk of the President's military aide, Major General Edwin Watson. One account suggests this occurred not once but twice, and that a precious document was found tossed into a wastepaper basket. A man linked to the codebreaking work, meanwhile, was caught in the act trying to sell information about it.

Then worry turned to nightmare. Thanks to the PURPLE intercepts, the diplomatic traffic they so prized, the custodians of MAGIC began to see messages indicating that the Japanese suspected their ciphers had been broken. On May 20th, suspicion seemed to become certainty. "Though I do not know which ones," Japan's ambassador to Washington advised Tokyo, "I have discovered the United States is reading some of our codes."

It looked as though it was only a matter of time until the Japanese switched to new cipher systems and brought down the curtain again. A few security warnings aside, however, the Japanese took no action. MAGIC continued to flow, as it would for the duration of the war. Tokyo's inaction seemed miraculous.

The panic in the United States that spring, however, resulted in a situation that—had it not been so serious—would have been comical. In light of the discovery that material had been handled irresponsibly at the White House, the general who headed Army Intelligence directed in May that the Army would no longer deliver MAGIC to the President's office. The following month, the Navy also decided that MAGIC decrypts and summaries were not to be delivered to the White House. Roosevelt's naval aide would merely be allowed to peruse the summaries, memorize them to the best of his ability, then brief the President orally.

The President of the United States, with his primary need to know what was in the Japanese correspondence, was thus for months reduced to receiving—in person—only a trickle of MAGIC. The ludicrous situation was to continue until November, when the Japanese crisis came to a head, Then, reportedly, Roosevelt would order his naval aide to "pay no attention to those dunderheads in the Army and Navy" and ensure that he receive MAGIC intercepts daily.

19

ADMIRAL KIMMEL KNEW nothing of the bizarre high-level to-ing and fro-ing about MAGIC in Washington. The word MAGIC, had it been used in the Admiral's presence at the time, might as well have been a reference to the movie about Dorothy and her adventures in the land of Oz.

The concern Kimmel had felt back in February, though, less than a month after taking over as commander in chief, had not gone away. Then, as noted earlier, he had written his first perplexed letter to Chief of Naval Operations Stark. An officer back from headquarters, Kimmel had noted, had told him there had been debate in Washington as to who should supply him with "information of a secret nature." The Admiral wanted to be sure he had not missed anything, hoped Stark would "fix responsibility."

Stark had merely hedged. The Office of Naval Intelligence, he wrote in an unusually stiff response, was aware of its responsibility to keep Kimmel "adequately informed." He let slip nothing about the constant stream of information that was MAGIC. Still uneasy, Kimmel had shared his worries with his Fleet intelligence officer, Lieutenant Commander Edwin Layton. "He repeatedly asked me," Layton recalled, "whether I thought that we were receiving all the diplomatic intelligence available in Washington." "Diplomatic intelligence"—the Admiral was cannily close to realizing what was being kept from him. It was agreed that Layton would try using his own contacts at headquarters.

Layton had the appropriate background for the task. Having twice served in the naval attaché's office at the U.S. embassy in Tokyo, he was familiar with the nature of the potential Japanese enemy. He spoke and read Japanese, had for a time headed the translation section of the Navy's codebreaking unit. Most relevantly in this instance, he and Commander Arthur McCollum, who now headed the Far East Section of ONI, had been colleagues in Tokyo.

So it was that, in March, Layton wrote to McCollum from Hawaii. "I told him," he would recall, "that Admiral Kimmel and I had been discussing intelligence—what we had, what we didn't have, and what we would like to be assured of receiving. I referred specifically to the 'Dip,' or diplomatic decrypts . . . My letter stated that we hadn't been receiving any, and the situation was getting tense. We thought we ought to be receiving some."

More than a month went by before McCollum replied, and his response was unhelpful.

> Dear Eddie,
>
> Sorry to be so late in replying . . . I thoroughly appreciate that you would probably be much helped in your daily estimates if you had at your disposal the DIP. This, however, brings up matters of security, et cetera, which would be very difficult to solve . . . I cannot agree that this material should be forwarded to you . . . The forces afloat must rely on the Department for evaluated views of political situations . . . I appreciate that all this leaves you in rather a spot . . . In other words, while you and the Fleet may be highly interested in politics, there is nothing you can do about it. Therefore, information of political significance, except as it affects immediate action by the Fleet, is merely a matter of interest to you and not a matter of utility.

For Layton, and by implication for his boss Admiral Kimmel, the rebuff was less than logical. If those at the sharp end would be "much helped" by having access to the "DIP," how could access also be of no "utility"? If it would have helped the commander in chief of the U.S. Fleet and his staff, moreover, should the security factor really have been insurmountable?

Integral to the problem, in early 1941, was the scenario being acted out by the top brass at Navy headquarters in Washington.

Years later, after he learned of the episode, Layton would characterize it as having been a facet of the "interdepartmental warfare . . .
conflict and jealousy that soured the spring air on Constitution
Avenue."

What Commander McCollum would have to say thirty years
later, when he felt free to do so, makes it clear that Layton's description was apt. "There had grown up in the Office of the Chief
of Naval Operations," McCollum recalled, "a coterie of officers,
Stark, of course, the head of it, and [Assistant CNO] Ingersoll and
Turner. They were a sort of triumvirate. Turner would bring in
the ideas, and these guys would execute them, frequently without
any staffing."

Turner was War Plans chief Kelly Turner, who persisted in asserting his belief that Kimmel did receive MAGIC. Assessments
of Turner vary greatly. To Stark, he was "one of the best men
ever . . . invaluable . . . a brilliant mind . . . There were not enough
superlatives in the dictionary for Turner." Admiral Thomas Hart,
commander of the Asiatic Fleet in the Philippines at the time,
admired him for "his mental power and his clearness of thought."

Others disagreed. Stark's flag secretary, Charles Wellborn, saw
Turner's merits but thought him "aggressive . . . a pretty tough
fellow to get along with for lots of people." Then–Commander
Walter Ansel, who served in War Plans, remembered him as "irascible." Others thought him "stubborn," a "bull in a china shop,"
"intolerant." Navy Secretary Knox's aide Admiral Frank Beatty
thought Turner "amazingly ignorant and ill-informed."

Subjective assessments aside, Turner's very presence led to a
change in the pecking order at the top of the Navy Department.
According to then–Lieutenant Commander William Smedberg, it
was actually Turner who wrote many of the CNO's dispatches, "although Admiral Stark usually managed to put something of himself into the final draft." At conferences, Knox's aide Beatty would
recall, Turner "always spoke for the Navy instead of Stark, although Stark was present . . . the opinions were those of Turner."
By late 1941, Beatty thought, Stark had come to rely "abjectly" on
Turner, who "was really Chief of Naval Operations."

In an unprecedented way, at a pivotal time, the turmoil at the top also changed the relationship between headquarters and the commanders in the field. In the past, information had flowed to the Fleet from the Office of Naval Intelligence. In the spring of 1941, Turner had seized that role, arguing at a key meeting—as then–ONI director Captain Alan Kirk recalled—that his department, War Plans, "should interpret and evaluate all information concerning possible hostile nations from whatever source received."

MAGIC, of course, was seen as the source of sources. There was, as Commander McCollum was later to put it, "a complex on secrecy." War Plans "didn't tell anybody what was going on, so O.N.I. was put in the unenviable position of having stuff going out about enemy intentions and what-have-you that they didn't know about at all." Admiral Turner had his "hand on the gullet . . . a stranglehold" on the interpretation of intelligence.

In June, when Admiral Kimmel traveled all the way from Hawaii to Washington precisely because he was so concerned that he was not being kept in the loop, Turner had assured him that he would indeed be kept informed. For just seventeen days the following month, whether by coincidence or not, headquarters did—out of the blue—briefly share some MAGIC material with Kimmel. Eight dispatches were sent to him, marked "Top Secret," reflecting Japanese diplomatic messages sent to and from Tokyo and foreign capitals. Most were summaries, while some included the numbers the Japanese had assigned to their messages, even some verbatim translations.

It was apparent to the Admiral and his staff that these messages drew on U.S. intercepts of Japanese traffic. No sooner had the flow of messages begun, though, than it stopped. They were the last messages based on intercepts that would be shared with Kimmel for the next four momentous months—until just days before the attack on Pearl Harbor.

On September 23rd, in a "P.S." to one of his long letters to the Admiral—letters that often took about two weeks to arrive—the Chief of Naval Operations mentioned a talk he had with Secretary of State Hull. "Conversations with the Japanese," Stark wrote, "have practically reached an impasse." Then, in a second postscript, he added that he had "again talked to Mr. Hull . . . He keeps me pretty fully informed, and if there is anything of moment I will, of course, hasten to let you know."

Stark closed, chummy as always, by saying he had just seen a photograph of a picture of Kimmel—probably the oil portrait of him, resplendent in the uniform of a four-star admiral. "It looks great," he wrote; "the boys will be proud of it always."

On September 24th, American codebreakers intercepted Tokyo's telltale message to its Hawaii consulate ordering the subdivision of Pearl Harbor into specified areas, and requesting reports on exactly where U.S. ships were moored and whether ships were moored together—the request that, as Kimmel would say when he finally saw it years later, had "no conceivable usefulness" other than for a potential attack on his Fleet.

Ironically, that pivotal message was intercepted by American operators working at a monitoring station in Hawaii, not far from Admiral Kimmel's headquarters—a station not equipped to decrypt it. Its story from there on—the tortoise speed at which it was processed, the ineptness with which it was evaluated—is yet another sorry tale within the greater tragedy.

First there were organizational delays. Like other non-priority messages, the September 24th intercept should, routinely, have been sent off to Washington aboard the next scheduled Pan Am Clipper flight. Because the next eastbound flight was delayed by weather, the shipment containing the message went by sea. It took two weeks to reach Army codebreakers on the East Coast. Once it did arrive, they had the message ready for evaluation within three days.

The head of Army Intelligence's Far East Section, Colonel Rufus Bratton, recognized at once that the September 24th message was unique. "I felt," he was to recall, "that the Japanese were showing unusual interest in the port at Honolulu." He took the report both to his Army superior and to his opposite numbers in the Navy. It was the rational thing to do.

Most of those he spoke with seemed not particularly impressed. His boss, Army Intelligence chief General Sherman Miles, would not recall having discussed the message. Perhaps, Miles mused in later testimony, the Japanese interest in moored ships had something to do with a desire to know how quickly the U.S. Fleet could leave harbor. It was not for him to say, the general implied. This was more a matter for the Navy than for him. When Bratton circulated the message at the War Department—to War Plans, Secretary of War Stimson, and Chief of Staff Marshall—it got minimal reaction. Marshall was to say he "had no recollection" of seeing the intercept. These were busy men, and it may not have caught their attention.

Likewise, few in the Navy Department expressed concern. "My consideration at the time," Bratton's opposite number in the Navy, Commander Alwin Kramer, would recall, was that the message might merely be "an attempt on the part of the Japanese diplomatic service to simplify communications." The Japanese, he said, were always trying to cut down on expenses.

The original of the intercept had been sixteen lines long. Commander Kramer's summary, or "gist," of the intercept ran to barely two:

Tokyo directs special reports on ships in Pearl Harbor, which is divided into five areas for the purpose of showing exact locations.

The Commander rated the message worthy of just one asterisk—for "interesting"—as distinct from two asterisks, denoting a message that was "especially important or urgent." Thus marked, and accompanied by the "gist," it then went to those on the Navy's MAGIC circulation list.

Chief of Naval Operations Stark, foremost among those who would have received the ominous message, would stumble through lengthy, muddled testimony on the subject. "We did not see it," he told Congress' Joint Committee. "I recall no such request from Tokyo . . . We did not see it." Referring to that message and to later related ones, he said, "I believe that I did not see them . . . I may have seen them. They may have been brought to me, and they may have slipped my mind, but I think I did not see them." That said, Stark acknowledged that the September 24th message had been significant:

> In the light of hindsight it stands out very clearly . . . as indicating the possibility or at least the groundwork for a Japanese air raid on Pearl Harbor . . . I do not recollect anyone having pointed it out. There was literally a mass of material coming in . . . If I had seen it myself, I do not know what I would have done. I might have said, "Well, my goodness, look at this detail" . . . It is very difficult to separate hindsight from foresight.

Head of War Plans Kelly Turner was also a fixture on the circulation list. Like Stark, though, he said his memory was blank. "As a matter of fact," he testified, "I have no recollection of ever having seen that dispatch of the 24th of September . . . I do not know why I did not see that. I believe that I would have remembered it."

Had Turner seen the intercept, he said, he thought he would have brought it to the attention of the director of the Office of Naval Intelligence. ONI, both Stark and Turner suggested, could have dealt with it.

Commander McCollum, the chief of ONI's Far East Section, would normally have seen the message. He had been away from headquarters at the time it reached the office. If he did see it, he was to say dismissively, "it did not make much impression on my mind."

The September 24th intercept came in at the time one director of ONI was about to leave and his replacement was phasing in. The new incumbent, Captain Theodore Wilkinson, would recall mentioning "to one or more officers that the Japs seemed quite curious as to the layout in Pearl Harbor . . . We did not, perhaps erroneously, recognize that that was an inordinate interest in Hawaii . . . I did not, I regret now, of course attribute to them the bombing target significance which now appears."

The official record is blank, however, on the position of the outgoing director of the Office of Naval Intelligence, Captain Alan Kirk. For some reason, although he would have been an important witness, he would not be called to testify before any of the Pearl Harbor inquiries. Much later, however, an insider was to claim that Kirk did see the September 24th intercept—and thought strongly that it should be sent to Admiral Kimmel.

Commander Laurance Safford, the veteran head of the Navy's codebreaking unit, would say—long after Pearl Harbor—that he knew the truth of this matter on which so many others claimed to have little or no memory. The reaction to the intercept, he would write in an unpublished manuscript, was "more violent" than ever became publicly known.

The truth, Safford asserted, was that the intercept's significance "was fully appreciated in the Navy Department by everyone who knew of it except Turner and Stark." He wrote, "O.N.I. Director Captain Kirk, supported by his assistant Captain Moore and his head of Foreign Intelligence, Captain Bode, had a showdown with Rear Admiral Kelly Turner as to whether enemy information was to be furnished to or to be denied to the Commander-in-Chief of the U.S. Pacific Fleet, Admiral Kimmel."

Kirk "demanded" that Kimmel be informed, Safford wrote, but "Admiral Stark decided in favor of Kelly Turner." In later testimony, Stark for his part claimed that if the "good men" in ONI studying the MAGIC intercepts had deemed an intercept significant, they had "full authority to send it out . . . This particular dispatch would have been of particular interest, if they had so considered it, to Admiral Kimmel."

By Commander Safford's account, of course, the Director of Naval Intelligence and his senior aides had *indeed* considered the September 24th intercept to be of special interest. They argued persistently for it to be sent to Hawaii, and were turned down.

Kimmel—as he had for months feared he might be—had been left purblind.

Had Kimmel and his senior staff had access to MAGIC messages, Fleet operations officer Captain DeLany was to say, they might have drawn logical conclusions from the material. It was for them, and them alone, to decide on appropriate action. The notion that Kimmel would not have reacted to the intercept, Fleet intelligence officer Layton said, was "malarkey."

Messages like this and other MAGIC traffic, Kimmel's chief of staff William "Poco" Smith would testify, "should certainly have been sent to the commander in the field . . . to permit him and his staff to evaluate the information they received. I think it is admitted that all the naval brains are not concentrated in Washington."

Admiral Kimmel himself was to say "without any reservation whatsoever" that to have been informed of Tokyo's September 24th request that Pearl Harbor be divided into specific zones "would have changed my ideas completely."

In Japan on September 11th, just thirteen days before the fateful request was sent to Hawaii, Admiral Yamamoto had gathered senior commanders at the Imperial Naval Staff College. On a game board, they had begun working through a series of simulated attacks on Pearl Harbor. Some officers had continued to think the plan fraught with risk. Yamamoto disagreed. His undoubted naval expertise aside, he excelled at *shogi* (a form of chess) and poker. "I like games of chance," he told one of the doubters. "You have told me that the operation is a gamble, so I shall carry it out."

The doubts about Yamamoto's plan evaporated. Following final deliberations and dinner, the meeting was formally adjourned on the 20th. Just four days later, Japanese naval intelligence sent out its September 24th request to the Honolulu consulate for the information on Pearl Harbor now seen as essential to planning the attack.

Hawai Sakusen, "Operation Hawaii," as the Japanese high command called it, was under way.

20

FOR A WEEK THAT SEPTEMBER, at 7:30 a.m. sharp, a celebrity guest joined Admiral Kimmel for a working breakfast. Lord Louis Mountbatten, a cousin of Britain's King George VI, was—though soon to be elevated to flag rank—a battle-hardened captain in the Royal Navy. He had seen action in World War I as a midshipman, commanded a destroyer in the 1930s, then—from the outbreak of World War II in Europe—achieved distinction with his leadership of a destroyer flotilla.

Mountbatten and his "Fighting Fifth" flotilla had sunk a German submarine, escorted convoys in the Atlantic, and survived bombs and torpedoes in the North Sea and the Mediterranean. On his arrival in the United States, the hero aristocrat had been feted, received by President Roosevelt at the White House, asked to give a talk at the Naval Academy, and had briefed correspondents.

Mountbatten had a reason to be in the United States—he was due to take command of an aircraft carrier currently under repair in a U.S. dockyard. He was also there, though, because British Prime Minister Churchill wanted him there. Roosevelt and his close military advisers, moreover, had been glad to welcome him.

There had been no certainty, two years earlier, that the United States and Britain would form what the world would come to call their "special relationship." Relations had been distant, sometimes strained, in the years between the wars. The Nazi onslaught on Europe had then changed everything.

Roosevelt's conviction that it was vital to U.S. interests that fascism be stopped, and his belief that fortress Britain must not fall—combined with the unique relationship that he and the

British leader developed—forged the lasting bond. His instincts aside, Churchill for his part had quickly understood that Britain could not survive without America's support and—as soon as possible—its participation in the conflict.

At the start of 1941, when Kimmel was appointed to head the Pacific Fleet, Roosevelt had dispatched to London his aide Harry Hopkins, who has been characterized as his "deputy President." "On January 10th," Churchill would write, "a gentleman arrived to see me at Downing Street . . . an envoy from the President of supreme importance to our life. With gleaming eye and quiet, constrained passion, he said: 'The President is determined that we shall win the war together. Make no mistake about it. He has sent me here to tell you that at all costs, and by all means, he will carry you through.'"

If there was a pivotal moment in Roosevelt's commitment to Britain, this may have been it. The relationship was central to his calculations about the conflict—in the Atlantic and the Pacific. The President's pledge to Churchill had been made very secretly. At home, he had no mandate from the U.S. Congress, no sure support from the public. For months to come—until Pearl Harbor—he would have to negotiate crosscurrents of opinion in politics and the press, even to a certain extent in the armed forces, that opposed involvement in the war.

Churchill, for his part, was the heroic ally leading a heroic country. In his secret messages to Roosevelt, however, and not only when discussing the war with Germany, he was a supplicant. A month after the meeting with Hopkins at Downing Street, he had pointed to signs that Japan might attack British territories. He asked the President to do "whatever you are able to do to instil in Japan anxiety as to a double war." In fact, in Tokyo a day or so earlier, an American diplomat had already quietly hinted to an official at the Japanese foreign ministry that the United States would probably come into the war on Britain's side.

The formal name of the "Lend-Lease Act," passed in March to make it possible for America to supply war matériel to Britain and other Allies, was "An Act to Promote the Defense of the United

States." To its many opponents, however, it was the "Dictator Bill." "If we do not watch our step," the chairman of the U.S. Maritime Commission wrote to Roosevelt a month later, "we shall find the White House en route to England with the Washington Monument as a steering oar."

"What would you rather do," retorted the President, "give away the White House and the Washington Monument and save civilization or have the White House and the Washington Monument taken over by people under a different regime. Think it over."

Top British and American commanders had since the start of the year been making contingency plans for how—*if* America joined the war—the two Allies would fight. The plans were kept strictly secret, as was the fact that the discussions had even taken place. Neither the President nor Churchill signed the resulting nonbinding document, the ABC-1 Staff Report (ABC stood for American, British, Canadian). In April in Singapore, with Dutch commanders also present, there were further talks between the U.S. and British military on planning for potential war in the Far East.

In the summer, the picture in the region changed radically. In defiance of a warning by Roosevelt not to do so, Japanese forces moved into southern Indochina. In late July and early August, the President responded with economic sanctions. What he had intended, he told Secretary of the Interior Harold Ickes at the time, was only to "slip the noose around Japan's neck and give it a jerk now and then." One effect, though, was to cut off oil exports to Japan.

The Japanese reaction was frantic, as a MAGIC intercept revealed. "Our Empire, to save its very life," the foreign minister cabled to the Washington embassy, "must take measures to secure the raw materials of the South Seas . . . must immediately take steps to break asunder this ever-strengthening chain of encirclement which is being woven under the guidance and with the participation of England and the United States, acting like a cunning dragon seemingly asleep."

Eighty-eight percent of Japan's oil was imported, most of it from the United States. Calculations indicated that the cutoff would shut down vital industries within a year, prevent the Imperial Navy from putting to sea in two years, and bring the Imperial Army's tanks to a halt. This was a hammer blow. No acceptable option remained to either nation. Should Japan not give in to American demands that it stop its aggression against neighboring countries, its economy would collapse. For its part, the United States had taken the last measure it could take short of war.

On August 3rd, Roosevelt made a show of setting off aboard the presidential yacht on what was billed as a cruise up the coast of Maine. Instead, at Martha's Vineyard off the Massachusetts coast, he transferred to a U.S. cruiser headed for Newfoundland and a meeting at sea with Winston Churchill. This would be only their second encounter—they had met briefly at a dinner more than twenty years earlier—and it was a crucial conference.

After a start that was more symbolic than substantive—one of the hymns at a religious service that everyone attended was "Onward, Christian Soldiers"—they and their diplomats and service chiefs gathered to discuss the worsening world situation. On August 14th, what had been top-secret meetings became worldwide news. In a resounding Joint Declaration, the two leaders spoke of "the dangers to world civilization" posed by Adolf Hitler, envisaged "the final destruction of the Nazi tyranny," and declared their aspirations for a postwar world. In a speech to the British nation on his return to London, the Prime Minister dubbed the document he and the President had produced the "Atlantic Charter."

Though replete with lofty language, the Charter was virtually devoid of factual detail. Privately, Churchill and his entourage were disappointed. They had exacted no firm commitments from the United States. "The Americans," an aide close to the British leader noted, "have a long way to go before they can play any decisive part in the war." As things turned out, Roosevelt acted within a month. On September 11th, in one of his "fireside chat" radio broadcasts, he told Americans of a clash a few days previously between a German U-boat and the destroyer USS *Greer*. The German submarine, the President said, had "fired first upon this American destroyer without warning and with deliberate design, to sink her." The *Greer* had not been damaged, but this was only the latest of several attacks on ships flying the American flag. Two U.S. merchant ships had been sunk.

The President said in the broadcast:

> The American people can have no further illusions . . . I am sure the Nazis are waiting, waiting to see whether the United States will by silence give them the green light to go ahead on this path of destruction . . . My obligation as President is historic . . . inescapable . . . From now on, if German or Italian vessels of war enter the waters, the protection of which is necessary for American defense, they do so at their own peril . . . The orders which I have given as Commander-in-Chief of the United States Army and Navy are to carry out that policy—at once.

For the time being, nevertheless, the United States remained nervously neutral.

This was the atmosphere when, following his visit to the East Coast, Britain's Lord Mountbatten headed for Hawaii. Though the trip to the Pacific was at his own request—Mountbatten wanted to learn more about aircraft carriers—Admiral Kimmel and his senior commanders made him welcome. He had the experience of conflict at sea that most of the officers and men of the Pacific Fleet did not. He got his experience on carriers during several days at sea aboard the USS *Enterprise* with Vice Admiral "Bull" Halsey. He flew in a carrier-launched plane taking part in a mock night attack on Pearl Harbor.

In return for ensuring he spent time on a carrier, Mountbatten noted in his later report, Admiral Kimmel asked for his considered views and advice. They discussed a number of detailed naval matters—and something else. During the visit, Mountbatten was to reflect years afterward, he had been "appalled" to see "how vulnerable Pearl Harbor was to a surprise attack . . . Admiral Kimmel agreed with me."

It is likely that the Admiral told him of the Fleet's problems. The list of concerns was long. The headlong drive to expand the U.S. Navy as a whole had meant a constant drain from Kimmel's command of not only ships but men. "In repeated correspondence," he would write in a letter to headquarters just weeks before the Japanese strike, "I have set forth to you the needs of the Pacific Fleet. These needs are real and immediate . . . This Fleet requires approximately 9,000 men to fill complements."

Those that Washington did send, he would recall later, were greenhorns. "With constantly changing personnel, both officers and enlisted men, and the induction of new personnel, there were times when 70% of the men on board individual ships had never heard a gun fired."

There were still chronic shortages of equipment. It was eight months since the Admiral's predecessor had asked for more airplanes, antiaircraft guns, and radar. Kimmel and the other commanders in Hawaii had been holding out the begging bowl to Washington ever since.

Kimmel and senior colleagues pleaded again and again for sufficient aircraft to fly long-distance patrols in search of an approaching enemy. In late 1941, though, there was still a severe shortage of the planes needed to conduct the 800-mile reconnaissance, covering 360 degrees, which the air defense chiefs for the Navy and Army had recommended earlier that year. In the fall, three dozen B-17 planes, which, other capabilities aside, would have been suitable for distant reconnaissance, had been sent not to Hawaii as requested but to the Philippines. The reasoning, Chief of Staff Marshall would say later, was to guard the Philippine islands and deter a Japanese thrust there. "We turned," Marshall testified, "and tried to do something for General MacArthur. Our struggle from that time on was to give the Philippines an adequate defensive setup."

Rear Admiral William Furlong, commander, Minecraft Battle Force Pacific, would remember coming upon Kimmel and his air force commander Admiral Bellinger as they pored over a chart, instruments in hand, planning how best to use the reconnaissance aircraft they did have. Because of the shortage of planes, Furlong said, they had to select a wedge of the reconnaissance arc here and there, then shift it again. "The picture of Admiral Kimmel and Admiral Bellinger trying to cut their cloth when there was really no cloth to cut," Furlong said, "was really too much."

So it was for land-based antiaircraft guns. Though these were primarily an Army concern, Kimmel had persistently complained that there were not enough of them. "I have frequently called to your attention," he would write to headquarters a few days before the Japanese attack, "the inadequacy of the Army's anti-aircraft defense in the Pearl Harbor area . . . Very little has been done to improve this situation."

Then there was the Aircraft Warning Service—radar. As reported earlier, commanders at Pearl Harbor had long been pushing for more radar equipment. There had been delays in delivery, failures that Congress' Joint Inquiry Minority Report on Pearl Harbor was one day to characterize as having been "inexcusable." By late September, when Lord Mountbatten visited, five land-based mobile radars had been installed and Army crews had begun training.

Mountbatten's experience in battle had taught him that radar was truly invaluable. With considerable prescience, he suggested to Kimmel and his senior officers that there should be "a permanent radar surveillance watch in case of an attack by the Japanese from aircraft carriers." The Admiral, who was himself alert to the importance of radar—though he was not responsible for the embryonic radar stations—assigned a Navy Reserve lieutenant commander, an officer with radar experience from his time attached to the British military, to work with the Army.

The lieutenant commander found the radar equipment Washington had supplied "inferior to any I had seen before," and the reporting system rudimentary. He had trouble, moreover, getting base defense officer Admiral Bloch and his officers—responsible with the Army for defense—to provide liaison officers. Admiral Kimmel's operations officer offered to help.

During exercises, the radar shield seemed to some to be working effectively. In drills coordinated with the Army's land-based radar, Fleet Base Force commander Rear Admiral William Calhoun was to say, no "enemy" planes got through.

Overall, Kimmel, was not complacent. His War Plans officer, "Soc" McMorris, thought he "was inclined to be somewhat more pessimistic in that regard than myself . . . There was much concern over the lack of radars and the requisite skill in their use . . . He undoubtedly recognized many weaknesses . . . We certainly felt there was much to be done, and all hands were working very hard to overcome deficiencies . . . in general, suitable representations had been made to higher authorities."

When Lord Mountbatten left Hawaii, Kimmel was there to see him off. Two months later, just after the Pearl Harbor attack, he would hasten to send Kimmel his condolences. The two men had established a relationship of friendship and mutual respect. At the end of the war, when Mountbatten had become a Vice Admiral and Supreme Commander South East Asia, he would help track down two members of the extended Kimmel family who had been captured by the Japanese and were missing.

Kimmel would still be under a cloud for his alleged failures at Pearl Harbor. Mountbatten, though, wrote: "I have never wavered in my admiration for you."

In October 1941, after Mountbatten's visit to Kimmel and the Fleet, President Roosevelt wrote to Winston Churchill to say how helpful it had been. As for the prospects in the Pacific, he told the Prime Minister: "The Jap situation is definitely worse."

21

THE WORD "JAPAN" had not appeared in the joint statement Roosevelt and Churchill issued after their August meeting at sea off Newfoundland. That omission, an unnamed Japanese diplomat quipped at the time, could mean only one thing—that Japan had been "one of the main points of discussion." He was right.

At the very time the President was conferring with the British leader, Japan's prime minister, Fuminaro Konoye, a moderate compared with the hawks in his cabinet, was pressing for a meeting of his own with the President. "We propose this step," his message to Washington said, "because we sincerely desire maintaining peace." Roosevelt would consider meeting Konoye, but senior aides thought the approach was a sham. They based their view not least on intercepted MAGIC messages indicating that Tokyo was duplicitous.

Japan's peace overtures, Secretary of War Stimson had written as the Roosevelt-Churchill talks began, were "a pure blind . . . They have already made up their minds to a policy of going [farther] south through Indo-China and Thailand. The invitation to the President is merely a blind to try to keep us from taking definite action. The papers show this right on their face."

During the talks at Newfoundland, Churchill had hoped that Roosevelt would agree to a statement designed to deter Japan from moves against British territories. Their joint declaration, as he envisaged it, would say that—were there such aggression—"the U.S. government would be compelled to take counter-measures, even though these might lead to war between the United States and Japan."

The British Prime Minister had not gotten the statement he wanted. Once back in Washington, however, Roosevelt sum-

moned Ambassador Kichisaburo Nomura to warn that should the
Japanese take further military action against their neighbors, the
United States would take "any and all steps which it may deem
necessary." The wording "any and all steps" implied the possibility of a military response.

What the President actually intended remained opaque even to
those close to him. "To some of my very pointed questions," Stark
wrote to Kimmel before the talks off Newfoundland, "I get a smile
or a 'Betty, please don't ask me that.' Policy seems to be something
never fixed, always fluid and changing."

Even after the meeting with Churchill, little or nothing had
been resolved. "If you do not get as much information as you
think you should get," Stark told Kimmel, the explanation was
probably that the situation "has just not jelled sufficiently for us
to give you anything authoritative . . . If England declares war on
Japan, but we do not, I very much suppose that we should follow
a course of action similar to the one we are now pursuing in the
Atlantic as a neutral."

While policy was still unclear, a letter Kimmel received in early
September suggested that tension was building. "I have not given
up hope of continuing peace in the Pacific," the CNO wrote, "but
I wish the thread by which it continues to hang were not so slender." The thread had become more slender by the day. In a new
message to Roosevelt, Prime Minister Konoye had warned that if
no progress was made at the negotiating table, there could be "unforeseen contingencies." One of those contingencies, the Americans had read that week in a MAGIC intercept quoting Hitler,
was that—should war break out between Japan and the United
States—Germany would also declare war against the United
States.

Japan's military, meanwhile, starved of oil by the American
sanctions, was impatient, eager to move not only against Britain's
Far East territories but also against the oil-rich Netherlands East
Indies. Konoye restrained it only by arguing that he might yet be
able to meet with Roosevelt, that they might yet agree on terms.

It was not going to happen. No version of Tokyo's proposals—

there were three in September—satisfied the conditions on which Washington was insisting. In sum, the United States insisted that Japan respect the sovereignty of other nations and not use force to change the status quo in the Pacific. Konoye's proposed terms did not renounce further conquest, nor agree to Japan's withdrawal from territories to the north—in China and Inner Mongolia— that it had invaded long since. Even so, he called on the United States to lift economic sanctions and halt reinforcement of British and Dutch territories, of China, and even of its own territory—the Philippines.

In early October, what hope Konoye had of a summit meeting with Roosevelt evaporated. On the 16th, after a protracted cabinet crisis, he resigned. The man appointed to replace him was former Minister of War Hideki Tojo, a man who said he did not see "any possible way" the crisis could be resolved by diplomacy. Japan's main English-language newspaper published the words of a new patriotic song:

> *Preparations are well done . . .*
> *Determination for defense is firm . . .*
> *We will win, we must win . . .*
> *We know no defeat.*

A formal dispatch now went out from the CNO in Washington to Admiral Kimmel in Hawaii. "Since the U.S. and Britain are held responsible by Japan for her present desperate situation," Stark told the Admiral, there was "a possibility that Japan may attack these two powers. In view of these possibilities you will take precautions, including such preparatory deployments as will not disclose strategic intention nor constitute provocative actions against Japan."

In a letter the following day, Stark sounded less concerned. "Personally," he wrote, "I do not believe the Japs are going to sail into us, and the message I sent you merely stated the 'possibility' . . . In any case, after long pow-wows in the White House it was felt we should be on guard."

Kimmel responded firmly to the formal message. He dispatched a dozen of his precious patrol planes and two submarines to Midway Island, situated between Hawaii and Japan, and deployed destroyers to Wake and Johnston islands. Two submarines were sent to Wake, and six made ready to leave for Japanese waters. The Battle Force was put on twelve-hour sailing notice. Additional security measures were put into effect in areas outside Pearl Harbor.

Already, two days before hearing from Stark, the Admiral had issued a revised Fleet security order, effective immediately. It provided for destroyer patrols at sea, air patrols as directed, and sweeps for mines, and for Navy ships to be ready to augment the Army's inadequate antiaircraft defenses. Ships were to be berthed in a way that maximized antiaircraft coverage. A minimum of four guns were to be "manned and ready" in each group of ships berthed in Pearl Harbor.

The Navy in Washington was satisfied with these precautions. Even after the Japanese strike, moreover, after Kimmel had been removed and publicly disgraced, his successor Admiral Nimitz would reissue the same security order, without change.

On the list of possible eventualities, Kimmel's order stated, was that—before any declaration of war—there could be "a surprise attack on ships in Pearl Harbor."

In Japan in October, the officers and crews of Yamamoto's fleet were working frenetically to complete preparations for just such a strike. At the Mitsubishi factory in Nagasaki, engineers toiled round the clock to produce the *gyorai*—"Thunderfish"—torpedo. Late that month, at Kagoshima Bay—a natural harbor off Kyushu, at the southern tip of Japan, that bears a resemblance to Pearl Harbor—pilots repeatedly practiced their bombing runs. The *gyorai*, modified with wooden fins, would prove capable of striking targets in a mere forty feet of water—as required for an attack on the anchorage at Pearl.

22

IN YOKOHAMA, ALSO in October, three Japanese naval officers boarded an ocean liner bound for Hawaii. They traveled incognito, one posing as an "assistant purser," another as a doctor, the third as an ordinary passenger. The liner, to all appearances simply a passenger ship, followed sea-lanes approximating part of the route the strike force would take. Its journey was a front for reconnaissance. The officers, each of whom had a separate area of expertise, logged sightings of U.S. air patrols, the movements of other ships, and weather conditions. Spotting air patrols was especially important—and none was seen until the liner was just two hundred miles from its destination.

During the liner's lengthy stopover at Honolulu, the officers did not disembark. They stayed on the ship, observing what they could through binoculars. When Consul Kita came on board—as a diplomat he could come and go as he wished—he was handed a list of some hundred questions. Among them: Where exactly were the airfields? How many planes took part in routine patrols? In what direction did they head, and at what times? Was there a day on which most ships would be in port? Was the entrance to Pearl Harbor protected by antisubmarine nets?

The consulate spy, Yoshikawa, had for months been filing intelligence responsive to many of these questions. Now, as Japanese Navy commanders started the countdown to action, they wanted the facts checked, double-checked, and fleshed out. Yoshikawa reconnoitred the harbor area by car yet again, collated earlier notes, prepared maps. Thanks to a recent "sightseeing" trip in a light aircraft, he also had aerial photographs. The information, concealed in bundles of newspapers, was smuggled aboard the liner and delivered to the waiting naval officers. It is said to have included the statement that more warships were in harbor on Sundays than on other days.

For the first time, meanwhile, Yoshikawa had been asked to take a real risk. On a Saturday afternoon that month, dressed as if going to the beach, he was driven to a point not far from the home of Otto Kühn, the German whom the FBI had months earlier pegged as a suspected enemy agent.

Having walked the final half mile to avoid being noticed, Yoshikawa arrived at Kühn's home unannounced. His conversation with the German was brief. He opened by saying he had something for Kühn from "Dr. Homberg," a fictitious name Japanese Intelligence had used in the past when sending Kühn money. The "something" that day was a cardboard box containing fourteen thousand dollars—at today's rates nearly a quarter of a million dollars.

There was also a typed letter asking Kühn to make a shortwave radio transmission test. A year earlier, the German had claimed he could use shortwave radio to transmit coded information on U.S. ship movements to the Japanese. He had proposed, too, to signal Japanese ships at night, using lights in a window or by burning garbage. He was now being taken up on his promise. According to Yoshikawa, he and Kühn discussed "a method by which he could signal to Japanese submarines off the windward coast by blinking his automobile headlights."

Yoshikawa had never been told in as many words that an attack on Pearl Harbor was in the works. Now, however, it was evident to him that "the hour of crisis was approaching."

FBI agents had been watching Kühn, and had been tipped off that Yoshikawa—under his alias Morimura—was an "outside man" for the consulate. Agents monitoring Kühn, however, were not watching on the day Yoshikawa came calling. The next FBI report on Kühn would say his recent activity did not indicate involvement in espionage.

Also in October, in Washington, a group of diplomats and their wives gathered for dinner in a suite at the Broadmoor, an upmarket apartment house on Connecticut Avenue that the Japanese embassy used. Its cohost was the embassy's First Secretary, Hidenari Terasaki, a man known for his perfect command of English, a wide range of contacts, and—rare in those days—an American wife, Gwen. Among the guests were several State Department officials, including Robert Smythe and Frank Schuler and their wives, Jane and Olive, respectively. All had served in the Far East, and the Smythes and Terasakis were old friends.

It seemed natural enough—according to Olive Schuler—when, following a sumptuous dinner, Gwen Terasaki suggested that she and Jane Smythe leave the main party and talk together in another room. When they returned, after some time, both women looked as though they had been crying. As the two American couples made their way home that night, Jane Smythe explained why.

Gwen Terasaki had burst into tears, she said, almost as soon as the two friends started talking. She said she had "a terrible problem." Faced with making a "decision between her country and her husband," she went on, she had resolved to "stand by her husband." She would not go into specifics. "All I can tell you," she said, "is that something terrible is going to happen between our two countries."

The Smythes and the Schulers chewed over what the episode could mean. That the situation between the two countries was on a knife-edge was public knowledge. Why, though, was Gwen Terasaki so distraught? It had been out of character for her to behave that way. Did she know something special? Could anything be done about it? The husbands decided to report what had happened to the head of State's Far East Division, Max Hamilton. He, however, reportedly dismissed the matter as "just a couple of hysterical women carrying on."

If the story was thus dismissed, that may have been a misjudgment. For a mass of FBI documents and MAGIC intercepts reveal a great deal about Terasaki and the role he played in the months before the attack on Pearl Harbor. As early as January, his name had featured in a foreign ministry message before he even arrived in the United States, when Tokyo decided to establish an "intelli-

gence organ" within its Washington embassy. Terasaki, the message said, would be the man to consult on the subject. He was
a significant figure, and U.S. intelligence agencies had rapidly
picked up on the fact.

"As a matter of interest," the Office of Naval Intelligence noted
in late summer, "Mr. Terasaki is head of the Japanese intelligence
network in the United States." As such, he was very much on the
FBI's radar. By mid-October, when Terasaki's wife broke down
sobbing and said that "something terrible" was soon to happen,
her husband's activity was the subject of a twelve-page Bureau report. Terasaki's primary mission, the report said, was "to maintain close contact with Japanese agents in the United States and
the entire Western Hemisphere." He traveled thousands of miles
setting up an intelligence network in Latin America, apparently
to establish a fallback position should Japan and the United States
sever relations.

The FBI watched the First Secretary when he made journeys by
air and by train, when he stayed at hotels, and when he met with
contacts. Some of his phone calls were tapped. On occasion, his
luggage was searched.

In July, when naval spy Itaru Tachibana had been arrested in
Los Angeles for soliciting espionage in Hawaii, it was Terasaki
who ensured he was not tried but swiftly deported. In September, significantly, when the Japanese consul in Hawaii responded
to the telltale request to divide Pearl Harbor into specific sectors
in sending espionage information about moored ships, the reply
went to Japan's Washington embassy as well as to Tokyo. The person directing intelligence from Washington was Terasaki.

In the fall, in Washington, Terasaki played on both sides of the
political fence. As tensions grew, he had sensitive exchanges with
U.S. government officials and courted key isolationists, Americans who opposed the United States' entry into the war.

Twice at least, FBI Director J. Edgar Hoover brought Terasaki's
activities to the attention of the State Department. Senior officials
at State, having discussed whether he should be declared persona non grata, decided—with what amounted to a bureaucratic

shrug—against taking that course. "This officer," one wrote, "has been assigned by his government to do a type of work which we do not like. If this officer does not do that type of work, some other officer will." Matter closed.

What had Terasaki's American wife learned from her husband that so distressed her during the soiree on Connecticut Avenue? Was it merely the fact that there might be conflict with Japan? Or had her husband, as his nation's intelligence chief in the United States, learned something of the plan to attack Hawaii—and shared it with his wife?

In Hawaii, at about the time of the dinner in Washington, a daily briefing report for Admiral Kimmel assessed the Japanese Navy's current activity. "With nothing definite to point to," it read, "the impression grows that a large-scale screening maneuver or operation, at least, is in progress."

The report was prescient.

Meanwhile, in Washington, Japan continued to negotiate. By now, though, negotiation was shot through with subterfuge.

23

ON NOVEMBER 4TH, Tokyo sent its ambassador in Washington, Kichisaburo Nomura, a slew of messages. All concerned the ongoing diplomatic exchanges, and the first was dramatic.

"This is our last effort," it read, as translated by U.S. codebreakers reading PURPLE, the Japanese diplomatic traffic: "If through it we do not reach a quick accord, I am sorry to say the talks will certainly be ruptured. The success or failure of the pending discussion will have an immense effect on the destiny of the Empire of Japan . . . We gambled the fate of our land on the throw of this die."

On analysis, the torrent of verbiage about negotiations added up to nothing. There were no significant concessions to American demands. The new regime in Japan had no intention of giving ground. "Those negotiations," the Prime Minister, General Tojo, would acknowledge, "were continued only for the sake of strategy."

One of the messages sent on November 4th advised Nomura that he was soon to be joined by a new right-hand man, special envoy Saburo Kurusu. Together, they were to try to arrange a meeting between Kurusu and President Roosevelt, and one would in due course take place. The new envoy would be bringing with him "no additional instructions," Nomura was told. The purpose was "to show our Empire's sincerity in the negotiations." The public would be told this was a further effort for peace, "to make it sound good." The truth, Lieutenant General Akira Muto, a senior official at Japan's war ministry, was to admit, was that Kurusu's mission to the United States was "nothing more than a sort of camouflage of events leading to the opening of hostilities."

A November 5th message to Ambassador Nomura had special

resonance. "Because of various circumstances," it told him, "it is absolutely necessary that all arrangements for the signing of [an] agreement be completed by the 25th of this month . . . This information is to be kept strictly to yourself only."

This raised obvious questions. Why was November 25th significant? Why was a deadline necessary? What might happen, or begin to happen, on or about that day?

There was, of course, no possibility that Japan's ambassador could keep the message about the deadline to himself. Unbeknownst to the Japanese, American codebreakers read it, as they did a number of other messages to Nomura at this time, the very day it was sent.

There is no evidence that the dispatch caught the attention of anyone at U.S. Navy or Army headquarters, or at the State Department, or at the White House. In the three weeks that followed, a further five messages would refer to the deadline, the last but one of them extending it slightly. All were available to U.S. officials either on the day they were sent or very soon afterward. The messages were available to those in Washington privy to MAGIC. None were available to Admiral Kimmel in Hawaii, and he was not briefed on any of them.

On November 15th, nine miles from the Admiral's headquarters, the consular spy Yoshikawa would receive an order to increase the frequency of his reports on what warships were moored in Pearl Harbor to "twice a week." Several more related requests would reach him before the attack. He in turn was urged to "take extra care to maintain secrecy."

Again, because of America's ability to read Japanese consular codes, no such secrecy existed. Four of Tokyo's requests to Yoshikawa would be decoded and translated in Washington before the attack. None of them were shared with Kimmel.

Though Chief of Naval Operations Stark's messages failed to ensure that the Admiral was informed of pertinent details, he kept up the flow of letters. On November 7th, Stark responded at length to Kimmel's recent concerns about the Fleet's needs. Otherwise, though two days had passed since the arrival of the first of the "deadline" messages, he wrote only:

> Dear Mustapha,
>   It was fine to hear from you and to learn that you are in fine fettle . . . The big question is—what next? . . . Things seem to be moving steadily towards a crisis in the Pacific. Just when it will break, no one can tell . . . it continually gets 'worser and worser'!"

The letter went off to Hawaii by Pan Am Clipper—for delivery a full week later.

Meanwhile, Admiral Yamamoto's strike force—six aircraft carriers, two battleships, nine destroyers, and their support ships—had been gathering off Kyushu. So tightly held was Admiral Yamamoto's plan that many of his ships' commanders still had not known what the target was to be. Now, on November 3rd, they were called together for a detailed briefing.

Over the past few days, in Tokyo, after the last doubters had been persuaded that the plan was feasible, the Navy general staff had approved the operation. The Army had followed suit, Then, on November 5th, the Chief of the Naval general staff went to the palace to brief Emperor Hirohito. The Emperor gave his approval.

Three days later, Yamamoto issued Combined Fleet Top Secret Order No. 1, a hundred-page document detailing all the Navy's contemplated operations. The order included plans for the moves against the Philippines, British Malaya, and the Netherlands East Indies. Only in the original, reportedly, did the following clauses appear:

> 1. The Task Force will launch a surprise attack at the outset of war upon the U.S. Pacific Fleet supposed to be in Hawaiian waters, and destroy it.

2. The Task Force will reach the designated stand-by point for the operation in advance.

3. The date of starting the operation is tentatively set for December 8 [December 7 by the U.S. calendar], 1941.

All was settled, pending a final decision to attack by Imperial General Headquarters and the government in Tokyo.

As of the second week of November, the Japanese Foreign Minister reiterated again and again the deadline for an end to negotiations. That date, November 25th, he told Ambassador Nomura on the 15th, was "absolutely immovable . . . Please, therefore, make the United States see the light." This message, like most diplomatic traffic to and from the embassy, was intercepted and read within days by U.S. officials in Washington.

Ambassador Nomura, who is generally regarded today as having been an honest broker doing his best in impossible circumstances, responded by urging patience. America was urgently preparing for "actual warfare," Nomura wrote, and would not hesitate to fight. "This little victory or that little victory," he warned, does "not amount to much . . . It is not hard to see that whoever can hold out till the end will be the victor."

His wisdom fell on deaf ears. The situation, the Foreign Minister replied the following day, put further patience "out of the question." On the 22nd, however, he pushed the deadline back by four days, to the 29th. If, the Minister wrote, an agreement could be made "by the 29th—let me write it out for you—twenty-ninth—if the pertinent notes can be exchanged, if we can get an understanding with Great Britain and the Netherlands, and in short if everything can be finished, we have decided to wait until that date. This time we mean it, that the deadline absolutely cannot be changed. After that, things are automatically going to happen."

There were, the Minister told Ambassador Nomura, "reasons

beyond your ability to guess" for the need to set a deadline. Officials in Washington also read these messages.

The reasons for the deadline were military. Five days before this last exchange, on November 17th, the Fleet that was to strike Pearl Harbor had started moving. One after another, the aircraft carriers and their accompanying warships had slipped away from their refuge in the Inland Sea and headed northeast.

Before the ships left, Admiral Yamamoto had addressed a hundred officers on the flight deck of the *Akagi*, the strike force's lead carrier. Unusually, he spoke without notes.

"Although we hope to achieve surprise," he said, "everyone should be prepared for terrific American resistance in this operation. Japan has faced many worthy opponents in her glorious history—Mongols, Chinese, Russians—but in this operation we shall meet the strongest and most resourceful opponent of all."

He spoke in detail, those listening would remember, of his opposing commander in chief, Admiral Kimmel. "The American commander is no ordinary or average man. Such a relatively junior admiral would not have been given the important position of Commander-in-Chief Pacific unless he were gallant and brave. We can expect him to put up a courageous fight. Moreover, he is said to be farsighted and cautious, so it is quite possible that he has instituted very close measures to cope with any emergency . . . You may have to fight your way in to the target."

Officers then assembled in the wardroom to drink a toast to the Emperor and the battle ahead: *"Banzai! Banzai! Banzai!"*

24

IN HAWAII EACH MORNING, Admiral Kimmel received a briefing on Japanese naval activity. At 8:00 a.m. sharp, Fleet intelligence officer Layton would deliver a written summary of the information gathered in the past twenty-four hours. Kimmel would mark it up, underline points he thought significant, and perhaps ask for clarification. Then he would add his initials: "H.E.K." For months, this had been a matter of routine.

The key information in the daily briefing came from the Combat Intelligence Unit, a group of forty-seven officers and enlisted men based in the Navy Yard. They worked in secrecy, behind an unmarked door, in basement quarters they called "the Dungeon." These were the men of Station Hypo, one of three units dealing with COMINT, communications intelligence. Hypo's workspace was divided into sectors according to different specialties: cryptanalysis—the unit's "meat and potatoes"—along with traffic analysis, direction finding, and translation.

Heading Station Hypo was Commander Joe Rochefort, an analyst whose skills would in months to come contribute mightily to the U.S. victory at the Battle of Midway, and—posthumously—earn him the Presidential Medal of Freedom. He was known for his brilliance, his prodigious working hours, and his sartorial eccentricity. Military correctness did not matter in his chilly fiefdom belowground. Rochefort was prone to wearing a maroon smoking jacket over his uniform and padding about in carpet slippers.

Though Rochefort's reports went to the Admiral through intelligence officer Layton, Hypo's principal mission had been ordained by Washington. The unit's standing orders were to concentrate on trying to break what U.S. analysts had called Japan's "Flag Officers' Code," so named because it was used for messages between headquarters in Tokyo and Japanese admirals. Though deemed very important, for obvious reasons, cracking it was a virtual impossibility. Hawaii intercepted only three or four such messages a day, and the code never would be broken in any meaningful way.

The Hypo team would have preferred, rather, to tackle the heavily used, and thus potentially far more breakable, "Fleet General Purpose Code." That task, however, had been assigned to Station Cast in the Philippines, on the reasoning that, being closer geographically to Japan, it was better positioned for the job. The experts working for Rochefort, meanwhile, also worked on areas that had been proving productive—traffic analysis and direction finding.

With little else available to supply Admiral Kimmel with timely intelligence, these were precious tools. From the number of radio messages, routing and call signs, traffic analysis could gauge the Japanese Fleet's organization and activity. There were clues to the source of a message—a known ship or land-based unit—in the way a familiar operator tapped the keys. An operator's "fist," as it was known, is said to have been as recognizable as handwriting.

Rochefort's direction finders, studying signals picked up by a far-flung network of antennae, could establish the direction from which a target's signals were coming. Successive fixes could plot the target's course and speed. For month after month in 1941, these skills had made it possible to figure out what the Japanese Fleet was up to.

On November 1st, however, as Yamamoto was gathering his strike force in the Inland Sea, the Japanese Navy changed its radio call signs. While it usually did so every six months, this switch came after only five. Though a little out of the ordinary, that in itself was not especially alarming. As analysts raced to figure out the new call signs, however, two of Rochefort's men made a discovery. They happened upon a dispatch directed to a previously unknown Japanese Navy addressee—*Itikoukuu Kantai*, or "First Air Fleet."

This, Hypo's daily summary told Kimmel two days later,

For Admiral Kimmel, February 1941 was a fateful month. President Roosevelt promoted him over forty-seven more-senior admirals to be Commander in Chief, U.S. Pacific Fleet. The change of command ceremony took place on the quarterdeck of the USS *Pennsylvania.(National Park Service & Kimmel family)*

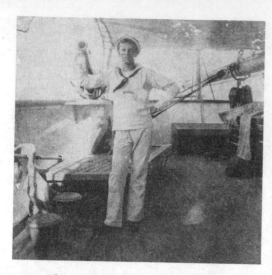

LEFT: The midshipman—Kimmel at age twenty, during his time at the Naval Academy. RIGHT: The lieutenant in combat—it was a narrow escape.

At thirty, after marriage to Dorothy, the daughter of a Navy officer—they would go on to have three sons.

Navy men together. Commander Kimmel, with sons Manning (*right*) and Tom in 1920. Both they and their brother, Ned, would serve in World War II. (*Kimmel family*)

The leaders confer. President Franklin Roosevelt and Prime Minister Winston Churchill met in August 1941 aboard a cruiser off Newfoundland. They agreed on their "Atlantic Charter," but the U.S. remained nervously neutral. *(National Archives)*

LEFT: Emperor Hirohito—his title meant "Enlightened Peace."
BELOW: Admiral Yamamoto, commander in chief of the Japanese Combined Fleet, conceived and directed the attack on Pearl Harbor. *(National Archives)*

Secretary of the Navy Frank Knox. (*National Archives*)

Chief of Naval Operations Admiral Harold "Betty" Stark. (*Naval History & Heritage Command*)

Secretary of War Henry Stimson (*right*) with Chief of Staff General George Marshall. (*Library of Congress*)

The Army commander-in-chief in Hawaii, Lieutenant General Walter Short. (*U.S. Army*)

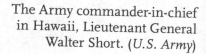

As early as 1940, in an attack against Italian battleships at Taranto (*above*), the British Navy had proved that torpedoes dropped from aircraft could be effective in shallow water. The U.S. Navy had inside information on the attack from its own observer, Lieutenant Commander John Opie, but failed to pass it on to Hawaii. The Japanese paid more attention. (*Christopher O'Connor*)

Double-agent Dusko Popov, whose loyalty was to the British, brought to the U.S. a questionnaire showing that Germany—Japan's close ally—wanted detailed naval information on Pearl Harbor. The FBI, the Office of Naval Intelligence, and G-2 failed to share this vital information with Hawaii. (*Marco Popov*)

Flottenstuetzpunkt Pearl Harbor:

1). Genaue Angaben und Skizze ueber die Lage der Staatswerft, der Pieranlagen, Werkstaetten, Tankanlagen, Lage des Trockendocks?
2). Nr. 1 und des in Bau befindlichen neuen Trockendocks? Einzelheiten ueber die Ubootstation (Lageplan). Welche Land-anlagen sind vorhanden?
3). Wo befindet sich die Station fuer Minensuchverbaende? Wie-weit sind die Baggerarbeiten (sic) an der Einfuhr und in Ost und South-East loch fortgeschritten? Wassertiefen?
4). Zahl der Liegeplaetze?
5). Befindet sich ein Schwimdock in Pearl Harbor oder ist die Verlegung eines solchen dorthin beabsichtigt?

Sonderaufgaben: Meldung ueber in britischer und U.S.A. Marine neu-eingefuehrte Torpedoschutznetze. Inwieweit in Handels- und Kriegs-Flotte bereits vorhanden? Benutzung in Fahrt? Durchschnittliche Fahrteinschraenkung bei Benutzung. Einzelheiten der Konstruktion d.a.-

1. Dringend erwuenscht sind genaue Angaben ueber die Panzerstaerke amerikan. Kampfwagen, besonders der Typen welche von den U.S.A. in letzter Zeit nach dem mittleren Osten geliefert worden sind.

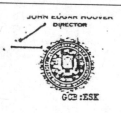

JOHN EDGAR HOOVER
DIRECTOR

GCB:ESK

SECRET

Federal Bureau of Investigation
United States Department of Justice
Washington, D. C.

October 31, 1941

Mr. E. A. Tamm
Mr. Clegg
Mr. Glavin
Mr. Ladd
Mr. Nichols
Mr. Tracy
Mr. Rosen
Mr. Carson
Mr. Coffey
Mr. Hendon
Mr. Quinn Tamm
Mr. Nettman
Mr. Harbo
Tele. Room
Your Room
Mr. Nease
Miss Beahm
Miss Gandy

MEMORANDUM FOR MR. LADD

DUSAN M. POPOV,
Confidential Informant
ESPIONAGE - G

There is attached hereto a two-page memorandum prepared by Lieutenant M. J. Perry of the Office of Naval Intelligence on the subject of the anti-torpedo defense nets. This was handed to the writer by Lieutenant Perry, who stated that it had been prepared at the request of Mr. Thurston and is to be used for counterespionage purposes. Lieutenant Perry advised that he could also provide sketches of a fictitious setup for the torpedo nets.

America's secret weapon—the machine the U.S. built to decrypt Japan's highest-level diplomatic message traffic—PURPLE. Admiral Kimmel did not see the intercepts. (*National Archives*)

```
From:  Tokyo
To:    Washington
December 7, 1941
Purple (Urgent -- Very Important)

#907.        To be handled in government code.

             Re my #902ᵃ.

             Will the Ambassador please submit to the United

States Government (if possible to the Secretary of State)

our reply to the United States at 1:00 p.m. on the 7th, your

time.

a - JD-1:7143 - text of Japanese reply.
```

Washington received a Japanese intercept pointing to possible imminent aggression in the Pacific, but its warning to commanders in the field arrived far too late.

In 1941, Rear Admiral Kelly Turner (*left*), the Director of War Plans, claimed— wrongly—that Hawaii was receiving Japanese code intercepts. Commander Arthur McCollum, head of the Far East section of ONI, knew Hawaii did not have access to the intercepts, and did not think it should. (*Naval History & Heritage Command*)

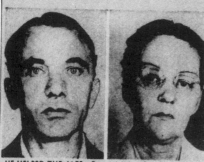

HE HELPED THE JAPS—Bernard Julius Otto Kuehn, Nazi-super spy, is doing 50 years at hard prison labor for collaborating in the Pearl Harbor sneak attack. He was originally sentenced to death. His wife, Friedel Kuehn, is interned for the duration.

Nazi Spy Helped Plot Pearl Harbor Attack

Devised System to Signal Japs, Gave Data On Our Fleet—Life Spared by U. S.

Trained spy Takeo Yoshikawa, posing as "chancellor" (*top right*), worked out of Japan's consulate in Honolulu. Nazi Otto Kühn and his wife, Friedel, were arrested after the attack—Kühn had been a sleeper agent. This cable (*right*), decrypted two months before the disaster, betrayed Japan's need for special intelligence on Pearl Harbor—yet went unnoticed in Washington. (*FBI, National Archives*)

From: Tokyo (Toyoda)
To: Honolulu
September 24, 1941

#83

Strictly secret.

Henceforth, we would like to have you make reports concerning vessels along the following lines insofar as possible:

1. The waters (of Pearl Harbor) are to be divided roughly into five sub-areas. (We have no objections to your abbreviating as much as you like.)

Area A. Waters between Ford Island and the Arsenal.

Area B. Waters adjacent to the Island south and west of Ford Island. (This area is on the opposite side of the Island from Area A.)

Area C. East Loch.

Area D. Middle Loch.

Area E. West Loch and the communicating water routes.

2. With regard to warships and aircraft carriers, we would like to have you report on those at anchor, (these are not so important) tied up at wharves, buoys and in docks. (Designate types and classes briefly. If possible we would like to have you make mention of the fact when there are two or more vessels along side the same wharf.)

23260
ARMY

Trans. 10/9/41 (S)

seemed to indicate the existence of "an entirely new organization of the Naval Air Force." Rochefort and Fleet intelligence officer Layton realized that this had to signify something. Just what it meant, however, would not become clear until after the strike on Pearl Harbor.

Meanwhile, everything they thought they knew about the configuration of the Japanese Navy suddenly became a jumble. "Each fleet circuit, which we called a 'mother,'" Layton was to recall, had until now "had certain 'chickens' under its radio 'wing.'" In the new situation, "Some of these chickens no longer turned up with their usual mother, but were calling the mother address of other fleets." There had been an inexplicable reorganization.

Rochefort remembered thinking, "Something was afoot . . . We couldn't put our hands on it, as to what it was to be, or any direction . . . but it was apparent there was something building up."

Trying to figure out just what was building up, and where, was an urgent priority. Months earlier, the Hypo unit had started working seven days a week. From now on, at least one officer—with enlisted men—worked around the clock. In the normal run of things, penetrating the seemingly impenetrable was what Rochefort and his team strove to achieve. The new puzzles, though, were diabolically difficult.

Much of the torrent of messages coming out of Tokyo, they reported to Kimmel, was "dummy traffic." That it was, and with a purpose. Yamamoto's trick in November was to make it appear that, long after the ships of his strike force had in fact sailed north, they remained in the Inland Sea. The airwaves crackled with phony messages between bases on land and planes in the air—in the south. Some Japanese operators whose "fists" were likely to be familiar to U.S. eavesdroppers had not sailed with the strike force. Instead they stayed ashore, sending deceptive messages purportedly generated by the force's aircraft carriers. Other fake chatter came from a venerable battleship, normally used for training purposes, cruising around the Inland Sea.

There would also be a baffling change in procedure. Instead of sending messages to individual recipients, Tokyo now transmitted to multiple recipients, indicating the intended addressee only in the encoded text. To U.S. eavesdroppers, Layton would wearily recall, these messages appeared to be "addressed to nobody from nobody. When they do that, nobody is being talked to that you can identify."

Admiral Kimmel, Layton remembered, became daily more interested in the obstacles the analysts were encountering. As Kimmel himself put it long afterward, he knew that simply changing a call sign—without any additional ploys—could make locating warships "practically impossible." On twelve separate occasions that year, the record shows, his intelligence people had been uncertain where the Japanese carriers were. The periods of virtual "blindness" had lasted as long as three weeks at a time. There was not, necessarily, any reason to think an attack was pending.

As they groped in the electronic darkness that November, Layton, Rochefort, and their colleagues guessed that the Japanese were readying for a push in two areas. Early that month, Kimmel drew Washington's attention to a buildup of activity in Micronesia, the string of islands and atolls at that time known as the Mandates. Some of them were within striking distance of the Philippines.

Given the hubbub of naval communications originating from the Inland Sea, the Admiral's intelligence staff in Hawaii anticipated—as had long been the case—that the Japanese were preparing to thrust south. "Those pieces of the puzzle that we possessed," as Layton recalled, "fit neatly into this framework. As we saw it, a Japanese offensive move was shaping up against Malaya. It was possible that it was also directed against the Philippines."

These guesses would turn out to be correct, but the analysts knew they were missing part of the puzzle. Station Hypo's reports of November 9th and 10th, which placed aircraft carriers in or near the Inland Sea, would turn out to be the last accurate reports on carriers until after the attack on Pearl Harbor a month later. On November 18th, in their estimate of the positions of Japanese carriers and battleships, Hypo's men would still hazard the guess that there had been "no movement from home waters." Wrong.

The previous day, as reported in Chapter 23, Yamamoto's warships had begun the roundabout voyage of well over four thousand miles that was to take them within striking distance of Pearl Harbor.

The first lap, a short hop by Pacific standards, took the strike force—thirty-three ships in all, not traveling as a group—to Hitokappu Bay, a remote spot in the Kurils, a northern archipelago that Japan at the time shared with Russia. To avoid telltale radio transmissions from the bay, essential messages between the strike force and Admiral Yamamoto and his staff were carried by couriers traveling by plane. Within days, total radio silence would be imposed. While the force would retain the ability to receive encoded messages, transmissions were prohibited. Even aboard the strike force flagship, the carrier *Akagi*, some keyboards were intentionally disabled, their circuit fuses removed.

Secrecy, Yamamoto's chief of staff noted in his diary, was "profound." So far as U.S. listeners at intercept stations across the vastness of the Pacific were concerned, the strike force was now invisible. Japan's deception had succeeded.

Once all the Japanese ships had arrived in the Kurils, senior commanders were briefed by one of the naval intelligence officers just back from their undercover fact-finding visit to Hawaii. He brought with him the most recent information on Pearl Harbor, as collated by the consulate's spy there, Yoshikawa. The officer showed his listeners the map the spy had prepared, and his sketches of U.S. installations, and briefed them on what he and his fellow officers had learned.

The strike force commander, Vice Admiral Chuichi Nagumo, weighed up the potential risks. Would the American Navy be alert to the possibility of attack? Would the weather, already bad at that northern latitude, hinder refueling operations en route to the target? Would the weather be too good, making Japan's ships only too visible to other shipping or U.S. patrol aircraft?

There were no good answers to such questions. Nagumo pushed ahead with preparations for the operation. The aspiration, senior officers were told, was to destroy all the U.S. Pacific Fleet's aircraft carriers and a minimum of four battleships, to neutralize American naval power for many months.

There remained the possibility that the strike might yet be called off, should a settlement be reached with Washington. The mood aboard the strike force warships, though, crew members would say after the war, was that this was only an outside chance.

On November 25th, Admiral Yamamoto sent the order to sortie. At dawn the following day, having paused in the Kurils for four days, the Japanese warships upped anchor and began steaming toward Hawaii.

On November 18th, when the strike force had begun its journey north, the spy Yoshikawa at the Honolulu consulate had received a fresh instruction, requiring him to report on areas that had not been part of his earlier brief. "Make your investigation," the message warned him, "with great secrecy."

The instruction, and the emphasis on secrecy, would have indicated that Pearl Harbor might soon be a target, had U.S. intelligence translated and read it—especially in the context of previous messages to the spy. Headquarters in Washington, however, had ordered that Hawaii forward consular intercepts—unread and by Clipper—to Washington. "We," Hypo's Commander Rochefort would recall, "were not to do any work on the diplomatic systems." U.S. analysts were not to decode and translate the new order to Yoshikawa until two days before the attack. It, like all previous messages to Yoshikawa, was not shared with Admiral Kimmel.

PURPLE, the other main stream of intercepted diplomatic traffic—communications between Tokyo and its embassy in the United States—was of course prioritized in Washington and read every day. Had Kimmel had access to PURPLE, he would have been ever more aware that Japan's continued negotiating was a charade. The leadership at U.S. naval headquarters knew this was so, but did not tell Kimmel.

The decision in Washington to give priority to PURPLE had a tragic result. Because of it, too few codebreakers had been assigned to work on the more intractable Japanese naval codes, like the Fleet General Purpose Code. Those Navy and Army analysts in Washington and the Philippines who were trying to break it were making virtually no progress. Headquarters did eventually decide that Station Hypo's specialists in Hawaii should have a crack at it. The documentation that would have made it possible for them to start work, however, did not reach the unit until after Pearl Harbor—because of a shipping snarl-up.

Of some two thousand Japanese Navy messages selected for decryption and translation after the war, almost two hundred—sent largely in the General Purpose Code—would be found to contain data relevant to the Pearl Harbor attack.

In a study half a century later, National Security Agency analyst Frederick Parker was to describe the material as "stunning." Had it been available before the attack, he thought, it would have identified not only the strike force but also—once analyzed—the objective. From October on, Parker's study shows, there were numerous references to the "Strike Force," and at least one to the "Striking Force Secret Operation." There was a reference to Hitokappu Bay, the strike force's holding point in the Kurils. There was a reference to "night and day" work on torpedoes for use at shallow depths, and, in early November, a reference to torpedoes that Japanese carriers were "to fire against anchored ships on the morning in question."

"Had Navy cryptanalysts been ordered to concentrate on the Japanese naval messages rather than diplomatic traffic," the NSA's Parker wrote, "the United States might . . . have avoided the disaster of Pearl Harbor."

25

IN WASHINGTON as November slipped by, there was much talk about what might or might not happen in the Pacific. President Roosevelt talked with his Secretaries of State, War, and the Navy. He talked with Japanese Ambassador Nomura and with the new envoy, Saburo Kurusu. On Constitution Avenue, Naval and Army intelligence officers talked and made their estimates. For all of the U.S. officials and military men privy to it, MAGIC continued to be a key source of information, one of the nation's most closely guarded secrets.

All the more astonishing, then, that on November 15th, when the war drums were beating loud, Marshall himself alluded to MAGIC less than prudently. That day, at a confidential briefing for correspondents of *Time* and *Newsweek* magazines, the *New York Times*, the *Herald Tribune*, and the main news agencies, he said that should war with Japan break out, the prospects for the United States were good. That was so, he said, in part because:

> We have access to a leak in all the information they are receiving concerning our military preparations, especially in the Philippines. In other words, *we know what they know about us, and they don't know that we know it* [authors' italics].

Marshall did not identify the nature of what he called the "leak." It was extraordinary, all the same, that the Chief of Staff should have come so close to revealing to reporters—even reporters he thought he could trust—what he deemed so precious a secret that it could not be shared with admirals and generals in the path of the coming storm.

MAGIC, and all but a few snippets of the intelligence provided by the intercepts, would remain unknown to Kimmel until long afterward. Marooned as he was in Hawaii, he knew nothing of the background it provided in the final three weeks before the attack on Pearl Harbor.

MAGIC aside, as he would later put it himself, Kimmel was "completely out of touch" with the details of the continuing talks between high Washington officials and Japan's representatives.

In the Philippines, Admiral Hart was also feeling the strain of the distance from events in Washington, of not knowing what was really going on. "War of Nerves," he wrote in a letter to CNO Stark of November 20th. "That's all we hear about. It's been on out here for a long time . . . Knowing that I must keep my Fleet healthy in mind and body, I have not kept them living under a state of high precaution and alarm. Have not been nearly as precautionary as the Navy is around Hawaii.

"Of itself, I don't think that has worn or tired me," Hart went on, "What has, however, is the rather chronic condition under which we don't get the word from Washington . . . [The] many indications that we are thought about last of all, and the disposition to think there is plenty of time."

Though Ambassador Nomura was shuttling between President Roosevelt at the White House and Secretary of State Hull at the State Department, and though both sides continued to make courteous noises, neither side was budging.

Nomura, who kept a diary, had noted after one meeting that the President thought a "general understanding" might yet save the situation. "There is no last word," Roosevelt had said, "between friends." He would, if asked to do so, see the Ambassador and his colleague Kurusu again.

There was no meaningful movement, however. At a session with Hull, there was no give on the U.S. side when Nomura floated the notion of returning to the situation that had existed before America froze oil exports. There was no give on the Japanese side when Hull emphasized the obstacle of Japan's alliance with Hitler's Germany. Tokyo's envoys got nowhere, either, when they made a five-point proposal that was essentially a rehash of the position Tokyo had taken months earlier.

Ambassador Nomura was by all accounts an honest man doing his best, not privy to the machinations of the high command in Tokyo but with a shrewd idea as to what was afoot. Acutely aware of the impasse the talks had reached, he at this point took drastic action behind the scenes. A retired admiral himself, he resorted to asking for a secret meeting with Chief of Naval Operations Stark.

A cloak-and-dagger episode, it took place on or about November 23rd, at the CNO's home. Nomura, the CNO said, was "extremely worried about the possibility of the war party in Japan making some drastic decisions." If the United States did not ease sanctions, he thought, the military would "do something desperate," and he begged Stark to alert the President and the State Department. Clearly upset, the Ambassador emerged from the meeting with tears in his eyes.

Stark, who spoke regularly with Roosevelt, almost certainly shared Nomura's dark premonition with the President. Roosevelt and his advisers, for their part, were debating how to respond to Japan's five-point proposal of November 20th.

The notion of accepting it, Hull would say later, was "clearly unthinkable." To do so, he wrote in his memoirs, would have "assured Japan's domination of the Pacific, placing us in serious danger for decades to come." Not to respond at all, though, might accelerate the outbreak of war. As State Department officials worked up a counterproposal, Hull consulted with the President, the Secretaries of War and the Navy, and the military.

Weeks earlier, in a long joint report on November 5th, Chief of Staff Marshall and Stark had warned Roosevelt that the Pacific Fleet was weaker than the Japanese Fleet and not capable of going to war in the western ocean. The bottom line, they had recommended, was that "no ultimatum be delivered to Japan." Now, when consulted about the State Department's draft counterproposal to Japan, the Army emphasized that it was "of grave importance" to find a way to prevent war with Japan.

During discussion of the draft with the envoys of U.S. allies, however, Hull made it clear that he was not optimistic. There was "probably not one chance in three that [the Japanese] would accept our reply."

Kimmel, in Hawaii, was not kept entirely out of the loop. On the heels of a letter saying that the Japanese and American positions seemed "impossible to reconcile," Stark sent the Admiral and several other commanders this dispatch:

TOP SECRET
NOVEMBER 24, 1941
FROM: CHIEF OF NAVAL OPERATIONS

Chances of favorable outcome of negotiations with Japan very doubtful X This situation coupled with statements of Japanese Government and movements their naval and military forces indicate in our opinion that a surprise aggressive movement in any direction including attack on Philippines or Guam is a possibility . . . Utmost secrecy necessary in order not to complicate an already tense situation or precipitate Japanese action X

This message told Kimmel and senior colleagues in the Pacific that things were coming to a head. What it did not give them was context or a sense, which Washington had from reading MAGIC, of *when* Japan might make a move. Kimmel was not told what high officials and analysts at headquarters knew: that Tokyo had warned its ambassador that, should there be no settlement by November 29th, things were "automatically going to happen."

What "things" were going to happen? Why would they occur "automatically"? And why had Tokyo told Nomura, in the same intercepted message, that a deadline was necessary for "reasons beyond your ability to guess."

This message alone should have set alarm bells ringing. It

would certainly have gotten the attention of Admiral Kimmel and General Short, whose air and ground forces were directly responsible for the defense of Hawaii. Though the message was decrypted in Washington two days before Stark's message of the 24th, its contents were not shared with either commander.

Early in the month, Tokyo had told Nomura that what was to become its five-point proposal would be its "last effort to prevent something [from] happening." Thanks to MAGIC, high U.S. officials had known this three *weeks* before Stark's message of the 24th. They had not told Kimmel or Short in Hawaii.

WITH THE DAYS passing and no response to Japan yet agreed on, the President showed that he too was pessimistic. On November 25th, at a meeting with the Secretaries of State, War, and the Navy; Chief of Staff Marshall; and the Navy's Stark, the President shelved other business and focused solely on Japan. He forecast, Secretary of War Stimson noted in his diary, "that we were likely to be attacked perhaps as soon as next Monday [December 1st], for the Japanese are notorious for making an attack without warning . . . The question was how we should maneuver them into the position of firing the first shot without allowing too much danger to ourselves."

The following day, when Stimson phoned the President, he passed on intelligence that Japanese transports loaded with troops had been seen on the move south of Taiwan. Roosevelt, the Secretary of War noted in his diary, "fairly blew up, jumped up in the air, so to speak, and said that he hadn't seen [the new information] and that that changed the whole situation, because it was evidence of bad faith on the part of the Japanese that while they were negotiating for an entire truce—an entire withdrawal (from China)—they would be sending this expedition down there to Indo-China."

The U.S. leadership had been considering responding to Japan's five-point proposal for a three-month breathing space—under certain strict conditions. During the breathing space, Japan would have gotten some of what it wanted—a limited amount of oil. In view of the new troop movements, however, and objections by Britain and China that the draft proposal would leave China vulnerable to further Japanese aggression, the American position hardened. Having consulted with the President, Secretary of State Hull framed a riposte that was shorter and sharper.

The document Hull handed Ambassador Nomura that after-noon, November 26th, called—other points aside—for a total withdrawal by the Japanese from Indochina and China. Nego-tiations on normalizing trade would begin only once that was agreed. For the bellicose regime in Tokyo, the U.S. message was anathema. "The United States," Foreign Minister Shigenori Togo would say after the war, "had served upon us what we viewed as an ultimatum."

The document took the form it did without the prior knowledge of Secretary of War Stimson, according to his diary entry for the following day. "First thing in the morning," he wrote, "I called up Hull to find out what his finale had been with the Japanese . . . He told me now that he had broken the whole matter off . . . 'I have washed my hands of it and it is now in the hands of you and [Sec-retary of the Navy] Knox—the Army and the Navy.' "

Nothing in the official record indicates that top Navy and Army officials saw the document before it was handed to the Japanese in its final blunt form. When they did see it, former CNO Stark would recall in testimony much later, it troubled them because they had been "playing for time." He could remember virtually no detail about the sequence of events, however; nor could Chief of Staff Marshall remember any. Their memory lapse—according to Navy War Plans chief Kelly Turner and Stark's aide Lieutenant Commander William Smedberg, speaking years later—obscured a failure of communication at the highest level.

Marshall, Stark, and their colleagues, Turner and Smedberg said, had been familiar with the document in its early draft form and had seen the final, curt version only after it had been deliv-ered to Nomura. Even the less peremptory draft had seemed to them "unwise," and they had urged that it not be sent. It was, after all, only three weeks since Marshall and Stark had written to Roosevelt stressing that U.S. forces were not ready for war. As a result of their comments, they had imagined, the President would have ordered that the draft be at least "softened in tone and de-mands."

On learning after the fact that a much tougher version had

been handed to the Japanese, the Navy and Army brass had all—in Turner's words—been "considerably upset." Smedberg put it more strongly: they had, he said, been "dumbfounded and aghast."

What had led to the decision to send the tough signal to Tokyo? Secretary of State Hull, for his part, may well have been emboldened by the oddly optimistic mind-set of his senior adviser on Far Eastern Affairs, Stanley Hornbeck. In a paper he was preparing at the time, Hornbeck wrote that in his opinion "the Japanese Government does not desire or expect to have *forthwith* armed conflict with the United States . . . Were it a matter of placing bets, the undersigned would give odds of five to one that the United States and Japan will not be at 'war' on or before December 15 . . . would wager even money that the United States and Japan will not be at 'war' on or before March 1."

Hull—according to Smedberg, quoting what Stark had told him—shared with the President his officials' further advice that "the Japanese respected firmness and if he gave in we would lose face . . . And the President said 'Okay,' and never notified the Army or the Navy that the position had changed." He had "changed his mind without telling them" and approved the peremptory document.

"In those days," said Smedberg, with considerable understatement, "there was a woeful lack of communication between the State Department and the War and Navy Departments."

On November 27th, the day after the uncompromising U.S. document had been handed to the Japanese, Stark and Marshall renewed their earlier advice to the President about avoiding "precipitance of military action." "The most essential thing now from the United States' standpoint," they wrote, "is to gain time."

Some six thousand miles away, Admiral Yamamoto's strike force was bucketing across the north Pacific, on its planned course for Hawaii. Negotiations in Washington had not been broken off—not in so many words—but the operation was going ahead.

27

THOUGH NAVY HEADQUARTERS learned of the U.S. government's uncompromising note to Tokyo within hours, and though U.S. military leaders feared it would provoke the Japanese, Kimmel was not told of it. He would not learn of its existence until well after the attack on Pearl Harbor. He had no reason to think such a note would be sent, having only a few days earlier received a copy of the appeal to the President by the Chief of Naval Operations and the Army's Chief of Staff *not* to confront Japan with an ultimatum.

Washington did not share with Kimmel, moreover, what the MAGIC intercepts and U.S. eavesdropping revealed of Japan's reaction to the note. It did not tell him that, in a despairing phone call, envoy Kurusu told Tokyo the United States *"will* not yield. . . . it is of no avail . . . I am unable to make any progress at all."

Nor did Washington tell Kimmel that—even before the State Department's stern note to Tokyo—MAGIC intercepts had shown that Japan was preparing for a complete break with the United States. As early as November 15th, its diplomatic missions abroad had been sent detailed instructions for the "order and method of destroying the code machines."

During the week leading up to delivery of Washington's note to Ambassador Nomura, headquarters had twice shared with Kimmel its sense of where Japan might make a hostile move. Options had included Thailand, the Burma Road, Malaya, the Netherlands East Indies, and the Russian Maritime Provinces. Possible targets, Stark had written, were the Philippines and Guam. There might be "a surprise aggressive movement in any direction."

One possible target not mentioned by anyone was Pearl Harbor.

———

The day after the note's delivery, November 27th, the Army and Navy leadership in Washington got together to frame a message that would alert commanders in the Pacific to the situation—and tell them what they should do about it. "In particular," Secretary of War Stimson noted, it was aimed at General MacArthur in the Philippines, who was "in the forefront of the threatened area." Stimson and his military colleagues wrestled for hours with the language, even consulting with the President. In the Secretary's words, the intention was that the communication should be "strictly accurate."

In view of claims and counterclaims made much later, the content of the November 27th messages matters. Two were transmitted, with slight adjustments according to the addressee—one for the Army's commanders, one for the Navy's admirals. The message to the Army in Hawaii, which arrived that afternoon over the Chief of Staff's signature, told General Short that talks with Japan appeared to be over, that "hostile action appeared possible at any moment," and that U.S. policy was that Japan should commit the "first overt act." That policy, however, should not hold the General back in any way that might jeopardize his defense.

Short was ordered to:

UNDERTAKE SUCH RECONNAISSANCE AND OTHER MEASURES AS YOU DEEM NECESSARY BUT THESE MEASURES SHOULD BE CARRIED OUT SO AS NOT COMMA REPEAT NOT COMMA TO ALARM CIVIL POPULATION OR DISCLOSE INTENT PERIOD REPORT MEASURES TAKEN PERIOD SHOULD HOSTILITIES OCCUR YOU WILL CARRY OUT THE TASKS ASSIGNED IN [War Plan] RAINBOW FIVE SO FAR AS THEY PERTAIN TO JAPAN.

The General responded within minutes by ordering Alert No. 1, the lowest of three alert levels, strengthening the guard at military installations and vital civilian facilities. At Army air bases, planes were bunched together for better protection, under guard. Three other messages from Washington, on that and the following day, emphasized—with Hawaii's large ethnic Japanese population in mind—that it was important to take measures to counter possible sabotage, espionage, or subversive propaganda.

Even before receiving the further messages, Short reported back, as requested, saying he had alerted his force "to prevent sabotage," and that he was liaising with the Navy. He made no reference to Washington's direction that he "undertake reconnaissance." He did, though, order that the embryonic "Aircraft Warning Service"—radar—should be operational during what were regarded as the "most critical" hours, from two hours before dawn until one hour afterward. There was to be training during the morning every day except Sundays. Radar, in Secretary of War Stimson's view, was the "most effective means of reconnaissance."

A memorandum prepared for a later investigation into the disaster establishes that Short's response to the warning, reporting that he was alerting his command only "to prevent sabotage," was routed not only to Chief of Staff Marshall but to key senior individuals in the War Department, including Secretary of War Stimson, Army chief of War Plans General Leonard Gerow, and others.

No one at the War Department raised any objection to the fact that Short responded to Marshall's order of November 27th merely by reporting that he was taking precautions against sabotage. The minutes of a staff meeting in Marshall's office on the preceding day reflect a concern not about Hawaii but about a sense that Japan would "soon cut loose and attack the Philippines."

The Chief of Staff's initial postattack testimony, moreover, indicates that his own assessment of the principal risk to Hawaii was identical to Short's. "I fully anticipated," he said, "a terrific effort to cripple everything out there by sabotage. I think that was almost axiomatic . . . that was going to come."

Much later, Marshall would say he had assumed Short would implement a higher alert. In the nine days remaining until the attack, however, neither he nor any of the other Army higher-ups who saw the traffic took steps to get their commander in Hawaii to amend the measures he had reported having taken. "I had an opportunity to intervene," Marshall would acknowledge, "and I did not take it . . . I was responsible."

At Navy headquarters in Washington the same day, Stark and his senior colleagues spent most of the morning discussing just what the corresponding message to the Pacific commanders—Kimmel in Hawaii and Admiral Hart in the Philippines—ought to say. It was eventually agreed that it should open—Navy War Plans chief Turner pressed for this—with the words "This is a war warning." The President agreed with the message as drafted. It read:

THIS DISPATCH IS TO BE CONSIDERED A WAR WARN-ING. NEGOTIATIONS WITH JAPAN LOOKING TOWARD STABILIZATION OF CONDITIONS IN THE PACIFIC HAVE CEASED AND AN AGGRESSIVE MOVE BY JAPAN IS EXPECTED WITHIN THE NEXT FEW DAYS. THE NUMBER AND EQUIPMENT OF JAPANESE TROOPS AND THE ORGANIZATION OF NAVAL TASK FORCES INDICATES AN AMPHIBIOUS EXPEDITION AGAINST EITHER THE PHILIPPINES THAI OR KRA PENINSULA [the neck of land between Thailand and Malaya] OR POS-SIBLY BORNEO. EXECUTE AN APPROPRIATE DEFEN-SIVE DEPLOYMENT PREPARATORY TO CARRYING OUT THE TASKS ASSIGNED IN [Navy War Plan] WPL-46. INFORM DISTRICT AND ARMY AUTHORITIES. A SIMI-LAR WARNING IS BEING SENT BY WAR DEPARTMENT.

No acknowledgment was requested, and there was no reference to a possible threat to Hawaii.

28

WHAT EXACTLY DID the November 27th message mean? It was the sixth message headquarters had sent to Kimmel that year alluding to possible war. Two, very similar to the one just in, had arrived over the past six weeks. One, in October, had warned of a possible Japanese attack somewhere—there was no suggestion as to where it might occur—and directed the Admiral to take precautions. Following up, CNO Stark had emphasized that he personally did not think the Japanese would attack—it was just a possibility.

The message of the 24th, just three days earlier, had also referred to the "possibility" of a "surprise aggressive movement" by Japan. There had been, as Kimmel later remembered, "a plethora of premonitions." Admiral Hart would characterize the messages as the "yakity-yak that went back and forth."

CNO Stark, in Washington, had himself wondered months earlier, in a postscript to one of his rambling letters to Kimmel, whether it was really worthwhile sending it. "One fellow's estimate," he had said wearily, "is as good as another's." If he sent more messages, aides told the CNO at one point, recipients in the Pacific might think he was crying wolf.

At the core of the dozens of words in the November 27th dispatch, just fourteen constituted an instruction from the high command:

EXECUTE AN APPROPRIATE DEFENSIVE DEPLOY-
MENT PREPARATORY TO CARRYING OUT THE TASKS
ASSIGNED IN WPL-46.

In four decades of service in the U.S. Navy, Kimmel had never seen the term "appropriate defensive deployment." What did Washington intend by that?

Long after the attack on Pearl Harbor, Admiral Turner would testify on one occasion that it meant that "all war scouting measures should be undertaken," that submarines, carriers, and destroyers should be sent to sea. On another day, he would say that deployment meant "to spread out . . . get into the best position from which to execute the operating plans against the enemy." The "operating plans" called for *offensive* action against the enemy. In the same testimony, however, Turner said that—in Hawaii—"an appropriate deployment" would have been *defensive*, the dispatch of warships "to cover certain sectors against approach."

Turner would later claim that at the time the November 27th directive was framed, he had felt there was "at least a 50-50 chance" that the Japanese would raid Pearl Harbor. The "war warning," he said, covered that concern. In fact, as Kimmel was to say, the message contained "not a hint" of danger to Hawaii.

Stark, for his part, would assert in testimony after the war that the language of the November 27th message called for taking "action against surprises" in Hawaii, for Kimmel to take "a position as best he could with what he had for the defense of his Fleet"— full security measures and long-distance air patrols. His deputy Rear Admiral Royal Ingersoll—who also took part in framing the message—would say, however, that the defensive deployment directive had been directed mainly not at Kimmel in Hawaii but at a coaddressee, Admiral Hart in the Philippines.

Before testifying on the subject, Stark had made clear in letters to Turner and Ingersoll that he really was not at all sure what "appropriate defensive deployment" had been intended to mean. In an earlier letter to another Navy colleague, he said of the "war warning," "I didn't know how to make it much stronger, but perhaps it could have been worded differently . . . Of course, the recipient's view at the other end of the line is what counts."

Turner, Stark, and Ingersoll were honorable men. Each spoke

long after the fact, however, in a time of controversy, when reputations were at stake.

To suggest that Admiral Kimmel in Hawaii should have interpreted the message as an order to focus on the defense of Pearl Harbor, his chief of staff Poco Smith was to say dismissively, was to distort the directive's wording.

The second part of the directive, however, was crystal clear. The "deployment," it told the Admiral and his chief of staff, was to be "preparatory to carrying out the tasks assigned in WPL-46." The formal War Plan, as adapted by Kimmel for the Pacific Fleet, had been approved in the early fall. It required the Fleet to be ready for action within four days of "general mobilization." That, once Japan began the war, was to involve "maximum patrol plane search" near Hawaii and a probable increase in patrol planes to the west— flying out of Johnston and Wake islands. The latter was to prepare for U.S. raids on Japanese forces in the Marshall Islands, and to draw enemy strength away from Malaya and territories to the south. As Poco Smith interpreted it, the war warning message meant the Fleet had to focus on how fast ships could "get out and go into battle."

The War Plan's requirement for "maximum patrol plane search," however, ignored the reality of the situation at Pearl Harbor, as would Stark's later assertion that he had expected Kimmel to order distant aerial reconnaissance. As we have reported more than once, the shortage of aircraft at Hawaii had been a chronic problem, an operational running sore. Some new planes had been delivered in recent months, but there were insufficient aircraft available to fly daily long-distance patrols to all points of the compass.

The man responsible for the Navy's contribution to defending Pearl Harbor, base defense officer Admiral Bloch, would within days of the "war warning" receive a letter from Stark informing him that there were "no additional airplanes available." Some new planes had been delivered for Admiral Kimmel's command, but they were having teething problems. Many other aircraft had cracked engine nose sections and were grounded. There were no substitute crews, and not enough mechanics. In those final days before the Japanese struck, the situation remained dire.

"As nearly as I could estimate and in view of our almost total lack of spare parts," said Lieutenant Commander Ramsey, the patrol wing's operations officer, "I believe that three weeks of intensive daily searches would have [meant] approximately a 75% reduction in material readiness of the entire outfit . . . We would have been placing planes out of commission and robbing them of spare parts to keep other planes going."

The head of the Pacific Fleet's patrol plane force, Rear Admiral Bellinger, would later be asked what he would have replied had Kimmel asked him—a few days before the attack—how long he could conduct "the fullest possible *partial* reconnaissance" [authors' italics]. The planes and pilots, Bellinger replied, might have managed 128-degree coverage, not the necessary 360 degrees, for two weeks—"perhaps."

The War Plan Kimmel was now ordered to prepare for, moreover, would itself mean drawing on the meager number of available airplanes. "I decided," he recalled, "that I could not fritter away my patrol plane resources by pushing them to the limit in daily distant searches of one sector . . . which within the predictable future would have to be discontinued when the patrol planes and crews gave out . . . I faced the peril of having these planes grounded when the Fleet needed them and the War Plan was executed."

In years to come, blame would be leveled at the Admiral—from the highest level—for not having ordered limited aerial reconnaissance in the specific area of the ocean, north and northwest of Hawaii, from which the Japanese attack in fact came. "The evidence indicates clearly," a future Secretary of the Navy, James Forrestal, would write, "that his most grievous failure was his failure to conduct long-range air reconnaissance in the most dangerous sectors." This was Monday-morning quarterbacking. Neither of the two detailed estimates of possible threat to Hawaii from the air, conducted in 1941, referred to north and northwest sectors as being most dangerous.

The airplane shortage was not the Admiral's only concern. In spite of multiple appeals to Washington, the Fleet required a further twenty thousand men to be brought up to strength. To satisfy the U.S. Navy's wider expansion program, Kimmel had every month been losing personnel to the mainland—including, not least, a dozen patrol plane crews.

If Kimmel had stopped training each time he received one of Washington's "alarming messages," he believed, on the outbreak of war his warships would have been "in a dangerously ineffective condition." He thought it "absolutely essential that we maintain training in the Pacific Fleet up until the last minute."

On November 27th, the day the war warning message arrived, the Admiral had been meeting with General Short and other senior staffers. At this point, he and Short were conferring frequently. That day, it was to discuss a request from Washington that fighter planes be transferred out of Hawaii to reinforce Wake and Midway islands. The assignment went to Admiral Halsey and the carrier *Enterprise*, which was to leave for Wake with the requested fighters within twenty-four hours. Days later, Rear Admiral John Newton, commanding a task force headed by the *Lexington*, would leave with planes for Midway.

Sending the carriers to the islands brought a bonus. Planes from the warships—*Enterprise* to the west, *Lexington* to the northwest—would conduct some of the distant air reconnaissance that shortages at Pearl Harbor made impractical. Other aircraft made sweeps out of Midway and Wake. Meanwhile, Catalinas out of Pearl would fly training missions in the week that followed, reaching some four hundred miles north and northwest of Hawaii. Every day at dawn, up to and including the morning of December 7, three PBYs continued to fly patrol over the Fleet's main operating area to a distance of some three hundred miles to the south.

Kimmel took other precautions. At Pearl, ships patrolled the immediate perimeter. At the entrances to the harbors at Pearl and Honolulu, the channels were swept daily. Sonar buoys reportedly were deployed to detect submarines. On the Admiral's initiative—though no instruction to that effect had come from Washington—commanders had orders to depth-charge any Japanese submarine found in the Fleet operating area.

At the joint meeting with Army commanders before the war warning message arrived, the order to move fighters from Hawaii to Wake and Midway had prompted a rational thought. Washington's request that Kimmel transfer scarce assets away from Hawaii suggested to him—he would recall in testimony—that HQ "did not consider hostile action on Pearl Harbor imminent or probable."

When one of General Short's officers expressed concern about sending the planes away, Kimmel asked whether he thought Pearl Harbor might be in danger of attack. The officer replied cautiously that the Japanese did have the "capability." The Admiral then asked his war plans officer, "Soc" McMorris, what he thought were "the prospects of a Japanese air attack." "None," McMorris replied, "absolutely none."

Kimmel did not leave the matter there. He made his way after the meeting—for the first time—to the place they called the "Dungeon," where the Hypo unit's chief Joe Rochefort presided over his codebreakers and traffic analysts. The Admiral, resplendent in his white uniform, four stars on the shoulders, and the Commander, in khakis, smoking his pipe, made an incongruous pair. Kimmel had Rochefort's respect, however, and they talked for an hour and a half.

Though briefed daily by his intelligence officer, Edwin Layton, Kimmel had wanted to hear directly from the Hypo unit's chief. He asked for his personal estimates, Rochefort would recall, on "the direction and location of the various Japanese forces."

As many as fifteen or twenty Japanese submarines, Rochefort thought, were in the Marshall Islands—the U.S. Navy's initial target should war break out. There might also be two carriers there. Where then were Japan's other carriers? Radio traffic, Hypo's chief said, indicated they were still at home, in or not far from the Inland Sea.

But where were the big beasts, the heavy carriers? There had been no identifiable transmissions from them for weeks, Rochefort said. There was no way to know for sure what that meant. "There was great unease in all our minds because of the lack of traffic," he was to recall, but: "no one thought in terms of Pearl Harbor at the time."

That same day, November 27th, the day of the "war warning" from Washington, the Hypo Unit analysts' best guess was that the heavy carriers were "still located in home waters."

29

IN FACT, THE carriers of the Japanese strike force were now some two thousand miles northwest of Hawaii. As they headed toward the target, cloaked in thick fog, those who controlled the operation were throwing up a new smoke screen of deceit.

As Kimmel huddled with Commander Rochefort to discuss where the heavy carriers might be, envoy Saburo Kurusu in Washington placed another radio-telephone call to a senior official at the Foreign Ministry in Tokyo. They chatted, at length, about "arranging a marriage" and two women: "Miss Fumeko" and "Miss Kimiko." For key U.S. personnel, who had a transcript of the call within twenty-four hours, it was a transparent pretense, simple to figure out.

The previous day, Washington had intercepted a list of code words the Japanese planned to use in phone calls, along with their true meaning. The word "marriage" stood for the Japanese-American negotiations. "Miss Fumeko" was the code for President Roosevelt, "Miss Kimiko" for Secretary of State Hull. The negotiations, Kurusu had again made clear in the call, had reached an impasse. His interlocutor in Tokyo, however, had told him—very firmly—not to break off the talks.

That was the striking point about the conversation; and in intercepts of other calls and coded communications between November 27th and December 1st—just six days before the attack—it was repeated. "I do not wish you to give the *impression* [authors' italics] that the negotiations are broken off," a Tokyo official wrote on the 28th. "Merely say to them that you are awaiting instructions."

Not only communications between Tokyo and Washington were of relevance. Two days later, Japan's ambassador in Germany

was ordered to tell Adolf Hitler that war with America might now
"come quicker than anyone dreams."

Then, in another phone call between Tokyo and Washington,
the conversation turned to the need to "stretch out" talks with the
United States. On December 1st, in yet another communication,
the Foreign Minister told his Washington envoys that:

> *the absolute deadline . . . has come and gone . . . The situation*
> *continues to be increasingly critical . . . To prevent the United*
> *States from becoming unduly suspicious we have been advising*
> *the press and others that . . . the negotiations are continuing.*
> *(The above is for your information only.)*

Previous exchanges, of course, had made it apparent that further talks were a charade. The fifth and last of the messages,
with its new reference to a deadline, to deliberate deception of the
press, and—above all—to concern that Washington not become
"suspicious," justified only one rational conclusion. Something of
moment was afoot, something that had to be concealed, something unexpected.

All these MAGIC intercepts, and the transcripts of the telephone calls, had obvious intelligence potential for the U.S. Navy
and Army in the Pacific. Like the vast majority of the intercepted
traffic over the months, however, none of them—not even the gist
of them—was shared with Admiral Kimmel or General Short.

In the coming crucial days, the commanders in chief—Kimmel
would recall—were compelled to take "into account" public information, the news broadcasts and wire service reports in the Honolulu newspapers. This included the phony news the Japanese
had concocted. Headlines on December 1st and 2nd announced:
"JAPAN ENVOYS RESUME TALKS" and "JAPAN GIVES TWO
WEEKS MORE TO NEGOTIATIONS." "The real situation," Kimmel would one day recall, "was then known to the Navy Department in Washington. But I was never advised that the resumption
of negotiations was a Japanese trick—as Washington knew it
to be."

What Kimmel had received was a further dispatch from the CNO. On the afternoon of the 28th, Stark had relayed the Army's cautionary message to Short of November 27th to the Admiral. Kimmel had already received a copy of the message, from Short. The officer who delivered it had informed him that the Army had "gone on alert." On the 28th, Kimmel conferred with Short himself.

Years later, in testimony before Congress' Joint Committee, Kimmel would say that he could not recall whether Short had mentioned the details of the "alert" he had ordered. At any rate, Kimmel testified:

> I knew that General Short had been ordered to report the measures he took in response to his message of the 27th from General Marshall. This meant the joint participation of General Marshall and General Short in the character of the alert assumed in Hawaii. I thought that General Marshall and General Short knew better than I what specific Army measures should be adopted to perform adequately the Army mission of defending the naval base at Pearl Harbor.

While forwarding the Army message to Kimmel, Stark took the opportunity to add to his own earlier warning—this time stressing that Kimmel should "undertake no offensive action until Japan has committed an overt act."

He advised Kimmel that a "shoot on sight" order, in force in the Atlantic, did not yet apply to the Pacific Fleet. The same day, Kimmel had ordered the Fleet to depth-bomb all suspect submarines found in its operating area. Though he had copied the message to the CNO, Stark did not demur—or respond in any way.

Also on the 28th, as Tokyo was urging its envoys to keep up the pretense that negotiations were not over, U.S. Navy and Army signals intelligence in Washington fired off a stream of orders to intercept stations across America and far beyond. A very significant

Japanese message was expected to be broadcast—possibly any day now—and special priority was to be given to searching the ether for it.

What had sparked the alert was a MAGIC intercept of the 19th telling Japan's envoys how—should normal communications links be severed—they could learn of an impending rupture of relations with the United States or other countries. In an emergency, it informed them, they should listen for a covert message. It would be hidden in the supposedly ordinary weather forecast segment of a regular shortwave news bulletin, and listeners would hear one of three possible predictions:

> (1) In case of a [sic] Japan-U.S. relations in danger: HIGASHI NO KAZEAME [which translates as EAST WIND RAIN].
> (2) Japan-U.S.S.R. relations: KITANOKAZE KUMORI [NORTH WIND CLOUDY].
> (3) Japan-British relations: NISHI NO KAZE HARE [WEST WIND CLEAR]
> 　　This signal will be given in the middle and at the end as a weather forecast and each sentence will be repeated twice. When this is heard please destroy all code papers, etc. This is as yet to be a completely secret arrangement.

This was only one of several Japanese messages about code destruction that were to come in—enough of them perhaps, to perplex even those Japanese waiting for them at embassies and consulates worldwide. They were certainly confusing, years later, for historians trying to disentangle the story of the drift to war.

Unlike messages between Tokyo and its envoys—to which the U.S. gave priority—the message setting up the "Winds" code, transmitted in a lower-level diplomatic code, was not decrypted and translated by analysts for more than a week. By then, the fact that relations with Japan were on the brink of severance was no longer news to U.S. intelligence. When Navy analysts did get around to translating the message, though, they inadvertently left out a salient phrase.

The message's Point 3—translated by the Navy as indicating danger to relations only between Japan and Britain—in fact also included the possibility that such a break might involve the "occupation of Thailand, the invasion of the Netherlands East Indies, [and] the invasion of Malaya." This was a significant part of the message that, in itself, could have indicated the scope of a coming attack.

Those in Washington who saw Tokyo's November 19th message about the anticipated Winds broadcast saw it as enormously important, a potential tip-off as to *when* they could expect a military development. The British had also intercepted the "Winds" message and seen its potential importance. The Australians spotted it, as did the Dutch, in the Netherlands East Indies. It had, as a senior Australian cryptanalyst would recall, "created quite a stir."

In Washington, Navy Communications codebreaking chief Commander Laurance Safford was to say, "everyone in authority from the President on down" believed that the "Winds" message, if and when it came, "would be the Japanese government's decision as to peace or war . . . That was our chance." Day after day, said G-2 chief General Sherman Miles, the broadcast was anxiously awaited. "It was," he recalled, "considered most important and of vital concern."

The U.S. Navy and Army committed every possible asset to listen for "Winds." Stations across the United States were tasked to intercept the broadcast, as were stations in the Panama Canal Zone and the Philippines, and Rochefort's Hypo team at Hawaii. At Hypo alone, four Japanese linguists did nothing else, around the clock, but listen for it. Even the Federal Communications Commission's intelligence division was co-opted.

In case the Winds broadcast was picked up, or believed to have been picked up, cards were printed bearing the key Japanese words in the expected text. Senior officers at headquarters kept the cards with them at all times.

The search for a "Winds Execute," as it would become known, taxed the abilities of staffers already stretched to the limit. Lieutenant Commander Alwin Kramer, chief translator of ONI's Far

Eastern Section, would recall that the volume of material sent in was "simply tremendous, swamping." Colonel Rufus Bratton, the Far Eastern Section chief for Army Intelligence, would remember being "waked up at all hours of the night" for what turned out, always, to be false alarms.

U.S. Army Intelligence's formal estimate, dated November 29th, of moves that foes might make in the foreseeable future listed nine territories where Japan might attack. Hawaii was not one of them. It was omitted, Bratton's immediate boss, General Hayes Kroner, was to say, because his staff had no information that Japan was "capable of" attacking Pearl Harbor or "planned to do so."

On November 30th, ONI's Far Eastern chief Arthur McCollum labored over the final details of a summary of Japan's recent machinations. It contained no reference to what the MAGIC intercepts had revealed of Japanese espionage in Hawaii.

Nor would that espionage be noted in an in-depth report on Japanese intelligence-gathering that ONI would start compiling days later and complete on the eve of the Pearl Harbor attack. That report, written by a member of ONI's counterintelligence staff, shows clearly that the author had been given access to some PURPLE intercepts. There is no indication in the report, though, that anyone had seen fit to share Tokyo's messages to its consular spy in Hawaii—even with the office charged with counterespionage.

The copious documentation and later testimony on those days of crisis contain nothing to indicate that anyone in the military— or at the highest political level—even considered the possibility that Japan might strike Pearl Harbor.

30

MONDAY, DECEMBER 1ST, HAWAII. On the stroke of midnight, the electronic eavesdroppers of Hawaii's Hypo unit picked up something they had not expected. Only a month after the Japanese Navy had changed its call signs, it changed them again. Normally, call signs were changed every six months.

In his report for the day, Commander Rochefort made no bones about what he thought the increased security meant. In his view, the Japanese were making it "appear as if nothing unusual was pending," while in fact "preparing for active operations on a large scale." He offered no new information on the whereabouts of Tokyo's aircraft carriers.

When given the report, intelligence officer Layton would recall, Admiral Kimmel showed "obvious concern." He underlined the sentence that predicted large-scale Japanese naval operations. As to the carriers, he worried aloud and pressed for more information. Rochefort asked for more time, saying the Japanese warships' positions seemed to be changing. He was told to work all night if necessary.

In the United States that day, one headline was: "F.D.R. RUSHES TO CAPITAL: FAR EAST CRISIS GRAVE." Three days after heading to his retreat in Georgia for Thanksgiving, President Roosevelt had returned to the White House. With intelligence continuing to come in indicating that Japanese forces were on the move, cabinet members had been talking of sending a further stern note to Tokyo. Roosevelt, however, was apparently not in a mood to listen to his principal advisers.

"He didn't even call us in," Secretary of War Stimson observed in his journal, "The only fault I have to find with the President is that he is so irregular in his consultations." Secretary of State Hull, who did see Roosevelt, looked worn. He had long been mulling resignation, and now complained to a colleague that "everybody was trying to run foreign policy."

Roosevelt had received an overnight message from Prime Minister Churchill suggesting the United States make a declaration—possibly accompanied by a similar British statement—that "any further act of aggression by Japan will lead immediately to the gravest consequences." London had instructed British Ambassador Lord Halifax, meanwhile, to inform Washington that Britain planned to counter any Japanese attack on Thailand and strategic points in the region—and wanted to be sure it would have the support of the United States.

At a meeting with Halifax, the President would say only that should Japan attack British or Dutch territories, they "should obviously all be in it together." Two days later, Halifax would report to London that Roosevelt had said America would offer "armed support" if—in the event that Japan attacked Thailand—Britain intervened militarily. The President was sailing close to the limits of his constitutional authority, however, and nothing could be formally agreed.

On December 1st, as intelligence continued to come in about Japan's southward military movements, Roosevelt issued an idiosyncratic order that reflected his penchant for impulsiveness. He ordered the Navy in the Philippines to see to it that three small, lightly armed vessels, commanded by U.S. naval officers but with Filipino crews, be sent to "observe and report by radio Japanese movements in west China Sea [off Vietnam] and Gulf of Siam [Gulf of Thailand]." He ordered, too, that he personally be briefed "as to what reconnaissance measures are being regularly performed at sea by both Army and Navy."

Over on Constitution Avenue, ONI's McCollum wrapped up the summary of the Japanese situation that he had begun the previous day, and delivered it to ONI Director Wilkinson. The two officers concluded, McCollum later testified, that "everything pointed to an imminent outbreak of hostilities between Japan and the United States." Around noon, Wilkinson took McCollum into

CNO Stark's office, where McCollum read the summary aloud to a group of senior officers that included Stark himself and War Plans chief Admiral Turner.

At the end of the presentation McCollum and Wilkinson—neither of whom had been shown the November 27th "war warning" that had been sent to Kimmel—urged that a warning be sent to the Fleet. Stark and Turner gave them a "categorical assurance," McCollum was to recall, that messages "fully alerting the fleet and placing them on a war basis had been sent."

31

TUESDAY, DECEMBER 2ND, PEARL HARBOR. Kimmel listened as Lieutenant Commander Layton delivered his morning briefing. Layton had as usual brought with him the Hypo unit's daily summary, and one sentence stood out:

> Almost a complete blank of information on the carriers today.

The Admiral had requested that Layton's own report offer speculations as to where a number of the Japanese carrier divisions, the CARDIVS, might be. The report contained nothing at all, however, on the whereabouts of CARDIVS 1 and 2. The Fleet intelligence officer had made no mention of them because, Layton would recall, "neither one of those commands had appeared in [radio] traffic for fully 15 and possibly 25 days."

Pressed by Kimmel as to where they were, Layton could only reply, 'I think they are in home waters, but I do not know where they are . . . We haven't heard from them in a long time and they may be refitting, as they finished operations only a month-and-a-half ago."

Kimmel looked at his subordinate in the way he sometimes did, "with somewhat a stern countenance and yet partially with a twinkle in his eye," according to Layton, "Do you mean to say that they could be rounding Diamond Head and you wouldn't know it?" Layton, as best he could remember, ventured a touch of black humor: "I hope they would be sighted before now."

Diamond Head was only a dozen miles as the crow flies from Fleet headquarters. Neither of the two men would forget their brief exchange. It reflected the Admiral's frustration over the lack of information about Japan's heavy aircraft carriers. He and Layton had not been seriously debating the likelihood—or un-likelihood—that the carriers were about to heave into view. The exchange during the meeting of the 2nd, though, was to live on—as a moment of awful irony.

In Washington that Tuesday, ONI's Commander McCollum talked with Captain Meijer Ranneft, the Dutch naval attaché. The attaché, a regular visitor, would recall McCollum discussing with him "two Japanese carriers that had left Japan on a south-easterly course." He pointed out their estimated position on the map, Ranneft would recall, "at the easterly edge of the Mandates," saying the carriers were probably there to defend against a possible U.S. attack on Japanese forces in the Mandates. "Neither any of the intelligence officers present nor I," Ranneft noted, "spoke of a possible attack by the carriers on Honolulu."

At the White House that same day, the President asked to see one of the previous day's MAGIC intercepts for the second time. This was the Japanese diplomatic message stating "very secretly" that the time of war with the United States and Britain "may come quicker than anyone dreams." It struck Roosevelt as particularly ominous, and he dictated a fresh, severe note for Tokyo. The sheer number of Japanese troops moving southward, the note said, suggested they were to be used against the Philippines, the Dutch East Indies, or British territories. Roosevelt asked for an immediate explanation. In response, Tokyo merely waffled. As instructed, its envoys in Washington continued to talk about negotiations—as if there were still hope they might be resumed.

At naval headquarters, meanwhile, analysts and translators pored over an unprecedented volume of MAGIC traffic. The priority focus remained the effort to pick up the "Winds Execute," the disguised message in a weather broadcast that would signal that relations were about to be broken off. Another intercepted message, meanwhile, presented the analysts with a new challenge.

Not content with the existing plan to tip off its diplomats, the Japanese had devised an alternative. It would involve a regular telegram that used hidden words which, for the recipient, would have a special meaning. To distinguish the message from all others, it would end not with the Japanese word "OWARI," as was normal, but with the English word "STOP."

So it was that, as of December 2nd, U.S. code experts began looking out for yet another indicator of an imminent rupture of relations. They worked, however, from a misleading template, because of a mistake by Navy translators. As they rendered it, the hidden word "HATTORI" would signify that "Relations with [name of country] are not in accordance with expectation." Correctly translated, this last phrase should have read, "on the brink of catastrophe." The mistranslation was a grievous error, not least because no one would catch it until after the Pearl Harbor attack.

On December 2nd in Hawaii, meanwhile, the efforts of U.S. intelligence agencies were disrupted by failures of coordination—and by sheer bad luck. All year, albeit against the law, Naval Intelligence had been tapping the Japanese consulate's phone lines. The FBI, for its part, had begun to listen both to trans-Pacific conversations between Honolulu and Japan, and to a consulate phone the Navy did not have covered. The eavesdropping had not yet produced anything sensational; there was nothing that betrayed Tokyo's timetable or Yoshikawa's espionage. During those days of overt tension, however, there remained a chance of catching some Japanese staff member in a verbal indiscretion.

Then, by pure mischance, a phone company technician doing routine work happened on a tap the FBI had also placed on the phone of a Japanese shipping company in Honolulu. The technician mentioned the tap to a Naval Intelligence agent, and that eventually led to words between his chief, Captain Irving Mayfield; and the FBI's Agent-in-Charge, Robert Shivers. Mayfield, incensed because he had not been consulted about the installation of the FBI tap, fearful that his own illegal tapping operation would be exposed—and mindful of orders from the top to avoid a diplomatic incident—ordered that all Navy taps on the Japanese consulate be removed at once.

Chief Ships Clerk Theodore Emanuel, who had been manning the taps for months, signed off on his final log entry with a cheery valediction: "In the 1941st year of Our Lord, December 2nd inst. I bade farewell to you my friend of 22 months standing. Darn if I won't miss you!!"

Mayfield did not inform the FBI that he had called off the Navy's coverage. "Had I known," the Bureau's Shivers said years later, "I would have caused FBI coverage in replacement." Mayfield's loss of nerve, and the agencies' dismal failure of coordination, had forfeited the potential of an eavesdropping operation that might yet have yielded gold.

An even better opportunity, one that really could have provided a last-minute breakthrough, also evaporated. In November, after months of trying to get commercial companies to ignore regulations and share Japanese consular cable traffic, Captain Mayfield had persuaded RCA to do so—as of December 1st. On the 2nd, as RCA began providing copies of encoded consular cables, Mayfield turned to Commander Rochefort and the Hypo unit for help. Would they please decrypt and translate the cables?

With his team already overwhelmed with work, Rochefort hesitated. His orders from Washington were clear. Japanese naval traffic, and the hunt for the "Winds Execute" message—not encoded diplomatic messages—were his priorities. He would eventually assign the work on consular cables to one of his codebreakers, but too late.

Had they been decoded in timely fashion, the United States—and Admiral Kimmel—would have seen a message that Tokyo sent to the Japanese consulate on the 2nd. It was for the spy Yoshikawa's attention, and virtually gave the game away:

> In view of the present situation, the presence in port of warships, aircraft carriers, and cruisers is of utmost importance. Hereafter, to the utmost of your ability, let me know day by day. Wire me in each case whether or not there are observation balloons above Pearl Harbor . . . Also advise me whether or not the warships are provided with anti-mine nets.

The message sat, undecoded, in the Hypo unit's "in" tray. A second copy of it, which went off to Washington by mail, would not be decrypted until three weeks after the strike on Pearl Harbor.

Meanwhile, Japanese trickery continued. Convoys heading south still gave the distracting impression that hostilities would begin not in the central Pacific but in Southeast Asia. On December 2nd, a passenger liner left Japan—as though all were normal—bound for Hawaii, then on to San Francisco. Before it pulled out, however, its captain was handed sealed orders. On opening them, as instructed at midnight on December 6th U.S. time, he would learn he was to abort the voyage and return to Japan. The liner's itinerary, never completed, was a ruse.

Also on the 2nd, a message went out to the Japanese Navy's Fleet at sea—a message not decrypted by U.S. analysts at the time because it was in a code that had not yet been broken. It read:

This dispatch is Top Secret. This order is effective at 1730 on 2 December. Climb NIITAKAYAMA 1208, REPEAT 1208.

Niitaka Yama, or Mount Niitaka, was the tallest mountain in the Japanese Empire. To the Pearl Harbor strike force, it was the signal that the attack was on, scheduled for "1208," December 8th Tokyo time—by the U.S. calendar, December 7th.

32

WEDNESDAY, DECEMBER 3RD, WASHINGTON. In the course of a single conversation during the day, President Roosevelt read the situation both wrong and right. Secretary of the Treasury Henry Morgenthau, who saw him that afternoon, was concerned that the United States should show no sign of appeasement toward Tokyo. Following his stiff message of the previous day, Roosevelt said he felt he "had the Japanese running around like a lot of wet hens." Not so. He was more correct than he knew, though, when he added that they were doing all they could to "stall until they are ready."

Secretary of State Hull, for his part, read the current temper of the opponent well. In his view, he told the Navy's liaison officer at State, the Japanese were "liable to run loose like a mad dog and bite." Having assured him that a war warning had been sent out, the officer reported what Hull had said to CNO Stark.

An indication came in that Japan might bite very soon. American analysts intercepted a new instruction to the Japanese embassy in Washington, one that it would circulate to other diplomatic missions. It read in part:

DECEMBER 2, 1941
FROM: Tokyo (Togo) [Foreign Minister Shigenori Togo]
TO: Washington
867 Strictly Secret

1. Among the telegraphic codes with which your office is equipped burn all but those now used with the machine . . . (Burn also the various other codes which you have in your custody.)

2. Stop at once using one code machine unit and destroy it completely.

3. When you have finished this, wire me back the one word "HARUNA."

4. At the time and in the manner you deem most proper dispose of all files of messages coming and going and all other secret documents . . .

At the White House, Captain John Beardall, the Navy officer who delivered MAGIC traffic to the President, drew the planned destruction of the codes and code machine to Roosevelt's attention. The President read the intercept carefully, then asked when Beardall thought "it"—war, presumably—would break out. "Most any time," Beardall thought, but the President expressed no view.

To Undersecretary of State Sumner Welles, seemingly the only close presidential adviser who recalled the development, news of the planned code destruction indicated that "the last stage" had been reached before a break and, probably, war. "Ordinarily" the move would have meant war, Chief of Staff Marshall would say years later, but destruction of codes did not necessarily mean Japan was about to go to war. His intelligence chief, General Sherman Miles, for his part, thought it could mean two things. "The inference," Miles thought, was that the Japanese had "planned to initiate a war, as they did, or feared war coming suddenly through . . . a clash of arms."

Asked whether the information on code destruction had resulted in the issuance of any orders, or any warning being given to the War Department, the Chief of Staff said he knew of none.

For the Navy, CNO Stark later said he had thought Japan's order about code destruction "one of the most telling items of information we ever received," and that it meant war was "just a matter of time." Turner, at War Plans, said he thought it "a definite and sure indication of war" and that a decision to destroy codes indicated "war within two or three days." Stark and Turner approved the sending of a brief message about the planned code destruction to

U.S. commanders in the Pacific. It included, however, neither a sense of the importance HQ gave to its message nor any suggestion as to what action the commanders ought to take:

> Highly reliable information has been received that categorical and urgent instructions were sent yesterday to Japanese diplomatic and consular posts . . . to destroy most of their codes and ciphers at once and to burn all other important confidential and secret documents.

Five minutes after this message had gone out to the Fleet, a second followed. It included not only the basic information on Japan's code destruction order but also—in an extraordinary slipup—the fact that Japanese missions were being ordered to "destroy PURPLE"—a word that had long been kept secret from Fleet commanders.

"Kimmel sent for me," intelligence officer Layton recalled, "and asked me what a PURPLE machine was. I told him I did not know." A security officer who had done a stint in Washington, who did know, explained that it was "an electronic coding machine." Only thus, just days before the end, did the commander in chief get a glimpse of what had been withheld from him all year.

Neither Kimmel nor his colleague Admiral Bloch, who was directly responsible for the Navy's contribution to the defense of the base at Pearl, thought the news as significant as headquarters staffers in Washington would later assert they did. Bloch would say vaguely that he had not been able to tell whether the code destruction was "something that was really filled with meaning, or not. It might be and it might not be."

Kimmel remembered the code destruction development as not having been of "vital interest." He and his senior staff noted that not all the Japanese codes were to be destroyed. To him and his colleagues, at a time when it seemed war might break out, partial destruction seemed consistent, with "routine diplomatic precautions." As for the bald, five-line dispatch he had received from Navy

HQ, Kimmel thought it might have been more valuable "had they enlarged somewhat on what they believed [the code destruction] meant." Nevertheless, he acknowledged, "if I had drawn different conclusions from what I got, we might have changed things."

The Admiral did not discuss the development with General Short, and would not be impressed by the argument—in years to come—that he should have done so. "If the War Department or the Navy Department had considered it of such vital importance," Kimmel would say, "they should at least have taken the precaution to tell me to give this message to General Short."

HQ's failure to articulate clearly its reading of events and to compose forthright messages to the Fleet was chronic.

In fact, Japan's destruction of secret material had immediately become known to Army Intelligence in Hawaii. The solitary tap on the consulate's phones that was still functioning, the FBI's, on December 3rd picked up a conversation in which a lowly staff member—the cook—mentioned that the Consul was burning "important papers." FBI Agent-in-Charge Shivers had promptly reported this to the assistant chief of Army Intelligence in Hawaii, Lieutenant Colonel George Bicknell.

Bicknell, however, did not pass the information on to General Short and other colleagues for days. He would get around to mentioning it, at a routine staff conference, only three days later, on December 6th—the eve of the Japanese attack.

In spite of the order to destroy certain codes, the Japanese consulate still had the ability to transmit information back to Tokyo. Two code systems remained in use. Perhaps anticipating the day when normal communications would be severed, the consulate's tame German, Otto Kühn, had meanwhile revised his ideas on how to get information out on the comings and goings of U.S. warships in Pearl Harbor. They included not only light signals, as he had suggested earlier, but also other imaginative notions.

An advertisement on local radio for a "Chinese rug for sale" would indicate that battleships had sortied. "Beauty operator wanted" would refer to the departure of aircraft carriers. And so on. A long message listing these proposals went out to Tokyo from the consulate on December 3rd. So did fresh reports on the movements of U.S. warships composed by the spy Yoshikawa. He would remain active, and assiduously observant, to the last possible moment.

Analysts in Washington would not decrypt and translate these consulate messages until days after the Pearl Harbor attack.

33

THURSDAY, DECEMBER 4TH, WASHINGTON. Sensation boiled around the White House, but not because of the crisis with Japan. The furor was over the publication, in anti-Roosevelt newspapers opposed to the United States' involvement in the war, of what was described as a U.S. blueprint for total war, "on an unprecedented scale." Its basis was a leaked copy of an estimate, prepared by the U.S. military in response to a request by the President, of what would be required to "defeat our potential enemies."

Only if the United States joined the conflict, the estimate flatly stated, could Germany and the Axis be vanquished. Defeating Hitler would involve putting American boots on the ground in Europe—millions of pairs of boots. There should be active collaboration with the British and other friendly nations. In Asia, to thwart Japan's ambitions, the high command foresaw using a wide spectrum of measures including—economic blockade aside—air raids and intervention to defend Malaysia. The overall effort would involve a program of armament manufacture and shipbuilding on a gargantuan scale. U.S. armed forces would be built up to an unprecedented total of some ten million men and women.

The press coverage was factually accurate and politically explosive. Little more than a year earlier, when running for election for a third term, Roosevelt had made a pledge: "I shall say it again and again and again," he had promised American parents. "Your boys are not going to be sent into any foreign wars." Now, the astonishing revelations in the newspapers sparked a clamor for explanation.

The White House press secretary, neither confirming nor denying the authenticity of the story, struggled to field a torrent of questions. At a press conference twenty-four hours after the story ran, the President himself declined comment—a failure to respond that would be unthinkable today. The uproar over the story seemed bound to continue, only to be stilled a few days later when the Japanese attacked Pearl Harbor.

Behind the scenes, while political Washington buzzed, the Navy and Army intelligence services were still focused on the search for the "Winds Execute" message, the anticipated phony Japanese weather forecast that would signal a break in relations— and perhaps, very rapidly afterward, military action.

That evening, it looked for a while as though the Federal Communications Commission, which was helping the armed forces hunt for "Winds Execute," might have picked up the planned forecast. An FCC monitoring station in Oregon picked up a Japanese weather bulletin that appeared possibly to fit the prescribed format. It contained the phrase "NORTH WIND CLOUDY," the signal for a break with the Soviet Union. Relayed to Washington, it reached the duty officer for the Navy's codebreaking unit, Lieutenant Junior Grade Francis Brotherhood. Brotherhood had his doubts.

"There seemed to be something missing," he would recall, "it did not contain the phrase in Japanese HIGASHI NO KAZEAME," which would have signified a diplomatic break leading—he assumed—to war with the United States. Brotherhood nevertheless contacted his superior, Communications chief Admiral Leigh Noyes. On going off duty at midnight, the lieutenant passed the intercepted broadcast, as logged, on to the night watch officer—it would echo into the next day.

From HQ in Washington to far-flung Pacific intercept stations, Far Eastern Section chief McCollum would recall, the analysts' workload was by now overwhelming. Hopes of picking up the "Winds Execute" aside, there was, constantly, the stress of handling incoming MAGIC and trying to deduce what exactly the Japanese were planning.

McCollum, who saw everything that came in, would recall having been "greatly concerned" all week. Worried, he drafted a message of warning that he proposed be sent to commanders in the Pacific. ONI Director Wilkinson told him to submit it to War Plans chief Turner.

Turner read the draft and edited it, "striking out" all but factual information. Then he showed McCollum the "war warning" that had been sent to Pacific commanders the previous week. "I said," McCollum would recall in testimony, " 'Well, good gosh, you put in the words 'war warning'. I do not know what could be plainer than that."

According to Turner in his testimony, McCollum—who appeared satisfied—tore up his proposed dispatch. McCollum did not recall it that way. He told Turner, he said, that he would nevertheless like his own dispatch to be sent. In that case, Turner countered, "Well, if you want to send it, you either send it the way I corrected it, or take it back to Wilkinson and we will argue about it."

McCollum said he did take it to Wilkinson, who told him to "leave it here with me for a while." So far as McCollum knew, the matter went no further. The proposed warning, McCollum recalled, "was merely my recommendation to my seniors, which they were privileged to throw in the waste basket."

At the imperial palace in Tokyo, Emperor Hirohito had received Admiral Yamamoto. The Emperor, Yamamoto thought, seemed "serene . . . fully realizing the inevitability of going to war."

Out in the north Pacific, meanwhile, the strike force had encountered bad weather. The warships were rolling and pitching heavily as they pushed on through high seas. Aboard one of the Japanese destroyers, the executive officer was keeping a record. News of what ships were where in Pearl Harbor, he noted—the fruits of Yoshikawa's spying—was continuing to arrive.

"Everyone prays God," the officer wrote in his journal, "to have the U.S. Fleet now in harbor stay a little longer."

34

FRIDAY, DECEMBER 5TH, WASHINGTON. A morning of muddled deliberations at Navy headquarters ended with an inept communication to Hawaii—one that achieved nothing. Word got around, at a very high level now, that "Winds Execute" had come in.

Around 9:30 a.m., it seems, Navy Communications chief Rear Admiral Noyes picked up the phone to speak to his Army opposite number in the Signal Intelligence Service, Colonel Otis Sadtler. As Sadtler would remember it, Noyes told him, "The message is in," saying it indicated an impending break with either Britain or the Soviet Union. Looking back, Sadtler could not clearly recall which of the two nations Noyes mentioned.

In another call, to War Plans' Kelly Turner, Noyes again declared that the weather message was in—but seemed to suggest it signaled a break not with Britain but with the Soviet Union. There was "something wrong," Turner commented, with the way Noyes was describing the broadcast, and Noyes did not demur. With that, they both got on with other business.

Not for nothing, however, did colleagues call Colonel Sadtler the "little dynamo." Far from getting on with other business, he was to say, he headed down the corridor to brief the Chief of Military Intelligence, General Sherman Miles. Miles, in turn, called in his head of Far East intelligence, Colonel Bratton. This might be a false alarm, Bratton thought, and suggested the message be double-checked.

Contacted again, according to Sadtler, Noyes said that he was due at a meeting and had no time to talk. He would check the information later.

Sadtler, for his part, thought "later" would be too late, and that if Japan was about to break with Britain, this would be tantamount to a break with the United States as well. He began hurrying from office to office—to General Miles again, then to Army War Plans chief Brigadier General Leonard Gerow, then to Colonel Walter Bedell Smith, who had direct access to Chief of Staff Marshall.

Sadtler, a thirty-year veteran, was so persistent because he thought Noyes's call to him that morning had been "the most important message I ever received . . . I was sure war was coming, and coming very quickly." In his opinion, word that the "Winds Execute" was in should go out at once to Hawaii, the Philippines, and the Panama Canal Zone. None of the very senior officers he approached, however, proved helpful. The commanders in the Pacific region, General Gerow reportedly said, already had "plenty of notification."

G-2's Bratton, however, did respond to Sadtler's entreaties. "Everybody was making such a hullaballoo about this Winds business," he was to recall. "I thought to be on the safe side, we might as well alert Hawaii." The go-to man on intercepts in Hawaii was the Hypo unit's Commander Rochefort, so—in a brief dispatch—G-2 in Hawaii was urged to contact Rochefort about a "broadcast from Tokyo reference weather." The deputy chief of Hawaiian G-2 did get in touch with Rochefort, only to be told that his team had in fact been listening for a "Winds Execute" for the past week.

With one imprecise initial call saying there had been such a broadcast, Admiral Noyes had started a fuss about nothing. There is no evidence that a "Winds Execute," in the precise language prescribed in advance, had really come in. A host of Army and Navy personnel continued to make it a priority. "We were continuing to look," ONI's McCollum would recall, until "after the bombs had started falling on the Fleet."

On the evening of the 5th, after all the hullaballoo of the past twenty-four hours, the FCC would call Army Intelligence with yet a further report on a possible "Winds Execute." Colonel Bratton, who took the call, recognized it as another false alarm. He sounded, though, not irritated but relieved. It meant, Bratton told his FCC contact, "that we have that much more time."

In fact, time had nearly run out—time in which less effort devoted to the search for a "Winds Execute," and more to connecting the dots in intelligence already in hand, could yet have avoided surprise at Pearl Harbor.

Had harried analysts not been so distracted, such intelligence was there to see. Messages to the Japanese consulate in Hawaii, available by that Friday, December 5th, made Tokyo's unnatural interest in Pearl Harbor obvious.

Even old messages, only now decoded and translated because of the backlog, should have set minds racing. They included requests by Tokyo from back in November, requiring the spy Yoshikawa to go out covertly and report where specific ships were anchored in a specific area of Pearl Harbor; to "investigate comprehensively Fleet — [word not decoded, probably "air"] bases in the neighborhood of the Hawaiian military reservation"; and, late that month, to send reports "even when there are no movements."

In those last days, Yoshikawa assiduously reported daily on any shipping movement he could see, from battleships to seaplane tenders. Sluggish U.S. processing of this type of message, however, meant that intelligence would read none of Yoshikawa's final messages until after Yamamoto's raiders had come, wreaked their havoc, and departed.

At the Foreign Ministry in Tokyo, officials had been wrangling over the text and timing of a final, formal message that would serve notice on the United States that negotiations were at an end. As of Wednesday that week, the draft of the planned message had included a statement that the United States would be "held responsible for any and all the consequences that may arise in the future."

That passage, tantamount to a declaration of war, had not satisfied those in the Japanese Navy who wanted to be certain their strike would come as a complete surprise. The compromise settled on was to hold back on informing Washington of a break in relations until the military was good and ready, the strike imminent.

The final sentence of the new draft message as of December 5th—very similar to the version that would eventually be delivered—merely stated that it was "impossible to reach agreement through further negotiations," unless the United States changed its attitude. By holding out the possibility that talks could yet be renewed, the final message was designed to continue Japan's deceitful diplomacy to the very last minute.

That Friday, from Washington, the Counselor of the Japanese Embassy had a query for the Foreign Ministry:

> We have completed destruction of codes, but since the U.S.-Japanese negotiations are continuing, I request your approval of our desire to delay for a while yet the destruction of the one code machine.

Ambassador Nomura and most of the embassy staff, historians believe, knew nothing of what was being plotted in Tokyo. The reference in this message to "continuing" negotiations and the request to "delay for a while" may have been innocent, expressing a practical concern that communication should not be severed prematurely. As part of the Tokyo-Washington diplomatic traffic that U.S. officials prized so highly, though, such language in an intercept fueled the notion that—for the moment—nothing was going to happen.

In the Pacific, the carriers and escorting warships of the Japanese strike force completed refueling, then forged on south toward the target.

Numerous submarines, meanwhile, were by now prowling the seas around Hawaii. On the afternoon of the 5th, two U.S. destroyers detected what was probably a submarine within five miles of Pearl Harbor. Kimmel had ordered all ships to be especially vigilant for submarines in the Fleet's operating area—and to depth-charge those judged not to be friendly. This contact was uncertain, however, and no depth charges were dropped.

Kimmel thought Japanese submarines might likely attempt a "mass attack" on shipping in the area around Hawaii.
He still, however, considered an attack from the air a "remote
possibility . . . The latest information I had from the Navy Department and other sources was that the greater portion of the
carrier forces were located in home waters."

35

SATURDAY MORNING, DECEMBER 6TH, WASHINGTON. At his routine briefing, the White House press secretary, Stephen Early, encouraged reporters to think they could relax. "The President," he said, "decided you fellows have been so busy lately, and Christmas is coming so close, that he would give you a day off to do some shopping."

During the morning meeting at the Navy Department, however, Secretary Frank Knox had a question for the admirals around him. "Gentlemen," he asked, "are they going to hit us?" "No, Mr. Secretary," one admiral responded. "They are not ready for us yet. They are going to hit the British." It is not clear which admiral said this.

It was in part from the British, later the same morning, that Washington learned that Japanese forces were on the move. A "Triple Priority" message for the President and Secretary Hull brought news that troop transports were heading south, as had long been thought probable, for the Kra Isthmus. The initial target might be either Thailand or Malaya—and would turn out within twenty-four hours to be both.

Of the very few appointments Roosevelt had on his schedule, none was about the diplomatic standoff with Tokyo. Budget Director Harold Smith was with him around 11:30 a.m, going through estimates, when Hull telephoned with news that the Japanese military had started moving south. Smith would note in his diary that, as the President hung up, he said, "We might be at war with Japan, although no one knows."

In Hawaii, five and a half hours behind Washington time, Admiral Kimmel was beginning his day. The headlines in the local papers that morning implied a continued stalemate with Japan. The *Honolulu Advertiser's* headline ran: "America Expected to Reject Japan's Reply on Indo-China"; the *Star-Bulletin* had "New Peace Effort Urged in Tokyo."

Though Kimmel did not much like dealing with the press, he had agreed to meet that day with Joseph Harsch of the *Christian Science Monitor.* When Harsch arrived at 8:00 a.m., he found the Admiral already conferring with his staff. Harsch, who had recently done a stint in Germany, initially found himself being peppered with questions. When at last he got in a question of his own, he asked whether Kimmel thought Japan would attack the United States in the Pacific.

In reply, the Admiral addressed the wider picture in the Pacific theater, and specifically Japan's expansionist ambitions in the easternmost Soviet Union. Because the war in the western Soviet Union had deadlocked—the German army had been held up in front of Moscow—the Admiral said he thought Tokyo unlikely to risk a war on two fronts. He did not expect an attack against the United States in the region.

On December 6th, this was sound strategic thinking. Later, however, Harsch was to wonder whether the Admiral had been entirely frank with him. "It may well have been what he considered prudent to say to a visiting reporter he did not know personally."

Everything known about December 6th indicates that, far from being complacent, Kimmel was intent on covering all the bases. There was palpable tension in Hawaii. The previous night, U.S. Marine and Navy guards had mounted an alert to counter possible sabotage—the threat considered most likely by the Army. American naval attachés in Tokyo, China, and Thailand, and outposts in the western Pacific, had meanwhile received orders to destroy secret material. HQ had authorized Kimmel to order the same precaution, should it be necessary, in remote island outposts.

With word in that the Japanese were moving toward the Kra Isthmus, Kimmel assessed the situation as serious. First thing that morning, yet again, he and Fleet intelligence officer Layton had discussed the whereabouts of the Japanese aircraft carriers.

As before, no radio transmissions by the carriers had been detected. Were they perhaps involved in the advance on Kra?

For a second opinion on the situation, Kimmel sent Layton out to the battleship USS *California* to get the views of his Battle Force commander Vice Admiral William Pye. Layton suggested to Pye that the Japanese would not risk leaving the Philippines on their flank. If they attacked the Thai-Malay region, they would surely also attack the U.S. forces in the Philippines. Pye demurred. "Oh no," Layton would remember him saying, "The Japanese will not attack America . . . we are too big, too powerful, and too strong." Pye's chief of staff seconded this view.

Back at headquarters, Layton told Kimmel what Pye had said. "He looked at me in a way he could look at people—straight through them," Layton would remember, and then he snorted, "as if disappointed." The Admiral was worried. Not long after noon, he told Fleet Marine officer Colonel Omar Pfeiffer and War Plans' "Soc" McMorris why.

"He felt he did not know the whole story," Pfeiffer recalled. "Capt. McMorris tried to allay the Admiral's concern, if not premonitions, by saying that the Japanese could not possibly be able to proceed in force against Pearl Harbor when they had so much strength concentrated in their Asiatic operations." Kimmel, Pfeiffer said, was not persuaded. He was "beside himself" about the whereabouts of Japan's heavy aircraft carriers.

Chief of Staff "Poco" Smith urged the Admiral to take a siesta for once, but his reply was curt: "Let's get back to work." On a Saturday afternoon in normal times, most senior staffers were off duty, but Kimmel kept the entire staff at headquarters until late in the day.

The focus of debate, as the day wore on, was whether, given the possible threat, warships still in Pearl Harbor should sortie. If they did, they would be hard for the Japanese to find. On the other hand, with the Fleet's own aircraft carriers away on missions to Wake and Midway, ships that sortied would have no air cover. "We were concerned," Kimmel would say later, "and didn't want to overlook anything." It was decided by day's end that the

Fleet would not sortie. Virtually everything he chose to do with such forces as he had, the Admiral would recall, "had its costs."

Just miles from Kimmel's HQ, at the Japanese consulate, the spy Yoshikawa was being pressed to respond to an outstanding request. Tokyo wanted to know, "immediately," not only what American warships were in port but whether they were equipped with torpedo nets. Also, had barrage balloons, a key defense against attack from the air, been deployed?

Yoshikawa rushed to reply. So far as he knew, he reported, the U.S. battleships were not protected by torpedo nets. This was true—it was ten months now since Navy headquarters had told Kimmel it hoped to supply nets "in the near future." There was no sign, the spy also correctly reported, that barrage balloons had been installed. Though there had long since been talk about the Army's getting barrage balloons "by the summer," none had arrived.

After the war, Yoshikawa would say that—not surprisingly—he had guessed the purpose behind Tokyo's demands. That may explain why, close to the end of this report, and after months of prudence, he included an astonishingly unguarded sentence. "I imagine," Yoshikawa wrote, "that in all probability there is considerable opportunity left to take advantage for a surprise attack."

Had that sentence been read in Washington, it would surely have jolted even the sleepiest analyst to attention. The code in which it was transmitted, however, had been given a low priority by U.S. intelligence. It would not be decrypted and read until the day following the Japanese attack.

36

SATURDAY AFTERNOON, DECEMBER 6TH, WASHINGTON. In the capital, diplomacy was grinding forward. There was a new message from London, again in connection with word of Japanese convoys moving toward Thailand and the Malay coast. The British were pressing again for clarity as to how involved militarily the United States was prepared to be. In late afternoon, President Roosevelt summoned British Ambassador Lord Halifax to the White House.

Halifax brought word that Churchill wished to assure Thailand of Britain's support should the Japanese attack. Roosevelt said he planned to send a similar message. Apparently, too, the President agreed that—absent satisfactory progress in his exchanges with Tokyo—he would warn Japan not to commit further aggression. The British and the Dutch, Roosevelt suggested, should follow suit.

First, however, he resolved to do what he had been mulling for more than a week. He would send a last-ditch message, from one head of state to another—to Emperor Hirohito.

On the afternoon of December 6th, working from a draft prepared by the State Department, the President began dictating a sixty-line letter filled with lofty verbiage.

Roosevelt was taking the unusual step of writing, he said in his message, because of the "deep and far-reaching emergency" and "developments that contain tragic possibilities." Americans had hoped that "a peace of the Pacific could be consummated in such a way that nationalities of many diverse peoples could exist side by side without fear of invasion." The sending now of huge numbers of Japanese forces to southern Indochina, however, could hardly be defensive, the President pointed out.

It was "unthinkable" that this situation could continue, Roosevelt went on. He urged the withdrawal from Indochina of "every Japanese soldier and sailor." "Both of us," he told the Emperor, "for the sake of the peoples not only of our own great countries but for the sake of humanity in neighboring territories, have a sacred duty to restore traditional amity and prevent further death and destruction in the world."

The letter to Hirohito was to be delivered at the imperial palace by Joseph Grew, the U.S. ambassador to Japan. As Roosevelt would relish saying in the hours that followed, it was a final message "from this son of man to the son of God."

All in vain. A ten-hour holdup of the letter in the Japanese censorship office, plus the protocol involved as Ambassador Grew tried and failed to obtain direct access to the Emperor, rendered the letter useless. Hirohito was not to receive it until a few minutes before his Navy attacked Pearl Harbor.

Days earlier, the Emperor had already issued his battle order. It exhorted his Fleet to "advance on the enemy to annihilate him . . . to prove to the whole world the greatness of our forces."

That day in Washington, top people in the government and the military did not behave as though there were a crisis. It was a Saturday, and almost everyone acted as though it was an ordinary Saturday. Though Secretary of War Stimson was to observe in his diary that "the news had got worse and worse and the atmosphere indicated that something was going to happen," he left his office before 2:00 p.m. "I went home, took a short lunch and took a horseback ride," Stimson wrote. "Then I went to meet Mabel at the train."

Secretary of the Navy Knox and his wife Annie planned dinner with friends at the Wardman Park, where they had an apartment. FBI Director J. Edgar Hoover, in charge of the nation's counterespionage, headed for New York City.

Top admirals and generals, too, deemed it unnecessary to stay in their offices. Chief of Staff Marshall believed, he was to say later, that he spent the evening at home with his wife Katherine. Having told a couple of his aides they could have Sunday off, Chief of Naval Operations Stark went to the National Theater to see a performance of *The Student Prince*, a show he had already seen several times.

War Plans' Turner was at home. Noyes, of Communications, went to the movies. ONI's Wilkinson and his wife had G-2's General Miles and other officers, including the President's naval aide Captain John Beardall, to dinner at their home in Arlington.

In the early evening at the White House, Roosevelt—who suffered from a chronic sinus infection—saw his doctor, Rear Admiral Ross McIntire. Then, following a chat over cocktails with an old friend, philanthropist Vincent Astor, it was on to a dinner party for some thirty guests. To one of the group, he appeared "very quiet . . . worn." In the morning, the President said, he planned to take it easy, work on his stamp collection perhaps. He had been collecting since he was a child and had accumulated more than a million stamps. The hobby, he would say, helped him relax. For the following afternoon, he said during dinner, he planned a snooze, then a drive in the Virginia countryside.

All that day, Navy and Army personnel had continued laboring on the cryptanalytic treadmill. Two of the MAGIC intercepts they handled were of immediate interest. The first, a notification from Tokyo to its Washington envoys, informed them that a fourteen-part message for the U.S. government was being prepared. Once the fourteen-part message had been delivered by the envoys—at a time yet to be fixed—the notification said, negotiations between the two nations would be broken off.

This was obviously a significant intercept, one that offered U.S. leaders advance notice that the crisis was nearing a climax. Distribution of the notification, however, was tardy. Some recipients, notably the President, would not receive their copies until the following morning—only hours before the attack on Pearl Harbor.

Both Marshall and Stark would say they never saw it. The apparent lapse has never been explained.

The fourteen-part message itself, meanwhile, had begun coming in, segment by segment, around lunchtime on the 6th. It embodied a long diatribe, to be handed to the U.S. Secretary of State, which crowed about Japan's supposed "spirit of conciliation" while castigating America for "imperialistic exploitation" and collusion with Britain and other Allies. Part 13 of the fourteen-part message revealed that—once the message had been delivered—Washington would learn that Japan was unable to accept the most recent U.S. proposal "as a basis of negotiation."

Down the decades since 1941, investigators and historians have wrangled over the significance of this message, over who received it and when, and how it was assessed or acted on. Witnesses' testimony and documents are hopelessly patchy, often contradictory. What is certain is that the President that evening read the thirteen parts of the message that had so far come in. What he read into them, however, remains uncertain.

Around 9:30 p.m., Roosevelt excused himself from the dinner table at the White House. Wheelchair-bound as ever because of the disability caused by polio, he was taken to his study—to be joined there by his adviser Harry Hopkins. As they talked, he pulled out the wooden box that housed part of his stamp collection. He was still riffling through it when his naval aide for the night, Lieutenant Lester Schulz, arrived with the latest batch of MAGIC intercepts. There were several documents, including the first thirteen parts of the message that Tokyo's embassy in Washington was instructed to deliver the following day.

As best Schulz could remember four years later, the President took ten minutes to read the transcript of the long message. Then, the officer would recall, he said something along the lines of, "This means war." After Hopkins in turn read the intercept, he agreed with the essence of what Roosevelt had said. Hopkins, as the lieutenant recalled it, thought the Japanese would "strike when they were ready." The President, Schulz said, "mentioned a message that he had sent to the Japanese Emperor." Though Indochina came up, Schulz added, "there was no mention of Pearl Harbor."

The comment Schulz attributed to the President—"This means war"—was to be quoted prominently down the years and assigned great importance. Schulz, though, at the time only a lieutenant new to the job, did not claim those were Roosevelt's exact words. Whatever the President said, as he remembered it years later, was more matter-of-fact than exclamatory. Nothing Schulz heard indicated that Roosevelt thought war would come "tonight, or tomorrow necessarily, or even in a few days."

The man who delivered the intercept to the White House, ONI's Lieutenant Commander Kramer, had then headed on to Navy Secretary Knox's apartment to show it to him. Knox called Stimson and Hull, and they arranged to meet at 10:00 a.m. the following day. Kramer, meanwhile, headed for the home of ONI Director Wilkinson, who was hosting General Miles of G-2 and the President's principal naval aide, Captain Beardall, for dinner.

All three read the latest Japanese intercept, but none would say he deemed it especially urgent or significant. Wilkinson thought the thirteen parts a "diplomatic paper," not of a military nature. General Miles judged them to be of "little military significance." He did not order that Chief of Staff Marshall, or General Gerow of War Plans, be alerted.

Colonel Bratton of Army Intelligence, whose responsibility it was to see that MAGIC intercepts got to the Chief of Staff, Gerow, and the Secretaries of State and War, made none of those deliveries. He merely left a copy of the thirteen-part message with the watch officer at the Department of State, then went home to bed. Kramer would also go home, having told his unit's duty officer to wake him should he be needed.

Chief of Naval Operations Stark, questioned later, would say repeatedly that he had no recollection of having been told of the thirteen-part message that Saturday night. The friends who had accompanied the CNO to the theater that evening, Captain Harold Krick and his wife Kathleen, would remember that when they got back to the Starks' home, a servant reported that there had been a call from the White House. Stark then went to his study, apparently to phone the President. He said when he returned, according to Captain Krick, that the situation with Japan was "critical, something of that sort." He did not go into detail.

Even with his memory refreshed, and on returning to testify again, Stark would say he remembered nothing about what he and Roosevelt had discussed. He could only assume, he told Congress' Joint Committee, "that when the President called me he mentioned this note that we had received from the Japanese, that he did not, certainly did not, impress me that it was anything that required action . . . I am certain that he gave me no directive."

Nothing in the accounts of that last evening, from Roosevelt's reaction on down, suggests that any senior official or military man thought there was anything in the latest Japanese intercept that could not wait till morning. While he had attempted to reach Stark—and may eventually have succeeded in doing so—the President had not deemed it necessary to reach out to Chief of Staff Marshall. No one, certainly, thought to keep the commanders in the Pacific up to speed on developments.

The White House log indicates that the President went to bed shortly before midnight Washington time. In Hawaii, it was 6:30 p.m.

37

EVENING, DECEMBER 6TH, HAWAII. At the consulate in Honolulu, Japan's agent Yoshikawa sent his final bulletin. "The following ships were observed at anchor," he told his masters:

> *9 battleships, 3 light cruisers, 3 submarine tenders, 17 destroyers, and in addition there were 4 light cruisers, 2 destroyers lying at docks (the heavy cruisers and airplane carriers have all left). It appears that no air reconnaissance is being conducted by the fleet air arm.*

Most of Yoshikawa's figures were right or almost right. There were no aircraft carriers in port, a pity from the Japanese point of view, a mercy so far as the Fleet was concerned. His tally of the number of battleships present was very nearly accurate—and they would suffer most the following day. And indeed, only limited air reconnaissance was being conducted.

The spy lingered at his desk until after nightfall, he would recall years later. It was clear to him, he said, that "the date was rapidly approaching . . . I strolled about the consulate grounds before turning in . . . The bright haze in the distance indicated that the lights were on at the Pearl Harbor naval base, and I could hear no patrolling aircraft aloft . . . I finally turned in and slept restlessly until morning."

Earlier in the evening, Fleet intelligence officer Edwin Layton had received a call from the Navy's local intelligence officer. He wanted to know whether Layton was expecting to come over to his office the next day. There was something about which he wanted Layton's opinion. It could wait till morning.

The something was a phone call the FBI had intercepted the previous day, a conversation between a local Japanese-born medical practitioner, Dr. Motokazu Mori—and his wife—and what had appeared to be a newspaperman in Tokyo. The exchange had lasted eighteen minutes, and—the transcript showed—included talk about airplane traffic; whether the U.S. military used searchlights at night; oddly, what flowers were currently in bloom in Hawaii; and much else. The FBI had thought it "peculiar," and alerted both Navy and Army Intelligence. G-2's local chief investigator took the transcript to Hawaii's G-2 chief, Lieutenant Colonel Kendall Fielder, who happened to be about to go out to dinner with General Short.

Short and Fielder spent an hour or more poring over the transcript. It looked "fishy," Fielder remembered, but "we couldn't make heads or tails of it." The two men could not see "any military significance," however, and headed off with their wives to their dinner at the officers' club.

At Fleet HQ, having driven his team hard all day, Admiral Kimmel had finally eased up. Old friends Admiral Fairfax Leary and his wife Marion had long since invited him to a dinner at the Halekulani Hotel. As befitted his position as commander in chief of the Fleet, Kimmel was seated at the head of the table.

As the meal got under way, Kimmel leaned across the table to tell a colleague, Rear Admiral Milo Draemel, about another, curious invitation he had received for that evening. The Japanese Consul, he said, had asked him to come and have a drink "without an aide—just himself." Draemel advised him to stay well away.

There was an incident, in hindsight chilling, as the Navy party dined. All of a sudden Frances, the wife of Admiral "Bull" Halsey—who was still away on his mission ferrying airplanes to Wake—loudly declared that she was "certain the Japs are going to attack." Those who heard her, Captain Joel Bunkley would recall, thought the prediction "crazy." As people in the know were aware, Frances Halsey had long suffered from manic depression.

Kimmel headed back to his quarters, a house overlooking the anchorage, soon after 9:00 p.m. There were points of light in the dark far below—navigation lights of vessels coming and going, lights in dry docks where men were laboring into the night, and the flickering neon lights of bars where men on liberty were carousing.

Elsewhere, at the recreation center, hundreds of sailors were attending the latest stage of a competition, the "Battle of Music 1941." They roared approval, according to shipboard loyalty, as bands from the *USS Pennsylvania* and the *USS Tennessee* blared out their routines. Both bands, and that of the *USS Arizona*, qualified to play in the finals.

At midnight, before dispersing, the crowd stood to sing "God Bless America."

More than five thousand miles to the west, in Manila, the U.S. admiral thought most likely to face a Japanese attack in the Pacific was puzzled. Admiral Hart, commanding the small U.S. Asiatic Fleet, had that day received information, which—if true—meant headquarters in Washington was keeping him out of the loop. The United States and Britain, a source told him, were now firmly agreed on mutual military assistance should Japan attack their territories.

Hart, who had received no such notification from headquarters, fired off a query to Washington. He, like Kimmel, had long complained that headquarters did not keep him informed. He wearied of "the rather chronic condition under which we don't get the word from Washington."

Again like Kimmel, Hart was concerned with his responsibilities under the War Plan. He had no carriers or battleships, only destroyers and cruisers, most of which he had dispersed for their protection. But he had opted to keep his greatest strength, a force of twenty-nine submarines, in harbor.

About the time Kimmel in Hawaii was turning in, Hart completed his diary entry for the 6th. "Guess war is just around the corner," he wrote, "but I think I'll go to a movie."

38

MORNING, DECEMBER 7TH, WASHINGTON. Unbeknownst to Kimmel and Hart in the Pacific, unbeknownst to anyone of senior political or military rank in Washington, four new Japanese messages had been intercepted by Navy operators in the United States during the night. All were significant, and one suggested the possibility of Japanese action somewhere in the Pacific at or close to a specified hour.

For mundane reasons, and in spite of the crisis, the new messages reached people in high places hours later than they should have done. When those people did see them, they first dillydallied, then wasted an opportunity to warn U.S. commanders in the Pacific.

The first message was the final, fourteenth part of Japan's rambling response to America's previous negotiating points. Japan, its ambassadors were to tell the Secretary of State at a time to be specified, considered it "impossible to reach an agreement through further negotiations." This air of finality was new.

Intercepted shortly after 3:00 a.m. Washington time, this dispatch should have been processed and promptly delivered to senior Washington officials and commanders. Instead, because the Navy's night duty officer did not rouse his boss, MAGIC specialist Kramer, as instructed, precious time was lost.

The second incoming message of the night was truly significant. It told Japanese envoys the precise hour—"1:00 p.m. on the 7th"—at which they were to deliver the fourteen-part message." The insistence on a specific time was ominous. Given that Japan's conduct thus far had been deceitful, it was rational to think that something—an attack?—was going to occur at the same time as the full fourteen-part message was delivered to the U.S. government or very soon afterward. There was a reason, one familiar to diplomats, why Japan would want to delay until *after* its diplomats had gone through the motions of cutting off negotiations. To make a military move totally by surprise would be to breach international law.

The "one o'clock message," as it is known, was intercepted around 4:30 a.m. Washington time on December 7th. Again, though, the sleeping Lieutenant Commander Kramer was not woken; and the message would not be decrypted, translated, and ready for delivery until 9:00 a.m. By then, more than four hours would have been lost.

The third of the overnight messages was also squandered. Codebreakers had been on the lookout since December 2nd for the preplanned "hidden word" message, designed to alert Japanese diplomats that a crisis with one or more named nations was imminent and that they should destroy remaining codes. Like its two predecessors of that night, and for the same reason, the "hidden word" word message was held up for hours.

Then at 10:30 a.m., in the rush of dealing with everything else—and though fluent in Japanese—Kramer made mistakes in translation. Perpetuating the original translation error, he rendered "relations between Japan and [name of country] are on the brink of catastrophe" as "relations . . . *are not in accordance with expectation.*" Astonishingly, too, he wrote only that the catastrophic break would be with "England," omitting the fact—plain to see in the text—that the break would in fact be with "England [*and*] the United States." A double mistake, perhaps excusable in a weary man, but a mistake all the same.

The fourth and last dispatch to be intercepted overnight and held up in the system, had its own special significance. It told the Japanese envoys in Washington that once the preceding three messages had been received and deciphered, they had to destroy the remaining cipher machine and all machine codes immediately; and, in like manner, all secret documents.

The order foresaw the imminent, total severance of the umbilical between Japan's diplomats in America and their masters in Tokyo.

These four overnight dispatches were to provide American readers of MAGIC with potent information. In sum, Tokyo was about to have its envoys make a "catastrophic" break with the United States, at a precise time on December 7th—a break so final that no further secret diplomatic communication would be possible.

Although these intercepts had been delayed by snarl-ups and fatigue, the men at the top of the U.S. government and the naval and military command would nevertheless receive virtually all this information in time to warn Army and Navy commanders in the Pacific that—to a virtual certainty—hostilities were imminent.

Those at the summit of power at home, however, were to prove insufficiently astute and dismally inefficient. They would fail to alert the men who, as things were about to turn out, had the most urgent need to know: General Short—the man most directly responsible for the defense of Pearl Harbor—and Admiral Kimmel.

On the morning of December 7th, the front pages of U.S. newspapers told of the continuing crisis with Japan. The late news in the *New York Times* and the *Washington Post* was that the President had sent a personal appeal directly to the Emperor. If there was any hope of peace, however, it was only a glimmer. *Times* readers were told of the "pall of the Far Eastern crisis," of America's "preparations for any eventuality." An article quoted Navy Secretary Knox, however, as saying the American people could "feel totally confident in their Navy." During a tour of naval bases, Senator Owen Brewster had declared that "The United States Navy can defeat the Japanese Navy at any place and at any time!"

Lieutenant Commander Kramer, meanwhile, got to the office early and found waiting for him the first of the dispatches received overnight. Japan's "fourteenth part," making it clear that Japan

saw negotiations as at an end. This was the message he should
have seen hours earlier. He began his regular MAGIC delivery
round at once—at first in-house.

With the fourteenth part in hand, ONI director Wilkinson
hurried off to tell Admiral Stark that the "fighting" tone of Tokyo's dispatch, in his opinion, suggested the Japanese military
was about to make a move—if not southward as expected, then
elsewhere in the Pacific. He thought the situation "very serious,"
suggesting to Stark that "the Fleet should be advised."

Wilkinson got the impression that the CNO agreed with him.
Stark did not, however, respond by sending such a message.
Rather, as Wilkinson recalled, he seemed to intend first to call
Chief of Staff Marshall. Nothing in the record indicates that he
did so.

It was now about 9:30 a.m., four hours before the strike on
Pearl. While Stark was being shown the fourteenth part, and doing nothing, Lieutenant Commander Kramer had headed to the
White House to get that part to the President. There, all was tranquil. In those days, 1600 Pennsylvania Avenue virtually closed
down on Sundays. Visitors were few; the clatter of typewriters
was stilled. Captain Beardall, the Navy aide who received the fourteenth part from Kramer, would recall having been perhaps—
domestic staff aside—the only person on duty in the mansion.
When Beardall took the latest MAGIC in to him, Roosevelt was
still in bed.

The President read the fourteenth part as Beardall waited.
Then, the aide would recall, he said merely, "It looks as though
the Japs are going to sever negotiations." Nothing in Roosevelt's
manner indicated alarm. Beardall departed.

The only other visitor to the bedroom that morning was the
President's doctor, Rear Admiral McIntire. Roosevelt's persistent
sinus trouble led his physician to remain with him all morning
and for at least part of the afternoon. The treatment that McIntire
used to clear the sinuses was painful and time-consuming. He
was alone with his patient until about noon.

Roosevelt shared some of his thinking on the Far East crisis with the physician. Though he thought Japan might strike a British possession, perhaps Singapore, he said nothing about a possible attack on any U.S.-governed territory; the President did not think Japan would risk war with the United States.

By 11:00 a.m., according to the record, the three other overnight Japanese dispatches had also been delivered to the White House. They included, of course, the highly significant instruction that the message breaking off negotiations was to be delivered to the State Department at 1:00 p.m. The record does not indicate, however, whether Roosevelt saw that or the other two delayed messages. The President of the United States was with his doctor and may have been effectively out of reach.

So too was the Chief of Staff, General Marshall. He had been at home during the early morning on the 7th, apparently not in crisis mode. "We had a late breakfast," his wife would recall, "George eating on a tray beside my bed. After breakfast he ordered his horse and said he would take his usual Sunday morning ride before going to the office."

Soon after nine, when G-2's Colonel Bratton was reading Tokyo's fourteen-part message, the ominous "one o'clock message" was handed to him. Bratton was—he would recall—"stunned into frenzied activity." He tried to raise Marshall, only to be told the General had "gone horseback riding." The minutes ticked by.

Around 10:20 a.m., at Navy, when Lieutenant Commander Kramer returned from his first round of morning deliveries, he too saw the "one o'clock message." Kramer had served in Hawaii, was familiar with the different time zones, and rapidly calculated what 1:00 p.m. Washington time—by now less than three hours away—would equate to at relevant points in the Pacific. On the Kra Isthmus and in the Philippines, Kramer figured, it would be two or three hours before dawn. At Pearl Harbor, it would be 7:30 a.m.

Before making his second round of MAGIC deliveries, Kramer headed for Admiral Stark's office. Of the several other officers present outside the office, one was ONI's Far Eastern chief, Commander McCollum. Together, the two men studied a large chart with time zones marked in blue, light blue, and pink. The chart showed that Kramer's initial calculations were correct, so they shared the finding with ONI chief Wilkinson. Then, as Kramer went off on his second delivery run, Wilkinson and McCollum approached Admiral Stark.

Stark "didn't seem to be very much perturbed," McCollum would recall. When Wilkinson asked whether the Pacific Fleet had been alerted, Admiral Stark said it had. When Admiral Turner showed up, at about eleven o'clock, McCollum and Wilkinson tackled him in turn. "At this time," according to McCollum, "we asked again whether the Pacific Fleet had been warned, and I believe Captain Wilkinson suggested to Admiral Stark that he pick up the phone and call Admiral Kimmel. I thought he was going to do it, but apparently he changed his mind and tried to get through to the White House—and was told the President wasn't available."

Meanwhile, the overnight messages had by now reached the Secretaries of State, War, and the Navy, who were meeting in Hull's office as agreed the previous night. Kramer made sure they understood the times in the Pacific that coincided with 1:00 p.m. Washington time. Hull, Stimson would note in his journal, said he was "very certain that the Japs [were] planning some devilry." The Secretaries wondered—impotently—"where the blow will strike."

All this time, the U.S. Army's Chief of Staff had been trotting and cantering around on horseback, winding up the ride on open ground where the Pentagon now stands. Only when he was home taking a shower and preparing to go to the office did Marshall start to play a role in the day's events. He got word at last that G-2's Bratton, frustrated in his earlier effort to reach the General, planned to bring an "important message" to him at home. Marshall briskly sent word that Bratton should stay where he was. He would be in the office shortly.

Between 11:15 and 11:30 a.m.—according to witnesses' varying memories, perhaps two hours after he had first been telephoned— the Chief of Staff reached his office and began to catch up. First, for long minutes, he read Japan's fourteen-part message—out loud. General Miles and Colonel Bratton, anxious to bring his attention to the matter of most concern, the "one o'clock" message, tried in vain to interrupt him.

When at last Marshall did take in the one o'clock message, they had his full attention. "General Miles and I," Bratton recalled, "both said that we were convinced that it meant Japanese hostile action against some American installation in the Pacific at or shortly after one that afternoon." Miles urged that "the Philippines, Hawaii, Panama, and the West Coast be informed immediately . . . to be on the alert."

Other officers had by now entered the office, and no one demurred. "There was no doubt in the minds of those present, certainly not in my mind, that the 'one o'clock' had some very definite significance," Marshall himself would recall. "Something was going to happen at one o'clock." Taking pencil and paper, he there and then drafted a message for commanders in the Pacific. Before sending it, however, he called Admiral Stark at the Navy Department.

"He said," Stark was to recall, "it would be a good thing to inform the people in the Pacific. My first reaction was that we had sent so much out . . . that it would be just as well not to send it." Had Marshall not phoned, the CNO was to say much later, he himself would probably have sent no warning.

As it turned out, Stark changed his mind. "I put the phone up and . . . in a matter of seconds, or certainly only a few minutes, thought, 'Well, it can't do any harm. There may be something unusual . . . there might be something.' And I turned back and picked up the phone—he [Marshall] had not yet sent the message—and I said, 'Perhaps you are right. I think you had better go ahead.' Stark asked Marshall to see that copies of the warning message also went to naval commanders in the Pacific.

As sent, the final telegram read:

THE JAPANESE ARE PRESENTING AT I P.M. EASTERN STANDARD TIME, TODAY, WHAT AMOUNTS TO AN ULTIMATUM. ALSO THEY ARE UNDER ORDERS TO DESTROY THEIR CODE MACHINE IMMEDIATELY. JUST WHAT SIGNIFICANCE THE HOUR SET MAY HAVE WE DO NOT KNOW, BUT BE ON ALERT ACCORDINGLY. IN- FORM NAVAL AUTHORITIES OF THIS COMMUNICA- TION. MARSHALL.

The Chief of Staff's use of the word "alert" was almost unique. It had not been used in any message to the Pacific since midsummer 1940, during what had turned out to be an exercise. This at last was a clear communication, impossible to misinterpret—and, by now, terribly, terribly urgent. By the time Marshall finished composing this dispatch it was 11:50 a.m.—just seventy minutes before Japan's envoys had been instructed to cut off negotiations.

Might the fastest way to get word to the Pacific have been to use the telephone—or radio? Testifying later, Marshall seemed unclear about that. Phoning in those days was a cumbersome business, he said, and not secure. Doing so was "not considered." Was he aware that the FBI had an efficient direct radio link to Hawaii? No. The Navy had a fast link to Hawaii, too, but Marshall— according to Stark—declined an offer to use it.

In the event, the Army relied on its own Message Center. There was an initial delay because the staff could not read Marshall's scribble. Bratton, who was able to make it out, then dictated the text to a clerk. The record indicates that it finally went for encryption and transmission at 12:00 noon. How long, Marshall wanted to know, would the message take to reach addressees? He was told: "Within thirty minutes at the latest."

Out in the Pacific, 230 miles due north of Pearl Harbor, the first wave of warplanes was already launching from the carriers of the Japanese strike force.

The rest is black farce. Messages to other Pacific commands, the Philippines, Panama, and San Francisco—the priority addressee was the Philippines—got through as intended. The warning to General Short in Hawaii, with a request that he inform "naval authorities," did not. When atmospheric conditions made connection impossible, the colonel in the Message Center in Washington resorted to more powerful commercial circuits.

So it was that the dispatch to the only place that immediately mattered went, at 12:17 p.m. East Coast time, first to Western Union in Washington by teletype, then across the street by pneumatic tube to RCA, thence to San Francisco, and from there by radio to the RCA offices in Honolulu—but not yet to the Army's Signal Center, because the circuit was down.

It was now 7:33 a.m. in Hawaii, already three minutes later than the hour when Tokyo had told its diplomats to deliver the final message to the State Department. The onslaught on the U.S. Fleet, the reason for the charade of which they were part, was only twenty minutes away.

The bombs began falling at 7:55 a.m. Hawaii time. Chaos reigned in Honolulu as an RCA messenger boy on a motorbike, the dispatch designed to forewarn General Short and Admiral Kimmel in his pouch, picked his way through a tangle of traffic.

The message—at this stage not even marked "Priority"—did not reach the Army Signal Office until four hours after the start of the attack. It was almost 3:00 p.m. by the time it was decoded and at last passed to General Short. By then, the Japanese airplanes were long gone. The Navy and the Army were counting their dead, succoring the wounded.

According to an Army captain present when Short received Marshall's message, he uncharacteristically swore like a sergeant.

Admiral Kimmel's copy of the warning dispatch reached him eight hours after the start of the attack. He balled it up and threw it into the trash.

PART II

CONSEQUENCE

39

THE HORRENDOUS DAY, and the nights that followed, blurred into one at Pearl Harbor. So great was the stress that barely anyone would later recall details about the rush of events. An officer who saw Kimmel at the height of the attack described his performance in command as having been "splendid."

For about forty-eight hours after the strike, meals were forgotten. No one showered or changed clothes. On the first night, Kimmel's sole concession to sleep was to move for a while to an armchair.

After nightfall on the 8th, Halsey—returning aboard the carrier *Enterprise* from the mission to reinforce Wake Island—found Kimmel and his staff "still wearing their Sunday uniforms, crumpled and spotted with mud. Their faces were haggard and unshaven but their chins were up. Kimmel himself was a marvel of cool efficiency, although the hysteria that surged around him mounted by the minute."

The Admiral and many senior officers thought it more than possible that the Japanese attack had been only the initial blow. In Washington, too, Secretary of War Stimson feared Tokyo might follow through by ordering an invasion of Hawaii. No invasion materialized, but there were major command decisions to be made.

Ships, and what planes could be scrabbled together, would for weeks to come conduct a prolonged search—in vain—for the enemy force that had struck on the 7th. Elements of the Fleet were already at sea, and Halsey headed out again almost at once. War plans to meet the new situation were urgently devised. Foremost among them was a major operation to relieve Wake, which had in turn come under prolonged enemy attack.

Kimmel resisted outright a suggestion from headquarters that Pearl Harbor was now barely serviceable as a major base for U.S.

warships. Damaged but seaworthy ships, Washington proposed, should be brought to the U.S. West Coast. Pearl should for the time being serve as a base only for submarines. Kimmel retorted that Pearl was still viable. The repair yards were functioning, and warships not terminally damaged—and that was most of them—could be put back into service. Most important of all, U.S. carriers, cruisers, and destroyers were still operational.

Though Kimmel could not be sure of it at the time, six of the nine battleships struck by the Japanese on the 7th were to be recovered and would fight again. What was really needed now, Kimmel made clear, was an infusion of planes, antiaircraft guns, and radar in the quantities Pearl had long lacked. "Repeated strong representations in the past," he wrote pointedly, "have only been partially heeded, but stronger support may now be expected."

All this over fourteen pages, in a document remarkable for the fact that it was composed amid the human loss and chaos that immediately followed December 7th. Kimmel continued working tirelessly, so tirelessly that his senior staff had to press him to take any rest. He was still, his chief of staff Poco Smith recalled, filled with "fight and determination." "What distressed him more than anything," Assistant Chief of Staff DeLany remembered, "was the loss of his personnel."

The Admiral strove to bolster the morale of the thousands of his men who toiled on amid the wreckage. "We Americans can sustain hard blows but can deliver harder ones" he told them days after the attack, "when we face the task that lies ahead with calm determination and unflinching resolve, it is truly great to be an American . . . Never have we been so proud as when we saw Sunday's magnificent response to the call of duty."

The response of the Fleet had been magnificent, and almost immediate. Later investigation would conclude that most antiaircraft guns aboard ships opened up within five minutes or less. "So prompt," Vice Admiral Chuichi Nagumo, the Japanese strike force commander, wrote in his after-action report "as to virtually nullify the advantage of surprise."

The gallantry of one officer, in charge of an antiaircraft battery aboard the USS *Nevada*, would deservedly become legendary in the Navy. A twenty-one-year-old fresh out of the Naval Academy, Ensign Joseph Taussig, went on directing fire after communications at the battery had been disabled and a missile passed through his thigh. The leg would eventually be amputated. For his "exceptional courage, presence of mind, and devotion to duty," he would be awarded the Navy Cross. There were many other stories of individual heroism—stories that tended to be obscured by the fog of loss and recrimination.

Unaccompanied, often unannounced, Kimmel made it his business after the attack to visit not only ships that had been badly battered but those that had escaped virtually unscathed. "The Admiral stepped aboard without any entourage," recalled an enlisted man who had served on the cruiser USS *Honolulu*. "He was in oil-stained, rumpled suntans.* No tie. No insignia. Bare headed. I shall always remember his face, so strained, so full of agony, so tired."

The ordeal was taking a toll.

From Washington, on the 8th, CNO Stark had written Kimmel a letter.

> Dear Admiral Kimmel,
> We are feeling for you just as hard as we can in just what you have gone through, biding our time until you can send us some details ... Hundreds of telegrams and messages are being received from the families ... We know that as soon as you can you will start sending us a list ... Very good wishes from us all.
>
> Sincerely,
> HAROLD R. STARK
> ADMIRAL, U.S.N.

---

* In both the Navy and the Army, hot-weather uniforms were referred to as suntans.

The note was oddly formal, coming as it did from a friend who most often signed himself "Betty" and addressed Kimmel as "Mustapha." Perhaps Stark sensed already that this was a time to be prudent, not to seem too close to the commander in chief Pacific.

The Secretary of the Navy himself carried the letter to Hawaii. Knox had resolved on making the trip rapidly, within hours of the attack, and the President had approved. The Secretary's task was to assess the scale of the catastrophe and find out how the Fleet could have been taken so totally by surprise. Knox was aware, too, that his own reputation was at serious risk. It was bad enough that, just hours before the Japanese strike, the press had reported him as boasting of the Fleet's competence. Worse, after it, at the White House and in the presence of senators and congressmen, he had been taunted over the fact that the Navy—the Navy for which he was responsible—had apparently been "asleep."

There was a prospect, Knox would recall, "of a nasty congressional investigation, and I made up my mind in a flash to go out there and get the actual facts." He was right about the imminence of a furor in Congress. Before he even boarded his plane, members of Congress were deriding the Navy, the Office of Naval Intelligence, and their Army counterparts. One U.S. senator would demand Knox's resignation.

There was a call, too, for five top Navy and Army commanders to be court-martialed, and Kimmel's name headed the list. He should be tried, a House member said, "to determine his guilt or innocence in the failure of Hawaiian defenders to beat off the surprise air attack before serious damage could be done . . . Hundreds of our boys have paid with their lives."

What would follow, then and for seventy-five years to come, would have little to do with justice. It was to be, rather, an absurdly prolonged exercise in damage control.

40

SECRETARY KNOX, ARRIVING at Pearl Harbor four days after the strike, declared himself "completely devastated" by what he saw. "Even as we looked on," recalled his aide, future vice admiral Frank Beatty, "bodies were being recovered from the oil-covered waters . . . Some 600 men killed in the raid had only recently been buried . . . At the Naval hospital, we saw hundreds of wounded, mainly suffering horribly from burns . . . Some were so terribly charred as to be beyond recognition."

Knox and Beatty were seeing what, two decades before satellite television, most Americans could barely imagine. In the hectic thirty-two hours of their stay in Hawaii, they saw all they could and talked to as many people as possible. Fleet intelligence officer Layton showed Knox images of the action and the aftermath taken by Navy photographers—they remain, today, virtually the only photos available. On Kimmel's orders, they had been locked in a safe pending Knox's arrival. Much time was spent talking with Kimmel and Short.

In the long hours of the flight back to Washington, alone in the navigator's compartment of his aircraft, Knox worked on his report to the President. Typed up by an aide during the journey, it ran to nineteen pages. The Secretary had once been a reporter, and what he wrote was a decent summary of what he had seen and heard.

In the report, Knox made a point of saying that neither Kimmel nor General Short had tried to "alibi the lack of a state of readiness for the air attack. Both admitted they did not expect it, and had taken no adequate measures to meet one if it came." Short had told him, reflecting his earlier reporting to Washington, that the measures he had taken had been against possible sabotage. He had bunched up his planes accordingly, to protect them, but with disastrous consequences. The Army's antiaircraft guns had not been manned. Its radar, which could have given some minimal warning, had been squandered.

As Secretary of the Navy, however, Knox had focused principally on the Fleet at Pearl. Kimmel's ships, he reported, had been "so dispersed as to provide a field of fire covering every approach from the air." At the time of the strike, they had been at Condition Three, which meant that "half the broadside and anti-aircraft guns were manned, and all of the anti-aircraft guns were supplied with ammunition and were in readiness." The Navy's "morning patrol," Knox wrote, "was sent out at dawn to the southward, where the Commander-in-Chief had reason to suspect an attack might come." The Navy had also taken "all necessary provisions" to counter submarines, which were thought to pose a threat.

The enemy, Knox reported with emphasis, had benefited mightily from "the most efficient fifth column to be found anywhere in the American possessions . . . The intelligence work done by this fifth column, before the attack, provided the Japanese Navy with exact knowledge of all necessary details." Exact charts, recovered from a downed plane and the wreck of a midget submarine, showed the "customary positions of ships when in Pearl Harbor, exact locations of all defenses, gun power and numerous other details."

On the first page of the report, and again near the end, Knox mentioned something else, something that impinged not at all on the commanders in Hawaii but on the high command in Washington. Neither Kimmel nor Short, he noted:

> *had any knowledge of the plain intimations of some surprise move, made clear in Washington—through the interception of Japanese instructions . . . in which a surprise move of some kind as clearly indicated by the insistence upon the precise time of [Ambassador] Nomura's reply to Hull, at one o'clock on Sunday.*

For all its tortured syntax, this was a direct reference to the knowledge Navy and Army chiefs in Washington had, thanks to the MAGIC intercept of the "one o'clock message," that an attack was likely somewhere in the Pacific—at almost the very time the Japanese did in fact hit Pearl Harbor. Pages later, and prominently, Knox noted with emphasis that "a *special* war warning, sent out by the War Department . . . to the Army was not received until some hours after the attack." This referred to the warning, based on the "one o'clock" intercept, that had reached Hawaii hopelessly late— having been fumbled by Chief of Staff Marshall and CNO Stark.

Knox's report focused attention at least as much on the military leadership in Washington as on Kimmel and Short. It was, however, to be rapidly suppressed. On his arrival in Washington late at night on the 14th, weary from what in those days was a twenty-two-hour journey, Knox hurried straight to the White House to bring his report to the President.

According to his appointments secretary Edwin Watson, Roosevelt was in very low spirits. The disaster in Hawaii had been followed by more bad news. In the Philippines, American forces had put up an ignominious defense to the initial Japanese attack. Japanese forces had begun landing there. Guam had been bombed and overrun. Malaya and Hong Kong had been invaded. The British Navy had suffered major losses. Invasion of the Dutch territories was imminent. The Japanese were on the rampage across the Pacific and beyond, so far with total success. Hitler and Mussolini, meanwhile, had declared war on the United States.

On the 15th, Secretary Knox returned to the White House twice more, to huddle with the President and debate what was to be done. His full report as he had written it, however, would not see the light of day until after the war. At one of the White House meetings, Roosevelt drafted notes that, as Knox's aide Beatty put it later, contained "all the information that could then, with the security of the nation at stake, be released to the public."

Then, during a hushed press conference in his office at the Navy Department, Knox issued a long statement. He devoted

most of it to graphic descriptions of what he had learned and
seen in Hawaii, and to admiration for what he had learned of the
Navy's gallant defense. "The whole spectacle," he said, had been
"the greatest spontaneous exhibition of cooperation, determination and courage that the American Navy has been called upon
to make . . . Without exception, all ships and stations rose to the
emergency."

Omitted from Knox's public statement, however, was any reference to the Washington high command having seen an intercept
indicating that an attack would occur somewhere in the Pacific—
at almost exactly the time it did occur. Omitted, too, was any mention of Washington having sent a warning that arrived too late.

In his public statement, as in his report to the President, Knox
attributed the effectiveness of the Japanese attack to the "most perfect" advance intelligence supplied by a supposed "fifth column"
of Japanese aliens in Hawaii. In fact, of course, the intelligence
had been gathered over the weeks not by any fifth column but by
consulate spy Yoshikawa. Most of his reports to Tokyo had been
intercepted, thanks to MAGIC, and several had been decoded and
circulated to U.S. analysts and senior military and political leaders. There is nothing in the record, though, to indicate that any of
them noted Tokyo's special preoccupation with Pearl Harbor.

Nothing about the MAGIC intercepts could be mentioned publicly, by Secretary Knox or anyone else, in the aftermath of Pearl
Harbor. It was essential to keep secret the fact that the United
States was reading Japan's diplomatic correspondence. That was
and would long remain a vital security asset.

The suppression of any hint of MAGIC in Knox's public report,
however, deprived the Hawaiian commanders—and the public—
of essential knowledge. Truth would from now on be distorted, at
the expense of Kimmel and Short.

At his press conference, before launching into his long paean
to the officers and men of the Fleet, the Secretary of the Navy
allotted a few sentences to a central truth and a consequence. The
central truth, he said, was that "United States services were not

on the alert against the surprise air attack." The consequence was that there would now be "a formal investigation, which will be initiated immediately by the President."

Further action, Knox said, would be "dependent on the facts and recommendations made by this investigation board." Pending the investigation, he added however, there would be "no changes in command." That situation held, so far as the public was concerned, for less than forty-eight hours. Behind the scenes, almost certainly, it changed even more rapidly.

For an hour the following afternoon, December 16th, Roosevelt set a whirlwind pace. First he told correspondents that, though "all Americans abhor censorship . . . some degree of censorship is essential in time of war, and we are at war. It is necessary to national security that military information that might be of aid to the enemy be scrupulously withheld." Effective at once, he was appointing a director of censorship.

Then, for less than a quarter of an hour, according to the White House appointments log, the President met with Secretary Knox and CNO Stark. Next, he conferred with Secretary of War Stimson and Chief of Staff Marshall. After twenty minutes, the log indicates, they were joined by Supreme Court Justice Owen Roberts. Their meeting apparently lasted a long time, perhaps as long as two hours.

Before the day ended, the White House announced that Justice Roberts would head a commission to "ascertain the facts" relating to the Pearl Harbor attack and "whether there were derelictions of duty or errors of judgment on the part of U.S. Army or Navy personnel . . . and who were responsible."

The next day, the 17th, Stimson and Knox each issued short, three-paragraph announcements. Contrary to what Knox had said two days earlier, changes at the top in Hawaii were being, had already been, made.

Stimson's announcement said that General Short had been

relieved, that his replacement, another general, had already arrived in Hawaii. The Army air force commander soon would be relieved.

Knox's announcement stated that Admiral Kimmel had also been relieved—by his own Battle Force commander, Vice Admiral William Pye—pending the arrival of a permanent replacement.

The news had reached Kimmel in Hawaii the previous day, in the form of a brief dispatch from Knox that CNO Stark initialed:

YOU WILL VERY SHORTLY RECEIVE DISPATCH ORDERS DETACHING YOU AS CINC PACIFIC AND COMMANDER IN CHIEF U.S. FLEET . . . INFORM PYE. HE WILL BE YOUR TEMPORARY RELIEF.

This was a body blow for Kimmel, but it was not wholly unexpected. "If I were in charge in Washington, I would relieve Kimmel at once," he had told "Soc" McMorris and another colleague within twenty-four hours of the Japanese attack. When he learned—from the Honolulu newspapers—there was to be an investigation, he had written to Stark telling him to "decide on the basis of what is best for the country. What happens to me is of no importance . . . Do not spare my feelings."

On the afternoon of the 17th, as the Admiral sat talking with his destroyer force commander, Rear Admiral Milo Draemel, there came a moment when he looked up at the clock. It was just before 3:00 p.m. Hawaii time. "I am to be relieved," he told Draemel, "at three." Disconcerted, Draemel offered to leave the room. "No, stay here," Kimmel replied.

Moments later, Vice Admiral Pye entered. He was one of the forty-seven more senior admirals who had been passed over, ten months earlier, when Kimmel had been appointed to head the Fleet. As Draemel sat in silence, the outgoing and the incoming admirals went through the ritual reading of the transfer of command orders—out loud.

A while later, when Fleet intelligence officer Layton went to Kimmel's office, there was no one there. The Admiral, an orderly told him, had "retired to his quarters."

When colleagues next saw him, he had shed the four-star shoulder boards he had worn as Commander in Chief, Pacific Fleet. The four stars had come with the job, but now he reverted to his permanent rank. He was, once again, a two-star rear admiral.

41

THE DECISION TO relieve Kimmel, the evidence suggests, had not been made by Secretary Knox. Knox directed that he be axed, CNO Stark was to recall, "shortly after coming from the White House." "A commander in chief," he added drily, "would not be removed without the President's permission." The sudden reversal of the assurance to the public that there would be *no* immediate change in command, however, is best explained by the machinations of Secretary of War Stimson, the Cabinet member responsible not for the Navy but for the Army.

Relations between the Army and the Navy had long been uneasy at best. This was very much the case in the aftermath of Pearl Harbor when, behind the scenes, finger-pointing began. In his diary entry of December 11th, Stimson had written that there was "bitterness on both sides over the failure at Hawaii . . . The younger and less responsible, and some of the irresponsible older men, are all trying to throw the burden off on the other Department." Later, in another journal entry, he wrote scornfully that the Navy was "shaken and panic-stricken after the catastrophe."

On the 11th, when Knox was far away starting his flying visit to Hawaii, Stimson had told the press it was "no time for accusations of blame . . . Anything like that, it seems to me, is a sign of an immature government." This statement, however, was less than forthright. Army records show that the previous day, well before any probe of Short's competence or incompetence, orders had been issued that the General be replaced. The fact that a replacement was on the way, Stimson told Roosevelt, was a "most confidential" matter, which "nothing should be said about."

Stimson evidently felt, though, that replacing Short would suggest that the Army rather than the Navy was deemed to have been responsible for the disaster. "My opinion," he told Roosevelt, "is that the housecleaning . . . should be synchronized with a similar housecleaning in the Navy command, and all announced at the same time."

So it was that, at the request not of his Navy superiors but of the Secretary of War and before any assessment of blame—Kimmel came to be relieved of his command.

During the wait for Justice Roberts and the members of the commission to arrive, the Admiral's mood fluctuated. Though he had half-expected to be relieved, the emotional effect of the reality swiftly became evident. Poco Smith, who knew him as well as anyone on the team, noticed that Kimmel had become unusually quiet, looked depressed. The old confidence had gone out of him. Patrol Wing 2's operations officer Logan Ramsey, a mere lieutenant commander, was astonished to be consulted by the Admiral about material he was preparing for the Roberts Commission.

From Washington, CNO Stark had forwarded a favorable comment on the Admiral in the *Congressional Record* along with a scrawled note: "Keep cheerful, good luck, we'll fight it out . . . Betty."

After the announcement that Kimmel had been replaced, and that there was to be an investigation, the chirpiness evaporated. "Dear Kimmel," Stark wrote on the 17th, "I wish there was something I could do for you, both officially and personally, but I know you will keep your chin up. My best to all hands, and good luck."

The CNO had always been something of a contradiction, a man who daily made tough decisions in his capacity as head of the Navy, yet mixed professional exchanges with chummy repartee. Just after sending the first of the notes cited here, he also fired off an effusive letter to Roosevelt:

Dear Mr. President:

I told Jack to tell you this morning, and I have been thinking about it seriously in these past tense days:

You are not only the most important man to the United
States today, but to the world. If anything should happen to
you, it would be a catastrophe. I do not say this to you because of my own personal relationship, but as a cold-blooded
fact.

I have said if I were Hitler and were timing it, and he
probably has timed it, that I would have ready a spectacular
raid on the United States—Washington, New York, or somewhere. Because he knows as well as any man what it would
mean were anything to happen to you.

Please, Mister, let Ben Moreell or somebody provide, and
provide as quickly as possible, a place where, in case of an
air raid or any other disturbance, not only your safety, but
the precious hours of sleep which you need and which are
probably too few, would be provided for against any disturbance of any kind, so far as we can humanly make it possible.

Sincerely,
BETTY

Stimson, at the War Department, was less than enthusiastic
about Stark. Of all Roosevelt's advisers, he had written in his journal, the Chief of Naval Operations was the "weakest one."

As the jockeying for influence went on in Washington, Kimmel—
toppled from his post—struggled to keep his emotional balance.
As he had been for the best part of a year, the Admiral was far
from his family. His wife Dorothy was living at an apartment hotel in Long Beach, California. Though the couple still maintained
a house on the East Coast, and though she was still separated by

more than two thousand miles from her husband in Hawaii, she felt somehow closer to him there.

Dorothy had spent much of her time in Long Beach with two other Navy wives, both also married to admirals serving at Pearl Harbor. One of them, Inez Kidd, was now a widow. Her husband Isaac had been on the bridge on December 7th when a Japanese bomb killed him, the ship's captain, and 1,175 others in the single cataclysmic explosion of the *Arizona*.

Dorothy and Kimmel had last seen each other in June, and then only briefly, when he was on the way back to Hawaii from his flying visit to Washington. The couple had for a long time barely seen their children at all. Manning was on the East Coast, waiting for a new submarine, on which he would serve as engineering officer, to be ready for action. Tom, who was executive officer aboard the submarine USS *S-40*, based in the Philippines, had been ordered to sea on the outbreak of war. He would soon be involved in dangerous hunt-and-be-hunted exchanges with Japanese warships. The one son able to respond effectively to news of the attack on Pearl Harbor had been twenty-year-old Ned, by then in his senior year at Princeton.

Ned had hurried across the country to California by train to be with his mother. Aware that there had been many casualties at Pearl, he would remember, he at first had no way of knowing whether his father was dead or alive. When he arrived to join Dorothy, he was carrying a newspaper with the headline "Japs Say Admiral Kimmel Killed."

On December 18th, having learned that his father had been removed from command, Manning wrote:

Dear Dad,
    There is so little to say at a time like this. But I do want you to know that I'm sure that your part of the job has been "well done"! My complete confidence and belief in you has not been shaken a bit, and I think you are the grandest Dad in the world.
                                                    MANNING

In a time of slow basic communications—there was no easy long-distance phone contact for most ordinary citizens—Kimmel family members had no clear idea how things were developing. In a letter to his in-laws later that month, Manning would write: "We have heard from several sources that Dad's reputation hasn't suffered, and that Secretary Knox doesn't feel that Dad's action in any way can bring discredit to him. But I imagine we will know more about this later."

In another letter, Manning told his father that Secretary Knox had sent word through an intermediary that he thought "no discredit would be attached to you as a result of the investigation."

42

"THE TRUTH, THE WHOLE TRUTH, and nothing but the truth," the *San Francisco Chronicle* declared, was what one could expect of the Roberts Commission. "Whatever it recommends will be just to the men concerned and fair and constructive for the efficiency and morale of the Army and the Navy." This, the first of what would be many inquiries and formal reviews, was conducted at a time when attention was riveted on the disaster. As a result, what the Roberts Commission would conclude was to be fundamental to what the nation came to believe.

Aside from Roberts himself, the Commission had four members: two from the Navy and two from the Army. From the Navy, there were retired admirals William Standley and Joseph Reeves; from the Army, Major General Frank McCoy, retired, and Brigadier General Joseph McNarney, who was still on active duty.

Whatever the probity of these individuals—and future criticism of some of them would be savage—the way the commissioners operated was flawed from the start. First, though one member was absent, they went to the War Department to receive directions on their task from Secretary of War Stimson. Knox, who was also present, briefed them on his visit to Hawaii. Then, over two days, they talked with Chief of Staff Marshall, CNO Stark, Admiral Turner, ONI Director Wilkinson, and G-2's General Miles and Colonel Bratton.

These headquarters officers were in a position to discuss vitally important information and greatly influence the Commission's direction. It was also entirely possible that they themselves might be found to bear responsibility for the failure at Pearl. Yet what they shared with the commissioners at this formative stage was neither said under oath nor formally transcribed. They could say or choose not to say whatever they wished, in the knowledge that it could not be held against them.

The Commission's Admiral Standley was to become its lone, vocal dissenter. Of its work in Washington, he would recall, he was "shocked" at the "irregularity of the procedure and the reliance on unsworn testimony." As a result of his objections, the way was cleared to subpoena witnesses and administer oaths. Even so, the Commission's procedure in Hawaii, where it questioned Kimmel, Short, and others, remained dubious.

The Pearl Harbor witnesses were sworn but not accorded various rights. Under naval regulations, Kimmel was to note, he would have had "the right to have counsel, to be present during the testimony of witnesses, to cross-examine other witnesses, and introduce evidence." He did not have counsel to advise and represent him when he appeared before the Commission. Fleet Marine officer Colonel Omar Pfeiffer, who had a law degree and volunteered to help, thought the proceedings unjust. "Admiral Kimmel," Pfeiffer would recall, "attempted to muster his forces to present his position and case in a fair and judicial manner . . . But the Commission settled the matter of counsel by prohibiting it and conducted a 'star-chamber' proceeding . . . Kimmel was not given the right of cross-examination, and was permitted only one person who could hand him documents that he might want while testifying."

That service was provided by Rear Admiral Robert Theobald, who had commanded one of Kimmel's destroyer flotillas. Preparing testimony, Theobald said years later, "was rendered most difficult for both of us by our total inability to find out what procedure the Roberts Commission was following."

During one of the hearings, Justice Roberts observed that the Commission was not a "trial of the Admiral, in any sense." No charges had been brought against Kimmel. Theobald, however, thought it "incomprehensible" that Kimmel was not given the rights of a defendant. He had, after all, been "partially condemned in the public eye as soon as the events of December 7th 1941 were known."

General Short had his staff available to assist and speak for him; by contrast, many key members of Kimmel's former team could not appear at the hearings—they were away at sea with the Fleet. Communications officer Maurice Curts, who was available, reportedly wanted to testify but was denied the opportunity.

Even when Kimmel was done testifying, his tribulations continued. "The stenographic staff hired by the Roberts Commission," Admiral Theobald wrote, "was unbelievably inept. When Admiral Kimmel's recorded testimony was submitted to him for verification, it was found to be filled with errors and at times was completely unintelligible . . . The questions and answers were frequently so badly garbled as to make no sense." So many errors were found, Theobald said, that it took two days and nights to work through the transcripts.

Admiral Standley recalled that "Admiral Kimmel asked permission to correct his testimony," but "the Commission voted to keep the record as originally made . . . At my urgent insistence, the Commission did finally authorize Admiral Kimmel's corrected testimony to be attached to the record as an addendum."

There came a point during the hearings when what Kimmel saw as unjust treatment drove him to distraction. Major Brooke Allen, a Hawaiian Air Force officer assisting with scheduling, recalled an encounter with the Admiral outside the hearing room. "What are they trying to do?" Kimmel asked, grabbing Allen by the shoulders: "Crucify me?"

The commissioners worked on in Hawaii until January 9th. Then they flew back to Washington to take some limited testimony, sworn this time, from senior headquarters officers. For reasons of national security, they allowed General Marshall to review and edit one of the commissioners' draft findings. One night, Stimson noted in his diary, he "sat up until twelve o'clock talking over with Roberts the views he had formed."

At Pearl Harbor, meanwhile, Kimmel's permanent replacement as commander in chief of the Fleet, Admiral Chester Nimitz, had taken command. Nimitz, who was to go on to defeat the Japanese in battle after battle and become an American hero, had let Kimmel know even before leaving Washington that he had the greatest respect for him.

By the time he reached Hawaii, Nimitz was becoming convinced it was wrong to blame Kimmel for the catastrophe. He told Kimmel on arrival, "The same thing could have happened to anybody."

Unlike those who thought Kimmel should have had his ships at sea on December 7th, Nimitz came to believe this would have risked even greater disaster. "Instead of having our ships sunk in the shallow protected water of Pearl Harbor," he wrote years later, "they could have been sunk in deep water—and we would have lost *all* of our trained men."

Nimitz retained Kimmel's headquarters staff and reissued, without change, the Kimmel standing order that prescribed appropriate states of readiness for warships in port. No information his predecessor had received from any source before the attack, he was to say, would have been cause to interrupt the urgent training Kimmel's force was undergoing in early December.

In a letter written as Kimmel prepared to leave Hawaii, Nimitz evinced no expectation that the current investigation would be definitive. "None of us," he wrote, "know all the facts connected with the Pearl Harbor incident, and I am doubtful personally whether all the facts will ever be known . . . "

Kimmel's next-door neighbor, Navy wife Grace Earle, would recall how—just before the Admiral left Hawaii—the officers who had been his staff came to say good-bye, then departed. "The young Marine sentry on duty said to me, 'Please go in. The old man is all alone' . . . I did, and he looked so forlorn I wanted to hug him."

Loneliness had added to the stress. Mail to Hawaii had been delayed in recent weeks, and supportive messages from family members had not reached him. He had, however, been in contact with his wife. Dorothy summed up her husband's personal tragedy in a letter to a sister-in-law. Life, she wrote, had become "one black cloud . . . Kimmel's lifetime work and brilliant career just wrecked, all in a few hours."

Kimmel left Hawaii for the mainland on January 14th. Admiral Harold Train, whose wife May had been a constant friend to Dorothy in California, accompanied Kimmel to the plane. "He told me," Train remembered, "that the United States was now at war and he didn't intend to do anything to vindicate himself as long as we were at war."

A MERE TWENTY-ONE PAGES LONG, the Roberts Report was delivered to President Roosevelt on January 24th, seven weeks after the Japanese attack. The accompanying testimony and exhibits, amounting to more than two thousand further pages, were to be withheld from the public until after the war.

The findings section of the Roberts Report opened with a vindication of the performance before Pearl Harbor of senior members of the government, the Navy, and the Army. Chief of Staff Marshall and Chief of Naval Operations Stark, it said, had fulfilled their command responsibility by sending appropriate warnings to Hawaii.

Not so Kimmel and Short. According to the report, they had not responded adequately to Washington's warnings. The Navy's state of readiness had not been "such as was required." Had orders been complied with, the report said, its distant air reconnaissance would have been maintained. As for the Army, Short's No. 1 Alert—an alert level restricted to countering possible sabotage— had not been adequate. The Army's radar should have been fully operating. The report censured both the Army and the Navy, in spite of the Navy's record in that regard, for the performance of their antiaircraft defense.

The most serious charge, though, was that the commanders at Hawaii had—according to the Commission—failed to "confer and cooperate" on their response to warnings issued by Washington. While acknowledging that the December 7th warning of possible imminent action had arrived too late to be of any use, the Commission said the warning had been "but an added precaution." Defense of Pearl Harbor had been less than effective, the report stated, because Kimmel and Short had failed to take adequate precautionary measures.

The Commission found both commanders culpable on the specific issues they had been asked to consider. The alleged failure to confer, the report concluded, amounted to "dereliction of duty." An alleged failure "properly to evaluate the seriousness of the situation," amounted to their having made "errors of judgment."

President Roosevelt perused the report with care, according to Roberts. "He read it line by line . . . carried his finger on the pages . . . Two or three times he would shake his head and say 'tsk, tsk,' or something of that sort." Then he asked, "Is there anything in this report that might give our enemies information they ought not to have?" Told there was not, the President said he saw no reason not to make the report public. Then he called in an aide, Marvin McIntyre, and said: "Mac, give that to the Sunday papers in full."

The headline in the *New York Times* the next morning read:

ROBERTS BOARD BLAMES KIMMEL AND SHORT: WARNINGS TO DEFEND HAWAII NOT HEEDED

Across the nation, the press howled with outrage. People had sensed from the start, one newspaper said, that "someone had been asleep at the switch." Roberts and his Commission had now confirmed that impression. Judging from their report, one Washington columnist wrote, there had been "practically no cooperation between Kimmel and Short." Another paper demanded that both commanders be "shorn of their rank and drummed out of the service . . . Those entrusted with the defense of Hawaii were the enemy's best ally."

The most serious charge, "dereliction of duty," seems to have been gratuitous, woven into the report because it had been a specific part of the Commission's brief to rule on the issue. Not one of the official probes that were to follow—over a period of more than half a century—would repeat such a charge. Nevertheless, once leveled in the Roberts Report, it was to linger over their reputations for the rest of their lives and long afterward.

Only a month after publication of the report, the Commission's Admiral Standley stepped out of line. The impression given to the public that the Army and Navy had not cooperated at Pearl Harbor, he told the Associated Press, was a "gross misinterpretation." He went on to say:

> The impression has been created that the relations between General Short and Admiral Kimmel were so estranged that they passed to opposite sides of the street to avoid meeting each other. The exact contrary was the fact, a careful reading of the report will show, that Kimmel and Short conferred for three hours on November 27th, and that they conferred again on December 1st—and again on the 2nd and on the 4th . . . Cooperation between Army and Navy was at the fullest—you can make that as strong as you want to. That was the fact.

Shortly after giving this interview, Standley left to become U.S. ambassador to the Soviet Union. According to his granddaughter Helen writing after his death, only President Roosevelt's personal intervention had prevented Standley from filing a dissenting minority report. The word in the family, the granddaughter said, was that he was offered the ambassadorship to Moscow "to get him as far away from Washington as possible."

While he was an ambassador, Standley made no further public statement about the Roberts inquiry. He took time, however, to respond privately to a letter from Delia Kimmel, a distant relative of the Admiral:

> I can well appreciate your feelings in regard to the treatment of Admiral Kimmel . . . Those of us who, like Admi-

ral Kimmel, were placed in responsible positions and who persistently but vainly urged and pleaded for a proper state of readiness, knew full well that—when the crisis came— we would be the ones to pay the penalty . . . It was inevitable that the doctrines of this era would eventually lead to crucifixions . . . Admiral Kimmel was a fine officer and he was doing a grand job and deserved a better fate.

A decade after the war, when Standley came to write his memoirs, he would return to this theme. Without clearing Kimmel and Short of all responsibility, he felt they had been "martyred." During the Roberts Commission's deliberations, he recalled, he had "acrimonious arguments" with his colleagues over holding the commanders solely responsible. He also addressed the report's most damaging charge against the commanders—"dereliction." In his opinion, "both would have been cleared of the charge of neglect of duty" had they been brought to trial. The years that were to pass before there was any public investigation, he concluded, "served to identify them in the public mind as jointly responsible for the disaster."

The Roberts Report, Standley wrote, had not presented the whole story. "Many sins of omission in the picture were omitted from our findings . . ." The Commission's instructions, he explained, had "precluded any investigations into the activities of high civilian officials in Washington . . . and such decisions or actions as they may have taken to inform the Hawaiian commanders as to their immediate danger or to order them to assume an adequate state of alertness."

Standley concluded, "Army and Naval officers and high civilian officials equally or more culpable," when compared with Kimmel and Short, had been permitted—unlike Kimmel and Short—to continue to serve with distinction during the war. He named, in particular, the two men who had headed the Navy and the Army—Admiral Stark and General Marshall—because of "all of the information available to them in Washington."

"All the information available to them . . ." Thereby hangs a tragic tale—of the honor of two good men jettisoned in the name of military necessity.

"The evidence," the *Roberts Report says* on its first page, "touches [on] subjects which in the national interest should remain secret." After all the years and all the investigations, however, it is still not clear what secrets had been entrusted to Justice Roberts and his commissioners.

The day Roberts was appointed, FBI Director Hoover had sent him a memo comprising "investigative suggestions." One referred to a lead the FBI had received, that coded intercepts—obtained in Hawaii but deciphered in Washington—had contained "substantially the complete plans for the attack on Pearl Harbor."

Given that the source was the Director of the FBI, Roberts did give this some attention. In Hawaii, the Commission's record shows, he asked Army intelligence officers whether they knew anything of such a coded intercept, and they said they did not. Did the Commission follow up when it interviewed military personnel in Washington? Questioned during the probe by Congress' Joint Committee in 1946, Roberts replied: "We asked for all the messages there were about any broken codes and we were told we had had all they had—except this MAGIC thing."

Pressed, he said he had known "that the Army or Navy or State Department had been cracking a super code of the Japanese for weeks or months and that they had been taking off all kinds of information . . . They did not show us the messages, any of them, and I didn't ask them to." Asked again, he insisted, "The MAGIC was not shown to us." And, astonishingly: "I would not have bothered to read it if it had been shown to us."

Instead, Roberts said, the commissioners had merely "asked the War Department and the Navy Department to tell us what they got from that and they told us." In an internal report at the time, Naval Intelligence director Wilkinson said he and others present had discussed MAGIC "freely" with the Roberts Commission.

This, on its face, could mean that commissioners were briefed on any number of the many MAGIC intercepts that had been de-crypted and circulated in 1941. It could in theory mean that the Commission was told about all the intercepted Japanese diplo-matic traffic—including the messages to and from the embassy in Washington about deadlines and deception, and the reports from the consulate in Hawaii reflecting intense intelligence interest in Pearl Harbor.

Roberts, however, did not admit to having been told any of this. The only intercept the Commission had been told about, he said on another occasion, was the "one o'clock" message of Decem-ber 7th—the message that led to a warning being sent, too late, to the commanders in Hawaii.

Roberts maintained, moreover, that he did not know that the President himself, as well as key government Secretaries, Chief of Staff Marshall, and CNO Stark, had access to MAGIC. He did not know that, he said, "and would not have been interested" because his one concern had been to establish whether or not officials and military men in Washington had done their duty by sharing and passing on intelligence about a threat.

These answers are puzzling. If Roberts and his colleagues had not seen the MAGIC intelligence for themselves, how could they state in their report that the civilian and military leadership had responsibly passed it on?

Over and above all this, something else, something with fatal implications for Kimmel's case, emerged during the later con-gressional probe. During their unsworn, unrecorded interviews with the Roberts Commission, it emerged, two of the Navy's most senior commanders in Washington apparently gave the commis-sioners the impression—entirely inaccurately—that MAGIC had been shared with Admiral Kimmel.

War Plans chief Admiral Turner was to testify that he had "prob-ably" told the commissioners that Kimmel had been "perfectly fa-miliar with all the intelligence information," MAGIC included. He had done so, he said, because he had been under the mistaken impression that MAGIC *was* being shared with Kimmel. Naval Intelligence director Captain Wilkinson, for his part, had noted in writing—following his meeting with the commissioners—that he had told them Kimmel "had as much information as we had."

Both Turner and Wilkinson may have said what they did say because—such was the confusion on the subject—they really thought Kimmel had been supplied with MAGIC. In fact, of course, he had not.

It would be years before Kimmel discovered that the Commission had been given this totally inaccurate information. He was aghast, appalled that the commissioners had not asked him just what intelligence he had received from Washington.

"It is impossible to imagine," he wrote, "how a just and honest allocation of responsibility for the Pearl Harbor disaster can be made without a thorough knowledge of the Japanese intercepts and of their distribution."

44

"THIS PEARL HARBOR business," the Navy's incoming commander in chief U.S. Fleet said, "has a terrible smell. Something went completely wrong with our intelligence activities." Admiral Ernest King, whom the President had elevated from his post as commander in chief of the Atlantic Fleet a few weeks after Pearl Harbor, ordered an immediate in-house review. "I want you to make a study," he told a senior aide; "interrogate people in the Department and come up with a report." He wanted results, and fast.

There was much that needed fixing—not least where MAGIC was concerned. It may initially have seemed appropriate to restrict circulation of the intercepted messages to the President, selected senior civilian officials, Chief of Staff Marshall, and CNO Stark, but that system had proved haphazard and inefficient. Sharing a torrent of raw intercepts with only a few overworked men had diminished the usefulness of a vital asset.

Not enough properly qualified personnel, moreover, had been tasked to evaluate the take from MAGIC. That, and the pressure of work, had meant that important intercepts had lain ignored and unbroken—notably in the final days before the Pearl Harbor attack. The insistence on secrecy, meanwhile, had also resulted in vital information not reaching some of those who most needed it.

Even before Admiral King was brought back to Washington from the Atlantic, the Navy was making major changes. Previously, War Plans chief Turner had had an iron grip on the intelligence reaching the Fleet. Within a week of Pearl Harbor, however, ONI Director Wilkinson was able to reassert his department's role in the effort to "collect, collate and reconcile all enemy information . . . whether directly by despatch or whether obtained by other means (including MAGIC) and to send out this information to the commanders-in-chief." Radical changes, which were to lead to important successes, were also being made in the Navy's codebreaking units. One success, the victory at Midway in the summer of 1942, turned the tide of the war in the Pacific.

The Army also made major changes. Three weeks after the strike on Hawaii, just as the Navy's Admiral King had done, Secretary of War Stimson commissioned an urgent study of how the Army could "improve the organization of our MAGIC information in such a way as to make it more valuable than it is at present." The Wall Street lawyer recruited to conduct the study, Alfred McCormack, proved enormously successful—he was later to be inducted into the Army as a lieutenant colonel and go on to head a key element of the Military Intelligence Service. No longer would it do, McCormack declared, for Stimson and Chief of Staff Marshall to have their time "wasted in reading odd and unchecked bits of information." The material they received was to be "carefully checked, evaluated and supplemented by all possible sources of intelligence."

Within three months of Pearl Harbor, McCormack's unit would be producing a daily summary and analysis of incoming MAGIC for key recipients. The Army was soon to take over all diplomatic MAGIC traffic—freeing up Navy cryptanalysts to concentrate on breaking key Japanese naval codes.

The changes in how MAGIC was handled also brought unprecedented rewards. In Europe, the U.S. high command was to learn of Hitler's military intentions before his forces moved. American and British forces were able to calibrate the timing of Allied offensives sooner than would otherwise have been feasible. Access to the intelligence gained from enemies' coded messages, the author Bruce Lee has written, "gave us the vital edge." Codebreaking has been credited with saving countless American lives. Unnamed "authoritative sources," quoted in the *New York Times* when peace came, said it "shortened the war by a year."

These were the MAGIC miracles to come. McCormack also looked backward, at what the earlier inefficient handling of

MAGIC had spawned. "When the sudden attack on Pearl Harbor occurred," he wrote, "it became apparent that the event had been clearly foreshadowed in the Japanese traffic of 1941. The Secretary of War and no doubt others then concluded that the traffic had not been given sufficiently close attention."

To America's terrible cost—and Admiral Kimmel's.

Another internal study, commissioned by the Office of Naval Communications in mid-1942, threw light on what might have been had MAGIC material been adequately analyzed and distributed in the fall of the previous year. Compiled by a junior officer, John Connorton, a former assistant history professor at Fordham University, it was—if not perfect—revelatory. Compiled as it was under conditions of tight security, few saw the study at the time.

Had Connorton's report been made public in 1942—and had Americans learned that none of the MAGIC information it contained was shared with Kimmel and Short before the strike—it would have made nonsense of the notion that they alone bore responsibility for the disaster. Though there had been intelligence-gathering exchanges between Tokyo and its agents at naval bases at Manila, Seattle, and Panama, there had been more with Hawaii. Only consulate spy Yoshikawa in Hawaii, moreover, had been tasked to divide the harbor into specific areas and send a stream of reports on where individual ships were positioned.

"It can safely be said," Connorton wrote, that the Japanese "had determined to attack Pearl Harbor as early as September 24th, if not before. Evidence for this last statement comes from the very detailed plans requested from Japanese agents in Honolulu, and the minute attention paid to every inch of Pearl Harbor in the instructions from Tokyo."

Later in the war, Connorton took part in the writing of a secret, five-volume expanded study: *The "Magic" Background of Pearl Harbor.* He retired in 1946 with the rank of lieutenant commander, and went on to become a city administrator and deputy mayor of New York City. When the second MAGIC report was made public in the late 1970s, National Security Agency Director Bobby Inman saw to it that Connorton received leather-bound copies.

"Pearl Harbor," Connorton wrote to Inman then, had "proved that too much security can lead to obscurity . . . We had a problem in even admitting the existence of the intelligence, never mind discussing its results." Admiral Kimmel, he told his eldest son, had been the "scapegoat for the Pearl Harbor attack—and the failures of many."

Neither Connorton's work nor the Army's McCormack report was made available to Kimmel during the numerous official investigations into Pearl Harbor or later, when he was fighting to clear his name. Not until 1953 would he become aware that Connorton's study existed, and he was denied access to it even then. The Admiral apparently never did learn of the McCormack report, which was not released until 1981.

Within less than a year of the strike, secret studies had handed senior Navy and Army officials irrefutable documentary evidence that MAGIC had been inefficiently handled in the months before Pearl Harbor. One of the studies had, for the first time, specifically pointed to the telltale messages between Tokyo and its Honolulu consulate. The information, however, was buried by the bureaucracy—and for years would stay buried.

"DON'T WORRY ABOUT our finding duty for you," Stark had written before Kimmel left Hawaii. The internal report the CNO filed on the Admiral, even following the Roberts Commission's findings, brimmed with confidence: "I have always considered Admiral Kimmel an outstanding officer in ability, integrity and character. I still do." Kimmel himself expected that he would soon be moving on to a new assignment. He spent a few days with Dorothy in Long Beach, then went north with her to his new temporary posting in San Francisco.

There was to be no new assignment for him or for General Short. The General, left to read in the newspapers of the Roberts Commission's "dereliction of duty" verdict, fended off a deluge of calls from reporters. He was, he remembered, "completely dumbfounded. To be accused of dereliction of duty after almost forty years of loyal and competent service was beyond my comprehension. I immediately called General Marshall on the telephone . . . I asked him what I should do, having the country and the war in mind, should I retire?" He replied, "Stand pat but if it becomes necessary I will use this conversation as authority." Short, however, did not "stand pat." That same day, January 25th, he mailed a formal application for retirement, for use at Marshall's discretion.

The following day, the Chief of Staff sent a memo to Stimson that seems out of kilter—given the affection that CNO Stark had long claimed to have for Kimmel. In light of Short's resignation, Marshall wrote, Stark now proposed "to communicate this fact to Admiral Kimmel in the hope that Kimmel will likewise apply for retirement."

Hours later, a phone conversation took place between Washington and San Francisco, an exchange that—very unusually—was recorded.

> *Admiral Jacobs* [*chief of the department dealing with personnel matters*]: Has Kimmel returned yet?
> *Admiral Greenslade* [*commandant in San Francisco*]: Yes, he's here.
> *Jacobs:* I've just been discussing the matter . . . with Admiral Stark, and they want Kimmel kept in a leave status until further disposition is made of the report . . . I was asked by Admiral Stark to inform you to tell Kimmel that General Short has applied for retirement.
> *Greenslade:* In leave status—you want me to tell him that?
> *Jacobs:* Yes.

Within hours, Greenslade duly passed on what Kimmel was to recall as "an official communication from the Navy Department . . . that General Short had submitted a request for retirement. That was the message."

For the Admiral, the suggestion was shattering news. "Up to that time," he would say, "I had not considered submitting any request for retirement; it never entered my head. I thought the matter over and decided that, if that was the way the Navy Department wanted to arrange this affair, I would not stand in their way."

He complied at once. The request for retirement, dated that same day, the 26th, reads:

> After forty-one years and eight months' service in the United States Navy, I hereby request that I be placed on the retired list . . . I hold myself in readiness to perform any duty to which I may be assigned.*

---

* Under U.S. Navy regulations, a retiree could be ordered back to active duty in time of war.

The transcript of a further phone call between Greenslade and Jacobs the following day makes it clear that Greenslade believed the highest authorities in the Navy Department "desired" a request for retirement from Kimmel. He duly reported to Jacobs that he now had the request in his hands.

A series of Machiavellian exchanges followed. Only twenty-four hours after telling Marshall he hoped Kimmel would retire—and now that he had confirmation that Kimmel had done just that— Stark rushed to backpedal. In a message to the commandant at San Francisco, he wrote: "I most positively do not want to influence Kimmel in his action." If the Admiral retired because he thought that was what was wanted of him, he went on, that could still be "corrected."

In another letter to Kimmel, Stark said he had shown the President himself the Admiral's message—sent soon after Pearl Harbor—saying that what happened to him was of little importance, that the one thing that mattered was "what is best for the country." People in Washington, he said, realized that Kimmel was "sitting on a question mark." No "definite action" had yet been taken.

The issue preoccupying the Washington leadership, though, was one Stark did not mention in his to-and-fro with Kimmel— court-martial. Merely to accept retirement by Kimmel and Short, Stimson had noted in his diary, would pose a political risk: "It might give the impression that we were trying to let off these people without punishment because we felt guilty ourselves." The President's view, he noted two days later, was to "wait about a week," then accept the retirements "with the distinct condition . . . that this does not in any way bar a subsequent court martial . . . The reason for this is the impossibility of a court-martial without the disclosure of military secrets."

"Court-martial," Stark wrote in a memorandum to Secretary Knox on January 31st, "is a practical impossibility at this time, because it would almost certainly disclose military secrets which must be kept from the enemy."

MAGIC—the miracle and the problem—in the end superseded all other considerations. Were Kimmel and Short to face trial in a military court, as the logical outcome of Roberts' finding of "dereliction of duty," witnesses testifying under oath might well reveal what Washington had known and the commanders had not. That would benefit the defense but be catastrophic for national security.

In San Francisco, waiting to know whether he would be recalled to duty, Kimmel was in a painful position. When reporters discovered that he and Dorothy were staying at the Fairmont Hotel, he brushed off questions with, "I don't want to see anyone and I can't see anyone. I am waiting for the Navy Department to tell me what to do next." Once his location became known, the couple began to suffer harassment. Anonymous callers phoned their room; other people sent letters, often unsigned, or slid notes under the door.

Local commandant Admiral Greenslade took pity on them. In a handwritten letter to Stark, he reported that Kimmel was "brooding, of course, trying to see bits of clear sky through the clouds. Mrs. Kimmel is with him . . . As you know, he is anxious to have this whole affair officially closed for good of country and of Navy."

Greenslade had a worthy suggestion. "Would it not be possible," he wrote, "for the President and Sec. Nav. to say something like this: 'We all—Administration to individual—feel a share of responsibility in the Pearl Harbor tragedy, and partake in it with those who—as the responsible military commanders—were relieved of their commands in the interests of military efficiency and morale? . . . The frank and high-spirited attitude of those commanders is worthy of recognition. And they will give active, responsible duty subsequent to acceptance of their retirement."

Some hope of that. In response, Stark hedged, mixing in a dollop of the customary breeziness. "I have every sympathy in the world for that fine shipmate of ours—and just as much respect as ever . . . I realize that whatever is done will have to go to the Secretary and possibly to the President. I feel, too, that their attitude is to cushion the blow . . . but there are so many angles to this—Naval, public, political . . . I just hope that Kimmel's great strength of character, his fundamental common sense, his fine fiber . . . will stand him in great stead to meet the tough situation he is facing."

Stark evidently had a sense of what was coming, and that it was not good. He would later claim that he had pleaded Kimmel's case with Roosevelt, urged that he be given a new command. Perhaps, though, Stark himself was no longer in the loop.

On the same day that Stark wrote his "shipmate" letter, Secretary Knox formally accepted Kimmel's retirement—Short would receive a similar letter—with a proviso. Retirement was approved "without condonation of any offense or prejudice to future disciplinary action."

In plain English, they could both be court-martialed.

46

KIMMEL'S SIXTIETH BIRTHDAY was only days away when he received this latest blow. Ever sentimental, Stark dashed off three letters in forty-eight hours. "On this occasion," he wrote, "instead of a wish for a happy birthday, knowing as I do that it will be just as happy as you choose to make it, and instead of wishing you the happiest year just ahead . . . I wish for you amid the clouds of uncertainty, **COURAGE**." Multiple aphorisms about courage, strength and wisdom followed.

In one of the trio of letters, Stark quoted Secretary Knox as having said lately, of the Admiral: "As for Kimmel, he has conducted himself in an exemplary fashion since this thing happened." To which view, Stark added, he thought the entire Navy "would give a hearty 'Aye, Aye!'"

Pending "something definite," Stark encouraged Kimmel, "there is no reason why you should not settle yourself in a quiet nook somewhere and let Old Father Time help this entire situation, which I feel he will . . . We realize how tough it is."

It does not seem likely that the decision makers in Washington knew just how tough it was to be Kimmel at that time. Of the letters he received that month, two were from judges. Twain Michelsen, of the San Francisco municipal court, wrote:

Dear Sir,

I am confident that the people of America will never forget the culpability that has been attached to both yourself and Short. Equally sure am I that history will forever point an accurate finger at both of you, and to your memory, when each has passed to the realm where so many of our men were so suddenly hurled because of your joint neglect and utter stupidity.

Surely, there isn't much for you and Short to live for—unless a general court martial would bring forth a page from the shameful chapter of Pearl Harbor . . . and thus, however possible, clean from the hands of both of you the blood of your unsuspecting victims . . .

> Sincerely . . .

From Saint Louis came a letter from George Mix, a former circuit judge:

Sir,

As an American citizen, taxpayer, graduate of Yale University, and one whose ancestors have fought in all the wars in which this country has been engaged, I suggest that *instead of your cowardly act in asking to be relieved from duty and placed on the taxpayers' payroll at $6000.00 per year, and in view of the millions of dollars of taxpayers' property destroyed at Pearl Harbor by reason of your carelessness, negligence and thoughtlessness,* that you try to show that you are a real man by using a pistol and ending your existence, *as you are certainly of no use to yourself nor the American people . . .*

On February 22nd, Kimmel wrote to Stark. The formal notice to him that retirement was conditional on "future disciplinary action," he surmised, was something that would shortly be "published to the country." He gave vent to his feelings:

Dear Betty,

I stand ready at any time to accept the consequences of my acts. I do not wish to embarrass the government in the conduct of the War. I do feel, however, that my crucifixion before the public has about reached the limit. I am in daily receipt of letters from irresponsible people all over the country taking me to task and even threatening to kill me. I am not particularly concerned except as it shows the effect on the public of articles published about me . . .

I have kept my mouth shut and propose to do so as long as it is humanly possible.

I regret the losses at Pearl Harbor just as keenly, or perhaps more keenly, than any other American citizen. I wish that I had been smarter than I was and able to foresee what happened on December 7th. I devoted all my energies to the job and made the dispositions which appeared to me to be called for. I cannot reproach myself for any lack of effort.

I will not comment on the Report of the Commission, but you probably know what I think of it. I will say in passing that I was not made an interested party or a defendant.

All this I have been willing to accept for the good of the country, out of my loyalty to the Nation, and to await the judgment of history when the facts can be published.

But I do think that in all justice the Department should do nothing further to inflame the public against me . . . You must appreciate that the beating I have taken leaves very little that can be added to my burden.

I appreciate your efforts on my behalf and will always value your friendship, which is a precious thing to me.

With kindest regards always,
H. E. KIMMEL

A week later, newspapers across the country carried headlines and stories that were as damaging as he had feared. In the *Washington Post*: "Short, Kimmel Must Stand Trial for Pearl Harbor Debacle; Dereliction Charged." In the *New York Times*, on the front page above the fold: "Kimmel and Short Will Stand Trial; Date Is Undecided. Courts-Martial on Charges of Dereliction of Duty at Pearl Harbor Ordered. Based on Roberts Report."

"The trial upon these charges," the *Times* quoted Secretary

Knox as saying, "would not be held until such a time as the public interest and safety would permit." Meanwhile, charges were being prepared.

By the time the news broke, Kimmel had left San Francisco and retreated to the family homestead in Henderson, Kentucky. A local reporter got through to him there and read out the news bulletin over the phone. "There was no answer," the reporter remembered, "but there was sound—the sound of deep, steady breathing." After a while, when the Admiral had still not spoken, the reporter asked if he was all right. Kimmel said he was, and asked, "Was there anything else?" The reporter asked for a comment on the news. The Admiral said, "No. Not even to the extent of saying 'No comment.' I thank you for your courtesy." Then he hung up.

The hate mail kept coming, even to Henderson, the home he had effectively left decades earlier. One person, addressing him pointedly as "Ex-Admiral Kimmel," told him to rest assured that "a time will come when you will have to face a tribunal from whose justice there will be no escape . . . and then you will have to answer for your miserable conduct. May the punishment fit the crime!"

Local malice, from the mouth of a senior member of Congress, was soon to make national news. Andrew J. May, a representative from the Admiral's home state who was chairman of the House Military Affairs Committee, said at an Army Day celebration that Kimmel and Short ought to face a "shooting match" court-martial. A "shooting match," according to a local newspaper editor, was "Kentucky language for a lawful execution."

By the time Representative May was sounding off, Kimmel had left Kentucky for Washington. There, in early April 1942, he had a momentous private meeting with Harold Stark. Stark's life had changed too, though in a far gentler way than Kimmel's. The reshuffle at the top after Pearl Harbor, with Admiral King being placed in overall command, had the previous month led to Stark's removal as Chief of Naval Operations. He was instead to become

Commander, Naval Forces Europe. As it would turn out, this would be a vitally important posting. Two years later, Stark would have a key part in coordinating the U.S. Navy's role in the D-Day landings that led to the liberation of Europe.

In the spring of 1942, however, there was no getting away from the fact that he was losing the post of Chief of Naval Operations, the top headquarters job in the Navy. He was the only man in the hierarchy to be removed from his job. In the order for his transfer, Secretary Knox praised Stark to the skies, telling him he was leaving with the good wishes of the "entire establishment."

Not everyone was so polite. "The President," Admiral King would recall, "said he did not give a damn what happened to Stark so long as he was gotten out of Washington as soon as practicable." In a postwar memo, King would indicate that the transfer had been an "administrative action" arising from Stark's role in the Pearl Harbor case.

Stark himself was downcast about the move. "He was hurt, disappointed and crushed," recalled Kathleen Krick, who with her Navy husband had been his longtime friend. "He just didn't believe that he could be treated that way."

It was then, in the early spring of 1942, that Stark phoned Admiral Kimmel to ask him to come to see him at his home in the Spring Valley section of Washington, D.C. Until then, and despite all the trials of recent months, Kimmel still trusted Stark. Their meeting on April 3rd, in the basement of Stark's house, changed everything.

"He was about to leave for Europe," Kimmel would recall years later. "I went up to his house and had breakfast with him . . . just the two of us, and I talked with him for about two hours. When I got through, I knew something was wrong . . . I was able to see that he was holding something out on me."

Aside from giving Kimmel the general impression that he was not being entirely straight with him, Stark posed a question that gave something away. "Stark asked me," Kimmel noted soon afterward, "if we were not intercepting the messages between

Washington and Tokyo during the progress of the negotiations. He presumed I had been getting them."

Kimmel, of course, had seen the content of only a minute number of intercepted messages—for a brief period months before the attack—and the subject had not been the details of the negotiations. For him now, sitting there in the basement with Stark—four months after Pearl Harbor, months during which he had been brought from the peak of his career to utter ignominy—this was a glimpse of the truth for the first time, of the fact that the intercepts had yielded far more than he had known—intelligence that Washington had not shared with him, the commander in chief.

Perhaps, as his question to Kimmel suggested and as other headquarters staffers would claim, Stark had until then genuinely assumed that the Admiral had been receiving MAGIC. What Kimmel would never forgive the former CNO for was that, though Stark learned at their breakfast that day that his commander in chief in the Pacific had not had the benefit of vital intelligence, he then failed to intervene on Kimmel's behalf—to help clear him of the charge of "dereliction of duty."

In the months and years to come, there would be much else Kimmel would not forgive.

Stark went off to the new post in Europe, having been honored with a Gold Star in lieu of a second Distinguished Service Medal. Chief of Staff Marshall, his reputation virtually untouched by the Pearl Harbor debacle, also headed for London, to discuss war plans with Churchill. Kimmel wrote to Navy Personnel, offering to do "any duty to which the Navy Department may see fit to assign me . . . anything to help." Personnel responded with a polite acknowledgment—and no work.

The man who had so recently commanded the Fleet moved with his wife to a modest home in a New York suburb. Using the engineering degree he had earned at the Naval Academy and his knowledge of the Pacific, he secured work with an engineering consultancy firm designing floating dry docks for the Pacific campaign.

Before starting this work, though, Kimmel spent many weeks in the Manhattan office of John Otterson, an old friend and roommate from Academy days who now headed a shipbuilding company. "I spend practically all my time on my own affairs . . . my personal work," he wrote to a brother in Kentucky. He was beginning the fight to restore his personal honor, the struggle to which he would devote the rest of his life.

Later, when Kimmel was representing his employers at an event in Georgia, a reporter tried to ask him about Pearl Harbor. "I'll talk about that plenty," he replied, "when the time comes."

47

THE COMING FOUR years—mid-1942 to mid-1946—were to be nightmarish for Kimmel. Fighting for his good name would take him into a legal and political labyrinth, from passionate hope to something like despair. As he waged his professional struggle, meanwhile, his family was to live through times of pride, anxiety, and devastating grief.

All three sons were now in the Navy, two of them aboard submarines in the Pacific. Manning, soon to become executive officer on USS *Drum*, survived three war patrols in 1942. During the first, off Tokyo Bay, the *Drum*'s torpedoes sank four ships. "I can't say much about the patrol—we think it successful," Manning wrote home. "I was thoroughly scared to death a couple of times. Suffice to say that we wriggled out of all the scrapes and got home just in time to participate in the tail end of the Midway battle." One scrape had involved being depth-charged by a Japanese destroyer for sixteen hours.

It had been the most successful mission thus far by any American submarine in the Pacific theater. There would be two more patrols aboard *Drum*, each lasting more than six weeks. In the eighteen months that were to follow, Manning would be promoted to lieutenant commander and given command of his own submarine. He would be awarded two Bronze Stars and a Silver Star. He earned the Silver Star, the nation's third-highest award for valor, the citation was to say, "for gallantry and intrepidity." Part of what drove him, a senior officer recalled, was the desire to restore the honor of the name Kimmel in the annals of the Navy.

His brother Tom was also serving with distinction. Tom's first submarine, USS *S-40*, evaded the enemy bombing of the Philippines that followed the attack on Pearl Harbor, was depth-charged during the Battle of Lingayen Gulf, and had a surface engagement with a Japanese sub. For his later service in the Pacific, he too would be awarded the Bronze Star—"for heroic achievement" and "outstanding seamanship" in sinking enemy ships.

Ned, the youngest brother, had to try hard to get into uniform. The Naval Reserve, the Marines, and the Army all initially turned him down because of his poor eyesight. In the midst of his own troubles after Pearl Harbor, though, the Admiral lobbied successfully to get Ned into the Navy. His classmates during the training period, Ned was to recall, were generally not "stupid enough" to believe ongoing lies and rumors about his father. He did not forget, however, an unsigned postcard he received. "It said, 'How dare you be in the Navy, you the son of an infamous traitor?' "

The "traitor's" son would rise to lieutenant commander and serve on the staff of the commander in chief Atlantic Fleet, and—aboard the aircraft carrier USS *Ranger*—with a task force operating in the North Atlantic. His presence on the *Ranger* would briefly cause his father concern—Kimmel kept the news away from Dorothy at the time—when Nazi propaganda broadcasts claimed falsely that a German submarine had sunk the carrier. (It was announced that Hitler personally had awarded the Knight's Cross to the submarine's captain.)

By the end of 1942, all three of Kimmel's sons were married. Tom's wedding had been a classic story of romance in wartime. He had met his bride two years earlier aboard a trans-Pacific steamer, he en route to his first posting outside the United States, she on her way home to her family in the Dutch East Indies. Though they had not thought they would meet again, fate brought them together. Many months later, having been evacuated in hair-raising circumstances as the Japanese invaded, she arrived in Perth, Australia, the very day Tom's submarine docked there. They met again by pure chance, then married after a whirlwind romance. The first the Kimmels knew of it was a telegram reading, "MARRIED TODAY. PHOTOGRAPHS AND LETTERS FOLLOW."

"These young ones," the Admiral wrote to a family member, "don't write often." There was that; there were poorer than usual communications on account of the war; and there was the fact that the sons serving in the Pacific had access to only minimal news. Theirs, though, was a family united. "Please do not feel," Manning had written after Pearl Harbor, "that you have let any of your sons down. The 'effect' upon us is the least of our thoughts—we think you're the best damn Admiral the Fleet will know for a long time."

Months later, when he chanced to encounter former members of Kimmel's command, Manning passed on word from them. Rear Admiral Frank Fletcher, who had served as a cruiser division commander at Pearl, asked him to "relay to Dad that the whole Navy was damn proud of him."

Of the three brothers, moving around as he was in the Pacific, Tom was the last to comprehend the full impact on his father of the strike on Pearl. Only when he got back on home leave, almost a year after Pearl, did he "realize what had really happened and the disgrace that had been heaped on my father. It was inconceivable to me that the Navy would allow such a public castigation to take place."

In his last days at Princeton before joining the Navy, the youthful Ned—he had just turned twenty—had sought the advice of people he thought might have reliable information. He asked Hanson Baldwin, the *New York Times'* naval correspondent, whether he thought the Admiral was really "as guilty as everyone says he is." "I felt so sorry for this youngster," Baldwin would recall. "I explained again what I had said in an article, that the job of defending the base was primarily the Army's, that I knew very little about the details of the attack or what went on before . . . I think there's been a national state of mind that it couldn't happen here, and that we reflected this."

Harold Sprout, a professor of politics at Princeton who had written an authoritative book on American naval power, offered comfort. "His first remark," Ned reported to his parents, "was, 'Why in the hell doesn't your father demand a court-martial and tell his side of the story which will expose some of the facts we don't know?'"

———

Kimmel was working toward just that. "What I have always wanted and hoped for," he would write, "was an impartial and judicial investigation." In the early days, however, he did not see how he could press for such a probe. For all the Roberts Commission's failings, he understood the "laudable desire to unify the American people in the face of the danger which threatened the country at that time. It was impossible for me to make any public statement until this danger had entirely passed."

So the Admiral worked at his new job in New York, designing dry docks for the Pacific Fleet, and waited. His son Manning's wife Gay reported in a letter that Kimmel and Dot "seemed well and quite happy—also that Dad is like his old self." Another acquaintance, however, noticed something "sad and quiet" about Kimmel's demeanor. In private, he spent time trying to gather what records he could, get sworn statements from former staffers now scattered across the Pacific, build the case for his defense. He saw a problem. With time passing, and the lives of many officers at risk in war zones, how long would witnesses be available?

There was another way in which time governed the situation, a way that controlled the decisions of both Kimmel and the government. If there was to be a court-martial, the statute of limitations required that it be held within two years of the attack—by December 7th, 1943. In late summer that year, with the deadline fast approaching, the Navy Department began pressing the government for a decision. The issue went right up to the President.

That August, Navy Secretary Knox sent Kimmel a request. While a trial could in theory now be held, Knox wrote, it would not be practical to bring essential witnesses back from war duty. On the assurance that a trial would be held as soon as possible, would Kimmel please not press for an immediate court-martial? On his honor "as an officer and gentleman," the Admiral agreed that he would not.

He accepted postponement, he responded, because he had all along been "anxious to subordinate my own interest to the national welfare." He emphasized, however, that he did wish to be tried "in open court" and as soon as possible.

Privately, Kimmel was anxious about where all this was going. In October, in a handwritten note to himself, he said that the government had known his side of the case from the start—"even though I was given no adequate chance to present it . . . The Administration had judged and sentenced me without a hearing. My only hope was to present my case publicly and depend upon the fairness of the American public to arrive at a verdict."

As it was, he went on, he had been unwilling:

> *to force a public investigation even had I been able to . . . It appeared probable that the Administration would have ordered me to trial before a secret court martial whose members could have been selected from those who would do the bidding of the Administration—either from hope of reward or from a conviction that I must be found guilty in order to save the Administration and the Nation . . . The public, prepared for this finding by the smear campaign started the day after the attack—maintained on the floors of Congress and in the press—would have accepted the findings.*

Then a bitter personal comment: "So long as Roosevelt is President he will not hesitate to use all the powers of his office to prevent a fair presentation of my side of the events and my actions prior to the attack." Resenting the way he had been treated, and groping for reasons, Kimmel had begun to see Roosevelt as his nemesis. As time passed, those who sought to blacken the President's name would come to infect him with their dark suspicions.

There was another reason for resentment. A congressional measure, signed into law by the President in late December 1943, extended the statute of limitations by six months—delaying the date of any theoretical court-martial, of anyone and everyone involved in the Pearl Harbor case, until mid-1944. Because of the late date on which the measure was processed, a future adviser to Kimmel was to note, it was probably invalid. If so, individuals other than Kimmel and Short—who had waived the statute—would remain beyond the reach of the law. The Admiral and the General, however, remained subject to prosecution because they had waived the statute of limitations when they had. The maneuver and Roosevelt's part in it, the adviser would observe, "had a cynical quality of artifice."

Months earlier, acutely aware that the struggle to clear his name was going nowhere, Kimmel had sought legal help—but initially in the wrong place, Accompanied by his predecessor Admiral Richardson, his former chief of staff Poco Smith, and his New York friend John Otterson—all trusted allies—he had met with a Washington attorney, Henry Leonard. A former Marine Colonel, Leonard was best known for his defense a year earlier of a Marine general. The strategy conference with Kimmel, however, misfired badly.

Within a week of the meeting, the *Washington Post* and other newspapers across the country had carried a sensational piece on Kimmel by the columnist Drew Pearson. Pearson had written that the Admiral was planning a letter designed to lay a "hot potato on the step of Secretary of the Navy Knox and the President which will be hard to handle." Because America now appeared to be winning the war, Kimmel was no longer prepared "to face the burden of obloquy alone," and was about to demand a "trial now." According to Pearson, the Admiral wanted access to records that might otherwise be "lost or misplaced," and said his defense would be that "higher authority" shared the blame for Pearl Harbor.

To air such plans publicly at this point was to make nonsense of the Admiral's agreement a month earlier that a court-martial should be delayed "in the public interest." The draft letter Pearson had cited had been dreamed up by attorney Leonard and shared with the columnist without Kimmel's knowledge or approval. Kimmel had promptly disowned the letter and told reporters that, while he certainly did want a trial, it should not be "at the expense of the war effort." He had fired Leonard.

On his own, though, the Admiral was floundering. His own efforts to obtain records from the Navy Department, and his attempts to get sworn statements from former members of his staff, had gotten nowhere. Something that might help his case was a procedure that had been mooted long since. In early 1942, soon after the Pearl Harbor attack, House Republicans had suggested that the matter should be investigated by Congress. There was "something the people want to know and feel they have a right to know," Republican representative William Ditter had said darkly. Even Democrat William Whittington had said the case could not be allowed to rest by merely finding Kimmel and Short derelict in their duty. He had concluded that "there also was dereliction in the War and Navy Departments." The months had passed, however, and Congress had not acted.

In December 1943, Kimmel found himself in legal limbo. On its face, "postponement" of a court-martial suggested that there would eventually be one. The government's maneuvering, however, prompted doubt, specifically doubt that a trial would occur within six months—the new deadline Congress had set. Behind the scenes, the record shows, the thinking in the Navy Department was that there could be no trial until after the war.

On the eve of the second anniversary of the disaster, Kimmel was, in his words, at his "wit's end."

48

THE ADMIRAL'S FORTUNES were about to change. With the start of 1944, some top-notch attorneys began working for him. Robert Lavender, a retired Navy captain who had served with Kimmel, was distinguished in his own right. He had served in both wars, commanded a destroyer, and been Fleet flag secretary. He did top-secret legal work for the Manhattan Project, which was building the atomic bomb that would be used against Japan. What Admiral Kimmel needed, Lavender could see, was a civilian trial lawyer unconstrained by ties to the Navy or the administration.

He took Kimmel to Charles Rugg, a former assistant attorney general of the United States who was to go on to be chief justice of the Massachusetts supreme court. With Lavender, he had worked on claims against the Navy Department. Rugg in turn was to bring in Edward Hanify, a former junior associate in his law firm now conveniently serving in the Navy—and made available to the Admiral to work on his defense.

"When I first met Admiral Kimmel," Hanify would recall, "I was struck by the authority and the forthrightness of his presence. He had the air of a man who knew how to plan and act thoughtfully and decisively. Pearl Harbor and the intervening years of strain and sadness had whitened his hair, but his carriage was erect, his bearing distinguished."

Rugg and Hanify listened as Kimmel told how events had unwound since the attack on Pearl Harbor. "To any self-respecting lawyer," Hanify remembered years later, "the notion that a conscientious man could be manipulated into a condition of permanent blame because of an alleged breach of duty, with no day in court, was repugnant. Particularly so in the case of a man whose whole life had been given to the service of his country . . . Rugg was appalled to learn of Kimmel's treatment by the Roberts Commission—denial to him of counsel although he was the plain target of the investigation, the later manipulated retirement and its consequences. He now sat in a Boston lawyer's office, two years after the charges publicly made against him, never having been permitted to read the transcript of the record."

In the American legal system, Hanify wrote, "a man accused had a right to his day in court. Here was a client who wanted that right above all else. Service in the United States Navy was not a consent to become a silent scapegoat."

Rugg took the case. Though he could command high fees, he charged Kimmel a minimal amount or nothing. Several years later, when Kimmel sent him money, the check was returned. The two men became firm friends. The bond between the Admiral and Hanify would be equally remarkable. Nearly six decades later, in old age and when the Admiral himself was long dead, Hanify would still be a powerful advocate for his former client's cause. He helped Kimmel's sons and grandsons continue the fight—for no charge.

Should the Admiral ever come to trial, it was realized, key testimony was likely to be incomplete or unobtainable. Two years after Pearl Harbor, memories had begun to dim. Some witnesses might die in combat before a court-martial could be held. So it was that in February 1944, after pressure had been brought to bear on the Navy Department, a senior officer was appointed to collect sworn testimony that—pending a future trial—would remain secret. The man chosen was Admiral Thomas Hart, the Navy's former commander in the Philippines, now retired. He was of two minds about becoming "a sort of judge." On the one hand, his diary shows, he thought the job was time "wasted on long-dead cats." He could also see, though, that the case was "full of dynamite." Hart was to feel "uncomfortable in the task . . . inadequate."

Early on, Kimmel went to Washington to meet with Hart informally. Hart's journal notes: "We had a two-hour, man-to-man, talk, all of which he requested should be strictly between us. He has aged considerably but is still forceful. Is bitter towards the powers that be, feels that he has been treated unjustly and is very distrustful."

Whether or not he shared it with Hart that day, Kimmel had just received explosive information from a totally unexpected source. This was Captain Laurance Safford, who in the months leading up to Pearl Harbor had headed the Navy's codebreaking unit. He had expected to be called to testify in the Kimmel case at some point—and not as a friendly witness. In light of the intelligence he assumed had been forwarded to the Admiral, he had initially believed the Fleet should have been more prepared for an attack.

Then, however, while preparing an internal history of Navy codebreaking, Safford had found that the documentation for some pre-attack Japanese intercepts was not where it should be. When staffers assigned to follow up also failed to locate the documents, he consulted with former MAGIC traffic coordinator Lieutenant Commander Kramer. It then dawned on Safford that numerous intercepts had never been shared with Kimmel. The Admiral had been blamed for ignoring information of which he had no knowledge.

Safford realized that to intervene in the Kimmel case would be to put his own Navy career at risk. In mid-January 1944, however, he decided to take the information he had learned to the man he now considered the victim of "a frame-up." On February 21st, 1944, without having made an appointment, Safford turned up at the office in New York where the Admiral was working. Soon, Kimmel was sitting, pencil and pad in hand, riveted to what the captain had to say.

He was, he would recall, "appalled and outraged as the events and actions leading to the attack on the Fleet at Pearl Harbor were disclosed to me." To credit what he was hearing of the intercepts of the last days and hours alone, he thought, was to conclude either that he had been denied intelligence "by design," or that "an unbelievable state of inefficiency prevailed in both the War Department and the Navy Department."

The facts, it is clear, suggest strongly that inefficiency was at the root of the failures to send key intelligence to the commanders in Hawaii. Kimmel, though, would come to believe he had been kept in the dark deliberately. What he learned from Safford, he would recall twenty years later, made him feel "almost sick." His sense of the injustice that had been done him in the aftermath of the Japanese attack became overwhelming. "I had never dreamed," he wrote, "that any administration in Washington would countenance for any citizen such treatment as that given to General Short and to me."

Within twenty-four hours of Safford's visit, the Admiral was meeting with his new legal advisers, Rugg and Lavender. At their behest, almost certainly, Safford drafted a memorandum summarizing the key elements of what he had told Kimmel. For security, the memorandum was consigned to a safe-deposit box that could be accessed only with Rugg's permission. In the weeks and months that followed, when MAGIC-related information came in from Safford, it was treated as top-secret.

For, as trust between Kimmel's team and Safford grew, Safford produced documentary evidence. "From time to time," attorney Hanify would recall, "he delivered to me as well as to Captain Lavender copies of the intercepted material." As it came in, and before being taken to the safe-deposit box, it was on occasion kept temporarily in a safe in which attorney Lavender kept legal documents connected to the Manhattan Project. Hanify, who handled much of the liaison with Safford, recalled how he handled incoming material when away from the office. "It never left my possession—I slept with it under my pillow."

There was every reason to protect the material. On the one hand, the existence of the MAGIC intercepts was still top-secret. By sharing the documentation, moreover, Safford was making himself vulnerable to punishment and jeopardizing his career.

Kimmel and his attorneys now realized the sheer scale of the intelligence that MAGIC had provided. "From Nov. 1 to Dec. 7 1941" alone, Safford wrote in his initial memo, "there were about 950 messages received in the Navy Dept in the Japanese diplomatic system which were considered important enough to fully translate . . . At least an equal number were only partially translated and discarded as of minor significance."

The material provided by Safford was treasure for the Kimmel camp, with the promise of more to come. How, though, to handle it? Possession of the information, the lawyers realized, presented them with a huge responsibility. They had, Hanify recalled, a dilemma—"how to preserve and record this material in the best interest of his client, yet protect Safford's career from destruction . . . Then there was the transcendent consideration of the national interest in protecting a vital national secret." The Japanese diplomatic code remained unchanged, a major, ongoing fount of intelligence in a war that was not yet won.

Rugg offered a canny solution. As a potential court-martial witness before Admiral Hart, Safford should make a point of referring to the MAGIC intercepts and their content. The fact that his testimony would be taken in secret would mean that both national security and Safford personally would be protected. Crucially for Kimmel, meanwhile, sworn testimony on the MAGIC intercepts would become part of the formal record.

The maneuver succeeded. Safford duly referred to the intercepts in testimony to Hart in late April 1944. What he revealed thus became part of the file, information designed to justify a demand by the Kimmel team for access to it in a future proceeding. For his part, on Rugg's advice, the Admiral declined to testify to Hart, not least because his inquiry was being held behind closed doors.

Hart himself remained uneasy with the entire procedure. He wound up his work after four months, having done a good deal of interviewing in the Pacific but having taken "purposely scant" testimony in Washington. He had not called former CNO Stark, whom he saw as "naturally on the other side of the fence" from Kimmel. Moreover, Hart noted in his diary, any further probe would "carry the investigation into very secret fields which must absolutely not be publicized . . . The plot thickens daily. The pot is boiling and the 'affair-Pearl Harbor-surprise' is a political foot-ball."

Pearl Harbor had always had political ramifications. From the start, the President's foes had hoped responsibility for the attack could be laid at the administration's door. Then, by heaping blame on the commanders in Hawaii, the Roberts Commission had effectively absolved the government of blame. Intermittently, though, partisan rumbling from senators and congressmen had continued. Kimmel's counsel Rugg, meanwhile, had been plotting a shrewd political move.

First, on April 22nd, he had conferred privately with David Walsh, the senior senator from Massachusetts, who was chairman of the Naval Affairs Committee. Congressional inaction, Rugg argued, would "head this entire matter into oblivion." Walsh, persuaded that the Admiral deserved help, then primed his colleagues to press for legislation that would again extend the period during which court-martials of Kimmel and Short could be postponed.

On its face, this seemed contrary to the speedy public trial that Kimmel wanted. In the weeks that followed, however, complex maneuvering led to a very different outcome—a joint congressional resolution that there be a "Navy Court of Inquiry," and what was to become known as the "Army Pearl Harbor Board." Both proceedings, conducted in secret, were to lead to dramatic developments—and, from the Navy Court, virtually total vindication for Kimmel.

Before triggering the action that led to the new probes, Hanify recalled, Rugg had warned the Admiral what they would mean. At a meeting weeks later in New York's Hotel Pennsylvania, he said his client would have to "bid a permanent farewell to tranquillity . . . face an indefinite period of strain, turmoil, harassment and bitter struggle." Kimmel told his lawyer to press ahead.

He and his wife were already suffering from a different kind of stress. Early that year, Dorothy had been diagnosed with "severe pernicious anemia." Then, with the discovery of a breast tumor, there was surgery followed by "X-Ray treatments." "I was so sick," Dorothy wrote to a sister-in-law. "Twice on the operating table, four blood transfusions and other things . . . I hope I'll soon be well and of some use to the world. It will be some months, I'm afraid."

While she was in the hospital, the Kimmels' son Tom, back briefly from sea duty, had come visiting with his new wife Nancy and their five-month-old baby boy. "I was too sick to see Nancy or the baby," Dorothy wrote, "and I felt cheated." She would be glad, she added, to get some news of her other submariner son, Manning: "It has been a long time since we have heard."

Weeks later, their eldest son did write:

Dear Mother and Dad,

   I had no idea how sick mother must have been. . . . We have had lots of action, a couple of close calls, my closest yet . . . Now I am waiting for the next run and more chances to get at 'em . . ."

                                                    Love,
                                              MANNING

49

DOGGED PERSISTENCE WON more ground for Kimmel during the
summer of 1944. The Navy Court of Inquiry, made up of three
admirals, got under way in late July with a clear brief. It was to
include in its findings "whether any offenses have been committed or serious blame incurred" by *anyone* in the Navy and, if there
had been offenses, recommend what further proceedings should
follow.

Of all the probes to investigate Pearl Harbor, this was the
first—and last—body to apply the "due process" concept of law.
As an "interested party," Kimmel and his counsel had the right
to participate fully, to examine and cross-examine witnesses, and
to call for evidence. Human testimony aside, what they fought for
from the start was access to the MAGIC intercepts. Safford had
gotten the fact of their existence into the record by referring to
them under oath before Admiral Hart. Kimmel's side now wanted
to get them before the Court.

A legal tussle ensued: Kimmel's counsel would submit a request; the Navy Department would seek to block it; and the Admiral's people would counter with a new move. The Navy stonewalled
at one point by repeatedly claiming that a relevant letter of request
was missing. Kimmel would recall riposting in person, by informing the deputy commander in chief U.S. Fleet that "it would
do no good for the Secretary of the Navy to lose my letters, as I
proposed to write a letter every day until I received an answer."

The Court itself asked the Department to make material available on a top-secret basis to the Admiral's naval counsel. The
Army, which was conducting its own parallel investigation, insisted that this could not be permitted. Eventually, however, Kimmel's Navy lawyer Lavender was told he could examine a limited

number of MAGIC intercepts for a strictly limited amount of time. From Safford, Lavender knew what record numbers to ask for, and thought he had a sense of what to expect. What he found, however, took him aback.

"I was astounded," he would recall, "when I was shown into a room and there was a stack of papers 2½ feet high of intercepted messages . . . I sat back in my chair and looked over the selected messages, and then at the piles of other messages, and became nauseated . . . I realized what the information in my hands would have meant to Kimmel and the men of the Fleet who died." As rapidly as possible, aware of the time limit, the Captain selected those intercepts he thought should have been shared with Kimmel, asked that they be copied for the Court, then left to join the Admiral and other members of the legal team for a prearranged meeting over dinner.

What he had seen had so upset Lavender that he barely touched his food that evening. "We were anxious to hear his report," his colleague Hanify remembered, but "there was no sense of satisfaction in Lavender, of 'mission accomplished' . . . What he was compelled to consider was evidence of perfidy and disloyalty in the very top echelon of the Navy, by having withheld from the Fleet this critical evidence of the enemy's intent." Lavender seemed "shattered and almost speechless."

Until now, Kimmel and his people had had only Safford's word, and such material as he had given them, as a basis for thinking Washington had had vital advance intelligence—information that, had it been properly analyzed, would have indicated that something game-changing was in the works. According to Safford, the intelligence included intercepts showing that three months before the attack, Tokyo had ordered special espionage to be conducted in Hawaii; that the month before the attack, Tokyo had insisted on receiving reports from Pearl Harbor not once but "twice a week"; that its negotiations in Washington had become a charade; and that it used delaying tactics because of something secret that was pending, something—Tokyo told its envoys to Washington—that was "beyond your ability to guess."

There had been, too, the repeated indication as the days passed that Tokyo was working toward a deadline that, by the end, applied to a specific day and hour—December 7th, 7:30 a.m.—when the Japanese attack aircraft would be in the air, their bomb-racks loaded, heading for Hawaii.

Safford had told Kimmel and his people of all this and more. What he told them, though, had been not hard evidence but based on fallible memory. Now that Lavender had examined the material and arranged to have it copied, however, revelation became reality. This was information of substance, ammunition to make the case that high officials in Washington must at the very least share the blame for the disaster at Pearl Harbor.

A legal hurdle remained. Kimmel's lawyer had been given permission, at the level of the Secretary of the Navy, only to *see* MAGIC intercepts, not to introduce them in evidence. "It was one thing to have the intercepts segregated and authenticated," Hanify wearily recalled. "It was quite another to get them before the Navy Court."

The Court asked for the material to be made available. Kimmel's counsel Rugg asked for it, time and again. Secretary of the Navy James Forrestal, in office since Knox's death in the spring, repeatedly refused. Rugg persisted. He told the Court that it would be "unable to arrive at any correct conclusions unless these documents are admitted. They are absolutely essential . . . For two and one half years, due to the report of the Roberts Commission, [Kimmel] has been pilloried by the press and the Congress and before the people of this country. It is now time that the true facts in this matter be brought out, and that Admiral Kimmel have a full opportunity to exonerate himself."

The government held out for the best part of three weeks. Then Lavender proposed that Kimmel himself pull a bluff. After the Court's next session, he suggested, and as people milled about in the corridor, the Admiral should declare in an exaggeratedly loud voice that the Secretary of the Navy was withholding information essential to determining responsibility for Pearl Harbor. If its introduction in evidence continued to be blocked, Kimmel should continue in stentorian tones, he would call a press conference, say as much, and withdraw from the Court's hearings.

Kimmel had no real intention of blabbing publicly about national secrets, but he played along as suggested. It worked. Clearance to introduce the intercepts in evidence came the following morning.

Duly read out in court on August 28th, the Japanese messages—Hanify remembered—left the three admirals sitting in judgment "shocked and shaken." Lavender, who was also present, thought the first intercept read out in court was the request

> to the spies in Honolulu saying that they wanted to get the names of the individual ships at the various docks at Pearl Harbor. Well, I never saw three officers, who were able officers, just simply blanch as they did when these things were read . . . Admiral Kalbfus simply shrunk and Admiral Andrews—I never saw anyone look so terrible . . . Admiral Murfin just threw his pencil down on his desk so hard that it bounced about ten feet.

Murfin, who was presiding, exclaimed, "Jesus Christ!" and adjourned the hearing for the day.

Evidence that Navy personnel in Washington had received vital intelligence—some of it suggesting imminent Japanese action in the Pacific, possibly at Pearl Harbor—but had failed to share it with the commanders in the Pacific, was now firmly on the record.

This was victory for Kimmel—but it was no time for celebration.

Some weeks before the breakthrough, Dorothy had had a premonition. According to a press report, the Japanese had claimed to have sunk two U.S. submarines. "It's strange how you feel things sometimes," the Admiral's wife recalled later, "but it went through me like a knife. I felt that one of them might be Manning's."

On August 22nd, while the Admiral was in Washington, his

trusted former operations officer Walter DeLany—now serving at headquarters—brought him news about his eldest son. Manning and the crew of the submarine *Robalo*, who had set out two months earlier on a third war patrol, had not returned to port. Nothing had been heard of them since a radio transmission in early July.

Kimmel, who had himself often sent others off on hazardous missions, was not given to displays of emotion. He hastened home to Dorothy in New York. They agreed not to call Manning's wife, Gay, until she had heard the news from the Navy herself. Forty-eight hours later, Gay Kimmel got the telegram all wartime wives fear receiving:

THE NAVY DEPARTMENT DEEPLY REGRETS TO IN-FORM YOU THAT YOUR HUSBAND LIEUTENANT COMMANDER MANNING MARIUS KIMMEL USN IS MISSING FOLLOWING ACTION IN PERFORMANCE OF HIS DUTY AND SERVICE TO HIS COUNTRY. THE DEPARTMENT APPRECIATES YOUR GREAT ANXIETY BUT DETAILS NOT NOW AVAILABLE.

Letters Gay had recently sent to her husband began coming back marked "Returned to Sender." A week or so later, news that Manning was missing was published in the press, coupled with the fact that his father faced a court-martial on charges that he had been derelict in his duty.

There remained, of course, Kimmel wrote to one of his brothers in Kentucky, "an outside chance that Manning may be still alive . . . I have not given up hope entirely."

Admiral Hart, who had a role in the ongoing Navy Court of Inquiry, wrote in his diary: "Hard luck certainly does endure. K's reputation blown to hell, wife seriously ill . . . now this!"

50

EVEN AS KIMMEL coped with the family crisis in late August 1944, a new libel was leveled at him. Senator Harry Truman, who was running as the vice presidential candidate in Roosevelt's bid to win an unprecedented fourth term, used an article on military unity in *Collier's* magazine to suggest—inaccurately—that Kimmel and General Short had liaised barely at all before Pearl Harbor. They had met, Truman wrote, only "if they happened to be on speaking terms, or exchange cables and radiograms." Though Kimmel had been "entrusted" with seeing that the Navy conducted long-distance air reconnaissance, Truman wrote, he had not done so. The Senator wrote of "neglects and derelictions" as though they were established fact.

Kimmel riposted with an open letter saying Truman had made false statements. "Until I am afforded a hearing in open court," he wrote, "it is grossly unjust to repeat false charges against me . . . I ask for nothing more than an end to untruths and half-truths about this matter." The "American sense of fair play," he thought, would ensure he got the hearing he wanted.

Instead of responding to the Admiral's letter, Truman issued a statement claiming that everything he had written "was correct." He was "certain the court-martial of officers commanding at Pearl Harbor on December 7th 1941 would bear out every assertion he had made and more."

The press noted the exchange—to Kimmel's benefit. "To date," the syndicated columnist Bill Cunningham wrote in the *Boston Herald* on August 22nd, "writers and commentators tiptoe as delicately around the subject as if it were a nest of sleeping rattlesnakes . . . Kimmel's conduct, and an examination of his public statements since he was relieved of his command, seem to paint him as a man at ease with his conscience, fearless of the future—if he can only get the chance to tell his story." This, he suggested, was "an American Dreyfus case."

There it was, the first reference to the struggle of Alfred Dreyfus, the Jewish French army officer who at the turn of the century had been convicted of treason and sentenced to jail for life— he was imprisoned for four years on Devil's Island off French Guiana—only, following a twelve-year ordeal, to be fully exonerated. The case had been a long-running international sensation, and in 1944 was still very much in the public memory. Soon, it would be evoked again.

Historian Rupert Hughes, a former U.S. Army officer, took to the airwaves to point out that Kimmel and Short, "charged with the most atrocious guilt for the most appalling disaster in our history, have never been brought to trial. . . . Suddenly Senator Truman comes out in an article, tries Kimmel and Short and pronounces them guilty . . . Dreyfus was on Devil's Island for four years. Kimmel and Short will have been in purgatory for three years in December."

Citing the *Army and Navy Journal*, Hughes noted that the case had become an issue in the current presidential campaign. If Governor Thomas E. Dewey of New York, the Republican candidate for the presidency, were elected, he predicted, "the fur will begin to fly." In fact, moves to get political fur flying were already afoot.

To have any hope of dislodging President Roosevelt, the Republican Party needed powerful issues. On the domestic front, there was little to set voters on fire. Though well-founded rumors swirled around Roosevelt's health, it was difficult to counter assurances by the White House that he was in good shape. In many ways, he seemed unassailable.

The tide of the war, once uncertain, was steadily going America's—and the administration's—way. The D-Day invasion had succeeded and Germany's armies were being rolled back. Paris was about to fall to the Allies. American sea power had reversed Japan's earlier gains. General Douglas MacArthur's forces were moving inexorably across the Pacific. American airplanes had bombed cities in the Japanese homeland. The conduct of the war was a success story, not an area on which Roosevelt could be attacked.

The defeat at Pearl Harbor that had started the conflict with Japan, however, had the potential to be a chink in the Democrats' armor. The proceedings of the Navy Court of Inquiry and the concurrent Army Board were secret, but developments were leaking. Would it be possible to cast blame for the disaster on people in high places—perhaps as high as Roosevelt himself?

Senators and representatives began sounding off. Cunningham's column, likening Kimmel to Dreyfus, was placed in the *Congressional Record*. On September 5th, a congressman declared that the administration was "afraid to let the facts be known" about Pearl Harbor. "As long as President Roosevelt remains Commander in Chief," he added, they probably never would be known.

Twenty-four hours later, another representative suggested: "Let the people know who was to blame . . . Let us have the truth, the whole truth, and nothing but the truth." "Since the commander in chief takes credit for the victories," said another, "he should certainly take the blame for defeats." Individual protests became a chorus, and they were aimed at the White House. There was a call in the Senate for a full inquiry by a committee tasked specifically to ascribe responsibility for Pearl Harbor.

Insinuations about the President's role aside, some speakers seemed to have an inside track on sensitive information. In a thinly veiled allusion to the MAGIC intercepts, Senator Hugh Scott, from Pennsylvania, asked whether Admiral Kimmel had been "informed of diplomatic developments" before the attack. Representative Forest Harness, from Indiana, made it obvious that he knew about the intercepts: he knew Washington had cracked the December 7th messages telling Japan's envoys when to destroy their code machines, and precisely when to break off negotiations.

All this made news in the most influential papers. On September 15th, an editorial in the *Washington Post* noted, "A first-

class political row appears to be brewing over the secrecy that
still shrouds many details of our disaster at Pearl Harbor nearly
three years ago." Americans, it said, had "a right to know the
background . . . And there is no reason that we know of for keeping them in the dark."

That was the nub of it. Neither the media nor the public at large
knew why, three years later, the full facts were still being covered
up. From his office in the new Pentagon building, Chief of Staff
Marshall had been watching all this with alarm. "A recent speech
in Congress," he told his Navy opposite number, Admiral King—
he was referring to Harness' speech—"had deadly indications . . .
I now understand much more is to be said, possibly by Governor
Dewey himself . . . The whole thing is loaded with dynamite . . . I
very much feel something has to be done."

So began a remarkable cloak-and-dagger approach to the Republican candidate. With King's approval, the Chief of Staff dispatched a full colonel, wearing civilian clothes, to carry a letter
to the Governor marked "TOP SECRET—FOR MR. DEWEY'S
EYES ONLY." It reached him on the stump in Tulsa, Oklahoma,
on September 26th, and its lengthy contents were blunt. Marshall wrote:

> The most vital evidence in the Pearl Harbor matter consists
> of our intercepts of the Japanese diplomatic communica-
> tions. Over a period of years our cryptograph people ana-
> lyzed the character of the machine the Japanese were using
> for encoding their diplomatic messages . . . A corresponding
> machine was built by us which deciphers their messages.
> Therefore, we possess a wealth of information regarding
> their moves in the Pacific.

The breakthrough, Marshall explained, had been key to American victories over the Japanese Navy. Partly thanks to the intercepts, Washington had learned not only Japan's plans but also
Hitler's. Then, repeatedly, he banged home his key point. The
European campaign and all operations in the Pacific were *still* "re-

lated in conception and timing" to intelligence gathered thanks to the intercepts. MAGIC was *still* saving American lives.

However, the Chief of Staff's letter told Dewey, current campaign activity posed a serious risk. The benefits of U.S. codebreaking would be "wiped out in an instant" should the leaks arouse suspicion in Tokyo. Marshall's fervent hope was that Dewey would see his way clear "to avoid the tragic results with which we are now threatened in the present political campaign."

The Republican candidate was wary of giving assurances. He was not prepared, on this initial approach, even to read Marshall's letter through. He did not want to be constrained to be silent about information he "already knew about Pearl Harbor," the intermediary reported to the Chief of Staff. Dewey suspected, too, that the President, not Marshall, was "behind this whole thing."

Marshall's messenger flew back to Washington, only to be sent again to see Dewey—this time at the statehouse in Albany—with a second letter, amended to convince him to read on. Dewey responded by stressing again that what Marshall was asking him not to reveal was already known to "at least twelve Senators." So far as the candidate was concerned, it was "the worst kept secret in Washington." "I'll be damned," Dewey said, "if I believe the Japs are still using those codes."

Marshall's messenger, who had long been privy to the existence of MAGIC, told Dewey that the code at issue was indeed still in use, that it was America's "lifeblood in intelligence," that the sole purpose of his mission was to try to "preserve the only worthwhile source of intelligence that this nation has."

During this second visit, Dewey broke off to make a phone call directly to the Chief of Staff. It is not known what Marshall said on his end of the line, and Dewey gave no assurances. Never at any point during the campaign, however, would he raise the matter of Pearl Harbor and U.S. codebreaking.

Marshall's successful appeal had included a statement that was at best misleading, at worst a deliberate untruth. The "wealth of information" received as a result of intercepting Japanese mes-

sages, the Chief of Staff's letter assured Dewey, had "unfortu-
nately made no reference whatever to intentions towards Hawaii
until the last message before December 7th."

The traffic between Tokyo and its consulate in Hawaii had of
course not referred to an attack plan. It had revealed more than
enough, though, to arouse suspicion.

During the summer of 1944, the Chief of Staff and other senior
officers tinkered with the truth in other ways. The work of the
Army's Pearl Harbor Board, which conducted its work at the same
time as the Navy Court of Inquiry, would remain classified for
months to come. A lengthy account written by one Board member, Major General Henry Russell, who in peacetime was a lawyer,
would surface only fifty-seven years later, in 2001. From the start,
he recalled, their work had been done in secrecy, under strictures
so stern that he likened them to a "kind of Gestapo technique."

"The most important information desired" by the Board, Russell wrote in his account, was what Marshall "knew about the intentions and plans of the Japanese in the fall of 1941 and what
part of this information he had passed on to General Short . . .
Marshall appeared somewhat vexed by my line of questioning and
manifested some signs of irritation."

After asking that everyone leave the room except the three
members of the Board, Marshall revealed a little about the breaking of the Japanese code—but virtually nothing of what it had
revealed of Japanese plans. "Marshall used a lot of words but said
little," Russell recalled, "The two main questions that the Board
wanted to ask Marshall had not been answered."

There were other matters, Russell realized, that Marshall "did
not wish to discuss"—in particular the limitations of the non-
specific "war warning" sent to the Army and the Navy in Hawaii
ten days before the attack. "Toward the end of the examination,
General Marshall lost interest in it. He began to watch the clock
rather regularly and stated that he had some meeting which he

was forced to attend . . . I realized that the brush-off technique had been applied."

Having heard Marshall, Russell and his colleagues took sworn testimony from numerous senior Army officers, including General Sherman Miles, who at the time of Pearl Harbor had headed Army Intelligence; General William Bryden, who had been senior Deputy Chief of Staff; and General William McKee, who had served in War Plans. McKee "seemed bored and indifferent" during questioning, withdrawing into a "cloak of ignorance," Russell wrote. He was "evasive" in a way that indicated that he "knew a great deal more than he was willing to tell." If Bryden's evidence was to be taken seriously, Russell thought, "his ignorance was dense and amazing." It was "perfectly evident" that he was "purposely avoiding all questions." His responses to the Board were "little short of contemptuous."

General Miles, for his part, was "a complete washout as a witness" according to Russell. What he said pointed to the "utter inadequacy" of G-2 at the time. Miles' testimony, today available in full, shows that he dodged answering questions that might have shed light on what the United States really knew of Japanese intentions. What the military learned of negotiations with Tokyo, he said, had been provided to the Army by the State Department— when in fact it had been largely the other way around. He told the Board only useless generalities.

A year later, during a secret internal follow-up by the War Department, Miles was to reveal why he had given such fatuous testimony. He had done so, he said, because intermediaries had relayed "instructions from the Chief of Staff that I was not to disclose to the Army Pearl Harbor Board any facts concerning the radio intelligence . . . or the existence of that form of intelligence . . . I obeyed that instruction." He had misled the Board, as ordered, to protect MAGIC.

Just over two weeks after Miles gave evidence, however, the deception was exposed—by none other than Admiral Kimmel. Though a Navy man, he testified to the Army Board at its request and when asked whether there was anything he wished to add, he said there was. Reading from a prepared statement, he revealed in a few crisp sentences that both the Army and the Navy had possessed "vital information" they had not shared with the commanders in Hawaii. The intelligence had indicated that Japan would strike and that "very probably, the attack would be directed against the Fleet at Pearl Harbor . . . and that early on 7th December 1941 the precise time of the attack was known . . . All this information was denied to General Short and to me. I feel that we were entitled to it."

Kimmel, who had just learned that his son was missing in action, was under evident emotional strain as he talked. The generals listened, and stared at each other. These were sensational charges. It was strange indeed, Russell reflected, that top Army officers had to discover from the Navy "things that should have been available from the files of the War Department."

The deception now unraveled. G-2 officers gave Russell access to the telltale intercepts—including intelligence that indeed led, Russell wrote, to "the inescapable conclusion that the Japanese Army and Navy had not lost interest in Pearl Harbor." The intercepts "reeked of war."

Chief of Staff Marshall had not authorized senior officers to give the Army Board the truth about MAGIC, Marshall would state in an affidavit as the war was ending, because—just as he told Dewey—public revelation of the secret would cause the Japanese to change their codes, cost American lives, and cut off a vital source of intelligence. The need to avoid that was indeed paramount, but the explanation did not wash with the Board's Russell. Not to have trusted three generals tasked with investigating Pearl Harbor, when many others—some of far junior rank—already knew about MAGIC, made no sense.

Deception over MAGIC aside, the Board's view of how the Army had performed before Pearl Harbor, or rather failed to perform adequately, caused it to censure Marshall and his close colleagues severely. Its report, just before the election, would lead to turmoil at the War Department and concern at the White House.

And ironically, in the end, it would have lasting adverse consequences not for Marshall and his officers but for Admiral Kimmel.

"THIS POSES A big problem," Secretary of War Stimson wrote in his diary on October 21st, 1944, only two weeks before the presidential election. He had just been briefed by an aide on the so far secret findings of the Army Pearl Harbor Board. Little he was told was good news.

Chief of Staff Marshall, the Board's report said, had failed to keep General Short in Hawaii advised of how seriously relations with Japan were deteriorating; had failed to send adequate directions when Short responded to the November 27th "war warning"; and had failed—although there had been "ample time"—to send him critical information on the eve of and on the day of the attack. Marshall's chief of War Plans, General Leonard Gerow, had failed to keep Short adequately briefed, failed to order him to be more prepared for war, and more. Short himself had failed to order sufficient war readiness, failed to implement joint Army-Navy plans, and failed to inform himself of the extent of the Navy's long-distance reconnaissance. The Board did not recommend that anyone be court-martialed, however—it proposed no action of any kind.

The Navy Court of Inquiry, which had reported the previous day, virtually cleared Admiral Kimmel of any failure, let alone dereliction. The presence of a large number of his warships in harbor at the time the Japanese struck had been "necessary." The notion that all antiaircraft guns should have been manned and U.S. Navy planes airborne—absent any knowledge that an enemy strike was imminent—was "questionable." Kimmel's decision that no routine long-distance reconnaissance be undertaken had been "sound." His cooperation with General Short had been "sufficient for all useful purposes."

By contrast, however, just as the Army Board had found fault with George Marshall, the Navy Court of Inquiry faulted former Chief of Naval Operations Stark. The "war warning" he sent Kimmel on November 27th, the Court ruled, had not conveyed the actual situation as it was seen in Washington. Though Stark possessed important information during the pre-attack period, especially on the morning of December 7th, he had "failed to transmit" it to Kimmel.

The Navy Court, like its Army counterpart, found that no further proceedings were necessary. It took the view, moreover, that "no offenses have been committed, nor serious blame incurred," by anyone in the Navy. It made no reference to possible courts-martial.

Both Navy and Army headquarters reacted with alarm to the reports. Secretary of the Navy Forrestal reacted by announcing a review to decide how much of the Navy Court's report could be publicly released and how much should be withheld for reasons of national security. At the War Department, a troubled Stimson consulted with his own people and with Forrestal. Two generals, one of them a close aide of Marshall's, Stimson recorded in his diary, told him "very strongly that those reports should not be made public during the war."

Even before the Army Board's report had been submitted, the President himself had contacted Stimson to say he had heard rumors about what it was going to conclude and wondered whether the report could be postponed until after the election. The election came and went, handing Roosevelt his fourth term in the White House. Then, for two more weeks, Stimson and his aides labored over various drafts of a possible statement about the report. Stimson twice conferred with Marshall, who at one point said he thought "his usefulness in the Army had been destroyed" by the report. "I told him that was nonsense," Stimson noted in his diary, "to forget it . . . He was very grateful for the work I had done on it and the fight that I was making for him."

The report became such a worrisome preoccupation that, nearly a month after its delivery, Stimson was calling it his "cross." It was the President, in the end, who carefully perused the Board's findings and cut through the deliberations. "When he saw the names they had criticized," Stimson noted, Roosevelt, "said 'Why, this is wicked! This is wicked!' . . . When I told him I feared the Congress would get after us, get at the papers and get at the facts, he said that we must take every step against that and that we must refuse to make the reports public. He said they should be sealed up . . . a notice made that they should only be opened on a joint resolution of both houses of Congress, approved by the President, after the War."

Further conferring with Roosevelt, Marshall, and Forrestal followed. Stimson complained that the Navy "had a Court of Inquiry which was doing its best, as was evident from its findings to acquit and whitewash Kimmel and all other Naval officers, where I have a Board that went just as much too far the other way." The wrangling and tinkering between Stimson and Forrestal continued, and only a telephone call to the President at his vacation retreat settled exactly what the public was to be told.

On December 1st, forty days after the reports had been delivered, the two Secretaries finally issued statements. Though the Army Board had recommended no disciplinary action, Stimson said, there had been "several officers in the field and in the War Department who did not perform their duties with the necessary skill or exercise the judgment which was required." So far as General Short was concerned, he said, "errors of judgment" had required his "relief from a command status." The evidence did not justify proceedings against any officers. It would, meanwhile, be prejudicial to the war effort and to American lives "to make public during the War the Report of the Army Pearl Harbor Board or the record on which it is based."

Forrestal, for his part, said no grounds had been found for a court-martial of anyone in the Navy. Reflecting not only the Court's report but also previous probes, he said there had been "errors of judgment" by officers in the Navy both at Pearl Harbor and in Washington. He referred to no one by name. In the interests of present and future U.S. operations, Forrestal said, the Court's records were to remain "Top Secret."

He promised further investigation.

The day Forrestal issued his statement, reporters who descended on Kimmel's home in the New York suburbs found him "smiling and obviously in good spirits." There was "an air of gaiety about the household." All was well with the Kimmels, if you believed the newspapers. They did say, though, that the Admiral had responded to questions with "No comment," and referred the reporters to his lawyer.

Kimmel was in fact seething with rage. Earlier, the moment it became known that the Navy Court's report had been delivered, his counsel Rugg had sent the Secretary of the Navy a lengthy telegram.

I REQUEST IMMEDIATE RELEASE OF FINDINGS OF NAVY COURT OF INQUIRY AS TO INNOCENCE OR GUILT OF ADMIRAL KIMMEL. FOR NEARLY THREE YEARS HE HAS BORNE PUBLIC BLAME FOR PEARL HARBOR DISASTER. HE HAS REQUESTED AND HAS BEEN DENIED COURT MARTIAL. HIS TREATMENT HAS BEEN UN-AMERICAN ... RELEASE OF FINDINGS OF COURT AS TO KIMMEL'S INNOCENCE OR GUILT CANNOT AFFECT WAR. PAST INJUSTICES CANNOT NOW BE REMEDIED. SIMPLE JUSTICE AND COMMON DECENCY REQUIRE IMMEDIATE PUBLIC ANNOUNCE-MENT OF COURTS FINDINGS.

Far from making public the simple fact that the Court had cleared him of blame, the Navy Secretary's opaque public statement—approved by the President in advance—said nothing of the kind. As Kimmel was to recall bitterly, it had "submerged" the Court's detailed findings. The Navy's and Army's statements, in the view of Admiral Harry Yarnell, who was a former commander of the naval yard at Pearl and had been Kimmel's adviser when the Court was in session, were "masterpieces of weasel wording, squirming to get out something that will prevent disclosure of the findings of the two courts and protect their own departments."

For Kimmel in December 1944, talk of vindication "someday" was small comfort. Disillusioned, and furious about officialdom's cynicism, he headed for Washington. There, on the 7th, he had meetings both with Admiral King, who now headed the Navy, and with Rear Admiral Thomas Gatch, head of the service's legal arm. Kimmel memorized what was said at the meetings.

King, Kimmel wrote, told him something of the internal to-and-fro that had gone on in recent weeks—but without being entirely frank with him. No, he would not let Kimmel even see the Navy Court's findings or the record of proceedings, let alone have a copy. The record, he promised, would not be destroyed but carefully preserved. Suppressing it until after the war, however, was essential so as to keep secret—especially—errors of judgment Marshall and Stark had made and so as to "imply, if not to state clearly" that Kimmel and Short had also made errors. It was necessary not to be specific about such putative errors—in order not to have to explain them.

Far from having cleared his name, Kimmel pointed out to King, the Court's work had rekindled slurs and false accusations against him. That same day, the prominent columnist Drew Pearson had published an article filled with snide allegations, purporting authoritatively to rebut the new "whitewash" of Kimmel.

Kimmel asked King how he could defend himself against such allegations. More important, how could he rebut the official suggestion that he was guilty of unspecified errors? Until the war was over, King told him, he would have "no redress." Though the Navy chief seemed friendly enough, Kimmel thought, his attitude was not what it had been on a previous occasion, when King had urged him to do his utmost to "blast out the truth, as he felt I had been treated vilely."

Before King and Kimmel met, the record shows, King had submitted a less than sympathetic "endorsement" of the Navy Court's report—an "endorsement" was a mandatory part of the bureaucratic process. Instead of giving the report King's backing, the endorsement stated that there had been "derelictions" by Kimmel—and CNO Stark—that, "faults of omission rather than commission" had shown a "lack of the superior judgment necessary for exercising command commensurate with their rank and their assigned duties."

The endorsement had been written not by King himself but by his deputy. In 1948, when he was retired, King would retract its most scathing points in a formal letter to a later Secretary of the Navy. His endorsement, he was to write, had not been "in accord with the realities" and he now wished to put right "continuing injustices." Later still, in a 1952 memoir, King would write that the initial Roberts Commission had merely "produced scapegoats to satisfy the popular demand," and that Kimmel, Short, and Stark "had been sacrificed to political expediency."

In his memorandum of the December 7th, 1944 meeting with King, Kimmel wrote, he got the impression that King's actions at the time were "at the behest of Mr. Roosevelt." What was said at his meeting that same day with Admiral Gatch, the Navy's Judge Advocate General, also led Kimmel to think the President had personally "dictated what was to be done with both the Navy Court and the Army Board."

Gatch told Kimmel he was glad to have played no part in the decision that had been made as a result of the Navy Court's report. Had he been asked, he would "never have gone along with it." According to Kimmel, the Advocate General thought the episode was having a "very bad effect on the morale of the service." He was "disgusted and discouraged and was hoping he could be sent to sea."

Asked for his legal view as to what would happen should Kimmel publish what he knew of the MAGIC background to the case, Gatch replied bluntly: "You would be brought to trial on charges that you had divulged secret matter and you would be convicted, thereby confusing the matter and absolutely discrediting your-self."

What if, Kimmel asked, he should publish something on the subject but without drawing on secret material? "In that case," Gatch replied, "the Navy Department would merely state that you are a liar, and you would be unable to prove any of your contentions unless you reverted to the secret matter."

Was there no way out of the Admiral's predicament, no way to vindicate himself? Gatch said there was not.

52

THE ANXIETY ABOUT his missing son, meanwhile, continued. For months now—week in, week out—the extended family had waited and hoped. One of Manning's former commanding officers had written to say of Manning, "He was tops. I gave him a straight 4.0 Fitness report, the only one I ever gave and probably ever will. I recommended him for a Gold Star in lieu of a second Silver Star . . . He rated one. The men thought a lot of him, called him Mr. K."

In the midst of his fight with officialdom, the Admiral had used contacts at Navy headquarters to get the names and addresses of the *Robalo*'s crew. Manning's wife Gay wanted to write to the next of kin of the men serving under him. Letters from anxious parents and wives came flooding back.

"We haven't been married very long, and we have a son fourteen months old. I just can't believe that anything would happen to my husband. He has always admired and respected his skipper. He was always a square-shooter . . . I can imagine how proud you are of him."

"We have received your most welcome letter concerning my son. You have given me new hope. I know that your husband Kimmel was an experienced submariner. If you do get any information about the *Robalo*, please let me know."

"Maybe they are captured and still alive . . . ?" "Harold, motor machinist, mate, first class, is my son . . . The Navy's message said 'missing,' not killed." "I have been crying and praying for Emile. He is my youngest . . . I was so glad to get your letter as you have informed me that your husband's first concern was always for his crew."

And: "A friend at home on leave after serving his time in the

Pacific told us that the subs operate very close to small islands, and that they have rescued a number of sub men off of these islands. Our son wrote home that the *Robalo* had the best skipper in the Navy. I know, if there was any chance, they are alive."

News of the sinking of the carrier on which Ned, the Kimmels' youngest son, was serving had, after all, turned out to be a false alarm. Tom, their second son, himself an officer on a submarine in the Pacific, counseled against despair. "We must not give up hope that he has been rescued," he wrote. "I know something of the circumstances, and there is some chance that he may have gotten out."

Dorothy, still weak from her illness, put a brave face on it. "My three boys have been my life and happiness," she wrote in a letter. "Life will never seem right to me without Manning—and just two boys. I try hard to hold on to some faint hope."

In early 1945, with the war moving into its final months, the Admiral resolved to continue the struggle to clear his name. The further investigations promised by the Navy and Army were to be internal, secret, like their predecessors, again frustrating his desire to see his guilt or innocence openly tested.

Support for a public airing of the case, however, was growing.

In light of the latest known developments, Arthur Krock, the influential winner of two Pulitzer Prizes, had recently summed up the situation in the *New York Times*. There was, he noted, "a fundamental conflict between the report on Pearl Harbor of the Commission headed by Justice Roberts and of those composed of admirals and generals . . . If Admiral Kimmel and General Short were guilty of 'dereliction of duty,' as the Roberts Commission concluded, it cannot equally be true, as the Secretaries of Navy and War appraised their officers' inquiries, that . . . no grounds exist for the courts-martial of the area commanders . . ."

This, Krock wrote, was an unsatisfactory situation for everyone concerned—not least the two commanders. Statements in Congress had revived suspicion that Washington bore more blame for the catastrophe at Pearl Harbor than had yet been made public. It now seemed that only a congressional investigation was likely to get to the truth.

Senator Homer Ferguson, a former circuit court judge, had long been calling for congressional action. The secret findings of the military boards, he had said two days before Krock's article appeared, should be provided to the Senate Military Affairs Committee. "The people," he said, "want to know how this thing at Pearl Harbor could possibly happen and yet nobody be to blame." Though Ferguson had significant support, the matter vanished from the news for some time. Then events changed the situation for the world—and for Kimmel and his legal team.

On April 12th, President Roosevelt suffered a massive cerebral hemorrhage and died. The length of his leadership of the nation, and the very personal role he had played as commander in chief during the years of war, made his death a momentous event worldwide. Harry Truman became President. Everywhere, German, Italian, and Japanese forces were crumbling. During April alone, 1.5 million Germans and Italians were taken prisoner, Mussolini was caught and killed by Italian partisans, and Hitler died in the Berlin bunker. One by one, the German armies surrendered.

Three months later, after the United States had dropped atomic bombs on Hiroshima and Nagasaki, Japan in its turn caved in. On September 2nd, aboard the battleship USS *Missouri* in Tokyo Bay, the Japanese political and military leadership formally surrendered.

In April, the day before Roosevelt died, Kimmel had received what seemed like bad news for his case. The Senate, his counsel Charles Rugg told him, had just quietly passed a bill that—if also passed by the House—would potentially outlaw the disclosure without permission of any information "derived from cryptanalysis of messages" from any foreign government. The penalty for disclosure would be draconian, a fine of $10,000—well over $100,000 at today's rates—or many years in jail.

"I was desperate," the Admiral would recall, "because if the House passed the Bill, that was the end of all disclosures about

Pearl Harbor." Kimmel still had entrée. In short order, he met with the publisher, the managing editor, and senior journalists of the *Washington Post*. Senator Ferguson, for his part, told the *Post* that the new law had the potential to impose press censorship and deprive Congress of the right to obtain information on military operations or foreign affairs.

On the morning of April 12th, hours before the President's death eclipsed other news, the *Post* covered the story on its front page. One casualty of the proposed law, Ferguson was quoted as saying, would be "the real truth about Pearl Harbor." The Roberts Commission report on the disaster, he suggested, had specifically mentioned coded messages. "If Congress should call Admiral Kimmel or General Short, these officers would be faced with ten years in jail if they disclosed any information which they had learned through these codes." Later, when the bill came before the House, it would be defeated.

Kimmel, meanwhile, pressed on. "Mr. Roosevelt's death," he wrote to his lawyer, "gives Mr. Truman a chance to air the whole Pearl Harbor affair. If we could get someone to advise Mr. Truman to do so, I really believe it would be in his interest in the long run." Four months later, a few days before the Japanese military formally surrendered, the new President acted as Kimmel had hoped. On August 29th, the reports of the Navy Court of Inquiry and the Army Board were released, making public in detail the findings that the high command in Washington shared the blame for the debacle.

At a press conference the following day, Truman reversed himself regarding his statements of the previous year about Kimmel and Short. "Things," he said, "come back to haunt you . . . It was not a statement of fact. I was speaking with the best information I had at the time." Asked whether the Admiral and the General should be allowed to defend themselves in open trial, Truman said he would have no objection. He wanted "everybody to be fairly treated."

He now thought that the catastrophe at Pearl Harbor had been a result of U.S. national policy at the time. "The country," he said, "was not ready . . . I think the country is as much to blame as any individual."

Newspapers across the nation gave the release of the reports extensive coverage. An editorial in the *New York Herald Tribune* said the public would find it hard to make sense "out of reports which, while conveying a vivid impression of over-all confusion, unawareness and 'buck-passing' in the Army, the Navy, the State Department and the White House, have nothing to say about the [late] President." The *Washington Post* said the picture presented was "a veritable masterpiece of snafu . . ." The *New Orleans Times-Picayune* pointed out that the findings left "the vital question of responsibility in doubt. That doubt should be cleared before the case is closed." The *Detroit Free Press* said the contents of the Army and Navy reports "should mean just one thing—a complete, unbiased, open investigation on the part of the Congress."

The following month, the House and Senate voted unanimously for a full congressional investigation of Pearl Harbor. In October, as it was getting under way, Truman approved release to the Joint Committee of all MAGIC material it might request, and cleared military witnesses to testify. This was a complete turnaround.

In the Senate's ornate caucus room on November 15th, Kimmel settled himself into a front-row seat well before proceedings began. Present, too, was General Short. For many attending, there was standing room only. This was a big event. Under klieg lights, newsreel cameras rolled. Soon after the chairman called the jam-packed room to order, the fuses blew, plunging the place into darkness for a time. In hindsight, it was a kind of omen. In the six months that followed, the Committee would make progress—but by no means illuminate all the mysteries of Pearl Harbor.

There would be blanket press coverage. This, as one newspaper put it, was "easily the year's biggest congressional show." The headline "Intercepted Messages Bared," right at the start, reflected the

Japanese airplanes readying for take-off from their carrier.

The first bombs strike Pearl Harbor, photographed by one of the pilots.

The USS *West Virginia*, struck by multiple torpedoes. *(Naval History & Heritage Command)*

"Like looking into hell on a sunshiny day." On the USS *Arizona* alone, 1,177 men died. (*National Archives*)

Name	Rank		Name	Rank		Name	Rank
R. N. FRIZZELL	S2c		W. W. HENDERSON	S2c		C. W. JOYCE	F2c
R. W. FULTON	AMSMTH1c		F. HENDRIKSEN	F2c		A. J. JUDD	COX
F. F. FUNK	BM2c		J. J. HERRING	SM3c			
L. H. FUNK	S1c		R. A. HERRIOTT, Jr.	S1c		H. L. KAGARICE	CSK
			D. M. HESS	FC1c		R. O. KAISER	F1c
R. A. GAGER	S2c		A. J. HESSDORFER	MM2c		E. L. KATT	S2c
E. R. GARGARO	S2c		R. A. HIBBARD	BKR2c		P. D. KELLER	MLDR2c
R. W. GARLINGTON	S1c		A. J. HICKMAN	SM3c		J. D. KELLEY	SF3c
O. V.				GM3c		W. L. KELLOGG	F1c
G. E.				PTR2c		R. L. KELLY	CEM
W. F.				OM1c		D. L. KENISTON	S2c
R. M.				GM1c		K. H. KENISTON	F5c
P. R.				S1c		K. F. KENNARD	GM3c
K. E.				F2c		C. C. KENNINGTON	S1c
K. F.				HA1c		M. H. KENNINGTON	S1c
M. F.				S2c		T. T. KENT, Jr.	S2c
S. H.				S1c		I. C. KIDD	RADM
R. G.				COX		BATTLESHIP DIV. COMMANDER	
B. E.				F3c		R. W. KIEHN	MM2c
K. A.				S1c		C. E. KIESELBACH	CM1c
R. E.				S1c		G. B. KING	S1c
M. J.			M. L. HORN	F3c		L. C. KING	S1c
H. R.						L. M. KING	F1c
A. GOBBIN	SC1c		H. H. HORRELL	SM1c		R. N. KING, Jr.	ENS
W. C. GOFF	S2c		J. W. HORROCKS	CGM		F. W. KINNEY	1stMUS
E. GOMEZ, Jr.	S1c		J. E. HOSLER	S1c		G. L. KINNEY	QM2c
L. GOOD	S1c		C. R. HOUSE	CWT		W. A. KIRCHHOFF	S1c
W. A. GOODWIN	S2c		J. J. HOUSEL	SK1c		T. L. KIRKPATRICK	CAPT
P. C. GORDON, Jr.	F1c		E. HOWARD	S1c		E. KLANN	SC1c
E. W. GOSSELIN	ENS		R. G. HOWARD	GM3c		R. E. KLINE	GM2c
J. A. A. GOSSELIN	RM1c		D. R. HOWE	S2c		F. L. KLOPP	GM3c
H. L. GOULD	S1c		L. HOWELL	COX		R. W. KNIGHT	EM3c
R. C. GOVE	S1c		H. HUBBARD, Jr.	MATT2c		W. KNUBEL, Jr.	S1c
R. E. GRANGER	F3c		C. F. HUFFMAN	F1c		W. E. KOCH	S1c
E. GRANT	Y3c		B. T. HUGHES	MUS2c		C. D. KOENEKAMP	F1c
. J. GRAY	S1c		L. B. HUGHES, Jr.	S1c		H. O. KOEPPE	SC3c
. M. GRAY	F1c		J. G. HUGHEY	S1c		B. KOLAJAJCK	S1c
V. J. GRAY, Jr.	S1c		D. C. HUIE	HA1c		A. J. KONNICK	CM2c
. H. GREEN	S1c		R. F. HUNTER	S1c		J. A. KOSEC	BM2c
. G. GREENFIELD	S1c		H. L.				S1c
O. GRIFFIN	EM3c		W. H.				MTH1c
A. GRIFFITHS	EM3c		W. R.				S1c
B. GRISSINGER	S2c		L. J.				GM2c
. W. GROSNICKLE	EM2c		A. A.				S1c
. H. GROSS	CSK		W. H.				S2c
G. GRUNDSTROM	S2c						QM2c
H. GURLEY	SK3c		J. C.				S1c
			H. B.				S1c
J. HAAS	MUS2c		R. F.				SC3c
W. HADEN	COX		T. "A"				RM3c
B. HAFFNER	F1c		D. A.				S1c
W. HAINES	S2c		O. A.				FC2c
R. HALL	CBM		L. J.				S1c
I. HALLORAN	ENS		E. H.				CLK
. HAMILTON	MM1c		N. K. IVERSEN	S2c		D. L. LAKIN	S1c
. HAMILTON	S1c		C. A.				S1c
H. HAMILTON	GM3c						S1c
. HAMMERUD	S1c		D. P. JACKSON, Jr.	S1c		G. S. LAMB	CSF
D. HAMPTON	F1c		R. W. JACKSON	Y3c		H. LANDMAN	AMM2c
. HAMPTON, Jr.	S1c		J. B. JAMES	S1c		J. J. LANDRY, Jr.	BKR2c

(Background: David Wall/Alamy; top: Hawaii State Archives; bottom: National Archives)

The Roberts Commission found that Admiral Kimmel had been guilty of "dereliction of duty." None of the other eight investigations did. (*Bettman*)

After the war, the Admiral and his attorneys exposed Washington's failures. He testified forcefully before Congress's Joint Committee. (*Bettman*)

December 18, 1941

Dear Dad,

There is so little to say at a time like this — but I do want you to know that I'm sure that your end of the job has been "well done"! My complete confidence and belief in you has not been shaken a bit and I think you are the grandest Dad in the world.

Manning

The eldest son, Manning Kimmel III (*left*), who served in submarines in the Pacific, wrote this letter to his father after Pearl Harbor. Manning won the Silver Star and two Bronze Stars, and rose to command the USS *Robalo*, but was lost in action in 1944.

The second eldest, Tom, also served with distinction in submarines. From the bridge of USS *Bergall*, after the war, he supervised a ceremony for all the men who had lost their lives at sea in the Pacific. (*Kimmel family*)

The youngest son, Ned, a lieutenant, served in the Atlantic. In 1945, he accompanied the Admiral to the congressional hearings. (*Getty*)

Following his Navy career, Tom Kimmel Sr. (*right*) became an executive for Westinghouse; his brother Ned, a senior attorney for Dupont. They both worked tirelessly to clear their father's name. (*Scott Thode*)

BELOW LEFT AND RIGHT: Tom Jr. served in the Navy and later as a senior FBI agent. Ned's son, Manning Kimmel IV, owns and runs radio stations. To this day, they are working to get their grandfather publicly vindicated. (*Kimmel family, Terry Roueche*)

The younger generation supports the family cause. In 2005, when Ned Kimmel was dying, the Admiral's great-grandson Nick Kimmel (*right*), then at the Naval Academy, donned his dress whites to pay his respects. On the wall is a portrait of the Admiral. (*Kimmel family*)

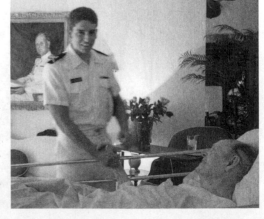

Resolution

Pearl Harbor Survivors Association

Whereas,

Admiral Husband E. Kimmel

had an excellent Navy service record and was carefully chosen for his respective command in Hawaii by persons of higher authority, and

Whereas, Admiral Kimmel shouldered the brunt of the blame for the national catastrophe that was Pearl Harbor December 7, 1941; and

Whereas, in the light of extensive documented writings on the subject many PHSA members feel that others, and the whole nation, should have shared the burden of these charges, and

Whereas, Admiral Kimmel cooperated fully with higher authority immediately following his removal from command, offered his resignation as requested, and generally displayed his soldierly training and love of country that had become a way of life for him from the moment he entered the military service, and

Whereas, because of the stated need for maintaining national security, Admiral Kimmel was not afforded the opportunity to clear himself of the charges leveled against him; he was never granted an official court martial through which medium he would have had full access to all forms of evidence, the right to counsel, to introduce, examine and cross-examine witnesses, to introduce matter pertaining to his examination, and to testify and declare in his own behalf, and in essence mount a full-blown defense of his actions and policies leading to the Pearl Harbor catastrophe, Now Therefore, Be It

Resolved, while there is still time in our generation, we members of the PHSA wishing to express a feeling of admiration and respect toward this officer do hereby request the Pearl Harbor Survivors Association to formally recognize, posthumously, Admiral Kimmel for his sincere and dedicated performance of duty and for carrying until his death, and thereafter, the unfortunate burden and stigma associated with the catastrophe at Pearl Harbor.

In Witness Whereof, I have hereunto set my hand and seal this 8th day of December, 1986.

Thomas J. Stockett
Thomas J. Stockett
National President

The support of the 10,000-member Pearl Harbor Survivors Association, in 1986, was a turning point for the Kimmels. Soon after, the Association called for the Admiral's posthumous restoration to four-star rank. (*Kimmel family*)

H. R. 4205

PUBLIC LAW 106-398

One Hundred Sixth Congress
of the
United States of America

AT THE SECOND SESSION

*Begun and held at the City of Washington on Monday,
the twenty-fourth day of January, two thousand*

An Act

To authorize appropriations for fiscal year 2001 for military activities of the Department of Defense, for military construction, and for defense activities of the Department of Energy, to prescribe personnel strengths for each fiscal year for the Armed Forces, and for other purposes.

Be it enacted by the Senate and House of Representatives of the United States of America in Congress assembled,

SECTION 1. ENACTMENT OF FISCAL YEAR 2001 NATIONAL DEFENSE AUTHORIZATION ACT.

The provisions of H.R. 5408 of the 106th Congress, as introduced on October 6, 2000, are hereby enacted into law.

SEC. 2. PUBLICATION OF ACT.

In publishing this Act in slip form and in the United States Statutes at Large pursuant to section 112 of title 1, United States Code, the Archivist of the United States shall include after the date of approval an appendix setting forth the text of the bill referred to in section 1.

Speaker of the House of Representatives.

President of the Senate. pro tempore

APPROVED

OCT 3 0 2000

In 2000, both houses of Congress passed a law urging posthumous restoration of the Admiral's four-star rank. Though President Clinton signed it, neither he nor any other president has moved to put the law into effect.

At the Naval Academy cemetery, in defiance of Navy bureaucracy, four stars are engraved on Admiral Kimmel's gravestone. His sons decided that this should be so. (*Chris Spencer*) surfacing of the intercepts that had been withheld from the commanders in Hawaii. "Kimmel Alarm Blocked Dec. 4—Disclosure of Authority Who Withheld Message May Solve Mystery" touched on the puzzle over why ONI's Commander McCollum's draft message to Hawaii had been aborted.

A story headed "Intercepted 'Wind' Code Put in Record" told of the intercept indicating that a phrase in a Japanese weather forecast would presage a break in relations with America. Then, weeks later, the headline "Navy's War Tip, Dec. 3, '41 Not in Files—Missing" referred to the notion that the "Winds" forecast had come in but since mysteriously vanished from Navy files.

The stories "Probers Talk to Dec. 7 Mystery Man," and "Navy Is Accused of 'Badgering' Dec. 7 Witness," focused on Alwin Kramer, former chief translator of the Navy's codebreaking unit. While he had earlier told the Navy Court of Inquiry that he recalled having seen a "Winds Execute" message referring to the United States, he had changed his mind. By the time the Committee was sitting, Kramer was a patient at Bethesda Naval Hospital, and—according to a Republican member of the Committee—the word from one of the doctors was that something unknown was "preying on his mind." Kramer would deny, though, an allegation that he had been "badgered into a breakdown by Naval officers trying to get him to change his testimony."

One by one, high Navy and Army officers took the witness stand. The headline "Turner Guessed Plan for Sneak Blow" reflected an assertion by Admiral Kelly Turner, the former War Plans chief, that he had thought "the chances were 50-50 that we would get a heavy raid in Hawaii." If he really had thought that, the Committee's chief counsel William Mitchell tartly pointed out, he was the only officer known to have had such foresight.

Then came a story headlined "Naval Expert Foresaw Pearl Harbor Attack." Captain Ellis Zacharias, who for years before the war had served in Naval Intelligence, told the Committee he had forecast not only that war would start with a raid on Pearl, but that it would come on a weekend and probably from the north. Zacharias claimed, moreover, that he had made this prediction nine months before the attack, in a conversation with Admiral Kimmel. The Admiral's chief of staff Poco Smith would, he was sure, remember that.

The news the next day, though, was "Zacharias Testimony Denied." While Smith certainly recalled the captain's visit to Kimmel's office—he had himself been present—he was positive Zacharias had made no such prediction. Kimmel himself recalled no such statement. The captain's claim, Smith said, was "clairvoyance in reverse."

A UP story headlined "Marshall Again Takes Blame for No Alert" reported that the Chief of Staff took overall responsibility for the failure to make General Short see that the November 27th "war warning" was more than a sabotage alert. It was clear, however, that the man who had done so much to win the war felt harassed during his testimony and could not remember details. Pressed on the point, Marshall snapped, "I had an immense amount of papers going over my desk every day . . . I am not a bookkeeping machine."

Why had Marshall not used the phone on December 7th to warn Hawaii that a Japanese attack was likely, somewhere in the Pacific, at 7:30 a.m. local time? The General did not exactly recall, but thought it might have been because the phones were insecure. The Germans, he said, had eavesdropped on calls between Roosevelt and Churchill.

The *New York Times* headline on the first day of 1946 read "Stark Says Kimmel Had Full Warning." The Admiral, former CNO Stark testified, had been sent "eleven specific warnings" of possible Japanese action in the final three months of 1941. The warnings he said he supplied to the commanders, though, showed that they had in fact been not specific but general—and that none had referred to Pearl Harbor. Why had Stark, for his part, not phoned Kimmel on December 7th to tell him of the intercept pointing to possible Japanese action somewhere in the area under his command, at 7:30 a.m. Hawaii time? It had not occurred to him, Stark told the Committee.

"Inquiry Charged with Politics—Roosevelt Is Central Figure"

had been a typical early headline. The primary question for the committee, the *Chicago Daily News* had said, was "Did President Roosevelt and his cabinet know in advance of December 7 when and where the Japs would strike?" Although the President and his high officials had access to the MAGIC messages, nothing in testimony or evidence before the committee indicated that they realized what might occur.

A subheadline, as the Committee got under way, had declared "Kimmel and Short Are 'Forgotten Men' as Congress Seeks to Untangle Blame." Their role in the disaster, the article suggested, now appeared to have been "a relatively minor one." The Admiral and the General had not made "basic, monumental errors like those that were committed in Washington."

Kimmel sat day after day, dressed in civvies—sober three-piece suits—as the hearings continued. His son Ned, still in uniform but soon to go to Harvard to study law, was occasionally at his side. In January 1946, the Admiral at last had the opportunity—five years after Pearl Harbor—to make his case in public. He testified over six days, went through every detail, and responded to a barrage of questions.

Understandably, Kimmel's main point was that the Navy withheld from him "information which indicated the probability of an attack on Pearl Harbor at the time it came." This in spite of the fact that, from the start of 1941, he had requested that he be supplied with all important intelligence. Given that MAGIC was being supplied to the British Navy, he was asked, did he think it could also safely have been entrusted to him in Hawaii? He had been "quite as much entitled" to MAGIC as was London, he replied. Intercepts could have been sent to him by courier in "complete security."

Had he received the withheld intercepts, Kimmel said, they would have "radically changed" his assessment of the situation. "Knowledge of a probable Japanese attack" would have given him an opportunity to "ambush the Japanese striking force as it ventured to Hawaii."

Did Kimmel accept responsibility for the loss of life and warships that had occurred? "I was Commander-in-Chief of the

Fleet," he replied. "I cannot escape the responsibility which goes with that position. But I have no responsibility due to any dereliction on my part."

Was he telling the Committee on his solemn oath that he had made neither mistakes nor errors of judgment in the days before the Japanese attack? "That is a reasonable conclusion," replied Kimmel, "and it is a conclusion that the Navy Court of Inquiry came to."

As the Admiral finished testifying, a Republican congressman told him he had acquitted himself magnificently. Spectators applauded.

The work of Congress' Joint Committee was less than complete. A number of significant witnesses did not testify. Documents were withheld, not least Secretary of War Stimson's diary entries for the days before the attack. Private letters exchanged before and after the Committee's proceedings by officers at the top of the U.S. high command—including Marshall and Stark—show that memories were at best confused on vital matters. As one senator put it, there were "certain twilight zones and brown-outs" into which the Committee had "not been permitted to penetrate."

The Joint Committee's findings came in July 1946. The Democratic majority, joined by two Republicans, found President Roosevelt and his cabinet blameless. A minority of two Republicans, however, felt they had failed to perform the "responsibilities essential to the defense of Pearl Harbor."

The Committee found that the Intelligence and War Plans divisions of both the Navy and the Army in Washington had failed to give "careful and thoughtful consideration" to the MAGIC messages intercepted over four months—notably those showing that Japanese espionage had specifically targeted the warships at Pearl Harbor. The intercepts, or the gist of them, should have been supplied to Admiral Kimmel and General Short.

Those who headed these divisions—Wilkinson, Turner, Miles,

and Gerow—were blamed by inference but not by name. Though both CNO Stark and Admiral Turner had said they "thought" Admiral Kimmel was getting MAGIC—the Committee's report noted pointedly—neither had made sure to establish that for a fact. On the morning of the 7th, Stark had at first "hesitated" to let the commanders know that the Japanese planned to confront the Secretary of State at precisely 1:00 p.m. Washington time—7:30 a.m. in Hawaii. Stark reasoned that he "did not want to confuse them," and while he was not censured for this, the report made it clear that—if there is any doubt—information should "always" be sent on.

"Had greater imagination and a keener awareness of the significance of intelligence existed," the report said, "it is proper to suggest that someone should have concluded that Pearl Harbor was a likely point of Japanese attack."

Notwithstanding all this, the Committee found that Admiral Kimmel and General Short—"adequately informed of the imminence of war"—had failed to "appreciate the significance" of the intelligence that was available to them, to coordinate and liaise sufficiently, and to "maintain a more effective reconnaissance within the limits of their equipment." Theirs, though, had been "errors of judgment and not derelictions of duty."

This was not the total vindication Kimmel would have wanted, but it was light-years away from the blackening of his name that the Roberts Commission had inflicted five years earlier. Public opinion had shifted, he thought, and his position was "immeasurably better."

The Admiral's own determination aside, the progress had been made thanks in large part to his legal team, which had been a force in the convening of the Joint Committee in the first place. A handful of citizens, the Admiral's Navy attorney Hanify would later write, had "stood up against the awful power of officialdom in wartime. They rescued truth from oblivion."

To a degree, honor had been satisfied.

Not that the congressional report was the end of it. "The fog of doubt and accusation" that had hung so long over Pearl Harbor, wrote William White, the *New York Times'* correspondent who covered the Committee's work from start to finish, had been "dispelled only in part. It is plain that Pearl Harbor will remain long in controversy, an unquiet and angry ghost."

53

A VERY REAL personal ghost had never left the Kimmel household, never really would leave. While the Admiral was testifying in Washington, a "Finding of Death" notice had come from the Navy Department. Following investigation, the notice told the family, it could now be presumed that the Kimmels' eldest son, Manning, had indeed perished.

The Admiral had hoped against hope for almost eighteen months. Confusion over USS *Robalo*'s fate had added to his torment. After a long period of no news, a report months earlier had suggested that the submarine had gone down off the Philippines, following an explosion. Manning and others had reportedly survived in the water for many hours, swimming toward a nearby island. He had last been seen swimming on his back, in a state of exhaustion, and was thought to have drowned.

Another report, however, included Manning's name in a list of four men said to have made it to the shore and been taken prisoner by the Japanese. Then Manning and another man had supposedly been shot dead while trying to escape. With the war in the Pacific over and with access to witnesses in captured territory, further fragments of information would come in.

Now, with notification that his son was presumed dead, the Admiral pressed the Navy for more information.

As harrowing details began to come in, he shared them with his sons Tom and Ned but not with Dorothy. What he was being told, he knew, might turn out to be inaccurate. "I see no good purpose," he told Ned in a letter, enclosing one of the reports, "in showing this to your Mother." But Kimmel harbored no lingering notion that Manning could still be alive. "I am afraid," he wrote to the mother of a *Robalo* crewman, that "this very definitely closes a chapter."

In little private ways, it never would do that. The Admiral could not bring himself to cross out the entry for Manning in his address book. There had been a moment, too, when grief mingled with bitterness, betraying his dark suspicion of what President Roosevelt's political maneuvering had been in the days before Pearl Harbor. "That son-of-a-bitch," he had exclaimed when he learned of Manning's probable death, "killed my son!"

On compassionate grounds Tom Kimmel, the other submariner brother, had been transferred to a shore job after Manning was listed as missing. Before the war ended, however, he was given a command of his own and went back to sea. As the conflict ended, he boarded and brought to port two surrendering German U-boats. A year later, back in the Pacific, he supervised from the bridge of his submarine as wreaths were strewn on the ocean in memory of Americans who had died at sea during the conflict. A Kimmel had returned to Pearl Harbor.

Through it all, ever since the catastrophe that had been blamed on her husband, Dorothy Kimmel had been quietly supportive of him. Like him, she had received threats and endured baseless lies and insinuations. There had been an allegation right after the attack that—asserting her privilege as the wife of the commander in chief—she had bumped two pregnant Navy wives off a flight from Hawaii to California. Dorothy had been able to reply, courteously and truthfully, that she had never set foot in Hawaii.

A story had gone the rounds, the Admiral had revealed while testifying to Congress' Joint Committee, that he got his job as commander in chief because Dorothy was—supposedly—the niece of Democratic Senator Alben Barkley, the Committee's Chairman. They had, Kimmel said, never met. Relatives today know of no connection between the two families.

The Admiral's wife had had enough, and liked to think her husband had too. "We are both fed up with this Pearl Harbor affair," she had written to relatives. "It is driving us crazy. It is wonderful to have the War over, but it has brought tragedy and sorrow to my family. I think of Manning every minute and wish a miracle would bring him back. It's hard to enjoy anything anymore."

As the Joint Committee wound up its work in early 1946, Tom Kimmel advised his father that it was time to ease up. "You have worked and slaved and suffered over this business," he wrote home. "You have done all that is humanly possible to bring out the truth. I think you should drop any further activities in connection with this case . . . You owe it to yourself and to Mother."

Kimmel himself said he meant "never again to become too much concerned over this affair." Perhaps he meant it. He would never let go, however, of some of the perceived lies that had been told, and of the personal hurt. There was one man, especially, whom he would never forgive.

During the hearings in Congress, there was a moment when Kimmel's lawyers and former CNO Stark's lawyers got together to discuss how tense the relationship was between their respective clients. They got Kimmel and Stark to shake hands. It was clear, though, one of the attorneys would recall, that Kimmel was just going through the motions and was "mad at Stark . . . bitter."

The bitterness went back to the one-on-one breakfast meeting between the two men in 1942, soon after Pearl Harbor, when Stark let slip the fact that Washington had received MAGIC intelligence that Kimmel had not. The souring of their relationship had begun then.

After the Japanese attack, but before that fateful meeting, Kimmel had told Stark in a letter that he appreciated what he was doing to help in his predicament. "I will always value your friendship," he had written, "which is a precious thing to me." In his reply, Stark had signed his letter, "As always, Sincerely, Affectionately, and Faithfully."

They had been friends for more than forty years, since their Naval Academy days. Stark described Kimmel as "one of the closest and finest" friends he ever had. "I had the highest regard for him," Kimmel for his part later said of Stark. "I felt that he was one of my best friends . . . I trusted him . . . But I can't forget the fact . . . well, the events that have occurred since then."

In the year or so following the 1942 meeting, "Betty" Stark had tried to repair the rift. At the height of the war, from London, he had sent an effusive note wishing Kimmel "Happy Birthday." His greetings, he wrote, came "with all the good old wishes, and affection, and esteem, and everything else that I have held for you—and then some. Best of luck, keep cheerful." Kimmel's files do not indicate that he replied.

In the fall of 1943, Stark tried again. He had recently had a chance encounter with the Admiral's son Ned, then serving aboard the USS *Ranger*, which was in harbor in Britain. "Dear Mustapha," Stark wrote, using Kimmel's old nickname: "On a trip north to the Fleet . . . a smiling face came in, and 'twas Ned. I could have hugged the boy, I was so glad to see not only him but just someone from the family . . . My thoughts are often with you and Dot and, as you know, they are loyal, happy thoughts . . . Here's hoping that when this old war is over we will all be together again. Keep cheerful, Betty."

When the two admirals next met, it would be outside the Navy Court of Inquiry as Stark—covered in glory after having successfully directed the U.S. Navy's part in the D-Day landings—was about to testify. It was clear at once that Stark's overtures had not placated Kimmel. Stark had entered the waiting area, lawyer Hanify remembered, "smiling and obsequious. Kimmel was serious, stern, and tight-lipped . . . Stark was obviously anxious for an opportunity to talk with Kimmel, learn his mood."

Kimmel's mood was "extremely bitter," Admiral Hart, who represented Stark before the Navy Court, told the former CNO in a letter before the proceedings began: "As the country seems to hold him as the Number 1 criminal, and way out ahead of Short in that respect, I personally think he has rather good grounds for said bitterness." Hart was bothered, he told Stark well in advance, that the former CNO had kept no diary. To describe that as "unfortunate," he told his client, was an understatement. His other concern was the need to keep certain "very secret" matters behind closed doors. For those reasons, Hart had hoped Stark would not be obliged to testify.

It would have been better had he kept a diary, Stark agreed. In the seven days he spent on the stand, the combination of protecting MAGIC and demonstrating a hopelessly poor memory—one of Kimmel's attorneys termed it "a curious amnesia"—did him no favors.

Time after time after time, Stark responded to questions with "I don't recall," "I don't know," "Not the slightest recollection," or "I couldn't say." Asked whether he recalled the events of December 6th, the eve of the attack, he replied with a flat "No." Had he received any information by telephone that night—when the White House had called saying President Roosevelt had been trying to reach him? "No," he responded; "I say I don't recall." Did he recall the matter of the much-anticipated "Winds" weather forecast, which for days before the attack had been the object of intense search by the Navy, by the Army, and others? That, he said, rang no bells at all.

With hindsight, read today, Stark's testimony seems on its face to be at best vacuous, at worst evasive. Kimmel's counsel Rugg was able to pose the questions he did thanks to the background he had gleaned, not least the leaks from chief codebreaker Safford. Stark, though, was by and large—at a moment when the MAGIC intercepts were not yet available even to the closed Navy Court—duty-bound to fend off many questions.

Less than three weeks later, on August 28th, the dozens of MAGIC intercepts—obtained after much persistence by Kimmel's legal team—were released into the Court record. Stark, called to testify again, was asked about the messages between Tokyo and its consulate in Hawaii that had betrayed a special, increasing focus on the exact position of U.S. warships in Pearl Harbor.

All the messages he was asked about had been decoded and translated in the days just before December 7th. One was a request for Japan's spy in Honolulu to report not once but twice a week; another asked for information on ships' positions at anchor in specific areas of Pearl Harbor; another asked for fullest possible details on Navy air bases. Stark responded no more than to say he "might" have seen a given intercept, or that he did "not recall it at this time." Had the intercepts been discussed at headquarters? They might have been, Stark said, but he did not remember.

Three weeks earlier, in the same hearing room, he had been asked whether he was aware of any "important development of which Admiral Kimmel was not advised, as it occurred, by the quickest secure means then available." Stark had replied: "I have searched my brain, my conscience, my heart, and everything I have got, since Pearl Harbor started, to see wherein I was derelict, or wherein I might have omitted something." He had been able, he said, to think of only one thing. He wished now that on the morning of December 7th he had personally warned Kimmel, perhaps by phone, that an attack was possible somewhere in the Pacific at 1:00 p.m. Washington time, 7:30 a.m. at Pearl Harbor.

"I may be reminded before this investigation is over," Stark had said on the stand, "of other things . . . something more I should have done." It had become clear, by the time he finished testifying, that there was much more that he—or others in the department—should have shared with Kimmel. The former CNO knew how badly his testimony had gone over. "Perhaps," he wrote afterward to Hart, he had been "trying too hard to be so one-hundred-per-cent-plus honest, so that in spots I may have made more or less a mess of it. I know I was depressed."

"Part of the trouble" while he was testifying, he told Hart, could have been "my fondness and loyalty to Kimmel, my actual desire to share the burden and protect him so far as I could." Against the background of the long, long friendship they had shared, coupled with the hard fact that Stark had failed to ensure that Hawaii had access to MAGIC, Stark's testimony had struck Kimmel as quite the opposite of sharing the burden. So far as he was concerned, his friend had turned out to be an "awful liar."

Stark's note of sympathy, handwritten following the announcement that Kimmel's son Manning was missing in action, failed to move Kimmel. The Admiral took time to respond to virtually all such letters, but not to that one. It still lies in the file today, marked: "No answer."

In December 1944, after the Secretary of the Navy had followed up the Navy Court's verdict with a statement that there would be no courts-martial—and with a public but less than ringing vote of confidence in Kimmel—Stark tried again.

Dear Mustapha,

While I know nothing can ever undo much that has been done to you, I want you to know that no one could have had greater satisfaction than I when I read the decision recently published in the papers, that there was no grounds for courts martial for Pearl Harbor; and I trust this gave you too at least some degree of satisfaction.

My every good wish, as always,

Keep cheerful.

Sincerely,
Betty

The ingratiating tone of this latest missive, referring to a public statement that Kimmel thought invidious, was the last straw. The Admiral restrained himself until after Christmas before attempting a reply. His first draft began, "As I read your note of 12 December 1944, I am forced to conclude that your mind is affected or that you think mine is." It ended, "May God forgive you for what you have done to me, for I never will."

In the last of three drafts, all of which survive in his files, the Admiral wrote—with no opening salutation (his handwritten additions are shown in brackets here):

I am astonished that you could and would write me such a letter as that of yours of 12 December and I can easily see why no one could have greater satisfaction than you upon the publication of the decision that there were no grounds for courts martial for Pearl Harbor.

You betrayed the officers and the men of the Fleet by not giving them a fighting chance for their lives and you betrayed the Navy in not taking responsibility for your actions; you betrayed me by not giving me information you knew I was entitled to and by your acquiescence in the action taken on the request for my retirement; and you betrayed yourself by misleading the Roberts Commission as to what information had been sent to me and by your [self serving lapse of memory] before the Court of Inquiry.

I hope that you never communicate with me again and that I never see you or [hear or see] your name again that my memory may not be refreshed of one so despicable as you.

Before mailing the letter, Kimmel consulted with his legal team. Senior counsel Charles Rugg doubted whether Stark's note to the Admiral merited a response. The drafts would be found years later, following Kimmel's death, still lying in his desk drawer. There is no evidence that the two friends ever had personal contact with each other again.

54

"**WHEN I FINISHED** the Pearl Harbor investigations," Kimmel was to write, looking back, to a former member of his staff, "I was a sadly disillusioned individual." What had hit him hardest, he said, had been the testimony by witnesses who either "failed to tell the whole story as they knew it" or flat out "lied."

The official inquiries were over. The urgency had gone out of the case. Blame for the catastrophe in Hawaii was not weighing quite so heavily on the Admiral's shoulders. What remained was the sense that the stain on his record had not been washed away entirely, that elements of the story remained untold.

Meanwhile, there was a vacuum in his life. In his mid-sixties, seemingly still fit, he left the New York area, which had been his base only for his wartime civilian work, and moved with Dorothy to the first of two homes in Connecticut. They wanted to be near their son Tom, now a commander, who was teaching at the New London submarine school.

In 1947, a hugely influential Navy voice was raised in Kimmel's defense. Admiral William "Bull" Halsey, who had after serving under Kimmel gone on to win a series of important victories in the Pacific, highlighted what he saw as gross injustice. He wrote in a memoir:

> I'll take my oath that not one of us would have guessed that the blame would fall on Kimmel, because not one of us thought he deserved it—any part of it. I want to emphasize my next statement. *In all my experience, I have never known a Commander in Chief of any United States Fleet who worked harder, and under more adverse circumstances, to increase its efficiency . . . Further, I know of no officer who might have been*

*in command at that time who could have done more than Kim-
mel* did . . . Even an ideal man can't do a job without proper
tools, and Kimmel did not have them.*

Who, then, is to blame? Look at it logically: the attack succeeded because Admiral Kimmel and General Short could
not give Pearl Harbor adequate protection. They could not
give it because they did not have it to give. They did not have
it because Congress would not authorize it . . . Instead of trying to dodge our responsibility by smirching two splendid
officers, we should be big enough to acknowledge our mistakes.

In a letter to Kimmel, Halsey told him he thought his treatment after Pearl Harbor had been "outrageous," that he had been
"left holding the bag for something you did not know and could
not control." If only, he went on, Kimmel and the Fleet had had
the MAGIC messages, had known of the intelligence the Japanese
had been gathering on Pearl, had known that something was
planned for December 7th . . .

One after another, other admirals made their voices heard. Admiral Yarnell, who had earlier commanded the Asiatic Fleet and
the Navy base at Pearl Harbor, said he thought Washington's treatment of Kimmel and Short had been "disgraceful," the flaws in official probes "a blot on our national history." CNO Stark and Chief
of Staff Marshall, he wrote to Kimmel's lawyers, should have admitted that the "cause of the disaster" had been their failure to
send vital information to Hawaii.

Admiral Raymond Spruance, who had found fame at the Battle of Midway, was to say he felt "Kimmel and Short were held
responsible for Pearl Harbor in order that the American people
might have no reason to lose confidence in their government in
Washington." That might have been possible to justify at the time,
with America in crisis, but it "did not justify damning forever

---

* Halsey's italics.

these two fine officers." The case had become "a dirty political proposition" and they should have been exonerated.

As the 1940s drew to a close, at his home in New London, Connecticut, Kimmel was not idle. He spent much of his time in a cramped upstairs room overlooking the old port, either corresponding about Pearl Harbor or working with the bulging boxes of documents he had accumulated. "We'd drive up there for a weekend," his son Ned's wife Harriott would recall, "and before we'd even get our suitcases in to the bedroom, Dad Kimmel would say, 'Ned, come on back here, I want to talk to you.' He'd show him all his papers—it was all he talked about. But he was a dear man."

The logical next step, the Admiral told a visitor in 1949, might be to write a book. He began working on it, but then—he explained in a letter—became "so emotionally upset I had to stop." Then, in the summer of 1950, a severe heart attack put the plan on hold for a matter of years. On the day of the attack, obstinate as ever, he insisted on walking to the ambulance and refused to lie on a gurney for the trip to the hospital. He would be there for months, then out of action for a long time.

In late 1954, when Kimmel's memoir did eventually appear, it was short and by and large factual, a military man's account. There in simple prose was the core of the story, told not in the complex language of government reports or in the tangle of lengthy testimony. No one who read it, however, could fail to be aware of the Admiral's lasting personal outrage.

"I deem it my duty to speak out," he wrote. "What took place in Washington must be so clearly placed on the public record that no group of persons in administrative power will ever again dare to invite another Pearl Harbor and then place the blame on the officers in the Fleet . . . I cannot excuse those in authority in Washington for what they did. And I do not believe that thousands of mothers and fathers whose sons perished . . . will excuse them. They will be judged at the bar of history." This last passage, predictably, greatly upset former Chief of Naval Operations Stark.

In spite of what Kimmel termed a "snotty" review in the *New York Times*, the book appeared on its best-seller list for a month. Good reviews in the *Wall Street Journal* and the *Chicago Tribune* pleased the Admiral. He was scornful of the *Washington Post* and the *New York Herald Tribune*, which gave the book "the brush-off or ignored it entirely." No newspaper however, challenged Kimmel's facts.

There had in recent months been an initiative to get the Navy to acknowledge in a practical way that an injustice had been done. Upon his removal as commander in chief, Kimmel had reverted to his previous two-star rank of rear admiral. Vice Admiral James Holloway, who headed the Bureau of Naval Personnel, proposed to the Secretary of the Navy that—"on the basis of information that has come to light"—Kimmel's four stars be restored.

A law passed after the war, Holloway pointed out, provided for all retired officers to be elevated—at the President's discretion—to the highest rank in which they had served. When the Navy Department had submitted a list of such officers to the White House, however, Kimmel had been the only flag officer omitted. "The pains of humiliation suffered by one of our country's finest officers," Holloway urged, should be eased. His proposal got nowhere.

Several years later, in a private letter to a fellow admiral, even the man Kimmel considered his nemesis, Admiral Stark, said he would be "glad" to see the four-star rank restored.

Kimmel had written his book, he said, for his grandchildren. There would soon be nine of them, frequent visitors to the roomy ranch-style house that he and Dorothy acquired at Groton—their last home. The grandchildren were to remember the house and their grandparents with lasting affection—Dorothy, large and welcoming, bountiful provider of food (not least peppermint-stick ice cream); the Admiral, formal but funny, attired in jacket and tie topped off by a seaman's knitted cap.

In the Kimmel household, the sea and the Navy were ever-

present. There was a dented silver canister that had once contained a bottle of champagne, a memento of the day when, as the
seagoing Navy's first lady, Dorothy helped launch the submarine
USS *Flying Fish*. The Admiral himself prowled about at dawn,
walking the perimeter of the house because he had been "used to
a ship's watch for so long."

At eighty, as the 1960s began, Kimmel was still a "commanding" figure. "He talked loud," one of the grandsons remembered,
"though I don't know if he talked loud because he could no longer
hear very well. But my impression was that when he talked you
listened." The boys found themselves listening, much of the time,
to the Admiral's thoughts about Pearl Harbor. "Though he was
enormously well versed on current events," one recalled, "a cover
to cover reader of newspapers and magazines of all stripes, he'd
start off on the news—but then almost inevitably get around to
Pearl Harbor." At least two of the grandchildren wrote high school
or college papers on the subject.

In the years just after the war, Kimmel had said that—in spite
of all the investigations—the full story of Pearl Harbor had yet to
be told. In old age, he still said that. Like thousands of others, but
more than most, he had been persuaded by all the early official
evasions that there was something about the case, something significant, that was still being covered up. "He spent the rest of his
life working on it," his grandson Manning remembered, "continuing to correspond with those of like mind."

A number of his Navy peers aside, those who were of like
mind—and eager to be in touch with Kimmel—were the Pearl
Harbor "revisionists," people pursuing the notion that President
Roosevelt had played a sinister role. By the late 1950s, by his own
account, Kimmel had read and been impressed by the works of the
principal revisionist authors. Though some were more reliable
than others, all targeted Roosevelt. All questioned whether the
truth had been told, and some were vitriolic. Their "facts" were
sometimes flimsy at best.

To speculate that something about the late President's role
remained hidden, however, was not the preserve of polemicists

or mischief-makers. At the cabinet meeting held a few hours after the attack, Secretary of Labor Frances Perkins had watched Roosevelt. Years later, she recalled having noted a look about him that she had seen often before. To her, the expression on his face that evening had suggested he was "making everything quite clear and open, when he was not exposing the total situation . . . There had been times when I associated that expression with a kind of evasiveness. I had a deep emotional feeling that something was wrong, that the situation was not all that it appeared to be."

Kimmel, moreover, was not the only admiral of his standing who came to think there was something about Roosevelt's actions before Pearl Harbor that had been concealed. In interviews published long after his death, his predecessor Admiral "Joe" Richardson declared himself "impelled to believe that sometime prior to December 7th the President had decided that only Marshall could send any warning message to the Hawaiian area. I do not know this to be a fact and I cannot prove it."

On the twentieth anniversary of the attack, Kimmel had spoken of new information, which he was "not at liberty to release," that showed the government in Washington "withheld information from us because they wanted the Japanese to attack." If there really was such evidence, it never did come out.

On the twenty-fifth anniversary, at the age of eighty-four, he went further. "My principal occupation—what's kept me alive—is to expose the entire Pearl Harbor affair. They wanted to get the United States into the War." "They?" a reporter asked.

"That was President Roosevelt and General George Marshall and others in the Washington high command," he replied. "FDR was the architect of the whole business—and I can't prove this categorically—that no word about Japanese fleet movements was to be sent to Pearl Harbor except by Marshall, and then he told Marshall not to send anything." Indeed, the Admiral could not prove it, nor has anyone ever succeeded in doing so. Though Kimmel had always been a stickler for hard facts, old age may have rendered him freer with his words than he should have been.

In the early 1960s, a historian who came to see him noted that he was "not too stable on his feet, merely shuffled along, pushing one foot on ahead of the other. A wave of sympathy swelled in me for this fine old gentleman who had suffered so much."

Kimmel did not have "any idea of dying any time soon," he told his son Tom in a 1963 letter, but he said that he believed in "preparing for the inevitable." He had begun to make arrangements for where his papers—there were fifty-six boxes of them—would eventually be deposited. It had to be somewhere, he said, "that the Government can't get their damned hands on them."

The Admiral was also thinking about where he wished to be interred—and where not. "Will you kindly make arrangements," he told his son, "to have a place reserved for Dot and me in the Naval Academy Cemetery? If you can't get a place there I don't care where I am buried so long as it is not in Arlington." Those he saw as having betrayed him and the Fleet—Stark and Marshall—were to be buried at Arlington.

Husband Kimmel died on May 14th, 1968, aged eighty-six, and was buried as he had wished at the Naval Academy. The large stone that marks the grave bears, on one side, an epitaph to his son Manning, lost at sea in 1944. On the other side, it bears the inscription:

HUSBAND EDWARD KIMMEL

ADMIRAL UNITED STATES NAVY

FEBRUARY 26, 1882–MAY 14, 1968

COMMANDER-IN-CHIEF, UNITED STATES FLEET

WHEN JAPAN ATTACKED PEARL HARBOR ON

DECEMBER 7, 1941

Above the inscription are four small stars.

Coda

OFFICIALLY, KIMMEL HAD died a *two*-star rear admiral. In spite of the law that provided for Navy officers' promotion to the highest rank at which they had served, Kimmel alone had been passed over. It was his sons, Navy veterans both, who drafted the inscription for his tombstone and determined that it would be topped by four stars. Four stars he had had, and so far as they were concerned, four stars he would have in perpetuity. No one at the Naval Academy raised any objection. The gravestone proclaims the fact that Kimmel had for a time been one of the very few four-star admirals of his generation.

After the war, on hearing that his sons wanted to go to Washington and fight his cause, Kimmel had told his son Tom, "I do not want you or Ned to be involved in any way so long as you are in the Navy." By the time the Admiral died, though, Tom was fifty-three years old, was retired from the Navy following his own long naval career, and working on secret projects for Westinghouse. As for Ned, he was now—at forty-six—a senior lawyer for the DuPont chemical company. Both were committed to clearing their father's name, and would be for the rest of their lives.

Tom made his feelings plain within three weeks of his father's death, when the Secretary of the Navy wrote to say that the Navy shared the Kimmels' loss. The Admiral, the Secretary ventured, had "played an important role . . . during some of the most trying times this country has known." His son responded with acid courtesy. Though the Secretary's letter was appreciated, Tom wrote, it was "to the everlasting discredit of the Navy Department" that his father's efforts to bring out the facts about Pearl Harbor had been obstructed. "It is to be hoped," he went on, "that the record will eventually be set straight to repair some of the damage done to the moral fiber of the Navy."

So began a family struggle that was continuing as this book went to press in 2016. From his home in Annapolis, after retirement from Westinghouse in 1976 to his death twenty years later, Tom fought to unearth hidden facts, wherever they might lead. When Ned in turn retired, in 1984, he threw all his energies—allied to his skills as a lawyer—into the fight.

The brothers' roots were in the Navy, and Tom had made the service his career. He was, one of his sons said, "loyal as a dog to the service." Yet they fought the Navy bureaucracy, seeking to right what they saw as the injustice to their father, to the end of their days.

In 1992, at seventy-eight, Tom could be found at his apartment a mile from the Naval Academy, seated behind a desk filled with data about Pearl Harbor, armed with phone, computer, and portable copier. He worked on, still lobbying the government, in his words, "for the name of the family and for the grandchildren." The room, a visitor thought, was his "small battle outpost for his father's place in history."

The military analogy applied equally to Tom's brother. At his home in Wilmington, Delaware, Ned labored on, virtually until he died, in a converted bedroom that all the family called his "war room." It contained a desk DuPont had given him when he retired, leather armchairs, two eight-foot tables, a couple of phones, and a fax machine. There were, too, shelves lined with books about Pearl Harbor and the forty volumes reflecting the work and findings of the nine official investigations. Ned would say, "My father .gave those to me in a laundry sack."

One of Ned's children remembered, "He'd sit there, for a long time, on a typewriter. We finally got him on to a computer." He worked on and on, day in day out, forty hours a week and more. "From when he retired," his widow, Harriott, recalled, "he went for it hook, line and sinker." "Bringing before the public the true circumstances," and "urging action which we believe, if taken, will restore my father's reputation and honor," Ned himself would write, "has consumed my full time."

Why were the brothers so powerfully motivated? "I think," Tom's daughter Ginger said, "they were brought up as red, white, and blue, the way my grandparents made them. Justice, duty, and honor were always taught in our family. It's the whole concept of 'It's the right thing to do.' The military in them said, 'You cannot leave a wronged man out there high and dry. You do things right. You do things with honor.' For my father and my uncle, it was part of their very being. You could not have met two more honest men."

The first major breakthrough for the family came in the mid-1980s, and not as a result of the brothers' work but from an entirely unexpected quarter. The ten-thousand-member Pearl Harbor Survivors Association, gathered in New York for its national convention, voted on a resolution calling for a tribute to honor both Admiral Kimmel and General Short. It was adopted unanimously by those attending. The brothers were invited to travel to Hawaii with their families for a reunion of the Association.

"We all went out there," Kimmel's grandson Tom Jr. remembered in 2016: "my Dad and my mother Nancy, my uncle Ned and his wife Harriott, both my brothers and their wives, my sister, and a bunch more of us. It was a big reunion—about eight hundred survivors and their families."

"We were wondering what kind of reception we would get from some of them," Tom Jr.'s brother Bill Kimmel said, "us being the children and grandchildren of Admiral Kimmel. Then, as we were walking down the street, one of the survivors came up to me and we talked a bit. I gave him my name, and he said, 'Any relation to *the* Kimmel?' I was wondering whether he was going to wag his finger at me and read me the riot act. Next thing I know he waves his friends over and says, 'You gotta meet this guy. This is Admiral Kimmel's grandson.' They asked us to pose with them for photos. They were so supportive of their former commander in chief!"

Later, in the convention hall, the Pearl Harbor Survivors roared applause as Tom and Ned Kimmel accepted awards on behalf of

their late father. The citation stated that it had been wrong that
the Admiral had taken the brunt of the blame, that others should
have shared it, and that he had not been allowed a court-martial
at which he could defend himself. "While there is still time in
our generation," it continued, the Association wished to recognize
Kimmel for his "dedicated performance of duty and for carrying
to his death the unfortunate burden and stigma associated with
the catastrophe."

Encouraged, the Kimmel brothers began lobbying for posthumous restoration of the Admiral's four-star rank. There began an
interminable round of reaching out to Secretaries of the Navy,
Secretaries of Defense, U.S. senators—and four U.S. presidents.

President George H. W. Bush's Secretary of the Navy recommended to Secretary of Defense Frank Carlucci that the rank issue be referred to the White House. Through a Deputy Secretary,
Carlucci declined to refer it. A request also went to Carlucci's successor Dick Cheney. Contacted through an intermediary, Cheney
suggested (among other things) that the Kimmels "seek help from
the voices of that time" and secure an appropriate resolution from
the Pearl Harbor Survivors Association.

At its 1990 convention, the Survivors Association voted a new
resolution, urging Cheney to recommend to President Bush that
he nominate Kimmel and Short for posthumous elevation to the
ranks they held until December 1941. The Association further
asked that Bush recommend the measure to the Senate. The Naval Academy Alumni Association and the Admiral Nimitz Foundation passed similar motions. Although the family had fulfilled
each and every one of the suggestions he had personally made,
Cheney was to turn the brothers' request down, stating that "the
promotion process is not the way to address the issue of your father's place in history."

In 1990, one distinguished survivor was a winner of the Navy
Cross: Joe Taussig, who as a twenty-one-year-old ensign aboard
the USS *Nevada* had continued to direct antiaircraft fire even after

suffering a wound that cost him one of his legs. "We who served under Admiral Kimmel," he wrote in 1990, "recognized him as an outstanding leader . . . It is time to return him to his four-star rank . . . It is never too late in our nation to do the right thing."

In 1991, five U.S. senators—Joe Biden, John McCain, William Roth, Alan Simpson, and Strom Thurmond—signed a letter asking President George H. W. Bush—a former Navy pilot who fought in the Pacific in World War II—to support the request. No fewer than thirty-six admirals—including a former chairman of the Joint Chiefs, four former Chiefs of Naval Operations, and ten former commanders in chief of the Pacific Fleet—all signed a petition urging him to recommend Kimmel and Short for posthumous promotion. The names on the petition, coupled with those of others who expressed their view before and since, show that dozens of admirals—Kimmel's peers—have expressly favored this course:

> We the undersigned retired senior officers respectfully urge you to nominate to the U.S. Senate Rear Admiral Husband E. Kimmel, USN for posthumous promotion to Admiral and Major General Walter C. Short, USA, for posthumous promotion to Lieutenant General.

> Very respectfully,

Thomas H. Moorer	Charles D. Griffin
Admiral, USN (Ret.)	Admiral, USN (Ret.)
Elmo R. Zumwalt Jr.	John J. Hyland
Admiral, USN (Ret.)	Admiral, USN (Ret.)
David H. Bagley	Robert L. J. Long
Vice Admiral, USN (Ret.)	Admiral, USN (Ret.)
William F. Bringle	Frederick H. Michaelis
Admiral, USN (Ret.)	Admiral, USN (Ret.)
Jeremiah A. Denton Jr.	Ulysses S. G. Sharp Jr.
Rear Admiral, USN (Ret.)	Admiral, USN (Ret.)

James B. Stockdale
Vice Admiral, USN (Ret.)

Steven A. White
Admiral, USN (Ret.)

Waldemar F. A. Wendt
Admiral, USN (Ret.)

James L. Holloway III
Admiral, USN (Ret.)

William J. Crowe Jr.
Admiral, USN (Ret.)

Lee Baggett Jr.
Admiral, USN (Ret.)

Thomas B. Hayward
Admiral, USN (Ret.)

Walter F. Boone
Admiral, USN (Ret.)

Worth H. Bagley
Admiral, USN (Ret.)

Donald C. Davis
Admiral, USN (Ret.)

Ralph W. Cousins
Admiral, USN (Ret.)

Noel A. M. Gayler
Admiral, USN (Ret.)

Sylvester R. Foley Jr.
Admiral, USN (Ret.)

Ronald J. Hays
Admiral, USN (Ret.)

Huntington Hardisty
Admiral, USN (Ret.)

Roy L. Johnson
Admiral, USN (Ret.)

William P. Lawrence
Vice Admiral, USN (Ret.)

Kinnaird R. McKee
Admiral, USN (Ret.)

Wesley L. McDonald
Admiral, USN (Ret.)

Horacio Rivero Jr.
Admiral, USN (Ret.)

David C. Richardson
Vice Admiral, USN (Ret.)

William N. Small
Admiral, USN (Ret.)

Harold E. Shear
Admiral, USN (Ret.)

Maurice F. Weisner
Admiral, USN (Ret.)

Stansfield Turner
Admiral, USN (Ret.)

Alfred J. Whittle Jr.
Admiral, USN (Ret.)

The Kimmel brothers, for their part, wrote to President Bush in the same vein. He replied through his military aide, noting that the Navy had repeatedly rejected the suggestion and asserting grandly that adopting it "would do no honor to the Admiral and might very well tear the tapestry that time and history have so thoughtfully woven."

During President Bill Clinton's first term, the Kimmels tried again. In 1994, however, Clinton replied that the record showed "no compelling justification for me to reverse prior decisions."

"In desperation," Ned Kimmel wrote, "I turned to Senator Strom Thurmond for help . . . We met with him and the Senator asked, 'What else can you do?' I answered that nobody in the Defense Department would meet or talk with me. To which the Senator replied, 'Well, I can take care of that.'" In early 1995, Thurmond, who was chairman of the Senate Armed Services Committee, convened a hearing. The Secretary of the Navy and the Deputy Secretary of Defense represented their departments, and Kimmel family members were given the opportunity to make their case. Undersecretary of Defense Edwin Dorn was then assigned to conduct a review.

From the family's point of view, the report Dorn produced late that year was a mixed bag. He led off with a finding: "Responsibility for the Pearl Harbor disaster should not fall solely on the shoulders of Admiral Kimmel and General Short; it should be broadly shared." On the other hand, he went on, "As commanders, they were accountable" and could not be absolved of responsibility. Dorn saw "no reason to contradict" previous findings that both commanders made "errors of judgment." There was, he said, "no evidence" that there had been efforts to make them scapegoats. He was unyielding on the issue of restoring their ranks. "Admiral Kimmel and General Short," he wrote, "suffered greatly for Pearl Harbor . . . But there can be no official remedy."

Neither the Kimmel brothers nor the members of the Survivors Association were prepared to throw in the towel. The Association asked veterans across the country to contact their senators and congressmen about the issue. "Nothing," it stated in a circular, "is more important to a career military person than their honor."

Meanwhile, one of the late Admiral's original team of lawyers, Edward Hanify, had for the past decade been quietly rustling up support for the restoration of rank. He had reached out early on to Senator Edward Kennedy, whose lead attorney Hanify had been following the accident at Chappaquiddick.

Kennedy had long expressed interest and now—at Hanify's urging—he put his weight behind getting action in the Senate. In April 1999, in Clinton's second term, Senators Joe Biden and William Roth sponsored a resolution to restore both Kimmel and Short to the ranks they had held in 1941. In Biden's words, it was unacceptable to forget "two brave officers whose true story remains shrouded and tarnished by fifty-seven years of official neglect of the truth."

Though the Senate approved the resolution, it initially died in the House. Then, a year later, new life was breathed into the measure when the House Armed Services Committee voted to include it as an amendment to the Defense Authorization Bill. The overall legislation was then passed by both House and Senate in the spring of 2000. All that was now necessary was presidential follow-through.

This was victory at long last, it seemed to the Kimmels. "I am still reeling with euphoria over the way things turned out," Ned wrote in a letter. "I was sitting quietly at my kitchen table Saturday afternoon when the phone rang and this voice said, 'This is Ted Kennedy.' You can imagine my surprise. The conversation ended with him pledging that he was going to do everything he could to see we got the result we wanted. It is my fervent hope we can muster enough clout with [President Bill] Clinton to get the ball over the goal line!"

Pressure was applied. Senators, including—not for the first time—Kennedy, as well as Biden, Roth, Strom Thurmond, and John Kerry, all wrote to the President urging the matter. So did several members of the House. Clinton, however, left office in January 2001 without fulfilling their request—apparently because of constitutional concerns.

For Ned Kimmel and the extended family, it was a huge disappointment. In the excitement after Congress passed the legislation, Ned had dictated the notional menu for a celebration dinner: "crab cakes, filet of beef," and—stern admonition—"no cheap whiskey." The invitees would have included nine admirals and seven U.S. senators.

At eighty, Ned would still be writing carefully argued letters, pressing the matter of rank restoration, to Clinton's successor George W. Bush. The Defense Department's advice, an aide responded, was that there was no cause to act. Senators who supported the Kimmels' campaign were told the same. "Dad had been hoping someone would get the doggone thing to the President himself," Ned's son Manning said: "But that wall around the President is very difficult to pierce."

Tom Kimmel had died in 1997 and Ned followed him in 2005. A year or so later, astonishingly, Ned's eighty-four-year-old widow Harriott did contrive to get material hand-delivered to President Bush, and got her congressman to write. The correspondence was forwarded to the Defense Department, which replied that its position remained unchanged. Before his death, Ned had said he hoped to get the Kimmel matter wrapped up, "so that I don't have to pass on the baton to my sons and nephews. But they are perfectly prepared to accept it should the need arise. This is a blotch on the family name and we're going to get rid of it."

The dozen family members interviewed during the writing of this book—all the Admiral's grandchildren and some of the great-grandchildren—support the continuing effort. The portrait of the patriarch, in uniform, with his four stars, hangs in many of their homes. His ceremonial swords are cherished by family members, two of them great-grandsons who are themselves now serving in the U.S. Navy.

"Our commitment is something handed down," said Singleton Kimmel, another great-grandson in his thirties, "and not as a burden. There's been a ripple effect down through the family. A lasting bond. And it is not only about the wrong that was done him. It is about respect, and the timeless truths of integrity and honor. Honoring the father and the father of the father, and on back. A lot of American ideals are inherent to our story and how the family responded to it."

Two men now lead the continuing struggle with officialdom—Tom Kimmel Jr., a former Navy lieutenant commander and senior FBI agent who during his career dealt with organized crime and foreign counterintelligence; and Ned Kimmel's son Manning Kimmel IV, the managing partner of a chain of several radio stations. When not working on the vast collection of file material related to the case, Tom Jr. travels around the country giving PowerPoint presentations about his grandfather's case. Manning, who also maintains a large archive, has continued the political lobbying his father pursued.

The wordy brush-offs from Washington continued into the first decade of the millennium. Tom Jr. echoes something his father once said: "You know the people who get me? . . . those damn blue-suit admirals. They never wanted to address it in all these years. They're the ones I have contempt for."

While most of the long, long stream of official correspondence on the case has been inflexible, there were exceptions. In the 1980s Arthur D. Baker III, then a Special Assistant to the Secretary of the Navy (Intelligence and Historical Matters), wandered off-message in a letter about the rank issue to a professor of history in the U.S. Southwest.

In spite of the "long-held tradition that the man in charge must accept responsibility," Baker wrote, "my own predisposition would be to make the reinstatement. . . . It's a small gesture, involving negligible expense, and unlikely to upset anyone. . . . Kimmel and Short were, given the character of the times (and the character of FDR), 'necessary' scapegoats."

In 2002, a Special Assistant to Deputy Secretary of Defense Paul Wolfowitz, Jim Thomas, was asked for his view. Though he thought the commanders in Hawaii had made errors of judgment, Thomas reported: "It is clear that others share at least as much—

and in my opinion even greater—responsibility for the magnitude of the defeat at Pearl Harbor."

Letters by the Kimmel family to the Secretary of Defense and the Navy Department during President Barack Obama's period in office had by mid-2016 elicited two turndowns, and in one case no reply. The family had every reason to think, however, that Vice President Joe Biden, who back in 2000 had led Congress's effort to get the Hawaiian commanders' ranks restored, might bring his influence to bear on Obama. In 2007, when he had last commented publicly on the case, he had described it as "the most tragic injustice in American military history."

In the final months of the administration, the Kimmels ensured that the matter got Biden's attention. Copies of the hardback edition of this book were sent to him, and the Vice President's response greatly raised their hopes. He returned one copy of the book, along with a note he had written inside it. On the title page, beneath the words *A Matter of Honor*, he had written "& it is— Keep the faith! . . . Joe Biden 11.1.16."

The Kimmels were filled with optimism. They waited all through the dying days of the Obama administration, a period during which outgoing U.S. presidents customarily take action on matters they favor—but waited in vain. Nothing happened.

After Obama and Biden had left office, the authors wrote repeatedly to the former Vice President and his Foundation. Had Biden in fact urged Obama to take action? If he did so urge him, how had the President responded? We received no answer to our questions.

Though deeply disappointed, the Kimmels remain undeterred. For their family's honor, and for posterity, they are battling on. In December 2016, forty-two of them—covering three generations—gathered to see a statue to the Admiral unveiled in his hometown of Henderson, Kentucky. As this book goes to press, the Kentucky State legislature has voted for a request to Congress and President Trump that they act on the rank restoration issue. An approach to the Trump White House is also underway.

———

Admiral Kimmel himself, one of his grandsons reflected recently, would be impressed and gratified by his descendants' loyalty and persistence. He might, though, think the effort to get his rank restored somewhat "vainglorious." He would, however, "encourage to the skies our effort to get the full Pearl Harbor story to the public."

A priority concern to the Admiral, always, was the men who had served under him. "The officers and men stationed in Hawaii in 1941," he wrote in a note to himself found after his death, "were fine upstanding young Americans whom the American people should ever remember with gratitude and honor. In the Japanese attack, they showed themselves fearless, resourceful, and self-sacrificing. I shall be proud always of having commanded such men."

As for his own honor, he had long been sure that the truth about the background to Pearl Harbor would eventually emerge. Within less than a year of the end of World War II, he had testified that "History, with the perspective of the long tomorrow, will enter the final directive in my case. I am confident of that verdict."

Acknowledgments

PEARL HARBOR, like our previous nine nonfiction books, demanded that we scale a mountain range of research. The focus on Admiral Kimmel led us to the thirty-six reels of microfilm of the former commander in chief's own papers, which were donated to the American Heritage Center of the University of Wyoming; to thousands of pages of information maintained by his grandson Thomas Kimmel Jr.; to hundreds of family letters and scrapbooks kept by another grandson, Manning Kimmel IV; to material collected by his daughter-in-law Harriott Johnson Kimmel; and to Kimmel family records dating back to prerevolutionary days shared by Dorothy Kimmel Newlin.

One and all, the Kimmels responded patiently to our myriad questions—in the case of Tom and Manning, questions that persisted until the book went to the printer. It was unique, in our experience, to come upon an extended family so committed—three generations on—to the search for vindication that their forebear pursued to the end of his life. Clearing his name, they fervently believe, is a cause justified not only by family loyalty but by the facts. Those most involved in fighting Kimmel's cause hoped our work would help that cause, but insisted that what matters above all is historical truth. "Let the chips fall where they may," one of the grandsons said to us at the outset. We have striven to bring out the facts, some of them hitherto unknown.

We thank all the family members named above, especially Harriott Kimmel, who—in her early nineties—twice submitted to interview. We thank, too, Virginia Kimmel Herrick and her husband Steven; Husband Kimmel II and his wife Susan; William Kimmel and his wife Gail; Harriott Kimmel Silliman and her husband Henry; Edward Kimmel Jr. and his wife Rebecca;

John Newlin; Cassin Kimmel Williams and her husband Paul; and Singleton Kimmel. Tom Kimmel Jr.'s wife Judy and Manning Kimmel IV's wife Sheilah both contributed in many ways—not least with endless hospitality.

More than seven decades after the Pearl Harbor attack, we expected few if any veterans of 1941 to have survived—let alone be available to share their thoughts on the details of the catastrophe. All the more welcome was it, then, to discover that centenarian Vice Admiral David Richardson was alive and cheerfully helpful. Richardson, who as a young pilot flew out of Pearl Harbor in 1940, had gone on to distinguish himself at Guadalcanal, eventually rise to command the U.S. Sixth Fleet, and then—his career took him full circle—to retire as Deputy Commander-in-Chief of the Pacific Fleet. He was a tireless advocate of posthumous restoration of Admiral Kimmel's four stars. Ambassador William van den Heuvel, who had been an aide to Office of Strategic Services chief William Donovan, corrected a published suggestion that Donovan told him that President Roosevelt indicated he had had a degree of foreknowledge of the attack on Hawaii.

John Hanify, whose father was a key member of the legal team that served Admiral Kimmel, shared both his recollections and his privately held documents. John Connorton Jr., son of the man who conducted a post–Pearl Harbor review of MAGIC intercepts of Japanese messages for the Office of Naval Communications, recalled his father's conclusion that the Admiral was a scapegoat. Michael Smith, a former codebreaker, now an author who has written on intercepts of Japanese traffic in World War II, offered guidance. Bruce Lee, coauthor with Henry Clausen of *Pearl Harbor: Final Judgement*—an account of the latter's one-man probe conducted for the Secretary of War—and later author of a book of his own, *Marching Orders*, was generous with his time. Both books contain pertinent information on MAGIC.

Of the very many books on or related in one way or another to Pearl Harbor, some are of special note. Gordon Prange, professor of history at the University of Maryland, studied the disaster for thirty-seven years, only to die before his work was published. His books *At Dawn We Slept* and *Pearl Harbor: The Verdict of History*, published in the 1980s with the collaboration of Donald Goldstein and Katherine Dillon, are indispensable—as are his papers, held by the university. The collection holds the product of the almost two hundred interviews conducted by Prange, and they are invaluable. Though compact, the 2001 book *Pearl Harbor Betrayed*, by Michael Gannon, Distinguished Service Professor Emeritus of History at the University of Florida, is also indispensable.

So too is *The Accused: The Ordeal of Rear Admiral Husband Edward Kimmel, U.S.N.* by Donald Brownlow, who benefited in 1968 from interviews with Kimmel himself and others—notably Admiral Stark. Roberta Wohlstetter's 1962 book *Pearl Harbor: Warning and Decision*, which won the Bancroft Prize, is renowned for its scholarship. Wohlstetter, an analyst at the Rand Corporation, interviewed among others former Pacific Fleet intelligence officer Edwin Layton; Commander Arthur McCollum, former chief of the Far Eastern Section of the Office of Naval Intelligence; and key cryptanalysts. The 1981 compilation of key oral history interviews by Paul Stillwell, of the U.S. Naval Institute's journal *Proceedings*, is a vital resource. David Kahn's *The Codebreakers*, a 1966 history of codes and ciphers, remains seminal.

Books like ours are made possible by the quiet help of those who manage archives across the nation. We thank: Matthew de Salvo of the LibTech section of the University of Central Florida; Anne Turkos and Jason Speck in the Department of Special Collections at the University of Maryland; Scott Reilly and Dara Baker at the U.S. Naval War College's Historical Collection; Dale "Joe" Gordon, reference archivist for the Naval History and Heritage Command at Washington's Navy Yard, and his colleagues John Hodges and Glenn Gray; Mark Savolis, archivist of Special Collections at the College of the Holy Cross in Worcester, Massachusetts; Kathryn Dundon of Special Collections at the University of California at Santa Cruz; Tammy Williams of the Harry S. Truman Presidential Library in Independence, Missouri; Steven Shafer and Nathaniel Patch of the National Archives at College Park; and those who helped us in the Manuscript Division of the Library of Congress. Special thanks are due for the help over many months of Sarah Malcolm and her colleagues at the Franklin Delano Roosevelt Library, Hyde Park, New York.

We acknowledge the willing cooperation of others in several countries. In the United States: Ruthanne Annaloro, who graciously arranged meetings with her father, Vice Admiral David Richardson; Paul Burtness and Warren Uber, authors of *The Puzzle of Pearl Harbor*, whose account of their interview with Admiral Stark was especially helpful; Christopher O'Connor, for his original research on the 1940 raid by British aircraft against Italian battleships at Taranto; attorney James Lesar, who introduced us years ago to the tangled tale of how Washington handled, or mishandled, early intelligence on a possible attack on Pearl Harbor.

In Canada: retired Lieutenant-Colonel Angelo Caravaggio, former director of the Centre for National Security Studies at the Canadian Forces College, conferred with us on the Taranto raid; and Alicia Floyd, Collections Technician at the City of St. Catherines Museum in Ontario, helped us to access documents relating to supposed foreknowledge of the Pearl Harbor attack. In the United Kingdom, Mark Dunton of the National Archives at Kew and Andrew Riley, Senior Archivist at the Churchill Archives in Cambridge, dealt patiently with our questions about alleged British foreknowledge, and about allegations that material is still being withheld; Chris Williams guided us toward archive material on Frederick Rutland, a former Royal Air Force officer who spied for the Japanese; John Simkin shared his information on British Security Coordination; and Sian Padgett, Archives Research Manager at the UK Hydrographic Office, supplied charts of the Italian port at Taranto. From France, Marco Popov worked with us—as he did years ago during research for our biography of J. Edgar Hoover—on the mission by his father, British double agent Dusko, to warn Washington of Japan's intentions.

Our own researchers served us handsomely. In particular, Jacob Williams, in Washington, proved indefatigable. Ariel Robinson went back and forth to the National Archives for us at an early stage. In the UK, we had the benefit of Dr. Kathryn Castle's experience in the successful effort to obtain a key document at the National Archives. In Germany, Josie Le Blond and Hannah Cleaver proved swift and able. In the Netherlands, our friend Tim van der Knaap relentlessly chased elusive Dutch leads.

We much appreciated the skill of Christopher Spencer, who directed the television documentary based on this book, ably assisted by Rebecca Hayman. We also thank producers Alan Handel of Handel Productions and Arrow's Tom Brisley in London, without whose initiative the film could not have been made.

In Ireland, the stalwart Sinéad Sweeney transcribed many hours of recording with sensitivity. Sam Brittain built a very large file system from scratch. Pauline Lombard maintained it, as she has on eight previous projects. Emma-Louise O'Shea and Caroline Virtue did marathon Xeroxing. Emily Evans did a stint as an intern and survived. Moss McCarthy of LED Technology continued to solve our computer problems. Ger Killalea kept the office functioning.

This has been, more than usually, a complex and highly pressured operation—one made possible by the people at our publisher HarperCollins. Claire Wachtel saw the potential at the outset, and Jonathan Jao steered the project to completion, ably assisted by Sofia Groopman. We owe much to the professionalism, experience, and wisdom of our editor, Roger Labrie. Copy editor Susan Gamer guided us on the last lap. Our publisher, Jonathan Burnham, understood the challenge of a subject that has sparked controversy for decades, and instilled confidence in us when the going was toughest. Yet a third Jonathan, who has seen *A Matter of Honor* from concept to publication, is our longtime agent and trusted friend, Curtis Brown chairman Jonathan Lloyd. (As all his clients know, his able assistant Lucia Walker really runs the show . . .)

We are indebted once again to friends and close family. Miles Kara, a former Army intelligence officer, read the manuscript—in the spirit of comradeship—and helped us avoid some military howlers. Jo Deutsch and Teresa Williams, in Washington, extended hospitality better than any hotel could offer. Robbyn's mother

Theresa saw us through the months as she always has done, and both she and Pete Swan even went to the FDR Library for us. Sons Ronan and Colm Summers were press-ganged to do vital work, and did it excellently well. Fionn and Lara put up with us—again.

Anthony Summers and Robbyn Swan
Ireland, 2016

Notes

Abbreviations

ANDERSON Papers of Vice Admiral Walter S. Anderson, Operational Archives, Naval History and Heritage Command, Washington, DC

BLOCH Papers of Claude C. Bloch, Naval Historical Foundation Collection, Manuscript Division, LOC

DKN Dorothy Kimmel Newlin papers

FDR Franklin D. Roosevelt

FDRL Franklin D. Roosevelt Library, Hyde Park, NY

GP Gordon Prange Papers, Special Collections, University of Maryland, College Park

HAAN Kilsoo Haan Papers, Special Collections and Archives, University of California at Santa Cruz

HANIFY Edward Hanify—Husband E. Kimmel Collection, Archives and Special Collections, College of the Holy Cross, Worcester, MA

HART Papers of Admiral Thomas C. Hart, Operational Archives, Naval History and Heritage Command, Washington, DC

HEK Papers of Rear Admiral Husband E. Kimmel (microfilm version of collection available at American Heritage Center, University of Wyoming), courtesy of Thomas K. Kimmel Jr. (papers cited by reel number, e.g., HEK R3)

HOWE Papers of Walter Bruce Howe (Roberts Commission recorder), Naval Historical Collection, Naval War College, Newport, RI

KING Papers of Admiral Ernest J. King, Operational Archives, Naval History and Heritage Command, Washington, DC

KIRK Papers of Admiral Alan G. Kirk, Naval Historical Foundation Collection, Manuscript Division, LOC

KNOX Papers of Frank Knox, Manuscript Division, LOC

LAYTON Papers of Admiral Edwin T. Layton, Naval Historical Collection, Naval War College, Newport, RI

LOC Library of Congress

MB *The "Magic" Background of Pearl Harbor*, ed. John Connorton et al., Washington, DC: U.S. Government Printing Office, 1980, Volumes I–V and related Appendixes

MMK Papers of Manning M. Kimmel IV including family papers of Edward R. (Ned) Kimmel and Agatha Kimmel

MCCREA Papers of John L. McCrea, Naval Historical Foundation Collection, Manuscript Division, LOC

NARA U.S. National Archives and Records Administration

NHHC Naval History and Heritage Command, Navy Yard, Washington, DC

NIMITZ Papers of Fleet Admiral Chester W. Nimitz, Operational Archives, Naval History and Heritage Command, Washington, DC

NYT *New York Times*

NWC U.S. Naval War College, Newport, Rhode Island

OFSTIE Papers of Vice Admiral Ralph A. Ofstie, Operational Archives, Naval History and Heritage Command, Washington, DC

PHA *Pearl Harbor Attack, Report, Hearings* and *Exhibits*, Joint Committee on the Investigation of the Pearl Harbor Attack, U.S. Congress, 79th Cong., 1st Sess., Washington, DC: U.S. Government Printing Office, 1946. Forty volumes, cited by volume and page number (e.g., PHA 3, p. 12)

    The volumes include Testimony, Exhibits, and Reports of the nine official Pearl Harbor Investigations and are broken down as follows:

PHA 1–11	Testimony before the Joint Committee 1946
PHA 12–21	Exhibits of the Joint Committee 1946
PHA 22–25	Proceedings of the Roberts Commission 1942
PHA 26	Proceedings of the Hart Inquiry 1944
PHA 27–31	Proceedings of the Army Pearl Harbor Board 1944
PHA 32–33	Proceedings of the Navy Court of Inquiry 1944
PHA 34	Proceedings of the Clarke Investigation 1944
PHA 35	Proceedings of the Clausen Investigation 1945
PHA 36–38	Proceedings of the Hewitt Inquiry 1945
PHA 39	Reports of the Roberts Commission, Army Pearl Harbor Board, Navy Court of Inquiry, and Hewitt Inquiry
PHA Report	Report of the Joint Committee 1946

POWELL Papers of Rear Admiral Paulus P. Powell, Operational Archives, Naval History and Heritage Command, Washington, DC

PRATT Papers of Admiral William V. Pratt, Operational Archives, Naval History and Heritage Command, Washington, DC

PRO Public Records Office, The National Archives [UK], Kew, Richmond, Surrey

RAMSEY Papers of Admiral Logan C. Ramsey, Operational Archives, Naval History and Heritage Command, Washington, DC

SIMPSON Papers of B. Mitchell Simpson, Naval Historical Collection, Naval War College, Newport, R.I.

STARK Papers of Admiral Harold R. Stark, Operational Archives, Naval History and Heritage Command, Washington, DC

STIM Henry Lewis Stimson Papers (MS 465), Manuscripts and Archives, Yale University

TKK Thomas Kinkaid Kimmel Jr.—includes Pearl Harbor papers of Edward R. Kimmel and Vincent Colan, and personal papers of Manning Marius Kimmel II

TOL John Toland papers, FDRL

TURNER Papers of Admiral Richmond K. Turner, Operational Archives, Naval History and Heritage Command, Washington, DC

WP Washington *Post*

Sources

Short citations of books (e.g., Stillwell, p. 211; Prange, *Dawn*) and of U.S. government publications refer to full citations in the Bibliography.

[Notes that appear within **bold brackets** are the sources for the information contained within that note.]

Prologue

1 **reminisce:** Interview with Harriott Johnson Kimmel, 2013; "My Most Unforgettable Character," by Harriott Kimmel, draft manuscript, 11/19/69.

2 **"dereliction of duty":** PHA 39, p. 21.

2 **"Please don't":** *Newsweek*, 12/12/66.

2 **"every moment":** Ibid.

3 **"betrayed the officers":** Undated draft letter, 1944, HEK R35; 12/28/44 draft, HEK R27.

CHAPTER 1

7 **"We will not participate":** FDR speech, 10/23/40, www.presidency.ucsb .edu.

7 **"surplus":** FDR speech, 6/10/41, ibid.

7 **"a fight":** FDR radio address, 12/29/40, ibid.

7 **Churchill-FDR correspondence:** "The Special Relationship," and correspondence, FDRL; voluminous correspondence in PREM 3/469, PRO.

7 **Churchill implored:** Dallek, p. 254.

7 **"more ships"/"an emergency"/"world control":** FDR radio address, 12/29/40, www.presidency.ucsb.edu.

8 **tension:** Prange, *Dawn*, pp. 3ff; Ted Morgan, pp. 575ff.

CHAPTER 2

9 **The sound of church bells:** Morison, pp. 98ff. Some descriptions rendered in the present tense in the quoted passages that follow—in this chapter only—are in the past tense in the original. The authors have altered tenses for consistency and compressed some quotes—but never changed the sense.

9 **At 7:54/"dots in the sky":** *Boston Globe*, 12/7/91.

9 **line of planes:** Stillwell, p. 211.

9 **Furlong:** Prange, *Dawn*, pp. 505ff.

9 **"flathatting":** PHA 32, p. 444.

10 **"Airraid on Pearlharbor":** Ramsey was to testify that he ordered this memorable broadcast. Other testimony, by Commander Vincent Murphy—Admiral Kimmel's duty officer that morning—indicates that he sent a virtually identical message. The record indicates that as many as three similar messages were transmitted within eleven minutes. The first, Ramsey's, appears to have been transmitted at 7:58 a.m. Pearl Harbor time—as a voice message (PHA 32, pp. 444, 458; PHA 26, pp. 209ff, 135; PHA 24, p. 1365, but see pp. 11, 535).

10 **"war planes"/call to arms:** Stillwell, p. 211.

10 **"stumbling"/"mackerel":** *Proceedings*, 12/68.

10 **"Rock of Ages":** Interview with Robert Dunlop, Series V.2, Box 13, GP.

10 **exercise:** La Forte and Marcello, p. xvi; Lord, pp. 66, 82.

10 **"Christ":** Ted Morgan, p. 615.

10 **war games:** Weintraub, p. 270.

10 **wife slumbers:** Interview with Robert Dunlop. Series V.2, Box 13, GP.

10 **"good imitation":** Stillwell, p. 264.

11 **Kimmel awake:** Kimmel, pp. 7ff, 76; PHA 23, pp. 1125, 1193; PHA 26, pp. 209ff.

11 **submarine:** The destroyer, USS *Ward*, had first been alerted to a possible submarine at 3:58 a.m., but at that time had been unable to locate one. At about 6:30 a.m., having sighted a sub in plain view—and in line with Kimmel's standing order—both the *Ward* and the patrol plane had attacked it. There had been numerous previous submarine sighting reports that had turned out to be baseless, and—though Kimmel said he would head for his office anyway—he wanted verification (PHA 26, pp.209ff; Kimmel, p. 7; Gannon, pp. 225ff; Prange, *Dawn*, pp. 495ff).

11 **"stricken":** Brownlow, p. 133.

11 **"something terrible":** Ibid., p. 507.

11 **tally:** Fact sheets, National WWII Museum and Pearl Harbor History Associates.

11 **devastation of fleet:** "Report of Action 7 Dec. 1941," 12/21/41, HEK R4; *Naval History,* Winter 1991.

11 **"Rising Sun markings":** John Burrill to John Toland, 7/29/79, TKK.

11 **Ten-Ten dock/***Utah:* PHA 1, p. 34; Gannon, pp. 1ff, 4.

12 *Oglala:* Commanding Officer to CINCPAC, 12/11/41, www.ibiblio.org.

12 *Pennsylvania:* Commanding Officer to CINCPAC, 12/16/41, ibid.; Prange, *Dawn,* p. 537.

12 **"tapping":** *Newsweek,* 12/12/66.

12 *Nevada:* Prange, *Dawn,* p. 536; Gannon, p. 245.

13 **"fireworks":** *Evansville Courier,* 12/1/91.

13 *Arizona:* Gannon, pp. 8ff; Prange, *Dawn,* pp. 513ff.

13 **"legs, arms"/"agony"/"hell":** Weintraub, pp. 244, 266.

13 **"no panic":** Landis and Gunn, p. 13.

13 **"shocked":** Interview with Edwin Layton, Series V.2, Box 58, GP.

13 **"cool and collected":** Crosley to Toland, 1/13/79, TKK.

13 **"very effectively executed":** Interview with William "Poco" Smith, Series V.2, Box 74, GP.

14 **"Goddamn":** Interview with Edwin Layton, Box 30, Folder 1, LAYTON.

14 **"exultant":** Brownlow, p. 134.

14 **"ping":** Major General Omar T. Pfeiffer, History and Museums Division, USMC, Washington, DC.

14 **"Too bad":** Brownlow, p. 134; and see PHA 23, p. 899.

14 **"Sailors jumping":** La Forte and Marcello, p. 123.

14 **"The oil":** Ibid., p. 55.

14 **"glob-like":** Ibid., p. 20.

14 **"Guys are screaming":** *Evansville Courier,* 12/1/91.

14 **"man crawling":** *Newsweek,* 12/12/66.

15 **"ashes blowing":** PoliticsDaily.com, 12/7/10.

15 **Valkenburgh:** Interview with Admiral William Smith, Series V.2, Box 74, GP.

15 **"disintegrate":** *Newsweek,* 12/12/66.

15 **"Two or three":** Weintraub, p. 285.

15 **"injured men":** La Forte and Marcello, p. 248.

16 **"We work":** *Boston Globe,* 12/7/91.

16 **Leary:** Fairfax Leary Jr. to Edward Kimmel, 2/2/90, MMK.

16 **whores:** *Naval History,* Winter 1991.

16 **"sterile"/"Limbs":** Weintraub, pp. 607ff.

16 **"hold the hand":** Stillwell, p. 241.

16 **"I take care"**: "A Priest's Memories of Pearl Harbor" www.susangaddis
.net.

17 **"A young man, filthy"**: *Naval History*, Winter 1991; interview with Admiral Logan Ramsey, Series V.2, Box 68, GP.

17 **"identification tags"**: Interview with General Robert Dunlop, Series
V. 2, GP.

17 **also suffered**: Dr. Richard Kelley, "PH Attack Killed Lots of Civilians,
Too," 12/11/10; Weintraub, p. 264.

17 **"jump rope"**: Interview with Elizabeth McIntosh, undated, Veterans
History Project.

17 **invade/rumors**: PHA 20, pp. 4523ff; Weintraub, pp. 270, 589ff.

17 **radio stations**: KGMB entry, www.ospreypearlharbor.com.

17 **Martial law/underground shelter**: Major General Thomas Green,
"Martial Law in Hawaii," Green Papers, LOC; interview with General
Robert Dunlop, Series V.2, GP.

18 **window painted/further attack**: PHA 20, pp. 4523ff; interview with
Poco Smith, Series V.2, Box 74, GP; interview with Walter DeLany,
Series V2, Box 12, GP.

18 **buses**: Interview with Walter DeLany, Series V.2, Box 12, GP.

18 **evacuating**: Roy Lynd to John Toland, 2/13/79, Box 118, TOL; *Naval History*, Winter 1991.

18 **"guards shoot"/"slit our wrists"**: La Forte and Marcello, pp. 248ff.

18 **"moonbow"**: Weintraub, pp. 534ff.

18 **2,403**: Prange, *Dawn*, p. 539.

18 **"Charred remains"**: Weintraub, p. 629; "Navy Medical Dept. Preparedness," 1941, www.ibiblio.org.

19 **DNA**: *Guardian* [London], 4/14/15.

CHAPTER 3

20 **The news had reached**: PHA 12, pp. 3828ff. Sources differ on exactly
when the message reached Knox and Stark. Our estimate is based on
the known time of transmission of the initial signal from Pearl Harbor,
and the rough time of Knox and Stark's meeting. Knox was the first
high U.S. government official to learn of the attack on Pearl Harbor.

In 1941, Pearl Harbor was designated a time five and a half hours
behind Washington, DC, time. Tokyo (across the international date line)
was fourteen hours ahead of Washington and nineteen and a half hours
ahead of Pearl Harbor. The attack on Pearl Harbor occurred at 7:55 a.m.
local, 1:25 p.m. in Washington, and 3:25 a.m. on December 8th in Tokyo.
(PHA 26, p. 135; PHA 8, pp. 3828, 3835; but see PHA 11, p. 535).

20 **"My God!"**: PHA 8, p. 3829.

20 **Hopkins and FDR "out of my hands"**: Sherwood, pp. 430ff.

20 **FDR calls Hull and Stimson:** Ibid., p. 431; Stimson diary, 12/7/41, cited in PHA 11, pp. 5437ff.

20 **Marshall:** PHA 14, p. 1411.

21 **"URGENT":** PHA 11, p. 5351; SECNAV to ALLNAV, 12/7/41, TKK; Simpson, p. 114.

21 **"HOSTILITIES":** PHA 24, pp. 1365, 1581.

21 **"flash":** Weintraub, pp. 268, 277; WP, 12/6/11.

21 **guard/machine guns:** Reilly, p. 5.

21 **knots:** WP, 12/6/11.

21 **crammed:** Correspondents of *Time, Life,* and *Fortune,* pp. 12ff.

21 **Tully/"anguish":** Tully, pp. 252ff.

22 **"visibly shaken":** Moreel to Barnes, 12/17/61, HEK R32.

22 **Churchill/"It's quite true":** Churchill, pp. 537ff.

22 **"tired and depressed":** Anthony Cave Brown, *C: The Secret Life,* p. 382.

22 **"So we had won":** Churchill, pp. 539ff.

23 **"My God":** Fields, p. 80.

23 **"I'm going":** Tully, pp. 256ff.

23 **updates:** Stillwell, p. 104.

23 **Bloch:** PHA 36, p. 371.

23 **"It's bad":** *Newsweek,* 12/12/66.

23 **Perkins:** Frances Perkins Oral History, Columbia University, 1955.

23 **cabinet meeting/FDR opens/"awfully serious"/"dead silence":** Stimson diary entry at PHA 11, p. 5439; PHA 19, p. 3502.

24 **Though news of:** Japan's bombing attacks in the Philippines, begun before the cabinet met at the White House, would continue after the meeting ended. During the night (Washington time), Japan also attacked the U.S. base on the island of Midway (Prange, *Verdict,* pp. 467ff).

25 **"Why did you":** Connally, p. 459. There had, in fact, been no "log chain" barrier. There was an antisubmarine net, but it was open at the time the attack began. No ships, however, left harbor during the attack (PHA 13, p. 494).

25 **Assumptions were already:** The assumptions about the whereabouts of officers and their activities were inaccurate: 70 percent of the officers and 90 percent of the men were on board their ships in the early morning of December 7th. Admiral Kimmel had ordered that an adequate complement of officers and men be on board ships at all times—including enough to man the antiaircraft batteries (PHA 32, p. 255; PHA 22, p. 537; "Air Raid Dec. 7 1941," memo prepared for Vice Admiral Pye, Commander Battle Force, Pacific Fleet, HEK 4; and Gannon, pp. 27ff).

25 **Perkins:** Perkins Oral History, supra.

26 **Knox would fly:** Ibid., p. 118.

26 **demand in Congress:** AP, 12/9/41.

CHAPTER 4

28 **"no dukes":** *Honolulu Star-Advertiser,* 2/1/41.

28 **first Kimmels/Husband family/flatboats:** "The Ancestors and Descendants of Husband Edward Kimmel," 1956; unpublished notes by Sibella Kimmel, 4/15/29; interviews with Thomas K. Kimmel Jr. and Manning M. Kimmel IV.

28 **Marius:** *Evansville Sunday Courier and Press,* 1/19/41; "Battle of Crooked Creek," Kansas State Historical Society, Vol. XII, pp. 312ff, TKK; Lee to Kimmel, 8/12/1866, MMK; Ashe, Weeks, and Van Noppen, pp. 185ff.

29 **"Hubbie" or "Kim":** E.g., Report card, Henderson Public Schools, 1/24/1892, TKK; family correspondence, MMK; genealogical records, DKN.

29 **North Green Street:** *Evansville Courier-Press,* 1/19/41.

29 **siblings not especially close:** Ibid.; interview with Thomas K. Kimmel Jr.

30 **Singleton/valedictorian/honesty:** *Evansville Courier-Press,* 1/19/41; "28th Annual Henderson High School Commencement," program, 6/15/1899, TKK.

30 **boating:** *Gleaner* [Henderson, KY], 4/23/39.

30 **So it was:** Annapolis officers in training were not styled "midshipmen" until 1904, the year Kimmel graduated (Gannon, p. 56).

30 **"Controlled":** Gannon, p. 56.

31 **Kimmel emerged from:** The Naval Academy began awarding the bachelor of science degree in 1933. By authority of Congress in 1937, however, all living Annapolis graduates became entitled to it (*A Brief History of USNA,* www.usna.edu).

31 **yearbook/"greaser":** *Lucky Bag,* Class of 1904.

31 **photograph:** TKK.

31 **"The Class the Stars Fell On":** Gannon, p. 57; *Sunday News* [Newark, NJ], 10/11/64; TKK.

31 **sword:** Interviews with Thomas K. Kimmel Jr., Manning M. Kimmel IV.

32 **Halsey's wedding:** Halsey and Bryan, p. 16.

32 **"balloon":** *Gleaner* [Henderson, KY], 4/23/39.

32 **"Proceed":** Chief, Bureau of Navigation (Nav.) to Kimmel, 6/14/04, TKK.

32 **gunnery:** Gannon, p. 58.

32 **Hart:** Brownlow, p. 26ff; Chief, Bureau of Nav. to Kimmel, 12/20/05, TKK.

32 **ensign:** Chief, Bureau of Nav. to Kimmel, 3/3/06, TKK.

32 **Cuba:** Brownlow, p. 27.

32 **white fleet/journal:** Kimmel diary 1908–1909, TKK.

34 **"one of the best turret officers":** Brownlow, pp. 27ff.

34 **The bride, twenty-one-year-old:** Wedding announcement, 1/31/12, MMK; marriage license, 1/18/12, TKK. Dorothy's father, Thomas W. Kinkaid, became a rear admiral in 1917.

34 **"never looked":** Brownlow, p. 169.

34 **called him "Kimmel":** Interviews with Ginger Kimmel Herrick, William Kimmel.

CHAPTER 5

35 **"This picture":** Postcard and photo, 8/19/14, TKK.

35 **Kimmel, now an aide:** The commander was Álvaro Obregón, who later became President of Mexico.

35 **commendation/medal:** Acting Sec. Navy to Kimmel, 9/11/14, TKK.

36 **lieutenant commander:** Chief, Bureau of Nav. to Kimmel, 1/8/17, TKK.

36 **"plotting":** CNO to Kimmel, 10/6/17.

36 **British adopted:** Brownlow, p. 30.

36 **German surrender:** HEK to Mother. 11/18, TKK.

36 **commander:** Bureau of Navigation to Kimmel, 6/4/21, TKK.

36 **captain:** CNO to Kimmel, 7/16/26, Chief, Bureau of Nav. to Kimmel, 8/4/26, TKK.

36 **Philippines:** CINC Asiatic to Comdt. 16th Naval District, 8/13/23, Cmdt. to Kimmel, 8/22/23, CINC Asiatic to Kimmel, 8/13/23 and 12/3/23, TKK.

36 **command of a destroyer division:** CINC Asiatic to Kimmel, 12/17/23 and 3/16/25, TKK.

36 **Army War College:** Bureau of Nav. to Kimmel, 3/19/26; Ely to Kimmel, 4/19/26, TKK.

36 **"humdinger":** Brownlow, p. 35.

37 **One young pilot:** The pilot was then–Lieutenant Logan Ramsey, who on December 7th, 1941, would be first to report that Japanese planes were attacking Pearl Harbor.

37 **radioman:** Hurst to Thomas K. Kimmel Sr., 12/8/89, TKK.

37 **family background:** Interview with Thomas K. Kimmel Jr., Harriott Johnson Kimmel.

37 **"Yesterday we reported":** Manning M. Kimmel III to Kimmel, 6/16/31, MMK.

38 "wonderful promotion": *Gleaner* [Henderson, KY], 4/23/39.

38 final assignments: Chief, Bureau of Nav. to Kimmel, 3/19/34; Commander, Battle Ships, Battle Force to Kimmel, 5/28/35; appointment certificate, 11/1/37, TKK.

38 "goodwill" tour: *South American Cruise of Cruiser Division Seven*, 1939; Dept. of Navy, "History of the USS *San Francisco*," 3/4/45.

39 storms/Hull: Brownlow, pp. 40ff, *Gleaner* [Henderson, KY], 1/19/41.

39 commander, Cruisers Battle Force: *Gleaner*, 6/24/60.

39 fitness reports: HEK R17.

39 temporary aide: CINC Pacific to Kimmel, 3/9/15, TKK.

39 met FDR again: PHA 6, pp. 2498ff.

39 "My dear Mrs. Kimmel": FDR to Delia Kimmel, 9/12/39, TKK.

CHAPTER 6

41 The proclamation made: The number most often given is forty-six, but forty-seven is the figure used by Kimmel in a 1945 letter to Admiral Harry Yarnell. Being promoted over so many others, he wrote, was "not such an unusual procedure." He declared himself puzzled that the press made much of the matter. [forty-six: E.g., *World War II* magazine, 1/2003. forty-seven: HEK to Yarnell, 8/13/45, TKK.]

42 summoned: Interview with Walter DeLany, Series V.2, Box 12, GP.

42 "perfectly stunned": PHA 6, p. 2498.

42 "faint": PHA 23, pp. 1227ff.

42 Knox: Interview with Husband Kimmel, Series V.2, Box 56, and interview with William Poco Smith, Series V.2, Box 74, GP.

42 final decision: PHA 16, p. 2144.

42 "Of course": Brownlow, p. 70.

42 "one of the greatest": *Military*, 11/98.

42 Kimmel's peers wholeheartedly: Nimitz, who at the time headed the Navy's Bureau of Navigation, had himself been the initial choice for the job, according to the historian Michael Gannon (Gannon, p. 62).

42 Halsey: Halsey and Bryan, p. 70.

42 "entire Navy": PHA 15, p. 1601.

42 one reason: PHA 16, pp. 2144ff.

43 Stark described: Simpson, pp. 1ff; Prange, *Dawn*, p. 41.

43 "honesty" and "integrity": E.g., Oral History interview by John T. Mason for US Naval Institute, 1975–1977. Courtesy of Naval Historical Collection, NWC; interview with John McCrea, Box 11, Folder 18, SIMPSON.

43 Pratt: Pratt quoted by Nomura, diary, Series V.2, Box 64, GP.

43 Shoemaker: Interview with James Shoemaker, Series V.2, Box 73, GP.

43 **Smedberg:** Smedberg Oral History, U.S. Naval Institute, 175, & NWC.

43 **Stark and Knox:** E.g., Stark to FDR, 4/29/44, and Knox to Stark, 3/21/42, Box 2, STARK.

43 **Stark and FDR:** E.g., Stark to FDR, 11/25/41, Box 2, and FDR Memorial Foundation to Stark, 3/5/48, Box 4, STARK; FDR to Stark, 3/25/33, President's Personal Papers, Folder 166, FDRL.

43 **Stimson:** Diary, 11/27/41, 11/30/41, STIM.

43 **Like many of his peers:** The eighteenth-century general John Stark was said to be one of CNO Stark's forebears. Before a battle in 1777, according to one account, Stark rallied his troops with the cry: "[The Redcoats] are ours, or this night Molly Stark sleeps a widow!" General Stark's wife Molly was actually named "Elizabeth" (www.mollystark byway.com).

43 **great ceremony/"forthright"/"5 feet 10"/"as modern":** *Honolulu Star-Advertiser,* 2/1/41.

44 **conferring:** Kimmel to Stark, 1/21/41, HEK R5; Stillwell, pp. 101ff.

44 **Richardson unhappy:** PHA 14, pp. 935ff; Simpson, p. 58.

45 **shamrock-shaped anchorage:** Prange, *Dawn,* p. 63.

45 **"Gibraltar":** E.g., *National Geographic,* 4/08; Gannon, p. 13.

45 **repairs/submarine base:** *Proceedings,* 12/71.

45 **San Pedro/dispatched:** Prange, *Dawn,* pp. 37ff.

45 **"training"/"double talk":** *Proceedings,* undated; TKK.

45 **support systems:** Morison, pp. 46ff; Brownlow, p. 66.

45 **"phony"/"nitwit":** Simpson, pp. 55ff.

45 **Richardson demurred/took concerns:** PHA 1, pp. 263ff.

45 **"Get rid":** Interview with George Dyer, Series V.2, Box 13, GP.

46 **did not bleat:** Kimmel, p. 7.

46 **"arbitrary power"/"loyally pull":** McCrea to Richardson, 12/30/41, Box 2, MCCREA.

46 **McCrea/"At night"/discussions:** Stillwell, pp. 98ff; McCrea notes and statement to Hart, 4/6/44 and 4/8/44, Box 3, MCCREA.

46 **most important strategy document:** *U.S. News and World Report,* 12/3/54; Simpson, pp. 65ff; Morton, *The U.S. Army in WWII: The War in the Pacific,* p. 81.

47 **"severely handicapped"/"immediate measures":** PHA 33, pp. 1349ff.

48 **"told the Gang":** PHA 16, pp. 2144ff.

48 **"paramount importance":** PHA 16, pp. 2225ff.

48 **The lamentable situation:** Prange, *Verdict,* pp. 384ff. Bloch had himself previously—from 1938 to 1940—served, with the temporary rank of full admiral, as commander in chief, U.S. Fleet. In his new position as commandant of the 14th Naval District, he had reverted to his perma-

nent rank of rear admiral. Aside from his own command, Bloch also served Kimmel as both base defense officer and commander of Task Force 4. Thus, somewhat confusingly, Bloch answered both to Kimmel and—in his role as commandant of the 14th District—to CNO Stark (PHA 28, p. 911).

48 **"any semblance"**: PHA 33, pp. 1194ff.

48 **"almost any length"**: PHA 16, pp. 1196ff.

48 **"The fullest protection"**: Marshall to Short, 2/7/41, Records of the War Plans Division, 4449-1, RG 65, NARA.

49 **Knox to Stimson/copied to Kimmel/Stark's note**: PHA 14, pp. 1000ff; PHA 5, p. 2127.

49 **The Navy had**: Toland, *Infamy*, pp. 260ff; Brownlow, pp. 60ff; Gannon, p. 304.

49 **An officer**: This was Commander (later Admiral) Arthur Radford.

CHAPTER 7

50 **Mitchell/"knows war"**: Davis, pp. 79ff, 89; Roger Miller, pp. 37ff, 53; correspondence Professor Mark Clodfelter.

50 **"Bombardment"**: Mitchell fact sheet, National Museum of the U.S. Air Force.

50 **His details were wrong**: Also, Mitchell expected the attack on Pearl Harbor to be carried out by planes launched not from carriers but from islands, such as Midway, that Japan would first seize.

51 **"pernicious"**: Hurley, p. 47.

51 **posthumous promotion**: The promotion finally went through in 2005. Long before, in 1946, Congress had honored Mitchell with the non-combatant equivalent of the Medal of Honor for his long effort to "achieve greater recognition of airpower as the major force in national defense." He is reportedly the only person after whom a U.S. military aircraft—the B-25 Mitchell—has been named.

51 **Bywater**: Bywater, author's biography and pp. 37ff, 44ff, 98ff, 118ff, 216ff, 262; *Insight*, 10/28/91; "Reporter Predicted Japanese Attack," www.lindseywilliams.org.

51 **Yamamoto**: Chronology 1920–1929, U.S. Naval War College; Prange, *Dawn*, pp. 9, 16; Gannon, pp. 38ff.

52 *Nichi-Bei*: *Sunday Morning Star* [Wilmington, DE], 4/7/40.

52 **"penny thrillers"**: *Wall Street Journal*, 12/5/91.

52 **stereotyped**: Toland, *The Rising Sun*, pp. 54ff; Madison, pp. 94ff.

52 **"The problem"**: Arthur McCollum Oral History, U.S. Naval Institute, 1971, NHHC.

53 **Haan to FDR/"war plan" book**: Cited in Asst. Secretary Sherwood to Haan, 2/7/41, Haan to Gephardt, 4/26/74, Box 133, TOL.

53 *Triple Alliance*/"new order"/"only the most trusted": *Investigation of Un-American Propaganda Activities in the U.S.*, pp. 1737ff; Matsuo, pp. 156ff, 190ff; *Argus* [Melbourne, Australia], 11/27/42; "Memorandum," Kilsoo K. Haan with aliases," 7/1/43, FBI 65–569, Box 133, TOL.

54 **Eleven months before:** Asst. Sec. Sherwood to Haan, 2/7/41, Box 133, TOL. Haan's papers show that the assistant secretary of the National Defense Council, Sidney Sherwood, went one better than merely sending a letter—he also met with Haan. The sizable file on Haan at FDRL indicates that most of his communications were forwarded to the State Department (2/7/41 letter Sherwood to Haan with handwritten note by Haan dated 7/16/66, TOL Box 133, Fldr. 2, President's Official Files, OF 3342).

54 **fire off letters:** E.g., Haan file, President's Official Files, OF 3342, FDRL.

54 **"Some of your facts":** Koster, p. 146.

54 **Haan biography/shady/real estate:** PHA 30, pp. 2861ff; Haan to Dodd, 11/8/54, Series, V.2, Box 22, GP; "Memorandum, Kilsoo K. Haan and aliases," undated, 1942, FBI 65-569-67, Box 133, TOL; *Pacific Historical Review*, Vol. 83, No. 2, 2104.

55 **"smooth talker"/shooting off mouth/"brushed off":** Hood to Ladd, 3/4/42, FBI 65-569-57, Ladd to Director, 4/15/42, FBI 65-569-70, Box 133, TOL.

55 **"impersonating":** "Memorandum, Kilsoo K. Haan and aliases," undated, 1942, FBI 65-569-67, Box 133, TOL.

55 **"persona non grata":** Ladd to Director, 4/15/42, FBI 65-569-70, Box 133, TOL.

55 **Meurlott/Haan:** Meurlott to Haan, 9/24/38, www.cia.gov; Haan to Dodd, 11/8/54, Series V.2, Box 22, GP.

55 **Meurlott background:** PHA 29, pp. 1999ff.

55 **looked into the "war plan" book:** PHA 35, pp. 109ff, 121ff, 348.

55 **Gillette/"understood"/"could not continue":** Spencer to Ladd, 4/16/42, FBI 62-60950-8-171, Box 133, TOL; "Predicted Pearl Harbor, Will U.S. Listen Now," undated clipping, HEK R15.

56 **"placed":** Kimmel to Haan and attachments, 6/8/44, HEK R26.

56 **"blueprints":** "Memorandum, Kilsoo K. Haan with aliases," 3/16/50, FBI 65-569-968, Hottel to Hoover, 10/7/43, FBI 65-569-622; AP, 2/19/42; FBI 65-569-35, Box 133, TOL.

56 **"stole"/Endo/"at risk":** Hood to Hoover, 3/4/42, FBI 65-569-45, McKee to Hoover, 2/24/42, FBI 65-569-37, Hoover to SAC, Washington, DC, 2/26/42; "Memorandum, Kilsoo K. Haan and aliases," undated, 1942, FBI 65-569-67, Box 133, TOL; *Milwaukee* [WI] *Journal*, 12/28/41.

56 **His overall operation:** According to FBI reports after the Pearl Harbor attack, *Triple Alliance* was not in bookstores in Hawaii as of June 1941, though a Japanese-language edition became available at some point.

Matsuo's book was published in English only after the attack on Pearl Harbor, as *How Japan Plans to Win (Investigation of Un-American Propaganda Activities in the U.S.*, p. 1737; memo re Kilsoo Haan, 4.30/42, FBI 65-569-67; PHA 35, p. 348; Tillman memo, 6/21/43, FBI 65-569-541).

56 **"the possibility"/"not translated":** Hood to Ladd, 4/16/42, FBI 62-60950-8-171, Box 133, TOL.

56 **contact the State Department repeatedly:** "Memorandum, Kilsoo K. Haan and aliases," undated, 1942, FBI 65-569-67, Box 133, TOL.

56 **Hull/Stimson/"agent"/optimum date:** Haan to Stimson, 10/28/41, Series V.2, Box 22, GP.

56 **Hornbeck:** Robert Thompson, p. 371, citing Hornbeck memo, Folder 197, Hornbeck Papers, Hoover Institution, Stanford University.

57 **Sevareid:** "Between the Wars," Part 16, Alan Landsburg Productions, 1978, PBS.

57 **In early October:** Prange, *Dawn*, pp. 255ff. On similar grounds—that relations with Japan were "extremely delicate"—Hull had earlier urged Martin Dies, chairman of the House Un-American Activities Committee, not to make public information that Haan had supplied. Long afterward, Dies would recall having told Hull that "it was a grave responsibility to withhold such information from the public. The Secretary assured me that he and Roosevelt considered it essential to national defense . . . I have never been able to understand why our government did not take the necessary precautions to protect our fleet from destruction after our Committee had furnished such precise information on the proposed attack." See further coverage in Chapter 16 (*American Opinion*, 4/64; Dies, p. 165).

57 **According to Gillette's nephew:** Toland, *Infamy*, pp. 349ff. By coincidence, Thomas Gillette was the son of Captain—later Admiral—Claude Gillette, who managed the Pearl Harbor Naval Shipyard at the time of the Japanese attack. Thomas himself served in the U.S. Navy in the 1950s.

57 **There is no record:** Raymond Teichmann to Anthony Summers, 6/16/92.

CHAPTER 8

58 **On January 27th, 1941:** PHA 14, p. 1042. Because of the international dateline, which runs through the central Pacific west of Hawaii, Tokyo time is often (though not always) a day ahead of the U.S. calendar. January 27, referenced in Grew's telegram, was the date of transmission by the Tokyo calendar. Where dates west of the date line are referenced in this book, however, the authors have by and large used the related U.S. date.

58 **"There is a lot of talk":** In his book *Ten Years in Japan*, Grew used the sentence: "Of course, I informed our Government." He did not use that sentence in his later book *Turbulent Era*, but inserted: "I rather guess that the boys in Hawaii are not precisely asleep."

The "talk around town" to which he referred in his diary, Grew would testify to Congress' Joint Committee, had come from various sources. What they were, he claimed, he had since forgotten. The Embassy's Third Secretary, Max Bishop, was to say in a 1993 interview that he heard about plans for the attack on Pearl Harbor from sources other than the Peruvian diplomat, "mostly American . . . the United Press correspondent in Tokyo . . . Harold O. Thompson . . . was one of my best sources." [**testify:** PHA 2, p. 561. **Bishop:** Interview with Ambassador Max Bishop, Oval History Project, Association of Diplomatic Studies, 2/26/93.]

59 "a rumor": PHA 32, p. 630.

59 "Peruvian Minister"/"personal friend": PHA 29, pp. 2145ff.

59 "utmost": PHA 32, p. 634.

59 secondhand/Bishop: Interview with Ambassador Max Bishop, Oral History Project, Association of Diplomatic Studies, 2/26/93; Toland, *Infamy,* p. 26.

59 He had detractors: A former specialist on Japan in the State Department's Division of Far Eastern Affairs, Frank Schuler, and his wife Olive, who had been a secretary in that division, were to claim that Bishop fabricated his supposed role. The Schulers said Bishop had been reassigned to Washington by late January 1941—and that his initials on a relevant document established this (correspondence and documents, Olive Schuler, 1993, in files of authors and James Lesar).

59 Crocker: Toland, *Rising Sun,* p. 151; Prange, *Dawn,* p. 31.

59 Schreiber biography: Rodriguez del Campo, refs.; interview with Teresa Kroll de Rivera Schreiber by Giovanni Volpi, TKK.

59 postwar account: *El Comercio* [Lima, Peru], 2/5/49.

59 affidavit: Affidavit of Teresa K. de Rivera Schreiber, 5/83, supplied to authors by Olive Schuler.

59 "I explained to him": As Rivera Schreiber recalled it, Grew followed up by sending a telegram "to President Roosevelt." This seems improbable—normal procedure would have been to report to the Secretary of State, and the record indicates that this is what Grew did (*El Comercio,* Lima, 2/5/49).

60 did not "recollect": PHA 2, pp. 570ff.

60 Bishop did not ask: Interview with Bishop, Association of Diplomatic Studies, supra.

60 Bohlen: Brownlow, pp. 100ff.

60 Fearey: *Foreign Service Journal,* 12/91.

60 Rivera Schreiber's account: *El Comercio,* 2/5/49; and see affidavit of Teresa K. de Rivera Schreiber, supra; Rodriguez del Campo, refs.

61 It was apparently common: A claim that there *was* a dispatch about the Rivera Schreiber–Grew information, a dispatch never made public,

came from the disaffected former Far Eastern Division staffers Frank and Olive Schuler.

61 **Claims that government:** Others assigned to the project, according to the memo, were Far Eastern Division head Maxwell Hamilton, and Alger Hiss, then a top aide in that division. Supervising the project was State Department historian Wilder Spaulding (Hornbeck to Secretary, 12/15/41).

61 **some reason to think:** Hamilton, Ballantine, and their colleague Stanley Hornbeck were described by Ladislas Farago, who wrote an early, insightful book about Pearl Harbor, as "sincere men of lofty principles whose patriotism and integrity were beyond a shadow of a doubt" (Farago, *Broken Seal*, p. 180).

61 **December 16th memo:** SKH to Secretary, 12/16/41, Department of State, supplied to authors by Olive Schuler.

61 **The State Department:** About the FRUS Series, www.history.state.gov.

62 **Asked by Thomas:** In the 1994 affidavit, both correspondent Thomas and former Far Eastern Division secretary Olive Schuler swore to having heard Shaffer make these allegations (correspondence and documents, Olive Schuler, files of authors and attorney James Lesar).

62 **"personal memoranda":** Bishop to Grew, 10/14/55, HEK R32.

62 **McCollum/"Japanese cook":** PHA 14, p. 973.

63 **The nascent plan:** That others on the Japanese navy's general staff were becoming aware of the plan at this time was reported by Ladislas Farago, who served in U.S. Naval Intelligence during the war. Farago cites a letter Admiral Yamamoto sent on February 1st, 1941, to Rear Admiral Takijiro Ohnishi, chief of staff of the 11th Air Fleet; he also cites Ohnishi's resulting consultation with Commander Minoru Genda (who went on to be a key planner of the operation). According to Farago, claims that the general staff was *not* made privy to the plan at this stage are less than convincing—these claims were made at a time after the war when it was in the interest of Yamamoto's surviving colleagues to avoid being seen to bear responsibility (Farago, *Broken Seal*, pp. 137, 404).

63 **timing of planning:** E.g., Prange, *Dawn*, p. 30; Farago, *Broken Seal*, pp. 136ff.

63 **"The Division":** PHA 33, p. 1390; McCollum Oral History, supra.

CHAPTER 9

65 **11 percent/70 percent:** Simpson, pp. 32, 39ff.

65 **titular authority:** PHA 33, pp. 924ff.

65 **three hundred ships:** Westcott, p. 343.

65 **"clatter":** *Honolulu Star-Bulletin*, 2/1/41.

65 **The Pacific Fleet:** These figures are for October 1941. The numbers fluctuated (PHA 17, pp. 2534ff).

65 **100,000:** Brownlow, p. 90.

65 **move to shore/office:** Interview with Poco Smith, Series V.2, Box 56, GP; *Proceedings*, 12/71; Prange, *Dawn*, p. 135.

65 **DeLany:** Interview with Walter DeLany, Series V.2, Box 12, GP.

65 **Veterans of Pearl Harbor:** DeLany and Christie went on to become vice admirals, Pullen to be a rear admiral.

66 **Christie:** *Honolulu Star-Bulletin*, 5/15/68.

66 **Pullen:** Prange, *Verdict*, p. 420.

66 **Pfeiffer:** Brownlow, p. 93.

66 **Fielder:** *Honolulu Star-Bulletin*, 5/15/68.

66 **Theobald:** Affidavit of Admiral Robert Theobald, 3/20/44, HEK R4.

66 **The pressure was:** Brownlow, p. 91. The Admiral's feeling that he should not enjoy the comfort of family while his men went without was cited by his neighbor at Pearl Harbor, Grace Earle. His aide Captain William "Poco" Smith, however, quoted him as saying: "I feel I could not do my job with my family present" (Earle letter, cited in Brownlow, p. 91; Smith interview, Series V.2, Box 74, GP).

67 **Dorothy/Long Beach/"can make herself at home":** Undated clippings, scrapbooks, courtesy of Harriott Johnson Kimmel; *WP*, 8/17/41; Kimmel to Edward "Ned" Kimmel, 5/8/41, Dorothy Kimmel to Ned Kimmel, 1/7/41, MMK; interview with Harold Train, Series V.2, GP; Kimmel, p. 185.

67 **"My first day":** Alfred Sidebottom to Gail Kimmel, 8/17/2002, courtesy of Gail Kimmel.

67 **Manning/letters:** Service Record of Lieutenant Commander Manning Marius Kimmel, U.S. Navy, Deceased, Bureau of Naval Personnel, 3/7/46; Manning Kimmel to Agatha and Oscar Swinford (in-laws), 6/18/39, 5/12/40, 9/11/40, 11/21/40, 12/25/40, 8/16/41, HEK to Manning M. Kimmel II (brother), 6/15/40, MMK; *Manchester* [NH] *Union*, 11/6/41.

68 **Tom:** Interview with Thomas K. Kimmel Sr., Box 120, TOL; interview with Thomas K. Kimmel Jr.; Husband Kimmel, "Adventures of Tom and Nancy Kimmel in the Early Days of the Japanese War," unpublished manuscript, TKK.

68 **Ned:** Biographical note by Vincent Colan, TKK; HEK to Ned K., 10/5/39, 6/16/40, 11/8/40, MMK.

68 **"No information":** Manning K. to Agatha and Oscar Swinford, 9/6/41, MMK.

69 **"I was greatly":** HEK to Ned K., 7/14/40, MMK.

69 **Grace Earle:** Brownlow, p. 91.

69 **"Sitting out here":** HEK to Edward Kimmel, 5/8/41, MMK.

69 **The Navy's "clear cut" job/WPL-46:** Morton, *The U.S. Army in World War II: The War in the Pacific*, pp. 80ff; Edward S. Miller, pp. 267ff,

280ff, 286ff; *U.S. News and World Report*, 12/3/54; PHA 33, pp. 927ff, 956ff; Kimmel, p. 24; Gannon, pp. 86ff.

70 **"to perfect":** PHA 33, pp. 1357ff.

70 **Kimmel's plan/approval/task forces:** *U.S. News and World Report*, 12/3/54; Edward S. Miller, p. 274; draft, Kimmel Statement to Joint Congressional Cttee., TKK; Prange, *Verdict*, p. 423; PHA 39, p. 296; PHA 17, p. 2476ff.

70 **Halsey:** Halsey and Bryan, p. 72.

70 **Hewitt:** Brownlow, p. 76.

70 **Kitts:** Gannon, p. 37.

70 **FTP 155:** "Joint Action of the Army and the Navy," Joint Board, 1927, revised 1935, J.B. 350, Washington, DC: US Government Printing Office, 1936; Kimmel, pp. 11ff.

70 **Bloch:** Prange, *Verdict*, pp. 384ff; Gannon, pp. 17ff.

71 **43,000:** PHA Report, p. 491.

71 **"I am either":** Stillwell, p. 102.

71 **at odds:** Brownlow, p. 89.

71 **no unity of command/major flaw/Navy allotted:** Prange, *Verdict*, pp. 543ff; *NYT*, 1/29/42; Clausen and Lee, pp. 229ff, 292; Marshall to Emmons, 12/20/41, HEK R25.

71 **"very direct":** Marshall to Short, 2/7/41, HEK R8.

71 **"I immediately":** Brownlow, p. 89.

71 **"highly cooperative":** *U.S. News and World Report*, 12/3/54.

71 **same words:** Ibid.; Short to Marshall, 2/19/41, HEK R8.

72 **golf:** Interview with Kimmel, Series V.2, Box 56, GP; Lau to Kimmel, 12/7/64, TKK; Prange, *Verdict*, p. 376.

72 **cordial relationship:** Interview with Robert Dunlop, Series V.2, Box 13, GP; Theobald affidavit, 3/20/44, HEK R4; Marshall to Short, 5/5/41, HEK R8; Brownlow, pp. 88ff.

72 **Truman:** *Collier's*, 8/26/44; AP, 8/22/44.

72 **Both man-to-man:** It was the body that first investigated the Pearl Harbor attack, the Roberts Commission, that initially suggested Kimmel and Short "failed to confer" properly in light of warnings they had received. This started a spate of rumors that the two commanders had been at odds; and the nature of their working relationship remained an issue during subsequent investigations. The Army Pearl Harbor Board found that they "did not accomplish fully the detailed working relationship necessary," while the Congress' Joint Committee found that they had failed to "command by mutual cooperation."

The Navy Court of Inquiry, by contrast, reported that there had been "no failure to cooperate on the part of either." Substantial testimony, much of it from close aides, supports that assertion.

Another claim had it that Kimmel should not have established as close a relationship with Short as he did—on the theory that doing so interfered with the liaison role that was more properly Admiral Bloch's. If so, the fault was that of Chief of Naval Operations Stark and Army Chief of Staff Marshall, who from the outset emphasized the importance of Kimmel and Short forging a good relationship. [**Roberts:** PHA 39, pp. 20ff; draft paper on Kimmel-Short relations by Robert Lavender (HEK lawyer), HEK 3. **rumors:** *Chicago Tribune,* 3/21/42. **Army Board:** PHA 39, 127, 175ff. **JCI:** PHA Report, p. 252. **Navy Court:** PHA 39, pp. 319ff. **testimony:** E.g., second endorsement to NCI by Adm. King, 11/6/44, HEK1; interview with Walter DeLany, GP V.2, Box 12; Gannon, pp. 285ff, n16. **interfered:** Prange, *Verdict,* pp. 390ff. **Stark/Marshall:** E.g., Marshall to Short, 2/7/41, HEK 8.]

72 **Kimmel thought the General:** This book does not attempt a detailed assessment of General Short's performance. Its focus is on Admiral Kimmel.

72 **security directive:** PHA 22, pp. 335ff.

72 **Two months after:** PHA 15, pp. 1429ff; PHA Report, pp. 81ff.

72 **Defense Plan:** More properly, the Joint Coastal Defense Plan, covering not only Hawaii but Midway, Wake, and other islands.

72 **CNO Stark:** *U.S. News and World Report,* 12/3/54.

72 **serious flaw:** PHA 26, p. 484; Prange, *Verdict,* pp. 301ff, 403.

72 **air forces/"It appears that":** PHA 33, pp. 1182ff.

73 **They would long plead:** PHA 36, pp. 286ff; interview with Poco Smith, Series V.2, Box 74, and "Interview with the President," 6/9/41, Series V.2, Box 56, GP; "Statement of Interested Party, Claude Bloch," Box 5, BLOCH.

CHAPTER 10

74 **eight thousand/six months/sixteen thousand/sixteen months/"urgently necessary"/"I always"/priority to the Atlantic/"the Navy Department viewed"/"After taking"/"flying fifty":** Richardson, pp. 190, 351, 353; PHA 9, p. 4289; PHA 37, pp. 961ff; PHA 26, p. 542; PHA 14, p. 1025.

75 **He had only sixty-odd:** In a report in August 1941, the Army air commander in Hawaii, Major Gen Frederick Martin, came up with a somewhat different estimate. He figured that a thorough search would require seventy-two planes every day (PHA 14, p. 1025).

75 **In the later months:** PHA 1, pp. 271ff; Gannon, p. 156. Richardson had initiated the reconnaissance in June 1940, after the Army in Hawaii received a perplexing message from Chief of Staff George Marshall that had the appearance of being an "alert" to counter a "trans-Pacific raid." There was no such raid, and whether this had been a real alert

or a training exercise was never established for sure. The doubt about the message exemplifies the failure of coordination that tended to afflict the Army and Navy high commands in Washington (Richardson, pp. 342ff; PHA 15, p. 1594; PHA 1, pp. 271ff).

75 "token": PHA 1, p. 273.

75 Moorer: Thomas Moorer Oral History, U.S. Naval Institute, NHHC.

75 "fly boys": George Dyer Oral History, U.S. Naval Institute, 1973.

76 "continued to accentuate"/"first priority": Richardson, p. 353.

76 "would give only": PHA 32, p. 571.

76 "It was a question": PHA 26, p. 207.

76 "the requirement": PHA 39, p. 338; Richardson, pp. 359ff.

76 "the force left": PHA 16, p. 2149.

76 As Stark's key aide: Smedberg Oral History, NWC. (Later Vice Admiral Smedberg.)

76 Not one of the hundred . . . patrol planes: Kimmel, pp. 14ff; PHA 36, p. 550.

77 Anderson: Introduction to Brownlow, p. 18.

77 "The Fleet's most desperate": Halsey and Bryan, p. 71.

77 "Radar was not trusted": Interview with David Richardson, 2014.

77 MacArthur: Prange, Verdict, p. 466 citing Admiral Hart memo.

77 "The possibilities": Halsey and Bryan, pp. 69, 72.

77 "wizard": "Churchill's Scientists," www.sciencemuseum.org.uk.

78 reciprocal exchange: Farago, Broken Seal, pp. 251ff; "Briefcase," BBC, 2/5/07.

78 "airplane detector": Terrett, p. 192; Farago, Broken Seal, p. 251.

78 Opie background/mission: O'Connor, pp. 46ff; correspondence Christopher O'Connor, 2015.

78 December/"Aircraft Warning Service": PHA 33, p. 1195; PHA 37, pp. 941ff; PHA 16, p. 1939; Theobald affidavit, 3/20/44, HEK R4.

79 February/"in June": PHA 5, p. 2128; Short to Marshall, 3/6/41, HEK R8.

79 National Park Service: Bryden to Short, 3/15/41, HEK R8.

79 "struggling with radar": Harvey Bundy Oral History, 10/7/59, George C. Marshall Foundation.

79 in May/"accelerated": PHA 22, pp. 360ff.

79 "terribly disturbed": PHA 16, pp. 2175ff.

79 By late September: PHA 24, p. 1788.

79 Martin: PHA 28, p. 981.

79 problem/equipment poached: PHA 27, pp. 156ff; PHA 7, pp. 2941, 3033ff.

79 **"I was very conscious":** PHA 26, pp. 149ff.

80 **Davis:** PHA 26, p. 107.

80 **On the day:** PHA 32, pp. 341ff; George Thompson et al., pp. 3ff; Gannon, pp. 230ff. The operators who spotted the incoming enemy planes were privates Joseph Lockard and George Elliott, manning the Army's Opana radar station. The unfortunate lieutenant who believed the planes were American was Kermit Tyler. This episode is well documented. The authors also noted claims made years later by a former Army private, Frank Tassinari, who served with one of the mobile radar units, that his team also picked up the incoming enemy planes. The details of Tassinari's accounts, however, are contradictory, and he acknowledged that he himself had been off duty, asleep, at the time. [Opana: PHA 32, pp. 341ff; Lord, pp. 41ff; Gannon, pp. 231ff. **Tassinari:** *Townsman* [Wellesley, MA], 12/4/86; *World War II* magazine, 1/98.]

80 **Kimmel grilled:** PHA 6, p. 2743.

80 **radar in Philippines:** George Thompson et al., pp. 10ff; Morton, *The U.S. Army in World War II: The Fall of the Philippines*, pt. 2, ch. 5.

81 **"certainly should have":** Ferrell, p. 43.

CHAPTER 11

82 **"Aerial Attacks"/Ramsey:** *Proceedings*, 8/37, pp. 1126ff.

82 **It was to be:** John F. De Virgilio, Pearl Harbor History Associates, "Japanese Thunderfish," *Naval History*, Winter 1991; and see Richardson, pp. 361ff. USS *Arizona*, on which 1,177 men died, was hit not by a torpedo but by a bomb. The authors have relied on De Virgilio's authoritative article.

82 **Torpedoes launched from aircraft:** Eleven torpedoes missed, failed to detonate, or became buried in the mud.

82 **Forrestal:** PHA 39, p. 377.

83 **Love/"took account":** Love, p. 664.

83 **"this torpedo business":** PHA 6, p. 2593.

83 **Mers el-Kébir/*Dunkerque*/Dakar:** Marder, refs.; David Brown, p. 33; Richardson, p. 363; Tute, p. 162; "Statement of Evidence," Box 5, RG 80, NARA.

83 **The truly big development:** In July 1941, the *Conte di Cavour* would be refloated and towed to Trieste—but it was never fully repaired (O'Connor, pp. 66ff, 68).

84 **These successes were:** *NYT*, 11/14/40. A 1938 British Admiralty chart, received by the U.S. Bureau of Navigation in April 1941, shows that the water in the Taranto harbor area ranged from 1–2 fathoms (6–12 feet) to 16 or more fathoms (96 feet or more). In planning for the Taranto raid, the British reportedly based their plans on ships anchored in

about 7 fathoms (40 feet) of water. Sources citing that figure include a 2006 article in the *Naval War College Review* and a 2014 article by Britain's Fleet Air Arm Officers Association. The historian Michael Gannon wrote that the British attacks were "generally" made at depths of "84 to 90" feet. The chart sent by Opie (the CNO's observer there) places targeted ships in depths of between 39 and 96 feet, most of them in depths ranging from 66 to 96 feet. [**Chart:** Emergency Reproductions of British Admiralty Charts (Italy), Stack Area 430, BA 1643, RG 37, NARA. **40 feet:** "On This Day," 11/11/14, www.fleetairarmoa.org; Lieutenant Colonel Angelo Caravaggio, "The Attack at Taranto," *Naval War College Review*, Summer, 2006; but see Lowry and Welham, p. 68; O'Connor, p. 33. **"generally":** Gannon, p. 174, but see p. 307n13.]

84 **Navies worldwide:** O'Connor, pp. 71, 73ff, 81; Prange, *Dawn*, p. 320.

84 **Months later, a Japanese:** A planner of the attack on Pearl Harbor, former Japanese staff officer Minoru Genda, was to claim years later that the Taranto raid had no influence on Japanese tactics. Whether or not that was the case, the raid was clearly of great interest to Japan—as a later chapter on Japanese espionage efforts will show (Gannon, p. 174; Stillwell, p. 74).

84 **Richardson/stop using:** Richardson, p. 361.

84 **"My concern":** PHA 1, p. 275.

85 **nets/"baffles":** Gannon, pp. 173ff.

85 **"neither necessary":** PHA 14, p. 975.

85 **McCrea:** Stillwell, p. 102.

85 **Opie:** "British Attack on Taranto," 11/14/40, Intelligence Division Secret Reports of Naval Attachés, 194–1946, File A-1-z, Entry 98B, Box 75, RG 38, NARA.

85 **Two torpedoes, marked:** ONI's British Empire section summarized Opie's report for distribution. Dated February 14, 1941, the summary contains no mention of the chart Opie sent. It does, however, state, "The British Navy has definitely given up high-level bombing attacks against ships. They believe that torpedoes are the best attack weapons." Although the summary is marked for distribution to multiple offices within the Navy Department—including those of both the CNO and CINCUS—there is no evidence that it reached the addressees. The summary did not surface during postattack inquiries (ONI, F-1—British Empire)—to multiple addressees, "Subject: Great Britain Navy Operations," 2/14/41; Intelligence Division Secret Reports of Naval Attachés, 1940–1946, Entry 98B, Box 75, RG 38).

86 **"I honestly feel":** O'Connor, p. 61.

86 **"reports from abroad":** PHA 14, p. 1000; PHA 5, p. 2127.

86 **"A minimum depth":** PHA 17, p. 2472.

86 **nine members:** "Narrative Statement of Evidence of the Navy, re Pearl Harbor Investigation," 1945, Box 5, RG 80, NARA.

86 **Kitts:** PHA 32, p. 391.

87 **"I don't think":** "Narrative Statement," supra.

87 **In view of Stark's letter:** PHA 26, p. 525. In 1944, Stark's successor as CNO, Admiral King, would comment in writing: "The decision not to install torpedo baffles appears to have been made by the Navy Department" (PHA 39, p. 338).

87 **"no minimum":** PHA 33, p. 1318.

88 **"negligible":** PHA 6, p. 2509.

88 **"7 fathoms"/"no indication":** "Narrative Statement," supra.

88 **Morehouse/"as shallow":** Intelligence Report, "Aviation Air Currents Vicinity Gibraltar" and attachments, 7/15/41, Entry 98B, Box 75, RG 38, NARA.

88 **A routing slip:** The routing slip also indicates that the report was to go to Op-10 (Stark), Op-11 (Stark's deputy), Op-12 (War Plans), Op-22 (Fleet Training), HO (Hydrographic Office), C&R (Bureau of Construction and Repair), Aero (Bureau of Aeronautics), Ord (Bureau of Ordnance), Eng (Engineering), and M&S (Bureau of Medicine and Surgery). To establish the above, the authors consulted the U.S. Navy's Naval History and Heritage Command (correspondence, Dr. Ryan Peeks, NHHC).

88 **Nor, though the existence:** Christopher O'Connor, author of the Taranto study, has theorized: "The reason why Morehouse's report disappeared may be typographical . . . Page 1 of the report listed the contents in four numbered items. The comment about depth of water was item #5 on page 3: it had been left out of the 'Contents' list. Busy staff officers may have just missed it." The report was not circulated to ONI's Far East Section, with its special interest in the Taranto raid— on account of the shallow water at Pearl Harbor—an odd omission that may add weight to O'Connor's theory (O'Connor, pp. 87ff; correspondence O'Connor).

89 **"Shortly after 7 December":** PHA 26, p. 108. The Navy's Bureau of Ordnance handled the development of aerial weapons.

89 **Ansel:** Walter Ansel Oral History, U.S. Naval Institute, 1970, NHHC.

CHAPTER 12

90 **began bleeding:** PHA 33, p. 1357; OPNAV to CINCPAC, 4/15/41, HEK R4; Gannon, pp. 31ff; Simpson, pp. 83ff.

90 **"obviously critical":** PHA 16, p. 2161.

90 **numerically superior:** PHA 39, pp. 302ff; Kimmel, pp. 22, 202ff.

90 **"I am telling you":** PHA 16, p. 2164.

90 **deterrent weakened:** Ibid.; PHA 6, p. 2566.

90 **"kiss of death":** Interview with Poco Smith, Series V.2, Box 74, GP.

90 **"taxicabs":** Interview with Edwin Layton, Series V.2, Box 58, GP.

91 **Stark-FDR relations:** Brownlow, p. 95, citing interview with Stark; Stark-FDR correspondence, e.g. PPF, Folder 166, FDRL; Box 2, STARK.

91 **direct line/weekends:** Interview with Charles Wellborn, Box 11, Folder 16, SIMPSON; Hoehling, p. 45.

91 **"wax cylinder"/"Now Betty":** Smedberg Oral History, NWC; Smedberg to Prange, 6/26/77, Series V.2, Box 74, GP.

91 **"Did you ever keep":** PHA 32, p. 86.

92 **Surprisingly, given what:** Smedberg kept secret the recording of the President's conversations until 1975, when he revealed it in the course of an oral history for the Naval Institute. Two years later, he wrote about it in detail in a letter to the historian Gordon Prange, but the recordings are not mentioned in either of Prange's books about Pearl Harbor. Excerpts from the Naval Institute oral history were published in 1981. One of the recordings, on which President Roosevelt could be heard ranting (about a naval matter unrelated to Pearl Harbor), may at least for a time have survived the initial destruction (interview with Vice Admiral Smedberg by John T. Mason, 10/2/75, Naval War College; Stillwell, pp. 88ff, 287; Smedberg to Prange, 6/26/77, GP, V.2, Box 74).

92 **"popping up":** PHA 16, p. 2163.

92 **"'lunger'":** Interview with Charles Wellborn, Box 11, Folder 16, SIMP-SON.

92 **"does not easily follow":** Andrew, p. 86.

92 **"send a carrier"/"we couldn't"/"I wouldn't":** PHA 16, pp. 2174, 2242; interview with Kimmel, Series V.2, Box 56, GP.

93 **"Keep cheerful":** E.g., PHA 16, p. 2163.

93 **"I have recently":** PHA 16, p. 2229.

93 **"officer fresh from Washington":** Kimmel would write in his 1954 book that this was Vice Admiral Wilson Brown (Kimmel, p. 79).

93 **"fully aware":** PHA 16, p. 2160.

93 **"getting the complete":** Interview with Walter DeLany, Series V.2, Box 12, GP.

94 **letter/"largely uninformed"/"in a very difficult":** PHA 16, p. 2233; PHA 32, p. 99; Kimmel, pp. 80ff; Prange, *Dawn*, pp. 136ff; Simpson, pp. 103ff.

94 **hand-carried:** Interview with Husband Kimmel, Series V.2, Box 56, GP.

94 **He made the journey:** Interview with Husband Kimmel, Series V.2, Box 56, GP. Kimmel told historian Gordon Prange, Prange's notes show, that he was "certain" he "initiated" the visit back to the United States. In his book, however, Prange wrote that Stark "summoned" Kimmel to Washington. The present authors find no evidence for that statement, or for the suggestion—in a study of U.S. military and po-

litical developments in 1941, previously seen as authoritative—that Kimmel arrived accompanied by more than one colleague. The study's author, Captain Tracy Kittredge, a former aide of Stark's, claimed no one had been "asked to approve" its text. Correspondence found by the present authors, however, shows that Kittredge consulted extensively with Stark and Stark's attorney. ["initiated"/"summoned": Interviews with Kimmel, Series V.2, Box 56, GP; Prange, *Dawn*, p. 138; Kittredge, *U.S. News and World Report*, 12/3/54; David Richmond to Stark and Kittredge, 7/29/54, to Stark, 8/5/54, Stark to Kittridge, 7/5/54, et al., ST, Boxes 2 and 29.]

95 **met with Stark:** Stark appointments book, 1941, Box 4, STARK.

95 **"doing the best":** Interview with Kimmel, Series V.2, Box 56, GP.

95 **"They didn't give"/Turner:** McCollum to Prange, 1/17/72, Series V/2, Box 60, GP.

95 **"complex on secrecy":** McCollum Oral History, supra.

95 **their brief encounters:** President's appointments diary, June 9, FDRL. See Chapter 5 supra.

95 **impressed/"tried to equate"/"very engaging"/"loved":** Brownlow, p. 83.

95 **The surviving record:** See Chapter 6 supra on the end of Admiral J. O. Richardson's time as CINCUS.

96 **memorandum/"for a hundred years"/"considerable"/"taking it":** "Interview with the President," 6/9/41, Operational Archives, File A3–1/NN-A3–2/QM, Navy History and Heritage Command; PHA 33, pp. 692, 696ff.

96 **big stick/freezing assets/oil:** U.S. Department of State, *Peace and War*, pp. 87ff; Minohari, Han, and Dawley, p. 99; Prange, *Verdict*, pp. 158ff, 166.

96 **malevolently:** Mauch, chs. 6–8; Prange, *Verdict*, p. 168.

96 **glimpse/battleships/"raiding"/"explode"/"crazy"/"silly"/"return"/"fanciful":** "Interview with the President," 6/9/41, File A3–1/NN-A3–2/QM, Navy History Heritage Command PHA 33, pp. 692, 696ff.

97 **The President relieved:** During his stay in Washington, Kimmel was to say, it was suggested a further three battleships might be moved to the Atlantic, along with another aircraft carrier, four cruisers, and two squadrons of destroyers (PHA 33, p. 696; Kimmel, p. 22).

97 **"Don't worry"/visit Japanese embassy/"banalities":** Brownlow, pp. 83ff.

98 **"The Fleet needs":** *Proceedings*, 6/95.

98 **"strongest fortress"/"impracticable":** PHA 3, pp. 1092ff.

98 **"grand conclusion":** McCollum Oral History, supra.

98 **In early spring:** Layton with Pineau and Costello, pp. 18, 70ff; "Translation of Japanese 'War-Novel'" (1932), Box 36, Folder 16, LAYTON; Edwin Layton Oral History, U.S. Naval Institute, 1970, NWC. (The book, *Warrera Moshi Tatakawaba*, had been published in Tokyo in 1933.

It is discussed in more detail, with slight differences, in Layton with Pineau and Costello, p. 70; and Stillwell, pp. 278ff. For a reference to relevant U.S. war games, see Chapter 6, supra.)

99 **"if they thought":** Weintraub, p. 231.

99 **McMorris:** Layton with Pineau and Costello, p. 74; PHA 36, p. 193; interview with Kimmel, Series V.2, Box 56, GP.

CHAPTER 13

100 **Tachibana/Kono/"Keeno" episode:** *NYT*, 6/10/41; PHA 10, pp. 4880ff; Layton with Pineau and Costello, pp. 106ff; *Time*, 6/23/41; Prange, *Dawn*, pp. 149ff, 248; PHA 1, pp. 234ff; PHA 13, pp. 424ff; Pedro Loureiro, "The Imperial Japanese Navy and Espionage: The Itaru Tachibana Case," *International Journal of Intelligence and Counterintelligence*, Vol. 3, No. 1; "Japanese Espionage and American Countermeasures in Pre–Pearl Harbor California," draft manuscript in authors' collection; *WP*, 12/6/81.

100 **It had been there:** See Chapter 7.

102 **Caught red-handed:** Investigators had to close down the sting operation, Kimmel's intelligence officer Layton was to recall, because Blake blew his own cover—he drunkenly bragged to a woman that he was working for U.S. intelligence (Loureiro, "Imperial Japanese Navy and Espionage," supra; Layton with Pineau and Costello, p. 108).

102 **Hull/"our conversations":** Hull, pp. 1011ff.

102 **Tachibana running:** E.g., Memorandum re Frederick Joseph Rutland, 7/2/43; interview of Rutland, 7/23/43, KV 2/336, PRO.

102 **Rutland on payroll:** Case summary, KV 2/337, PRO.

102 **information on the movements:** Advisory Committee to Consider Appeals Against Orders of Detention, Appellant—Frederick Joseph Rutland, Interview 1/15/42, KV 2/333, PRO.

102 **Hawaii/whiskey business:** Biographical summary, Frederick Joseph Rutland, copy found in PF 37966, KV 2/332, PRO.

102 **"consolidate":** DNI Tokyo to Japanese Naval Attaché, London, 7/4/35, KV2/339.

102 **What exactly Rutland:** Thurston to Gibbs, 7/10/43, and Memorandum re Frederick Joseph Rutland, 7/2/43, KV2/336; biographical summary, Frederick Joseph Rutland, copy found in PF 37966, KV 2/332, PRO. Having agreed with their British counterparts to send Rutland back to Britain, U.S. Intelligence officers lost the opportunity to interrogate him on his years of working for the Japanese. He was interned by the British after the Pearl Harbor attack but was never tried. Released late in the war, he died—an apparent suicide—in 1949.

102 **"except vicinity":** Loureiro, "Imperial Japanese Navy and Espionage," supra.

103 **"The role played":** PHA Report, p. 150.

103 **The FBI and Naval Intelligence:** On wider espionage matters, Army Intelligence—G-2—was also involved (PHA 31, pp. 3176ff).

103 **Japanese interest:** PHA 35, p. 554.

104 **160,000:** "Japanese Intelligence and Propaganda in the U.S. During 1941," 12/4/41, Office of Naval Intelligence, supplied to the authors by Lee Allen; www.internmentarchives.com; PHA 35, pp. 559ff; Farago, *Broken Seal*, p. 406.

104 *joho kyoku:* Farago, *Broken Seal*, p. 141.

104 **The arrangement had:** Farago, *Broken Seal*, pp. 83ff; "Japanese Intelligence and Propaganda in the U.S. During 1941," 12/4/41, Office of Naval Intelligence, supra.

104 **naval attaché:** The attaché was Colonel Hiroshi Oshima.

104 **Kühn background:** Re Bernard Julius Otto Kühn, Hoover O&C File 164, FBI; Press Release, Office of War Information, 6/4/43; FBI 65–1574–130, Affidavit of Otto Kühn, 1/1/42; Doc. 6256A, Series V.2, Box 58, GP.

105 **Bund:** Shivers to Director, 4/10/41, FBI 65–1574–23.

105 **entertained/Army officers/"espionage agents":** Hoover to [name redacted], 2/11/39, and Tamm to Director, 2/11/39, FBI 65–1574.

105 **$70,000:** Re. Bernard Julius Otto Kuehn, Hoover O&C File 164, FBI.

105 **"considered for":** Shivers to Director, 4/10/41, FBI 65–1574–23.

105 **"It is not conceivable"/"eliminated":** Ladd to Director and attached report of Sterling Adams, 10/19/45, citing Shivers report of 3/11/41. The recommendation that the offending passage be omitted was of a piece with the notorious FBI mantra of the day: "Don't embarrass the Bureau." In an obsequious letter to Director Hoover, reporting that he might be called to testify during the first investigation into the attack, Hawaii agent-in-charge Robert Shivers made clear where his priorities lay. "I want you to know," he wrote, "that I have upheld the Bureau in all its interests since the beginning of the attack on December 7, 1941 . . . My first loyalty, thought and obligation is to and for you—next comes the Bureau and after that the general welfare." [mantra: Summers, *Official and Confidential*, p. 71; **"I want":** Shivers to Director, 12/30/41, FBI 65–42502–21, TKK.]

105 **new report/citizenship:** Title: Friedel Barta Augusta Kuehn, with aliases, etc., 11/24/41, FBI 65–1574–27.

105 **Not until after:** In February 1942, a military court would find Kühn guilty of espionage. He received the death sentence, though this was later commuted to fifty years in prison. He was deported after the war. The role he and his wife played prior to Pearl Harbor is described in Chapter 22 ("Re Bernard Julius Otto Kühn," FBI O&C file, Vol. 164; Press Release Office of War Information, 6/14/43; FBI 65–1574–130).

CHAPTER 14

107 **Gardner/special attention/solved puzzle/shared with FBI:** Memorandum, FBI to Stott, 5/5/44, KV2/2632, PRO; Hyde, *Room 3603*, pp. 79ff; "Joe K," undated, #14A, and Security Officer, Bermuda to Asst. Director Postal and Telegram Censorship, undated, KV2/2630, PRO.

108 **"closest possible marriage":** Hyde, *Secret Intelligence Agent*, foreword by Sir William Stephenson, p. xvi.

108 **Von der Osten killed:** FBI to Stott, 5/5/44, KV2/2632 and "Most Secret" transcription B.466, 3/20/41, KV2/2630, PRO; Hyde, *Room 3603*, p. 83.

108 **experienced/Shanghai:** Zacharias, pp. 159ff; Farago, *Foxes*, pp. 493ff; Summary of Joe K and Sawyer Trials, 5/21/42, KV2/2632, PRO; UP 2/7/42, 2/10/42, 2/12/42.

108 **duplicates:** Security Officer, Bermuda, to Asst. Director Postal and Telegram Censorship, undated, 14A, KV2/2630, PRO.

108 **Himmler:** Farago, *Foxes*, p. 470; AP 3/7/41.

108 **arrest of Ludwig:** UP 9/4/41.

109 **"Pacific insular":** AP 2/19/42.

109 **sending his letter:** PHA 30, pp. 3082ff.

110 **The postmark on:** PHA 31, Item no. 60. The letter appears, obscurely, only as an exhibit in a volume of Congress' Joint Committee's inquiry into the Pearl Harbor attack. Many reports have suggested it was written in 1941, but the envelope in which it was contained—reproduced as an exhibit in the record of the Committee's probe—shows clearly that it was mailed in February 1940. So does the fact that Von der Osten's Hawaii report refers to the presence of the USS *Saratoga*—the *Saratoga* was not at Pearl Harbor as of early January 1941, but in dry dock on the U.S. West Coast. The letter had been obtained by the U.S. naval attaché in Shanghai, and passed to the FBI. [**letter appears:** PHA 30, pp. 3082ff. **suggested:** E.g., *Foxes*. pp. 494ff; UPI, in *San Bernardino County Sun*, 2/9/42. **envelope:** PHA 31, Exhibit 53, Items 60 and 61. *Saratoga:* Ship's history, www.uscarriers.net. **obtained:** FBI to Stott, 5/5/44, PRO KV 2/2632.]

110 **map:** UP 2/7/42.

110 **Godfrey/"expressed himself"/"fortnight"/no collaboration:** Godfrey, pp. 132ff.

111 **In an effort:** The coordinator was Colonel William Donovan, whom President Roosevelt had earlier assigned to make informal contacts with British leaders, including Churchill, and his intelligence chiefs. Because of territorial rivalries, Donovan's first year as U.S. coordinator of information was to see only limited success. He was close to BSC's William Stephenson, however, and was to flourish once America joined the war. In 1942, he would head the Office of Strategic Services—OSS—the forerunner of the CIA. (Thomas Troy, "Donovan's Original Marching Orders," and Arthur B. Darling, "Origins of

Central Intelligence," both at www.cia.gov; Ranelagh, pp. 37ff. On BSC and Hoover-Donovan relations see Stephenson, refs.: authors' citations draw from the unpublished draft, shared privately in 1989. See also Batvinis, *Hoover's Secret War*, pp. 22ff; Summers, pp. 117ff; Andrew, pp. 85ff, 93ff; PHA 4, p. 2016.)

111 **"Roosevelt's folly":** Ranelagh, p. 52; and see Chalou, p. 80; Batvinis, *Hoover's Secret War*, pp. 133ff.

111 **"always conditioned":** Stephenson, "BSC History," unpublished manuscript, p. 8.

CHAPTER 15

112 **"presently of assistance":** Memorandum for the Director, 6/5/41, FBI 65-36994-1, RG 65, NARA. The Popov episode has been a subject of lasting controversy in the forty years since elements of the story first surfaced. The authors' analysis here is informed principally by contemporary records released only since the millennium. The British Intelligence file "Dusko Popov, Codename Tricycle" was released into London's Public Record Office in 2002. FBI documents, previously available only in heavily redacted form, were released to the National Archives in 2007.

112 **"chief"/"leading":** Masterman, pp. 79, 55; interview with T. A. "Tar" Robertson, 1990.

112 **Double-Cross Committee:** See Macintyre, refs.; Batvinis, *Hoover's Secret War*, pp. 43ff.

112 **godfather:** Interview with Marco Popov, 2015.

112 **D-Day:** Numerous references to Popov in British security files, KV 2/856, KV2/858-859, KV 2/864, KV 2/867, PRO; Macintyre, pp. 174–231ff; Russell Miller, pp. 207ff.

112 **rank/decorations:** Interview with Marco Popov, 2015; Russell Miller, pp. 246ff.

112 **The businessman son/satisfied British:** Summary of Tricycle Case 7/28/41, KV2/849, PRO; Masterman, pp. 55ff, 79ff. The Abwehr officer's real name was Kremer von Auenrode (*Der Spiegel*, 8/18/75).

113 **list of questions:** Summary of Tricycle Case, supra; and, e.g., Traffic Summary, KV2/849, PRO.

113 **decided to send/August:** Tricycle, Revised Summary up to departure from Lisbon to USA, 8/11/41, KV2/852; Guy Liddell diary, 3/15/41, KV4/187, PRO; Masterman, p. 95.

113 **As on previous missions/questionnaire/"microdots"/plain text:** Tricycle to T. A. Robertson, undated, August 1941, and translation and Cowgill to Robertson, 8/19/41, KV2/849, PRO; To Director, re. Dusan M. Popov, Confidential Informant, 8/26/41, FBI 65-36994-17; and Laboratory Report, 9/3/41, FBI 65-36994-7, RG 65, NARA.

When he left Portugal by air on August 10th, Popov apparently had with him both a typewritten copy of the questionnaire and the hidden text in the form of microdots. Then, following a stopover in Bermuda, he passed the material to a British agent assigned to escort him on the final leg of the journey to New York. The British agent, in turn, passed the material on to the FBI. It may seem odd that Popov carried the German transcript in clear as well as in microdot form, for that would appear to negate the secrecy of the microdot version. FBI documents, however, mesh with Popov's account in the book he was to write in 1974. They establish, moreover, that the FBI had the questionnaire by the 14th, two days after Popov's arrival, rather than—as another FBI document suggests—not until five days later.

The questionnaire may initially have reached the British earlier. Popov had passed it to an MI6 agent in Lisbon—probably Major Ralph Jarvis, who was assigned to handle double agents. British records show that it was certainly in London, being passed to Popov's handler, Major T. A. Robertson, by August 19th. [**Popov:** Popov, pp. 132ff. **FBI:** Memo for the Director, 8/1/4/41, FBI 65–36994–19, Connelly to Director, 8/21/41, FBI 65–36994–5, RG 65, NARA. **Jarvis:** White to Cowgill, 8/2/41, Dusko Popov file, KV 2/849, PRO; Jeffrey, refs. **reached British:** Popov, supra; Cowgill to Robertson, 8/19/41, Dusko Popov file, KV 2/849, PRO.]

115 **FBI laboratory's random assembly:** Laboratory Report, 9/3/41, FBI 65–36694–7, RG 65 NARA.

115 **Popov himself/Jebsen/Taranto:** Popov, pp. 126ff, 141. As described in Chapter 11, British aircraft flying off carriers had months earlier sunk one Italian battleship and disabled two others at Taranto. The British planes had achieved this using aerial torpedoes—the weapon that was soon to cause havoc at Pearl Harbor.

115 **"specific instructions":** Popov, p. 132.

115 **"first thing":** Ibid., p. 144.

115 **Three decades later:** The FBI was riled, too, by Popov's claim in the book that he had seen Director Hoover during his visit to the United States, that Hoover had called him a "bogus spy" and had virtually thrown him out of the office. In his complaint to Popov's publisher, Kelley maintained that Popov never did see Hoover. In interviews for Anthony Summers' 1993 biography of Hoover, *Official and Confidential*, however, Popov's principal British Intelligence handler, Major T. A. Robertson, and Chloe McMillan, who worked for Intelligence in Portugal, both recalled Popov's mentioning his encounter with Hoover when he returned to Europe. In a 1978 book, Commander Ewen Montagu of British Naval Intelligence, who handled aspects of the Popov case, referred to the encounter as fact. [**"bogus":** Popov, p. 149. **Kelley:** *Washington Post*, 4/29/74; and Kelley to Dunn, 10/1/73, FBI 65–36994, NARA. **interviews:** Summers interviews, 1990. **Montagu:** Montagu, p. 75.]

116 **Did Popov embroider:** Likewise, the British written record does not show that Popov shared these additional details with his British associates. In his 1978 memoir, however Commander Montagu recalled a "verbal report" from Popov on what he had learned of the Japanese naval mission to Taranto. The report may have come through MI6's Major Jarvis (see note, supra, for present chapter, "As on previous missions"; Montagu, p. 74; "Tricycle," doc. 456B, Dusko Popov file, KV 2/852, PRO).

116 **Various facts support:** Popov's explanation of why his contact Jebsen had been assigned to liaise with the Japanese mission—because German military intelligence used his family's companies in the Far East as cover—is plausible. The family shipping firm, Jebsen and Jebsen, had indeed long traded in the Far East. There is doubt, however, about a statement by Popov, quoting Jebsen, that the German air attaché in Tokyo, Baron Wolfgang von Gronau, joined the Japanese mission to Taranto. In a postwar memoir, the former air attaché mentioned no travel to Europe in 1941. It does seem possible, however, that Jebsen and von Gronau knew each other. The attaché's daughter was to become romantically involved with Jebsen. She told U.S. interrogators after the war that she was aware of secret meetings between Jebsen and Popov. [explanation: Popov, pp. 126ff. traded: "Dramatis Personae," Dusko Popov file, KV 2/849, PRO; MacIntyre, pp. 8ff. Gronau: Ibid.; Gronau; and "Wartime Activities of the German Diplomatic and Military Services," U.S. Army European Command, www.foia.cia.gov; "Tricycle Recycled," *Intelligence and National Security*, Vol. 7, No. 3, 1992. interview with Gronau's granddaughter Marlise Karlin. daughter: Interrogation of Marie Luise von Gronau, 9/19/46, in FBI 65-36994, RG 65, NARA.]

116 **Japanese naval mission Fioravanzo:** *Proceedings*, 1/56; Prange, *Dawn*, p. 320; Naito Takeshi (Japanese naval attaché, Berlin) visits Taranto, cited in "A General Handbook on Japanese Army and Navy," www.axishistoryforum.com.

116 **"enthusiastic":** Connelly to Director, 8/19/41, FBI 65-36994-4, RG 65, NARA.

116 **"satisfied":** Signature illegible to Robertson, 8/18/41, KV2/849, PRO.

116 **He "did not believe":** Foxworth to Director, 9/8/41, FBI 65-36994-24, RG 65, NARA.

116 **"unhesitatingly":** Hoover to Connelly, 8/21/41, FBI 65-36994-1, RG 65, NARA.

116 **agents bugged:** Connelly to Director, 9/5/41, FBI 65-36994-49, RG 65, NARA; Tricycle in America, August 1941–October 1942, #457a, KV2/852.

117 **listened to his phone calls:** Connelly to Director, 8/20/41, FBI 65-36994-3, and 9/2/41, FBI 65-36994-21, RG 65, NARA.

117 **watched:** Memo for Foxworth, 9/18/41, FBI 65–36994–36, RG 65, NARA.

117 **high on the hog/playboy:** Connelly to Director, 8/19.41, FBI 65–36994–4, 9/27/41, FBI 65–36994–30, 8/25/41, FBI 65–36994–29 and 9/2/41, FBI 65–36994–21, Memo for Foxworth, 8/21/41, FBI 65–36694–18, RG 65, NARA; Tricycle, Revised Summary up to departure from Lisbon to US, 8/11/41, KV2/852.

117 **former colleague:** Interview with Chloe McMillan, 1990.

117 **puritanical:** Summers, pp. 47ff.

117 **"serious doubt":** Connelly to Director, 9/9/41, FBI 65–36994–25, RG 65, NARA.

117 **more than a year:** Report on the Eastbound Atlantic Clipper, Bermuda Travellers Censorship, 10/12/42, KV2/850.

117 **"Revelations":** Guy Liddell diary, 9/19/41, KV4/186, PRO.

117 **Liddell:** Liddell headed MI5's "B," or counterespionage, section in 1941.

117 **"get their double agent":** Tricycle in America, #457a, KV2/852, PRO.

117 **"meddling":** Carson to Foxworth, 8/23/41, FBI 65–36994–22, RG 65, NARA.

117 **FBI set up transmitter ineptly:** Tricycle in America, #467a, KV2/852, PRO.

117 **"not been taken":** Memorandum for Mr. Tamm, 3/25/42, FBI 65–36994–276; memo #457K, KV2/852, PRO.

118 **Florida:** Connelly to Director, 9/27/41, FBI 65–36994–30.

118 **did not go to Hawaii:** Popov, 144ff.

118 **"there were indications":** Tricycle in America, #457a, KV2/852, PRO.

118 **risk/"cold-blooded":** Montagu, pp. 80ff.

118 **Naval/Army Intelligence/pumping/call off:** Sharp to Asst. Chief of Staff, G-2, 8/15/41; authors' files, obtained under FOIA, 1988; Tamm to Director, 8/16/41, FBI 65–36994–12, Carson to Foxworth, 8/15/41, FBI 65–36994–15 and Connelly to Director, 8/20/41, FBI 65–36994–3, RG 65, NARA; Tricycle in America (further information), 4/10/44, KV2/852, PRO.

118 **Some weeks later/Army began to oblige/Naval Intelligence/armored netting:** Thurston to Ladd, 9/20/41, FBI 65–36994–33, Carson to Connelly, 9/13/41, FBI 65–36994–47, Fletcher to Foxworth, 9/12/41, FBI 65–36994–48 and 9/18/41, FBI 65–36994–36, Little to Foxworth, 9/25/41, FBI 65–36994–49x2 and 49x3, Connelly to Director, 9/26/42, FBI 65–36994–41 and 9/27/41, FBI 65–36994-30, Fletcher to Director, 9/30/41, FBI 65–36994-27, Thurston to Ladd, 10/1/41, FBI 65–36994-49x1, Fletcher to Ladd, 10/5/41, FBI 65–36994-42, 10/13/41, FBI 65–36994-50 and 11/8/41, FBI 65–36994-77, Hoover to Connelly, 10/3/41, FBI 65–36994-45, Foxworth to Director, 10/13/41 and attachments, FBI 65–36994-54, Burton to Ladd, 10/31/41, FBI 65–36994-75

and 11/8/41, FBI 65–36994-76, Hoover to Lanman, 11/8/41, FBI 65–36994-77, RG 65, NARA.

119 **Clearly, each of:** In 1972, when former British spymaster John Masterman made elements of the Popov episode public, a newspaper report quoted "FBI sources" as claiming that—in 1941—"the importance of [Popov's] information was clearly seen and processed through domestic intelligence channels to military officials in Hawaii." The FBI record contains nothing to indicate that this was so, and the claim has not been repeated (*International Herald Tribune*, 1/3/72).

119 **paraphrased summaries:** Fletcher to Ladd, 10/20/41 and attachment, FBI 65–36994-74, Thurston to Ladd, 10/1/41 and attachments, FBI 65–36994-45.

119 **"We ought":** Masterman, p. 80.

120 **Robertson/"not to take":** Interview with T. A. Robertson, 1990.

120 **brag:** Summers, pp. 99ff.

120 **"I thought"/wrote again/more minuscule:** Hoover to Watson, 9/3/41 and attachments, FBI reports,#906 and 10/1/41, #2372, Box 28, OF 10B, FDRL. After the war, moreover, in a 1946 article for *Reader's Digest*, Hoover would claim the FBI had discovered the microdots—not been handed them on a plate. The article was factually misleading in other ways (*Reader's Digest*, 4/46).

120 **There was, though:** Hoover would yet again remind Roosevelt, the month after the attack on Hawaii, of his September 1941 message about the microdots. That third message, too, would make no mention of the questionnaire's Pearl Harbor content (Hoover to General Watson, 1/13/42, FBI 65–36994-103, RG 65, NARA).

121 **Future CIA Director:** William Casey, pp. 10ff. For all Casey's biting comment about Hoover's personal competence as of mid-1941, the FBI was to have major successes—especially in counterintelligence—during World War II (Batvinis, *Hoover's Secret War*).

121 **"another American fumble":** Layton with Pineau and Costello, p. 105.

121 **It was an unforgivably:** Neither Popov's name nor his operational codename "Tricycle" appear in the volumes of the Joint Committee's investigation of Pearl Harbor, which include the records of other probes. There is, too, only a passing reference to the Von der Osten case (see Chapter 14). Asked whether he had been aware of the case, Lieutenant Colonel Kendall Fielder of G-2 in Hawaii said he had not. The record suggests that neither military intelligence in Hawaii nor the FBI's Honolulu office was ever told of the Von der Osten case (PHA 28, p. 1562; Honolulu to Director, 9/10/44, FBI 100–97–1–213).

CHAPTER 16

122 **"one of the most":** Gordon Prange, "The Truth About Japan's Pearl Harbor Spy," Draft mss., Series V.2, Box 68, GP.

122 **"goldfish bowl":** Prange, *Dawn*, p. 156.

122 **"go up in the hills":** PHA 6, p. 2575.

122 **"common knowledge":** Prange, *Dawn*, p. 70.

122 **The consulate . . . was:** Brief history, www.honolulus.us.emb-japan. go; Thurston Clarke, "The Ghosts of Pearl Harbor" *Los Angeles Times*, 10/20/91.

123 **media coverage:** Farago, *Broken Seal*, pp. 148ff; Prange, "The Truth About Japan's Pearl Harbor Spy," supra.

123 **Seki:** PHA 35, pp. 353ff; Farago, *Broken Seal*, 147ff.

123 **vice consul:** Analysis of the Japanese Espionage Problem in the Hawaiian Islands, 4/20/43, Box 2, Entry UD-11W 41, RG 38, NARA.

123 **March arrivals:** PHA 355, p. 355; Report on Honolulu, TH, 5/10/41, attached to Hoover to Berle, 5/23/41, Box 1949, RG 59, NARA.

123 **"chancellor":** Prange, "The Truth About Japan's Pearl Harbor Spy," supra.

123 **"expatriation matters":** PHA 35, p. 363.

123 **Yoshikawa's background:** Takeo Yoshikawa, "Top Secret Assignment," *Proceedings*, 12/60; Report on Honolulu, TH, 9/7/42, Doc. 40; www .internmentarchive.com; Farago, *Broken Seal*, pp. 156ff, 239ff; Prange, "The Truth About Japan's Pearl Harbor Spy," supra.

124 **Such claims are ludicrous:** Yoshikawa's less than credible versions of his story appeared between 1960 and 1991. The authors have followed the more believable record of interviews conducted in 1950 and 1955 by the historian Gordon Prange. [**less than credible:** *Proceedings*, Vol. 86, 1960; *WP*, 12/10/1978; "Intrigue in the Islands," *American History Illustrated*, Vol. 26, No. 3, 1991. **Prange interviews:** "The Truth About Japan's Pearl Harbor Spy," 12/1978; Prange, *Dawn*, citing interviews, 1950, 1955.]

124 **opportunity to work:** *Proceedings*, 12/60.

124 **desk/accommodations:** Prange, *Dawn*, p. 75.

124 **"indulge only":** PHA 35, p. 555.

124 **cruise around:** PHA 35, pp. 355ff; Prange, *Dawn*, 75ff.

124 **carried a camera:** PHA 35, pp. 362, 366.

124 **"not to get caught":** Ibid., p. 366.

124 **sugarcane fields/Shuncho-ro:** Prange, *Dawn*, p. 76.

125 **womanizer:** Ibid.; Farago, *Broken Seal*, pp. 235ff.

125 **"frequently drunk"/"mystery man":** PHA 35, p. 363.

125 **soda stand:** *America History*, July–August, 1991.

125 **seamen/kendo:** Farago, *Broken Seal*, pp. 235, 238.

125 **"The key information":** *Proceedings*, 12/60.

126 **Shivers-Kita meeting:** Prange, *Dawn*, p. 155.

126 **"outside man":** Report on Japanese Consulate, Hawaii, T.H., 7/15/41, attached to Hoover to Berle, 8/7/41, Box 1949, Department of State Decimal files 1940–1944, 702.9411A/35, RG 59, NARA.

126 **Apparently, however:** Records made available during the inquiries suggest that Yoshikawa aka Morimura was identified as having been an espionage agent for the first time only a month after the attack. That the FBI had been told he was an "outside man" was evidently forgotten or, perhaps, suppressed. It was not until 1953 that Yoshikawa was linked under his real name to his intelligence work—in a Japanese newspaper article. With other staff, he was interned after the Pearl Harbor attack, and later repatriated. He died in 1993.

Robert Stinnett, author of the book *Day of Deceit*, claimed that FBI and ONI agents in Hawaii had identified Yoshikawa as a spy months before the Pearl Harbor attack. According to *Day of Deceit*, the FBI both surveilled him and placed a wiretap on a phone he used. In support of these claims, Stinnett cited an interview he said he had conducted with former FBI agent Frederick Tillman, and supporting documentation. During several months of correspondence, the present authors asked to see a transcript or notes of that interview but Stinnett—mentioning pressure of work—did not comply. Some documents related to the Japanese consulate's activity and cited by Stinnett could not be found by the present authors. A cited entry in the diary of Assistant Secretary of State Adolf Berle, which we did locate, turned out to be on another subject. The FBI has still not fully released all files relevant to Pearl Harbor into the National Archives. One of the items not in the archives is file 65-414, which contains intelligence the FBI gathered on the Honolulu consulate in 1941. It was in one document from that file, located by the authors in State Department records, that consular spy Yoshikawa was identified as "an outside man." Other documents in file 65-414 may be equally relevant to understanding the nature of the FBI's pre-attack intelligence. There can be no reasonable excuse for continuing to withhold this material seventy-five years after the event. The authors' Freedom of Information Act request for file 65-414 was still pending at the time of this writing. **[Records made available:** Shivers to Mayfield, 1/4/42; "Investigative Report," 6/15/42; PHA 35, pp. 336, 506ff. **real name linked:** Farago, *Broken Seal*, p. 240. **interned/died:** *Proceedings*, Vol. 86, 1960; Hastedt, p. 831. **Stinnett claimed:** Stinnett, pp. 85ff, 89ff, 95ff. **Stinnett did not comply:** Correspondence, 7/24, 7/29, 8/25, 9/8/15. **documents not found/ another subject:** E.g., Stinnett, p. 97n42, citing "Adolf Berle entry, p. 196, 6/3/41, FDRL." The referenced citation does not appear on that page. Nor has the quotation been located elsewhere in the diary for 1941, author correspondence FDRL archivist Sarah Malcolm, 8/21/15.]

126 **Shivers/Mayfield/Bicknell:** PHA 23, p. 914.

126 **tapping phones:** PHA 35, p. 84.

126 **tap of Consul's home/not much more:** Farago, *Broken Seal*, p. 239.

126 **Federal law:** Affidavit of J. Edgar Hoover, FBI Director, 8/25/44; PHA 31, pp. 3189ff; PHA 36, p.331.

126 **"consular staffers":** PHA 23, pp. 859ff; PHA 31, pp. 3180ff).

127 **The Navy's view:** PHA 6, p. 2575; PHA 31, p. 3185.

127 **Putting the consular agents "in the jug":** This was Kimmel's casual way, years later, of referring to the recommendation by Admiral Bloch, his defense officer, that consular agents who were committing offenses should be prosecuted.

127 **"unduly alarm":** PHA 31, p. 3184.

127 **In Washington:** Prange, *Dawn*, p. 255; and see Chapter 7, regarding Gillette and Haan.

127 **"The Japanese consulate here":** *Honolulu Star Bulletin*, 10/3/41.

127 **to conduct:** PHA 23, p. 862; PHA 31, p. 3185.

128 *shikyu:* Laurance Safford, "The Kita Message, No Longer a Mystery," unpublished manuscript, TKK; PHA 35, p. 475.

129 **This message, expressed:** PHA 12, p. 261. In books and articles about Pearl Harbor, it is often referred to as the "bomb plot" message, a somewhat confusing description that is not used in this book. The request to Hawaii to divide the harbor into specific segments had been initiated by none other than Itaru Tachibana, who had earlier been deported from the United States because of his espionage activity and was now back in Tokyo working for the intelligence section of the naval general staff (Prange, "The Truth About Japan's Pearl Harbor Spy," supra; Prange, *Dawn*, p. 248).

129 **new way/segments/three weeks/calling into question:** PHA Report, p. 516.

129 **collected basic information:** Ibid., pp. 186ff; Farago, *Broken Seal*, p. 230.

129 **Nowhere else, moreover:** A 1942 Navy Department study lists sixty-eight ship movement reports from Hawaii, fifty-five from Manila, eighteen from Panama, and six from Seattle. As will be fully reported in Chapter 44, the list was not made available to Admiral Kimmel or his legal team during postattack investigations. Other sources, citing versions of the intercepts published by Congress' Joint Committee, suggest more ship movement requests were made for information about Manila than about Pearl Harbor. Sources agree, though, that *only* the Japanese mission in Honolulu was required to divide the harbor into sections in its reports, or to indicate where ships were moored ("SRH 012: The Role of Radio Intelligence in the Japanese-American Naval War, Aug. 1941—June 1942," Vol. I, aka "RIP 87Z," RG 457, entry AI 9002, Boxes 6 and 7, NARA; and, e.g., Greaves, p. 109; PHA 2, pp. 794ff).

130 **Kimmel/Short not told:** PHA Report, pp. 184ff, 188ff, 516ff; PHA 7, pp. 2956ff.

130 **"pointed to an attack"/"I was entitled":** PHA 6, p. 2543. See Chapter 8 for an analysis of the January 27th report sent to Washington by Ambassador Joseph Grew.

CHAPTER 17

131 **"Gentlemen":** Stimson's "Gentlemen" quote is from his 1948 memoir, but this had already been his view in 1929. The Federal Communications Act of 1934 made it illegal to intercept radio or cable traffic between the United States and other nations (Stimson and Bundy, p. 188).

131 **law:** Federal Communications Act, 1934, Section 605, www.fcc.gov.

131 **codebreakers worked on:** David Kahn, pp. 5ff, 11ff.

131 **rivalry:** Budiansky, pp. 82ff, 87; Parker, pp. 12ff, 16ff.

131 **"Most of the time":** Kahn, p. 21.

131 **OP-20-G:** Ibid., p. 10.

131 **able to read naval operating code:** Parker, pp. 16ff; Budiansky, p. 88; Carlson, pp. 103ff.

131 **foreign ministry codes/basic groups:** History of OP-20-3-GYP, Box 116, RG 38, NARA; Kahn, pp. 14ff.

132 **Darkness fell:** William Friedman, "Preliminary Historical Report on the Solution of the 'B' Machine," top-secret unpublished manuscript, 10/14/40, NSA; Parker, pp. 18ff; Budiansky, p. 88.

Foreign ministry messages of high importance *other* than PURPLE—like the espionage messages to and from the Honolulu consulate—were usually sent in code U.S. cryptanalysts called the "J series." It remained readable, as did other lower-level foreign ministry codes, used mainly for administrative messages.

Following the naval code changes, the Japanese Navy's main operating code was its Fleet General Purpose Code—which would eventually be known as JN-25. Over time, as the Japanese instituted changes to the code, Americans renamed it to mark the changes—JN-25b, JN-25c, and so on. In the months before Pearl Harbor, the General Purpose Code carried almost half of the Japanese navy's messages. Revisionists have long suggested that JN-25b (the derivation of the code in use in the months before the attack) had been broken—thus giving the U.S. authorities foreknowledge of the impending Japanese moves. The best evidence, however, indicates that such claims are ill founded, that—in the period before the attack—at most 10 percent of any message in JN-25b could be understood. An internal history of naval codebreaking, released in the 1990s, states that "JN-25 played no part in the Radio Intelligence story of Pearl Harbor." Would that it had. (See Chapter 24.)

Evidence suggests that British codebreakers, with whom from early 1941 the Americans were sharing information, also failed to break JN-25b in such a way as to yield usable intelligence prior to Pearl Harbor. A history of Britain's Far East codebreaking unit states that work on JN-25 did not produce "operational intelligence" until early 1942. Another British internal history of naval intelligence, not declassified until 1994, states firmly that the British "had not penetrated the Japanese plan to attack Pearl Harbor." The report makes clear that in the weeks prior to the attack, like their U.S. counterparts, they relied on other forms of intelligence to track the movements of the Japanese Fleet, and had not been able in the final weeks to accurately locate the position of many of the Japanese ships. [**foreign ministry codes:** Kahn, pp. 14ff; Parker, pp. 21ff. **JN-25b/best evidence:** PHA 10, pp. 4674, 4678; Gannon, p. 206; History of OP-20-3-GYP, Box 116 and The Activities and Accomplishments of GY-1 During 1941, 1942, and 1943, Box 115, RG 38, NARA; and see analysis of JN-25, *Cryptologia*, April 2000; *Crytolog*, Winter 2000; Hanyok and Mowry (cited as Hanyok), p. 9; Budiansky, pp. 7ff, 12ff, 21ff, 364n8; *Naval War College Review*, Autumn 2008; Parker, pp. 35, 43. **Revisionists:** E.g., Stinnett, refs.; Timothy Wilford, "Decoding Pearl Harbor: USN Cryptanalysts and the Challenge of JN-25b in 1941," *Northern Mariner*, Vol. 12, 1/02. **British:** "History of HMS Anderson," HW4/25, PRO; "Pearl Harbor and the Loss of the Prince of Wales and Repulse," ADM 223/494; Michael Smith, pp. 106ff, 125; Hanyok, pp. 13ff.]

132 **would remain impenetrable:** Carlson, pp. 121ff; Kahn, pp. 562ff; Budiansky, pp. 8ff.

132 **for many months:** Friedman manuscript, supra.

132 **"Alphabetical Typewriter 97":** Kahn, pp. 18ff.

132 **Munitions Building:** *World War II* magazine, "Pearl Harbor" commemorative edition, 2001.

132 **thought the code was unbreakable:** Layton with Pineau and Costello, p. 80; Farago, *Broken Seal*, pp. 198ff.

132 **brutal toll/nervous collapse:** "The U.S. Army in World War II: The Signal Corps," draft mss, Box 116, TOL, p. 769; Kahn, p. 23; Budiansky, p. 175.

132 **Hurt/"the psychological":** John Hurt, "A Version of the Japanese Problem in the Signal Intelligence Agency," Washington, DC: Army Security Agency, 9/48, SRH-252, NARA, p. 10.

132 **"A cryptanalyst, brooding":** Kahn, p. 22.

133 **build a machine:** Parker, pp. 21ff; "Pearl Harbor Review—Red and Purple," www.nsa.gov; Kahn, p. 22.

133 **"rat's nest":** Layton with Pineau and Costello, p. 81.

133 **"whizzing":** Dundas Tucker, "Rhapsody in Purple," *Cryptologia*, 7 and 10/82.

133 **"Solving the secret":** *World War II* magazine, supra.

133 **"boogie-woogie":** Clausen and Lee, p. 64.

133 **"magicians":** Layton with Pineau and Costello, p. 81.

133 **Soon, insiders:** MAGIC would become the common usage. More formally, cryptographic intelligence was styled, as in Britain, ULTRASE-CRET or ULTRA ("U.S. Army in World War II: The Signal Corps," draft manuscript, Box 116, TOL; Layton with Pineau and Costello, p. 81).

133 **valuable intelligence:** E.g., Kahn, pp. 31ff; Farago, *Broken Seal*, p. 211.

133 **Marshall sought:** Farago, *Broken Seal*, p. 101.

133 **"horrendous":** Clarke to Prange, 9/4/76, Series V.2, Box 11, GP; Ober to Barnes, 1/19/62, Series V.2, Box 75, GP; Lavender to Kimmel, 8/1/61, HEK R32; and see, regarding oath, PHA 5, p. 2468; Smedberg Oral History, NWC; Stark to Barnes, 8/62, TKK.

133 **"TOP SECRET":** Interview with David Richmond, Box 14, Folder 1, SIMPSON.

133 **"solemnly swear":** E.g., oath of Malcolm Johnson, 11/14/45, Box 85, STARK.

134 **basic list/Hopkins:** Kahn, p. 24; Farago, *Broken Seal*, pp. 100ff, 194ff.

134 **Numerous others, however:** An odd omission at a senior level was William Donovan, appointed in June 1941 to coordinate the efforts of intelligence agencies (Anthony Cave Brown, *Last Hero*, pp. 192ff).

134 **copies destroyed:** PHA 4, p. 1601; Wohlstetter, p. 180.

134 **To handle the PURPLE:** Sources differ on how many machines went where, and when. The authors here rely on figures cited by Laurance Safford, the head of the Navy's cryptanalytic section. In July 1941, he wrote later, there had been a possibility that a machine might go to Hawaii. Because this would have been "at the expense of Washington," however, there was no follow-through. [differ: E.g., Prange, *Dawn*, p. 81; Kahn, pp. 23, 25; Farago, *Broken Seal*, pp. 102ff. **Safford:** Laurance Safford, "Rhapsody in Purple," draft manuscript, TKK.]

134 **FBI:** PHA Report, p. 261; PHA 31, p. 3189; Ladd to Director, 5/17/46, FBI 100–97–1–458, TKK; Prange, *Verdict*, pp. 270ff.

134 **Like the vast majority:** "The U.S. Army in World War II: The Signal Corps," draft mss, Box 116, TOL; Kahn, p. 24. For just over two weeks in July, inexplicably, Washington shared a jumble of either paraphrased or verbatim versions of intercepts of diplomatic traffic. See Chapter 19 (PHA 14, pp. 1397ff).

135 **Because of their proximity:** PHA 36, p. 46; Wohlstetter, pp. 180ff. There are contradictory claims regarding how much and what diplomatic traffic was available in the Philippines. Laurance Safford, the head of the Navy's codebreaking unit, wrote later that though Navy codebreakers there had a PURPLE machine, their instructions for using it were to concentrate on locally relevant information—as opposed to the Washington-Tokyo traffic.

General MacArthur, when shown some significant PURPLE and

other decoded intercepts during a later Pearl Harbor investigation, would deny ever having seen them before. Two of his senior aides, however, while denying having seen those particular intercepts, acknowledged having seen other MAGIC traffic, including some produced by PURPLE. An officer with the Army intercept team who delivered MAGIC messages to MacArthur's headquarters, for his part, recalled that certain intercepts were selected "to take . . . in to the General." [locally relevant: Safford to Hiles, 1/17/64, TKK; and see Lavender to Kimmel, 12/28/44 HEK R27. MacArthur: PHA 35, pp. 41, 84ff; "SRH 045, Reminiscences of LTC Howard W. Brown," Washington, DC: Signal Intelligence Agency, 8/4/45, Entry A1 9002, Container 16, RG 047, NARA; Costello, pp. 260ff; Willoughby and Chamberlain, pp. 22ff.]

135 **"The U.S. authorities"**: William Friedman, "Certain Aspects of Magic in the Cryptological Background of the Various Official Investigations into the Attack on Pearl Harbor," 5/8/57, Folder 199, www.nsa.gov, p. 46.

135 **The Director of Naval Intelligence**: PHA 24, p. 1361; PHA 4, pp. 1844ff.

135 **Turner was to assert**: PHA 33, p. 806; PHA 32, pp. 619ff; Hanify draft memoir, p. 12, HANIFY; Edward Hanify, Memorandum for the Director of Naval History, 12/23/87, TKK. Knox's aide was Captain Frank Beatty (Frank E. Beatty, "Another Version of What Started War with Japan," *U.S. News and World Report*, 5/28/54; interview with Beatty, Series V.2, Box 6, GP).

136 **"that goddamned Kimmel"**: Interview with Edwin Layton, Box 30, Folder 1, LAYTON.

136 **Stark "inquired"**: PHA 5, pp. 2175ff.

136 **"On three occasions"**: PHA 4, pp. 1975ff, 2019, 2040.

136 **"Noyes" was Rear Admiral Leigh Noyes**: Wohlstetter, p. 172. Turner's biographer, Vice Admiral George Dyer, would say Noyes "lied" about the exchange with Turner. According to Dyer, Noyes had not known whether the Navy at Pearl had MAGIC or not. By twice responding "Yes" to Turner's question, he misled him (interview with Dyer, Series V.2, Box 13, GP).

136 **"No"/"not intentionally"**: PHA 33, pp. 897ff.

136 **"to the best"/"confused"**: PHA 10, pp. 4714ff.

136 **Safford**: PHA 8, pp. 3715, 3858ff; Kimmel to Clarke, 3/20/60, TKK; Brownlow, p. 152.

137 **Kramer**: PHA 9, pp. 4195ff.

137 **"evasive"**: Russell, article in *U.S. News and World Report*, 5/7/54.

137 **possible/"unwise"**: PHA 29, p. 2328; and see PHA 9, pp. 4594ff.

137 **affidavit**: PHA 35, p. 104; and see PHA 33, p. 824.

137 **He had not**: Wohlstetter, pp. 183ff.

137 **Miles**: PHA 35, p. 102.

CHAPTER 18

138 **barely a thousand/far-flung stations:** Parker, p. 30; Kahn, pp. 10ff; Wohlstetter, pp. 174, 171.

138 **static:** Safford to Hiles, 1/8/64, Series V.2, Box 6, GP.

138 **PURPLE had priority/not radioed/by mail:** Ibid.; Kahn, pp. 12ff.

138 **delays/eight weeks:** Laurance Safford, "The Kita Message: No Longer a Mystery," TKK; Wohlstetter, pp. 173ff; "U.S. Army in World War II: The Signal Corps," *supra,* pp. 773ff.

138 **Telegraphic Japanese/"Any two":** Kahn, p. 29; Safford to Hiles, 1/8/64, Series V.2, Box 6, GP.

138 **"the whole matter"/"opportunity":** PHA 37, pp. 998ff; Baecher to Correa, 10/17/45, Box 15, RG 80, NARA.

139 **total of six:** Kahn, p. 29.

139 **Army found fewer:** John Hurt, "A Version of the Japanese Problem," supra; Wohlstetter, p. 174.

139 **unprecedented traffic:** Parker, p. 30.

139 **little time off:** PHA 9, p. 4168.

139 **odd and even days:** "U.S. Army in World War II: The Signal Corps," p. 772; Wohlstetter, pp. 174ff; Parker, pp. 16ff.

139 **named officer/delivered/odd-numbered months/folder/locked pouch:** PHA 33, pp. 850ff; PHA 11, p. 5475; PHA 3, pp. 1195ff, 1324ff, 1575ff; PHA 8, p. 3681; PHA 9, p. 4584; PHA 34, p. 94; Kahn, p. 30; Wohlstetter, pp. 176ff; "U.S. Army in World War II: The Signal Corps," *supra,* pp. 776ff.

139 **summaries:** PHA 33, pp. 848ff; PHA 9, p. 4584; Kahn, p. 30.

139 **red-pencil/paper clips:** PHA 33, pp. 851ff; PHA 4, pp. 1735, 1927; PHA 5, p. 2173; PHA 9, p. 4582.

139 **asterisks:** PHA 33, pp. 848ff, 861ff; PHA Report, p. 184.

139 **not required to sign:** PHA 26, p. 391; Edward Morgan, p. 266, but see dissenting recollection by Wilkinson, Statement of Theodore Wilkinson, 2/19/45, TKK.

140 **look rapidly/retrieve:** PHA 4, p. 1601; Wohlstetter, p. 180.

140 **more than a hundred:** PHA 33, p. 848.

140 **"put the pieces":** Friedman, "Certain Aspects of Magic," supra, p. 59.

140 **Joint Army-Navy committee:** PHA 2, pp. 529ff, 909ff; PHA 4, pp. 2020ff; PHA 34, p. 44; Prange, *Dawn,* p. 293.

140 **As it was, the system:** Sources differ on exactly what the security breaches were, and who was to blame (e.g., PHA 11, pp. 5475ff; Kahn, p. 26; Farago, *Broken Seal,* pp. 195, 200; Clausen and Lee, pp. 45ff).

140 **nightmare/"Though I do not":** Kahn, pp. 26ff; Farago, *Broken Seal,* p. 189; and see *Pacific Historical Review,* 2/81.

141 **It looked as though:** Even after Japan's defeat in 1945, Tokyo would continue to believe the PURPLE code was secure, and continue using it. For that reason, the fact that the United States could read it remained top-secret (Clausen and Lee, p. 48; Lee, pp. 545ff).

141 **In light of:** PHA 11, pp. 5268ff, 5475; Kahn, p. 30; Farago, *Broken Seal*, pp. 200ff, 276. The general was Sherman Miles. He felt that intercepted diplomatic messages were principally the concern of the State Department, which continued to see MAGIC and could decide what MAGIC content should be broached with the President.

CHAPTER 19

142 **He let slip nothing:** The February exchange is reported in full in Chapter 12.

142 **"He repeatedly":** Layton with Pineau and Costello, p. 91.

142 **Layton's background/McCollum:** Ibid., pp. 57ff, 495ff.

143 **"I told him":** Layton Oral History, supra.

143 **"Dear Eddie":** PHA 10, pp. 4845ff.

144 **"interdepartmental warfare":** Layton with Pineau and Costello, p. 95.

144 **"had grown up"/Turner:** McCollum Oral History, supra.

144 **"one of the best":** Prange, *Verdict*, p. 214.

144 **"brilliant":** Interview with Harold Stark by James Leutze, Box 41, STARK; and see Stark to McCrea, 2/27/61, Box 9, MCCREA.

144 **"not enough superlatives":** Prange, *Verdict*, p. 214.

144 **"mental power":** Hart diary, 4/7/44, Box 9, HART.

144 **"aggressive":** Wellborn to Prange, 5/1/69, Series V.2, Box 85, GP; interview with Charles Wellborn, Box 11, Folder 16, SIMPSON.

144 **"irascible":** Oral History of Walter Ansel, Naval Institute, 1970, NHHC.

144 **"stubborn":** Interview with Claude Bloch, Series V.2, Box 8, GP.

144 **"bull"/"intolerant":** Prange, *Verdict*, p. 294; interview with Joseph Rochefort, Series V.2, Box 70, GP; Hoehling, p. 53.

144 **"amazingly ignorant":** Interview with Frank Beatty, Series V.2, Box 6, GP.

144 **"although Admiral Stark":** Smedberg to Prange, 7/29/77, Series V.2, Box 74, GP.

144 **"always spoke"/"abjectly":** Interview with Frank Beatty, Series V.2, Box 6, GP.

145 **Turner had seized:** PHA 4, pp. 1913ff; Wellborn to Prange, 5/1/69, Series V.2, Box 85, GP; Statement of VADM Theodore Wilkinson, 4/19/45, HEK R12; Wohlstetter, pp. 315ff; Prange, *Verdict*, pp. 290ff; Dyer, pp. 181ff; Kirk to Wilkinson, 12/19/45, Wilkinson to Ingersoll, 12/20/45, TKK; and see PHA 15, p. 1864.

145 **"should interpret":** PHA 4, pp. 1925ff.

145 "a complex on secrecy"/"hand on the gullet": McCollum Oral History, U.S. Naval Institute 1973, NHHC.

145 **In June, when Admiral Kimmel/Eight dispatches/"Top Secret":** PHA 14, pp. 1397ff; Edward Hanify, Draft Report for the Minority, TKK; interview with Edwin Layton, Series V.2, Box 58, GP. The Admiral's visit to Washington is reported at length in Chapter 12. Two of the Japanese messages shared with Kimmel in July included the word "PURPLE," revealing the code in which they had been obtained by U.S. codebreakers. Kimmel and his staff, however, had no knowledge of what PURPLE was—and seemed at that stage not to notice the word (copy of 7/19/41 message from OPNAV, PHA 14, p. 1399).

145 **"Conversations with the Japanese":** PHA 16, pp. 2212ff.

146 **intercepted message to Hawaii/delays/Clipper:** Interview with Husband Kimmel, Series V.2, Box, 56, GP; Farago, *Broken Seal*, pp. 227ff, 166ff.

146 **Bratton/"I felt":** PHA 9, pp. 4534, 4526.

147 **Miles would not recall:** PHA 2, pp. 826ff.

147 **Stimson/Marshall/"had no recollection":** PHA 2, p. 1102; PHA 9, p. 4526; Gannon, pp. 193ff; Prange *Dawn*, pp. 249ff. Harvey Bundy, who was an assistant to Stimson in the fall of 1941, would say eighteen years later: "I read the MAGIC about where the Japanese were counting the ships and where they were located in Pearl Harbor, and my recollection is that I mentioned this to G-2—the MAGIC man in G-2—and his reply was, 'Oh, the Japs are doing that all over the world.'" Colonel Bratton, who handled MAGIC for Army Intelligence, could well have said—accurately—that Japan collected information on U.S. ships in many ports. Bratton, though, had been alerted by what was unique about the September 24th intercept—that Tokyo wanted Pearl Harbor information divided into specified sections, and detail on moored ships (Bundy oral history, 10/7/59; George C. Marshall Foundation).

147 **"My consideration":** PHA 9, p. 4177.

147 **"gist"/"Tokyo directs"/asterisk:** Ibid., pp. 4176ff, 4195ff.

147 **Stark/"We did not see"/"In the light of":** PHA 5, pp. 2173ff.

148 **Turner/"As a matter of fact"/brought to the attention of ONI:** PHA 4, pp. 1921ff.

148 **"it did not make":** PHA 8, p. 3391.

148 **replacement phasing in/"to one or more officers":** PHA 4, pp. 1746–1939ff.

149 **Safford/"more violent"/"was fully appreciated"/Kirk "demanded":** Safford himself, he claimed in his unfinished manuscript, tried to get word of the intercept to Kimmel but was blocked by his boss Admiral Noyes. If Safford's account is accurate, in the authors' view it may indicate that some of the principals later covered up their failure to see the significance of the September 24th intercept—and of related

messages. Alternatively, the episode may be a further example of the turf wars in the Navy Department. Conspiracy theorists, however, later seized on Safford's account as evidence of a plot within the Roosevelt administration to withhold vital information. Though Safford himself came to subscribe to that view, there is no reason to doubt the essence of his account. Our assessment comports with that of Pearl Harbor historian Professor Gordon Prange. "One can understand," Prange wrote on this issue, "why some individuals have cried 'Villain!' instead of 'Fool!'" (Laurance Safford, "The Kita Message: No Longer a Mystery," TKK; Prange, *Verdict*, pp. 278ff).

149 **Stark/"full authority":** PHA 5, p. 2174.

150 **DeLany:** Interview with Walter DeLany, Series V.2, Box 12, GP.

150 **"malarkey":** Interview with Edwin Layton, Box 39, Folder 1, LAYTON.

150 **"should certainly":** PHA 7, p. 3364.

150 **Admiral Kimmel himself:** PHA 6, p. 2610. It seems that no maps of Pearl Harbor divided into zones were recovered from downed Japanese aircraft after the attack—a fact that some have contended indicates that the information requested on September 24th was not intended for use by strike force pilots. That conclusion, however, appears to be at odds with other evidence. Very detailed maps showing where Fleet warships were moored, though without actual reference to the zones, were indeed recovered from Japanese airplanes after the attack. Japanese officers involved in the attack, moreover, would later credit the information supplied by the spy Yoshikawa as having been valuable. [**contended:** Carlson, citing Hanyok, p. 491; Kittredge in *U.S. News and World Report*, 12/3/54. **detailed maps:** "U.S. Pacific Fleet and Pacific Ocean Areas," *Weekly Intelligence*, Vol. 1, No. 22, 12/8/44; A-1 Entry 167F, Box 40, RG 80, NARA; PHA 16, p. 2257. **Japanese officers:** E.g., Fuchida in *Proceedings*, 9/52; Tomioka and Chigusa, cited in Prange, *Dawn*, pp. 453ff, 479, 774, 776.]

150 **Yamamoto had gathered/"I like games":** Prange, *Dawn*, pp. 180ff, 223ff 258ff.

150 *Hawai Sakusen:* Proceedings, 12/55; Ken Kotani, *Japanese Intelligence in World War II*, Tokyo: National Institute for Defense Studies, 2009.

CHAPTER 20

151 **Mountbatten's background:** Hough; Adrian Smith.

151 **feted:** FDR diary, 8/25/41, FDRL, re White House dinner; Adrian Smith, p. 167.

151 **Churchill wanted:** Adrian Smith, p. 165.

151 **There had been/"special relationship":** Colman, p. 2; Ted Morgan, p. 579. Churchill would first use the term in 1944, then again in 1945, and—most famously—in 1946, in his landmark speech at Fulton, Missouri.

151 **Roosevelt's conviction:** Roosevelt and Churchill exchanged 1,700 letters and telegrams between 1939 and 1945. They met nine times during the war. It may be relevant that they were distantly related, and that Churchill's mother had been American (Churchill, eulogy on Roosevelt's death, 4/17/45).

152 **"deputy President":** Ted Morgan, p. 578.

152 **"On January 10th":** Churchill, pp. 20ff; Colville, p. 346.

152 **"whatever you are able":** Churchill to FDR, 2/14/41, PREM 3/469, PRO.

152 **Lend-Lease:** Ted Morgan, pp. 579ff; Gannon, p. 76.

153 **"If we do not watch":** Ted Morgan, p. 581.

153 **ABC-1 Staff Report:** Matloff and Snell, ch. 3, pp. 32ff; PHA 3, pp. 993ff; Prange, *Verdict*, pp. 69ff; Simpson, pp. 74ff; Wohlstetter, p. 111.

153 **Japanese forces moved/economic sanctions/oil:** Prange, *Dawn*, p. 165; Gannon, p. 92; Morison, pp. 63ff.

153 **"slip the noose":** Layton with Pineau and Costello, p. 121.

153 **"Our Empire":** Tokyo to Washington, 7/31/41, MB, Vol. III, Appendix, pp. 9ff.

154 **Roosevelt made a show/meeting with Churchill/"Onward, Christian Soldiers"/Joint Declaration:** Memorandum of Trip to Meet Winston Churchill, 8/23/41, PSF, Box 1, FDRL; Stark to Katie, 8/21/41, Box 8, Folder 2, SIMPSON; Press Release, 8/14/41, PSF Safe Files, FDRL; AP, 8/14/41; Freidel, pp. 384ff; "The Atlantic Conference and Charter," www.state.gov; Simpson, pp. 92ff; Ted Morgan, pp. 597ff.

154 **"Atlantic Charter":** E.g., *Bakersfield Californian*, 8/25/41.

154 **"The Americans,"** The aide was Colonel Ian Jacob, the Military Assistant Secretary to the war cabinet (Rose, p. 342).

155 **The German submarine/"The American people":** Fireside Chat 18, 9/11/41, www.millercenter.org; PHA 5, pp. 2295ff. The submarine, U-652, did fire torpedoes at the *Greer*. The story of the action, however, also involved two British Royal Air Force bombers, which had earlier attacked the submarine with depth charges. Having been torpedoed, the *Greer* in turn dropped depth charges, thus becoming the first U.S. ship to engage the Germans ("A Brief History of U.S. Navy Destroyers," www.navy.mil; "USS *Greer*," http://destroyerhistory.org).

155 **made welcome/Halsey/Kimmel asked/views:** Mountbatten to Pott, 10/9/41; Remarks by Capt. Mountbatten Armoured or Un-Armoured Carriers, undated, Papers of Earl Mountbatten of Burma, with permission of the Hartley Library, University of Southampton, UK.

156 **"appalled":** Terraine, ch. 5 [Kindle edition].

156 **"In repeated":** PHA 16, p. 2253.

156 **"With constantly changing":** PHA 6, p. 2500.

156 **begging bowl/severe shortage:** PHA 16, pp. 2181, 2242ff; PHA 16, pp. 2206, 2241; PHA 33, pp. 1280ff; Kimmel, pp. 15ff.

156 **In late 1941:** See Chapter 10.

156 **B-17s:** PHA 3, pp. 1119ff; Costello, pp. 86ff, 90ff.

157 **"The picture":** Interview with William Furlong, Series V.2, Box 56, GP.

157 **"I have frequently":** PHA 16, p. 2254.

157 **"inexcusable":** PHA Report, p. 549.

157 **"a permanent radar":** Mountbatten to Simpson, 9/14/78, Mountbatten papers, supra.

157 **Kimmel alert to importance:** CINCPAC to Fleet, 11/17/41, Entry P91, Container 40, RG 313, NARA. On November 17, 1941, Kimmel issued an order to the Fleet in anticipation of what he hoped would soon be a large number of radars being installed aboard his ships. "It is imperative," he wrote, "that each man trained either as an operator or maintenance man, be employed in connection with the subject equipment and that his wherabouts be known at all times."

157 **Kimmel assigned/"inferior"/Bloch/offered to help/exercises:** Statement of Claude Bloch, Box 5, BLOCH; PHA 23, pp. 1195ff; PHA 27, pp. 360ff; PHA 26, pp. 379ff; PHA 29, pp. 1983ff; PHA 36, pp. 270ff; PHA 39, pp. 109ff, 309ff; PHA 22, pp. 367ff; Kimmel, p. 9; and see Prange, *Verdict*, pp. 367ff, 393ff.

158 **Calhoun:** PHA 22, p. 593.

158 **"was inclined":** PHA 26, p. 247.

158 **When Mountbatten left:** Mountbatten to Potts, 10/9/41, Mountbatten papers, supra.

158 **condolences:** Mountbatten to Kimmel, 12/9/41, HEK R25.

158 **track down/"I have never wavered":** Mountbatten to Kimmel, 9/18/45, 11/1/45, 11/19/45, Kimmel to Mountbatten, 9/4/45, Mountbatten papers, supra.

158 **"The Jap situation":** FDR to Churchill, 10/15/41, PSF Box 34, FDRL.

CHAPTER 21

159 **"one of the main points":** AP, 8/14/41.

159 **"We propose":** MB, Vol. III, Appendix, p. A-8.

159 **duplicitous:** E.g., ibid., pp. A-97ff, A-106ff; Ted Morgan, p. 607; Mauch, pp. 190ff.

159 **"a pure blind":** Stimson diary, 8/8/41, STIM.

159 **"the U.S. government":** Draft of Parallel Communications to the Japanese Government, PSF Box 1, FDRL.

160 **"any and all steps":** U.S. Department of State, *Papers Relating* . . . Vol. II, pp. 556ff.

160 **military response:** PHA 2, p. 511.

160 **"To some":** PHA 33, p. 1356.

160 **"If you do not":** PHA 16, pp. 2182ff.

160 **"I have not given up":** PHA 16, p. 2208.

160 **"unforeseen contingencies":** U.S. Department of State, *Paper Relating . . .* Vol. II, p. 573.

160 **One of those contingencies:** MB III, Appendix, p. A-400.

160 **starved of oil/eager to move/three in September/In sum/did not renounce:** MB, Vol. I, p. 15ff; Gannon, pp. 92, 95, 90ff, 293.

161 **Konoye resigned/"Preparations are well done":** Toland, *Rising Sun,* pp. 110ff, 116; MB, Vol. III, Appendix, p. A-158.

161 **A formal dispatch:** The tenor of a message from the adjutant general, Major General Emory Adams, to General Short was less alarmist: "Tension between United States and Japan remains strained, but no, repeat no, abrupt change in Japanese foreign policy appears imminent" (PHA 14, p. 1327).

161 **"Since the U.S.":** PHA 26, p. 487.

161 **"I do not believe":** PHA 16, p. 2214.

162 **Kimmel responded/additional measures:** PHA 16, p. 2249; PHA 33, pp. 699ff.

162 **revised security order:** Pacific Fleet Confidential Letter No. 2CL-41 (revised) 10/14/41, reprinted in Kimmel, pp. 19, 189ff; PHA 33, p. 709ff; PHA 32, p. 400.

162 **satisfied:** PHA 16, p. 2219; *U.S. News and World Report,* 12/3/54.

162 **working frenetically/"Thunderfish":** *Naval War College Review,* Vol. 67, No. 1, Winter 2014; Prange, *Dawn,* pp. 320ff, 323; Parker, p. 56; *Naval History,* Winter 1991.

CHAPTER 22

163 **"assistant purser"/followed sea-lanes/two hundred miles/stayed on board/hundred questions:** Prange, *Dawn,* pp. 314ff.

163 **The consulate spy, Yoshikawa/"sightseeing"/smuggled:** Ibid., pp. 317ff; Farago, *Broken Seal,* p. 246.

163 **Sundays:** As the Fleet's schedule makes clear, Yoshikawa was making a broad statement that was not really accurate—on December 7th, for example, elements of two carrier divisions were *not* in harbor. As early as April, CNO Stark had circulated a message to all U.S. Navy outposts and the governors of Guam and Samoa, noting that, in the past, the Axis powers had often taken action "on Saturdays or Sundays or on national holidays of the countries concerned." Navy outposts should therefore "take steps on such days to see that proper watches and precautions are in effect." In the case of Hawaii, this message had gone to the base defense officer, Admiral Bloch. It is not clear whether or not

Bloch passed this information to General Short, who with him was primarily responsible for the defense. Kimmel did not see the message until sometime after the attack, he testified to Congress' Joint Committee (PHA 39, p. 298; PHA 17, p. 2476ff; PHA 14, pp. 139ff; PHA 6, pp. 2620, 375ff; PHA 22, p. 97).

164 **going to the beach:** Farago, *Broken Seal*, p. 242.

164 **walked/"Dr. Homberg"/fourteen thousand/letter/radio/lights/"a method":** Affidavit of Otto Kuehn, 1/1/42, Doc. 6256A, Series V.2, Box 58, GP; PHA 35, pp. 331ff; *Proceedings*, 12/50; Farago, *Broken Seal*, pp. 242ff.

164 **"the hour":** Prange, *Dawn*, p. 317.

164 **FBI agents had:** The meeting between Kühn and Yoshikawa is believed to have taken place on October 25th. An FBI document indicates that Kühn was watched only on four other days that month (Prange, pp. 310ff; Honolulu report re. Kühn, 11/24/41, FBI 65-1574-27, RG 65, NARA).

164 **"outside man":** Japanese Consulate, Honolulu, T.H., 7/15/41 attached to Hoover to Berle, 8/7/41, Box 1949, Department of State, Decimal Files 1940–1944, 702.9411A/35, RG 59, NARA.

164 **diplomats gathered for dinner:** Olive Schuler to Summers, 1993.

165 **Among the guests:** Frank and Olive Schuler have been mentioned in the notes for Chapter 8. The incident described here is as recalled years later by Olive Schuler in a draft manuscript she shared with the authors (mss. and correspondence, Olive Schuler to Anthony Summers, 1993).

165 **Terasaki-Smith friendship:** See Memorandum for Mr. Wilson, re Japanese Activities, 8/22/41, Box 1887, Department of State, Decimal Files, 701.9411, RG 59, NARA.

165 **name featured/"intelligence organ":** MB I, pp. A-76ff; MB II, pp. 100ff; MB II, Appendix, pp. A-72, A-124ff, A-203ff; MB III, pp. 113ff, 143, 150, 188, 189; MB III, Appendix, pp. A-57, A-60, A-155, A-215, A-235ff, A-324ff, A-466; MB IV, pp. 46ff, 76, 92ff, 121, 126ff, 135, 137, 139; MB IV, Appendix, pp. A-60, A-96, A-184ff, A-213, A-222ff; and see re background, Dossier with Questionnaire of Hidenari Terasaki, Entry A1 134-B, Container 780, ARC 645054, RG 316, NARA.

166 **"As a matter of interest":** Memorandum for Mr. Wilson, 8/22/41, supra.

166 **twelve-page FBI report/"to maintain"/traveled thousands/watched/ calls tapped:** Japanese Activities in Washington, DC, 10/24/41, FBI report attached to Department of State Division of Far Eastern Affairs, 12/1/41, Box 1887, Department of State, Decimal Files 701.9411, RG 59, NARA.

166 **luggage searched:** MB III, p. 150.

166 **Tachibana:** Japanese Activities in Washington, DC, 10/24/41, supra.

166 **Hawaii responded:** PHA 12, p. 262.

166 **sensitive exchanges:** E.g., MB IV, p. 76, 92.

167 **Hoover/"This officer":** Hoover to Berle, 10/18/41, 11/14/41, 11/29/41, 12/2/41; Berle to Welles, 12/1/41; Warren to Berle, 12/1/41; MMH [Hamilton] to Hornbeck and Welles, 12/4/41; Memo to Hamilton, 12/3/41.

167 **What had Terasaki's:** In 1956, Gwen Terasaki would write a celebrated book, *Bridge to the Sun*, about her marriage and the couple's experiences during the war. She portrayed her husband as having been a moderate, a man who loved the United States and had been appalled by his nation's attack on Pearl Harbor.

CHAPTER 23

168 **slew of messages/"This is our last":** MB IV, Appendix, pp. A11ff.

168 **"Those negotiations":** Cited in Majority Judgement, International Military Tribunal for the Far East, Boister and Cryer, p. 527.

168 **"no additional"/"to show"/"sound good":** MB IV, Appendix, p. A11ff.

168 **Muto:** Boister and Cryer, p. 527.

169 **November 25th deadline:** MB IV, Appendix, p. A-22.

169 **further five messages:** MB IV, Appendix, pp. A-39, A-58ff, A-89.

169 **None were available to Kimmel:** British intelligence, however, did have access to Japanese messages sent in the PURPLE code. As reported in Chapter 17, Washington had supplied London with the PURPLE machine that had originally been destined for Kimmel's Fleet in Hawaii. Revisionist authors have long used the fact that the British had the machine—and access to other intelligence sources—to substantiate the notion that Prime Minister Churchill knew of the coming Pearl Harbor attack before it occurred, and let it go ahead to ensure that the United States would enter the war. British analysts reading PURPLE, revisionist books suggest, may have obtained telltale pre-attack messages that Washington missed—or did not read until too late.

It is a fact, as research in the British National Archives makes clear, that London did read *some* PURPLE intercepts before Washington did. It is also a fact that in his memoir *Grand Alliance*—published in 1950, when the details of American-British intelligence cooperation were still top-secret—Churchill was less than truthful on the subject. Instead of acknowledging that the United States had supplied Britain with a decoding machine, he maintained that Japan's diplomatic messages were merely passed on to London by Washington after "an inevitable delay—sometimes of two or three days—before we got them." Documents in the British archives show that some intercepts were in fact decrypted days *before* U.S. analysts decoded the identical intercepts on their side of the Atlantic. Churchill's scribbled comments appear on a number of the intercepts.

The authors' research in London, however, also uncovered what is probably the first evidence that—far from London's being overall *better* informed than Washington, and contrary to the revisionists' suppositions—there were great gaps in what was read by the British. In a handwritten report made at Churchill's request in 1949, a senior British cryptanalyst, Nigel de Grey—who served as deputy director at GCHQ—concluded from the files that "we did not have all the Americans had." Had they had the "deadline" intercepts at the time, de Grey wrote, "Mr. Churchill would have been better informed." According to de Grey, "none" of Tokyo's "deadline" messages appeared in London's collection of PURPLE intercepts.

According to de Grey's report, London also failed to intercept the to-and-fro between Tokyo and the Honolulu consulate's spy, Yoshikawa. That said, several individuals who were once in a position to be well informed have made statements that might appear to indicate Britain had some sort of foreknowledge. Future CIA Director William Casey, who had been a top intelligence officer in Europe in World War II, wrote in a 1988 memoir that, before the attack, "The British had sent word that a Japanese fleet was steaming east toward Pearl Harbor." To what may this undated, opaque reference refer?

In 1975, the wartime chairman of Britain's Joint Intelligence Committee (JIC), Victor Cavendish-Bentinck, told an author that he recalled a December 5th meeting of the Committee at which there was discussion of information that "a Japanese fleet was sailing in the direction of Hawaii." An unnamed individual at the meeting, Cavendish-Bentinck said, stated that Washington had been informed. It is not clear, however, that there was a JIC meeting on December 5th. Professor Richard Aldrich has written that there was not—and that, at meetings on the 3rd and 9th, Pearl Harbor was not discussed.

Another fragment of information on JIC discussions comes from Sir Julian Ridsdale, who was not a committee member but attended one of its meetings on or about November 27th. Participants at that meeting, he wrote in a draft for a memoir, discussed the fact that both U.S. and British monitoring "had begun losing track of the movements" of the Japanese fleet. Because of radio silence, he wrote, "we concluded that the Japanese Fleet was now in a position to be considered a major threat to the American Fleet in Pearl Harbor. It was agreed we should alert the President of the United States." In 1987, Ridsdale wrote, Cavendish-Bentinck "assured me that he had passed the message on."

If the JIC discussion of November 27th did occur as described, and if a message was passed to President Roosevelt, nothing about it has surfaced in American archives. The London discussion as recalled, moreover, reflects, not specific intelligence about a threat to Pearl Harbor, but merely a general sense that the Japanese fleet was at large in the Pacific, its whereabouts unknown. Concern on that point was exactly what Admiral Kimmel and the head of the Pacific Fleet's Combat Intelligence Unit, Lieutenant Commander Rochefort, met to discuss on the same day as the JIC meeting in London (see Chapter 28).

None of this information, taken together, indicates that the British expected an attack or had any foreknowledge of the strike on Pearl Harbor. A final tidbit from the official history—compiled, apparently, by someone with "free access to official documents"—suggests the very opposite. "In a paper issued on 28 November," F. H. Hinsley wrote, "the JIC implicitly excluded the prospect of a direct Japanese attack on U.S. possessions."

It calculated that if Japan broke off the negotiations it would move against *Thailand* [authors' italics] very early in 1942, in order to be ready for an attack on Malaya. [**British intercepts:** See HW 12/270, HW 12/271, PRO. **Casey:** Casey, p. 7. **Churchill/"delay":** Churchill, *Grand Alliance*, p. 536. **de Grey:** Paper prepared for Winston Churchill on "Info. Available to British Cabinet Before Pearl Harbor," HW 50/52, PRO. **Cavendish-Bentinck/Aldrich:** Fitzgibbon, p. 255; *Intelligence and National Security*, Vol. 7, No. 3, 1992; and see JIC (41) 460, 12/5/41, CAB 79–16–14, PRO. **Ridsdale:** unpublished manuscript. Box 1, Papers of Sir Julian Ridsdale, Churchill Archives Centre, Cambridge. **Hinsley:** Hinsley, et al., pp. 76ff.]

169 **November 15th/"twice a week"/Several more/four requests decoded:** PHA 12, pp. 262ff.

169 **none shared with Kimmel:** Husband Kimmel, "Facts About Pearl Harbor," Groton, CT: self-published, 1958.

170 **"Dear Mustapha":** PHA 16, p. 2219.

170 **Meanwhile, Admiral Yamamoto's:** Carlson, pp. 135ff; Naval Analysis Division, *Campaigns of the Pacific War*, ch. 2, Appendix 1; and see "The Ships That Attacked Pearl Harbor and Their Fate," NavSource Naval History.

The strike force would be joined by three submarines. Twenty-five other submarines (five of which carried midget submarines) would also be sent to Hawaiian waters—separate from the main force. Two other submarines would head for the U.S. West Coast (Wilmott, refs.; "Japanese Submarines at Pearl Harbor," www.ww2pacific.com).

170 **detailed briefing:** Prange, *Dawn*, p. 327.

170 **general staff approved:** Naval Analysis Division, *Campaigns of the Pacific War*, p. 15; PHA 12, p. 400; Gannon, pp. 171ff.

170 **Hirohito's approval:** Bix, pp. 425ff; Wetzler, p. 30; Bartsch, *Every Day a Nightmare*, p. 7.

170 **Top Secret Order No. 1:** PHA 13, pp. 431ff; Prange, *Dawn*, pp. 331ff.

170 **The order included:** Though datelined November 5th, the order was issued on the 8th. In the seven hundred *copies* of the order that were printed, there was no reference to the plan to attack Pearl Harbor. The three points about the attack appear only in a surviving fragment of the original (PHA 13, pp. 431ff; Prange, *Dawn*, pp. 329ff; Gannon, pp. 172ff).

171 **"absolutely immovable":** MB IV, Appendix, p. A-58.

171 **"actual warfare"/"This little victory":** Ibid., pp. A-56ff.

171 **"out of the question"**: PHA 12, p. 138.

171 **"by the 29th"/"reasons beyond"**: MB IV, Appendix, p. A-89.

172 **"Although we hope"/"The American"/"*Banzai*"**: Prange, *Dawn*, pp. 343ff.

CHAPTER 24

173 **Kimmel briefed**: PHA 10, pp. 4831ff; Layton with Pineau and Costello, p. 183; Carlson, p. 113.

173 **forty-seven officers/"the Dungeon"**: *Naval Intelligence Professionals Quarterly*, 10/91; Carlson, pp. 89ff.

173 **These were the men**: The other two units were Station Negat, at head-quarters in Washington; and Station Cast in the Philippines (interview with Joseph Rochefort by Gordon Prange, GP).

173 **Rochefort skills/medal**: Carlson, pp. 1ff, 307ff, 321ff, 335, 455; Layton with Pineau and Costello, pp. 410ff, 464.

173 **brilliance/smoking jacket**: Carlson, pp. 95ff, 102.

173 **Flag Officers' Code/never broken**: Interview with Joe Rochefort, Series V.2, Box 70, GP; *Naval Intelligence Professionals Quarterly*, 10/91; Kahn, p. 7; Carlson, pp. 120ff.

174 **assigned to Station Cast**: History of OP-20-3-GYP, Box 116, 5750/199, RG 38, NARA; Carlson, pp. 120ff, 122.

174 **traffic analysis/direction finding defined**: *Foreign Affairs*, Winter 1991/1992; PHA 6, p. 2522.

174 **"fist"**: Kahn, p. 32; interview with Joe Rochefort, Series V.2, Box 70, GP.

174 **far-flung network**: Carlson, pp. 115ff.

174 **changed call signs**: *Naval War College Review*, Autumn 2008.

174 ***Itikoukuu Kantai*/"an entirely new"**: PHA 35, p. 63.

175 **"Each fleet circuit"**: Layton with Pineau and Costello, p. 183; PHA 10, p. 4834.

175 **"Something was afoot"**: PHA 23, p. 679.

175 **seven days/around the clock**: Carlson, p. 132.

175 **"dummy traffic"**: PHA 35, p. 63.

175 **phony messages**: PHA 1, p. 185.

175 **"fists"/stayed ashore**: PHA 23, p. 1273; *Naval War College Review*, Autumn 2008.

175 **fake chatter**: Carlson, p. 136.

176 **"addressed to nobody"**: PHA 10, p. 4893.

176 **more interested**: PHA 10, p. 4834.

176 **"practically impossible"**: PHA 6, p. 2522.

176 **twelve occasions**: PHA 23, p. 1273.

176 **Kimmel drew Washington's attention:** PHA 16, p. 2251; Parker, p. 37; Layton with Pineau and Costello, p. 181.

176 **Some of them were within:** The westernmost Mandates, the Caroline Islands, are less than a thousand miles from the Philippines. Truk, at the heart of the archipelago, had an excellent deepwater anchorage. The easternmost Mandates, the Marshalls, are some 2,400 miles from Hawaii.

176 **"Those pieces of the puzzle":** Layton with Pineau and Costello, p. 183.

176 **reports of November 9th and 10th:** PHA 35, p. 66.

177 **"no movement":** PHA 35, p. 71.

177 **The first lap/radio silence/"profound":** *Intelligence and National Security*, Winter 2004; *Cryptologia*, 4/05; *Cryptolog*, Winter 2000; SRH-406, Pre-Pearl Harbor Japanese Naval Despatches, Box 183, RG 38, NARA; *Naval War College Review*, Autumn 2008; *Intelligence and National Security*, Winter 2004; PHA 13, p. 717; Carlson, p. 137.

Whether the Japanese strike force really did maintain strict radio silence has been an issue down the years. Revisionist authors contended that some ships in the strike force continued to transmit as they headed toward Pearl Harbor, and that their transmissions were detected by the United States, tipping off Washington that an attack was imminent. The authors have found no evidence to support these claims.

One such claim, which featured in John Toland's 1982 book *Infamy*, arose from a story told by "Seaman Z," later identified as former seaman first class Robert Ogg. Ogg was attached to the ONI office in San Francisco in early December 1941 and was tasked—he said, as paraphrased by Toland—"to collate reports from commercial ships in the Pacific." In the course of doing that job, he said, he picked up some "queer signals," then worked with his superior officer to plot the source of the signals. They then passed on the resulting information to Admiral Richard McCullough, who headed ONI in San Francisco. Later in the week leading up to the attack, Ogg said he and the officer managed to identify the signals as coming from a position "approximately 400 miles north-northwest" of Pearl Harbor. There "was now no doubt at all. Pearl Harbor was going to be raided the next morning." As before, he and his superior passed the latest information on to their boss, McCullough. McCullough, they assumed, in turn passed it on not only to ONI at headquarters in Washington but to President Roosevelt—who was supposedly his "personal friend."

The story does not stand up to scrutiny. In a later oral history interview for the National Security Agency, Ogg was much vaguer about what he had heard. The transmissions he heard, he said, might have been from a Soviet Russian source—not from a Japanese source at all. The authors have established, moreover, that Admiral McCullough was a friend, not of Franklin Roosevelt, but of his distant cousin, former president Theodore Roosevelt. There is no evidence that McCullough knew FDR.

Since his days at the Naval Academy, though, McCullough had been close to Admiral Kimmel. The authors' checks in Kimmel's papers located letters between Kimmel and McCullough—and they contain nothing about the "queer signals" episode. [**Ogg's story:** Toland, *Infamy*, pp. 293ff, 299, 331, 341, 345; oral history interview of Robert Ogg, SRH 255, RG 457, NARA. **McCullough:** *Newark News*, 10/65. **correspondence:** E.g., McCullough to "My dear Hub," 5/16/42, HEK R25.]

177 **Kurils:** Prange, *Dawn*, pp. 365ff; Carlson, p. 130.

177 **commanders briefed:** Prange, *Dawn*, pp. 365ff; SRH 406 Pre-Pearl Harbor Japanese Naval Despatches, p. 17, Box 183, RG 38, NARA.

177 **gathered for briefings/aspiration:** Prange, *Dawn*, pp. 373ff.

177 **yet be called off:** Ibid., pp. 373, 387; PHA 13, p. 420.

178 **order to sortie:** PHA 13, p. 418.

178 **upped anchor:** Prange, *Dawn*, pp. 390ff.

178 **"Make your investigation":** PHA 12, p. 263.

178 **"We," Hypo's Commander Rochefort:** Interview with Joe Rochefort, Series V.2, Box 70, GP. Interception of diplomatic traffic was done in Hawaii by the Army's local intercept station, under an arrangement agreed on between the Army and the Navy in Washington. As the Army in Hawaii had no decrypting facility, its raw intercepts were forwarded to Washington by airmail (PHA 10, p. 4697; Farago, *Broken Seal*, p. 227; Carlson, p. 153).

179 **The decision/Of some two thousand:** History of OP-20-3-GYP, Box 116, RG 38, NARA; SRH 406 Pre-Pearl Harbor Japanese Naval Despatches, Box 183, RG 38, NARA; Parker, pp. 1ff, 43ff, 47, 53ff; Carlson, pp. 156ff, 202. On claims that the fleet's main operating code, its General Purpose Code, or JN-25b, was being read *during* 1941, see note in Chapter 17, "Darkness fell."

179 **"Had Navy cryptanalysts":** Parker, p. 1.

CHAPTER 25

180 **We have access:** The quotation is from a copy of an in-house memorandum at *Time*, found by the Pulitzer Prize-winning author Hanson Baldwin in 1949. Marshall's purpose in holding the press briefing, the historian David Kaiser has written, was to intimidate the Japanese. He told those listening that the United States was "preparing for an offensive war against Japan, whereas the Japs believe we are preparing only to defend the Philippines" (Sherrod to Hulburd, 11/15/41, Sherrod to Baldwin, 6/27/50, Baldwin Collection, George C. Marshall Research Foundation; Kaiser, p. 214).

181 **"completely out of touch":** PHA 33, p. 700.

181 **"War of Nerves":** Hart to Stark, 11/20/41, Box 15, STARK.

181 **diary/"general understanding"/no give/got nowhere:** Admiral Nomura's Diary, 11/17, 11/18, 11/19 11/20/41 IPS Document Division, trans. 7/18/46, Series V.2, Box 64, GP; Morton, *Command Decisions*, pp. 115ff; Hull, p. 1069.

182 **five-point proposal:** Prange, *Verdict*, pp. 178ff, 650; Prange, *Dawn*, p. 363. The five-point proposal has been referred to in previous books as Japan's "Proposal B" or "modus vivendi," as delivered by Nomura (e.g., Wohlstetter, p. 233; Prange, *Verdict*, p. 135).

182 **A cloak-and-dagger:** Smedberg Oral History, NWC; Smedberg to Prange, 7/29/77, Series V.2, Box 74; Simpson, pp. 107ff. It was Smedberg who, as reported in Chapter 12, later revealed that—with Stark's knowledge—he recorded many of the CNO's phone conversations with President Roosevelt. Neither Stark nor Smedberg mentioned the secret meeting with Nomura when testifying to future Pearl Harbor boards of inquiry.

182 **"clearly unthinkable":** PHA 2, p. 432.

182 **"assured Japan's domination":** Hull, p. 1069.

182 **"no ultimatum":** PHA 116, p. 2223.

182 **"grave importance":** PHA 14, p. 1106.

183 **"not one chance":** PHA 14, p. 1123.

183 **"impossible to reconcile":** PHA 16, p. 2221.

183 **"Top secret, November 24, 1941":** MB IV, Appendix, p. A-90.

183 **This message alone:** See Chapter 23.

184 **"last effort":** MB IV, Appendix, p. A-16.

CHAPTER 26

185 **"that we were likely":** Stimson diary, 11/25, PHA 11, pp. 5433ff. Down the years, this diary entry has sparked controversy and fueled conspiracy theory. Revisionists have seized on the word "maneuver," citing it as evidence that Roosevelt wished to provoke a Japanese attack. If the President made such a remark, however, it ran counter to what is known of his position. During the 1940 presidential campaign, he had pledged more than once not to take the nation into war. In 1941, Secretary of the Navy Knox repeatedly cautioned military chiefs that he and the President "were determined that the Navy should take no action that would provoke Japan."

Chief of Staff George Marshall, for his part, was to testify after the war that it had been the wish of the cabinet and of the military, "and I am quite certain of the President of the United States, that the Japanese be given no opportunity whatever to claim that we had taken some overt act which forced a state of war upon them."

Concern not to be first to provoke conflict was not merely a political issue. Other considerations aside, the U.S. high command had made clear to Roosevelt that neither the Army nor the Navy was yet ready for war. One Navy pilot serving in Hawaii, future chairman of the Joint

Chiefs Admiral Moorer, would recall having been "admonished over and over again, 'Now don't do anything provocative.'" Days after the November 25th cabinet meeting described in the Stimson diary entry, the same concern was expressed in the war warning messages that Washington sent to Kimmel and Short.

Almost a year earlier, after Germany, Italy, and Japan declared they were forming a military alliance, ONI's Far Eastern section chief Commander Arthur McCollum had acknowledged that the public opposed involvement in the conflict. "It is not believed," he had written in October 1940 in one of his periodic estimates, "that in the present state of political opinion the United States is capable of declaring war against Japan."

Should Britain be defeated however, McCollum speculated, the Axis powers would at once focus on attacking America. Britain could be strengthened, he suggested, by actions the U.S. Navy could take to divert or neutralize Japan. "If by these means Japan could be led to commit an overt act of war," he concluded, "so much the better."

In a 2000 book that received considerable attention, author Robert Stinnett used the McCollum memo to posit a complex conspiracy by Roosevelt and others designed to goad Japan into war. To Stinnett, it was suspect that, asked under oath after the war whether he knew of anyone in the Navy "who attempted to trick or maneuver the Japs into attacking the United States," McCollum replied, "No, sir."

That response was less than frank, given that McCollum had proposed doing just that. To suggest that his memo triggered a conspiracy, however, is a stretch that cannot be justified, that is unsupported by the weight of the evidence. Only one of the three senior colleagues in ONI who reviewed the Commander's memo, Rear Admiral Dudley Knox, indicated that he concurred with McCollum's ideas. He opined, nevertheless, that the United States should not "precipitate anything in the Orient" that would hamper its ability to continue to send substantial supplies to Britain. [**controversy:** E.g. Morgenstern, pp. 292ff. **Knox:** Prange, *Verdict*, p. 95. **Marshall:** PHA 3, p. 1173. **"admonished":** Stillwell, p. 204. **war warnings:** PHA 14, p. 1407, and see Chapters 27 and 28. **McCollum estimate:** Estimate and Summary, 10/7/40, Bode to DNI, 10/9/40, and James to DNI, 10/11/40, Record of the Office of the CNO, ONI, Foreign Intelligence Branch, Box 2, Entry UD2, RG 38; draft of Estimate, 10/7/40, and Comment by Dudley Knox, TKK; Stinnett, pp. 7ff, 271ff, 324n29. **asked under oath:** PHA 8, p. 3447ff.]

185 **The following day:** Stimson diary, PHA 11, p. 5434. In 1941, Taiwan was still known as Formosa.

185 **leadership had been considering:** U.S. Government Printing Office, *Foreign Relations . . .*, Vol. IV, pp. 600ff; Wohlstetter, pp. 233ff; Gannon, pp. 121ff.

185 **objections by Britain and China:** PHA 14, pp. 1139ff; Churchill to FDR, 11/25/41, PREM 3/469, PRO.

185 **consulted with the president:** PHA 14, pp. 1176ff; Wohlstetter, p. 242.

186 **The document Hull:** U.S. Department of State, *Papers Relating . . . ,* Vol. II, pp. 768ff. In testimony to the congressional Joint Committee in 1945, Hull was angered by the suggestion that the U.S. riposte "started the war." The notion that the United States ought to have made concessions to keep the peace, he said, ignored the reality of the situation at the time. It had been obvious, he went on, that Japan was on a "march of invasion in the Pacific area to get supreme control . . . They were off on this final attack and no one was going to stop them . . . We would have been cowards to have lain down."

This principled justification of the November 26th message to Tokyo has been rejected by those who proposed that Roosevelt deliberately took the nation into the war. The uncompromising message, according to the theory, was calculated to force Japan into a position in which its only recourse was to fight. There is no good evidence that this was so.

One anecdote suggests that, contrary to his own sworn testimony, Hull sent the stern message under pressure from "madmen" at the White House. It is unreliable hearsay, passed on after the fact.

There is also the theory proposed by some authors that—sometime late on November 25th or early on the 26th—British Prime Minister Churchill shared with Roosevelt intelligence that led the President to adopt a much harder position. In support of this notion, author John Costello expressed suspicion that relevant evidence had been suppressed. In a 1994 book, he wrote, "A whole section of the Prime Minister's secret office file relating to Japan is marked 'closed for 75 years'." In that book, the file in question was identified as PREM 3/252/5. Earlier, in a 1985 book of which he was a coauthor, Costello identified the file in question as PREM 3/252/6b. The former was opened to the public in 1997, the latter in 1993.

The subject of PREM 3/252/5 is "Contact Between Lord Sempill and the Japanese Embassy." Two pages remain redacted; but the file does not, as Costello suggested, cover the month of November. The subject of File PREM 3/252/6b turns out on inspection to be, in fact, "Japanese Oil Stocks in the Philippines." The only document for November 26th has nothing to do with the stern U.S. message for that date. It is, rather, a report on Japanese commercial shipping movements from July to November 1941. [**Hull:** PHA 2, pp. 614ff. **hearsay:** Bishop to Grew, 10/14/55, HEK R32. **Costello:** Costello, pp. 313, 325; Layton with Pineau and Costello, pp. 204, 416. **files:** PREM 3/252/5, PREM 3/252/6b, PRO, Dunton to Swan, 1/15/16.]

186 **"The United States":** Gannon, p. 126.

186 **"First thing":** Stimson diary, 11/27/41, PHA 11, pp. 5434ff.

186 **Nothing in the official record/"playing for time"/no detail/nor could Marshall:** PHA 32, pp. 90ff; PHA 6, pp. 2322ff; PHA 3, pp. 1168ff, 1412ff; PHA 2, pp. 1091ff; Hanify draft manuscript, p. 78, Box 24, HANIFY. General Gerow of War Plans, who had been standing in for

Marshall during his absence at maneuvers, said only that he was "informed" (at some unspecified point) of Hull's November 26th document (PHA 29, p. 2210; and see PHA 3, p. 1017).

186 **Turner/"unwise"/"considerably upset":** Interview with R. Kelly Turner by Stark, 10/16 and 10/17/45, Box A9, STARK; and see U.S. Government Printing Office, Foreign Relations . . . , Vol. IV, pp. 630ff.

187 **Smedberg put it/"dumbfounded"/"In those days":** Smedberg to Prange, 7/29/77; Smedberg Oral History, NWC.

187 **Hornbeck/"the Japanese Government":** PHA 5, pp. 2089ff; and see Hornbeck to Hull, 11/27/41, Hull to Hornbeck, 11/28/41, DM 16, 160, Reel 21, Container 49, LOC.

187 **the day after:** PHA 14, pp. 1083ff. Marshall, who had been out of town, signed the document only on November 28th. It was delivered to the President, however, on the 27th.

CHAPTER 27

188 **Kimmel not told:** PHA 6, p. 2761; PHA 33, pp. 700ff.

188 **received a copy/*not* to confront:** PHA 16, pp. 2220ff, 2223.

188 **"*will* not yield":** MB IV, Appendix, p. A-105.

188 **"order and method":** MB IV, Appendix, p. A-197.

188 **twice shared/"a surprise aggressive movement":** PHA 16, pp. 2219ff; PHA 14, p. 1083.

189 **"In particular":** Stimson diary, 11/27/41, PHA, p. 5423.

189 **wrestled/consulted President:** Stark to Hart, 6/2/44, Box 4, HART; McCrea to Hart, 8/4/44, Box 3, MCCREA; Clausen and Lee, pp. 287ff; interview with R. Kelly Turner by Stark, 10/16 and 10/17/45, Box A9, STARK; Baecher to Hidalgo, 3/14/45, TKK.

189 **"strictly accurate":** PHA 11, p. 5423.

189 **Two were transmitted:** The initial message to Short went out at 6:11 p.m. DC time, and the message to Kimmel was sent at about 6:37 p.m. There has been some confusion in the literature as to these times, probably because Navy records used Zulu (or Greenwich) time (PHA 14, pp. 1328ff, 1406; PHA 18, p. 3171; PHA 33, p. 1150).

189 **Short responded/Alert No. 1:** PHA 7, pp. 2941ff; Baecher to Hidalgo, 3/14/45, TKK.

190 **Three other messages:** PHA 14, pp. 1329ff.

190 **radar/"most critical"/except Sundays:** PHA 7, p. 2941; PHA 22, pp. 214ff.

190 **"most effective":** PHA 11, p. 5425.

190 **memorandum/routed:** Baecher to Hidalgo, 3/14/45, TKK.

190 **"soon cut loose":** Bartsch, *December 8*, pp. 185ff, 467.

190 **"I fully anticipated":** PHA 39, p. 1081; and see Anderson, pp. 91ff.

190 **Marshall assumed/"I had an opportunity":** PHA 7, pp. 1420ff.

191 **spent morning:** PHA 26, pp. 423ff; McCrea to Hart, 4/8/44, Box 3, MCCREA; Stillwell, pp. 103ff; interview with Richmond Kelly Turner by Stark, 10/16 and 10/17/45, Box A9, STARK.

191 **President agreed:** Stark cited by Brownlow, p. 109.

191 **"EXECUTE":** PHA 14, p. 1406.

CHAPTER 28

192 **sixth message:** PHA 14, pp. 1402ff; PHA 6, pp. 2512ff.

192 **The message of the 24th:** For the message of November 24th, see Chapter 25.

192 **"plethora":** PHA 6, p. 2514.

192 **"yakity-yak":** Brownlow, p. 110.

192 **"One fellow's estimate":** PHA 16, p. 2177.

192 **crying wolf:** Stark to Hart, 6/2/44, Box 4, HART; interview with Harold Stark by Forrest Pogue, Box 31, STARK.

193 **never seen the term:** PHA 32, p. 236.

193 **"all war scouting":** PHA 26, p. 280.

193 **"to spread out"/"to cover":** PHA 4, p. 1950.

193 **at the time:** Then–Lieutenant Commander Charles Wellborn, CNO Stark's flag secretary, would say Turner had thought an attack on Hawaii "quite probable," and that some other officers thought it "entirely possible" but "less probable" than did Turner. The CNO and his deputy Ingersoll, he said, took the latter view (PHA 4, pp. 2007, 1963, 1984ff, 1990ff; PHA 26, pp. 423ff).

193 **"action against surprises"/"a position as best":** PHA 5, pp. 2149ff, 2152; and see PHA 32, p. 52.

193 **Ingersoll would say:** PHA 26, p. 463.

193 **Stark not at all sure:** Stark to Turner, 10/11/45, Stark to Ingersoll, 10/11/45, Box A4, Richmond to Turner and Ingersoll, 10/4/45, Box 29, Ingersoll to Stark, 10/9/45, STARK.

193 **"I didn't know":** Stark to Hart, 6/2/44, Box 4, HART.

194 **formal War Plan:** PHA 37, pp. 837ff, 841, 862.

194 **"get out and go into":** PHA 32, p. 415; Hanify draft memoir, pp. 176ff, Box 24, HANIFY.

194 **As we have:** See Chapters 9, 10, and 20.

194 **The man responsible:** This in reply to an October 17th letter to Stark from Bloch pleading for antisubmarine patrol planes. British failures in battle at sea, Bloch had noted, had been caused by supply that had been "too little and too late" (PHA 33, pp. 1280ff).

195 **teething problems:** Gannon, p. 303.

195 **remained dire:** Ibid.; PHA 33, p. 708; PHA 6, pp. 2754ff; *Proceedings*, 12/91.

195 **"As nearly":** PHA 32, p. 442.

195 **"the fullest possible":** PHA 6, p. 2534.

195 **would itself mean:** Kimmel, pp. 59ff.

195 **"I decided":** PHA 6, p. 2535.

195 **"The evidence":** PHA 39, p. 368, and see p. 338.

196 **detailed estimates:** PHA 33, pp. 1182ff; PHA 14, pp. 1019ff. The detailed estimates were the Martin-Bellinger Report of March 31st, 1941, and the Farthing Report of August 20th, 1941. The historian and author Professor Gordon Prange wrote in *Pearl Harbor: The Verdict of History*, one of the best-known books on the disaster, "Carefully reasoned estimates, such as the Martin-Bellinger and Farthing reports, existed postulating that the most dangerous sectors were the north and northwest." Excellent though Prange's work was in many respects, this assertion is wrong. As a later historian, Professor Michael Gannon, pointed out in his 2001 book *Pearl Harbor Betrayed*, those reports in fact identified *no* such most dangerous sector. **[Martin-Bellinger:** PHA 33, pp. 1182ff; **Farthing:** PHA 14, pp. 1019ff; **Prange:** Prange, *Verdict*, p. 441; **Gannon:** Gannon, pp. 280, 323; *Proceedings*, 12/94.]

196 **twenty thousand/"absolutely essential":** PHA 32, pp. 219ff.

196 **Kimmel and Short conferring:** PHA 7, pp. 2950, 2984, 3228; PHA 6, p. 2882; PHA 32, p. 414.

196 **That day:** PHA 17, pp. 2479ff; PHA 16, pp. 2253ff; PHA 33, pp. 701ff; Halsey and Bryan, pp. 72ff. Though Washington's request was to transfer Army fighters—half their pursuit planes—commanders decided at the joint meeting that more suitable Marine aircraft should be transferred instead.

196 **Sending the carriers/dawn patrol/other precautions:** PHA 6, pp. 2531ff; PHA 33, pp. 703ff; Gannon, pp. 165ff, citing Admiral Bloch's testimony.

197 **"did not consider":** PHA 6, p. 2517.

197 **"capability":** Prange, *Dawn*, p. 401.

197 **McMorris:** Ibid.; PHA 22, p. 526; PHA 27, p. 412; PHA 28, p. 1497; PHA 7, p. 2942.

197 **Rochefort:** Carlson, pp. 146ff; PHA 22, pp. 33ff.

198 **"There was great unease":** PHA 26, p. 221.

198 **"still located":** PHA 35, p. 62ff.

CHAPTER 29

199 **strike force/two thousand miles:** Layton with Pineau and Costello, pp. 220ff.

199 **"arranging a marriage"/"Miss Fumeko"/transcript of the call:** PHA 12, pp. 178, 188ff; MB IV, Appendix, p. A-113ff.

199 **"I do not wish":** MB IV, Appendix, p. A-118.

199 **Not only communications:** A letter from William Donovan to the President of November 13th and a MAGIC intercept of the 29th show that Germany had reiterated its resolve to fight alongside Japan should war break out between Japan and the United States (Donovan to Roosevelt, 11/13/41, PSF, Box 128, FDRL; MB IV, Appendix, p. A-383).

200 **"come quicker":** MB IV, Appendix, pp. A-384ff.

200 **"stretch out":** PHA 12, pp. 206ff.

200 **"the absolute deadline":** MB IV, Appendix, A-120.

200 **Previous exchanges, of course:** In order, the exchanges described above occurred on November 27th (phone call), November 28th, November 30th, (coded messages), November 30th (phone call), and December 1st (coded message) (MB IV, Appendix, pp. A-113ff, A-118, A-120ff, A-384ff; PHA 12, p. 206).

200 **none shared with Kimmel/press:** Kimmel, p. 95; PHA 33, p. 703.

200 **Headlines:** PHA 30, p. 2974ff.

200 **"The real situation":** PHA 33, p. 703.

201 **Stark had relayed:** PHA 14, p. 1407.

201 **Kimmel had already received/"gone on alert"/conferred with Short/"I knew":** PHA 6, pp. 2580ff.

201 **"undertake":** PHA 14, p. 1407; Wohlstetter, pp. 261ff.

201 **He advised Kimmel:** PHA 6, pp. 2537ff, 2662; PHA 33, p. 1286; and see PHA 39, p. 305. "Shoot on sight" was order WPL-52, under which U.S. forces had authority to fire on Axis ships encountered in the western Atlantic.

201 **stream of orders:** Hanyok and Mowry (cited as Hanyok), pp. 31ff; Carlson, pp. 158ff; Layton with Pineau and Costello, p. 219.

202 **"In case of a":** In fact, the Japanese created *two* weather-related codes. One, as explained, was to be transmitted by voice. The second, an abbreviated version of the winds code, was to be used in the General News Broadcast, a Japanese news bulletin transmitted in Morse code (MB IV, Appendix, p. A-81; PHA 18, Exhibit 142; Hanyok, pp. 25ff).

202 **HIGASHI/not translated for a week:** MB IV, Appendix, p. A-81; PHA 12, p. 154; Hanyok, pp. 15ff, 122.

203 **Point 3:** Hanyok, pp. 25, 116, 118; Wohlstetter, pp. 215ff; Newby to Ladd, 3/18/46, FBI 100–97–1-Sec16 and "The 'Winds' Message, 2/13/46, FBI analysis, FBI 100–97–1–459, TKK.

203 **British had also intercepted:** Intercept 2353, decoded 11/25/41, HW 12/270, PRO; PHA 29, pp. 2368ff; Michael Smith, p. 99.

203 **Australians:** Pfennigwerth, p. 175. The cryptanalyst was Eric Nave.

203 **Dutch:** PHA 29, p. 2369; PHA 18, p. 3303; Hanyok, pp. 26ff.

203 **"everyone from the President":** PHA 8, p. 3640.

203 **anxiously awaited:** PHA 3, p. 1374; PHA 29, p. 2430; Statement of
     Lt. D.W. Wigle, 12/11/45, 5830/69, Box 166, RG 38, NARA.

203 **"It was considered":** PHA 35, p. 102.

203 **stations tasked/four linguists:** Hanyok, pp. 33ff.

203 **cards printed:** PHA 10, p. 4726; Layton with Pineau and Costello,
     pp. 264ff.

204 **"simply tremendous":** PHA 36, p. 81.

204 **"waked up":** PHA 9, p. 4520.

204 **Army Intelligence's estimate/Kroner:** PHA 34, pp. 47ff, 176ff. Dean
     Rusk, then serving in Army Intelligence, would later recall an incident
     on or shortly after December 7th. According to Rusk, he was shown a
     memo prepared five days earlier by the Japanese section of G-2, listing
     potential Japanese targets. Pearl Harbor was not on the list. Rusk's
     chief, Colonel James Compton, told him copies of the memo were be-
     ing "gathered up and destroyed" (Rusk, p. 102).

204 **McCollum labored:** PHA 36, p. 19; PHA 15, pp. 1839ff.

204 **ONI report:** "Japanese Intelligence and Propaganda in the U.S. During
     1941," 12/4/41, Office of Naval Intelligence, supplied to the authors by
     Lee Allen, www.internmentarchives.com.

CHAPTER 30

205 **call signs changed/"appear"/"preparing":** Communications Intelli-
     gence Summary, 21/1/41, cited in PHA 35, p. 78.

205 **"obvious concern"/worried:** Oral History of Edwin Layton, U.S., Naval
     Institute, 1969, NHHC; PHA 10, pp. 4837ff; Layton with Pineau and
     Costello, pp. 237ff.

205 **As to the carriers:** According to a passage in Layton's posthumously
     published 1985 memoir, Kimmel shared Layton's concern that the
     carriers "would be the most dangerous element of a striking force
     that might already be assembling in the Marshalls for an offensive
     move *against Pearl Harbor*" [authors' italics]. In his sworn testimony,
     however, Layton made no reference to having such concern. On the
     contrary, he said he did not suggest such a possibility "at any time."
     The authors have found nothing along those lines in transcripts of
     his interviews for the memoir archived at the Naval War College or
     in his oral history for the U.S. Naval Institute. Noting that the mem-
     oir was edited by others after Layton's death, the authors have relied
     on his sworn testimony of 1946. [**memoir:** Layton with Pineau and
     Costello. pp. 237ff. **testimony:** PHA 10, p. 4840. **transcripts:** Box 30,
     Folder 1, Layton Papers, Naval War College. **oral history:** Stillwell,
     p. 281.]

205 **headline:** *San Francsco Chronicle,* 12/1/41.

205 **further stern note/not in a mood to listen/"He didn't even call":** Stimson diary, 11/30/41, STIM.

205 **Hull/"worn"/"trying to run":** Adolph Berle diary, 12/1/41, FDRL, Prange, *Verdict*, pp. 145ff.

206 **Churchill's message:** Former Naval Person to President, 11/30/41, PREM 3/469, PRO.

206 **Halifax:** Woodward, pp. 185ff; Prange, *Verdict*, pp. 78ff, 846ff; Kaiser, pp. 324ff.

206 **"all be in it":** 124th Conclusions, Minute 4, Confidential Annex, 12/4/41, Minutes of the War Cabinet, CAB 65/24, PRO.

206 **On December 1st:** PHA 14, p. 1407. The President's order was dated December 1st, contrary to references in Pearl Harbor literature that date it to the 2nd. In years to come, when it became public knowledge, Roosevelt's detractors would claim that his purpose in ordering the patrol was to provoke Japan into firing the first shot—thus starting the war. Admiral Hart, who received the order, would be quoted as having said years later—over lunch—to the former captain of one of the patrol vessels involved that he thought they had been "bait." He would later say in a letter, however, that he had "only opinion, no real fact."

As mentioned in these pages, President Roosevelt was known for sudden, impulsive initiatives, and the explanation of the order may lie in other episodes of the relatively recent past, when his close friend the millionaire Vincent Astor was running "The Room," an informal intelligence-gathering group. In 1938, on the President's instructions according to Astor, he had taken his luxury yacht on a Pacific cruise to gather intelligence on Japanese naval activity.

The experience of cavalier adventures in less dangerous times may perhaps have prompted the December 1st, 1941, order to Hart to send small vessels reconnoitering off the coast of southeastern Asia. Hart, at any rate, obeyed orders only reluctantly. The operation, he said long afterward, "was risking some personnel to no end whatsoever." [**Roosevelt's order**: Landis and Dunn, p. 45; and, with date, PHA 14, p. 1407; Stillwell, p. 123. **wrong date:** E.g., Farago, *Broken Seal*, p. 317; Layton with Pineau and Costello, p. 549, n. 35. **Hart:** Hart to Tolley, undated, 1967, and 2/14/67, TKK. **"bait":** Landis and Dunn, p. 49. **Astor:** Andrew, pp. 83ff. **"risking":** Reminiscences of Admiral Thomas Hart, oral history, 1962, Columbia University.]

207 **"categorical assurance":** PHA 8, pp. 3384ff; PHA 36, p. 19; McCollum to Kimmel, 5/21/44, HEK R26; Memorandum of Interview with Arthur McCollum, 5/18/45, HEK R12.

CHAPTER 31

208 **"Almost a complete":** PHA 35, p. 80.

208 **Layton's report:** PHA 17, pp. 2666ff.

208 **"neither one":** PHA 10, p. 2839.

208 **Kimmel looked at:** PHA 36, pp. 127ff, 152ff; PHA 6, pp. 2623ff, 2597ff. Layton would tell and retell his account of this exchange. The authors have used his testimony to the 1945 Hewitt Inquiry.

209 **In Washington that Tuesday:** Johan Meijer Ranneft, later a rear admiral in the Netherlands Navy, was a respected figure in Washington naval and political circles. In 1982, in his book *Infamy*, John Toland made much of the Ranneft episode, implying that it reflected possible U.S. foreknowledge of the whereabouts of the aircraft carriers that were to strike Pearl Harbor. Fresh translation and research in Dutch archives have turned up no evidence that this was the case. [Toland: *Infamy*, pp. 282ff, 294, 298, 301, 317.]

209 **regular:** E.g., Rear Admiral Walter Anderson, ONI, datebook entries, Anderson Papers.

209 **would recall:** Ranneft note attached to letter, Netherlands Embassy Washington to Minister of Foreign Affairs, 9/18/44, No. 6390/1752, Toegang 2.05.80, Archiefbloknummer Z27018, Dutch National Archives; and Ranneft to Furstner, 10/9/45, Losse Stukken 057, Inventory nr 2424 and diary of Ranneft, Collection Marine Biographies WWII, Section EC-1, Institute of Military History, The Hague. Ranneft's granddaughter Danielle believed the original handwritten version of his diary was probably destroyed in a fire before his death (interview with Danielle Ranneft, 2016).

209 **President asked to see:** Farago, *Broken Seal*, pp. 316ff.

209 **"very secretly":** MB IV, Appendix, p. A-385.

209 **severe note:** U.S. Department of State, *Peace and War*, pp. 821ff.

209 **waffled:** *U.S. News and World Report*, 12/3/54.

209 **volume of MAGIC:** Laurance Safford, "The Kita Message, No Longer a Mystery," unpublished manuscript, TKK; Memorandum of February 23, 1944 [by Safford], Box 24, File 1, HANNIFY; *Foreign Affairs*, Winter 1991.

209 **hidden words/"brink of catastrophe":** PHA 36, p. 307ff; Wohlstetter, pp. 205, 224ff; Hanyok, pp. 38ff, 43; and see British translation, BJ 098602, HW 12/271, PRO.

210 **The FBI, for its part:** PHA 35, pp. 43, 84; Farago, *Broken Seal*, pp. 314ff; PHA 31, p. 3186. The FBI had only recently received permission from the Justice Department to do this, having pressed for it for months.

210 **pure mischance/led to words/removed:** PHA 35, pp. 44, 48ff; PHA 36, pp. 222ff, 336ff; Clausen and Lee, pp. 119ff.

211 **cheery valediction:** PHA 35, p. 206.

211 **RCA:** PHA 31, p. 3189.

211 **Mayfield turned to Hypo/Rochefort hesitated:** Carlson, pp. 172ff; PHA 23, pp. 685ff; PHA 10, pp. 4698ff; Layton with Pineau and Costello, pp. 277ff; Safford, "The Kita Message, No Longer a Mystery," supra.

211 **"In view of":** PHA 12, p. 266.

212 **passenger liner:** Prange, *Dawn,* p. 444; Farago, *Broken Seal,* p. 298.

212 **Also on the 2nd:** SRH-406, Pre-Pearl Harbor Japanese Naval Despatches, pp. 32ff, Box 183, RG 38, NARA. The message was sent in JN-25b, a naval code that had not been readably broken as of 1941. It was decrypted in 1945, but was not passed on to Congress' Joint Committee investigation. Because the Niitaka Yama order had been obtained separately from captured Japanese documents and diaries, however, it did appear in the inquiry's volumes, published in 1946 (PHA 1, p. 185; Gannon, pp. 189, 309; Prange, *Dawn,* pp. 445, 773; Parker, 65).

CHAPTER 32

213 **"wet hens":** Henry Morgenthau diary, 12/3/41, Vol. IV, FDRL.

213 **"liable to run loose"/assured:** PHA 26, p. 451.

213 **"#867 Strictly Secret":** MB IV, Appendix, p. A-122; MB IV, pp. 92, 135ff.

214 **"Most any time":** PHA 11, p. 5284.

214 **To Undersecretary Welles:** PHA 2, p. 513. Welles—and Secretary of State Hull—have been quoted, in error, as having said the destruction order meant that "the chances had diminished from one in a thousand to one in a million that war could be avoided." Welles, not Hull, did make such a comment, but not with reference to the code destruction. He referred, rather, to Japanese naval movements of December 6th. [**Welles misquoted:** Kahn, p. 43. **ascribed to Hull:** *Proceedings,* 12/99.]

214 **"Ordinarily":** PHA 3, pp. 1426ff.

214 **"The inference":** PHA 2, p. 841.

214 **"one of the most":** PHA 5, p. 2131.

214 **"a definite and sure":** PHA 4, p. 2002.

214 **brief message:** PHA 14, p. 1407.

215 **second message/"destroy PURPLE":** Ibid., p. 1408.

215 **"Kimmel sent for me":** PHA 10, p. 4842.

215 **Neither Kimmel nor:** Kimmel and Bloch were not alone in thinking that Tokyo's code destruction message did not necessarily mean war was imminent. Britain's counterintelligence chief Guy Liddell, who had access to the same MAGIC intercepts, did not think it was clear what the development signified. "Presumably in the future," Liddell wrote in his diary on December 4, "they will be communicating through naval or military ciphers. It is difficult to see whether this is just nervousness, or whether it is part of a pre-arranged plan to declare war on a given date" (Liddell diary, KV/4/189, PRO, BJ 098540, 12/4/41, including distribution list).

215 **"something that was really":** PHA 26, p. 27; PHA 27, pp. 789ff.

215 **"vital interest":** PHA 6, p. 2764.

215 **"routine":** PHA 33, pp. 704ff.

216 **"had they enlarged"/"if I had drawn":** PHA 22, p. 379.

216 **"If the War Department":** PHA 6, p. 2764.

216 **solitary tap/cook/Bicknell failed to pass:** PHA 35, pp. 43, 30.

216 **two code systems:** Carlson, p. 174.

216 **Perhaps anticipating the day:** PHA 12, p. 267; PHA 35, pp. 322, 330ff, 492ff; *Proceedings*, 12/78; Prange, *Dawn*, p. 450. On Kühn, see Chapters 13 and 22.

217 **Yoshikawa reports:** MB IV, Appendix, p. A-153.

217 **Analysts in Washington:** Yoshikawa's two ship movement reports of December 3rd were not decrypted and distributed by the Navy until December 10th. Conspiracy theorists were later to seize on the testimony of Navy translator Dorothy Edgers, who said she produced a "rough draft translation" of Kühn's revised signal plans as early as December 6th—before the Japanese strike. Had the message with Kühn's plans really been available then, its suspicious nature would have been obvious. The evidence, however, suggests that the version of the intercept Mrs. Edgers started to tackle on the 6th was badly garbled and incomplete. Analysts were under pressure dealing with vital PURPLE traffic that day, and work on the Kühn intercept was held over until a more complete version of it had been obtained. The message was eventually decoded by both Station Hypo and Washington on December 10th and December 11th respectively (PHA 36, pp. 303ff, 345ff; PHA 38, Item 51; and especially Laurance Safford, "The Kita Message: No Longer a Mystery," unpublished manuscript, TKK. Kühn's message of December 3rd is often referred to as the "Kita Message," after Consul Kita, its official sender. But see Toland, *Infamy*, pp. 3ff).

CHAPTER 33

218 **blueprint/explosive:** *Chicago Daily Tribune*, 12/4/41; *American Heritage*, 12/87; Stimson diary, 12/4/41, STIM.

218 **"I shall say it":** Address in Boston, 10/30/40.

219 **FCC in Oregon/"NORTH WIND"/Brotherhood/Noyes:** PHA 33, p. 839ff; PHA 18, p. 3305ff; PHA 34, p. 173ff; PHA 10, p. 4732; Hanyok, pp. 36ff.

219 **On going off duty:** Captain Laurance Safford, the Navy's respected codebreaking chief, was to testify that an *actual* "Winds Execute" message—signifying a break with the United States—was indeed intercepted on December 4th. Having first claimed, in a private conversation with Admiral Kimmel in 1944, that an "Execute" had been received, he was to stick to that certainty for the rest of his life. Safford's version of the language in which the "Execute" came, however, was inconsistent with the format prescribed in Tokyo's earlier setup message.

A witness whom Safford thought would confirm his recollection, ONI's Lieutenant Commander Kramer, first testified that he had recalled an "Execute" message regarding a break in relations between Japan and the United States, but later said he thought it had referred to a break not with the United States but with Britain.

There was also the account of Ralph Briggs, who in 1941 had served as an intercept operator at the Navy's station in Cheltenham, Maryland. In 1977, in an oral history interview, Briggs claimed to have himself intercepted a "Winds Execute" message on December 4th—the same date as in Safford's account. What he said seemed at first to corroborate Safford, but it falls apart on scrutiny. Like Safford's version of the supposed "Execute" message, what Briggs described did not match the prescribed format.

There was also a dating problem with Briggs' story. Years after the war, Briggs claimed, he had searched in official files for a record of the intercept—which according to him he had made on December 4th—but it was missing. He had noted that fact, he said, in the file. The file in the National Archives containing records from Cheltenham does include such a note by Briggs. It relates, however, not to December 4th but to December 2nd.

Finally, there is the matter of Daryl Wigle, another former Cheltenham operator. Wigle, Briggs said, could corroborate his claim. Interviewed about the "Winds" message at the end of the war, however, Wigle had said he did not "handle or observe" a "Winds Execute" at any time. [**Safford:** Hanyok, pp. 66ff; PHA 8, pp. 3578ff; Edward Morgan, Appendix C, pp. 283ff. **Kramer:** PHA 36, pp. 81ff; PHA 33, pp. 853ff; PHA 9, pp. 3950ff; Gannon, p. 201; Hanyok, pp. 77ff. **Briggs:** SRH-051, Oral History Interview of Ralph Briggs, National Security Agency, 1977; *Cryptolog*, Fall 1986; Hanyok, pp. 85ff. **files:** Entry 1030, Folder 5830/61, Box 165, RG 38, NARA. **Wigle:** Statement of Lt. D. W. Wigle, 12/11/45, Folder 5830/69, Box 166, RG 38, NARA.]

219 **McCollum/"greatly concerned"/drafted a message:** McCollum to Kimmel, 5/18/44, HEK R26; Memorandum of Interview with Capt. McCollum, 5/18/45, HEK R12; McCollum Oral History, U.S. Naval Institute, 1971, NHHC; Edward Morgan, p. 208; PHA 8, pp. 3387ff, but see PHA 4, pp. 1969ff; Wohlstetter, pp. 330ff.

220 **imperial palace/Out in the north Pacific/"Everyone prays":** Prange, *Dawn*, pp. 456, 453ff.

CHAPTER 34

221 **9:30/"The message":** PHA 29, pp. 2427ff; PHA 10, pp. 4628ff.

221 **Turner:** PHA 4, pp. 1968ff.

221 **Noyes:** PHA 10, p. 4732ff.

221 **Miles:** PHA 35, p. 102.

221 **Bratton:** PHA 9, pp. 4520ff.

221 **Gerow:** PHA 34, p. 37.

222 **Smith:** PHA 35, p. 91.

222 **"the most important":** PHA 10, p. 4630.

222 **None of the very senior:** Miles, Gerow, and Smith would later say that
they did not remember this episode. Admiral Noyes said he did not recall the phone conversation with Sadtler but "wouldn't say it didn't occur." An official Army history, however, accepted that it had occurred
essentially as recounted by Sadtler and corroborated by Bratton. **[Miles:**
PHA 35, p. 102. **Gerow:** PHA 34, p. 37. **Smith:** PHA 35, p. 91. **Noyes:**
PHA 10, p. 4733. **history:** "U.S. Army in World War II: The Signal
Corps," Vol. 1, p. 785, TOL, Box 116.]

222 **"plenty of notification":** PHA 29, p. 2430.

222 **"Everybody was making":** PHA 9, pp. 4520ff, 4543.

222 **Rochefort/dispatch:** Ibid., p. 4542ff; PHA 18, p. 3305; PHA 29, pp.
2337ff; PHA 34, pp. 5, 21; PHA 35, pp. 23ff, 29.

222 **"We were continuing":** PHA 8, p. 3411. American, British, and Dutch
forces did indeed continue listening for a "Winds Execute" for some
time after the attack on Pearl Harbor. The British in Southeast Asia
appear to have heard one almost two hours after the strike. Britain's
Director of Naval Intelligence received a message reading: "Information received at 2010Z 7th by Hong Kong that severance of Japanese
relations? [garbled in decoded text] admitted imminent." "2010Z"
[Zulu] equates to 9:40 a.m. Hawaii time. A history of Britain's Far East
Combined Bureau refers to a "priority message from Hong Kong" reporting "that the broadcast mentioning "East" and "West" winds had
been heard." "EAST WIND RAIN," if that is what was indeed heard,
was the coded language for an imminent break in relations with the
United States. If the British history is accurate, it represents the only
known record of the receipt anywhere of a "Winds Execute" referring
to a break with the United States.

About five and a half hours after the attack, FCC monitors in Oregon and Hawaii also picked up an Execute—though it included only
the code for an imminent break in relations with Britain. The G-2 officer to whom this was reported responded that the information was
"too late." **[British:** "History of HMS Anderson," PRO HW 4/24; "The
Evidence for: Paper Prepared for Winston Churchill's History of Information Available to the British Cabinet Before Pearl Harbor," PRO
HW 50/52; C.O.I.S. Singapore to Admiralty, 2312Z/7, Exhibit 1, item Q,
Entry 167cc, Box 9, RG 80, NARA; and see Hanyok, pp. 82ff. **five and
a half hours later:** PHA 18, pp. 3302ff; Hanyok, pp. 47ff.]

222 **yet a further report/"that we have":** PHA 34, pp. 17, 173ff.

223 **Had harried analysts:** The "Winds" matter aside, the Navy—which by
virtue of the odd days–even days agreement with the Army had responsibility for MAGIC intercepts on December 5th—had a slew of other
messages to process that day. Most of these were in the high-level PUR-
PLE code requiring immediate attention. Analysts were still working
their way through several long messages received earlier in the week,

and a couple from the week before. Almost two dozen messages, most of them in PURPLE, were then intercepted that day alone. Previously, many such messages had been decrypted on the same day, but for whatever reason—the pace of work; the fact that one man was on leave—the Navy codebreakers did not manage to get to a single one of the messages intercepted that day for at least twenty-four hours. One PURPLE sat unbroken until 1945. [**slew:** MB IV, Appendix, pp. A-127ff, A-171ff, A-221ff, A-271ff, A-327ff, A-387ff, A-403ff, A-421ff, A-449ff, A-541; **still working:** PHA 12, pp. 185ff, 209ff, 227ff. **on leave:** Laurance Safford, "The Kita Message: No Longer a Mystery" draft manuscript, TKK.]

223 **old messages/"investigate comprehensively":** PHA 12, p. 263; MB IV, Appendix, p. A-147ff.

223 **In those last days:** According to a former Japanese intelligence officer speaking after the war, information on U.S. warships was also passed to Tokyo by phone, in the guise of business conversations (Prange, *Dawn*, p. 479).

223 **Yoshikawa reported:** PHA 12, pp. 268ff, 270; PHA 35, p. 389.

223 **At the Foreign Ministry:** Law professor Takeo Igushi, the counselor's son, was to study his nation's diplomacy for years. His revelatory analysis of Japan's chicanery just before Pearl Harbor was published at and after the millennium (*NYT*, 12/9/99; *Japan Times*, 12/7/99; *Japan News*, 12/9/14; and see Mauch, pp. 212ff.)

224 **"We have completed":** PHA 12, p. 236.

224 **refueling/submarines prowling:** Prange, *Dawn*, p. 463.

225 **"mass attack":** Gannon, p. 165; and see PHA 26, p. 51.

CHAPTER 35

226 **"The President":** Press Conference, 12/6/41, Box 41, Stephen Early Papers, FDRL.

226 **During the morning meeting:** Knox's former aide, Vice Admiral Frank Beatty, who offered this account in 1954, thought the speaker was Rear Admiral Turner. As Turner was to claim he had believed for months that conflict between the United States and Japan was imminent, it seems unlikely that it was he who voiced the opinion. Turner's testimony suggests the speaker may have been ONI chief Theodore Wilkinson. [**Beatty:** *News and World Report*, 5/23/54. **Turner:** PHA 4, pp. 1984ff; and see Wilkinson, PHA 4, p. 1876.]

226 **"Triple Priority":** PHA Report, p. 424.

226 **few appointments:** Appointments Diary, 12/6/41, FDRL.

226 **Smith/"We might":** Hoehling, p. 115.

226 **local headlines:** PHA 10, pp. 5123ff.

227 **Harsch/"It may well":** Harsch to Beach, 4/18/96, TKK; Stillwell, pp. 263ff, 269.

227 **mounted an alert:** Interview with Admiral James Shoemaker, Series V.2, Box 73, GP.

227 **destroy secret material/remote island outposts:** PHA 14, p. 1408; Prange, *Dawn*, p. 465.

227 **Japanese were moving:** PHA 15, pp. 1680ff.

227 **Kimmel and Layton discussed:** Layton with Pineau and Costello, p. 274; Communications Intelligence Summary, 12/6/41, HEK R3.

228 **Layton suggested to Pye:** Layton Oral History, U.S. Naval Institute, 1970, NWC; interview with Edwin Layton, Box 30, Folder 1, LAYTON; interview with Edwin Layton, Series V.2, Box 58, GP; PHA 6, p. 2537; PHA 10, p. 4859.

228 **"beside himself":** Clark to Bundy, 3/10/60, TKK.

228 **siesta:** Brownlow, p. 126.

228 **sortie:** Layton with Pineau and Costello, p. 275; interview with Walter DeLany, Series V.2, Box 12, GP.

228 **"We were concerned":** Brownlow, p. 127.

229 **"had its costs":** PHA 6, p. 2536.

229 **Yoshikawa/"immediately"/"I imagine":** PHA 12, pp. 269, 266.

CHAPTER 36

230 **diplomacy was grinding/Halifax warn Japan:** Woodward, pp. 187ff; Halifax diaries, 12/6/41, University of York, UK; PHA 11, pp. 5165ff; PHA Report, pp. 424ff.

230 **First, however, he:** U.S. Government Printing Office, *Foreign Relations . . .* , Vol. IV, pp. 688ff, 697ff; PHA Report, pp. 427ff. The official record indicates that it was the President himself who initially, during a cabinet meeting on November 28th, voiced the idea of writing to the Emperor. Another account has it that the Japanese special envoy Kurusu and Second Secretary Terasaki independently discussed the notion on November 29th, and that Terasaki then got a U.S. intermediary to suggest it to Roosevelt. Is it possible that the concept of a letter to the Emperor was conceived separately, by the President on one day and by Japanese diplomats on the next?

The account crediting Terasaki with having played a major role first appeared in a book by his widow that depicted him as sympathetic to the United States. If he really did play a role in the "letter to the Emperor" episode, though, was it as a genuine would-be peacemaker? There is another possibility. Terasaki headed Japanese intelligence in the United States and, as noted in Chapter 23, had long been under investigation by the FBI. It may be that his role—like other Japanese "deception diplomacy"—was a delaying tactic to facilitate his nation's military preparations. [**cabinet meeting:** Stimson Diary, Series V.2, GP. **Terasaki:** Terasaki, pp. 59ff.]

231 **"from this son"**: Halifax diaries, 12/6/41, University of York, UK; Freidel, p. 402.

231 **ten-hour holdup**: Prange, *Dawn*, p. 477.

231 **battle order**: SRH-406 Pre-Pearl Harbor Japanese Naval Dispatches, p. 108, Box 183, RG 38.

231 **Stimson/"the news"**: Stimson diary, 12/6/41, STIM.

231 **Knoxes' dinner**: Hoehling, p. 134ff.

231 **Hoover**: Summers, p. 147; Batvinis, *Hoover's Secret War*, pp. 12ff.

231 **Marshall at home**: PHA 11, pp. 5193ff; PHA 3, pp. 1110ff.

232 **Having told a couple/Stark to theater**: Smedberg Oral History, U.S. Naval Institute, 1975, NHHC; PHA 11, pp. 5543ff, 5555ff; interview with Kathleen Krick by John Toland, TOL. The aides told they could take Sunday off were William Smedberg and Charles Wellborn.

There has been enduring uncertainty as to where Stark and Marshall actually were on the evening of December 6th, triggering speculation that they were in fact at a secret White House meeting with President Roosevelt. The best Marshall could do, he said in testimony after the war, was to assume he had been at home. The *Washington Times-Herald* of December 7th reported, however, that he attended a World War I veterans' reunion at the University Club that evening. Marshall's response, in sworn testimony, was that no such function was listed in the family engagement book. In 2016, when the authors attempted to check with the University Club, a spokeswoman said no relevant records existed.

Doubts as to Stark's whereabouts that Saturday evening were sparked by the fact that, for a long time, he too could not remember where he had been. That he was at the theater emerged only when a longtime friend, Captain Harold Krick, reminded him that he and his wife Kathleen had accompanied Stark and his wife to see *The Student Prince*. That he was indeed at the theater is corroborated by Lieutenant Lester Schulz's earlier sworn testimony about what had happened at the White House—that when FDR had attempted to call Stark, the President had been told that the CNO was "at the National Theater."

The jumble of memory over what senior officials did late on December 6th led to conjecture that, late that Saturday, the President and key officials had held a meeting at the White House. The notion was encouraged by two letters written in the 1970s by publisher James Stahlman, who had been a friend of the late Navy Secretary, Frank Knox. In one letter, in 1973, Stahlman quoted Knox as having told him that he and "Stimson, Marshall, Betty Stark, and Harry Hopkins had spent the night before [Pearl Harbor] at the White House with FDR, all waiting for what they knew was coming after those intercepts." In a second letter, in 1975, Stahlman's list of supposed participants in the late-night meeting expanded to include Knox's aide Frank Beatty and Stark's aide John McCrea.

Told of Stahlman's claim, however, McCrea categorically denied having been at such a meeting. By the time Stahlman made his claims, Stark and Marshall were dead. Both, though, had in 1946 denied in testimony that they had been at any White House meeting on the night of December 6th. [**Marshall had to assume:** PHA 11, pp. 5193ff; PHA 3, p. 1110. **reunion:** *Times-Herald*, 12/7/41; correspondence Sheila Katoff, 2016. **Stark:** PHA 11, pp. 5555ff. **Krick:** PHA 11, pp. 5555ff; Toland interview with Kathleen Krick, 1979, TOL. **Schulz:** PHA 10, p. 4663. **meeting:** E.g., Costello, p. 209ff; Toland, *Infamy*, p. 335. **Stahlman:** Stahlman to Tolley, 11/26/73, Stahlman to Slosson, 4/28/75, TKK. **McCrea denied:** Interview with John McCrea, Box 11, Folder 18, SIMPSON. **Stark and Marshall had denied:** PHA 11, pp. 5232, 5193.]

232 **Turner:** PHA 4, pp. 1970ff.

232 **Noyes:** Farago, *Broken Seal*, pp. 4ff.

232 **Wilkinson, Miles, and Beardall:** PHA 11, pp. 5271ff; PHA 33, p. 857; Hoehling, p. 135.

232 **McIntire/Astor:** White House Ushers' Logs, 12/6/41, FDRL; Hoehling, pp. 134ff.

232 **dinner party:** PHA 15, pp. 1633ff.

232 **"very quiet":** Hoehling, p. 147.

232 **cryptanalytic treadmill:** Farago, *Broken Seal*. pp. 340ff; Prange, *Dawn*, pp. 464ff.

232 **first message:** MB IV, Appendix, p. A-129.

232 **Distribution/President:** PHA, 11. p. 5481; Edward Morgan, pp. 211ff.

233 **Marshall and Stark would say:** PHA 3, pp. 1176; and see PHA 3, p. 1366, PHA 5, p. 2183.

233 **segment by segment:** PHA 14, pp. 1414ff.

233 **"spirit"/Part 13 "as a basis":** MB IV, Appendix, p. A1–130ff.

233 **Roosevelt/Hopkins/Schulz:** PHA 10, pp. 4659ff; PHA 11, p. 5481; PHA 8, p. 3901; Toland, *Infamy*, p. 316.

234 **"tonight, or tomorrow":** Interview by Hoehling cited in Hoehling, p. 151.

234 **Kramer to Knox/Knox called Hull:** PHA 8, pp. 3902ff; Hoehling, pp. 152ff.

234 **Kramer to Wilkinson's home/"diplomatic paper":** PHA 8, pp. 3902ff; PHA 4, pp. 1762ff; PHA 11, pp. 5271ff; Statement of VADM Wilkinson to Kimmel, Lavender, and Rugg, 2/19/45, HEK R12.

234 **General Miles also:** PHA 2, pp. 925ff. Though admirals Turner and Ingersoll were to testify that they saw the thirteen-part intercept that evening, Kramer would insist he did not take it to either of them. [**Turner:** PHA 4, p. 1970. **Ingersoll:** PHA 9, p. 4263. **Kramer:** PHA 8, p. 3903; and transcript of Kramer note supplied by Mary Kramer, 12/3/70, Series V.2, GP.]

234 **Bratton left copy/went home:** PHA 10, pp. 4607ff; PHA 9, pp. 4515ff; PHA 35, pp. 25ff, 96ff; Edward Morgan, p. 213.

234 **Kramer would also go home/duty officer:** PHA 8, pp. 3903ff, 3906.

234 **Stark had no recollection:** PHA 33, pp. 729ff; PHA 5, pp. 2183ff.

235 **Krick/"critical":** PHA 11, pp. 5555ff, 5557; and see interview with Kathleen Krick by John Toland, TOL, and also PHA 11, p. 5482.

235 **"that when the President":** PHA 11, p. 5545.

235 **Nothing in the accounts:** Edward Morgan, pp. 217, 219ff.

235 **Marshall:** PHA 11, p. 5193.

235 **President went to bed:** White House usher's diary, 12/6/41, FDRL.

CHAPTER 37

236 **Most of Yoshikawa's figures:** PHA 12, p. 270; PHA 35, p. 390. But Yoshikawa's figure on the number of destroyer-type ships—nineteen—was badly skewed; there were in fact twenty-nine.

236 **spy lingered/"the date":** *Proceedings*, Vol. 86/12/694, 12/60.

236 **call to Layton:** PHA 10, p. 4870; Layton with Pineau and Costello, p. 276; and see PHA 36, pp. 337ff.

237 **Mori call:** PHA 31, pp. 3186ff; PHA 10, p. 5106.

237 **"peculiar":** Honolulu to Director, undated, 12/41, TKK.

237 **FBI alerted:** PHA 27, pp. 737ff; PHA 10, p. 5099.

237 **Short and Fielder spent:** PHA 28, pp. 1542, 1558; PHA 22, p. 175. The Army's chief investigator in Hawaii, Lieutenant Colonel George Bicknell, recalled a mere five-minute discussion of the Mori transcript. Fielder, however, was clear that he and Short perused the transcript for more than an hour, and that the conference made them an hour late for dinner. In 1946, Congress' Joint Committee was to include the reaction to the Mori call in its criticisms of Short and the Navy.

Did the call in fact have anything to do with espionage? Maybe so, but very possibly not. Dr. Mori's father, also a medical man, was considered an elder statesman of the Japanese community in Hawaii, and did have contacts with the Japanese consulate. Was it coincidence that the supposed newspaperman on the Tokyo end of the call was named Ogawa—the same name as that of the man who headed the U.S. section of Japanese naval intelligence? Why did the lengthy exchange with Dr. Mori contain—along with much innocuous chat—questions about airplane traffic, about whether the American military in Hawaii used searchlights at night, and about what flowers were in bloom? Were the flowers, people have wondered, some sort of code?

Immediately after the attack on Pearl Harbor, both Dr. Mori and his wife Ishiko were arrested, never charged, but interned until the end of the war. More than a decade later, Mrs. Mori—a doctor like her

husband and still living in Honolulu—offered an innocent explanation of the phone call. In December 1941, when—her medical quali-
fication aside—she had been a contributor to the newspaper *Yomiuri
Shimbun*, she had been asked to get leading members of the local
Japanese community to give interviews about the current situation.
Failing to find anyone willing to talk, given the sensitive atmosphere
at the time, she had recruited her own husband to take the newspaper's call. Her account has substance. *Yomiuri Shimbun* did publish
an article—based on the supposedly suspect conversation—the day
after the call, a fact not mentioned in the Joint Committee Report.
Dr. Mori's son Victor, who was alive as this book went to print, has
written a book defending his family's innocence in the matter.

Close study of the call transcript today suggests that Ishiko Mori's
explanation, which seems to have been ignored in the Pearl Harbor
literature, may well have been truthful. The person *initiating* the call
from Tokyo, however, may have had more than a mere journalistic interest.

There is a sidebar to this episode. The FBI was to tell the Army's
Pearl Harbor Board that the call's contents, having been recorded on
Friday, December 5th, first became available in transcript form only
on Saturday the 6th. Interviewed in 1990, however, two retired FBI
agents said the intercept had in fact been made as early as Wednesday, December 3rd. Former agent George Allen said he was personally
involved, and that a transcript was sent to the Bureau's headquarters
in Washington as early as Thursday. If this was so, it would indicate
that the FBI's handling of the call was less than timely. [**Bicknell:** PHA
10, pp. 5091. **Fielder:** PHA 28, p. 1542. **Joint Committee:** PHA Report,
p. 137. **espionage:** PHA 29, pp. 1666ff; Prange, *Dawn*, pp. 150, 226;
Honolulu Star-Bulletin, 12/5/57, 12/7/01; Soga, p. 39; Mori, pp. 31ff, 44,
80ff. **sidebar:** Summers, pp. 132ff.]

237 **dinner Halekulani/Draemel/"certain the Japs":** Brownlow, pp. 127ff;
Kimmel, p. 7; and see Borneman, pp. 344, 520.

238 **men laboring/carousing/"Battle of Music"/"God Bless America":**
Weintraub, pp. 153ff; Anderson, p. 102; *Life*, 12/91.

238 **More than five thousand miles:** Hart's information, which apparently
originated with a British source in Singapore, was premature. There
was *soon* to be such an arrangement, following the imminent Japanese
attacks on Pearl Harbor and the Philippines, but documents suggest
that—in line with constitutional restrictions—nothing had yet been
formally agreed.

238 **Hart fired off query:** PHA 14, p. 1412; Prange, *Verdict*, pp. 83ff.

238 **"chronic condition":** Hart to Stark, 11/20/41, Box 15, STARK; Hart diary, 2/20/42, Box 4, HART.

238 **dispersed/opted to keep/"Guess war":** pp. 39ff; Parker, pp. 47ff; Blair,
pp. 129ff; United States Asiatic Fleet Locations December 7, 1941, Nav-
Source.

CHAPTER 38

239 **first message/fourteenth part:** PHA 12, p. 245; PHA 14, p. 1415; Edward Morgan, pp. 221ff; PHA 9, pp. 4514ff; Kahn, p. 55.

239 **Intercepted shortly after:** Though the night duty officer, Lieutenant Junior Grade Brotherhood, did not phone Kramer during the night, he may not simply have ignored the senior officer's instruction. There may, rather, have been crossed wires because of a temporary work-sharing arrangement that night between the Navy and the Army.

Army testimony about the fourteen-part message, meanwhile, is inconsistent and conflicting. Colonel Bratton, responsible for distribution to Army recipients and the Secretaries of War and State, initially testified that he had during the evening delivered the first *thirteen* parts to the Secretary of the Army general staff, who in turn was to pass it on to Chief of Staff Marshall. Bratton also took it, he said, to generals Miles and Gerow. Later, when Marshall, Miles, and Gerow all denied having received the material from him, he corrected himself, saying he had delivered it only to the State Department duty officer.

Bratton's assistant Colonel Clyde Dusenbury said in a 1945 affidavit that Bratton had left it to him to receive and distribute the fourteenth part when it came in. When it did arrive—"about midnight," he asserted—he did not see any "implication of immediate hostilities" in it, and so he chose to wake neither Bratton nor "the usual recipients." He too had gone home to bed. Colonel Bratton said he first saw the fourteenth part only when he arrived at the office early the following morning.

Were it accurate, Dusenbury's account would mean that the fourteenth part sat neglected for more than eight hours. The Army investigator who took Dusenbury's affidavit, then-Major, later–Lieutenant Colonel, Henry Clausen, would write in a 1992 book that, had Hawaii been alerted during those lost hours, disaster could have been avoided. According to Clausen, who had conducted a one-man probe for Secretary of War Stimson, Dusenbury's account of the timing was supported by both Army and Navy witnesses.

The present authors, however, reviewed the affidavits and testimony on this matter cited by Clausen, and found that they do not support Dusenbury's account. The record, moreover, indicates that the fourteenth part was not even transmitted from Tokyo until 2:38 a.m. Washington time. According to testimony, it was intercepted in the United States around 3:00 a.m. If these times are correct, then Dusenbury's stand-alone account must be skewed. [**Brotherhood:** PHA 33, pp. 764, 844ff; PHA 10, p. 4930; PHA 36, p. 317; Memorandum of 2/23/44 re interview with Safford, HANIFY. **Bratton testified/corrected himself:** PHA 9, pp. 4515ff; PHA 35, pp. 97ff; Clausen and Lee, pp. 81, 178ff. **Dusenbury:** PHA 36, pp. 25ff; Clausen and Lee, pp. 78ff. **Army witnesses:** Clausen and Lee, pp. 106ff, 212ff; PHA 35, pp. 34ff, 105ff; affidavits of Doud, Rowlett, Dunning, Prather, and Martin. **Navy wit-**

nesses: Clausen and Lee, p. 216; PHA 36, p. 532. **2:28 a.m.**: PHA 14, p. 1415. **3:00 a.m.**: PHA 36, p. 532; PHA 10, pp. 4929ff.]

239 **The second incoming:** PHA 12, p. 248; PHA 14, p. 1416; Kahn, pp. 1ff, 55, 978, 984; Wohlstetter, p. 223. Under the Hague Convention of 1907, of which the United States and Japan were both signatories, hostilities could "not commence without previous and explicit warning." In this instance, it might have been hard to argue, after the fact, that Japan's final message had amounted to "explicit warning." There had, though, been lengthy debate on the issue between the more and less militant parties in the Tokyo regime, and the fixed timetable was the outcome ("Opening of Hostilities," Hague Convention III, 1907).

240 **Codebreakers had been:** PHA 12, p. 251; PHA 11, p. 5481; PHA 36, p. 504; Hanyok, pp. 44ff. See Chapter 31.

240 **fourth dispatch/destroy at once:** PHA 12, p. 249; Edward Morgan, pp. 223ff; Wohlstetter, p. 223.

241 **front pages/"feel totally confident":** NYT, 12/7/41.

241 **Brewster:** Hoehling, p. 160.

241 **Kramer arrived early/"fourteenth part":** PHA 8, p. 904; Edward Morgan, p. 222.

242 **"very serious":** PHA 4, pp. 1766ff, 1798.

242 **Rather, as Wilkinson:** As Wilkinson recalled it in 1945, he was accompanied on the visit to Stark's office by Commander McCollum, head of ONI's Far East section. McCollum's various statements also indicate that this was so. That said, McCollum's memory—like that of many officers speaking years later—was less than perfect. He was to cause a stir, for example, by stating that Chief of Staff Marshall had been present in Stark's office when he and Wilkinson entered it that morning. Other information indicates that Marshall was not even contactable at the time, let alone in the CNO's office. McCollum was later to admit that his earlier testimony had been in error. [**Wilkinson:** PHA 4, p. 1766. **McCollum caused a stir:** PHA 36, p. 27; and, e.g., Memorandum of Interview McCollum, 5/18/45, HEK 12; Shafroth to Kimmel, 5/4/61, HEK 32; Shafroth to Kimmel, 3/9/67, HEK R13. **not contactable:** E.g., PHA 9, p. 4517; PHA 4, pp. 1766ff. **in error:** PHA 8, p. 3432.]

242 **fourteenth part to the president/Beardall/"It looks":** PHA 11, pp. 5481, 5269ff, 5283.

242 **all tranquil:** Reilly, p. 3.

242 **McIntire:** McIntire, pp. 136ff; Farago, Broken Seal, pp. 373ff; Hoehling, pp. 179ff.

242 **Roosevelt shared some:** In addition to the medical treatment, Roosevelt did, at 12:30 p.m., for half an hour, receive the Chinese ambassador, Dr. Hu Shih. He then lunched in his study with Harry Hopkins ("FDR Day by Day," FDRL).

243 **three other overnight messages:** PHA 11, p. 5481.

243 **Marshall/"We had a late":** Katherine Tupper Marshall, pp. 98ff.

243 **"stunned"/"gone horseback riding":** PHA 9, p. 4524.

243 **Around 10:20 a.m./"one o'clock message"/Kramer calculated:** PHA 8, pp. 3908ff.

244 **large chart/Wilkinson and McCollum approached Stark/"didn't seem to be very much"/"At this time":** McCollum Oral History, U.S. Naval Institute, 1971, NHHC.

244 **Kramer made sure:** PHA 8, p. 3911.

244 **Stimson was "very certain":** Stimson diary, 12/7/41, PHA 11, p. 5437.

244 **cantering:** Pogue to Prange, 8/22/77, Series V.2, Box 67, GP; PHA 3, p. 1184.

244 **shower/Bratton/"important message":** PHA 3, p. 1327.

245 **Between 11:15:** Marshall himself twice testified that he got to the office around 11:00 a.m. In his 1992 book, Clausen wrote—citing witnesses' statements—that Marshall in fact reached his office forty-five minutes to an hour earlier than the 11:15–11:30 time frame. The present authors have examined the testimony and affidavits on this issue but are not persuaded that the weight of evidence supports Clausen's thesis. [**Marshall:** PHA 29, p. 2309, PHA 3, p. 1431. **1992 book:** Clausen and Lee, p. 180, citing affidavits, PHA 35, pp. 90ff, 116, 139. **11:15–11:30:** PHA Majority Report, p. 223; PHA 9, p. 4517; PHA 2, p. 933; PHA 14, p. 1409—but see Deane on p. 1411.]

245 **"General Miles and I":** PHA 9, p. 4518.

245 **Miles urged:** PHA 2, p. 929.

245 **"There was no":** PHA 29, pp. 2309ff.

245 **drafted a message/called Stark:** PHA 29, p. 2309; and see PHA 9, pp. 4518ff.

245 **"He said"/Had Marshall not phoned/"I put":** PHA 5, pp. 2184ff.

246 **"The Japanese":** PHA 14, p. 1334.

246 **midsummer 1940:** Gannon, p. 223.

246 **seemed unclear:** PHA 3, pp. 1432ff.

246 **not secure:** PHA 3, p. 1213; PHA 39, p. 1081; and see PHA 33, p. 882.

246 **"not considered":** PHA 29, p. 231.

246 **FBI link:** PHA 3, p. 1433.

246 **Marshall declined:** PHA 5, p. 2185. Marshall would deny having discussed with Stark anything about rapid communication. At the time, very soon after the attack, the Chief of Staff appears to have become concerned about the facts surrounding his alert to Short and other commanders. He ordered staff members involved to submit notes for the record about the writing and transmission of the message. [**Stark:** PHA 33, p. 87. **notes:** Interview with David Richmond, Box 14, Folder

1, SIMPSON; PHA 14, pp. 1409ff, citing memos of December 15, 1941; PHA 34, p. 19.]

246 **In the event/delay/"Within thirty":** PHA 14, pp. 1409ff, 1411; PHA 3, pp. 1042ff.

246 **planes launching:** *Proceedings*, 9/52; Prange, *Dawn*, p. 435.

247 **black farce/"naval authorities"/atmospheric conditions/circuit down/ motorbike/almost 3:00 p.m.:** PHA 15, p. 1640; PHA Report, pp. 223ff; PHA 14, pp. 1409ff; PHA 11, pp. 5296ff; PHA 7, pp. 3163ff; PHA 35, pp. 211ff; PHA 22, pp. 46–217; Gannon, pp. 224ff; Farago, *Broken Seal*, pp. 381, 432.

247 **It was now 7:33 a.m.:** The Japanese envoys were in fact held up— they would enter Secretary of State Hull's office not at 1:00 p.m., as planned, but at 2:20 p.m. News of the attack on Pearl Harbor had by then reached Washington, and Hull told the envoys bluntly what he thought of the fourteen-part document. It was, he said, filled with "infamous falsehoods and distortions on a scale so huge that I never imagined until today that any government on this planet was capable of uttering them" (PHA Report, pp. 440ff).

247 **Short swore:** Anderson, pp. 104.

247 **balled up:** Interview with Poco Smith, Series V.2, Box 74, GP.

CHAPTER 39

251 **"splendid":** Halsey and Bryan, p. 81.

251 **meals forgotten/armchair:** Interview with Poco Smith, Series V.2, Box 74, GP.

251 **"still wearing":** Halsey and Bryan, p. 81.

251 **only the initial blow:** Interview with Poco Smith, Series V.2, Box 74, GP; interview with Raymond Spruance, Series V.2, Box 74, GP.

251 **Stimson/invasion:** Stimson diary, 12/8/41, STIM.

251 **command decisions:** Interview with Poco Smith, Series V.2, Box 74, GP; interview with Walter DeLany, Series V.2, Box 12, GP.

251 **prolonged search:** Gannon, pp. 263ff.

251 **Halsey headed:** Halsey and Bryan, p. 82.

251 **Foremost among them:** Kimmel had long seen Wake not only as defensible but as a place where Japan could be lured into a costly battle at sea. Soon after he was relieved of command, however, the operation would be called off. On December 23rd, after having ferociously resisted the Japanese onslaught, and having taken heavy casualties, the U.S. garrison on Wake was forced to surrender (Gannon, 269ff; Robert Cressman, "A Magnificent Fight," www.ibiblio.org).

251 **Kimmel resisted/Washington proposed:** OPNAV to CINCPAC, CINCPAC to OPNAV, Nimitz Gray Book, CINCPAC files, Vol. 1, pp. 6ff; Gannon, pp. 268ff; Prange, *Dawn*, p. 737.

252 **Though Kimmel could not:** Gannon, pp. 268ff; Prange, *Dawn*, p. 737. Of the battleships, only the *Arizona* and the *Oklahoma* were write-offs. The *Utah* had long been used only as a target ship (Wallin, chs. XIIff).

252 **"Repeated strong":** Wallin, pp. 8ff, 14.

252 **rest/"fight and determination":** Interview with Poco Smith, Series V.2, Box 74, GP.

252 **"was the loss":** Interview with Walter DeLany, Series V.2, Box 12, GP.

252 **"We Americans can":** Kimmel issued this statement, jointly with Admiral Bloch, the base defense officer, on December 10th ([Louisville] *Courier-Journal*, 12/12/41).

252 **five minutes or less:** PHA 1, p. 46; PHA 39, p. 307.

252 **"So prompt":** Michael Gannon, "Admiral Kimmel and the Question of Pacific Fleet's State of Readiness," TKK; and see Fuchida in *Proceedings*, 9/52. By contrast, the response time of the Army's antiaircraft batteries was very poor. Congress' Joint Committee report would in 1946 describe it as an "extraordinary lack of readiness . . . occasioned largely by the time required for moving into position and the fact that ammunition was not really accessible to the mobile batteries" (PHA Report, pp. 67ff).

253 **Taussig:** Commanding Officer, USS *Nevada* to CINCPAC, 12/15/41, BB36/A9/A16.

253 **"The Admiral stepped":** Sidebottom to Gail Kimmel, 12/31/91, courtesy of Gail Kimmel.

253 **"Dear Admiral":** Stark to Kimmel, 12/8/41, STARK.

254 **Knox's trip/reputation/taunted:** *National Review*, 12/13/66; PHA 19, p. 3506.

254 **"of a nasty":** Knox to Mowrer, 12/18/41, Box 4, KNOX.

254 **members of Congress deriding/resignation:** *St. Louis Post-Dispatch*, 12/9/41; Prange, *Verdict*, pp. 285ff.

254 **court-martialed/"to determine":** E.g., *San Bernadino County Sun*, *St. Louis Post-Dispatch*, NYT, 12/9/41.

CHAPTER 40

255 **"completely":** *National Review*, 12/13/66.

255 **showed Knox images:** Interview with Edwin Layton, Box 30, Folder 1, LAYTON.

255 **Knox worked on his report:** *National Review*, 12/13/66.

255 **In the report/"alibi":** PHA 24, pp. 1749ff.

256 **Its radar, which:** See Chapter 10.

256 **"so dispersed":** PHA 24, pp. 1749ff.

256 **The Navy's "morning patrol":** Knox apparently confused the regular dawn air patrol—which was indeed flown southward on December

7th—with additional patrols Kimmel had ordered carried out by his Wake and Midway task forces. Intelligence Kimmel had received from his analysts in recent days, meanwhile, suggested a buildup of Japanese naval forces—including perhaps two carriers—in the Marshalls, some 2,400 miles southwest of Pearl. According to Fleet intelligence officer Layton, the Admiral surmised that the air patrols he had ordered carried out by his Wake and Midway task forces would spot a Japanese approach from that direction (Gannon, pp. 165ff; Laytoni, pp. 225ff).

256 **Knox mentioned:** PHA 24, pp. 1749ff.

257 **Pages later, and prominently:** The first question Secretary Knox had put to Kimmel on arriving in Hawaii on December 11th had been: "Did you receive my message on Saturday night?" He asked the same question of General Short and other officers in Hawaii: Had they received a message from Washington on the night of December 6th? The reply from all of them was that they had not—and no such message has turned up in the record. Down the years, revisionists have seized on this as a possible indication that some dark force in Washington blocked the sending of a timely warning to Hawaii. That notion is dispelled by the testimony of Kimmel's chief of staff, Poco Smith, who said later that when Knox asked the question in Hawaii, he referred to a message sent after Washington learned from MAGIC that Tokyo's envoys were under orders to end negotiations at precisely 1:00 p.m. That intercept was not seen in Washington until the morning of December 7th. That being the case, it seems virtually certain that, probably in a muddle over time zones, and after a long, exhausting journey, Knox misspoke when he asked whether Hawaii had received a message sent on "Saturday night." He was surely referring, in fact, to the message Marshall sent on the morning of Sunday the 7th—the ill-fated message that did not reach commanders until after the Japanese strike was over. This interpretation of Knox's question is supported by the testimony of two other witnesses in Hawaii—and by Knox's own written report. [first question/Short: Kimmel, p. 3, *U.S. News and World Report*, 5/28/54; PHA 24, p. 1750; interview with Edwin Layton, Box 30, Folder 1, LAYTON. See also similar question by Marshall, PHA 22, p. 173. they had not/no such message: PHA 32, p. 429; Kimmel, p. 3; Affidavit of Ernest Blake, 1/22/62, and Affidavit of William Smith, 1/18/62, HEK R32. dark force: E.g., Beach, p. 112; Toland, *Infamy*, p. 335. Smith: PHA 32, pp. 428ff. two witnesses: Interview with Edwin Layton, Box 30, Folder 1, LAYTON; Beatty testimony, PHA 8, p. 3816. report: PHA 24, p. 1750.]

257 **Knox hurried:** Roosevelt Day by Day, 12/14/41, FDRL.

257 **low spirits:** Prange, *Dawn*, p. 588.

257 **On the 15th Knox returned twice:** Roosevelt Day by Day, 12/15/41, FDRL.

257 **"all the information":** *National Review*, 12/13/66.

257 **hushed press conference:** Toland, *Infamy*, p. 23.

258 **"The whole spectacle":** Brief Report on the Conduct of Naval Personnel During Japanese Attack, Pearl Harbor, December 7, 1941, 12/15/41, Navy Department Communiqués and Pertinent Press Releases, 12/10/41–3/5/43, U.S. Navy Office of Public Relations, 1943; AP, 12/15/41; UP, 12/15/41.

258 **There is nothing:** See Chapters 16 and 35.

258 **central truth/"a formal investigation"/"no changes":** Brief Report on the Conduct of Naval Personnel, supra; AP, 12/15/41; UP, 12/15/41.

259 **whirlwind pace/"all Americans abhor":** Press conference #792, 12/16/41, President's Press Conferences, Series 1; and Roosevelt Day by Day, 12/16/41, FDRL.

259 **Roberts to head:** *NYT*, 12/17/41; *Arizona Republic*, 12/17/41.

259 **"ascertain":** PHA 39, p. 1.

259 **announcements:** *Pittsburgh Post-Gazette*, 12/18/41.

260 **brief dispatch:** SECNAV to CINCPAC, 12/16/41, HEK R12; PHA 5, pp. 2429ff.

260 **"If I were":** Kimmel to Stark, 12/15/41, STARK.

260 **Draemel:** Hoyt, p. 14.

261 **"retired to his":** Layton with Pineau and Costello, p. 338.

261 **shoulder boards:** Brownlow, p. 141.

CHAPTER 41

262 **"shortly after":** PHA 5, p. 2430.

262 **Army-Navy relations:** E.g., *NYT*, 1/19/42; Marston, p. 62.

262 **"bitterness":** Stimson diary, 12/11/41, STIM.

262 **"shaken":** Ibid., 12/14/41.

262 **"no time":** AP, 12/11/41.

262 **Army records show:** The initial intended replacement was Major General Herbert Dargue. Though he did leave for Hawaii, he was killed en route on December 12th when his plane crashed in California. When news of Dargue's death arrived, a substitute was quickly found. This was Lieutenant General Delos Emmons, who by December 17th had arrived to replace Short. [**replacement/crash:** Army Section, Personnel Records Center, GSA, 10/29/63, cited by Professors Paul Burtness and Warren Ober, "Secretary Stimson and the First Pearl Harbor Investigation," *Australian Journal of Politics and History*, Vol. 14, 4/68; and Stimson to Roosevelt, PHA 7, p. 3260. **by December 17th:** Pittsburgh *Post-Gazette*, 12/18/41.]

262 **"most confidential"/"My opinion":** PHA 7, p. 3260.

263 **depressed:** Interview with Poco Smith, Series V.2, Box. 74, GP; Brownlow, p. 140.

263 **Ramsey:** Interview with Logan Ramsey, Series V.2, Box 68, GP.

263 **"Keep cheerful":** Stark to Kimmel, 12/11/41, HEK R3.

263 **"I wish":** Stark to Kimmel, 12/17/41, STARK.

264 **"Dear Mr. President":** Stark to Roosevelt, 12/12/41, PSF, Box 59, FDRL.

264 **"weakest one":** Stimson diary, 12/1/41, STIM.

264 **Dorothy was living in Long Beach/closer to him:** Dorothy Kimmel to Lucille Kimmel, 12/30/41, MMK.

265 **spent much of her time/Inez Kidd:** Interview with Harold Train, Series V.2, GP.

265 **Manning:** Interview with Thomas K. Kimmel Jr., 2015.

265 **Tom/S-40:** Tom Kimmel Sr. to Tolley, undated/2/72, TKK; Husband Kimmel, "Adventures of Tom and Nancy Kimmel in the Early Days of the Japanese War," unpublished manuscript, TKK; Blair, p. 150.

265 **Ned/had hurried:** Interview with Edward "Ned" Kimmel, Box 120, TOL; Edward Kimmel, "How History Has Touched Me," 11/4/99, unpublished manuscript, TKK, interview with Harriott Kimmel, 2014.

265 **headline:** UP, 12/13/41; Brownlow, p. 149.

265 **"Dear Dad":** Manning Kimmel to Kimmel, 12/18/41, HEK R25.

266 **"We have heard":** Manning Kimmel to Agatha and Oscar, 12/30/41, MMK.

266 **In another letter:** Manning Kimmel to Kimmel, 12/30/41, HEK R25. The intermediary was Admiral Russell Willson, superintendent of the Naval Academy.

CHAPTER 42

267 **"The truth":** Prange, *Dawn*, p. 594.

267 **the Commission had:** *NYT*, 12/17/41.

267 **criticism:** E.g., Prange, *Dawn*, p. 594.

267 **receive directions:** Stimson diary, 12/17/41, STIM.

267 **two days/not under oath:** PHA 22, pp. 1ff.

268 **"shocked":** Standley and Ageton, p. 82.

268 **Pearl Harbor witnesses were sworn:** E.g., PHA 22, pp. 31, 317, 374.

268 **"the right":** Kimmel, p. 146.

268 **"Admiral Kimmel":** Brownlow, p. 145; and see Kimmel, p. 151.

268 **Theobald/"was rendered":** affidavit of Robert Theobald, 3/20/44, HEK R4.

268 **not a "trial of":** PHA 22, p. 375.

268 **"incomprehensible"/"condemned":** Affidavit of Robert Theobald. 3/20/44, HEK R4.

269 **General Short had his staff:** Standley and Ageton, p. 83.

269 **Curts:** Brownlow, pp. 145ff; PHA 22, p. 375.

269 **"The stenographic staff":** Theobald, p. 154.

269 **Admiral Standley recalled:** Standley and Ageton, pp. 84ff; Kimmel, pp. 139ff. Years later, testifying to Congress' Joint Committee, Justice Roberts would say the Commission's stenographers had been competent, and the transcript accurate. On reviewing it today, the authors did find errors—some significant, some minor. [**Roberts:** PHA 7, p. 3268.]

269 **Brooke Allen:** Prange, *Dawn*, pp. 595ff.

269 **limited testimony, sworn:** E.g., PHA 23, pp. 1082, 1075.

269 **Marshall:** Ibid., pp. 1076ff.

269 **"sat up":** Stimson diary, 1/20/42, STIM.

269 **Nimitz:** Stillwell, pp. 258, 261, Potter, pp. 13, 17, BUNAV to CINCPAC, 12/16/41, HEK, PHA32, p. 400, Nimitz to Kimmel, 1/15/42, NIMITZ, Box 102.

270 **"The young Marine":** Brownlow, p. 141.

270 **mail delayed:** Manning Kimmel to Kimmel, undated, December 41, HEK R25.

271 **"black cloud":** Dorothy Kimmel to Lucille Kimmel, 12/30/41, MMK.

271 **"He told me":** Interview with Harold Train, Series V.2, GP.

CHAPTER 43

272 **Roberts Report/delivered to President Roosevelt/withheld/findings:** PHA 39, p. 1ff, 19ff; Prange, *Dawn*, p. 599.

273 **"He read it"/"Mac, give that":** PHA 7, pp. 3265ff.

273 **headline:** *NYT*, 1/25/41.

273 **press/"someone"/"practically"/"shorn":** Washington *Times-Herald*, 1/6/42, Washington *Star*, 1/26/42 and 1/27/42.

273 **Not one of the official:** CNO Stark's successor, Admiral King, did use the word "derelictions" in a 1944 "endorsement" (opinion) of the Naval Court of Inquiry decision that had effectively cleared Kimmel. See Chapter 51 (PHA 16, p. 2269).

274 **"gross misinterpretation":** AP, 2/27/42. As reported in Chapter 9, the relationship between Short and Kimmel certainly was by all accounts good, and they did confer often. By contrast, the relationship between General MacArthur and Admiral Hart, in the Philippines, was—in the same period—appalling. Though the two men had been close for forty years, they proved professionally incompatible. In October 1941, MacArthur had written privately to Stark complaining about Hart's supposed assumption of authority over elements of the Army when ashore in China. Hart, for his part, wrote in a November letter of his own to Stark that it had become "plain enough that [MacArthur] did

not want to have much to do with me . . . Our last confab was a month back . . . I suppose MacA resents my rank." (Hart was a four-star admiral; MacArthur—at the time—a three-star lieutenant general.) He thought the General had "prima donna complexes . . . a mental superiority complex" and an "erratic mind . . . it is to be feared that an imbalance will appear which may be dangerous."

Following the savaging of MacArthur's air force in the Japanese strike hours after U.S. forces had been told of the attack on Pearl Harbor, invasion and the General's legendary retreat soon followed. On December 24th, MacArthur had an emissary inform Hart that he was declaring Manila an "open city" and would be evacuating his troops within twenty-four hours—leaving Hart scrambling to evacuate his men and matériel. It was, perhaps, the most egregious evidence of the ill will that by then existed between the two commanders. There was no investigation of the humiliation in the Philippines. While Kimmel and Short were disgraced, MacArthur was promoted and awarded the Medal of Honor. The citation referred to his "conspicuous leadership in preparing the Philippines islands to resist conquest." [**MacArthur to Stark/Hart to Stark:** 10/19/41 and 11/20/41, Box 15, STARK. **"open city":** Leutze, pp. 244ff; Hart, p. 50. **citation:** www.militarytimes.com.]

274 **Helen:** Heinrich to Von Freund, 12/3/91, TKK.

274 **"I can well":** Standley to Delia Kimmel, 2/10/43, HEK R25.

275 **memoirs:** Standley and Ageton, pp. 8off.

276 **"The evidence":** PHA 39, p. 1.

276 **The day:** Hoover to Roberts, 12/18/41 and attachments, documents from Hoover and Nichols Official Files, TKK. The detail in the memo suggests that this was in the main a garbled reference to the message giving recipients advance notice of the "Winds" code—the elusive phony Japanese weather forecast that U.S. intelligence had tried so hard to pick up. Hoover's memo, research shows, summarized in a muddled way what an FBI agent had learned from G-2's head of counterintelligence, Colonel John ter Bush Bissell (Ladd to Hoover, 12/11/41, "Documents from Hoover and Nichols Official Files"; and Thomas K. Kimmel and J. A. Williams, unpublished manuscript, "Supreme Court Justice Owen Roberts' Performance," TKK).

276 **asked Army intelligence officers:** PHA 22, pp. 175ff, 192ff.

276 **"We asked for"/he had known/"I would not"/"asked the War Department":** PHA7, pp. 3274ff, 3278, 3280, 3284ff.

276 **had discussed "freely":** PHA 4, p. 1848.

277 **Turner:** PHA 32, pp. 614ff.

278 **"had as much":** PHA 4, pp. 1846ff. A note in the Commission's files, indeed, confirms that Wilkinson said both commanders in Hawaii "had available to them the same information . . ." (PHA 24, p. 1361).

278 **Both Turner and:** See Chapter 17.

278 **It would be years:** PHA 6, p. 2553.

278 **"without":** Kimmel, p. 150.

CHAPTER 44

279 **"This Pearl Harbor business":** Oral History Interview of George Dyer, U.S. Naval Institute, 1969, NHHC. There was a gradual reorganization at the top of the Navy after Pearl Harbor. In late December 1941, King, who had been commander in chief Atlantic Fleet, was brought to Washington to be commander in chief U.S. Fleet—the post previously known by the acronym CINCUS, now changed to COMINCH. In March, King replaced Stark as Chief of Naval Operations (CNO), and took overall command as COMINCH-CNO.

279 **Previously, War Plans chief:** See Chapter 19.

279 **iron grip/to "collect, collate":** Dyer, p. 194, citing DNI to DWP, OP-16, 12/15/41, "Dispatches Regarding Intelligence of Enemy Activities."

280 **urgent study/McCormack/"wasted"/"checked":** Stimson diary, 12/31/41, STIM; Lee, pp. 8ff, 25ff, 35ff; SRH-116 Origin, Functions, and Problems of the Special Branch, MIS, 4/15/43, RG 457, NARA; Clausen and Lee, pp. 46ff.

280 **Army soon to take over:** Safford to Barnes, 3/8/62, HEK R33; Kahn, p. 574.

280 **rewards/"vital edge"/saving countless lives:** Lee, p. xv; Clausen and Lee, pp. 47ff; NYT, 12/9/45.

281 **"When the sudden":** SRH-116 Origin, Functions, and Problems of the Special Branch, MIS, 4/15/43, RG 457, NARA.

281 **Navy study/Connorton/"It can safely be":** SRH 012 The Role of Radio Intelligence in the American-Japanese Naval War, August 1941–June 1942, Vol. 1, September 1942, RIP 87Z, Entry A1 9002, Boxes 6 and 7, RG 457, NARA; Safford to Kimmel, 8/7/53, HEK R15; Redman to Connorton, 9/12/42, and letter of reference from Dean Thomas Hughes, Fordham University, 6/18/42, courtesy of John V. Connorton Jr.

281 **Compiled by a junior:** Because Connorton had only the documents that had at that stage been supplied to him, he placed messages decrypted overnight on December 6th/7th—listed as relating to the 7th—in the section of his report covering "Messages received after the attack." Some intercepts, meanwhile, were omitted (see Safford to Barnes, 1/29/62, HEK R32; Harrison to Safford, 11/10/54, HEK R30; Greaves to Barnes re Redman interview 5/13/62, HEK R15; and see Wohlstetter, p. 180, re filing).

281 ***"MAGIC" Background*/Inman:** Interview and correspondence with John V. Connorton Jr., 2015; Connorton to Inman, draft letter, undated, courtesy of John V. Connorton Jr.

282 **not available/not until 1953:** Safford to Kimmel, 8/7/53, 9/29/53, HEK R15; Kimmel to Hanify, 9/6/53, and Kimmel to Rugg, 9/17/53, HEK

R30; Carney to Kimmel, 10/5/53, HEK R13; Laurance Safford, "The Kita Message, No Longer a Mystery," unpublished mss, TKK.

282 **McCormack report released in 1981:** Lee, p. 35.

282 **Within less than a year:** Connorton's 1942 study was titled "The Role of Radio Intelligence in the American-Japanese Naval War, August 1941–June 1942," Vol. 1. (It was also known as RIP 87Z.) Of seven original copies, three were kept in the safe of the Office of Communications and two others in the custody of that office's senior commanders. One was lodged with ONI, another with the Navy's General Board. In 1945, copies were made available to the Navy's Hewitt Inquiry and to Congress' Joint Committee. There is only one reference to the study in the Committee's volumes. [**seven copies:** Memo for Admiral Joseph Redman, 6/21/43, provided to authors by John V. Connorton Jr. **Hewitt:** Laurance Safford, "The Kita Message, No Longer a Mystery," unpublished manuscript, TKK. **one reference:** John Baecher memo, 4/29/46, Box 21, Pearl Harbor Liaison Office files, NARA: PHA 11, pp. 5477ff.]

CHAPTER 45

283 **"Don't worry":** PHA 17, p. 2733.

283 **"I have always":** Report on Fitness of Officers, October 1–December 17, 1941, HEK R17.

283 **Long Beach/temporary posting:** Kimmel to Jacobs, 1/21/42, 2/22/42, Box 102, NIMITZ; Bloch to Kimmel, 1/14/42, HEK R12.

283 **deluge of calls:** Anderson, p. 117; AP, 1/25/42.

283 **"dumbfounded":** PHA 7, pp. 3133ff.

283 **That same day:** Gordon Prange, the history professor who made chronicling Pearl Harbor his lifework, raised some doubt as to whether Short's reaction to the Commission's finding was the first time the idea of retirement had been raised at the top of the War Department. Scrawled notes, apparently written by Marshall and Stimson, reflect an exchange between the two men about the wording that might be used to accept Short's retirement, and the timing of such a statement. The notes, curiously, appear in the War Department files for January 13th, more than a week before the Commission issued its findings. Was Marshall mulling Short's removal from active duty at that early date? That is possible. On the other hand, and since the notes themselves are undated, they may have been misfiled (PHA 19, pp. 3780, 3797ff).

283 **The following day:** PHA 7, p. 3139. At a meeting the same day, an entry in Stimson's diary shows, Marshall told him that Stark was "hoping that Kimmel would do the same thing" as Short—retire. The apparent fact that Stark expressed such a wish, when discovered by Kimmel years later, would contribute to his later view that Stark had been two-faced (Stimson diary, 1/26/42, STIM).

283 **"to communicate":** PHA 7, p. 3139.

284 *Admiral Jacobs:* Transcript, 1/26/41, Box 102, NIMITZ. Jacobs headed the Bureau of Navigation—shortly to be renamed the Bureau of Naval Personnel.

284 **"an official":** PHA 6, pp. 2561ff.

284 **"Up to that time":** PHA 6, pp. 2561ff; PHA 17, pp. 2728ff.

284 **"forty-one years":** Kimmel to SECNAV, 1/26/42, HEK R12.

285 **"desired":** transcript 1/27/41, Box 102, NIMITZ.

285 **"I most positively"/"corrected":** Stark to Greenslade, 1/27/42, Box 102, NIMITZ.

285 **shown the President:** Stark to Kimmel, 1/27/42, TKK; and see Kimmel to Stark, 12/15/41, STARK.

285 **The issue:** Stimson to Marshall, 2/13/42, Hilldring to Attorney General, 2/14/42, and Attorney General to Stimson, 2/14/42, HEK R12; Stimson diary entries, January–February 1942, STIM.

285 **"It might give":** Stimson diary, 1/26/42, STIM.

285 **"wait":** Stimson diary, 1/28/42, STIM.

285 **"Court-martial," Stark wrote:** Stark to SECNAV, 1/31/42, Box 20, Pearl Harbor Liaison Office files, NARA—supplied to authors by TKK.

286 **"I don't want"/harassment:** Prange, *Dawn*, p. 610.

286 **"brooding":** Greenslade to Stark, 2/13/42, STARK.

286 **"I have every":** Stark to Greenslade, 2/16/42, HEK R4.

287 **pleaded Kimmel's case:** Interview with Harold Stark by Forrest Pogue, Box 31, STARK.

287 **Short would receive a similar letter:** PHA 19, p. 3804.

287 **"without condonation":** Knox to Kimmel, 2/16/42, HEK R12.

CHAPTER 46

288 **"On this occasion":** Stark to Kimmel, 2/21/42, STARK.

288 **trio of letters/"As for Kimmel"/"something definite":** Ibid. and (second letter, same date) Stark to Kimmel, 2/21/42, Stark to "Mustapha," 2/23/42; PHA 17, p. 2729.

288 **It does not seem:** Kimmel, pp. 171ff. Checks confirm that the men who saw fit to send these letters really were judges (Michelsen; *Journal of Criminal Law and Criminology*, Vol. 31, Winter 1940).

289 **Mix:** *St. Louis Post-Dispatch*, 8/2/28.

289 **"Dear Betty":** PHA 17, pp. 2729ff.

290 *Washington Post:* WP, 3/1/42.

290 *New York Times:* NYT, 3/1/42.

291 **"no answer":** Prange, *Dawn*, p. 612.

291 **"Ex-Admiral":** Kranz to Kimmel, 3/8/42, HEK R25.

291 **May/"shooting match":** UP, 4/7/42, HEK R2.

291 **Stark/reshuffle/D-Day:** Simpson, pp. 127ff, 129, 132, 135.

292 **Knox "entire establishment":** Knox to Stark, 3/31/42, Box 2, STARK.

292 **"The President":** Richardson, p. 442.

292 **"administrative action":** King to Sullivan, 7/14/48, Box 4, Stark.

292 **"He was hurt":** Interview with Kathleen Krick by John Toland, TOL.

292 **Spring Valley/"He was about to leave"/"Stark asked me"/would never forgive Stark for:** Memo of meeting, 4/3/42, HEK R15; Brownlow, p. 149; Brownlow to Kimmel, 5/1/66, HEK R34; Stark to Kimmel, 3/20/42, TKK.

293 **Gold Star:** Simpson, p. 132.

293 **Marshall:** Prange, *Verdict*, pp. 231ff; Mosley, p. 202.

293 **"any duty"/acknowledgment:** PHA 17, p. 2728.

293 **modest home:** Unidentified letter to Ned Kimmel, circa 1942, TKK.

293 **secured work/Otterson:** Kimmel to Singleton Kimmel, 4/24/42, and Kimmel to Jacobs, 6/11/42, HEK R25; *NYT*, 7/15/42; Brownlow, p. 150.

294 **"I spend":** Undated clipping, "Kimmel Here, Bars Talk of Pearl Harbor 'Sneak Attack,'" HEK R14.

CHAPTER 47

295 **Manning/three war patrols/Bronze/Silver Stars:** History of the USS *Drum*, Navy Department; Jacobs to Kimmel, undated 11/44 and 11/29/44, Report on Fitness of Officers, 3/28/43, 7/13/43, MMK.

295 **"I can't say":** Manning K. to Kimmels, 6/16/42, HEK R25.

295 **desire to restore:** Blair, p. 626.

295 **Tom/"outstanding":** Interviews with Thomas K. Kimmel Jr., 2015, Blair, pp. 137ff, 147, 149ff, brief biography, with citation, TKK.

296 **Ned/try hard/lobbied:** Kimmel to Jacobs, 1/21/42, 2/22/42, and Jacobs to Kimmel, 1/24/42, Box 102, NIMITZ; Jacobs to Kimmel, 2/25/42, HEK R25.

296 **"stupid"/"How dare?":** Interview with Ned Kimmel by John Toland, Box 120, TOL.

296 **Ranger/sunk:** Ibid.; Reuters flash, 4/25/43; brief biography by Vincent Colan, 8/31/98, TKK.

296 **married:** Interviews with Harriott Kimmel, Thomas K. Kimmel Jr., 2014, 2015.

296 **Tom's bride:** The bride was Nancy Stanley Cookson (Tom Kimmel Sr. to Kimmels, 6/11/42, MMK; interview with Thomas K. Kimmel Jr.;

Nancy Kimmel to friend, undated, TKK; Husband Kimmel, "Adventures of Tom and Nancy Kimmel in the Early Days of the Japanese War," 8/1/45, TKK; correspondence Susan Cookson Stretch, 2014; *Shipmate*, 4/04.

296 **"These young ones":** Kimmel to Singleton, 4/24/42, HEK R25.

297 **"Please do not":** Manning Kimmel to Kimmels, undated 1941, HEK R25.

297 **Fletcher:** Manning Kimmel to Kimmels, 7/10/42, HEK R25.

297 **"realize what had really":** Undated notes by Tom Kimmel Sr., TKK; interview with Tom Kimmel Sr., Box 120, TOL.

297 **Baldwin:** Stillwell, p. iii.

297 **Sprout:** Ned Kimmel to Kimmels, 2/2/42, HEK R25.

298 **"What I have always":** Husband Kimmel, Memorandum of Events in Connection with Pearl Harbor Investigation, 6/6/46, TKK.

298 **"seemed well":** Manning Kimmel to Kimmels, 9/24/42, HEK R25.

298 **"sad":** Unidentified letter to Ned Kimmel, 1942/1943, TKK.

298 **gather records:** Kimmel to Knox, 11/26/43, Box 4, KING.

298 **sworn statements:** E.g., Kimmel to Pye, 10.11/43, Kimmel to McMorris, 12/29/43, HEK R25; re Memorandum of May 18, 1942, 12/19/43, HEK R13.

298 **statute of limitations:** *Washington Times-Herald*, 9/14/43; WP, 9/15/43.

298 **That August, Knox:** Jacobs to SECNAV, 8/17/43, Box 102, NIMITZ; memo by Judge Advocate Gatch, 9/22/44, TKK. General Short, for his part, received a similar request from the Secretary of War, and agreed to it (Joint Army-Navy Statement, 10/2/43, Box 5, BLOCH).

298 **"as an officer"/"in open court":** Knox to Kimmel, 8/27/43, Kimmel to Knox, 9/7/43, HEK R25.

299 **"even though":** Memorandum, undated, 10/43, HEK R15.

299 **There was another reason:** The measure, Public Law 208 (78th Cong.), was approved by Congress and signed by the President on December 20th, 1943. Kimmel's adviser Edward Hanify deemed this ex post facto—passed after the statute of limitations had run out on December 7th, the second anniversary of Pearl Harbor—and thus unconstitutional. [measure: *Extending the Time Limit for Immunity (Pearl Harbor)*, Calendar No. 948, Report No. 935, U.S. Senate, 78th Cong., 2nd Sess., 6/1/44. adviser: Draft memoir, ch. 2, pp. 1off, Box 24, HANIFY.]

300 **Months earlier, acutely:** Press release, 10/11/43, Leonard to Kimmel, 10/13/43, HEK R25. The Marine general, war hero Smedley Butler, had publicly alleged that Italy's dictator Mussolini had killed a child in a hit-and-run accident. The charge, essentially, was that Butler had caused an international incident. As a result of Colonel Leonard's negotiation, and amid a wave of popular support for the colonel, the

court-martial had been canceled and the General was let off with a reprimand (Schmidt, p. 208).

300 **Pearson's column:** E.g., *Lincoln* [NE] *Star*, 10/11/43.

300 **draft letter:** Kimmel to SECNAV, 10/6/43, unsigned and unsent, HEK R13.

300 **promptly disowned:** AP, 10/11/43.

300 **fired Leonard:** Kimmel to Leonard, 10/11/43, HEK R25ff).

301 **Ditter/Whittington:** *NYT*, 1/28/42.

301 **"postponement":** Hanify draft memoir, p. 27, Box 24, HANIFY.

301 **after the war:** King to SECNAV, 12/23/43, Box 4, KING.

301 **"wit's end":** Hanify draft memoir, p. 9, Box 24, HANIFY.

CHAPTER 48

302 **Lavender:** Hanify draft memoir, pp. 16ff, Box 24, HANIFY; *WP*, 7/15/76; Alex Wellerstein, "Patenting the Bomb," *ISIS*, 2008; Kimmel to Lavender, 1/19/44, HEK R25.

302 **Rugg:** Hanify draft memoir, pp. 32ff, Box 24, HANIFY; interview with Edward Hanify, Box 118, TOL.

302 **Hanify/"When I first":** Hanify draft memoir, pp. 1ff, 4, Box 24, HANIFY; and Edward Hanify, "Pearl Harbor: The Effort to Preserve the Truth for History," address to Union Club, Boston, 12/6/79, TKK.

302 **"To any self-respecting":** Hanify draft memoir, p. 21, Box 24, HANIFY.

303 **"He now sat":** Kimmel had at that stage not been permitted to see the testimony or evidence gathered by the Roberts Commission—except his own. The citations of Hanify in this book are from an unedited draft manuscript that he dictated. The authors have on occasion made small adjustments, while always maintaining the sense (Hanify draft manuscript, Box 24, HANIFY).

303 **check was returned:** Kimmel to Rugg, 1/29/44, HEK R25, and 1/8/47, HEK R28.

303 **powerful advocate:** Interviews with Thomas K. Kimmel Jr., Manning Kimmel IV, John Hanify, 2015; Edward Kennedy to Hanify, 12/13/00, courtesy of John Hanify.

303 **Hart chosen:** Navy Department press release, 2/25/44, Box 5, BLOCH; SECNAV to Hart, 2/12/44, HEK R13.

303 **"sort of judge"/"dynamite":** Hart diary, 1/27/44, 2/16/44, Box 9, HART.

303 **"long-dead cats":** Hart Oral History, Columbia University, 1961/1962.

303 **"We had a two-hour":** Hart diary, 2/26/44, Box 9, HART.

304 **In light of the intelligence he assumed:** Safford thought, in particular, that Kimmel had received a warning message which had been drafted by ONI's Commander McCollum on December 4th, 1941, but which—following discussion—had not in fact been sent. (See Chap-

ter 34.) Safford thought too that an authentic Japanese "Winds Execute" weather forecast—signaling a break with the United States—had been intercepted and that Kimmel had been so advised. As reported earlier, however, Safford's notion that a "Winds Execute" was intercepted is not supported by other testimony or evidence. See Chapter 34 (PHA 8, pp. 3858ff, 3878ff).

304 **Then, however, while:** After a search, a file containing many of the missing intercepts would be found in the office safe previously used by Commander Kramer—who had since been transferred to duty overseas. The present authors, however, believe that there may be an innocent explanation for the discovery of the folder in Kramer's safe. Testimony suggests that in late December 1941, when Secretary Knox was in Hawaii, Assistant Navy Secretary James Forrestal—who had not been on the MAGIC distribution list—asked to be briefed. A file had been prepared for him, read, returned, and then placed in the safe—there to lie forgotten until found by Safford in 1943. This background may also partially explain why some key intercepts known to have existed are not listed in the report by Lieutenant Connorton—see Chapter 46—which was prepared in the months following Pearl Harbor. [**Forrestal:** PHA 36, pp. 71, 83ff, 503, 505. **found in 1943:** Safford to Kimmel, undated, 9/53, Safford to Kimmel, 9/29/53, HEK R15; "Memorandum of Feb. 23, 1944." HEK R 13; Harrison to Safford, 1/10/54, HEK R 30; Kimmel to Clark, 3/20/60, TKK.]

304 **internal history/Safford/failed to locate/"a frame-up"/turned up:** Kimmel, pp. 130ff; Hanyok, p. 55; Seamans to Beach, 9/29/97, TKK; PHA 8, pp. 3858ff; Safford to Kramer, 1/22/44, HEK R25; Kramer to Safford, 12/28/43, HEK R13; Brownlow, p. 152; Kimmel to Clark, 3/20/60, TKK; Gannon, 314; Toland, *Infamy*, p. 69.

304 **"as the events"/"I had never":** Undated memorandum, HEK R4.

305 **"almost sick":** Prange, *Dawn*, p. 622.

305 **meeting with advisers:** Hanify draft memoir, p. 100, Box 24, HANIFY.

305 **memorandum:** Memorandum of February, 23, 1944 (as revised May 16, 1944), and affidavit of Laurance Safford, 5/18/44, HEK R13.

305 **"he delivered"/safe/"pillow":** Hanify draft memoir, pp. 16, 99ff, Box 24, HANIFY.

305 **"950 messages":** Ibid., p. 102.

306 **"how to preserve"/unchanged/canny solution:** Ibid., pp. 32ff.

306 **Safford duly referred:** PHA 26, pp. 387ff.

306 **Kimmel declined:** Hanify draft memoir, p. 31, Box 24, HANIFY; Kimmel to SECNAV, 2/29/44, 3/16/44 and SECNAV to Kimmel, 3/4/44, HEK R13.

306 **uneasy:** Hart Oral History, Columbia University, 1961/1962.

306 **"purposely scant":** Hart to Stark, 6/28/44, Box 28, STARK.

306 **"naturally on the other"**: Hart Oral History, Columbia University, 1961/1962.

306 **"carry the investigation"**: Hart to Stark, 6/28/44, Box 28, STARK.

306 **"plot thickens"**: Hart diary, 6/16/44, Box 9, HART.

307 **political ramifications**: E.g., UP, 5/17/44; AP, 5/8/44; Hanify draft memoir, p. 45, Box 24, HANIFY.

307 **conferred privately/Walsh**: Hanify draft memoir, pp. 42ff; Memorandum of Conference Saturday May 27, 1944, Between Sen. David Walsh, Lt. Edward Hanify, and Charles Rugg, HEK R13.

307 **"head this entire"**: Hanify draft memoir, p. 44, Box 24, HANIFY.

307 **press for legislation/maneuvering**: Ibid., pp. 46, 48ff.

307 **At a meeting**: Ibid., pp. 46ff; Hanify, address to Union Club, supra.

308 **"severe pernicious anemia"**: Kimmel to Singleton Kimmel, 3/25/44, Kimmel to Manning Kimmel (son), 4/1/44, HEK R26.

308 **"I was so sick"/baby boy/"It has been"**: Dorothy Kimmel to Lucille Kimmel, 5/4/44, MMK.

308 **"lots of action"**: Manning Kimmel to Kimmels, 6/6/44, MMK.

CHAPTER 49

309 **The Navy Court of Inquiry**: The three admirals were Admiral Orin Murfin, presiding; Admiral Edward Kalbfus; and Vice Admiral Adolphus Andrews.

309 **late July/"whether any offenses"/recommend**: PHA 39, p. 297ff.

309 **"due process"/tussle**: Hanify draft memoir, pp. 58ff, Box 24, HANIFY.

309 **missing/"do no good"/Army insisted not/Lavender was told/limited time/record numbers**: Ibid., pp. 69ff; Husband Kimmel, Memorandum of Events in Connection with Pearl Harbor Investigation, TKK.

310 **"I was astounded"**: Brownlow, p. 153.

310 **dinner/"We were anxious"/"It was one thing"**: Hanify draft memoir, pp. 71ff, 36ff, Box 24, HANIFY.

311 **Rugg persisted/told the court**: Ibid., p. 36; and see, e.g., PHA 32, p. 130.

311 **proposed a bluff**: Hanify draft memoir, pp. 36, 75, Box 24, HANIFY, Brownlow, pp. 154ff.

312 **"shocked and shaken"**: Hanify draft memoir, p. 75, Box 24, HANIFY.

312 **Lavender, who was**: Brownlow, p. 157. The exhibits list of forty-six copies of intercepts filed in the Navy Court of Inquiry does not include the September 24th, 1941, message relating to Tokyo's request that spy reports on Pearl Harbor be categorized by "sub-areas." Safford had, however, described that intercept, and Lavender appears to refer to it here—it is of course an authentic MAGIC message. (See Chapter 16.) Its absence from the exhibits list is an unexplained anomaly. **[exhibits:**

PHA 33, pp. 1346ff. **Safford described:** Edward Hanify, "Pearl Harbor: The Effort to Preserve the Truth for History," address to Union Club, Boston, 12/6/79, TKK.]

312 **"Well, I never saw":** Toland, *Infamy*, p. 91; and see PHA 33, pp. 1346ff.

312 **Murfin, who was presiding:** Toland, *Infamy*, p. 95. Admiral Murfin had once commanded the Asiatic Fleet and the base at Pearl Harbor. Kalbfus had been director of War Plans and had headed the War College. Andrews, who at one point had commanded in Hawaii, still headed the Navy Manpower Survey Board (Prange, *Dawn*, pp. 620ff).

312 **"It's strange":** Dorothy Kimmel to Gay Kimmel, 8/30/44, MMK.

312 **On August 22nd:** Ibid., 9/21/44, MMK.

313 **DeLany:** Toland, *Infamy*, p. 89.

313 **third patrol:** Entry for *Robalo*, U.S. Submarine Losses in World War II, MMK.

313 **hastened home/agreed not call:** Dorothy Kimmel to Gay Kimmel, 9/21/44, MMK.

313 **telegram:** Jacobs to Agatha Gay Kimmel, 8/24/44, MMK.

313 **"Returned":** E.g., letters of 7/27/44, 8/4/44, MMK.

313 **in the press:** UP, 9/6/44.

313 **"an outside chance":** Kimmel to Singleton Kimmel, 9/8/44, HEK R26.

313 **"Hard luck":** Hart diary, 8/24/44, Box 9, HART.

CHAPTER 50

314 *Collier's:* 8/26/44.

314 **They had met:** They had in fact conferred regularly. They played golf every other weekend, and Kimmel was a frequent social guest in Short's home (PHA 26, p. 44; PHA 32, p. 283; Gannon, pp. 17ff).

314 **"Until I am afforded":** Kimmel, pp. 183ff.

314 **Truman's statement:** AP, 8/22/44.

314 **"To date"/Dreyfus:** *Boston Herald*, 8/22/44.

315 **"charged with":** Radio address of 8/30/44 reprinted in *Indiana Gazette*, 9/16/44.

315 **dislodging Roosevelt/rumors:** Freidel, pp. 557ff; Ted Morgan, pp. 738ff; Toland, *Infamy*, p. 129.

316 *Congressional Record:* Prange, *Dawn*, p. 627.

316 **"afraid to let":** Ibid., p. 629.

316 **"Let the people":** UP, 9/6/44; INS, 9/6/44.

316 **"Since the commander in chief":** *Chicago Daily Tribune*, 9/12/44.

316 **Scott/"informed":** UP, 9/6/44.

316 **Harness/messages:** *Chicago Daily Tribune*, 9/12/44.

316 **"A first-class":** *WP*, 9/15/44.

317 **"A recent speech":** Mosley, p. 303.

317 **TOP SECRET/"The most vital"/"related in conception":** Messenger's account reproduced in *Cryptologia*, Vol. 7, No. 2, April 1983; PHA 3, pp. 1127ff.

317 **The Republican candidate:** In testimony in 1945 Marshall would deny that Roosevelt had anything to do with the approach to Dewey in Tulsa. It had, he said, been entirely his own initiative (PHA 3, p. 1139).

318 **"already knew about Pearl"/"behind this"/"preserve"/successful appeal:** Messenger's account reproduced in *Cryptologia*, Vol. 7, No. 2, April 1983; PHA 3, pp. 1127ff.

318 **deliberate untruth:** PHA 3, p. 1128.

319 **Army's Board:** PHA 29, pp. 23ff.

319 **Russell/"Gestapo"/"The most important":** Russell, pp. 9, 13, 46ff.

319 **Marshall's testimony:** PHA 27, pp. 11ff.

320 **Miles:** Ibid., pp. 54ff.

320 **Bryden/McKee:** Ibid., pp. 57, 58ff.

320 **A year later:** Miles owned up to the deception in an affidavit taken by Henry Clausen, the officer who the following year, 1945, was to conduct a secret further investigation for Secretary of War Stimson. The intermediaries who passed on the order by the Chief of Staff that he not tell the truth had been Brigadier General Russell Osman and Colonel Carter Clarke of G-2 (PHA 35, p. 101).

320 **Kimmel's testimony:** PHA 28, pp. 946ff; Brownlow, p. 159; Kimmel, pp. 124ff.

321 **strain:** Russell, p. 99.

321 **"things that should":** Ibid., p. 100.

321 **"the inescapable":** Ibid., pp. 92ff, 94.

321 **Marshall had not authorized:** PHA 35, p. 104; Clausen and Lee, p. 202.

CHAPTER 51

323 **"This poses":** Stimson diary, 10/21/44, STIM.

323 **Army Board report:** PHA 39, p. 173ff.

323 **Navy Court had reported:** PHA 39, pp. 297ff.

324 **Forrestal reacted:** UP, 10/22/44; AP, 10/21/44.

324 **"very strongly":** Stimson diary, 11/1/44, STIM.

325 **President contacted/labored/"his usefulness"/"cross"/"When he saw"/"had a Court"/wrangling:** Stimson diary, entries from 9/26/44 through 12/11/44, STIM.

325 **"several officers"/Short/"to make public":** AP, 12/1/44.

325 **Forrestal/"errors"**: Ibid.

326 **"Top Secret"**: UP, 12/1/44.

326 **"smiling"/"air of gaiety"**: Ibid.

326 **"I request"**: Rugg to Forrestal, 10/24/44, HEK R26.

326 **"submerged"**: Husband Kimmel, Memorandum of Events in Connection with Pearl Harbor Investigation, TKK.

327 **"masterpieces"**: Yarnell to Kimmel, 12/2/44, HRK R26; and see Kimmel, p. ix.

327 **furious**: Kimmel to Rugg, 11/27/44, HEK R26.

327 **meeting with King**: Memorandum of Interview, 12/7/44, TKK.

327 **Far from having cleared**: Drew Pearson, "Washington Merry-Go-Round," 12/7/44. Pearson's column cataloged a number of points that, as presented, made Kimmel—and the Navy—look as bad as possible. It stated, for example, that Naval Intelligence at Pearl had "been not interested" in a last-minute warning from the FBI, and that the Navy had "laughed off" the sighting of a Japanese submarine just before the attack. The last-minute FBI warning was a reference to the "Mori call," covered in Chapter 38 of this book. Fleet intelligence officer Layton had never been briefed on the Mori matter; he had merely been asked—on the eve of the attack—to come to the local ONI office the following morning to discuss an undisclosed matter. He had agreed to do so. A Japanese submarine (probably a midget sub) had been sighted south of Pearl, then fired at and depth-charged, at 6:40 a.m. on December 7th—in line with a Kimmel standing order. The episode had not been "laughed off" but reported up the line. The information reached Kimmel by 7:00 a.m. To the extent that there was a delay, it had been in light of numerous previous false submarine sightings. [**"Mori call"**: Layton with Pineau and Costello, pp. 276ff. **submarine**: Prange, *Dawn*, pp. 496ff.]

328 **Before King and Kimmel met**: PHA 39, pp. 344ff. King also wrote in 328 endorsement that, although no court-martial was warranted, both Kimmel and Stark should be relegated to "positions in which lack of superior judgment may not result in future errors."

328 **written by his deputy**: Simpson, p. 265.

328 **1948 retraction**: King to Sullivan, 7/14/48, Box 4, STARK.

328 **memoir**: King and Whitehill, pp. 355ff.

328 **Gatch**: Memorandum of Interview with RADM Gatch, 12/7/44, HEK R12.

CHAPTER 52

330 **"He was tops"**: Davis to Kimmel, 9/1/44, MMK. As noted in Chapter 46, a Gold Star is awarded in lieu of a second award of an existing honor. In Manning Kimmel's case, it would have been the equivalent

of a second Silver Star (Kimmel to Davis, 10/5/44, Davis to Gay Kimmel, undated, 1944, MMK.

330 **used contacts:** Kimmel to Davis, 10/5/44, Jacobs to Kimmel, 8/30/44, and Jacobs to Gay Kimmel, 9/13/44, MMK.

330 **"We haven't":** Wilkerson to Gay Kimmel, 10/23/44, MMK (all names spelled phonetically).

330 **"We have received":** Wlodarczyk to Gay Kimmel, 11/17/44, MMK.

330 **"Maybe they are":** Gleason to Gay Kimmel, 9/16/44, MMK.

330 **"Harold":** Ramfier to Gay Kimmel, 9/22/44, MMK.

330 **"I have been crying":** Johnson to Gay Kimmel, 10/6/44, MMK.

330 **"A friend":** Bailey to Gay Kimmel, 9/21/44, MMK.

331 **"We must not":** Tom Kimmel Sr. to Kimmels, 9/7/44, MMK.

331 **"My three boys":** Dorothy Kimmel to Davis, 11/12/44, MMK.

331 **The Admiral resolved:** E.g., Kimmel to Rugg, 4/14/45, HEK R27.

331 **The further investigations:** UP, 12/2/44; AP, 12/1/44. For two months in the spring of 1945, a further one-man Navy inquiry was conducted by Vice Admiral Kent Hewitt, to look into matters arising from the Navy Court's probe. Kimmel did not participate. Numerous witnesses were heard for the first time, with the emphasis on what had been gleaned from intelligence. No solid basis was found for Safford's insistence that a "Winds Execute" message had been intercepted before the Japanese strike. Hewitt faulted Admiral Stark for having failed to send Kimmel "important information," yet said Kimmel had had "sufficient information" on the "unusually serious" nature of the situation. Hewitt maintained, moreover, that the "most probable approach" sector from which an attack might come could have been covered by "partial air reconnaissance." As noted in Chapter 28, expert advice supplied to Kimmel had specified no approach that posed the most peril.

For the Army, Deputy Chief of G-2 Colonel Carter Clarke focused on the handling of secret documents, briefly pursued the issue as to whether a "Winds Execute" message had ever come in, and found that none had. (During the 1944 election campaign, Clarke had been the go-between used by Chief of Staff Marshall to make contact with the Republican candidate Thomas Dewey.) Much more thoroughly, throughout 1945 and focusing above all on MAGIC, Lieutenant Colonel Henry Clausen interviewed ninety-two witnesses worldwide. He also obtained voluminous documentary evidence. Though his report made no finding as such, he would tell Congress' Joint Committee in 1946 that there had been a failure to share or properly evaluate MAGIC. Clausen advocated the creation of one agency to coordinate intelligence. "Otherwise," he testified, "we are liable to have Pearl Harbor all over again." In 1992, he assembled his views in book form. In the book, he asserted that Kimmel had "withheld vital information from Short and his own command." He faulted the Admiral for not having shared information that the Japanese were destroying their codes and code machines, and for not having asked headquarters for "clarification of what Washington really knew or what Washington wanted him to do." [**Hewitt:** PHA 39, pp. 393ff, 523; Prange, *Dawn*, pp. 662ff. **Clarke:** Ibid., pp. 669ff. **go-between:** See Chapter 50. **Clausen:** PHA 9, pp. 4437ff, 4469; PHA 35, 1ff; Clausen and Lee, pp. 223, 300ff.]

331 **In light of:** *NYT*, 12/5/44. Krock was honored by the Pulitzer Prize Board three times during his long career. He won the prize in 1935 and 1938, and in 1951—when he was himself a member of the Pulitzer Advisory Board—was given a Special Citation (www.pulitzer.org).

332 **Ferguson had long been calling:** *WP*, 6/7/44.

332 **findings should be provided:** AP, 12/1/44.

332 **"The people":** UP, 12/2/44.

332 **bill/"cryptanalysis"/"I was desperate"/met publisher/Ferguson/Bill defeated:** Kimmel, pp. 127ff; Husband Kimmel, Memorandum of Events Leading to the Congressional Investigation of Pearl Harbor Behind the Scenes, TKK; Brownlow, pp. 163ff; Prange, *Dawn*, pp. 670ff; S. 805, A Bill to Insure Further the Military Security of the U.S., 79th Cong. 1st Sess.; *WP*, 4/12/45.

333 **"Mr. Roosevelt's death":** Kimmel to Rugg, 4/14/45, HEK R27.

333 **reports released:** *NYT*, 8/30/45.

333 **press conference:** News conference, 8/30/45.

334 **Newspapers:** Cited in *NYT*, 8/31/45.

334 **voted unanimously:** *New York Herald Tribune*, 9/12/45.

334 **October/Truman approved:** McCrea to Dietrich, 10/31/45, TKK; Hanyok, p. 62.

334 **Senate's caucus room/Kimmel/Short/"easily"/"Intercepted Messages":** *New York Sun*, 11/15/45.

335 **"Kimmel Alarm":** *Chicago Herald*, 12/10/45. See Chapter 33.

335 **"Intercepted 'Wind' ":** Unidentified clipping, 11/16/45, HEK R14.

335 **"Navy's War Tip":** Unidentified clipping, 12/12/45, HEK R14.

335 **"Probers Talk":** *New York Daily News*, 11/10/45.

335 **"Navy Is Accused":** *New York Herald Tribune*, 11/13/45.

335 **Kramer had earlier told/denied being "badgered":** PHA 33, pp. 853ff; PHA 9, pp. 3942ff, 3964ff.

335 **"Turner Guessed":** Unidentified clipping, 12/20/45, HEK R14.

335 **"Naval Expert":** [Columbus, IN] *Republic*, 1/28/46.

336 **The news the next day:** *Arizona Republic*, 1/30/46. Zacharias did reportedly say he expected an attack on Pearl in November 1941—to Curtis Munson, a civilian on an information-gathering mission to the Pacific for the State Department; and to Lorrin Thurston, editor of the *Honolulu Advertiser*. A 2008 article by David Pfeiffer of the National

Archives described Zacharias as a "colorful and controversial figure" who did not receive the recognition he deserved. His claim to have discussed the possibility of a Japanese raid on Pearl Harbor with Kimmel in February 1941 is neither provable nor disprovable. [**State Department:** PHA 6, pp. 2679ff. **David Pfeiffer:** "Sage Prophet or Loose Cannon?" *NARA Magazine*, Vol. 40, No. 2, 2008.]

336 **Kimmel recalled no such:** PHA 6, p. 2639.

336 **"Marshall Again":** *Tennessean*, 12/13/45.

336 **"I had an immense":** *NYT*, 12/13/45.

336 **Why had Marshall not:** *Pittsburgh Press*, 12/9/45.

336 **"Stark Says Kimmel":** *NYT*, 1/1/46.

336 **had not occured to Stark:** PHA 5, p. 2260.

336 **"Inquiry Charged":** *New York Sun*, 11/16/45.

337 **"Did President Roosevelt":** *Chicago Daily News*, 11/14/45.

337 **Ned on occasion:** *Washington Times-Herald*, 12/11/45.

337 **to make his case:** *NYT*, 1/22/46.

337 **"information":** PHA 6, p. 2498.

337 **"quite as much":** PHA 6, p. 2835.

337 **"complete security":** PHA 6, p. 2834.

337 **"radically"/"Knowledge"/"ambush":** PHA 6, p. 2543.

337 **"I was Commander-in-Chief":** PHA 6, p. 2752.

338 **"That is a reasonable":** PHA 6, p. 2751.

338 **magnificently/applauded:** *NYT*, 1/22/46.

338 **a number of significant:** E.g., Index of Witnesses, PHA; Edward Hanify, Draft Report for the Minority, TKK.

338 **memories were confused:** E.g., Stark to Ingersoll, 10/11/45, Stark to Turner, 10/11/45, Stark to Wellborn, 10/31/45, and Marshall to Stark, 12/3/45, Box A4, STARK.

338 **"certain twilight zones":** PHA 11, p. 5538.

338 **findings:** PHA Report, p. 251ff.

338 **blameless:** *NYT*, 2/24/46; *Life*, 9/24/45.

338 **"responsibilities":** *NYT*, 7/21/46; PHA Report, pp. 573ff.

338 **"careful"/"hesitated"/"Had greater":** PHA Report, pp. 251ff.

339 **Notwithstanding all this:** For the Committee's full report, of necessity truncated here, see the majority's "Conclusions and Recommendations," PHA Report, pp. 251ff.

339 **"immeasurably":** Kimmel to Singleton Kimmel, 10/16/46, HEK R27.

339 **"stood up":** Hanify draft memoir, p. 42, Box 24, HANIFY.

339 **"The fog":** *NYT*, 2/24/46.

CHAPTER 53

341 **"Finding of Death":** Signed by Forrestal, 1/17/46, MMK.

341 **report months earlier:** King to Kimmel, 5/6/45 and attachments, MMK.

341 **Another report, however:** Ibid. Captain Marshall Austin, former commander of the submarine USS *Redfin*, which had been sent into the area at the relevant time, would many years later provide a cogent account to Manning's daughter. A freed U.S. prisoner of war he questioned, Austin said, had talked with Ensign Samuel Tucker, who had survived the sinking and had been captured. By Tucker's account, he and Manning and some others "on the bridge at the time the *Robalo* struck a mine, were blown into the water as the submarine sank . . . Manning made it to the water's edge on Cameron Island and was shot as he was walking ashore. He was sure that Manning died as a result of being shot . . . Tucker and at least one sailor were taken prisoner and transported to the Puerta Princesa prison camp."

An Ensign Tucker had indeed served aboard *Robalo*, and captured Japanese documents indicated that he and three other crewmen did survive the sinking and were captured. None of the four men, however, emerged alive at the end of the war.

A 1975 account, drawing on interviews with Rear Admiral Ralph Christie, commander of the task force of which the *Robalo* was part, had it that Manning Kimmel and perhaps *six* men survived and were imprisoned at Puerta Princesa. Manning supposedly died when, following a U.S. air raid, enraged Japanese soldiers "pushed Kimmel and some other POW's in a ditch, then poured gasoline into the ditch and set it on fire." This story was published in a 1975 book on submarine warfare in the Pacific by author Clay Blair—contrary to the wishes of Manning's brother Tom, himself a former submarine commander. This horrific account of Manning's supposed death aside, Tom Kimmel judged Christie's overall analysis of the loss of the *Robalo* inaccurate.

The authors' reading of the extensive file in Kimmel family archives on the *Robalo*'s fate produced no evidence that Manning and six men survived to become prisoners. Nor was there information to support Christie's account of Manning's alleged death at Puerto Princesa. Dennis Wrynn, author of a detailed account of events at the prison camp and the December 1944 massacre of American prisoners there, considered Christie's assessment "incorrect." [**Austin:** Gay Kimmel to Marshall Austin, undated, 10/86, Austin to Agatha Kimmel, 10/30/86, MMK. **Tucker:** King to Kimmel, 5/6/45, attaching Rear Admiral Daubin report, Kimmel to Ned Kimmel, 6/4/45 and attachment re Palawan POWs, MMK. **Tucker/None:** Atkinson to Kimmel, 11/30/45, Kimmel to Wurzler, 1/30/46, MMK. **Christie:** Blair, pp. 687ff; Blair to Kimmel, Blair to Tom Kimmel Sr., 7/9/73, Tom Kimmel Sr. to Blair, 7/14/73, and Tom Kimmel Sr. reply to Blair's questions, 11/17/72, TKK. **Wrynn:** Wrynn to Tom Kimmel Jr., 9/10/97; *World War II*, magazine, 11/87; *Barnes Review*, 9/97.]

341 **made it to the shore/shot:** Kimmel to Ned Kimmel, 6/4/45 and Extracts from files of Palawan Military Police Detachment, Interrogations 1/8–10/10/44, MMK, USS *Robalo*, www.subsowespac.org.

341 **further fragments:** Kimmel to Chief, Naval Personnel, 11/3/45, Connell to Bolster, 12/9/45, Martin to Kimmel, 12/26/45, MMK.

341 **pressed for more information:** Kimmel to Chief, Naval Personnel, 1/24/46.

341 **"I see no good":** Kimmel to Ned Kimmel, 6/4/45, MMK; Kimmel to Tom Kimmel Sr., 5/10/45, HEK R27.

341 **"I am afraid":** Kimmel to Wurzler, 1/30/46, MMK.

342 **address book:** MMK.

342 **"son-of-a-bitch":** Interview with Ned Kimmel by John Toland, Box 120, TOL.

342 **Tom transferred/given a command:** Tom Kimmel Sr. to Blair, 11/72, TKK; Memories of Thomas K. Kimmel, website of SS320; Kimmel to Singleton Kimmel, 10/16/45, HEK R27.

342 **U-boats:** *New York Daily News*, 5/16/45.

342 **wreaths:** U.S. Navy photo 496257, 10/28/46.

342 **Dorothy/lies/bumped:** Interview with Harriott Kimmel, 2014; Kimmel, pp. 185ff, 91.

342 **Barkley:** *NYT*, 1/19/46.

342 **"We are both":** Dorothy Kimmel to Lucille and Manning Kimmel, 10/23/45.

343 **"You have worked":** Tom Kimmel Sr. to Kimmel, 3/9/46, HEK R28.

343 **"never again":** Kimmel to Singleton Kimmel, 1/25/46, HEK R28.

343 **During hearings/shake hands/"mad":** Interview with David Richmond, Box 14, Folder 1, SIMPSON. See Chapter 46.

343 **"I will always":** PHA 17, pp. 2729ff.

343 **"As always":** Stark to Kimmel, 3/20/42, TKK.

343 **"one of the closest":** PHA 5, pp. 2451ff.

343 **"I felt that":** *NYT*, 1/17/46.

344 **effusive note:** Stark to Kimmel, 2/12/43, HEK R25.

344 **In the fall:** Stark to Kimmel, 9/27/43, HEK R25. Ned Kimmel would one day recall this shipboard encounter with Stark. The older man's reaction, he said, had in fact been "formal . . . cool." Stark, who was in the *Ranger*'s barbershop when approached by Ned, may merely have been taken aback, astonished to meet a Kimmel family member so far from home (interview with Edward Kimmel, TOL, Box 120).

344 **"smiling and obsequious":** Draft memo by Edward Hanify, 2/4/45, courtesy of John Hanify.

344 **Kimmel's mood was:** Hart to Stark, 6/28/44, Box 28, STARK. Admiral Hart, the former commander in the Philippines, not only earlier collected testimony from many witnesses—as reported in Chapter 50—but went on immediately afterward to act as Stark's counsel during the Navy Court process.

344 **"unfortunate"/"very secret":** Hart to Stark, 6/28/44, Box 28, STARK.

345 **better had he kept a diary:** Stark to Hart, 6/2/44, Box 4, HART; Stark to Hart, 7/15/44, Box 28, STARK.

345 **seven days:** PHA 32, p. 11ff, 21ff, 54ff, 69ff, 93ff, 121ff, 145ff.

345 **"curious amnesia":** Hanify draft memoir, p. 78, Box 24, HANIFY.

345 **"I don't recall":** PHA 33, pp. 729ff; PHA 32, pp. 55ff, 132ff.

345 **Less than three weeks:** See Chapter 49.

345 **called to testify again/All had been decoded:** PHA 16, p. 2388; PHA 33, pp. 793ff; PHA 32, p. 527.

346 **"important development"/"I may be":** PHA 32, p. 99.

346 **"Perhaps":** Stark to Hart, 9/20/44, Box 28, STARK.

346 **"awful liar":** Kimmel to Singleton Kimmel, 2/15/46, HEK R28.

346 **note of sympathy/"No answer":** Stark to Kimmel, 8/24/44, HEK R26.

347 **"Dear Mustapha":** Stark to Kimmel, 12/12/44, HEK R26.

347 **"I am astonished" Kimmel consulted:** Kimmel to Lavender, 12/28/44, drafts Kimmel to Stark, 12/28/44, Kimmel to Yarnell, 12/28/44, 1/19/45, Kimmel to Rugg, 12/28/44, 1/8/45, Rugg to Kimmel, 12/29/44, 1/9/45, Yarnell to Kimmel, 1/2/45, HEK R27; undated drafts, Kimmel to Stark, HEK R35.

    In his book on the case, Michael Gannon wrote that Kimmel drafted this letter "in the last year of his life"—1968. The multiple drafts in the Kimmel file indicate that they were in fact written in late December 1944 and early 1945 (Gannon, p. 282).

CHAPTER 54

349 **"When I finished":** Kimmel to Blake, 1/8/51, TKK.

349 **moved to Connecticut:** Kimmel to Blake, 4/7/55, TKK.

349 **Halsey:** Halsey and Bryan, pp. 82, 70.

350 **"outrageous":** Kimmel, p. 168.

350 **Yarnell/"disgraceful":** Barnes, p. 423.

350 **"cause of the disaster":** Yarnell to Rugg, 7/5/46, TKK.

350 **Admiral Raymond Spruance:** Spruance to Morison, 11/29/61, TKK. Admiral Thomas C. Kinkaid would say he thought Kimmel was a scapegoat who had "had to take the rap . . . was very unjustly treated." Because Kinkaid was Dorothy Kimmel's older brother, his view might be thought not to be impartial. For that reason only, his comments

have not been included in the main text (Thomas C. Kinkaid oral history, Columbia University, 1961).

351 **"a dirty":** Interview with Raymond Spruance, Series V.2, Box 74, GP.

351 **cramped room:** [New London, CT] *Evening Day,* 2/28/49.

351 **"We'd drive":** Interview with Harriott Kimmel, 2014.

351 **logical next step:** [New London, CT] *Evening Day,* 2/28/49.

351 **"so emotionally":** Kimmel to Blake, 1/30/55, TKK.

351 **heart attack:** Kimmel to Blake, 1/8/51, Dorothy Kimmel to Anderson, 7/26/50, Box 10, ANDERSON.

351 **ambulance:** Interview with Harriott Kimmel, 2014.

351 **In late 1954:** The 200-page book, *Admiral Kimmel's Story,* was dedicated to "The Officers and Men Who Fought and Died at Pearl Harbor."

351 **"I deem":** Kimmel, p. 2.

351 **"I cannot":** Ibid., p. 169.

351 **greatly upset:** McCrea to Turner, 12/17/54, TKK.

352 **"snotty":** Kimmel to Tom Kimmel Sr., 12/31/60, HEK R32.

352 **reviews/"brush-off":** Kimmel to A.J., 4/7/55, TKK.

352 **No newspaper challenged:** Kimmel to Clemens, 10/2/55, HEK R29.

352 **rank/Holloway:** Chief Naval Personnel to SECNAV, 4/27/54, TKK.

352 **A law passed:** The relevant section of the 1947 Officer Personnel Act stipulated, "Any officer of the Navy . . . in the discretion of the President, by and with the advice and consent of the Senate, when retired, [may] be placed on the retired list with the highest grade or rank held by him." The same applied to Army officers—General Short's name had likewise been the only one omitted from the equivalent Army list. Later, some years after the law was enacted, members of Congress raised the matter of Kimmel's and Short's anomalous ranks. Navy Secretary Thomas Gates, however, responded that he did not think it would be "in the best interest of the Nation," or of Kimmel, to raise him to four-star rank in retirement. [law: Public Law 381, 80th Congress, 1st Session, 8/7/47, Sections 413, 414, 504. **Congress:** E.g., Shafroth to Smith, 7/30/55, Kimmel to Rugg, 7/31/55, HEK R29, Rankin to Smith, 6/24/57, Morton to SecNav, 7/8/57, Cooper to SecNav, 7/31/57, TKK. **Gates:** Gates to Cooper, 8/27/57, TKK.]

352 **Several years later:** Evidence that Stark concurred with the notion, which would be under discussion once more in 1960, derives from two letters—one to Admiral Arleigh Burke and another to Kimmel himself—written by Admiral Charles "Savvy" Cooke, who had been corresponding with Stark. [discussion: E.g., Wedemeyer to Secretary of the Army, 12/15/60, Judd to Wedemeyer, 12/23/60, Sec. Army to Wedemeyer, 1/9/61, HEK R32. **Stark:** Cooke to Burke, 12/2/60, Cooke to Kimmel, 12/7/60, HEK R32.]

352 **written for grandchildren:** Kimmel to A.J., 4/7/55, TKK.

352 **visitors/bountiful/"ship's watch"/"commanding"/"talked loud"/"well versed"/papers:** Interviews and correspondence, Thomas Kimmel Jr., Manning Kimmel IV, Dorothy Kimmel Newlin, Husband Kimmel II, Edward Kimmel Jr., Harriott Kimmel Silliman, William Kimmel, Virginia Kimmel Herrick, 2015, 2016.

353 **full story had yet to be told:** [New London, CT] *Evening Day*, 2/28/49.

353 **still said:** [Chicago] *American*, 12/7/61; AP, 5/15/68.

353 **"He spent":** Interviews with Manning Kimmel IV, Harriott Kimmel, 2015; *Daily News*, 12/7/66.

353 **A number of his:** Even before the end of the war, author and columnist John Flynn had produced a pamphlet on the theme that Roosevelt and his advisers had been plotting war with Japan since as early as January 1941. An early revisionist author was George Morgenstern, an editorial writer for the anti-Roosevelt *Chicago Tribune*, who assailed the Roosevelt administration's handling of negotiations with Japan. Charles Beard, an influential historian and author, had been a prominent voice opposing U.S. involvement in the war. He and another historian, Charles Tansill, suggested that Roosevelt intentionally lured Japan into opening hostilities. Harry Elmer Barnes, a former historian turned freelance writer, was not only an isolationist but an apologist for Nazi Germany. He suggested that Roosevelt had intentionally provoked the strike on Hawaii.

A 1954 book by Rear Admiral Robert Theobald, who had been commander, Battle Force, at the time of Pearl Harbor, falls into a somewhat different category. Theobald suggested that Roosevelt had "enticed" Japan into initiating hostilities. Both Kimmel and Admiral Halsey wrote forewords to this book. In his foreword, Kimmel wrote that the book was "convincing." Halsey's comments were favorable but noncommittal. [**Flynn:** Flynn, *The Final Secret of Pearl Harbor*; Mintz, pp. 18ff. **Morgenstern:** Morgenstern, *Pearl Harbor* and, e.g., *New York Herald Tribune*, 2/9/47; Kimmel to Rugg, citing letter from Morgenstern, 1/8/47, HEK R28; Mintz, pp. 10, 19ff. **Beard:** Beard, *President Roosevelt and the Coming of the War*; Mintz, pp. 1ff, 19; *Foreign Affairs*, 10/48. **Tansill:** Tansill, *Back Door to War*; Mintz, pp. 1ff, 20, 26ff; *Foreign Affairs*, 10/52; *American Historical Review*, Vol. 58, No. 1, 10/52. **Barnes:** Barnes, pp. 639ff, 631ff; Mintz, pp. 1ff, 50ff. **Theobald:** Theobald, pp. vff, viiff.]

353 **by his own account:** Husband Kimmel, *Facts About Pearl Harbor*, Groton, CT: self-published, 1958, p. 7.

354 **Perkins:** Reminiscences of Frances Perkins, Oral History Project, Columbia University, 1955.

354 **Richardson/"impelled":** Richardson as told to Dyer, p. 451.

354 **"not at liberty":** *NYT*, 12/7/61.

354 **"My principal":** *New York Daily News*, 12/7/66.

354 **stickler:** Thomas Kimmel Sr., Impressions of My Father, 1966, TKK.

355 **"not too stable":** Observation of Gordon Prange, Kimmel interview, Series V.2., Box 56, GP.

355 **"any idea":** Kimmel to Tom Kimmel, 9/5/63, TKK.

355 **papers:** Kimmel to Tom and Ned Kimmel, 8/11/65, University of Wyoming to Tom Kimmel Sr., 12/19/91, TKK.

355 **"that the Government":** Interview with Edward Kimmel Jr., 2015. Kimmel chose the University of Wyoming. The Admiral's son Tom maintained the collection for some time following his father's death, pending its deposit at the university. The papers are available on microfilm, and the authors perused them extensively in 2015 (interview with Thomas Kimmel Jr.).

355 **"Naval Academy cemetery":** Kimmel to Tom Kimmel Sr., 9/5/63.

355 **died:** Death certificate, 5/14/68.

355 **The large stone:** USNA cemetery documentation project, section 02–0243A. Dorothy Kimmel, who lived until 1975, is buried with her husband.

CODA

357 **four stars:** Correspondence Tom Kimmel Jr.

357 **"I do not want":** Kimmel to Tom Kimmel Sr., 6/25/45, HEK R27.

357 **Tom retired/Westinghouse:** Interview with Tom Kimmel Jr., 2015; obituary 12/97, TKK.

357 **Ned/DuPont:** Interview with Manning Kimmel IV; [Wilmington, DE] *News-Journal*, 7/6/05.

357 **"played an important":** SECNAV to Dorothy Kimmel, 5/28/68, Tom Kimmel Sr. to SECNAV, 6/7/68, TKK.

358 **hidden facts, wherever:** Tom Kimmel Sr. to Greaves, 3/4/83, Box 13, Folder 1, HANIFY.

358 **"loyal as a dog":** Interview with Tom Kimmel Jr., 2014.

358 **"for the name":** [Annapolis, MD] *Intelligencer-Record*, undated, 1991, TKK.

358 **Ned labored/"war room":** Interviews with Harriott Kimmel, Manning Kimmel IV, Edward Kimmel Jr., Dorothy Kimmel Newlin, Harriott Kimmel Silliman, 2015.

358 **"My father gave":** [Louisville, KY] *Courier-Journal*, 4/28/02.

358 **"He'd sit there"/forty hours:** Interviews with Manning Kimmel IV, Edward Kimmel Jr., 2014.

358 **"hook":** Interview with Harriott Kimmel, 2014.

358 **"Bringing":** Edward Kimmel, "How History Has Touched Me," 11/4/99, TKK.

359 **"I think"**: Interview with Virginia Kimmel Herrick, 2015.

359 **Pearl Harbor Survivors/resolution/invited:** Cobb to Tom and Ned Kimmel, 5/7/86, 6/4/86, Tom Kimmel Sr. to Cobb, 5/11/86, 8/2/86, 11/10/86, 12/15/86; *Florida Times-Union*, 12/7/87.

359 **"We all"**: Interview with Tom Kimmel Jr., 2014.

359 **"wondering"**: Interview with William Kimmel, 2014.

359 **roared:** Interview with Tom Kimmel Jr., 2014; Tom Kimmel remarks, 12/8/86, TKK; *Navy Times*, 12/8/86.

360 **"While there is"**: Pearl Harbor Survivors Association, resolution, 1986, TKK.

360 **Encouraged, the Kimmel brothers:** Interviews with Tom Kimmel Jr., Manning Kimmel IV. In 1987, the Kimmels wrote to the Board of Correction of Naval Records, asserting that their father had been singled out for unjust treatment when—after the war—he had been the only Navy officer excluded from retirement at the highest rank at which he had served. The Board declined to review the case, stating that a review was not within its authority. The Army's Board of Correction, however, responded favorably in 1991 to a similar application by General·Short's family. There had been "injustice," the board said. That finding, though, was in turn overruled by the then–Deputy Assistant Secretary of Defense.

The Kimmel brothers also wrote to presidents Ronald Reagan, George H. W. Bush, Bill Clinton, and George W. Bush. [**Navy board:** Application, 4/7/87, Pfeiffer to Susman, 6/9/87, TKK. **Army board:** Goldberg to Van Alstyne and attachments, 8/9/01, Finding 12, TKK. **presidents:** E.g., Ned Kimmel to Reagan, 5/16/88; Tom and Ned Kimmel to George H. W. Bush, 10/16/91; Ned Kimmel to George W. Bush, 2/6/02 and 11/1/02; Manning Kimmel IV to Clinton, 12/21/94, TKK.]

360 **Secretary of the Navy recommended:** Ball to SECDEF, 12/7/88, TKK.

360 **Carlucci declined:** Taft to Thurmond, 2/21/89, TKK.

360 **Contacted/Cheney suggested/"seek"**: Ned Kimmel to Cheney, 5/5/8, Cheney to Montgomery, 10/23/89, Edward Kimmel Jr. To Cheney, 12/28/89, TKK.

360 **1990 resolution:** PHSA to Ned Kimmel, 1/14/91, TKK.

360 **Academy:** Resolution, 10/25/90, TKK.

360 **Nimitz Foundation:** Resolution, 5/30/91.

360 **fulfilled/"the promotion process"**: Tom and Ned Kimmel to Cheney, 5/29/91, Cheney to Ned Kimmel, 8/21/91, TKK.

360 **Taussig:** Unidentified clipping, 1/13/90; Taussig to Editor, *Navy Times*, undated 1990; *Navy Times*, unidentified clipping 1990, TKK.

361 **five senators:** Biden et al. to George H. W. Bush, 10/17/91, MMK.

361 **No fewer than thirty-six:** The former Chairman of the Joint Chiefs who signed the petition was Admiral William Crowe. The CNOs were admirals Thomas Moorer (himself a Pearl Harbor veteran), James Holloway III, Elmo Zumwalt, and Thomas Hayward. Admiral Arleigh Burke wrote separately to the Secretary of Defense in support of promotion. The Pacific Fleet commanders in chief were Donald Davis, Sylvester Foley Jr., Noel Gayler, Huntington Hardisty, Ronald Hays, John Hyland, Roy Johnson, Robert Long, Ulysses Sharp, and Maurice Weisner. Admiral James Lyons added his name later. Admiral Carlisle Trost, who as CNO in 1988 had declined to support the Kimmel sons' request that their father be posthumously promoted, reversed himself on reviewing the evidence. Accordingly, he wrote to the Secretary of the Navy withdrawing his earlier rejection of promotion. [**petition:** Signatories to Bush, 10/22/91, TKK. **Burke:** Burke to Cheney, 7/24/91, TKK. **Trost declined:** Trost to SecNav, 1/19/88, TKK. **Trost reversed himself:** Trost to SecNav, 10/4/94.]

362 **Kimmel brothers wrote:** Ned and Tom Kimmel to Bush, 10/16/91, TKK.

363 **"do no honor":** Trefry to Ned Kimmel, 11/19/91, TKK.

363 **Clinton's first term:** Clinton to Manning Kimmel IV, 12/1/94, and Manning Kimmel IV to Clinton, 12/21/94, TKK.

363 **"In desperation":** Ned Kimmel, "Watershed Events," supra.

363 **Thurmond convened a hearing/Secretary of the Navy:** Transcript of meeting, 4/27/95; remarks of Tom, Ned, and Manning Kimmel, 4/27/95; interviews with Manning Kimmel IV, Tom Kimmel Jr., William Kimmel, 2015; Thurmond to Perry, 5/17/95; *Naval History,* July/August 1995.

363 **Dorn's report:** Dorn to Kimmel, 12/29/95, White to Thurmond, 12/27/95, and Memorandum for the Secretary of Defense by Edwin Dorn, 12/15/95, TKK.

363 **Survivors Association/"Nothing":** Press release, circa 3/16/98.

364 **Hanify had been quietly:** Hanify to Tom and Ned Kimmel, 11/20/86, TKK.

364 **He had reached out:** AP, 9/2/69; *Chicago Tribune,* 10/9/69. There had been a national furor in 1969 after an accident in which the last surviving Kennedy brother, then a young senator, drove off a bridge on Chappaquiddick Island in Massachusetts. A young woman, Mary Jo Kopechne, who had for a time been on his brother Robert's staff, drowned.

364 **Kennedy had long:** Hanify to Susman, 12/16/88, Hanify and Susman to Kennedy, 1/3/89, Kennedy to Clinton, 10/15/99, Kennedy to Podesta, 1/20/99, Kennedy to Ned Kimmel, 12/17/99, Asst. SECNAV to Kennedy, 12/20/99, TKK.

364 **Biden and Roth sponsored:** Press release, re resolution re amendment 388 as part of S.1059, 5/25/99; Ned Kimmel, "Watershed Events," supra.

364 **Senate approved/died in House:** Ned Kimmel, "Watershed Events," supra. Roll call vote, 5/25/99, Temp. Cong. Record p. S-5915, TKK.

364 **House Armed Services Committee:** Ned Kimmel, "Watershed Events," supra.

364 **Defense Authorization Bill/passed:** Ibid.; Floyd D. Spence National Defense Authorization for Fiscal Year 2001, 106th Cong., 2nd Sess, Section 537; Ned Kimmel to Opinion Page Editors, 9/13/00, and memo, undated, TKK.

364 **"still reeling":** Ned Kimmel to Spratt, 6/12/00, Ned Kimmel to Kennedy, 6/26/00, TKK.

364 **Senators wrote:** Biden et al. to Clinton, 12/15/00, TKK.

364 **House members:** Spratt et al. to Clinton, 12/12/00, TKK.

364 **Clinton, however, left office:** In an October 2000 statement on the overall bill, Clinton suggested that certain matters—including "congressional members' requests for the review and determination of proposals for posthumous or honorary promotions"—were "precatory rather than mandatory." In other words, whether or not a president responds to the request is discretionary (Clinton Statement on Signing Floyd D. Spence National Defense Authorization Act for Fiscal Year 2001, 10/30/00).

365 **"no cheap whiskey":** Notebook, undated 2000, MMK; interviews with Harriott Kimmel, Manning Kimmel IV, 2014.

365 **letters to George W. Bush:** 1/10/02, 2/6/02, 11/1/02, 6/3/04, TKK.

365 **aide responded:** Card to Ned Kimmel, 11/4/02, TKK.

365 **"doggone thing":** Interview with Manning Kimmel IV.

365 **Tom/Ned died:** Tom Kimmel, obituary 1/23/97, TKK; [Wilmington, DE] *News-Journal*, 7/6/05.

365 **widow did contrive:** Manning Kimmel IV to Tom Kimmel Jr. et al., 1/26/07, Harriott Kimmel to Colan, 4/29/07, Colan to Harriot Kimmel, 4/30/07, Harriott Kimmel to Rove, 5/14/07, Hipp to Harriott Kimmel, 7/2/07.

365 **remained unchanged:** Carr to Harriott Kimmel, 7/18/07.

365 **"so that I don't":** Gannett News Service, 9/7/98.

365 **swords:** Correspondence Tom Kimmel Jr., 2016.

365 **"Our commitment":** Interview with Singleton Kimmel, 2015.

366 **Two men now lead:** Interviews with Kimmel family, 2014, 2015, 2016.

366 **brush-offs:** E.g., Carr to Manning Kimmel IV, TKK.

366 **"blue-suit":** *Life*, 12/91.

366 **Baker/"long-held":** Baker to Carr, 3/17/87, 4/8/87, Box 13, Folder 2, HANIFY.

366 **Thomas:** Thomas to Wolfowitz, 4/3/02, TKK.

367 **Obama presidency:** Correspondence Tom Kimmel, 2016, Tom Kimmel to Moran, 12/7/14, Moran to Tom Kimmel, 1/26/15, Tom Kimmel to Hagel, 8/2/13, 12/7/14, Tom Kimmel to Navas, 3/18/13, Beyler to Kimmel, 4/22/14 TKK.

367 **"most tragic":** Biden conversation with Manning Kimmel IV, 10/1/07; correspondence Manning Kimmel IV, 2016.

367 **In the final months:** Correspondence & phone exchanges with Manning Kimmel IV, Tom Kimmel Jr., & Fran Person, 2016.

367 **Biden note:** Attachment to email from Manning Kimmel IV, 11/4/15, & facsimile in Irish Echo, 12/14-20/16.

367 **Authors wrote:** Authors to Biden, 3/27/17, authors to Terrell enc. letter to Biden, 3/29/17, 4/10/17.

367 **Statue:** authors were present at unveiling, 12/3/16.

367 **KY legislature/approach to White House:** Correspondence Manning Kimmel IV, & Steven Ray, 4/17.

368 **Grandson reflected:** interview with Tom Kimmel Jr., 2015.

368 **"The officers":** Draft notes for article, HEK R29.

368 **"History":** PHA 6, p. 2554.

Bibliography

Books

Aldrich, Richard J. *Intelligence and the War Against Japan: Britain, America, and the Politics of Secret Service.* Cambridge: Cambridge University Press, 2000.

Anderson, Charles R. *Day of Lightning, Years of Scorn—Walter C. Short and the Attack on Pearl Harbor.* Annapolis, MD: Naval Institute Press, 2005.

Andrew, Christopher. *For the President's Eyes Only: Secret Intelligence and the American Presidency from Washington to Bush.* New York: HarperCollins, 2005.

Arnold-Forster, Mark. *The World at War.* London: Pimlico, 2001.

Ashe, Samuel, Stephen Weeks, and Charles Van Noppen, eds. *Biographical History of North Carolina from Colonial Times to the Present,* Vol. II, Greensboro, NC: CL Van Noppen, 1905.

Barnes, Harry, ed. *Perpetual War for Perpetual Peace.* Caldwell, ID: Caxton, 1953.

Bartsch, William. *December 8, 1941: MacArthur's Pearl Harbor.* College Station: Texas A&M Press, 2003.

———. *Every Day a Nightmare.* College Station: Texas A&M Press, 2010.

Batvinis, Raymond. *Hoover's Secret War Against Axis Spies.* Lawrence: University of Kansas Press, 2014.

———. *The Origins of FBI Counter-Intelligence,* Lawrence: University of Kansas Press, 2007.

Beach, Edward L. *Scapegoats A Defense of Kimmel and Short at Pearl Harbor.* Annapolis, MD: Naval Institute Press, 1995.

Beard, Charles. *President Roosevelt and the Coming of the War, 1941.* New Haven, CT: Yale University Press, 1948.

Beasley, Maurine H. *Eleanor Roosevelt: Transformative First Lady.* Lawrence: University of Kansas Press, 2010.

Bird, Kai. *The Chairman: John J. McCloy—The Making of the American Establishment.* New York: Simon and Schuster, 1992.

Bix, Herbert. *Hirohito and the Making of Modern Japan*. New York: Harper-Collins, 2000.

Blair, Clay, Jr. *Silent Victory: The U.S. Submarine War Against Japan*. Annapolis, MD: Naval Institute Press, 2001.

Boister, Neil, and Robert Cryer, eds. *Documents of the Tokyo International Military Tribunal*. Oxford: Oxford University Press, 2008.

Borch, Fred, and Daniel Martinez. *Kimmel, Short, and Pearl Harbor: The Final Report Revealed*. Annapolis, MD: Naval Institute Press, 2005.

Borneman, Walter R. *The Admirals: Nimitz, Halsey, Leahy, and King—The Five-Star Admirals Who Won the War at Sea*. New York: Back Bay, 2012.

Brown, Anthony Cave. *The Last Hero*. New York: Times Books, 1982.

———. *C: The Secret Life of Sir Stewart Graham Menzies*. New York: Macmillan, 1987.

Brown, David. *The Royal Navy and the Mediterranean*, Vol. 1. London: Royal Navy, 1952.

Brownlow, Donald G. *The Accused: The Ordeal of Rear Admiral Husband Edward Kimmel, U.S.N.* New York: Vantage, 1968.

Bryden, John. *Fighting to Lose: How the German Secret Intelligence Service Helped the Allies Win the Second World War*. Toronto: Dundurn, 2014.

Budiansky, Stephen. *Battle of Wits: The Complete Story of Codebreaking in World War II*. New York: Touchstone, 2000.

Burtness, Paul S., and Warren U. Ober. *The Puzzle of Pearl Harbor*. Elmsford, NY: Row, Peterson, 1962.

Bywater, Hector C. *The Great Pacific War: A History of the American-Japanese Campaign of 1931–1933*. Bedford, MA: Applewood, 1925.

Carlson, Elliot. *Joe Rochefort's War*. Annapolis, MD: Naval Institute Press, 2011.

Casey, William, *The Secret War Against Hitler*. Washington, DC: Berkley, 1989.

Chalou, George, ed. *The Secrets War: The OSS in World War II*. Washington, DC: National Archives, 1992.

Churchill, Winston. *The Second World War*, Vol. III, *The Grand Alliance*. London: Houghton Mifflin, 1986.

Clausen, Henry C., and Bruce Lee. *Pearl Harbor: Final Judgement*. New York: Da Capo, 2001.

Colman, Jonathan. *A Special Relationship*. Manchester: Manchester University Press, 2004.

Colville, John. *The Fringes of Power: Downing Street Diaries, 1939–1955*. New York: Norton, 1985.

Connally, Thomas. *My Name Is Tom Connally*, New York: Crowell, 1954.

Correspondents of *Time, Life,* and *Fortune. December 7: The First Thirty Hours.* New York: Knopf, 1942.

Costello, John. *Days of Infamy.* New York: Pocket Books, 1994.

Culbertson, Charles. *War in the Pacific: End of the Asiatic Fleet—The Classified Report of Admiral Thomas C. Hart.* Staunton, VA: Clarion, 2013.

Dallek, Robert. *Franklin D. Roosevelt and American Foreign Policy, 1932–40.* New York: Oxford University Press, 1979.

Davis, Burke. *The Billy Mitchell Story.* Philadelphia: Chilton, 1969.

Dies, Martin. *Martin Dies' Story.* New York: Bookmailer, 1963.

Donovan, Robert J. *Conflict and Crisis.* New York: Norton, 1977.

Dyer, George. *The Amphibians Came to Conquer,* Vol. 1. Washington, DC: U.S. Government Printing Office, 1972.

Farago, Ladislas. *The Broken Seal: "Operation Magic" and the Secret Road to Pearl Harbor.* New York: Random House, 1967.

———. *Burn After Reading.* New York: Walker, 1961.

———. *The Game of Foxes: British and German Intelligence Operations and Personalities Which Changed the Course of the Second World War.* London: Pan, 1973.

Ferrell, Robert, ed. *The Eisenhower Diaries.* New York: Norton, 1981.

Fields, Alonzo. *My 21 Years in the White House.* New York: Coward-McCann, 1961.

Fitzgibbon, Constantine. *Secret Intelligence and the Twentieth Century.* London: Granada, 1978.

Flynn, John. *The Final Secret of Pearl Harbor.* New York: privately printed, 1944.

———. *The Roosevelt Myth.* New York: Devin-Adair, 1948.

Freidel, Frank. *Franklin D. Roosevelt: A Rendezvous with Destiny.* Boston: Little, Brown, 1990.

Gannon, Michael. *Pearl Harbor Betrayed.* New York: Henry Holt, 2001.

Godfrey, John. *The Naval Memoirs of Admiral J. H. Godfrey,* Vol. V, *1939–1942,* Cambridge, UK: privately published, Cambridge Archives, 1964.

Goldstein, Donald, and Katherine Dillon. *The Pearl Harbor Papers.* Herndon, VA: Potomac, 1999.

Greaves, Percy L., Jr. *Pearl Harbor: The Seeds and Fruits of Infamy.* Auburn, AL: Ludvig von Mises Institute, 2010.

Grew, Joseph. *Turbulent Era: Diplomatic Record of Forty Years, 1904–1945,* Boston: Houghton Mifflin, 1952.

Gronau, Wolfgang von. *Weltflieger: Errinnerungen 1926–1947.* Stuttgart: Deutsche Verlags Anstalt, 1955.

Grose, Peter. *Gentleman Spy: The Life of Allen Dulles*. Boston: University of Massachusetts Press, 1994.

Halsey, William, and J. Bryan, III. *Admiral Halsey's Story*. New York: McGraw-Hill, 1947.

Hanyok, Robert J., and David P. Mowry. *West Wind Clear: Cryptology and the Winds Message Controversy—A Document History*. Fort George Meade, MD: Center for Cryptologic History, 2008.

Hart, Thomas and Charles Culbertson. *War in the Pacific: End of the Asiatic Fleet—The Classified Report of Admiral Thomas C. Hart*. Staunton, VA: Clarion, 2013.

Haslach, Robert. *Nishi no kaza, hare*. Weesp, Netherlands: Van Kampen and Zn, 1985.

Hastedt, Glenn, ed. *Spies, Wiretaps, and Secret Operations*. Santa Barbara, CA: ABC-CLIO, 2011.

Hastings, Max. *The Secret War: Spies, Codes and Guerrillas, 1939–1945*. London: William Collins, 2015.

Haynes, John Earl, and Harvey Klehr. *VENONA: Decoding Soviet Espionage in America*. New Haven and London: Yale University Press, 1999.

Helms, Richard, with William Hood. *A Look over My Shoulder, A Life in the Central Intelligence Agency*. New York: Random House, 2003.

Herzstein, Robert E. *Roosevelt and Hitler: Prelude to War*. New York: Paragon House, 1989.

Hinsley, F. H., E. E. Thomas, C. F. G. Ransom, and R. C. Knight. *British Intelligence in the Second World War: Its Influence on Strategy and Operations*, Vol. 2. New York: Cambridge University Press, 1981.

Hirata, Shinsaku. *Warera moshi tatakawaba*. Tokyo: Kodansha, 1933.

Hoehling, A. A. *The Week Before Pearl Harbor*. New York: Norton, 1963.

Holmes, Richard. *The World at War*. London: Ebury, 2011.

Hough, Richard. *Mountbatten: Hero of Our Time*. London: Book Club Associates, 1981.

Hoyt, Edwin. *How They Won the War in the Pacific*. Guilford, CT: Lyons, 2013.

Hull, Cordell. *The Memoirs of Cordell Hull*, Vol II. New York: Macmillan, 1948.

Hurley, Alfred. *Billy Mitchell, Crusader for Air Power*. Bloomington: Indiana University Press, 2006.

Hyde, Montgomery. *Room 3603: The Story of the British Intelligence Center in New York During World War II*. New York: Farrar, Straus, 1962.

———. *Secret Intelligence Agent*. London: Constable, 1982.

Jeffrey, Keith. *MI6: The History of the Secret Intelligence Service*. London: Bloomsbury, 2010.

Kahn, David. *The Codebreakers: The Story of Secret Writing*. London: Weidenfeld and Nicolson, 1966.

Kaiser, David. *No End Save Victory*. New York: Basic Books, 2014.

Kelly, C. Brian. *Best Little Stories from World War II*. VA: Montpelier, 1989.

Kimmel, Husband E. *Admiral Kimmel's Story*. Chicago: Regnery, 1954/55.

King, Ernest, and Walter Whitehill. *Fleet Admiral King*. New York: Norton, 1952.

Knightley, Phillip. *The Second Oldest Profession: The Spy as Bureaucrat, Patriot, Fantasist and Whore*. London, André Deutsch, 1986.

Koster, John. *Operation Snow*. New York: Regnery History, 2012.

La Forte, Robert S., and Ronald E. Marcello. *Remembering Pearl Harbor*. Wilmington, DE: Scholarly Resources, 1991.

Lambert, John W., and Norman Polmar. *Defenseless: Command Failure at Pearl Harbor*. New York: Motorbooks International, 2003.

Landis, Lieutenant Commander Kenneth, USNR (ret.), and Staff Sergeant Rex Gunn USAR (ret.), *Deceit at Pearl Harbor: From Pearl Harbor to Midway*. Self-published, 2001.

Larrabee, Eric. *Commander in Chief*. New York: Harper and Row, 1987.

Layton, Edwin T., Rear Admiral, with Captain Roger Pineau and John Costello. *And I Was There: Pearl Harbor and Midway—Breaking the Secrets*. New York: Quill, 1985.

Lee, Bruce. *Marching Orders: The Untold Story of World War II*. Boston, MA: Da Capo, 2001.

Leutze, James. *A Different Kind of Victory: A Biography of Thomas C. Hart*. Annapolis, MD: U.S. Naval Institute, 1981.

Lewis, Jonathan, and Ben Steele. *Hell in the Pacific: From Pearl Harbor to Hiroshima and Beyond*. London: Channel 4 Books, 2001.

Littell, Norman M. *My Roosevelt Years*. Seattle: University of Washington Press, 1987.

Lord, Walter. *Day of Infamy*. New York: Henry Holt, 1957.

Love, Robert. *History of the U.S. Navy*. Harrisburg, PA: Stackpole, 1992.

Lowry, Thomas, and John Welham. *The Attack on Taranto*. Mechanicsburg, PA: Stackpole, 2000.

MacDonald, Bill. *The True Intrepid: Sir William Stephenson and the Unknown Agents*. Vancouver: Raincoast, 2001.

Macintyre, Ben. *Double Cross: The True Story of the D-Day Spies*. London: Bloomsbury, 2012.

Madison, Nathan. *Anti-Foreign Imagery in American Pulps and Comic Books, 1920–1960*. Jefferson, NC: McFarland, 2013.

Manchester, William. *American Caesar: Douglas MacArthur, 1880–1964*. Boston: Little, Brown, 1978.

———. *The Glory and the Dream*. Boston: Little, Brown, 1973.

Marder, Arthur. *From the Dardanelles to Oran*. London: Seaforth, 1974.

Marshall, Katherine Tupper. *Together: Annals of an Army Wife*. New York: Tupper and Love, 1946.

Marston, Daniel. *The Pacific War Companion*. Oxford, UK: Osprey, 2005.

Masterman, John C. *The Double-Cross System: In the War of 1939 to 1945*. London: Granada, 1979.

Matloff, Maurice, and Edwin Snell. *Strategic Planning for Coalition Warfare, 1941–1942*. Washington, DC: U.S. Army, 1990.

Matsuo, Kinoaki. *How Japan Plans to Win*. London: Harrap, and New York: Little, Brown, 1942.

Mauch, Peter. *Sailor Diplomat: Nomura Kichisaburō and the Japanese-American War*. Cambridge, MA: Harvard University Asia Center, 2011.

McIntire, Ross. *White House Physician*. New York: Putnam, 1946.

Miller, Edward S. *War Plan Orange: The U.S. Strategy to Defeat Japan, 1897–1945*. Annapolis, MD: Naval Institute Press, 1991.

Miller, Roger. *Billy Mitchell, Stormy Petrel of the Air*. Washington, DC: Office of Air Force History, 2004.

Miller, Russell. *Codename Tricycle: The True Story of the Second World War's Most Extraordinary Double Agent*. London: Pimlico, 2005.

Minohari, Tosh, Tze-ki Han, and Evan Dawley, eds., *The Decade of the Great War: Japan and the Wider World in the 1910s*. Leiden, Netherlands: Brill, 2014.

Mintz, Frank Paul. *Revisionism and the Origins of Pearl Harbor*. New York: University Press of America, 1985.

Montagu, Ewen. *Beyond Top Secret U*. Newton Abbot, UK: Readers Union, 1978.

Morgan, Ted. *FDR: A Biography*. New York: Simon and Schuster, 1985.

Morgenstern, George. *Pearl Harbor: The Story of the Secret War*. New York: Devin-Adair, 1947.

Mori, Victor. *East Meets West: A Family History*. Honolulu: self-published, 2012.

Morison, Samuel Eliot. *The Rising Sun in the Pacific, 1931–April, 1942*. New York: Little, Brown, 1948.

Morton, Louis. *Command Decisions*. Washington, DC: U.S. Army, 1990.

———. *The U.S. Army in World War II: The Fall of the Philippines*. Washington, DC: U.S. Army, 1953.

———. *The U.S. Army in World War II: The War in the Pacific, Strategy and Command—The First Two Years*. Washington, DC: U.S. Army, 2000.

Mosley, Leonard. *Marshall: Hero for Our Times*. New York: Hearst Books, 1982.

O'Connor, Christopher. *Taranto: The Raid, the Observer, the Aftermath*. Indianapolis, IN: Dog Ear, 2010.

Parker, Frederick. *Pearl Harbor Revisited: United States Naval Communications Intelligence, 1924–1941*. Fort George Meade, MD: Center for Cryptologic History, 1994.

Pfennigwerth, Ian. *A Man of Intelligence*. Australia: Rosenberg, 2006.

Popov, Dusko. *Spy/Counterspy*. London: Weidenfeld and Nicolson, 1974.

Potter, E. B. *Nimitz*, Annapolis, MD : Naval Institute Press, 1976.

Powers, Richard Gid. *Broken: The Troubled Past and Uncertain Future of the FBI*. New York: Free Press, 2004.

Prados, John. *Combined Fleet Decoded: The Secret History of Naval Intelligence and the Japanese Navy in World War II*. New York: Random House, 1995.

Prange, Gordon, with Donald Goldstein and Katherine Dillon. *At Dawn We Slept: The Untold Story of Pearl Harbor*. New York: McGraw-Hill, 1981.

———. *Pearl Harbor: The Verdict of History*. New York: Penguin, 1986.

Ranelagh, John. *The Agency: The Rise and Decline of the CIA*. New York: Simon and Schuster, 1986.

Reilly, Michael, as told to William Slocum. *Reilly of the White House*. New York: Simon and Schuster, 1947.

Richardson, James, as told to George Dyer. *On the Treadmill to Pearl Harbor: The Memoirs of Admiral James O. Richardson*. Washington, DC: Department of the Navy, 1973.

Rodriguez del Campo, Juan. *Pearl Harbor, la Historia Secreta: La Diplomacia Peruana y la Misión Rivera Schreiber en Japón Durante la II Guerra Mundial*. Lima: Asociación de Funcionarios del Servicio Diplomatico del Perú, 2010.

Rose, Lisle. *Power at Sea*. Columbia: University of Missouri Press, 2007.

Rusbridger, James, and Eric Nave. *Betrayal at Pearl Harbor: How Churchill Lured Roosevelt into War*. New York: Michael O'Mara, 1991.

Russell, Henry. *Pearl Harbor Story*. Atlanta, GA: Mercer University Press, 2001.

Schecter, Jerrold, and Leona Schecter. *Sacred Secrets: How Soviet Intelligence Operations Changed American History*. Washington, DC: Brassey's, 2003.

Schmidt, Hans. *Maverick Marine*. Lexington: University of Kentucky Press, 1998.

Sherwood, Robert. *Roosevelt and Hopkins*. New York: Harper, 1948.

Simpson, B. Mitchell, III. *Admiral Harold R. Stark: Architect of Victory, 1939–1945*. Columbia: University of South Carolina Press, 1989.

Smith, Adrian. *Mountbatten: Apprentice War Lord*. London and New York: I. B. Tauris, 2010.

Smith, Michael. *The Emperor's Codes: Bletchley Park's Role in Breaking Japan's Secret Ciphers*. London: Biteback, 2000.

Soga, Keiho. *Life Behind Bars*. Honolulu: University of Hawaii, 2008.

Standley, William, and Arthur Ageton. *Admiral Ambassador to Russia*. Chicago: Regnery, 1955.

Stephenson, William, ed. *British Security Coordination: The Secret History of British Intelligence in the Americas, 1940–45*. New York: Fromm, 1999.

Stevens, Janice. *Stories of Service: Valley Veterans Remember World War II*. Fresno, CA: Craven Street, 2007.

Stillwell, Paul. *Air Raid: Pearl Harbor—Recollections of a Day of Infamy*. Annapolis, MD: Naval Institute Press, 1981.

Stimson, Henry, with McGeorge Bundy. *On Active Service in Peace and War*. New York: Harper, 1948.

Stinnett, Robert B. *Day of Deceit: The Truth About FDR and Pearl Harbor*. New York: Touchstone, 2000.

Summers, Anthony. *Official and Confidential: The Secret Life of J. Edgar Hoover*. New York: Putnam, 1993.

Tansill, Charles. *Back Door to War: The Roosevelt Foreign Policy 1933–1941*. Chicago: Regnery, 1952.

Terasaki, Gwen. *Bridge to the Sun*. Casper, WY: Rock Creek, 2009.

Terraine, John. *The Life and Times of Lord Mountbatten*. London: Bloomsbury Reader, 2013.

Terrett, Dulany. *U.S. Army in World War II: The Technical Services, the Signal Corps—The Emergency*. Washington, DC: U.S. Army, 1994.

Theobald, Robert A., Rear Admiral. *The Final Secret of Pearl Harbor*. Old Greenwich, CT: Devin-Adair, 1954.

Thompson, George, Dixie Harris, Pauline Oakes, and Dulany Terrett. *U.S. Army in World War II: The Signal Corps—The Test*. Washington, DC: U.S. Army, 1957.

Thompson, Robert. *A Time for War*. New York: Prentice-Hall, 1991.

Thorpe, Elliott R., Brigadier General. *East Wind, Rain*. Boston: Gambit, 1969.

Toland, John. *Infamy: Pearl Harbor and Its Aftermath*. New York: Berkley, 1983.

———. *The Rising Sun*. New York: Modern Library, 2003.

Tully, Grace. *FDR: My Boss.* Chicago: People's Book Club, 1949.

Tute, Warren. *The Deadly Stroke.* London: Collins, 1973.

Victor, George. *The Pearl Harbor Myth: Rethinking the Unthinkable.* Washington, DC: Potomac, 2007.

Wallin, Homer. *Pearl Harbor: Why, How, Fleet Salvage, and Final Appraisal.* Washington, DC: Department of the Navy, 1968.

Wedemeyer, Albert C. *Wedemeyer Reports!* New York: Henry Holt, 1958.

Weinstein, Allen, and Alexander Vassiliev. *The Haunted Wood: Soviet Espionage in America—The Stalin Era.* New York: Random House, 1999.

Weintraub, Stanley. *Long Day's Journey into War—December 7, 1941.* New York: Truman Talley, 1991.

West, Nigel. *VENONA: The Greatest Secret of the Cold War.* London: Harper-Collins, 1999.

Westcott, Allan. *American Sea Power Since 1755.* Chicago: Lippincott, 1947.

Wetzler, Peter. *Hirohito and the War.* Honolulu: University of Hawaii Press, 1998.

Willoughby, Charles A., and John Chamberlain. *MacArthur, 1941–1951.* New York: McGraw-Hill, 1954.

Wilmott, H. P. *Empire in the Balance.* Annapolis, MD: Naval Institute Press, 1982.

Wohlstetter, Roberta. *Pearl Harbor: Warning and Decision.* Stanford, CA: Stanford University Press, 1962.

Woodward, Sir Llewellyn. *British Foreign Policy in the Second World War.* London: Her Majesty's Stationery Office, 1962.

Zacharias, Ellis M., Rear Admiral. *Secret Missions.* New York: Paperback Library, 1946.

U.S. Government Publications

Investigation of Un-American Propaganda Activities in the U.S., Appendix VI, *Report on Japanese Activities.* Hearings Before a Special Committee on Un-American Activities, House of Representatives, 77th Cong., 1st Sess., Washington, DC: U.S. Government Printing Office, 1942.

Morgan, Edward. *Confidential Report: An Approach to the Question of Responsibility for the Pearl Harbor Disaster: Respectfully Submitted at the Suggestion of the General Counsel for the Consideration, Assistance, and Sole Personal Use of the Joint Congressional Committee on the Pearl Harbor Attack.* Joint Committee on the Investigation of the Pearl Harbor Attack, U.S. Congress, 79th Cong. 1st Sess., Washington, DC: U.S. Government Printing Office, 1946.

Naval Analysis Division. *The Campaigns of the Pacific War: United States Strategic Bombing Survey (Pacific).* Washington, DC: U.S. Government Printing Office, 1946.

Pearl Harbor Attack, Report, Hearings and *Exhibits,* Joint Committee on the Investigation of the Pearl Harbor Attack, U.S. Congress, 79th Cong., 1st Sess., Washington, DC: U.S. Government Printing Office, 1946.

U.S. Department of State. *Papers Relating to the Foreign Relations of the United States, Japan: 1931–1941,* Vol. II. Washington, DC: U.S. Government Printing Office, 1943.

U.S. Department of State. *Peace and War: U.S. Foreign Policy, 1931–1941.* Washington, DC: U.S. Government Printing Office, 1943.

U.S. Government Printing Office. *Foreign Relations of the U.S.: Diplomatic Papers, 1941—The Far East,* Vol. IV. Washington, DC: U.S. Government Printing Office, 1956.

Index

Note: Pages numbers after 375 refer to notes.

About the Authors

ANTHONY SUMMERS is the author of nine acclaimed nonfiction books. *The Eleventh Day*, on the 9/11 attacks, was a finalist for the 2012 Pulitzer Prize for History and the winner of the Golden Dagger—the Crime Writers' Association's top nonfiction award. He is the only author to have won that award twice. Educated at Oxford University, Summers traveled worldwide for the BBC, becoming a deputy editor of the flagship program *Panorama*. His books on President Nixon, FBI director J. Edgar Hoover, the assassination of John F. Kennedy, and Marilyn Monroe have been the basis for major television documentaries. The feature film *Scandal*, starring John Hurt, was based on Summers' book on the Profumo sex/espionage scandal.

A Matter of Honor is ROBBYN SWAN's fifth book. With Summers, she was a Pulitzer Prize finalist for *The Eleventh Day* and the winner of the Golden Dagger Award. Swan has explored many of the seminal events of the past century, including the rise of the American Mafia, the assassination of John Kennedy, Watergate, and the 9/11 attacks. A graduate of Smith College, she early on worked as a researcher for John le Carré. She has written for *Salon*, the *National Journal*, the UK's *Daily Telegraph*, the *Observer*, the *Independent*, and the *Irish Times*. She has contributed to documentaries for PBS, A&E, The History Channel, CNN, and the BBC. Swan and Summers have both written for *Vanity Fair*.

They are married and live in Ireland.